The Handbook of Emotional Intelligence

Theory, Development, Assessment, and Application at Home, School, and in the Workplace

Reuven Bar-On
James D. A. Parker
Editors

JOSSEY-BASS
A Wiley Company
San Francisco

Published by

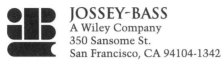

JOSSEY-BASS
A Wiley Company
350 Sansome St.
San Francisco, CA 94104-1342

www.josseybass.com

Jossey-Bass books and products are available through most bookstores. To contact Jossey-Bass directly, call (888) 378-2537, fax to (800) 605-2665, or visit our website at www.josseybass.com.

Substantial discounts on bulk quantities of Jossey-Bass books are available to corporations, professional associations, and other organizations. For details and discount information, contact the special sales department at Jossey-Bass.

We at Jossey-Bass strive to use the most environmentally sensitive paper stocks available to us. Our publications are printed on acid-free recycled stock whenever possible, and our paper always meets or exceeds minimum GPO and EPA requirements.

Library of Congress Cataloging-in-Publication Data
The Handbook of emotional intelligence
  [edited by] Reuven Bar-On and James D. A. Parker.—1st ed.
     p. cm.
  Includes bibliographical references and index.
  ISBN 0-7879-4984-1 (hardcover : alk. paper)
    1. Emotional intelligence. 2. Emotional intelligence tests.
  I. Bar-On, Reuven, 1944– II. Parker, James D. A.
  (James Donald Alexander), 1959–
  BF576.H36 2000
  152.4—dc21
                                      00-031550
                                         CIP

FIRST EDITION
HB Printing   10 9 8 7 6 5 4 3 2

CONTENTS

FOREWORD

Daniel Goleman

There are distinct stages in the evolution of scientific theories, from the seminal conception, through hypothesis generation and testing, to successive refinements and modifications as the theory matures. From that perspective the publication of *The Handbook of Emotional Intelligence* marks a coming-of-age (perhaps a bar mitzvah, of sorts) for this body of theory.

It has been a remarkably rapid progression. In the 1980s Reuven Bar-On first used the abbreviation *EQ* to refer to aspects of this range of abilities. In 1990 Peter Salovey and John Mayer published their landmark conceptualization of what was described for the first time as "emotional intelligence." And in 1995 the idea was carried out into the world at large with the publication of my book *Emotional Intelligence.*

Although the concept of emotional intelligence as such has been taken as new by many, its historical roots are well embedded in psychological thought over the past century. Yet the recent rash of attention seems to have catalyzed a ferment of interest in this way of conceiving human abilities. Since the publication of my book in 1995, I, like others who have done the pioneering work in this fledgling field, have received a steady stream of inquiries from graduate students and academic researchers seeking to undertake research on emotional intelligence.

Now, with the publication of the *Handbook*, those who want to pursue such research have a solid source book, one that offers access to the leading thought and tools in the field. That access should play a role in propelling emotional intelligence theory into its next stage of evolution, generating grounded theory. As is inevitable for any emerging theory, the first round of theorizing has been extrapolated from findings that do not directly test hypotheses about emotional intelligence. That has begun to change only in very recent years, as researchers have had the time to do research guided directly by this body of thought.

But now the process of testing, clarifying, and modifying emotional intelligence theory can accelerate, because researchers have easier access to the thinking and methods of those who have gone before. That access, in turn, should yield a flowering of findings in the future.

Readers will find in these pages many issues raised, disputations of theory, and varied points of view. All that signifies a field in healthy ferment, a sign of growth. That growth can be seen in the connections made with other psychological theories, such as the theory of practical intelligence, the five-factor theory of personality, and theories of creativity. New insights are offered from neurology, particularly insights into the mechanisms at work in emotional self-awareness and in the role of emotions in information processing. Implications are drawn for a new understanding of alexithymia and related psychological disorders that may in part reflect a deficit in emotional intelligence abilities.

Another sign of the field's maturation is the handful of sound measures that have emerged for assessing emotional intelligence, each from a unique theoretical perspective. Practical applications of this body of theory are represented in the realm of business and organizational life, for physical health and adaptation to stress, and for psychotherapy. Certainly one of the most promising integrations documented here focuses on how children develop emotional competence and the hopeful data emerging from school-based programs for promoting social and emotional competence.

The *Handbook* itself provides a rich feast of seminal findings and an even richer range of challenging questions that should stimulate important research. It will likely prove invaluable for those who seek to pursue the research that will carry this field to its next level of depth and clarity.

ACKNOWLEDGMENTS

We would like to acknowledge the contributions made by a number of people who have facilitated the writing of this book.

First of all, we thank Alan Rinzler at Jossey-Bass for inviting us to write a textbook on emotional intelligence. He made this challenging request after he attended a symposium we gave, together with Peter Salovey and John Mayer, at the 1998 American Psychological Association Annual Conference in San Francisco.

Our immediate gratitude goes out to the thirty-seven authors who contributed the twenty-two chapters included in this volume. Without these internationally recognized experts in emotional intelligence and related fields there would be no *Handbook of Emotional Intelligence*. We thank them for their cooperation in helping us meet the publisher's challenge. In addition to summarizing the essence of their work in this wide area, many of the contributing authors gave us invaluable advice about how to bring the project together. The ongoing exchange has also provided an interesting and enjoyable learning experience that has helped to enrich our collective knowledge of emotional intelligence.

We would like to express a word of thanks to our colleagues in the Collaborative to Advance Social and Emotional Learning and in the Consortium for Research on Emotional Intelligence in Organizations. Our discussions with them have been both helpful and encouraging.

We thank Steven Stein and Gill Sitarenios at Multi-Health Systems (MHS) in Toronto for sharing with us findings from a number of studies that they have conducted over the past few years. MHS is the world's leader in emotional intelligence assessment based on the shear numbers of people that the company tests annually with instruments it has published and is presently developing.

Graeme Taylor and Michael Bagby from the University of Toronto and Jan Derksen from the University of Nijmegen in the Netherlands have also provided important research findings that have found their way into the *Handbook*. We also thank Claus Moller at Time Manager International (TMI) in Denmark, who shared with us findings from his pioneering work in organizational emotional intelligence, an area sure to attract research interest. TMI has provided a laboratory for studying ways to improve human effectiveness in the workplace.

We thank Tonya Bauermann, Kimberly DaSilva, Sarah Majeski, and Dana Reker for their library assistance.

Numerous other colleagues and friends have contributed to the *Handbook* in one form or another. Our humble gratitude goes out to them even though space limits our ability to recognize them individually for their contributions.

Last but not least we thank our families, who have been with us every step of the way on this project. They bore the brunt of the sacrifices of these past two years and provided a home environment that enabled *The Handbook of Emotional Intelligence* to come together.

INTRODUCTION

Reuven Bar-On and James D. A. Parker

The primary reason for publishing *The Handbook of Emotional Intelligence* is to provide a scholarly and informative book on what is popularly referred to as *emotional intelligence*. In that such a textbook does not yet exist, the *Handbook* is designed to meet the growing needs of researchers, practitioners, educators, and students who want to learn more about this topic. Interest in this concept emerged in dramatic fashion following the publication in 1995 of *Emotional Intelligence* by Daniel Goleman. One of the myths that emerged from the "media fallout" surrounding this bestseller was that emotional intelligence is a "new" field. What the reader of the *Handbook* will discover is that this concept is not new at all. Emotional intelligence, and related concepts, have been around for most of the twentieth century. These concepts have generated a rather large body of theoretical and empirical literature over the past eighty years (see Bar-On, 1997, and Taylor, Bagby, & Parker, 1997, for discussions on some of this history).

The spirit behind the *Handbook* is interdisciplinary and multimodal. We have woven this spirit into the fabric of the book by stressing the importance of varied empirical methodologies and diverse levels of analysis in the study of emotional intelligence and related constructs. The reader will find, for example, that individual chapters explore the neurobiology of emotion abilities, the role of early childhood history, and the development of emotional abilities, as well as the relationship between emotional abilities and interpersonal relationships at home or at work. Specific research findings reported in a chapter may have utilized behavioral observations or the latest brain imaging technology, as well as information gained from structured interviews, standardized performance mea sures, or self-report instruments.

One of the most important goals in creating the *Handbook* was to bring together a set of chapters, written by recognized leaders in the field, on the most prominent conceptual models of emotional intelligence and related concepts. The list of related concepts includes topics such as alexithymia, levels of emotional awareness, emotional competence, openness to experience, practical intelligence, psychological mindedness, social competence, and social intelligence. Along with providing a forum for a discussion of different theoretical approaches, we also wanted to bring together, in a single volume, a set of chapters that review and evaluate the most valid and reliable methods for assessing emotional intelligence and related constructs. There is a growing interest by researchers, clinicians, and educators in being able to assess emotional intelligence and related concepts. The information presented in several chapters in this book will help readers decide which test or instruments might be useful for their particular research or assessment need.

Another important goal for the *Handbook* was to examine the growing literature concerning the relationship between emotional intelligence (and related constructs) and a variety of outcome variables: personality factors; creativity; mental and physical health; and the quality of interpersonal relationships at home, school, and work. Specific chapters focus on these types of outcome variables. Given the important relationship between emotional intelligence and various quality of life and health variables, several chapters examine the growing literature on intervention programs and techniques developed to improve or enhance emotional intelligence or related abilities.

The first part of this book deals with the conceptualization of emotional intelligence and closely related constructs. This section begins with a presentation by Sabrina Zirkel on a conceptual model that is linked with a construct originally described by Thorndike in 1920: social intelligence. According to contemporary theory, social intelligence involves a set of abilities related to how people try to make sense of the world around them; it is a set of skills and abilities that guide adaptive and purposive behavior. This chapter is followed by a discussion from Keith Topping and colleagues on the related concept of social competence. This is a construct that has been popularized in recent years by individuals associated with the social and emotional education movement.

Drawing on a substantial clinical and medical literature that goes back to the 1940s and 1950s, Graeme Taylor and Michael Bagby present a detailed overview of alexithymia, which shares a number of important features with the emotional intelligence construct. Although originally of interest to researchers working in the area of psychosomatic disorders, this personality variable has attracted considerable interest from health care professionals working with a diverse range of medical and psychiatric problems.

Carolyn Saarni's chapter follows with an overview of the concept of emotional competence, particularly those emotional competencies or skills involved in various types of interpersonal behaviors. Emotional intelligence and relevant skills or mental abilities are expanded on in the next chapter by John Mayer and colleagues, who present a detailed overview of their unique model of emotional intelligence. These authors also explore the broad range of meanings that have been attached to the concept of emotional intelligence in the past decade.

The next chapter is by Mary McCallum and William Piper, who explore the conceptual overlap between the concept of psychological mindedness and the core features of several established models for emotional intelligence. The concept of psychological mindedness evolved from clinical research that sought to identify individuals likely to benefit from insight-oriented psychotherapy. The last chapter of this section, by Jennifer Hedlund and Robert Sternberg, compares the concept of practical intelligence with other concepts closely related to emotional intelligence. Reviewing many of the interrelated concepts explored in previous chapters, these authors attempt to identify the core dimensions relevant to the scientific study of emotional intelligence.

The second section explores the diverse literature focusing on the development of various mental abilities and skills relevant to emotional and social intelligence. The section begins with a chapter by Richard Lane, who examines the empirical literature in search of the anatomical and physiological foundations of abilities linked with his model of levels of emotional awareness—a model with close ties to the emotional intelligence construct. The *Handbook* continues with a related chapter by Antoine Bechara and colleagues, who examine the neurological factors related to the problem-solving component of emotional and social intelligence.

The next chapter is by Robert Sternberg and Elena Grigorenko, who examine the literature that has explored various factors involved in the development (or lack of development) of practical intelligence. The model of practical intelligence proposed by these authors involves a broad range of skills related to how individuals shape, select, or adapt to their physical and social environments. Elaine Scharfe, in the following chapter, summarizes the research on how children learn to express, recognize, and understand emotional behavior. She also examines the literature on the relationship between competency in these types of emotional abilities and the quality of interpersonal relationships.

The next chapter in this section is by Robert McCrae, who examines the relationship between basic personality and various models proposed for the emotional intelligence construct. With reference to the five-factor model of personality, McCrae argues that many of the dimensions associated with emotional intelligence share conceptual overlap with basic personality dimensions such as openness to experience. James Averill, in the concluding chapter of this section, examines the relationship between cognitive intelligence and emotion. In addition, he examines the special role played by emotion in creativity.

The third section of the *Handbook* focuses on assessment methods and issues related to emotional intelligence and related constructs. Graeme Taylor and his colleagues discuss a multimodal approach to the assessment of alexithymia. They describe the validity and reliability of several alexithymia measures using different assessment strategies (such as self-report versus observer-rated techniques). John Mayer and colleagues describe a task-performance methodology for measuring the components in their specific model of emotional intelligence. Richard Boyatzis and colleagues describe a recently developed multirater measure for measuring emotional competence in the workplace.

In the concluding chapter of this section, Reuven Bar-On describes the development of a self-report measure of emotional and social competence: the Bar-On Emotional Quotient Inventory (EQ-i). This chapter describes the psychometric properties of the EQ-i, as well as summarizing what we presently know about emotional and social intelligence from research using the EQ-i.

The fourth and last section of the book discusses specific ways emotional intelligence and related constructs can be applied in preventive and remedial work. A number of approaches are explored that are designed to help people become more effective in the educational, corporate, and clinical settings. The first chapter of this section, by Patricia Graczyk and colleagues, describes the work of the Collaborative to Advance Social and Emotional Learning (CASEL), which has developed education programs designed to promote social and emotional competence in children of various ages. The next chapter is by Keith Topping and colleagues, who critically evaluate (from a review of over 700 empirical reports) the effectiveness of intervention programs such as those developed by CASEL.

The relationship between social and emotional competence and the workplace is discussed by Cary Cherniss in the next chapter of this section. Although the concept of emotional intelligence is a relatively new concept in business and industry, there is a long history in this area of training and development interventions for improving emotional competence and work performance. Cherniss critically evaluates a cross section of these intervention programs.

In the next chapter, Gerald Matthews and Moshe Zeidner examine the empirical literature on the relationship between various facets of the emotional intelligence construct and physical and mental health. They recommend that researchers continue to study this link but strive to use the most reliable and valid measures available. The last chapter in this section is by James Parker, who describes a number of important clinical and therapeutic implications of emotional intelligence and related concepts. In particular, these constructs appear to be related to various psychotherapy outcome variables.

References

Bar-On, R. (1997b). *BarOn Emotional Quotient Inventory (EQ-i): Technical manual.* Toronto, Canada: Multi-Health Systems.

Goleman, D. (1995). *Emotional intelligence.* New York: Bantam Books.

Taylor, G. J., Bagby, R. M., & Parker, J. D. A. (1997). *Disorders of affect regulation.* Cambridge, U.K.: Cambridge University Press.

Thorndike, E. L. (1920). Intelligence and its uses. *Harper's Magazine, 140,* 227–235.

PART ONE

CONCEPTUALIZATION
OF KEY CONSTRUCTS

CHAPTER ONE

Social Intelligence

The Development and Maintenance of Purposive Behavior

Sabrina Zirkel

INTRODUCTION

The concept of social intelligence provides a way of understanding individual personality and social behavior. The central thesis of the social intelligence perspective is that people are reflective, thinking beings and their behavior can be understood in terms of the ways that they actively seek to engage in their social environment and pursue desired outcomes in the important domains of their lives (see also Cantor & Kihlstrom, 1987, 1989; Cantor et al., 1991; Cantor, Norem, Niedenthal, Langston, & Brower, 1987; Cantor & Zirkel, 1990). Social intelligence is a model in which it is presumed that researchers can best understand people if investigations focus on the adaptive and purposive aspects of behavior and it is assumed that individuals are actively trying to make sense of the world in which they live and are directing their behavior accordingly (Cantor & Zirkel, 1990). Such research is related to work in the areas of multiple intelligences and emotional intelligence in that people's behavior is best understood in terms of its adaptability and functionality (Gardner, 1983; Goleman, 1994; Saarni, 1999). In this framework, we focus our attention on what people are "trying to do"—attending more to the goals and plans they are pursuing than to simple assessments of their behavior (see also Cantor, 1990). In concentrating on the relation between motivation and behavior and the processes by which individuals work toward desired outcomes, we can make sense of people in a way that we cannot if we focus simply on broad behavioral tendencies, such as aggressiveness.

A social intelligence model presumes several core assumptions about human behavior. First, behavior is *purposive* and *strategic*, that is, it is oriented toward the achievement of some purpose or goal. Studies of the development of goal-directed or planful behavior have revealed that in their third year, children develop the ability to direct their behavior toward desired outcomes (Lysyuk, 1998). Focusing on what people are "trying to do" has proven a powerful framework for understanding their actions (see Cantor, 1990 and Cantor & Zirkel, 1990 for reviews). Second, people are *active* rather than passive participants in their own lives. They actively interpret the meaning of their social surroundings and the opportunities and risks presented to them. Third, behavior is inherently *social* and *contextualized* in that all action takes place within a given cultural context in which actions take on socially defined meanings. Theoretical work in the area of cultural psychology has helped us articulate how cultural frames of reference shape our behavior in important ways (see Markus & Kitayama, 1991; Shweder & Sullivan, 1990; Triandis, 1997). Fourth, behavior is *developmental* in that individuals (and by extension, the societies comprising those individuals) make sense of their own lives within a given framework that defines appropriate behaviors, tasks, and goals in terms of a person's place or stage in the life cycle (see Elder, 1974, 1975, 1985, 1998; Sroufe, 1996; Sroufe, Carlson, Levy, & Egeland, 1999). Finally, the social intelligence perspective places a premium on *cognition* in that people's adaptive efforts are creative and imaginative, which can be most easily seen in people's ability to cognitively transform their surroundings and the meanings they attach to them (Cantor & Norem, 1989; Mischel, Shoda, & Rodriguez, 1989; Showers & Cantor, 1985).

Comprehensive reviews of the theoretical basis of the social intelligence perspective can be found elsewhere (Cantor, 1990; Cantor & Kihlstrom, 1987, 1989), and so a thorough articulation of this view is neither needed here nor possible within the space limitations of this chapter. Instead, I begin with a brief review of the intellectual roots of social intelligence, followed by a review of how the social intelligence perspective can provide a framework for our understanding of current research in the areas of goal and identity development.

HISTORICAL ROOTS

Social intelligence has its historical roots in the traditions of Kelly (1955), Rogers (1961), Rotter (1966, 1975), and the "new look" movement of the 1950s (see Bruner, 1990). In his theory of personality, Kelly (1955) proposed a model in which one's anticipation of events, or expectations, play the central role in determining one's behavior. His model is cognitive to the core, placing its emphasis on the expectations, interpretations, and "personal constructs," or schemas, one brings to one's understandings about the way the world works. In Kelly's model, behavior can best be understood to originate in these cognitive processes and in the understandings that individuals develop concerning the social world in which they live. Similarly, Rotter (1966, 1975) placed a premium on understanding the opportunities individuals perceive in their surroundings. He transformed the researchers' question from, What do I see is possible for this person in this situation, and how can that help me to understand him? to, What does the *individual* see as possible for *himself or herself* in this situation, and how can *that* help me to understand him or her? Similarly, Thorndike's (1905) "law of effect" is an important part of the social intelligence perspective: the focus is less on the behavior itself and more on the effect it is designed to produce. The "new look" of the 1950s (G. A. Miller, Galanter, & Pribram, 1960) and the "new, new look" (Bruner, 1990) demonstrated the ways in which individuals' own creative power of interpretation plays an important role in their understanding of the world in which they live and the behavior that results from that understanding. The social intelligence model presumes this creativity and places emphasis on individuals' interpretations of situations and their cognitive reframing of problems in need of solution. Roger's (1961) trust in the transformative potential of individuals is also inherent in the social intelligence perspective. By linking behavior to the social context and the individuals' understanding of that social context, social intelligence is a model in which peoples' potential for change and increasing adaptiveness are of central importance (see also Cantor & Kihlstrom, 1987, 1989).

In personality psychology, there is a long tradition of looking at motivation and purpose when trying to understand individuals. The focus of theorists in this area has been to look behind the behavior to the outcomes that the behavior is directed at achieving, including the fulfillment of basic human needs such as sexual gratification (Freud, 1940/1989), affiliation, achievement, autonomy, and intimacy (Atkinson, 1981; McClelland & Koestner, 1992; Murray, 1938). These theorists have focused their attention on what people were trying to achieve rather than on the specific behaviors they engaged in to achieve that end, and the social intelligence perspective draws heavily on such models of human behavior.

CURRENT RESEARCH: GOALS, PLANS, AND PURPOSIVE BEHAVIOR

This chapter is primarily a review of the current psychological literature from the perspective of social intelligence just outlined. In particular I focus on the ways that an understanding of social intelligence can inform our comprehension of purposive behavior, and the discussion centers on four themes. First is a review of a series of studies that contribute to our understanding of the assessments that individuals make of their environment, and how these assessments affect their perceptions of the opportunities and risks in "taking on" different goals. Next is a review of the larger social and developmental context in which goal setting takes place. To what extent can we see our goals or tasks as being defined by our culture and the biologically and socially defined tasks of a given developmental stage? The third section concerns the role of the self and identity in purposive behavior. I review studies that indicate the ways we use goals to define and solidify our sense of self or identity. Finally, in the last section I concentrate on the strategies people use to achieve their goals.

Goal Development: Assessment of Opportunities and Risks

People use cues from their environment to judge what kinds of goals and opportunities to pursue—which are likely to lead to good outcomes and which are not. One aspect of goal formation is making an assessment of the likelihood of success in achieving that goal and the costs such success would entail. Sometimes the processes by which people choose which goals to pursue are quite conscious and rational. For example, many undergraduates think carefully about their choice of major: Will this area of study give me satisfaction? Will I be good at it? What kinds of job opportunities are likely? Other times, our choices are anything but conscious or rational. There may not even be any clear decision point. In reflecting on such decisions, we sometimes say things like, I just always knew, or, I don't know; I never really thought about it. Nevertheless, a close examination of these less consciously thought-through decisions often reveals implicit reasoning processes based on our own understanding of the world. In this section, I review a wide range of research on the adoption of goals and plans. In these studies, a careful assessment of individuals' internal beliefs or aspects of the social world in which they live showed that these influence their perceptions of the opportunities and risks inherent in choosing different paths. These assessments—both conscious and unconscious—in turn shaped the development of different goals or pursuits.

Learning Orientations. In an extensive series of studies, Dweck and her colleagues (Dweck, 1996; Dweck, Chiu, & Hong, 1995; Mueller & Dweck, 1998) have demonstrated that we can understand much about the kind and amount of effort people put into learning and achievement if we assess some of their beliefs about intelligence. Two distinctly different orientations to the meaning inherent in learning and performance situations were identified. People with a "learning" orientation to intelligence perceive intellectual prowess to be a function of learning and make no assumption that any individual performance is a measure of that intelligence or one's worth as a person. Because the "learners" presume that intellectual growth is both possible and typical, performance situations are not threatening. Instead, they are seen as an opportunity to assess one's current knowledge and plan future learning.

In contrast, those with an "entity" orientation to intelligence believe that intelligence is primarily a fixed attribute that individuals are either born with or come to very early in life. Intelligence is assumed to be a measurable, and fairly constant, attribute of the person, rather than something that grows and develops with effort and new learning. This means performance situations—situations in which one's intelligence might be assessed—are risky and threatening and thus are to be avoided if at all possible. Because intellectual assessments can provide only a measure of one's worth or intellect, rather than a measure of one's potential, the risks presented by the possibility of a less than perfect performance are enormous. Thus, a "learning" orientation is likely to lead to the adoption of learning goals, with intermediate assessments of performance along the way, whereas an "entity" orientation is likely to lead to an attempt to have few, relatively low-risk performance opportunities and fewer learning goals.

These orientations can be clearly connected back to early experiences in which children learn to presume that adults expect that a good performance is indicative of either a good effort or a high intelligence (Mueller & Dweck, 1998). When children were praised for their intelligence rather than their efforts, there was a negative impact on their achievement motivation. The implication of a message about intelligence rather than effort seems to be that intelligence is some predetermined aspect of the self—rather than the effort one puts into learning—that people care about. This message undermines young people's sense that their success is something that they are responsible for and can influence. Moreover, when children who were praised for intelligence rather than effort did fail in an activity, this failure had debilitating effects; they withdrew effort very easily and showed less enjoyment of the activity in question. Together, these data suggest both the power of beliefs and the risks of an "entity" orientation to intelligence because, from the beginning, these attitudes do not encourage the development of goals, and they allow people very little resilience for a rebound after a poor performance.

Similarly, Ryan and Pintrich (1997) found young adolescents' willingness to ask for help from teachers was related to their own beliefs about the implications that a request for help would have on teachers' and peers' perceptions of their ability. Perceived costs or threats that were predictive of not asking for help included the belief that "a need for help is construed as evidence of low ability and thus will incur negative reactions or judgments from others" (p. 333). Students made internal assessments of the costs and benefits of asking for help and weighed the learning they would gain against the potential costs to self-esteem that they perceived would result from asking for help. Moreover, these effects held regardless of students' actual competence in math, as measured by standardized tests, indicating that students' perceptions of the social costs of asking for help were not dependent on any actual assessment of their own ability in this domain.

Academic Identification and the Development of Achievement Goals

Researchers exploring the academic achievements of women and members of ethnic minority groups have focused their attention on the origins and development of students' goals and plans and on the development of achievement-oriented or academic identities. Steele (1997) and Eccles (1989; Eccles & Jacobs, 1986) noted that ethnic and gender differences in academic achievement do not exist in the early years of schooling; they emerge, instead, later—after extended periods of time in school. Several different but related lines of research and theoretical work in this area have begun to help us explain how ethnic and gender differences in achievement emerge. At the center of the theoretical framework of this research is the idea that all students do not face the same "situation" in school and that the experiences of young women and minority students differ in important ways from the experiences of majority men.

Several research programs (Steele, 1997) have documented the increased risks or threats that students of color face in academic situations. For example, students of color have to assess if academic or achievement situations are likely to be a place where they are welcomed, or if committing to such goals is likely to lead to a cold and lonely life in which they spend all their time in a place where they are "not wanted." In a longitudinal study of early adolescence, I found that for students of color, investment in academic goals and academic work could be directly tied to the extent to which those students felt that school was a place where they felt welcome and one where they could expect to find friends (Zirkel, 1999a). Specifically, their commitment to and perceptions of the value of school and schoolwork were positively correlated with the number of school friends they reported having. Among students of color, the number of friends at school a student reported was strongly and positively related to the number of achievement goals he or she reported and to how important, fun, and easy he or she reported working on academic tasks to be. This pattern did not hold for European American students, for whom friendships at school were correlated with their appraisals of their social goals rather than their assessments of the importance and feasibility of academic goals.

Steele (1997, 1999) articulated the ways that negative stereotypes provide a specific threat to those to whom they refer. He called this threat a *stereotype threat*, that is, the threat that stereotyped individuals feel at the prospect of confirming a negative stereotype as self-characteristic. Steele and Aronson (1995) noted "the existence of such a stereotype means that anything one does or any of one's features that conform to it make the stereotype more plausible as a self-characterization in the eyes of others, and perhaps even in one's own eyes"

(p. 797). In a comprehensive series of experiments, Steele and his colleagues (Spencer, Steele, & Quinn, 1999; Steele, 1997, 1999; Steele & Aronson, 1995) demonstrated the costs that this threat poses for members of stigmatized groups. When negative stereotypes about intellectual performance (for African American students) or mathematical ability (for women) were primed so that they were present in consciousness, members of the stigmatized group showed impaired performance relative to when these stereotypes were not present. Earlier experiments conducted by Gougis (1986) also demonstrated that performance by African American participants was negatively affected by the presence of discriminatory or racist messages.

Further research has explored whether this decrement in performance can be experimentally induced in participants who belong to groups that do not typically experience negative stereotypes in the relevant domain. Steele and his colleagues (Aronson et al., 1999) were able to elicit a decrement in performance (relative to students' own baseline performance) in male European American students by invoking stereotypes about the superior mathematical ability of their Asian American peers.

Shih, Pittinsky, and Ambady (1999) conducted two follow-up studies to this work; they tested whether positive and negative stereotypes could be primed at different times in the same individual and whether priming the two stereotypes would influence performance. These studies demonstrated that a high-ability group of Asian American women showed higher math performance (relative to their own baseline) when their Asian American identity was activated and positive stereotypes about the ability of Asian American students were made salient. The same group of participants showed lower performance (again, relative to their own baseline) when their identity as women was activated and negative stereotypes about women's mathematical ability were made salient. A replication of this study was conducted in Canada, because Canadians do not possess a parallel stereotype about the superior mathematical abilities of Asian Canadian students relative to other Canadian students. In the Canadian version of the study, the priming of Asian Canadian students' identity as Asian did not have the same positive effect on performance that it had for Asian American students, thus confirming that when stereotypes are present in a culture, they can have a powerful effect on performance.

These studies demonstrate the importance of stigmatization with regard to our understanding of the academic performance of different groups of students. Steele (1997) and Steele and Aronson (1998) noted two implications of this finding: (1) it provides a means for understanding the increasing gap between minority and majority students the longer they stay in school (as the stakes grow higher and the stereotypes clearer throughout students' development), and (2) it demonstrates one of the processes by which minority students (and, in different situations, women) may withdraw their efforts from certain academic domains (because this withdrawal is a means of protecting oneself from the threat of confirming a stereotype).

Eccles (1989; Eccles & Jacobs, 1986) argued that as women and girls think about the opportunities presented by math and science, they worry about the implications for the self of pursuing advanced studies in these areas. She noted that girls perform as well or better than boys in math and science until the point at which these courses become voluntary. Once voluntary, girls drop out of advanced math and science classes in large numbers, and they never catch up. These high school choices, in turn, lead to difficult barriers to a math or science major in college. As in Steele's (1997) analysis of African American students reviewed in the preceding paragraph, Eccles pointed out that a psychologically based rather than an ability-based explanation is required to account for this pattern. In trying to understand the process by which capable young girls choose to forgo coursework in math and science—areas in which they have succeeded—she suggested that we must attend to the social context in which these choices are made. Specifically, she argued that some girls see the implications of a career in math or science as having negative implications for their identity, and that concerns about stereotypes of the "cold" scientist or the "geeky" mathematician conflict with many young girls' sense of who they want to be. Thus, pursuing majors in these fields presents particular challenges—a different kind of stereotype threat—for young women that young men do not face.

I found a similar pattern in a longitudinal study of women in engineering, a field with a very low percentage of women (Zirkel, 2000). Many women left the field between college and their late thirties, and women who stayed in engineering were largely able to do so only by developing an identity different from the "typical" engineer, who they perceived as cold, insincere, and lacking in creativity and initiative. Men, in contrast, did not show this pattern; they had more positive perceptions of the typical engineer, and most saw themselves as relatively like the typical engineer. Women developed something akin to what Ogbu (1988, 1991) and Gibson and Ogbu (1991) referred to as an "oppositional culture" (see the following discussion): the women denigrated the orientations and values of the dominant "culture" of engineering, positioning themselves "in opposition to" those values by arguing for the relative merits of a different value system. Some took this opposition to the point of leaving the profession altogether, sometimes intentionally choosing something very different (for example, nursing). Others were able to keep an oppositional stance *within* the profession.

John Ogbu, an anthropologist, has conducted ethnographic studies of adolescent identity development, as well as cross-cultural studies of the relationship between stigma and intellectual achievement (Gibson & Ogbu, 1991; Ogbu, 1991). He has found a consistent pattern across the world in which members of stigmatized minority groups perform less well on measures of intellectual ability, regardless of their status and performance in other cultures where they do not experience stigmatization.

In his work with African American adolescents in the United States, he has focused more concretely on the strategies young people use to cope with this stigma and the cultural expectations that they have less potential than nonstigmatized, "white" adolescents. One strategy he has identified includes the development of an oppositional culture, based loosely on the logic of the statement, If they don't want me, I don't want them. In other words, one response to the social stigma of racism is to opt out of the relevant domain—in this case, schooling (see also Steele, 1997, 1999 regarding disidentification). In this model, a focus on school, achievement, and expectations about pursuing higher education are dismissed as "white" pursuits, not for "us." This attitude, Ogbu argues, develops at least in part from a real assessment of the barriers such students face in high school, college, and professional life after college. Some African American students, of course, do choose to adopt achievement goals, and Ogbu argued that these students sometimes need to develop a range of strategies to avoid looking as if they are trying to "act white." Such strategies include, but are not limited to, hiding one's interest in school; making sure one doesn't stick out by raising one's hand in class; not staying after school; and making sure that more traditionally African American school-related pursuits (for example, sports) are also adopted. Still others work to find a way of defining academic achievement as a "black" pursuit, to directly counter the idea that adopting such goals represents "acting white." This work identified some of the issues and concerns that nonstigmatized students do not face as they make choices about where to invest their energies. It highlights some of the threats or risks faced by racially stigmatized students and also reviews some of the strategies such students have used to overcome those threats. The model is a powerful one for highlighting the ways that individuals can bring their own creative social intelligence to bear in a difficult and stressful situation to address questions that have no easy answers.

Examining the threats or risks inherent for some in adopting achievement goals is only one way of examining how individuals use cues from their social world to make choices about which goals to adopt and which to avoid. Alternatively, one might look for the cues that tell people that these same goals might have *positive* implications. The study of the relationship between friendships at school and the adoption of academic goals by students of color could be turned around and examined in this way: friendships at school provide a positive indicator of one of the positive aspects of adopting such goals (Zirkel, 1999a).

In my own study of early adolescent development described here, students indicated whether they had a race-and-gender role model. This was measured by their indication of whether they knew someone of the same gender and ethnicity who worked in an area in which they would like to work someday. In this way, the measurement of their role models was idiographically centered on their own professional ambitions, no matter what those ambitions were. Overall, about half of the sample reported having a race- and gender-matched role model defined in this way. All students—but particularly students of color—who reported having a race- and gender-matched role model were more likely to indicate an interest in and motivation to pursue academic goals, were more likely to rate such goals as important and enjoyable, and performed better in their academic work in subsequent school years (Zirkel, 1999b). I interpreted these matched role models as a concrete measure of the extent to which these young people saw positive outcomes as possible for them, and matched role models appeared to provide students with an incentive to invest themselves and their energy in academic pursuits.

Cultural and Developmental Context of Goal Development

Two of the most important influences on the development and patterning of individuals' goals are the cultural context in which one operates and the culturally defined, age-graded definitions of the patterning of life span development. Each culture defines the developmental trajectory of the life course, defining stages, or "ages," each with its own defining goals or developmental tasks. An examination of "what people are trying to do" necessitates that we pay careful attention to both the life stage and culture in which this behavior occurs.

Erikson. Whereas many theorists have noted the developmental nature of personality, Erikson (1950/1963) was one of the first and most thorough at identifying stages of life span development and clarifying the relationship between development and the age-graded tasks or goals that arise out of different developmental stages. In this model, each life stage presents a set of corresponding developmental tasks or goals. For example, Erikson (1950/1963) noted that early infancy is focused on the development of basic trust, adolescence is associated with the development of identity, middle adulthood is concerned with generativity, and later life is focused on ego integrity. Erikson argued that "the human personality in principle develops according to steps predetermined in the growing person's readiness to be driven toward, to be aware of, and to interact with a widening social radius" (p. 270). Thus, identity becomes the focus of the life stage during which young people are asked to make decisions about occupational goals, and ego integrity is the concern of later life when concerns about mortality and the tying together of one's life become salient.

Several researchers have empirically tested Erikson's proposed patterns and the development of different goals at set points in the course of life. Much attention has been given to an examination of the development of identity in adolescence and young adulthood. Although the precise stages by which Erikson argued we develop that identity have not held up to empirical tests, the notion that identity negotiation is particularly important in adolescence and early adulthood has stayed relatively constant (Baumeister, 1986, 1997; Marcia, 1966; McAdams, 1985, 1993; Zirkel, 1992; Zirkel & Brown, 1999; Zirkel & Cantor, 1990). McAdams (1998) demonstrated in several studies that concerns about generativity and caring for the next generation emerge strongly in midlife. Stewart and McAdams and their colleagues (Helson & Stewart, 1994; Mansfield & McAdams, 1996; Peterson & Stewart, 1996; Stewart & Ostrove, 1998; Stewart & Vandewater, 1998) provided extensive documentation of Erikson's patterning of developmental tasks in both idiographic case studies and nomothetically oriented studies of the typical patterning of goals and concerns across the life span.

Other theorists have, however, argued that Erikson missed the culturally bound nature of the stages he identified. Several (Gilligan, 1982; Helson, Pals, & Soloman, 1997; J. B. Miller, 1986) have noted that the developmental path of women may differ from that of men. Differences in the early developmental experiences of boys and girls (see Chodorow, 1978) may, for example, lead women to approach the task of intimacy before that of identity, a reverse of the order Erikson proposes (Gilligan, 1982). Helson and her colleagues (Helson, Mitchell, & Moane, 1984; Helson, et al., 1997) noted that differences in the normative expectations about women's and men's lives may lead to differences in their "social clocks," or the organization and timing of the developmental tasks they face.

Historical Context of Goal Development. Stewart and Healy (1989) and Elder (1975, 1998) have provided elegant arguments for the position that an understanding of developmental tasks and goals must also take into account historical and cultural influences on individual development. Historical events such as the Great Depression of the 1930s and cultural changes such as those prompted by the women's movement of the 1960s and 1970s are also important in the shaping of personality and goals. Those who experience such changes during adolescence and early adulthood (when much of adult identity is formed) show dramatic changes in the nature and kind of goals they pursue. For example, Stewart and Healy (1989) demonstrated that women who were born in the 1950s, and who thus experienced the women's movement during their teens and twenties, were far more affected by that experience than were women who were born earlier (and thus formed some of their core goals and values before the women's movement) or later (and thus formed their core goals and values in a world in which many more opportunities for women were taken for granted). Similarly, in a classic study of the psychological effects of surviving the depression, those who went through the depression as adults were less likely to have it shape every aspect of their lives as were those who experienced it at an earlier point in their lives (Elder, 1998; Stewart & Healy, 1989).

Culture and the Development of Goals and Orientations. In the 1990s, psychologists displayed a resurgence of interest in understanding the relationship between culture and personality. Early work in the area of culture and personality focused on cross-cultural assessments of personality, that is, looking for broad differences between peoples of different cultures. Interest in this area lessened for several decades because many expressed the concern that the analyses the work provided seemed fragmented and did not contribute to a theoretically driven whole that would help us understand either personality or development in a coherent way (see Shweder & Sullivan, 1990). Subsequent work in the area, which is now often referred to as cultural psychology rather than cross-cultural psychology, focused on using cultural differences to answer basic questions about the way people think, define themselves, and organize their social relationships (see Goldberger & Veroff, 1995; Kitayama & Markus, 1994; Kitayama, Markus, & Lieberman, 1995; Markus & Kitayama, 1991; Miller, 1997, 1999; Shweder & Sullivan, 1990; Triandis, 1997).

One of the core cultural differences that has been explored concerns the extent to which a given culture is oriented toward individuality and independence or collectivity and interdependence (see Crocker, Luhtanen, Blaine, Broadnax, 1994; Markus & Kitayama, 1991; Miller, 1997, 1999; Triandis, 1997). In these analyses, Western cultures are seen as more oriented toward individuality and independence, whereas Eastern cultures are seen as more oriented toward collectivity and interdependence. This difference in emphasis on independence versus interdependence is interesting in its own right, but it's importance in this chapter stems from the ways this difference in orientations shapes the goals, values, interpretations of events, and affective experience of members of these different cultures. Markus and Kitayama (1991) demonstrated in a series of studies how our very conceptions of what is self and what is other are shaped by this cultural frame. In other studies Kitayama and Markus (1994) have also established that our sense of what is right and wrong, desirable and undesirable—and thus our affective experience—is also shaped by these two cultural frames. Similarly, Miller and her colleagues (Miller, 1997) conducted a series of experiments in India and the United States illustrating that these independent and interdependent cultural frames shape our evaluations of responsibility and accountability.

In a different vein, those operating in cultures with different expectations and experiences will encounter different developmental demands, and thus the structure and nature of the life tasks associated with their respective stages will also vary. For example, the "identity versus role confusion" developmental task identified by Erikson (1950/1963) presumes a Western industrial society in which young people are expected to make choices about their professional paths and the goals and values they adopt. Such a task will not hold the same power in a preindustrial world in which young people are expected to take on more prescribed roles (see also Baumeister, 1997). Thus, the very nature and meaning of development and the appropriateness and relevance of different goals vary with the cultural framework in which one lives.

Self-Definition, Identity, and Goals

Goals represent a fundamental means by which we develop, solidify, maintain, and protect our sense of identity and self. In this section I review studies that inform our understanding of the ways that goals and identity confirm one another. In this research we can see some of the ways that purposive behavior helps to define our own sense of who we are: we are not just a particular person or kind of person, rather, we are persons striving toward some ideal. In these identity goals, we can see the ways in which individuals use their environment to shape themselves and use their conceptions of themselves to shape and give meaning to the world around them. Some goal constructs (such as possible selves) are inextricably linked to self and identity. Possible selves are essentially goals represented as images of the self projected into the future (Markus & Nurius, 1986; Markus & Ruvolo, 1989). Identity and conceptions of the self are, in fact, defined by the goals one chooses to adopt or not adopt. We also saw some examples of this process in the studies (previously described) of the development achievement goals of stigmatized students. Some of the theorists whose work is reviewed in this section speak of some of the more concrete means by which we define our identities through our goals—by adopting the dress, manners, attitudes, and "props" of those we are trying to become (see Gollwitzer & Wicklund, 1985). Identities and identity-related goals provide a means for linking cognition and motivation (Gollwitzer & Bargh, 1996).

Possible Selves. Markus and Nurius's (1986) possible selves are concrete depictions of anticipated outcomes for the self that inform our current actions. Possible selves "represent individuals' sense of what they might become, what they would like to become, and what they are afraid of becoming, and thus provide a conceptual link between cognition and motivation" (p. 954). In a wide-ranging series of studies, the content of individuals' possible selves was shown to have implications for the achievement of children (Day, Borkowski, Punzo, & Howespian, 1994; Leondari, Syngollitou, & Kiosseoglou, 1998) and adults (Ruvolo & Markus, 1992), career planning (Chalk, Meara, & Day, 1994; Freeman, 1997; Meara, Day, Chalk, & Phelps, 1995), and problem-solving and persistence in goal-directed behavior (Cross & Markus, 1994). Several studies have shown that as with other goal constructs, individuals' possible selves change throughout the life course as the developmental demands faced in different stages of the life course present changes in the goals people pursue (Cross & Markus, 1991; Hooker & Kaus, 1994).

Self-Identifications. Goals can be self-defining—forming a core aspect of our identity or self (Carroll, Durkin, Hattie, & Houghton, 1997; Gollwitzer & Kirchhof, 1998). King (1998) introduced the concept of "life dreams" as coherent frames within which more proximal goals are used to direct energies toward fulfilling more long-term goals. These life dreams can serve as a source of personal agency and meaning in life and are directly related to subjective well-being and life satisfaction. We can see this in something as simple and seemingly meaningless as allowing the young premedical student to wear a lab coat when participating in an experiment, and the corresponding rise in self-esteem this causes (Steele, 1988). "Identity goals," as Gollwitzer (Gollwitzer & Brandstatter, 1997; Gollwitzer & Kirchhof, 1998) refers to them, are enduring over time, and their function is more about guiding behavior and choices than about achieving a specific end.

Identities form a means by which we locate ourselves within our social environment. They are both public and private, providing a link between how we see ourselves and how we present ourselves to the world. We exert great energy to manage the impressions we make to others in the service of protecting those identities (Schlenker, Britt, & Pennington, 1996). Schlenker and his colleagues argued convincingly that impression management is not "superficial, deceptive, or an afterthought" (Schlenker, et al., p. 646), rather, it is precisely the means by which we place ourselves within self-defining social circles and solidify those values and goals we have identified as important.

Protecting Identities in the Face of Failure. Given the value and importance we place on our identities, it is not surprising that we will go to great lengths to protect them. Although we are responsive to our social environments, we are not slavishly so. We do not easily let go of important self-conceptions; instead, we exert effort to protect them. This protection is often active and functional rather than self-deceptive and manipulative. Both Brunstein and Gollwitzer (1996) and Zirkel (2000) have shown that when important identities are threatened by a failure experience, people will perform even better than their standard on subsequent tasks. In one set of studies, these effects could be demonstrated to be the result of increased persistence and effort on the subsequent task, implying that when important identities are threatened, people step up their efforts, perform better, and thus consolidate the identity rather than relinquish it. It would not be very adaptive to give up important and self-defining goals at the very first sign of failure; most long-range goals require extended effort and persistence through both relatively successful periods and through more difficult times. Deaux and Ethier (1998; Ethier & Deaux, 1994) have identified a similar process when a cultural identity is threatened. They have documented that when Latino students with a strong cultural identity enter an Ivy League school, they exert effort to keep their cultural identity intact by joining relevant groups and engaging in culturally relevant activities. On the less adaptive side, Swann and his colleagues (Swann, 1987; Swann, Hixon, & de la Ronde, 1992) have shown that people work hard to protect even negative identities. A series of laboratory and field studies showed that people will choose people and activities that confirm identities that are familiar and negative even over those that are positive but unfamiliar.

Strategies for Goal Achievement

The social intelligence perspective also speaks to the *means* by which people work toward their goals. A central tenet of the social intelligence model is that behavior is *strategic,* that behavior can best be understood to be in the service of purposes, and that if behavior does not seem to make sense on the surface, it often does when examined in the context of the individuals' own knowledge of their strengths and weaknesses and the goals they wish to accomplish. This section focuses on strategies people use to achieve those outcomes identified as desirable in the processes just described.

Defensive Pessimism. In a series of studies including lab experiments, field experiments, and longitudinal field research, Norem and her colleagues (Cantor et al., 1987; Norem & Cantor, 1986a, 1986b; Norem & Illingsworth, 1993; Showers, 1992) identified and outlined the strategy of defensive pessimism. Some people with a history of success and for whom success in a given domain is an important goal find that as they approach new challenges, the best way to manage their anxiety is to anticipate and prepare for each possible problem that could occur. Research documenting the merits of an optimistic approach to life and stressful situations would suggest that pessimistically focusing on every possible bad outcome in a stressful situation would be a poor strategy for achieving desired outcomes (see Taylor & Brown, 1988). However, this presumes that the only "goal" is the stated outcome one is working toward, such as getting good grades, solving problems in an experiment, or winning a competition. The social intelligence perspective assumes that people's efforts make sense, and those studying defensive pessimism have found that defensive pessimists have a parallel goal of managing anxiety. By using their pessimist thinking-through of all possible "worst case scenarios," they are able to manage that anxiety and use it to fuel increased efforts toward the "stated" or overt goal. Moreover, when defensive pessimists are encouraged to "think positively," their strategy is undermined and their performance suffers as a result. Showers (1992) demonstrated that this strategy can also be used in the social domain, which is an area where greater effort does not show such a direct link to better performance. In this study, social defensive pessimists who were encouraged to use the pessimistic strategy performed better in conversations than did pessimists who were discouraged from thinking about what could go wrong and instead were encouraged to "think positively."

Self-Handicapping. Self-handicapping is a strategy that received substantial attention in the 1980s and 1990s (see Higgins, Snyder & Berglas, 1990, for a review). Self-handicapping refers to situations in which a person develops an excuse for a poor performance in advance of the actual performance itself. Examples are many and include staying out late and getting drunk the night before the SAT exams or other major exam and not studying for an exam. Those who use this strategy do so as a means of protecting self-esteem: because of the (albeit self-inflicted) handicap, a poor or less than ideal performance does not really reflect badly on one's abilities. In other words, the self-handicapper can maintain the belief that he or she could have done well on the test or other performance if only he or she had gotten enough sleep the night before, had studied, or had otherwise been better prepared. Self-handicapping also holds open the possibility of the boost to self-esteem that would result should the individual be able to perform well *despite* the handicap. The person who gets drunk the night before his or her SAT exams and *still* performs well may fantasize about how *amazingly* well he or she might have done without a hangover and with more sleep.

Self-handicapping serves both a public and a private function; it is sometimes a public performance one puts on for others, sometimes a private performance strictly for one's own internal benefit, and sometimes both. It is also possible to use the public aspect of self-handicapping (excuse making) without actually engaging in the self-destructive behavior. One can announce that one "hardly studied" for the exam, thereby creating an excuse in case one's performance is a disappointment, even if one actually did study quite hard. Of course, such a strategy is not self-protective in the sense that one has shielded oneself from the truth; the individual must internally, at least, accept the poor performance as an accurate measure of his or her abilities.

Clearly, self-handicapping represents one of the most potentially costly strategies one could choose. It can help protect one's self-esteem, but at the cost of risking poor performances in a very real way. Moreover, those events that are most threatening to self-esteem, for example, taking a major exam, an important sports event, or taking an SAT or graduate entrance exam, are the situations that are most likely to invite self-handicapping *and* those that are most likely to have the highest costs as a consequence of a poor performance caused by the handicap. However, the use of this strategy has been linked to implicit beliefs about intelligence and ability that are similar to those identified by Dweck and her colleagues described earlier, and thus the potential risks of an "unprotected" poor performance are also quite high. Rhodewalt (1994) has demonstrated that self-handicappers are more likely to hold beliefs that approximate the "entity" models of intelligence described by Dweck and are more likely to see performances as a demonstration of a rather fixed ability level. For those who hold such beliefs but are very uncertain of their abilities or even suspect that they are not very capable, performance opportunities represent an extremely threatening situation.

It seems less emotionally costly to risk a performance where one does not expect to perform very well rather than risk the potential costs to self-esteem and identity that putting in a strong effort and not performing well might entail.

Choosing Situations. Another strategy that individuals use to help them achieve their goals and operate effectively in the world is to choose carefully the people they spend time with and the situations or activities that they pursue (Buss, 1987; Ickes, Snyder, & Garcia, 1997; Snyder, 1981). Part of the agenda of social psychology is to document the effects that different situations and social contexts have on the behavior of individuals, whereas part of the agenda of personality psychology is to demonstrate how individuals' behavior can be linked to processes internal to the person (see also Snyder & Cantor, 1998). One area where these two points of view come together is in the documentation of the relationship between individuals' personality or goals and their choices about the situations they choose to spend time in, the ways that they shape the nature of the situations, and what kinds of behavior they elicit from others in their social environment. Essentially, the point being made by these scholars is that although situations may influence individuals' behavior and experience, situations are not randomly distributed. People have a great deal of control over what kinds of situations they engage in. This ability to choose situations has been demonstrated in many areas of life, including, for example, the number and kind of friends one chooses to spend time with (Snyder, 1987), who one dates (Buss, 1987), the kind of job one chooses (Snyder, 1987; Ickes et al., 1997), the affective nature of the situations one chooses or avoids (Emmons, 1986), and the college major one chooses.

Parties represent a clear example of the kind of situation that individuals may choose to enter or avoid. We all have a pretty good idea what to expect at a party and how that experience will differ depending on whether it is a "dance 'til dawn" party or a cocktail party. We also have strong intuitions about what it will mean for our experience to show up at the party alone or with a good friend. And we have choices about all of these different activities. We can decide to go to neither, one, or both of these parties, and we can choose to go alone or with someone else. These choices, moreover, can be linked to our own understanding about ourselves and our expectations about what those different experiences are like. Looking more carefully at the party choices, one can make a choice based solely on what feels comfortable—in which case, the shy person may choose to spend his social time in smaller groups that don't activate that shyness. Or, conversely, the shy person may do the opposite—forcing himself to go to parties, and to even go alone—precisely because he believes this is the only way he can force himself to get out and meet new people.

How people choose the situations in which they want to spend time and focus their energies is a perfect example of social intelligence at work. The research in this area shows that people use their knowledge of themselves and of their social worlds to find appropriate matches between the two. These matches, moreover, may serve any number of functions; situations may be chosen for emotional self-regulation, as a means of expressing and confirming the self, in order to accomplish certain self-relevant goals, or as a means of self-development or personal change. The precise choices individuals make at any given moment, then, are not simple computations of a metric of the fit between the person and the situation. Instead, these decisions represent active choices based on one's own needs, goals, and purposes and one's knowledge of the social world and how to achieve desired ends.

CONCLUSION

Social intelligence can be described as a model of personality and individual behavior in which people are presumed to be knowledgeable about themselves and the social world in which they live. Individuals actively use this knowledge to manage their emotions and direct their behavior toward desired outcomes. This model incorporates work from both personality psychology and social psychology—focusing on individuals in their social contexts—and builds on the traditions laid out by theorists such as George Kelly (1955) and those in the "new look" movement in cognitive psychology (Bruner, 1990).

In this chapter I reviewed the literature of personality and social psychology for examples of the socially intelligent nature of *purposive* behavior. The purposive and essentially adaptive nature of our actions is one of the fundamental assumptions of the social intelligence model. The four main ways to examine purposive behavior are through (1) the assessment of opportunities and risks inherent in the self-defining goals and how this shapes individuals' choices about which goals to pursue, (2) the culturally and developmentally bound nature of goals, (3) the relationship of goals to self-definition and identity and the means by which we protect our important self-conceptions, and (4) the strategies individuals use to pursue important goals, regulate their affective experiences, and achieve desired ends in a wide variety of situations. In this work we see how people actively shape their own lives to achieve the ends that they find meaningful and desirable.

References

Aronson, J., Lustina, M. J., Good, C., Keough, K., Steele, C. M., & Brown, J. (1999). When White men can't do math: Necessary and sufficient factors in stereotype threat. *Journal of Experimental Social Psychology, 35,* 29–46.

Atkinson, J. W. (1981). Studying personality in the context of an advanced motivational psychology. *Psychologist, 32,* 117–129.

Baumeister, R. F. (1986). *Identity: Cultural change and the struggle for self.* New York: Oxford University Press.

Baumeister, R. F. (1997). Identity, self-concept, and self-esteem: The self lost and found. In R. Hogan, J. Johnson, & S. Briggs (Eds.), *Handbook of personality psychology* (pp. 681–710). San Diego, CA: Academic Press.

Bruner, J. (1990). *Acts of meaning.* Cambridge, MA: Harvard University Press.

Brunstein, J. C., & Gollwitzer, P. M. (1996). Effects of failure on subsequent performance: The importance of self-defining goals. *Journal of Personality and Social Psychology, 70,* 395–407.

Buss, D. M. (1987). Selection, evocation, and manipulation. *Journal of Personality and Social Psychology, 53,* 1214–1221.

Cantor, N. (1990). From thought to behavior: "Having" and "doing" in the study of personality ad cognition. *American Psychologist, 45,* 735–750.

Cantor, N., & Kihlstrom, J. (1987). *Personality and social intelligence.* Englewood Cliffs, NJ: Erlbaum.

Cantor, N., & Kihlstrom, J. (1989). Social intelligence and cognitive assessments of personality. In R. S. Wyer & T. K. Srull (Eds.), *Advances in social cognition* (Vol. 2, pp. 1–59). Hillsdale, NJ: Erlbaum.

Cantor, N., & Norem, J. K. (1989). Defensive pessimism and stress and coping. *Social Cognition, 7,* 92–112.

Cantor, N., Norem, J. K., Langston, C. A., Zirkel, S., Fleeson, W., & Cook-Flannagan, C. (1991). Life tasks and daily life experience. Special issue: Personality and daily experience. *Journal of Personality, 59,* 425–451.

Cantor, N., Norem, J. K., Niedenthal, P. M., Langston, C. A., & Bower, A. M. (1987). Life tasks, self-concept ideals, and cognitive strategies in a life transition. *Journal of Personality and Social Psychology, 53,* 1178–1191.

Cantor, N., & Zirkel, S. (1990). Personality, cognition, and purposive behavior. In L. A. Pervin (Ed.), *Handbook of personality: Theory and research* (pp. 135–164). New York: Guilford Press.

Carroll, A., Durkin, K., Hattie, J., & Houghton, S. (1997). Goal setting among adolescents: A comparison of delinquent, at-risk, and not-at-risk youth. *Journal of Educational Psychology, 89,* 441–450.

Chalk, L. M., Meara, N. M., & Day, J. D. (1994). Possible selves and occupational choices. *Journal of Career Assessment, 2,* 364–383.

Chodorow, N. (1978). *The reproduction of mothering: Psychoanalysis and the sociology of gender.* Berkeley, CA: University of California Press.

Crocker, J., Luhtanen, R., Blaine, B., & Broadnax, S. (1994). Collective self-esteem and psychological well-being among White, Black, and Asian college students. *Personality and Social Pscyhology Bulletin, 20,* 503–513.

Cross, S. E., & Markus, H. (1991). Possible selves across the lifespan. *Human Development, 34,* 230–255.

Cross, S. E., & Markus, H. R. (1994). Self-schemas, possible selves, and competent performance. *Journal of Educational Psychology, 86,* 423–438.

Day, J. D., Borkowski, J. G., Punzo, D., & Howespian, B. (1994). Enhancing possible selves in Mexican-American students. *Motivation and Emotion, 18,* 79–103.

Deaux, K., & Ethier, K. A. (1998). Negotiating social identity. In J. K. Swim & C. Stangor (Eds.), *Prejudice: The target's perspective.* San Diego, CA: Academic Press.

Dweck, C. (1996). Implicit theories as organizers of goals and behavior. In P. M. Gollwitzer & J. A. Bargh (Eds.), *The psychology of action: Linking cognition and motivation to behavior* (pp. 69–90). New York: Guilford Press.

Dweck, C., Chiu, C., & Hong, Y. (1995). Implicit theories and their role in judgments and reactions: A world from two perspectives. *Psychological Inquiry, 6,* 267–285.

Eccles, J. S. (1989). Bringing young women to math and science. In M. Crawford & M. Gentry (Eds.), *Gender and thought: Psychological perspectives* (pp. 36–58). New York: Springer-Verlag.

Eccles, J. S., & Jacobs, J. E. (1986). Social factors shape math attitudes and performance. *Signs: Journal of Women in Culture and Society, 11,* 367–380.

Elder, G. H., Jr. (1974). *Children of the Great Depression.* Chicago: University of Chicago Press.

Elder, G. H., Jr. (1975). Age differentiation and the life course. *Annual Review of Sociology, 1,* 165–190.

Elder, G. H., Jr. (1985). Perspectives on the life course. In G. H. Elder Jr. (Ed.), *Life course dynamics: Trajectories and transitions, 1968–1980* (pp. 23–49). Ithaca, New York: Cornell University Press.

Elder, G. H., Jr. (1998). The life course as developmental theory. *Child Development, 69,* 1–12.

Emmons, R. A. (1986). Personal strivings: An approach to personality and subjective well-being. *Journal of Personality and Social Psychology, 51,* 1058–1068.

Erikson, E. H. (1963). *Childhood and society.* New York: Norton. (Original work published 1950)

Ethier, K. A., & Deaux, K. (1994). Negotiating social identity when contexts change: Maintaining identification and responding to threat. *Journal of Personality and Social Psychology, 67,* 243–251.

Freeman, K. (1997). Increasing African Americans' participation in high education: African American high school students' perspectives. *Journal of Higher Education, 68,* 523–550).

Freud, S. (1989). *Outline of psychoanalysis* (James Strachey, Trans.). New York: Norton. (Original work published 1940)

Gardner, H. (1983). *Frames of mind: The theory of multiple intelligences.* New York: Basic Books.

Gibson, M., & Ogbu, J. (1991). *Minority status and schooling.* New York: Garland.

Gilligan, C. (1982). *In a different voice: Psychological theory and women's development.* Cambridge, MA: Harvard University Press.

Goldberger, N. R., & Veroff, J. B. (1995). *The culture and psychology reader.* New York: New York University Press.

Goleman, D. (1994). *Emotional intelligence: Why it can matter more than IQ.* New York: Bantam Books.

Gollwitzer, P. M. (1996). The volitional benefits of planning. In P. M. Gollwitzer & J. A. Bargh (Eds.), *The psychology of action: Linking cognition and motivation to behavior* (pp. 287–312). New York: Guilford Press.

Gollwitzer, P. M., & Bargh, J. A. (Eds.). (1996). *The psychology of action: Linking cognition and motivation to behavior.* New York: Guilford Press.

Gollwitzer, P. M., & Brandstatter, V. (1997). Implementation intentions and effective goal pursuit. *Journal of Personality and Social Psychology, 73,* 186–199.

Gollwitzer, P. M., & Kirchhof, O. (1998). The willful pursuit of identity. In J. Heckhausen & C. S. Dweck (Eds.), *Motivation and self-regulation across the life span* (pp. 389–423). New York: Cambridge University Press.

Gollwitzer, P. M., & Wicklund, R. A. (1985). The pursuit of self-defining goals. In J. Kuhl & J. Beckman (Eds.), *Action control: From cognition to behavior* (pp. 61–85). New York: Springer-Verlag.

Gougis, R. A. (1986). The effects of prejudice and stress on the academic performance of Black Americans. In U. Neisser (Ed.), *The school achievement of minority children: New perspectives* (pp. 145–158). Hillsdale, NJ: Erlbaum.

Helson, R., Mitchell, V., & Moane, G. (1984). Personality and patterns of adherence and non-adherence to the social clock. *Journal of Personality and Social Psychology, 46,* 1079–1096.

Helson, R., Pals, J., & Solomon, M. (1997). Is there adult development distinctive to women? In R. Logan, J., Johnson, & S. Briggs (Eds.), *Handbook of personality psychology* (pp. 291–314). San Diego, CA: Academic Press.

Helson, R., & Stewart, A. J. (1994). Personality change in adulthood. In T. F. Heatherton & J. L. Weinberger (Eds.), *Can personality change?* (pp. 201–225). Washington, DC: American Psychological Association.

Higgins, R. L., Snyder, C. R., & Berglas, S. (1990). *Self-handicapping: The paradox that isn't. The Plenum series of social/clinical psychology.* New York: Plenum Press.

Hooker, K., & Kaus, C. R. (1994). Health-related possible selves in young and middle adulthood. *Psychology and Aging, 9,* 126–133.

Ickes, W., Snyder, M., & Garcia, S. (1997). Personality influences the choice of situations. In R. Logan, J. Johnson, & S. Briggs (Eds.), *Handbook of personality psychology* (pp. 165–195). San Diego, CA: Academic Press.

Kelly, G. A. (1955). *A theory of personality: The psychology of personal constructs.* New York: Norton.

King, L. A. (1998). Personal goals and personal agency: Linking everyday goals to future images of the self. In M. Kofta, G. Weary, & G. Sedek (Eds.), *Personal control in action: Cognitive and motivational mechanisms.* New York: Plenum Press.

Kitayama, S., & Markus, H. R. (1994). *Emotion and culture: Empirical studies of mutual influence.* Washington, DC: American Psychological Association.

Kitayama, S., Markus, H. R., & Lieberman, C. (1995). The collective construction of self-esteem: Implications for culture, self, and emotion. In J. A. Russell, J. M. Fernandez-Dols, A. S. R. Manstead, & J. C. Wellenkamp (Eds.), *Everyday conceptions of emotion: An introduction to the psychology, anthropology, and linguistics of emotion* (pp. 523–550). Dordrecht, Netherlands: Kluwer Academic.

Leondari, A., Syngollitou, E., & Kiosseoglou, G. (1998). Academic achievement, motivation, and possible selves. *Journal of Adolescence, 21,* 219–222.

Lysyuk, L. G. (1998). The development of productive goal-setting with 2- to 4-year-old children. *International Journal of Behavioral Development, 22,* 799–812.

Mansfield, E. D., & McAdams, D. P. (1996). Generativity and themes of agency and communion in adult autobiography. *Personality and Social Psychology Bulletin, 22,* 721–731.

Marcia, J. E. (1966). Development and validation of ego identity status. *Journal of Personality and Social Psychology, 3,* 551–558.

Markus, H. R., & Kitayama, S. (1991). Culture and the self: Implications for cognition, emotion, and motivation. *Psychological Review, 98,* 224–253.

Markus, H., & Nurius, P. (1986). Possible selves. *American Psychologist, 41,* 954–969.

Markus, H. R., & Ruvolo, A. (1989). Possible selves: Personalized representations of goals. In L. A. Pervin (Ed.), *Goals concepts in personality and social psychology* (pp. 211–241). Hillsdale, NJ: Erlbaum.

McAdams, D. P. (1985). *Power, intimacy and the life story: Personological inquires into identity.* New York: Guilford Press.

McAdams, D. P. (1993). *The stories we live by: Personal myths and the making of the self.* New York: Morrow.

McAdams, D. P. (1998). *Generativity and adult development: How and why we care for the next generation.* Washington, DC: American Psychological Association.

McClelland, D.C., & Koestner, R. (1992). The achievement motive. In C. P. Smith, J. W. Atkinson, D. C. McClelland, & J. Veroff (Eds.), *Motivation and personality: Handbook of thematic content analysis.* New York: Cambridge University Press.

Meara, N. M., Day, J. D., Chalk, L. M., & Phelps, R. E. (1995). Possible selves: Applications for career counseling. *Journal of Career Assessment, 3,* 259–277.

Miller, G. A., Galanter, E., & Pribram, K. H. (1960). *Plans and the structure of behavior.* New York: Holt, Rinehart, & Winston.

Miller, J. B. (1986). *Towards a new psychology of women* (2nd ed.). Boston: Beacon Press.

Miller, J. G. (1997). Taking culture into account in social cognitive development. *Psychology and Developing Societies, 9,* 9–34.

Mischel, W., Shoda, Y., & Rodriguez, M. L. (1989). Delay of gratification in children. *Science, 244,* 933–938.

Mueller, C. M., & Dweck, C. S. (1998). Praise for intelligence can undermine children's motivation and performance. *Journal of Personality and Social Psychology, 75,* 33–52.

Murray, H. A. (1938). *Explorations in personality.* New York: Oxford Press.

Norem, J. K., & Cantor, N. (1986a). Anticipatory and post hoc cushioning strategies: Optimism and defensive pessimism. *Cognitive Therapy and Research, 10,* 347–362.

Norem, J. K., & Cantor, N. (1986b). Defensive pessimism: "Harnessing" anxiety as motivation. *Journal of Personality and Social Psychology, 51,* 1208–1217.

Norem, J. K., & Illingsworth, S. (1993). Strategy-dependent effects of reflecting on self and tasks: Some implcations of optimism and defensive pessimism. *Journal of Personality and Social Psychology, 65,* 822–835.

Ogbu, J. U. (1988). Cultural diversity: A human development perspective. *New Directions for Child Development, 42,* 11–28.

Ogbu, J. U. (1991). Minority coping responses and school experience. *The Journal of Psychohistory, 18,* 433–456.

Peterson, B. E., & Stewart, A. J. (1996). Antecedents and contexts of generativity motivation at midlife. *Psychology and Aging, 11,* 21–33.

Rhodewalt, F. (1994). Conceptions of ability, achievement goals, and individual differences in self-handicapping behavior: On the application of implicit theories. *Journal of Personality, 62,* 67–85.

Rogers, C. R. (1961). *On becoming a person* (2nd ed.). Boston: Houghton Mifflin.

Rotter, J. B. (1966). Generalized expectancies for internal versus external control of reinforcement. *Psychological Monographs, 80,* 1–28.

Rotter, J. B. (1975). Some problems and misconceptions related to the construct of internal versus external control of reinforcement. *Journal of Consulting and Clinical Psychology, 40,* 313–321.

Ruvolo, A. P., & Markus, H. R. (1992). Possible selves and performance: The power of self-relevant imagery. Special issue: Self-knowledge: Content, structure, and function. *Social Cognition, 10,* 95–124.

Ryan, A. M., & Pintrich, P. R. (1997). "Should I ask for help?" The role of motivation and attitudes in adolescents' help seeking in math class. *Journal of Educational Psychology, 89,* 329–341.

Saarni, C. (1999). *The development of emotional competence.* New York: Guilford Press.

Schlenker, B., Britt, T. N., & Pennington, J. (1996). Impression regulation and management: Highlights of a theory of self-identification. In R. M. Sorrentino & E. T. Higgins (Eds.), *Handbook of motivation and cognition: Vol. 3. The interpersonal context* (pp. 118–147). New York: Guilford Press.

Shih, M., Pittinsky, T. L., & Ambady, N. (1999). Stereotype susceptibility: Identity salience and shifts in quantitative performance. *Psychological Science, 10,* 80–83.

Showers, C. (1992). The motivational and emotional consequences of considering positive or negative possibilities for an upcoming event. *Journal of Personality and Social Psychology, 63,* 474–484.

Showers, C., & Cantor, N. (1985). Social cognition: A new look at motivated strategies. *Annual Review of Psychology, 36,* 275–305.

Shweder, R. A., & Sullivan, M. A. (1990). The semiotic subject of cultural psychology. In L. A. Pervin (Ed.), *Handbook of personality psychology: Theory and research* (pp. 399–416). New York: Guilford Press.

Snyder, M. (1981). On the influence of individuals on situations. In N. Cantor & J. Kihlstrom (Eds.), *Personality, cognition, and social interaction* (pp. 309–329). Hillsdale, NJ: Erlbaum.

Snyder, M. (1987). *Public appearances/private realities: The psychology of self-monitoring.* New York: Freeman.

Snyder, M., & Cantor, N. (1998). Understanding personality and social behavior: A functionalist strategy. In D. T. Gilbert & S. T. Fiske (Eds.), *The handbook of social psychology* (Vol. 2, 4th ed., pp. 635–679). Boston: McGraw-Hill.

Spencer, S. J., Steele, C. M., & Quinn, D. M. (1999). Stereotype threat and women's math performance. *Journal of Experimental Social Psychology, 35,* 4–28.

Sroufe, L. A. (1996). *Emotional development: The organization of emotional life in the early years. Cambridge studies in social and educational development.* New York: Cambridge University Press.

Sroufe, L. A., Carlson, E. A., Levy, A. K., & Egeland, B. (1999). Implications of attachment theory for developmental psychopathology. *Development and Psychopathology, 11,* 1–13.

Steele, C. M. (1988). The psychological of self-affirmation: Sustaining the integrity of the self. In L. Berkowitz (Ed.), *Advances in experimental social cognition* (Vol. 21, pp. 261–302). New York: Academic Press.

Steele, C. M. (1997). A threat in the air: How stereotypes shape intellectual identity and performance. *American Psychologist, 52,* 613–629.

Steele, C. M. (1999). Thin ice: "Stereotype threat" and black college students. *Atlantic Monthly, 284,* 44–54.

Steele, C. M., & Aronson, J. (1995). Stereotype threat and intellectual test performance of African Americans. *Journal of Personality and Social Psychology, 69,* 797–811.

Steele, C. M., & Aronson, J. (1998). Stereotype threat and the test performance of academically successful African Americans. In C. Jencks & M. Phillips, (Eds.), *The Black-White test score gap* (pp. 401–427). Washington, DC: Brookings Institution.

Stewart, A. J., & Healy, J. (1989). Linking individual development and social change. *American Psychologist, 44,* 30–42.

Stewart, A. J., & Ostrove, J. M. (1998). Women's personality in middle age: Gender, history, and midcourse corrections. *American Psychologist, 53,* 1185–1194.

Stewart, A. J., & Vandewater, E. A. (1998). The course of generativity. In D. P. McAdams & E. de St. Aubin (Eds.), *Generativity and adult development: How and why we care for the next generation* (pp. 75–100). Washington, DC: American Psychological Association.

Swann, W. B., Jr. (1987). Identity negotiation: Where two roads meet. *Journal of Personality and Social Psychology, 53,* 1038–1051.

Swann, W. B., Jr., Hixon, J. G., & de la Ronde, C. (1992). Embracing the bitter "truth": Negative self-concepts and marital commitment. *Psychological Science, 3,* 118–121.

Taylor, S. E., & Brown, J. (1988). Illusion and well-being: Some social psychological contributions to a theory of mental health. *Psychological Bulletin, 103,* 193–210.

Thorndike, E. L. (1905). *The elements of psychology.* New York: A. G. Seiler.

Triandis, H. C. (1997). Cross-cultural perspectives on personality. In R. Hogan, J. Johnson, & S. Briggs (Eds.), *Handbook of personality psychology* (pp. 439–464). San Diego, CA: Academic Press.

Zirkel, S. (1992). Investing the self in the concerns of the day: Developing independence in a life transition. *Journal of Personality and Social Psychology, 62,* 506–521.

Zirkel, S. (1999a). *Is there a place for me? Role models and academic identity among majority and minority youth.* Manuscript submitted for publication.

Zirkel, S. (1999b). *What will you think of me? Social integration and achievement among minority and majority youth.* Manuscript submitted for publication.

Zirkel, S. (2000). *Protecting identities: Persistence in the face of failure.* Unpublished manuscript, Saybrook Graduate School and Research Center, San Francisco.

Zirkel, S., & Brown, D. (1999). *Identity commitment and life satisfaction: Studying commitments over time.* Unpublished manuscript, Saybrook Graduate School and Research Center, San Francisco.

Zirkel, S., & Cantor, N. (1990). Personal construal of a life task: Those who struggle for independence. *Journal of Personality and Social Psychology, 58,* 172–185.

CHAPTER TWO

Social Competence

The Social Construction of the Concept

Keith Topping, William Bremner, and Elizabeth A. Holmes

How to define *social competence* has been a vexing question for decades. Arguments on the issue are often characterized by a lack of shared vocabulary and conceptual frameworks between protagonists. Certainly the whole issue is much more complex than might be assumed by the naive onlooker. This complexity was highlighted decades ago by Bandura (1977, 1986), whose experimental studies indicated that social learning was a function of many variables. Chief among these were attentional, retentional, motor reproduction, and motivational processes.

What is attended to depends on the characteristics of the model, the characteristics of the situational context, and the characteristics of the observer. The selectivity of the observer's attention might be dysfunctional. Having attended, whatever meaning is made of the event might or might not be retained, more or less accurately. Differential efficiency in "social encoding" suggests a "social memory" to parallel the notion of "social intelligence." Beyond this, perceiving and recalling a behavioral constellation does not automatically enable reproduction of all the component behaviors simultaneously, especially in a novel context requiring transfer and generalization of learning. Repeated practice might be necessary to achieve any degree of fluency or automaticity, especially when feedback in response to early attempts is mixed. Even if all the previous processes are mastered, and the socially competent behavior is firmly ensconced within the repertoire of the actor, the motivation for its emission might be absent. This might again depend on the actor's perceptions of the social context and the antecedents and contingencies operating within it. Sometimes different contingencies will be in conflict.

So who can we reliably and validly label "socially incompetent"? Is it those who do not attend to social behavior and situations, those who attend but do not perceive accurately, those who attend and perceive but cannot produce the needed performance, those who attend and perceive and can perform but choose not to do so, or all of them? It seems that social competence comprises multiple variables, each of which varies along a dimension, rather than being categorical in a simple binary way.

Over the years, such questions have preoccupied those who have struggled to define social competence.

SOCIAL COMPETENCE: CONCEPTUAL EVOLUTION

Early attempts to define social competence tended to fixate on social behavior. Later, cognitive and behavioral aspects came to be seen as equally important. Most recently the emotional or affective component has come to greater prominence. Thus current conceptions of social competence give equal weight to the behavioral, cognitive, and affective domains.

The early emphasis on behavior led to much discussion of social skills, rather than the broader concept of social competence. Paradoxically, the term *social competence* was in use as early as the 1930s, before the introduction of the term *social skills*, and the latter was originally reserved for the purely behavioral components of effective social interaction. Beck and Forehand (1984) observed that even social skills had been conceptualized both from a molecular perspective (including specific behaviors such as eye contact and voice intonation) and from a more molar perspective (with the emphasis on more global behaviors such as assertiveness). Similarly, Gesten, Weissberg, Amish, and Smith (1987) differentiated between microskills, such as eye contact and smiling behavior, and more complex skills, such as those involved in conversing or in joining a group.

Asher and Taylor (1983) noted evolutionary shifts in the terminology used in the literature but commented on a continuing lack of consistency, finding that the terms *social competence* and *social skills* were still sometimes used as if interchangeable. Gesten et al. (1987) suggested that *social competence* is "the most general or overarching term, which represents a summary judgement of performance across a range of interpersonal situations," whereas *social skills* refers to "the highly specific patterns of learned observable behavior, both verbal and non-verbal, through which we influence others and attempt to meet our needs" (p. 27). This suggests that both terms can be used concurrently (with care) to describe different perspectives and levels of analysis of social behavior.

Although many researchers have reported a lack of any agreed definition of social skills or social competence (see Hubbard & Coie, 1997; Hughes & Sullivan, 1987; Ogilvy, 1994), thinking has moved from focusing on the acquisition and demonstration of behavioral skills by the individual, to placing greater emphasis on the ability to achieve social outcomes. Obviously, possessing skills does not necessarily mean that the skills are actually deployed, let alone deployed to good effect. Social outcomes might include peer acceptance, acceptance by significant adults (see parents, teachers), school adjustment, mental health status, and absence of negative contact with the legal system. Signs of successful socialization have also included establishing and maintaining positive social relationships; refraining from harming others; serving as a constructive, contributing member of one's peer group, family, school, workplace, and community; engaging in health-enhancing and health-protective behaviors; and avoiding engaging in behaviors that may lead to negative consequences (such as substance abuse, unwanted pregnancy, social isolation, AIDS, and dropping out of school) (Consortium on the School-Based Promotion of Social Competence, 1994).

Increasingly, authors acknowledged the importance of both social skills and social outcomes in defining social competence. This was true at an early stage of determining a definition and can be seen in the frequently cited definition of Combs and Slaby (1977), which described the ability to interact with others in a given social context in specific ways that are socially acceptable or valued and at the same time personally beneficial, mutually beneficial, or beneficial primarily to others, that are at least minimally acceptable according to societal norms, and that are not harmful to others. In addition to social skills (abilities) and social outcomes (benefits), this definition makes reference to criteria in relation to which the social outcomes are valued (locally prevailing social norms).

However, it was not until the 1980s that the importance of affect as a major contributor to social behavior was fully recognized. Research identified affective factors that influenced social behavior, such as anxiety (see Wheeler & Ladd, 1982) and low self-esteem (Lochman & Lampron, 1986). This raised the question of whether affective states were a consequence of social skill capabilities or deficits, or whether social skills capabilities and deficits were a consequence of affective states, or both. By 1997, Hubbard and Coie were suggesting that the behavioral and cognitive components of social behavior had received greater research focus than the affective component, and that the historical developments in social competence research demonstrated the successive introduction and emphasis of each of the three components in turn. They asserted that the study of social competence had focused primarily on behavioral skills, with social behavioral correlates of sociometric status having been investigated as early as the 1930s. During the 1980s and 1990s a new dimension had been added, namely, social cognitive processes that antecede behavior. During the

1990s there was a growing interest in the emotional functioning of children, specifically in the ability of children to think about emotions and to regulate their emotions.

Rinn and Markle (1979) had earlier expressed caution regarding the affective component, noting that the expression of feelings could be considered to be a behavioral component, and that such expression may not always accurately reflect the true underlying affective state.

By the late 1980s, theoretical models that could account for the interaction of the cognitive, affective, and behavioral components of social competence were beginning to be constructed. Interestingly, these bore a remarkable similarity to those of Bandura from many years before. Thus the RGA social information processing model proposed by Hughes (1988) referred to three stages described as reading, generating, and applying, and suggested that the achievement of socially competent outcomes requires "that an individual accurately interpret social cues (*Read* the situation), generate appropriate social responses *(Generate)*, and effectively implement the selected response in the situation *(Apply)*" (p. 170).

A five-stage social information processing model was proposed more recently by Crick and Dodge (1994), suggesting a sequence of information processing whereby a child is considered to (1) encode cues that are both internal (feelings) and external (observed actions of others), (2) interpret these cues (causal and intent inferences), (3) clarify goals, (4) decide on a response, and (5) enact the behavior. These stages might be alternatively expressed as perception, analysis, prioritization of both goals and responses, and action. The emphasis on the ability to perceive and analyze both internal states and external behavior is useful. In some individuals, the internal capability might operate at a very different level from the external capability.

These models avoid the value issues in relation to outcomes by using words such as *appropriate,* which imply (but perhaps unhelpfully do not state) local and specific subjectivity. That social behavior and achievement of social outcomes are judged to be competent only according to the prevailing or dominant values and norms of the social environment in which the behavior is being performed is all too often left implicit (although Combs and Slaby clearly flagged the importance of social valuation of outcomes in their 1977 definition of social competence). This value relativity was expressed eloquently by the Consortium on the School-Based Promotion of Social Competence (1994), which asserted that social competence comprises a set of core skills, attitudes, abilities, and feelings that are given functional meaning by the contexts of culture, neighborhood, and situation. Thus social competence could be viewed in terms of the life skills used for adaptation to diverse ecologies and settings.

The value issues assume special importance in the design of interventions. Many early social skills interventions were predicated on a deficit model, assuming that the subject or client lacked certain skills that remedial intervention would implant. Such a crude (quasi-medical) model often largely neglected the cognitive and affective domains and the cultural and contextual relativity of social competence. It also seemed to regard the client as an empty vessel to be filled (or blank canvas to be painted), ignoring previously overlearned behaviors likely to interfere with new behaviors. Increasing dissatisfaction with such simplistic models of social skills training (see Gresham, 1998) has led to recent interventions that place much greater emphasis on the promotion of self-management skills that integrate cognitive, affective, and behavioral aspects (see self-control or social problem-solving skills) and make few assumptions about the purposes for which these skills will be applied. Social skills are thus conceived of in parallel with what might be termed *metasocial* skills. These newer approaches often explicitly explore, acknowledge, and build on the previous learning histories of the client. Gresham (1998) also emphasized the importance of *fluency*, which he defined as the extent to which effective social responses are automatized through frequent practice (with consequent feedback or reinforcement), thereby lowering the threshold and speed of elicitation of such responses in the future.

The conceptual evolution of social competence has been paralleled in recent years by the development of various models of emotional intelligence, with some disagreement between those who favor narrower cognitive-affective models, and those who favor broader mixed models that include a wide range of personality variables. An example of a narrower model is that of Mayer and Salovey (1997) and Mayer, Salovey, and Caruso (2000), which proposed an information processing element (perception, appraisal, and expression of emotion), integrated cognitive-affective elements (analysis and understanding of emotion, with emotional facilitation of cognition and vice versa), and a skill or performance aspect (the ability to regulate emotion in the self and others). The relative predictive value of these models is beginning to be explored empirically, a welcome step that is perhaps less apparent in the field of social competence. However, the contextually relativistic nature of the construct of social competence suggests it is broader than any notion of social intelligence.

Given all these complexities, and in order to achieve some resolution and basis for progression, we now offer our own current definition of social competence.

A CURRENT DEFINITION OF SOCIAL COMPETENCE

Our definition of social competence is the possession and use of the ability to integrate thinking, feeling, and behavior to achieve social tasks and outcomes valued in the host context and culture.

In a school setting, these tasks and outcomes might include accessing the school curriculum successfully, meeting associated personal social and emotional needs, and developing transferable skills and attitudes of value beyond school. However, very different social competencies are required and valued in different contexts. Behaviors that are dysfunctional and disapproved of in one context might be functional and approved of in another.

Through thinking and feeling, socially competent people are able to select and control which behaviors to emit and which to suppress in any given context, to achieve any given objective set by themselves or prescribed by others. This relativistic definition deliberately omits any specification of a particular outcome. This is in contrast to populist conceptions of social competence, which often assume specific outcomes, implying but not making explicit culturally based value judgments.

This definition suggests that social competence is not only knowledge and information processing capability, but also a set of component skills or procedures applied conditionally. These might include perception of relevant social cues, interpretation of social cues, realistic anticipation of obstacles to personally desired behavior, anticipation of consequences of behavior for self and others, generation of effective solutions to interpersonal problems, translation of social decisions into effective social behaviors, and the expression of a positive sense of self-efficacy.

A social information processing model of social behavior is implied by this definition, with an input (decoding) stage, a central processing and decision-making stage, and an output (encoding) stage. However, it does not imply a predominantly cognitive model, and in particular, the importance of feeling at all stages should not be underestimated. In this it is similar to models of emotional intelligence. Feelings can relate to the self, other people, groups and affiliations, objects, places, and activities, as well as specific events and behaviors. Feelings can stimulate, mediate, and reinforce thoughts and behavior. Feelings can be problematic when in excess, in deficit, or distorted or inappropriate. Feelings might inhibit or otherwise damage accurate cognition, and vice versa. Feelings may need to be managed directly through the emotions, rather than circuitously through thinking and behavior.

Although social competence implies intentionality, of course there might be several effective pathways to the same outcome in any context. Also sometimes, successful outcomes might be attributed by the child to random chance or external factors, validly or otherwise. Thus it is very simplistic to define social competence only in terms of specific skills or only in terms of specific outcomes, especially when the latter are valued very differently by different groups and cultures. Traditional operational definitions of desirable skills and outcomes are likely to be highly adult-centered and might neglect the child's own objectives. It follows that peer definition and assessment of social competence might be equally or more valid than adult assessment. Similarly, children perceived by adults as having a "poor self-image" within an adult-dominated context might feel very differently about themselves in a peer-dominated context; children have multiple self-concepts as well as multiple intelligences. Contentiously, it might be speculated that middle-class children who have acquired social competence, as narrowly construed by the controlling adults in schools, almost unconsciously by osmosis, might be disadvantaged by a limited capacity for generalization to novel contexts, should they ever encounter any.

Although different cultures and contexts value different social behaviors, there is nevertheless some broad consensus in most societies about what is desirable, for example, establishing and maintaining a range of positive social relationships; refraining from harming others; contributing collaboratively and constructively to the peer group, family, school, workplace, and community; engaging in behaviors that enhance and protect health; and avoiding behaviors with serious negative consequences for the individual or others or both.

However, it is significant that a number of these putative components of social competence are expressed negatively, which defines social competence as the absence of social incompetence. This highlights the need to term specific behaviors as socially competent or incompetent, not to so label children. Although it might in principle be meaningful to term persons socially competent as a function of the number of social skills they possessed, the number of contexts in which they could demonstrate them, and the number of different objectives they could thereby achieve, quantifying these performance indicators would prove very difficult.

Given the very important role of feelings and culture- and group-specific values and norms in the perception of social competence, it seems that the conception, definition, and stereotype of social competence is actually socially constructed within each group or culture in a way that is more or less specific to that grouping. When different groups with differently socially constructed conceptualizations of social competence need to interact in order to achieve some task salient to both, problems might arise. This is of course what happens in schools, among other places.

Next we consider how the construct of social competence is actually operationalized in schools.

THE SOCIAL CONSTRUCTION OF SOCIAL COMPETENCE IN SCHOOLS

In this section, we seek to express some of the main theoretical issues and problems in language that is accessible to a wide readership, in a way that is intended to relate to the needs and preoccupations of teachers. We hope that this will facilitate practical exploration of such issues among those who have direct day-to-day caring contact with children. This section also provides concrete examples to substantiate and elaborate the discussion to this point.

Within schools, it is important to bring teachers (and other staff) to the realization that social competence is socially constructed and relativistic, not least in the hope that this will have a moderating influence on the way behaviors perceived by teachers as socially incompetent are managed.

What Is Social Competence?

We would all like to think of ourselves as socially competent, but are we equally socially competent with people who are younger and older, who are the same or different gender, who we know well or who are new to us, over whom we have power or who have power over us, at work and at play, and so on? Very different social competencies are required and valued in different contexts. Social competence includes being aware of what to do and also of what not to do, as well as awareness of the undesirable effects of passively doing nothing at all. Everyone is socially competent in at least one situation, and no one is socially competent in all situations. We tend to regard a person as generally socially competent if he or she manages to get along with a fairly wide range of people in a fairly wide range of situations.

However, if one sees a person only in a single situation, one might tend to make assumptions about that person's social competence in other situations based on his or her social competence in the familiar situation—and one might well be wrong. For teachers, there is always a danger that a child's social functioning in class may be taken as indicative of the child's social competence in other classes, elsewhere in school, outside of school, and in the home. There is also the danger that conformity in class may be taken as indicative of social competence. In fact, social competence is not a single homogeneous attribute that is within the child, but a constellation of thoughts, feelings, skills, and behaviors that vary from situation to situation.

Some people are good at the thinking element—they know what they should do to be considered socially competent in a situation. However, dealing with the feelings and emotions involved in social interaction might not be easy—especially for those who have never learned to do this—so such people do not necessarily actually behave in a socially competent way. Others might have mechanistically learned a few socially competent behaviors to cope with routine situations but have never really thought about them and so are confused when the situation changes and adaptation is needed. Still others might possess quite well developed social skills but choose not to use them in certain situations, perhaps because of peer group or other pressure.

Teachers might wish to consider the definition of social competence offered here and appraise it prior to collaborating with colleagues to brainstorm a better or more locally relevant one.

Why Is Social Competence Important?

School, in particular, is very much a social environment, with many demands on social competence. In schools, young people who cannot get along with their peers in the classroom are likely to be perceived as distractible or even disruptive; their performance and progress is likely to suffer, and there might be unpleasant aftereffects outside of class. In short, a child gets in trouble, does not learn, and gets picked on. If a child's search for a context in which he or she can feel socially competent and accepted leads to illegal activities, that child's social competence in relation to police officers might soon be tested.

The world of work, with few exceptions, also has many social demands. Social competence is one of the transferable skills constantly in high demand by employers, who are not as interested in what a person knows as what that person can do and be quickly trained to do, and the doing will almost always be in a social environment.

Social competence is also essential in the successful conduct of everyday life—from minor but high-frequency community activities such as shopping, through establishing and enjoying the support and benefits of friendship and neighborliness, to major but low-frequency home-based activities such as bonding with a partner and raising children. Relating to the extended family in a large gathering is another example of a situation that makes considerable demands on social competence.

Social competence is also a factor in resilience. Those who are socially competent and socially integrated are likely to be more able to withstand the stresses of life, and probably more able to withstand temptations to become involved in self-damaging behavior such as taking drugs.

Clarifying Values

Children need to feel valued and secure. So do teachers. However, one teacher does not necessarily fully share a value system with the next, whatever the school's policy concerning shared values may be. Paradoxically, if teachers in a school do not feel valued and secure, differences in basic values between them can remain a hidden agenda and contribute to fragmentation. These issues must be discussed openly, remembering that no one is "right" about things that are a matter of opinion. When one's values come under question, it is easy to feel personally attacked—but the "no blame" approach should be taken with colleagues as well as with pupils.

Considering Ethos

In recent years, much attention has been paid to school "ethos" as a contributory factor in school effectiveness. However, in some schools, the visitor observes that every classroom seems to have its own individual ethos, varying across a very wide spectrum, or that the ethos in a classroom is very different from the ethos in the corridors or other areas of the school. Students might need very well developed social competence to cope with the differences between teachers, let alone the differences in the peer group from one class session to the next. Children and young people value consistency and fairness, which require shared values between pupils and teachers, and a cohesive commitment from pupils and teachers alike to put these into practice in everyday behavior. Only when this stage has been reached can one talk meaningfully about a whole-school ethos.

Channels for Information and Communication

Communication is an essential component of the educational process and is also essential for the management and development of educational processes. This is especially true of the promotion of social competence, much of which is itself about communication between people.

A useful step is to conduct a social competence audit. In doing this, one needs to identify and target a range of levels of analysis and operation of social competence (individual children, small groups, whole classes, entire schools) and consider how to gather information at and about all these levels. It is necessary to identify existing stakeholders and key players. The major stakeholders are the pupils themselves. How are their views to be heard? Such communication is essential because an attempt to impose a monocultural version of social competence from the top down is doomed to failure. Equally, input from all teachers is essential, but it is not immediately clear how their input should be grouped. There are attendance registration or form teachers, departmental subject teachers, specialist teachers, senior management, and so forth. Some members of the staff will fall into more than one group, but the groupings might determine how communication and consultation processes are accessed. In addition, there are part-time and temporary teachers and peripatetic teachers who serve several schools. Nonteaching staff members, who often make shrewd observations regarding social competence in contexts other than the classroom and also present a role model to pupils, whether intentionally or not, should also be involved in the audit process.

Stakeholders external to the school should also be considered and may include the school's advisers, educational or school psychologists, local authority behavior support team, and other relevant professional agents, as well as members of the school board and those who have a responsibility for communicating with both the school and the community. In addition, stakeholders may well include parents and caretakers of the students, as well as local employers, who might have very strong views about which kinds of transferable social competencies make young people more or less employable. These external stakeholders are also part of the solution.

Through these channels for information and communication, a local definition of social competence that is relevant to the world view and goals of all key stakeholders can be socially constructed, and the process may well be more important than the product.

CONCLUSION

Our review of the concept of social competence concludes that it is not a single homogeneous entity. It has component variables that vary along continuous dimensions and is value laden and socially constructed through social interaction. Different stakeholders in cooperative communities need to communicate to socially construct their own shared understanding of social competence. The concept should not be reified or used to label people. The complexity of social competence facilitates rather than hinders the design of successful interventions to enhance it, and these interventions are now considerably more sophisticated than in former years (see chapters 19 and 20). However, direct empirical tests of theoretical models of social competence themselves are still awaited.

References

Asher, S., & Taylor, A. (1983). Social skill training with children: Evaluating processes and outcomes. *Studies in Educational Evaluation, 8,* 237–245.

Bandura, A. (1977). *Social learning theory.* Englewood Cliffs, NJ: Prentice-Hall.

Bandura, A. (1986). *Social foundations of thought and action: A social cognitive theory.* Englewood Cliffs, NJ: Prentice-Hall.

Beck, S., & Forehand, R. (1984). Social skills training for children: A methodological and clinical review of behavior modification studies. *Behavioral Psychotherapy, 12,* 17–45.

Combs, M. L., & Slaby, D. A. (1977). Social-skills training with children. In B. B. Lahey & A. E. Kazdin (Eds.), *Advances in Clinical Child Psychology* (Vol. 1, pp. 161–201). New York: Plenum.

Consortium on the School-Based Promotion of Social Competence (1994). The school-based promotion of social competence: Theory, research, practice and policy. In R. J. Haggerty, L. Sherrod, N. Garmezy, & M. Rutter (Eds.), *Stress, risk and resilience in children and adolescents.* New York: Cambridge University Press.

Crick, N. R., & Dodge, K. A. (1994). A review and reformulation of social information-processing mechanisms in children's social adjustment. *Psychological Bulletin, 115,* 47–101.

Gesten, E. L., Weissberg, R. P., Amish, P. L., & Smith, J. K. (1987). Social problem-solving training: A skills-based approach to prevention and treatment. In C. A. Maher & J. E. Zins (Eds.), *Psychoeducational interventions in the schools: Methods and procedures of enhancing student competence* (pp. 197–210). New York and Oxford: Pergamon.

Gresham, F. M. (1998). Social skills training: Should we raze, remodel, or rebuild? *Behavioral Disorders, 24,* 19–25.

Hubbard, J. A., & Coie, J. D. (1997). Emotional correlates of social competence in children's peer relationships [On-line]. Available: http://www/udel.edu/psyc/fingerle/article1.htm.

Hughes, J. N. (1988). *Cognitive behavior therapy with children in schools.* Oxford, U.K.: Pergamon Press.

Hughes, J. N., & Sullivan, K. A. (1987). Outcome assessment in social skills training with children. *Journal of School Psychology, 26,* 167–183.

Lochman, J. E., & Lampron, L. B. (1986). Situational problem-solving skills and self-esteem of aggressive and non-aggressive boys. *Journal of Abnormal Child Psychology, 14,* 605–617.

Mayer, J. D., & Salovey, P. (1997). What is emotional intelligence? In P. Salovey & D. J. Sluyter (Eds.), *Emotional development and emotional intelligence* (pp. 3–31). New York: Basic Books.

Mayer, J. D., Salovey, P., & Caruso, D. (2000). Emotional intelligence. In R. J. Sternberg (Ed.), *Handbook of intelligence* (2nd ed.). New York: Cambridge University Press.

Ogilvy, C. M. (1994). Social skills training with children and adolescents: A review of the evidence. *Educational Psychology, 14,* 73–83.

Rinn, F. C., & Markle, A. (1979). Modification of social skill deficits in children. In A. Bellack & M. Hersen (Eds.), *Research and practice in social skills training* (pp. 61–83). New York: Plenum Press.

Wheeler, V. A., & Ladd, G. W. (1982). Assessment of children's self-efficacy for social interactions with peers. *Developmental Psychology, 18,* 795–805.

CHAPTER THREE

An Overview of the Alexithymia Construct

Graeme J. Taylor and R. Michael Bagby

Alexithymia is a personality construct that is conceptually similar and exhibits some overlap with the emotional intelligence construct. It has emerged, however, from a very different context and generated a considerably greater body of empirical research that has examined its validity and its relevance in clinical situations. In this chapter we first review the historical background and clinical features of the alexithymia construct. We then discuss some similarities and differences between alexithymia, emotional intelligence, and other conceptually related constructs and also review findings from empirical studies that have examined the relationships between alexithymia and these other constructs. Although research concerning the psychology and neurobiology underlying individual differences in alexithymia is still in an early explorative stage, we consider the current knowledge and speculations about these areas. We conclude the chapter with a proposal that alexithymia and low emotional intelligence originate, at least in part, from failures in early caregiver-child relationships that adversely affect the development of neural and cognitive systems involved in the processing of emotional information.

HISTORICAL BACKGROUND

The origins of the alexithymia concept can be traced back at least a half century to clinical reports by Ruesch (1948) and Maclean (1949), who observed that many patients suffering from so-called classical psychosomatic diseases show an apparent inability to verbalize feelings. Ruesch noted also that such patients tend to be unimaginative, use direct physical action or bodily channels for emotional expression, and respond poorly to insight-oriented psychotherapy. Maclean (1949) and Ruesch (1948) attributed these characteristics to a deficit in representing emotions symbolically, a function Maclean (1949) assigned to the neocortex.

A few years later, Horney (1952) and Kelman (1952) reported similar characteristics in certain psychiatric patients whom they were finding difficult to treat with psychoanalytic psychotherapy because of a lack of emotional awareness, paucity of inner experiences, minimal interest in dreams, concreteness of thinking, and an externalized style of living in which behavior was guided by rules, regulations, and the expectations of others rather than by feelings, wishes, and personal values. These psychiatric patients were prone to developing "psychosomatic" symptoms and often engaged in binge eating, alcohol abuse, or other compulsive behaviors, seemingly in an attempt to regulate distressing inner states.

Marty and de M'Uzan (1963), who were working in the field of psychosomatic medicine in France, subsequently reported a similar operational thinking style—*la pensée opératoire*—among physically ill patients. Unable to access an inner life of feelings and fantasies, these patients were preoccupied with physical symptoms and the minute details of external events, and they showed an affectless way of relating to other people.

The significance of these various reports became more evident in the early 1970s when Nemiah and Sifneos (1970) began to systematically investigate the cognitive and affective style of patients suffering from two of the classical psychosomatic diseases. The results of their investigations seemed to confirm that many psychosomatic patients have a marked difficulty in describing subjective feelings, an impoverished fantasy life, and a cognitive style that is literal, utilitarian, and externally oriented. Sifneos (1973) coined the term *alexithymia* (from the Greek: *a* meaning *lack, lexis* meaning *word,* and *thymos* meaning *emotion*) to denote this cluster of cognitive characteristics.

Quite independently, but in parallel with Sifneos's research, other investigators were reporting similar characteristics in patients with posttraumatic states (Krystal, 1968) and in patients with substance use disorders (Krystal & Raskin, 1970). Wurmser (1974) also described deficits in the verbal affective expression and imaginal capacity of those addicted to drugs, which he referred to as *hyposymbolization*. And in the field of eating disorders, Bruch (1973) observed that patients with anorexia nervosa lack an awareness of inner experiences and are often unable to describe their feelings.

Following a series of presentations and debates on alexithymia at the 11th European Conference on Psychosomatic Research held in Heidelberg, Germany, in 1976 (Bräutigam & von Rad, 1977), it was concluded that clinicians and researchers should agree on a precise formulation and definition of the alexithymia construct. This was facilitated by the concurrent publication of a seminal article on alexithymia by Nemiah, Freyberger, and Sifneos (1976).

SALIENT FEATURES OF THE ALEXITHYMIA CONSTRUCT

Since the Heidelberg conference, there has been a consensus in the literature on the definition of the alexithymia construct. The salient features of the construct are (1) difficulty identifying feelings and distinguishing between feelings and the bodily sensations of emotional arousal; (2) difficulty describing feelings to other people; (3) constricted imaginal processes, as evidenced by a paucity of fantasy; and (4) a stimulus-bound, externally oriented cognitive style (Lesser, 1985; Lolas & von Rad, 1989; Nemiah, 1977, Sifncos, 1996; Taylor, Bagby, & Parker, 1991, 1997). Although some so-called alexithymic individuals appear to contradict this definition of the construct because they experience chronic dysphoria or manifest outbursts of weeping or rage, intensive questioning usually reveals that "they know very little about their own feelings and, in most instances, are unable to link them with memories, fantasies, or specific situations" (Taylor et al., 1991, p. 155).

Several additional characteristics, which we have discussed elsewhere (Taylor, Bagby, & Parker, 1997), were included among some of the early clinical observations and have sometimes been associated with the alexithymia construct. These include a tendency to social conformity, a tendency toward action to express emotion or to avoid conflicts, poor dream recall, a somewhat stiff, wooden posture, and a paucity of facial expressions (Krystal, 1979; Nemiah et al., 1976; Ruesch, 1948; Sifneos, Apfel-Savitz, & Frankel, 1977). However, although these characteristics are sometimes manifested by individuals with a high degree of alexithymia, they are not part of the theoretical core of the alexithymia construct. Moreover, in the process of validating the construct, social conformity, a tendency toward action, and the ability to recall dreams did not emerge as essential features of the construct (Bagby, Parker, & Taylor, 1994). Clinical experience suggests that it is the structural features of dreams more than the ability to recall them that best characterizes alexithymia. When dreams are recalled they either contain explicit mental content (for example, scenes of violence) or they merely replay a daytime experience without the usual dream work of symbolization, condensation, and displacement (Levitan, 1989; Taylor, 1987).

Even without these additional features, alexithymia is a multifaceted construct comprising the four salient features outlined above, which are conceptually distinct but logically interrelated. The ability to communicate feelings to others verbally is obviously contingent on the cognitive skill of identifying and labeling one's feelings; and an externally oriented cognitive style reflects a paucity of fantasy and other inner experiences as well as a low range of emotional expressiveness. Alexithymia is conceptualized not as a categorical phenomenon, but as a dimensional construct that is distributed normally in the general population.

Despite the clear definition of the alexithymia construct, some clinicians and researchers have the misconception that individuals with alexithymia are totally unable to express emotions verbally and that they may even fail to acknowledge that they experience emotions (see, for example, Oxman, Rosenberg, Schnurr, & Tucker, 1985; Simon & Von Korff, 1991). Although this misconception may stem from a literal translation of the term *alexithymia* as meaning *no words for feelings,* even before coining the term, Sifneos (1967) reported that his patients commonly mentioned anxiety or complained of depression; however, the patients displayed a limited vocabulary for describing their emotions: when questioned further about their anxiety, they talked "only about nervousness, agitation, restlessness, irritability, and tension"; when asked about depression, they talked about "sensations of emptiness, void, boredom, and pain" (pp. 3–4). In other words, the emotions of alexithymic individuals are poorly differentiated and not well represented mentally, an observation made initially by Ruesch (1948) and Maclean (1949), as noted earlier.

During the past decade, findings from research studies conducted with a variety of clinical populations have confirmed the earlier observations that alexithymia is associated strongly with substance use disorders (Taylor, Parker, & Bagby, 1990), eating disorders (Taylor, Parker, Bagby, & Bourke, 1996), posttraumatic stress disorder (Yehuda et al., 1997; Zeitlin, Lane, O'Leary, & Schrift, 1989), and a tendency to somatization (Taylor, Parker, Bagby, & Acklin, 1992); there is empirical evidence also that high degrees of alexithymia may be present in a substantial number of patients with inflammatory bowel disease (Porcelli, Zaka, Leoci, Centonze, & Taylor, 1995), essential hypertension (Jula, Salminen, & Saarijärvi, 1999; Todarello, Taylor, Parker, & Fanelli, 1995), or functional gastrointestinal disorders (Porcelli, Taylor, Bagby, & De Carne, 1999). For an extensive review of these studies, see Taylor et al. (1997).

Before examining the relationship between alexithymia and emotional intelligence and other constructs that appear conceptually similar, it is important to emphasize that the psychometric properties of the Twenty-Item Toronto Alexithymia Scale (TAS-20) (Bagby, Parker, & Taylor, 1994), which is described in detail in Chapter Fourteen, have provided strong support for the validity of alexithymia as a multifaceted construct. The three-factor structure of the TAS-20, which has been replicated in numerous confirmatory factor analytic studies (Beresnevaite, Taylor, Parker, & Andziulis, 1998; Pandey, Mandal, Taylor, & Parker, 1996; Parker, Bagby, Taylor, Endler, & Schmitz, 1993; Taylor, et al., 1997), and the finding of significant parameter estimates for the relationships among the three factors, confirm that difficulty identifying feelings, difficulty describing feelings, and externally oriented thinking (that is, a cognitive style characterized by a preoccupation with the minute details of external events, rather than by feelings, fantasies, and other aspects of inner experience) are subordinate components of the construct that can be distinguished conceptually and measured separately from one another, despite being related to each other empirically. The limited fantasy and other imaginal processes aspect of the construct is encompassed by the externally oriented thinking factor of the TAS-20, which correlates significantly and negatively with a measure of fantasy (Bagby, Taylor, & Parker, 1994). Given the positive relationships between the components of the construct, one would expect the TAS-20 and its three factors to be related in similar ways to measures of conceptually similar constructs. As with other multifaceted constructs, however, one would expect to find some facets of alexithymia to sometimes relate to other constructs better than the broader construct, and for some facets to even be unrelated to other constructs (Carver, 1989).

RELATIONSHIP BETWEEN ALEXITHYMIA AND EMOTIONAL INTELLIGENCE

In exploring the relationship between alexithymia and emotional intelligence, one is drawn first to Gardner's (1983) concept of personal intelligences and to his description of two subtypes: *intrapersonal intelligence* and *interpersonal intelligence*. In elaborating on the concept of intrapersonal intelligence, Gardner (1983) noted the following:

> The core capacity at work here is *access to one's feeling life*—one's range of affects or emotions: the capacity instantly to effect discriminations among these feelings and, eventually, to label them, to enmesh them in symbolic codes, to draw upon them as a means of understanding and guiding one's behavior. In its most primitive form, the intrapersonal intelligence amounts to little more than the capacity to distinguish a feeling of pleasure from one of pain and, on the basis of such a discrimination, to become more involved in or to withdraw from a situation. At its most advanced level, intrapersonal knowledge allows one to detect and to symbolize complex and highly differentiated sets of feelings. (p. 239)

Whereas intrapersonal intelligence involves the examination and knowledge of one's own feelings, interpersonal intelligence is the ability to read the moods, intentions, and desires of others and potentially to act on this knowledge. Awareness of and sensitivity to the feelings of others is generally referred to as *empathy*, which is guided by an awareness and appraisal of the subjective feelings evoked in oneself by others, and also by the perception and appraisal of spontaneous nonverbal expressions of others. That is, the two forms of personal intelligence are intimately related; through attention to one's subjective feelings, affects can function as a "sixth sense" to provide information about others (Solms, 1997). Moreover, acquiring knowledge of one's own emotions is dependent on the ability to learn from observations of other people (Gardner, 1983).

It is immediately evident that the concept of alexithymia overlaps considerably, albeit inversely, with Gardner's (1983) concept of intrapersonal intelligence, in particular with the ability to identify, label, and discriminate among feelings and to represent them symbolically. Although difficulty in monitoring the feelings and emotions of others is not included in the definition of the alexithymia construct, there is clinical and empirical evidence that individuals with high degrees of alexithymia experience difficulties in accurately identifying emotions in the facial expressions of others (Lane et al., 1996; Parker, Taylor, & Bagby, 1993) and also manifest a limited capacity for empathizing with the emotional states of others (Beckendam, 1997; Davies, Stankov, & Roberts, 1998; Krystal, 1979; McDougall, 1989; Taylor, 1987).

Although the concept of emotional intelligence stems in part from Gardner's contributions, the construct has been defined in several different ways, which has made it difficult for researchers to evaluate its validity or its relationship with alexithymia and other conceptually similar constructs (see, for example, Davies et al., 1998). In an initial theoretical paper, Salovey and Mayer (1989/1990) defined emotional intelligence as "the ability to monitor one's own and others' feelings and emotions, to discriminate among them and to use this information to guide one's thinking and actions" (p. 189). Although this definition encompasses emotional self-awareness and empathy, Mayer and Salovey (1997) recently argued that it gives insufficient emphasis to "thinking about feelings." This is somewhat surprising because the definition clearly refers to the ability to use emotional information to guide cognition and behavior. Nonetheless, Mayer and Salovey (1997) introduced a revised and more complex definition that identifies four central components of the construct: the perception, appraisal and expression of emotion; emotional facilitation of thinking; understanding and analyzing emotions, and employing emotional knowledge; and reflective regulation of emotions to promote emotional and intellectual growth. Noticeably absent from this revised formulation of the construct is any direct reference to interpersonal intelligence.

In an attempt to operationalize the emotional intelligence construct, Schutte et al., (1998) based their writing of items for a self-report scale on Salovey and Mayer's (1989/1990) original definition on the grounds that it lends itself better to conceptualizing the various facets of an individual's current level of emotional development. The scale has a single factor with 33 items that assess the appraisal and expression of emotions in self and others, regulation of emotion in self and others, and utilization of emotions in solving problems. In a small sample of 25 students, the 33-item scale correlated strongly and negatively with the self-report Toronto Alexithymia Scale ($r = -.65, p < .0001$).

In a more recent study with a large community population ($N = 734$), Parker, Taylor, and Bagby (forthcoming) explored the relationship between alexithymia and emotional intelligence using the revised Twenty-Item Toronto Alexithymia Scale (TAS-20) and the BarOn Emotional Quotient Inventory (EQ-i). Developed over many years, and based on a very broad conceptualization of emotional intelligence, the EQ-i includes not only the intrapersonal and interpersonal intelligences among its five second-order factors, but also adaptability, stress management, and general mood (Bar-On, 1997). In our view, the last three factors encompass a cluster of traits (and one state, namely, happiness) that could be considered *outcomes* of emotional intelligence rather than essential components of the construct. Table 3.1 presents the Pearson correlations between the TAS-20 and its three factors and the EQ-i total score, the five second-order factors of the EQ-i, and the various subscales that comprise these factors. As one would predict on theoretical grounds, the TAS-20 correlated strongly and negatively with the total score on the EQ-i and also with the intrapersonal and interpersonal factors. Interestingly, significant negative correlations were obtained also with the second-order factors assessing adaptability, stress management, and general mood. Moreover, consistent with the theoretical coherency of the facets of the alexithymia construct, all three factors of the TAS-20 correlated significantly with the EQ-i and its various subscales and factor scales.

Overall, these findings are consistent with clinical observations and some empirical evidence that alexithymic individuals not only lack emotional self-awareness and empathy, but also have difficulty establishing warm, intimate

Table 3.1. Correlations Between the TAS-20 and the EQ-i (N = 734).

	DIF	DDF	EOT	TASTOT
EQ-i total	−.64	−.61	−.42	−.72
Intrapersonal	−.58	−.62	−.35	−.66
Emotional self-awareness	−.46	−.72	−.41	−.67
Assertiveness	−.38	−.51	−.31	−.50
Self-regard	−.47	−.38	−.13	−.43
Self-actualization	−.46	−.43	−.34	−.53
Independence	−.41	−.32	−.19	−.40
Interpersonal	−.38	−.47	−.41	−.54
Empathy	−.29	−.37	−.41	−.46
Interpersonal relationships	−.34	−.50	−.32	−.49
Social responsibility	−.35	−.35	−.36	−.45
Adaptability	−.59	−.46	−.37	−.62
Problem solving	−.36	−.32	−.34	−.44
Reality testing	−.60	−.44	−.25	−.56
Flexibility	−.40	−.30	−.26	−.42
Stress management	−.54	−.33	−.20	−.47
Stress tolerance	−.47	−.34	−.19	−.43
Impulse control	−.42	−.21	−.15	−.35
General mood	−.53	−.44	−.22	−.51
Happiness	−.48	−.41	−.17	−.46
Optimism	−.46	−.38	−.22	−.46

Note: DIF = difficulty identifying feelings; DDF = difficulty describing feelings; EOT = externally-oriented thinking; TASTOT = TAS-20 total score. All correlations are significant at $p < 0.05$.

relationships, manifest a propensity to dysphoric states, and are unable to think about and use emotions to cope with stressful situations (Beckendam, 1997; Krystal, 1988a; Parker, Taylor, & Bagby, 1998; Schaffer, 1993; Taylor et al., 1997).

CLINICAL VIGNETTES

The following clinical vignettes further illustrate the conceptual overlap of the alexithymia and emotional intelligence constructs. Both patients had been referred for consultation because of an apparent lack of psychological minded-ness and an unresponsiveness to insight-oriented psychotherapy.

Case 1

Dr. Brown is a middle-aged male university professor with coronary heart dis-ease and a past history of substance abuse and depression. He is intelligent, well-educated, and holds two doctoral degrees. Although he reported that he could experience feelings of anger and fear, Dr. Brown was unaware of the nuances of various emotions and claimed to have never experienced any plea-surable emotions other than a mild feeling of enjoyment. He stated that he had no feelings when his father died four years ago and had no emotional response when his sister committed suicide soon thereafter. Dr. Brown described a lack of emotional connection with other people; he reported that when he embraces his daughter, for example, he experiences no subjective feelings. Over the course of his life, however, he had learned to imitate emotional expressions such as tenderness and love by watching movies and television shows. He has no imag-inative fantasies and rarely recalls dreams.

Dr. Brown scored in the high alexithymia range on the TAS-20. On the EQ-i, he obtained an overall score that placed him in the lower 2 percent of the pop-ulation for emotional intelligence. Consistent with the clinical impression of lim-ited skills in the domains of intrapersonal and interpersonal intelligence, he scored in the low average range on the EQ-i scale assessing emotional self-awareness, and in the very low range on the interpersonal relationship and empathy scales.

Case 2

Mr. Thomas is a forty-two-year-old single man who initially sought psychiatric treatment because of difficulty in making friends. Although he has an under-graduate university degree, he had been employed mostly in clerical or secre-tarial jobs and earned only a modest income. He had suffered from ulcerative colitis for many years. Mr. Thomas claimed not to experience depression, but wondered if he might be depressed as he mostly experiences a sense of inner emptiness and low motivation. He always smiles and behaves pleasantly toward other people but, without authentic feelings, his attempts at being friendly lack depth and fail to engage others in any meaningful way. Mr. Thomas obtained a very high score on the TAS-20, but only a mildly elevated score of 19 on the Beck Depression Inventory. On the EQ-i, he obtained low scores on every sub-scale, and an overall score that placed him in the lower 1 percent of the population for emotional intelligence. The three lowest subscale scores were on assertiveness, self-actualization, and independence, but very low scores were also obtained on the emotional self-awareness, self-regard, and stress tolerance subscales.

RELATIONSHIP BETWEEN ALEXITHYMIA AND OTHER CONSTRUCTS

During the Heidelberg conference, Singer (1977) suggested that the cluster of characteristics comprised in the alexithymia construct closely resemble the characteristics usually subsumed within the more familiar concept of psychological mindedness. As outlined by Taylor (1995), however, the construct of psychological mindedness (like that of emotional intelligence) has been defined in both broad and narrow ways. This has led to a variety of different methods for assessing an individual's capacity for psychological mindedness, and therefore to difficulty in comparing findings across studies.

Perhaps closest to Gardner's (1983) concept of intrapersonal intelligence, but formulated a decade earlier, is Appelbaum's (1973) definition that psychological mindedness is "a person's ability to see relationships among thoughts, feelings, and actions, with the goal of learning the meanings and causes of his experiences and behavior" (p. 36). This and other similar broad definitions of the construct were used by Conte et al., (1990) in developing the self-report Psychological Mindedness Scale (PMS). In a study with a group of 85 university students, the results of the PMS correlated strongly and negatively with those of the TAS-20 and its three-factor scales (see Table 3.2) (Bagby, Taylor, & Parker, 1994). This finding is consistent with numerous clinical reports that individuals with marked alexithymic characteristics are poor candidates for insight-oriented forms of psychotherapy (Horney, 1952; Krystal, 1982/1983; McDougall, 1972; Nemiah et al., 1976; Sifneos, 1975; Taylor, 1987).

A less familiar construct, but one that also overlaps conceptually with aspects of alexithymia and emotional intelligence, is the affective orientation construct. This construct is defined as "the degree to which people are aware of their emotions, perceive them as important, and actively consider their affective responses in making judgements and interacting with others" (Booth-Butterfield & Booth-Butterfield, 1994, p. 332); people who test low for affective orientation seem to

Table 3.2. Correlations Between the TAS-20 and Measures of Other Constructs.

Variable	N	DIF	DDF	EOT	TASTOT
Psychological mindedness	85	−.44**	−.51**	−.54**	−.68**
Affective orientation	210	−.24**	−.36**	−.28**	−.37**
Need for cognition	85	−.40**	−.36**	−.44**	−.55**
Openness to experience	85	−.28*	−.30**	−.61**	−.49**

Note: DIF = difficulty identifying feelings; DDF = difficulty describing feelings; EOT = externally-oriented thinking; TASTOT = TAS-20 total score.

*p < 0.05; **p < 0.01.

weigh logic and facts more heavily than affects in guiding their behavior (Yelsma, 1996). The Affective Orientation Scale (AOS) is a 20-item self-report measure that assesses awareness of emotion, implementation of emotion, importance of emotion, and intensity of emotion (Booth-Butterfield & Booth-Butterfield, 1990). In a study with a mixed sample of normal adults and victims and perpetrators of verbal and/or physical abuse, the AOS results correlated negatively and significantly with the TAS-20 results and with those of each of its three factors (Table 3.2) (Taylor, 1994; Yelsma, 1996).

Consistent with the view that alexithymia and emotional intelligence involve a set of cognitive skills that facilitate introspection, reflection, and the effective regulation of emotions, a strong negative relationship has been found between alexithymia and the need for cognition construct, which is the tendency to engage in and enjoy effortful and analytical cognitive endeavors (Cacioppo, Petty, Feinstein, & Jarvis, 1996). Table 3.2 shows the correlations between the results of the TAS-20 and its three factors and those of the short form of the Need for Cognition Scale (Cacioppo, Petty, & Kao, 1984) in the same group of university students who completed the PMS (Bagby, Taylor, & Parker, 1994).

Several studies have examined the relation between alexithymia and the major personality dimensions in the five-factor model of personality (Bagby, Taylor, & Parker, 1994; Luminet, Bagby, Wagner, Taylor, & Parker, 1999; Wise & Mann, 1994; Wise, Mann, & Shay, 1992). Of particular interest is the consistent finding of a moderately strong negative relationship with the openness to experience dimension (O). One set of correlations between O and the TAS-20 and its factors is shown in Table 3.2; these results were obtained with a sample of university students (Bagby, Taylor, & Parker, 1994). The elements of O include active imagination, aesthetic sensitivity, attentiveness to inner feelings, curiosity, preference for variety, and independence of judgment (McCrae & Costa, 1985). It is evident, as McCrae and Costa (1985, 1987; Costa & McCrae, 1987) have commented, that there is considerable conceptual overlap between O and the alexithymia and psychological mindedness constructs. And like emotional intelligence, O is not equivalent to general intelligence; indeed, "many people score high in O without having a corresponding high IQ" (McCrae & John, 1992, p. 198).

Although Salovey, Hsee, and Mayer (1993) place alexithymia at the extreme lower pole of the emotional intelligence construct, they and their collaborators have sometimes misconstrued alexithymia as "a psychiatric diagnosis" (Mayer & Stevens, 1994) or "diagnostic category" (Mayer, DiPaolo, & Salovey, 1990) rather than a personality trait and have even suggested that the Toronto Alexithymia Scale (an earlier version of the TAS-20), because it correlates positively with measures of neuroticism and depression, should probably be regarded as a measure of general distress rather than introspective ability (Mayer et al., 1990). There is empirical evidence, however, that alexithymia (as measured by the TAS or TAS-20) corresponds not to any single dimension or lower-order trait within the five-factor model, but is captured by a complex admixture of narrow personality traits (Bagby, Taylor, & Parker, 1994; Luminet et al., 1999). Moreover, several longitudinal studies have shown that alexithymia scores remain stable after general distress or depression have subsided (Keller, Carroll, Nich, & Rounsaville, 1995; Martinez-Sánchez, Ato-García, Adam, Medina, & España, 1998; Pinard, Negrete, Annable, & Audet, 1996; Porcelli, Leoci, Guerra, Taylor, & Bagby, 1996; Salminen, Saarijärvi, Äärelä, & Tamminen, 1994).

Bonanno and Singer (1990) suggested that alexithymia might be part of the repressive coping style, which is identified by high scores on social desirability scales (indicating high defensiveness) and low scores on measures of anxiety despite high levels of physiological arousal (Weinberger, 1990). Empirical investigations have revealed, however, that these are distinct constructs. Those with a repressive coping style score low on measures of alexithymia, and the data indicate that alexithymia is actually more similar to the sensitizing style of highly anxious individuals who acknowledge negative emotional experiences but have difficulty regulating them (Myers, 1995; Newton & Contrada, 1994). As Newton and Contrada (1994) point out, however, individuals with alexithymia are distinguished from individuals with high anxiety by their diminished fantasy life and externally oriented cognitive style. Thus, whereas those with repressive responses often believe that they are not upset despite objective evidence to the contrary (Weinberger, 1990), individuals with alexithymia acknowledge that they are upset but have difficulty in elaborating on the nature of their distress (Nemiah et al., 1976; Sifneos, 1967).

THE PSYCHOLOGY AND NEUROBIOLOGY OF ALEXITHYMIA

Although alexithymia and emotional intelligence reflect individual differences in emotional awareness, neurobiological studies over the past fifteen years suggest that subjective feelings are an outcome product of a more basic emotional processing system that operates independent of and outside of conscious experience (LeDoux, 1996). The key structure in this system (at least for the emotions of fear and anger) is the amygdala, which is part of a neural network that computes the affective significance of stimuli an individual encounters, including stimuli from within the brain (thoughts, images, and memories) and stimuli from the internal or external environment (LeDoux, 1989). Separate affective and cognitive computational systems have been identified: the affective system provides a rapid appraisal of a stimulus that often leads to a rapid response in the peripheral autonomic, endocrine, and motor systems of the body; the cognitive system performs a more detailed appraisal of a stimulus, including its relationship to other stimuli and to representations of past experiences, which leads to a more modulated response. Neural pathways between the amygdala and brain areas involved in cognition allow affect to influence cognition and cognition to influence affect, all of which can occur without conscious awareness (LeDoux, 1986, 1989).

LeDoux (1989, 1996) suggests that emotional feelings are experienced when representations of the affective and cognitive computations of stimuli, along with representations of the triggering stimuli, enter working memory and become integrated with representations of past experiences and representations of the self. Cognitive scientists and neuroscientists (Baddeley, 1992; Goldman-Rakic, 1994; Kihlstrom, 1987; Kosslyn & Koenig, 1992) consider working memory the basis of all conscious experience and part of an essential information-processing system that allows behavior to be guided by ideas, thoughts, and other symbolic representations rather than by immediate emotional reactions to stimuli. There is accumulating evidence that working memory and the selection of information that will be attended to and held "on line" at any given time involve the lateral prefrontal cortex, the anterior cingulate cortex, and the orbitofrontal cortex (LeDoux, 1996).

Given current knowledge of cognitive and emotional processing in the brain, any theory that attempts to explain individual differences in alexithymia (or emotional intelligence) must consider variations in the level of complexity of representations of emotional states and in the neural organization associated with working memory. Although some nonhuman animals have the capacity to form symbolic representations and to be consciously aware of their emotional responses, the unique feature of humans is the ability to make distinctions between different emotional states and to reflect on the meanings of these subjective experiences. This capacity has evolved with the acquisition of language, which according to Rolls (1995), requires the same or very similar brain systems as those that underlie consciousness. An important aspect of linguistic processing is the ability to think about one's thoughts and other mental experiences (Rolls, 1995), an ability that developmental psychologists and attachment researchers have referred to as *metacognitive monitoring* (Main, 1991), the *reflective-self function* (Fonagy, Steele, Steele, Moran, & Higgit, 1991), or simply the *reflective function* (Fonagy & Target, 1997). As LeDoux (1996) pointed out, "feelings will be different in a brain that can classify the world linguistically and categorize experience in words than in a brain that cannot" (p. 302).

A similar view was taken by Gardner (1983), who attributed the evolutionary origin of the personal intelligences to the emergence of symbol systems, in particular language, which he referred to as "the pre-eminent symbol system" (pp. 256–257). Gardner commented that "without a symbolic code supplied by the culture, the individual is confronted with only his most elementary and unorganized discrimination of feelings" (p. 242). This is the level of emotional organization that Sifneos (1973) accurately captured when he coined the term *alexithymia*—an absence of *words* for feelings!

In conceptualizing stages in the normal development of representations of emotions, Piaget (1981), Krystal (1974), and Lane and Schwartz (1987) all proposed epigenetic sequences in which the progressive learning of language skills leads to the formation of cognitive schemata of increasing complexity that gradually elevate the conscious experience of emotions from an awareness of peripheral manifestations of emotional arousal only (namely, undifferentiated bodily sensations and/or a tendency to action) to an awareness of blends of feelings, an ability to make subtle distinctions between nuances of emotions, and a capacity to appreciate the emotional experience of others. Higher levels of representation of emotions in the working memory and associative memory systems not only enhance the conscious appraisal and self-regulation of states of emotional arousal (the latter via neural pathways from the prefrontal cortex and hippocampus to the amygdala), but also enable the person to intentionally communicate feelings to others via language and images. In addition, the mental representation of affective experiences of the self interacting with others fosters the creation of memories, fantasies, and dreams, which further help in containing and modulating states of emotional arousal (Brown, 1993; Mayes & Cohen, 1992).

Without imaginative fantasies and subjective feelings to think about and use to guide behavior, the alexithymic individual is subject to "the tyranny of external [and internal] stimuli" (Goldman-Rakic, 1994, p. 354) and an activated amygdala unchecked by feedback from the consciously and unconsciously operating cognitive systems (LeDoux, 1986, 1996). Not surprisingly, empirical studies have confirmed an association between alexithymia and medical and psychiatric disorders in which emotions are poorly regulated; these include panic disorder (Parker, Taylor, Bagby, & Acklin, 1993), posttraumatic stress disorder (PTSD) (Yehuda et al., 1997; Zeitlin et al., 1989), substance use disorders (Taylor et al., 1990), essential hypertension (Jula et al., 1999; Todarello et al., 1995), functional gastrointestinal disorders (Porcelli et al., 1999), and a propensity to somatization (Taylor et al., 1997).

Evidence that the neural correlates of emotional awareness include a part of the brain associated with selective attention and working memory was provided by a recent functional brain imaging study with a small group of healthy women. As described in Chapter Eight, Lane, Quinlan, Schwartz, Walker, and Zeitlin (1990) developed the Levels of Emotional Awareness Scale (LEAS) to assess individual differences in the cognitive skill of recognizing and describing emotions in oneself and others; higher scores on this scale are thought to indicate greater differentiation in the mental representations of emotion and greater awareness of emotional complexity in self and others. In a study with a small group of healthy women, Lane et al., (1998) found a positive relationship between LEAS scores and increased activity in the anterior cingulate cortex (measured by changes in blood flow) when emotions were induced either by films or by recall of personal experiences. This finding led Lane, Ahern, Schwartz, and Kaszniak (1997a, 1997b) to speculate that alexithymia, which corresponds to low scores on the LEAS, might be associated with a deficit in anterior cingulate cortex activity during emotional arousal. Given that the anterior cingulate cortex not only plays a role in conscious experience, but also helps orchestrate the autonomic, endocrine, and motor responses to emotional stimuli (Vogt, Finch, & Olson, 1992), Lane et al. (1997b) suggests that some altered functioning in this part of the brain might contribute to exaggerated and persistent autonomic arousal that could lead to somatic symptoms.

As LeDoux's (1996) research has demonstrated, however, the anterior cingulate cortex and other parts of the limbic system do not operate in isolation but are functionally intertwined with higher areas of the brain. Indeed, there is evidence that interhemispheric communication also plays a role in consciousness, including the conscious awareness of important aspects of emotional processing. In the well-known studies of patients whose corpus callosum had been surgically severed to control intractable epilepsy, Sperry, Gazzaniga, and Bogen (1969) demonstrated that each hemisphere could work and function outside the conscious realm of the other. Although the right hemisphere is preferentially involved in the perception and expression of nonverbal emotion behavior (facial expressions, prosody, gestures), and the left hemisphere preferentially involved in verbal functioning, the left hemisphere also functions as the "interpreter" of information it receives (Gazzaniga, 1992, 1995) and is involved therefore in assigning causal meanings to conscious emotional experiences, even when it is unaware of the stimulus that has triggered an emotional response (Pally, 1998). This interpreter system relies largely on language to process information and perform its reflective function (Gazzaniga, 1992), but the right hemisphere is not uninvolved in language; according to Ornstein (1997), it has a superior ability to understand the figurative or metaphorical meanings of words, as well as the meanings of nonverbal cues, and is thereby able to hold alternative meanings and grasp a broader understanding of situations and experiences. The integration and conscious awareness of these different left and right hemisphere functions are central to emotional intelligence but appear to be deficient in highly alexithymic individuals who become confused by interoceptive stimuli (Taylor et al., 1996), misperceive nonverbal cues in others (Lane et al., 1996; Parker, Taylor, & Bagby, 1993), respond to the literal rather than the metaphorical meanings of words (Krystal, 1988b), and consequently misinterpret their own and others' emotions (Taylor et al., 1997). As Ornstein (1997) pointed out, neither side of the brain does anything on its own but, like everything biological, individuals may differ in how well their hemispheres communicate.

The possibility that alexithymia might be associated with a functional impairment in interhemispheric communication was proposed by Hoppe (1977) more than two decades ago after observing that "split-brain" patients manifest alexithymic features (Hoppe & Bogen, 1977). This proposal has now been supported by two experimental studies conducted with subjects with intact brains. Using a tactile finger localization task to assess interhemispheric communication, Zeitlin et al. (1989) demonstrated a significant bidirectional transfer deficit in combat veterans with PTSD and alexithymia. Parker, Keightley, Smith and Taylor (1999) later replicated this finding in a study comparing the performance of the finger localization task among university students with alexithymia with the performance of those without alexithymia.

Although the results of these studies apply only to the transfer of sensory information and need to be replicated with regard to the transfer of emotional information, the discovery that the interhemispheric deficit is bidirectional supports the hypothesis that the salient features of the alexithymia construct reflect a limited capacity to coordinate and integrate the activities of the two hemispheres. Although each hemisphere is specialized for different functions, it is now known that emotional processing, imaginal activity, and most other cognitive tasks normally require a varying amount of interhemispheric cooperation (Banich, 1995; Christman, 1994). As Teicher, Ito, Glod, Schiffer, and Gelbard (1996) indicated, "our capacity to appropriately [sic] identify and evaluate the affect of others, and in turn to communicate affect, depends on a healthy interaction between right-hemisphere emotional perception, and left hemisphere linguistic processing and reason" (p. 65).

In proposing a psychobiological model of alexithymia, we differ from Lane et al. (1997b) who doubted the usefulness of the "functional commissurotomy" model of alexithymia and suggested that researchers focus primarily on a disturbance in the selective attention function of the anterior cingulate cortex. We suggest a more comprehensive model in which the neural correlates of alexithymia include an interhemispheric transfer deficit, thereby reducing coordination and integration of the specialized activities of the two hemispheres, as well as underactivity of that part of the anterior cingulate cortex associated with selective attention and working memory. In our model, states of emotional arousal evoked by activation of the amygdala may remain unregulated for two reasons. First, the unconscious inhibitory feedback from the orbitofrontal cortex to the amygdala is reduced because of an impoverished representational world that limits the ability of this part of the prefrontal cortex to perform a more detailed cognitive appraisal of complex emotional stimuli. Second, the limited ability to represent and contain emotions with words and fantasies and to reflect on their meanings restricts the use of conscious cognitive processes to modulate arousal by way of corticoamygdala pathways. Instead of consciously experiencing a range of differentiated subjective feelings, the individual will be aware of unidimensional feelings and/or elementary and unorganized representations of bodily sensations and *impulses* to action when the amygdala is activated by emotional stimuli.

Lane et al. (1997b) questioned how a failure to transfer emotional information from the right to the left hemisphere could contribute to the pathophysiology that is often associated with alexithymia. Although there is evidence that the right hemisphere is preferentially involved in mediating autonomic nervous system responses to emotional stimuli (Spence, Shapiro, & Zaidel, 1996), patients with lesions of the left hemisphere have a greater autonomic response than normal subjects (Heilman, 1997). It thus appears that the left hemisphere can modulate an individual's arousal response, perhaps by maintaining, as Heilman (1997) suggested, some type of inhibitory control over the right hemisphere. Consequently, impaired interhemispheric communication could lead to extreme dominance of the right hemisphere in controlling the level of activity of the autonomic nervous system.

It must be emphasized that the findings from the neurobiological studies of alexithymia are correlational only and do not imply any cause-effect relationships. Indeed, we must consider the possibility that individual differences in alexithymia and the associated variations in brain organization are both caused by something else. Findings from developmental research are pointing in this direction.

DEVELOPMENTAL CONSIDERATIONS

Although we have stressed the role of symbolic systems, in particular language, in the development of emotional awareness and imaginal capacities, it must be remembered that the first language of the infant for communicating needs comprises nonverbal facial expressions and other behavioral displays of emotion (Emde, 1988; Osofsky, 1992). Of particular importance as the infant grows is the attention the mother gives to her child's facial expressions; it is the mother's perception of these facial cues that enables her to appraise the child's internal state and to respond with her own emotional expressions including prosodic vocalizations. The infant also keeps a close eye on the mother's facial and other behavioral expressions as a signal of her own internal state and as a "mirror" reflecting back to the infant an image of his emotional state; such signals may serve to amplify or dampen the infant's affective state (Schore, 1996). The development of affect awareness and affect regulating skills is therefore facilitated by the mutual sharing and mirroring of emotional expressions with the mother, and later by engaging in pleasurable playful interactions and being taught words to name and talk about feelings (Dunn, Brown, & Beardsall, 1991; Gergely & Watson, 1996; Taylor et al., 1997).

The emotional state of the mother is therefore an important factor in the infant's emotional development. A mother who is very emotionally expressive will communicate very different signals to her infant than a mother who is depressed, anxious, or alexithymic. But even without any psychiatric disorder, parents differ in their level of attunement to their infants' emotional states and ability to respond to the infants' nonverbal emotional communications (Osofsky & Eberhart-Wright, 1988; Stern, 1985). Given that the limbic system evolved as mammals nurtured their young, and that affect is inseparable from attachment and social relations (Watt, 1998), a logical way of investigating differences in emotional development has been to compare mother-infant pairs with different attachment styles.

In a study of healthy one-year-old infants and their mothers, Goldberg, MacKay-Soroka, and Rochester (1994) found that the mothers of infants with an avoidant attachment style responded minimally to their child's expressions of negative affect; mothers of resistant/ambivalent infants were responsive to negative affect but gave less attention to positive affect; and mothers of securely attached infants were responsive to positive, negative, and neutral affect expressions. Whereas the mothers of the secure infants often commented verbally about their infants' emotions (for example, "you are in a good mood today"), the mothers of the avoidant and resistant infants made very few comments. In turn, the securely attached infants were found to express a full range of emotions; the avoidant infants were the least emotionally expressive; and the resistant infants fussed and cried a lot. Although avoidant children learn to suppress displays of negative affect, they are emotionally aroused; after short separations from their mothers, they show elevated heart rates and increased cortisol secretion (Spangler & Grossman, 1993).

Although there are a variety of reasons why a mother may not respond to her infant's emotional signals, there is evidence that some mothers have difficulty accurately decoding the facial expressions of their infants. As part of Goldberg et al.'s (1994) study of one-year-old infants, Myhal and Goldberg (1995) assessed maternal responses to infant facial expressions of emotion and found that the mothers of avoidant infants had difficulty distinguishing between expressions of sadness and distress and were likely to perceive neutral expressions as expressions of interest.

Another characteristic that influences the development of a child's emotional intelligence is the caregiver's capacity for reflective self-awareness and her ability to transmit this capacity to the child. The reflective function, which was linked with linguistic processing and metacognition in our discussion above, includes the caregiver's ability to reflect on the infant's emotional and mental states after she has correctly recognized them. As Fonagy and Target (1997) explained, it is the child's experience of himself or herself as represented in the parent's mind as feeling, thinking, and behaving in particular ways that promotes development of the child's capacity to reflect on and find meaning in his own emotions and behavior as well as in other people's behavior. Using a scale derived from the Adult Attachment Interview, Fonagy et al. (1991) found that both fathers and mothers who were rated high in the capacity for self-reflection were three or four times more likely to have securely attached children than parents whose reflective capacity was poor. The mothers of children with a resistant attachment style scored only slightly lower on reflective function, but mothers of avoidant children scored a great deal lower.

Because the child's experience of the parent's reflective function influences how well this capacity develops in the child, we would expect alexithymia to be associated with insecure attachment styles and with maladaptive affect regulating strategies (such as bingeing on food or developing a somatic symptom), rather than with strategies that involve contemplation and/or talking to other people. These associations have been demonstrated in studies of adults from both clinical and nonclinical groups in which attachment styles were measured with self-report scales (Beckendam, 1997; Schaffer, 1993). More recently, Scheidt et al. (1999) used the Adult Attachment Interview to assess the mental representation of attachment and found that the TAS-20 correlated positively with dismissing (avoidant) attachment and negatively with secure attachment.

Although the development of certain mental capacities in the infant is influenced by emotional interactions with the caregiver, there is accumulating evidence that the caregiver also has a regulatory influence on the maturation of parts of the brain that are involved in emotional awareness and emotion regulation. It is possible to reliably identify an infant's attachment style at around one year of age, which corresponds to a critical time in the maturation of the prefrontal cortex (Schore, 1994). Of particular interest is the orbital area of the prefrontal cortex, which is intimately connected with the amygdala and other parts of the limbic system and is involved in affect regulation, appraisal, directed attention, and the processing of nonverbal emotional signals that are necessary for initiating attachment behaviors (Schore, 1996). Research findings suggest that the maturation of the orbitofrontal cortex occurs in stages and is dependent on the high levels of neurotransmitters that are released in the infant's forebrain by the emotion-laden interactions with the caregivers (Pally, 1997; Schore, 1994, 1996).

Based on an extensive review of animal and human studies, Schore (1994, 1996) suggested that when caregivers fail to regulate excessive levels of low emotional arousal and/or excessive levels of high negative emotional arousal, there can be permanent alterations in the morphological development of the orbitofrontal cortex. For example, excessive states of hyperarousal could lead to excessive pruning of descending neural pathways and reduce the capacity of the cortex to modulate excitatory processes in the amygdala and other subcortical structures.

There is evidence also that the development of other parts of the neocortex can be impeded by emotional trauma. In a recent investigation of school-age children with histories of psychological, physical, or sexual abuse, Teicher et al. (1996) found evidence of a greater prevalence of left-sided frontotemporal electroencephalogram (EEG) abnormalities when compared with nonabused children, and also a higher prevalence of right-left hemispheric asymmetries. In a later investigation of children with histories of severe physical or sexual abuse, Ito, Teicher, Glod, and Ackerman (1998) used the method of measuring EEG coherence to test the hypothesis that early childhood abuse affects cortical maturation and laterality. Subjects were excluded from the study if they had suffered any physical abuse to the head or other form of head trauma. Compared with nonabused children, the abused children had greater coherence in the left hemisphere, and a reversed asymmetry, with left hemisphere coherence significantly exceeding right hemisphere coherence. The findings suggest reduced differentiation of the cortex in the left hemisphere, presumably a consequence of effects of early severe abuse on brain maturation. According to van der Kolk (1998), Teicher and his colleagues are now using magnetic resonance imaging to investigate the brains of abused children and have some preliminary findings that suggest the possibility of abnormalities in the corpus callosum.

CONCLUSION

Alexithymia is a precisely defined and extensively investigated construct that has been applied mostly in the fields of psychosomatic medicine, psychoanalysis, general psychiatry, and personality psychology. Although the construct is derived from clinical observations, alexithymia is conceptually similar to the lower pole of Gardner's (1983) concept of intrapersonal intelligence and overlaps considerably with the more broadly defined construct of emotional intelligence. Theoretical conceptions and research findings from developmental psychology, neurobiology, cognitive science, and studies of attachment suggest that individual differences in alexithymia (and presumably in emotional intelligence as well) can be attributed partly to early environmental influences, especially variations in the caregiver's capacity for attunement, self-reflection, and ability to facilitate a pattern of secure attachment behavior in her child. In addition, there is accumulating evidence that extreme degrees of alexithymia might be a consequence of early trauma, including emotional deprivation and neglect, which appears to alter the maturation of some of the brain structures as well as the mental capacities that are associated with emotional processing and emotional intelligence.

References

Appelbaum, S. A. (1973). Psychological-mindedness: Word, concept, and essence. *International Journal of Psychoanalysis, 54,* 35–45.

Baddeley, A. (1992). Working memory. *Science, 255,* 556–559.

Bagby, R. M., Parker, J.D.A., & Taylor, G. J. (1994). The Twenty-Item Toronto Alexithymia Scale: Part I, Item selection and cross-validation of the factor structure. *Journal of Psychosomatic Research, 38,* 23–32.

Bagby, R. M., Taylor, G. J., & Parker, J.D.A. (1994). The Twenty-Item Toronto Alexithymia Scale: Part II, Convergent, discriminant, and concurrent validity. *Journal of Psychosomatic Research, 38,* 33–40.

Banich, M. T. (1995). Interhemispheric interaction: Mechanisms of unified processing. In F. L. Kitterle (Ed.), *Hemispheric communication: Mechanisms and models* (pp. 271–300). Hillsdale, NJ: Erlbaum.

Bar-On, R. (1997). *BarOn Emotional Quotient Inventory (EQ-i): Technical manual.* Toronto, Canada: Multi-Health Systems.

Beckendam, C. C. (1997). *Dimensions of emotional intelligence: Attachment, affect regulation, alexithymia and empathy.* Unpublished doctoral dissertation, The Fielding Institute, Santa Barbara, CA.

Beresnevaite, M., Taylor, G. J., Parker, J.D.A., & Andziulis, A. (1998). Cross-validation of the factor structure of a Lithuanian translation of the 20-Item Toronto Alexithymia Scale. *Acta Medica Lituanica, 5,* 146–149.

Bonanno, G. A., & Singer, J. L. (1990). Repressive personality style: Theoretical and methodological implications for health and pathology. In J. L. Singer (Ed.), *Repression and dissociation: Implications for personality theory, psychopathology and health* (pp. 435–470). Chicago: University of Chicago Press.

Booth-Butterfield, M., & Booth-Butterfield, S. (1990). Conceptualizing affect as information in communication production. *Human Communication Research, 16,* 451–476.

Booth-Butterfield, M., & Booth-Butterfield, S. (1994). The affective orientation to communication: Conceptual and empirical distinctions. *Communications Quarterly, 42,* 331–344.

Bräutigam, W., & von Rad, M. (Eds.). (1977). *Proceedings of the 11th European Psychosomatic Research Conference: Toward a theory of psychosomatic disorders.* Basel, Switzerland: Karger.

Brown, D. (1993). Affective development, psychopathology, and adaptation. In S. L. Ablon, D. Brown, E. J. Khantzian, & J. E. Mack (Eds.), *Human feelings: Explorations in affect development and meaning* (pp. 5–66). Hillsdale, NJ: Analytic Press.

Bruch, H. (1973). *Eating disorders: obesity, anorexia nervosa, and the person within.* New York: Basic Books.

Cacioppo, J. T., Petty, R. E., Feinstein, A. & Jarvis, W.B.G. (1996). Dispositional differences in cognitive motivation: The life and times of individuals varying in need for cognition. *Psychological Bulletin, 119,* 197–253.

Cacioppo, J. T., Petty, R. E., & Kao, C. F. (1984). The efficient assessment of need for cognition. *Journal of Personality Assessment, 48,* 306–307.

Carver, C. S. (1989). How should multifaceted constructs be tested? Issues illustrated by self-monitoring, attributional style, and hardiness. *Journal of Personality and Social Psychology, 56,* 577–585.

Christman, S. D. (1994). The many sides of the two sides of the brain. *Brain and Cognition, 26,* 91–98.

Conte, H. R., Plutchik, R., Jung, B. B., Picard, S., Karasu, T. B., & Lotterman, A. (1990). Psychological mindedness as a predictor of psychotherapy outcome: A preliminary report. *Comprehensive Psychiatry, 31,* 426–431.

Costa, P. T., & McCrae, R. R. (1987). Personality assessment in psychosomatic medicine: Value of a trait taxonomy. *Advances in Psychosomatic Medicine, 17,* 71–82.

Davies, M., Stankov, L., & Roberts, R. D. (1998). Emotional intelligence: In search of an elusive construct. *Journal of Personality and Social Psychology, 75,* 989–1015.

Dunn, J., Brown, J., & Beardsall, L. (1991). Family talk about feeling states and children's later understanding of others' emotions. *Developmental Psychology, 27,* 448–455.

Emde, R. D. (1988). Development terminable and interminable: Part I, Innate and motivational factors from infancy. *International Journal of Psychoanalysis, 69,* 23–42.

Fonagy, P., Steele, M., Steele, H., Moran, G. S., & Higgit, A. C. (1991). The capacity for understanding mental states: The reflective self in parent and child and its significance for security of attachment. *Infant Mental Health Journal, 12,* 201–218.

Fonagy, P., & Target, M. (1997). Attachment and reflective function: Their role in self-organization. *Development and Psychopathology, 9,* 679–700.

Gardner, H. (1983). *Frames of mind: The theory of multiple intelligences.* New York: Basic Books.

Gazzaniga, M. S. (1992). *Nature's mind: The biological roots of thinking, emotions, sexuality, language, and intelligence.* New York: Basic Books.

Gazzaniga, M. S. (1995). Consciousness and the cerebral hemispheres. In M. S. Gazzaniga (Ed.), *The cognitive neurosciences* (pp. 1391–1400). Cambridge, MA: MIT Press.

Gergely, G., & Watson, J. S. (1996). The social biofeedback theory of parental affect-mirroring: The development of emotional self-awareness and self-control in infancy. *International Journal of Psychoanalysis, 77,* 1191–1212.

Goldberg, S., MacKay-Soroka, S., & Rochester, M. (1994). Affect, attachment, and maternal responsiveness. *Infant Behavior and Development, 17,* 335–339.

Goldman-Rakic, P. S. (1994). Working memory dysfunction in schizophrenia. *Journal of Neuropsychiatry and Clinical Neuroscience, 6,* 348–357.

Heilman, K. M. (1997). The neurobiology of emotional experience. *Journal of Neuropsychiatry and Clinical Neuroscience, 9,* 439–448.

Hoppe, K. D. (1977). Split brains and psychoanalysis. *Psychoanalytic Quarterly, 46,* 220–244.

Hoppe, K. D., & Bogen, J. E. (1977). Alexithymia in twelve commissurotomized patients. *Psychotherapy and Psychosomatics, 28,* 148–155.

Horney, K. (1952). The paucity of inner experiences. *American Journal of Psychoanalysis, 12,* 3–9.

Ito, Y., Teicher, M. H., Glod, C. A., & Ackerman, E. (1998). Preliminary evidence for aberrant cortical development in abused children: A quantitative EEG study. *Journal of Neuropsychiatry and Clinical Neuroscience, 10,* 298–307.

Jula, A., Salminen, J. K., & Saarijärvi, S. (1999). Alexithymia: A facet of essential hypertension. *Hypertension, 33,* 1057–1061.

Keller, D. S., Carroll, K. M., Nich, C., & Rounsaville, B. J. (1995). Alexithymia in cocaine abusers: Response to psychotherapy and pharmacotherapy. *American Journal on Addictions, 4,* 234–244.

Kelman, N. (1952). Clinical aspects of externalized living. *American Journal of Psychoanalysis, 12,* 15–23.

Kihlstrom, J. F. (1987). The cognitive unconscious. *Science, 237,* 1445–1452.

Kosslyn, S. M., & Koenig, O. (1992). *Wet mind: The new cognitive neuroscience.* New York: Macmillan.

Krystal, H. (1968). *Massive psychic trauma.* New York: International Universities Press.

Krystal, H. (1974). The genetic development of affects and affect regression. *Annual of Psychoanalysis, 2,* 98–126.

Krystal, H. (1979). Alexithymia and psychotherapy. *American Journal of Psychotherapy, 33,* 17–31.

Krystal, H. (1982/1983). Alexithymia and the effectiveness of psychoanalytic treatment. *International Journal of Psychoanalytic Psychotherapy, 9,* 353–388.

Krystal, H. (1988a). *Integration and self-healing: Affect, trauma, and alexithymia.* Hillsdale, NJ: Analytic Press.

Krystal, H. (1988b). On some roots of creativity. *Psychiatric Clinics of North America, 11,* 475–491.

Krystal, H., & Raskin, H. (1970). *Drug dependence.* Detroit, MI: Wayne State University Press.

Lane, R. D., Ahern, G. L., Schwartz, G. E., & Kaszniak, A. W. (1997a). Alexithymia: A new neurological model based on a hypothesized deficit in the conscious experience of emotion. In A. Vingerhoets, F. van Bussel, & J. Boelhouwer (Eds.), *The (non)expression of emotions in health and disease.* Tilburg, Netherlands: Tilburg University Press.

Lane, R. D., Ahern, G. L., Schwartz, G. E., & Kaszniak, A. W. (1997b). Is alexithymia the emotional equivalent of blindsight? *Biological Psychiatry, 42,* 834–844.

Lane, R. D., Quinlan, D. M., Schwartz, G. E., Walker, P. A., & Zeitlin, S. B. (1990). The Levels of Emotional Awareness Scale: A cognitive-developmental measure of emotion. *Journal of Personality Assessment, 55,* 124–134.

Lane, R. D., Reiman, E. M., Axelrod, B., Lang-Sheng, Y., Holmes, A., & Schwartz, G. E. (1998). Neural correlates of levels of emotional awareness: Evidence of an interaction between emotion and attention in the anterior cingulate cortex. *Journal of Cognitive Neuroscience, 10,* 525–535.

Lane, R. D., & Schwartz, G. E. (1987). Levels of emotional awareness: A cognitive developmental theory and its application to psychopathology. *American Journal of Psychiatry, 144,* 133–143.

Lane, R., Sechrest, L., Reidel, R., Weldon, V., Kaszniak, A., & Schwartz, G. (1996). Impaired verbal and nonverbal emotion recognition in alexithymia. *Psychosomatic Medicine, 58,* 203–210.

LeDoux, J. E. (1986). Sensory systems and emotions: A model of affective processing. *Integrative Psychiatry, 4,* 237–248.

LeDoux, J. E. (1989). Cognitive-emotional interactions in the brain. *Cognition and Emotion, 3,* 267–289.

LeDoux, J. E. (1996). *The emotional brain: The mysterious underpinnings of emotional life.* New York: Simon and Schuster.

Lesser, I. M. (1985). Alexithymia. *New England Journal of Medicine, 312,* 690–692.

Levitan, H. (1989). Failure of the defensive functions of the ego in psychosomatic patients. In S. Cheren (Ed.), *Psychosomatic medicine: Theory, physiology, and practice* (Vol. 1, pp. 135–157). Madison, CT: International Universities Press.

Lolas, F., & von Rad, M. (1989). Alexithymia. In Cheren, S. (Ed.), *Psychosomatic medicine: theory, physiology, and practice* (Vol. 1, pp. 189–237). Madison, CT: International Universities Press.

Luminet, O., Bagby, R. M., Wagner, H., Taylor, G. J., & Parker, J.D.A. (1999). The relationship between alexithymia and the five factor model of personality: A facet level analysis. *Journal of Personality Assessment, 73,* 345–358.

Maclean, P. D. (1949). Psychosomatic disease and the "visceral brain": Recent developments bearing on the Papez theory of emotion. *Psychosomatic Medicine, 11*, 338–353.

Main, M. (1991). Metacognitive knowledge, metacognitive monitoring, and singular (coherent) vs. multiple (incoherent) model of attachment: Findings and directions for future research. In C. M. Parkes, J. Stevenson-Hinde, & P. Marris (Eds.), *Attachment across the life cycle* (pp. 127–159). London: Routledge.

Martinez-Sánchez, F., Ato-García, M., Adam, E. C., Medina, T.B.H., & España, J. S. (1998). Stability in alexithymia levels: A longitudinal analysis on various emotional answers. *Personality and Individual Differences, 24*, 767–772.

Marty, P., & de M'Uzan, M. (1963). La "pensee operatoire." *Revue Francaise de Psychanalyse, 27*, 1345–1356.

Mayer, J. D., DiPaolo, M., & Salovey P. (1990). Perceiving affective content in ambiguous visual stimuli: A component of emotional intelligence. *Journal of Personality Assessment, 54*, 772–781.

Mayer, J. D., & Salovey, P. (1997). What is emotional intelligence? In P. Salovey & D. J. Sluyter (Eds.), *Emotional development and emotional intelligence: Educational implications* (pp. 3–34). New York: Basic Books.

Mayer, J. D., & Stevens, A. A. (1994). An emerging understanding of the reflective (meta-) experience of mood. *Journal of Research in Personality, 28*, 351–373.

Mayes, L. C., & Cohen, D. J. (1992). The development of a capacity for imagination in early childhood. *Psychoanalytic Study of the Child, 47*, 23–47.

McCrae, R. R., & Costa, P. T. (1985). Openness to experience. In R. Hogan & W. H. Jones (Eds.), *Perspectives in psychology: Theory, measurement, and interpersonal dynamics* (Vol. 1, pp. 145–172). Greenwich, CT: JAI Press.

McCrae, R. R., & Costa, P. T. (1987). Validation of a five-factor model of personality across instruments and observers. *Journal of Personality and Social Psychology, 52*, 81–90.

McCrae, R. R., & John, O. P. (1992). An introduction to the five-factor model and its applications. *Journal of Personality, 60*, 175–215.

McDougall, J. (1972). The anti-analysand in analysis. In S. Lebovici & D. Widlocher (Eds.), *Ten years of psychoanalysis in France.* New York: International Universities Press.

McDougall, J. (1989). *Theaters of the body: A psychoanalytic approach to psychosomatic illness.* New York: Norton.

Myers, L. B. (1995). Alexithymia and repression: The role of defensiveness and trait anxiety. *Personality and Individual Differences, 19*, 489–492.

Myhal, N. K., & Goldberg, S. (1995, March). *Infant attachment and maternal perceptions of facial emotions.* Paper presented at the Society for Research in Child Development, Indianapolis, IN.

Nemiah, J. C. (1977). Alexithymia: Theoretical considerations. *Psychotherapy and Psychosomatics, 28,* 199–206.

Nemiah, J. C., Freyberger, H., & Sifneos, P. E. (1976). Alexithymia: A view of the psychosomatic process. In O. W. Hill (Ed.), *Modern trends in psychosomatic medicine* (Vol. 3, pp. 430–439). London: Butterworths.

Nemiah, J. C., & Sifneos, P. E. (1970). Affect and fantasy in patients with psychosomatic disorders. In O. W. Hill (Ed.), *Modern trends in psychosomatic medicine* (Vol. 2, pp. 26–34). London: Butterworths.

Newton, T. L., & Contrada, R. J. (1994). Alexithymia and repression: Contrasting emotion-focused coping styles. *Psychosomatic Medicine, 56,* 457–462.

Ornstein, R. (1997). *The right mind: Making sense of the hemispheres.* New York: Harcourt Brace.

Osofsky, J. D. (1992). Affective development and early relationships: Clinical implications. In J. W. Barron, M. N. Eagle, & D. L. Wolitzky (Eds.), *Interface of psychoanalysis and psychology* (pp. 233–244). Washington, DC: American Psychological Association.

Osofsky, J. D., & Eberhart-Wright, A. (1988). Affective exchanges between high risk mothers and infants. *International Journal of Psychoanalysis, 69,* 221–231.

Oxman, T. E., Rosenberg, S. D., Schnurr, P. P., & Tucker, G. J. (1985). Linguistic dimensions of affect and thought in somatization disorder. *American Journal of Psychiatry, 142,* 1150–1155.

Pally, R. (1997). How brain development is shaped by genetic and environmental factors. *International Journal of Psycho-Analysis, 78,* 587–593.

Pally, R. (1998). Bilaterality: Hemispheric specialisation and integration. *International Journal of Psycho-Analysis, 79,* 565–578.

Pandey, R., Mandal, M. K., Taylor, G. J., & Parker, J.D.A. (1996). Cross-cultural alexithymia: Development and validation of a Hindi translation of the Twenty-Item Toronto Alexithymia Scale. *Journal of Clinical Psychology, 52,* 173–176.

Parker, J.D.A., Bagby, R. M., Taylor, G. J., Endler, N. S., & Schmitz, P. (1993). Factorial validity of the 20-Item Toronto Alexithymia Scale. *European Journal of Personality, 7,* 221–232.

Parker, J.D.A., Keightley, M. L., Smith, C. T., & Taylor, G. J. (1999). Interhemispheric transfer deficit in alexithymia: An experimental study. *Psychosomatic Medicine, 61,* 464–468.

Parker, J.D.A., Taylor, G. J., & Bagby, R. M. (1993). Alexithymia and the recognition of facial expressions of emotion. *Psychotherapy and Psychosomatics, 59,* 197–202.

Parker, J.D.A., Taylor, G. J., & Bagby, R. M. (1998). Alexithymia: Relationship with ego defense and coping styles. *Comprehensive Psychiatry, 39,* 91–98.

Parker, J.D.A., Taylor, G. J., & Bagby, R. M. (forthcoming). The relationship between alexithymia and emotional intelligence. *Personality and Individual Differences.*

Parker, J.D.A., Taylor, G. J., Bagby, R. M., & Acklin, M. W. (1993). Alexithymia in panic disorder and simple phobia: A comparative study. *American Journal of Psychiatry, 150,* 1105–1107.

Piaget, J. (1981). *Intelligence and affectivity.* Palo Alto, CA: Annual Reviews.

Pinard, L., Negrete, J. C., Annable, L., & Audet, N. (1996). Alexithymia in substance abusers: Persistence and correlates of variance. *American Journal on Addictions, 5,* 32–39.

Porcelli, P., Leoci, C., Guerra, V., Taylor, G. J., & Bagby, R. M. (1996). A longitudinal study of alexithymia and psychological distress in inflammatory bowel disease. *Journal of Psychosomatic Research, 41,* 569–573.

Porcelli, P., Taylor, G. J., Bagby, R. M., & De Carne, M. (1999). Alexithymia and functional gastrointestinal disorders: A comparison with inflammatory bowel disease. *Psychotherapy and Psychosomatics, 68,* 263–269.

Porcelli, P. Zaka, S., Leoci, C., Centonze, S., & Taylor, G. J. (1995). Alexithymia in inflammatory bowel disease. A case-control study. *Psychotherapy and Psychosomatics, 64,* 49–53.

Rolls, E. T. (1995). A theory of emotion and consciousness, and its application to understanding the neural basis of emotion. In M. S. Gazzaniga (Ed.), *The cognitive neurosciences* (pp. 1091–1106). Cambridge, MA: MIT Press.

Ruesch, J. (1948). The infantile personality. *Psychosomatic Medicine, 10,* 134–144.

Salminen, J. K., Saarijärvi, S., Ääirelä, E., & Tamminen, T. (1994). Alexithymia—State or trait? One-year follow-up study of general hospital psychiatric consultation outpatients. *Journal of Psychosomatic Research, 38,* 681–685.

Salovey, P., Hsee, C. K., & Mayer, J. D. (1993). Emotional intelligence and the self-regulation of affect. In D. M. Wegner & J. W. Pennebaker (Eds.), *Handbook of mental control* (pp. 258–277). Englewood Cliffs, NJ: Prentice Hall.

Salovey, P., & Mayer, J. D. (1989/1990). Emotional intelligence. *Imagination, Cognition, and Personality, 9,* 185–211.

Schaffer, C. E. (1993). *The role of adult attachment in the experience and regulation of affect.* Unpublished doctoral dissertation, Yale University, New Haven, CT.

Scheidt, C. E., Waller, E., Schnock, C., Becker-Stoll, F., Zimmerman, P., Lucking, C. H., & Wirsching, M. (1999). Alexithymia and attachment representation in idiopathic spasmodic torticollis. *Journal of Nervous and Mental Disease, 187,* 47–52.

Schore, A. N. (1994). *Affect regulation and the origin of the self: The neurobiology of emotional development.* Hillsdale, NJ: Erlbaum.

Schore, A. N. (1996). The experience-dependent maturation of a regulatory system in the orbital prefrontal cortex and the origin of developmental psychopathology. *Development and Psychopathology, 8,* 59–87.

Schutte, N. S., Malouff, J. M., Hall, L. E., Haggerty, D. J., Cooper, J. T., Golden, C. J., & Dornheim, L. (1998). Development and validation of a measure of emotional intelligence. *Personality and Individual Differences, 25,* 167–177.

Sifneos, P. E. (1967). Clinical observations on some patients suffering from a variety of psychosomatic diseases. *Acta Medicina Psychosomatica, 7,* 1–10.

Sifneos, P. E. (1973). The prevalence of alexithymic characteristics in psychosomatic patients. *Psychotherapy and Psychosomatics, 22,* 255–262.

Sifneos, P. E. (1975). Problems of psychotherapy of patients with alexithymic characteristics and physical disease. *Psychotherapy and Psychosomatics, 26,* 65–70.

Sifneos, P. E. (1996). Alexithymia: Past and present. *American Journal of Psychiatry, 153,* 137–142.

Sifneos, P. E., Apfel-Savitz, R., & Frankel, F. H. (1977). The phenomenon of "alexithymia": Observations in neurotic and psychosomatic patients. *Psychotherapy and Psychosomatics, 28,* 47–57.

Simon, G. E., & Von Korff, M. (1991). Somatization and psychiatric disorder in the NIMH epidemiological catchment area study. *American Journal of Psychiatry, 148,* 1494–1500.

Singer, M. T. (1977). Psychological dimensions in psychosomatic patients. *Psychotherapy and Psychosomatics, 28,* 13–27.

Solms, M. (1997). What is consciousness? *Journal of the American Psychoanalytic Association, 45,* 681–778.

Spangler, G., & Grossman, K. E. (1993). Biobehavioral organization in securely and insecurely attached infants. *Child Development, 64,* 1439–1450.

Spence, S., Shapiro, D., & Zaidel, E. (1996). The role of the right hemisphere in the physiological and cognitive components of emotional processing. *Psychophysiology, 33,* 112–122.

Sperry, R. W., Gazzaniga, M. S., & Bogen, J. E. (1969). Interhemispheric relationships: The neocortical commissures; syndromes of hemisphere disconnection. In P. J. Vinken & G. W. Bruyn (Eds.), *Handbook of clinical neurology* (Vol. 3). Amsterdam: North Holland Publishing.

Stern, D. N. (1985). *The interpersonal world of the infant.* New York, Basic Books.

Taylor, G. J. (1987). *Psychosomatic medicine and contemporary psychoanalysis.* Madison, CT: International Universities Press.

Taylor, G. J. (1994). The alexithymia construct: Conceptualization, validation, and relationship with basic dimensions of personality. *New Trends in Experimental and Clinical Psychiatry, 10,* 61–74.

Taylor, G. J. (1995). Psychoanalysis and empirical research: The example of patients who lack psychological mindedness. *Journal of the American Academy of Psychoanalysis, 23,* 263–281.

Taylor, G. J., Bagby, R. M., & Parker, J.D.A. (1991). The alexithymia construct: A potential paradigm for psychosomatic medicine. *Psychosomatics, 32,* 153–164.

Taylor, G. J., Bagby, R. M., & Parker, J.D.A. (1997). *Disorders of affect regulation: Alexithymia in medical and psychiatric illness.* Cambridge: Cambridge University Press.

Taylor, G. J., Parker, J.D.A., & Bagby, R. M. (1990). A preliminary investigation of alexithymia in men with psychoactive substance dependence. *American Journal of Psychiatry, 147,* 1228–1230.

Taylor, G. J., Parker, J.D.A., Bagby, R. M., & Acklin, M. W. (1992). Alexithymia and somatic complaints in psychiatric out-patients. *Journal of Psychosomatic Research, 36,* 417–424.

Taylor, G. J., Parker, J.D.A., Bagby, R. M., & Bourke, M. P. (1996). Relationships between alexithymia and psychological characteristics associated with eating disorders. *Journal of Psychosomatic Research, 41,* 561–568.

Teicher, M. H., Ito, Y., Glod, C. A., Schiffer, F., & Gelbard, H. A. (1996). Neurophysiological mechanisms of stress response in children. In C. R. Pfeffer (Ed.), *Severe stress and mental disturbance in children* (pp. 59–84). Washington, DC: American Psychiatric Press.

Todarello, O., Taylor, G. J., Parker, J.D.A., & Fanelli, M. (1995). Alexithymia in essential hypertensive and psychiatric outpatients: A comparative study. *Journal of Psychosomatic Research, 39,* 987–994.

van der Kolk, B. A. (1998, May). *The psychobiology of developmental trauma.* Paper presented at the 151st Annual Meeting of the American Psychiatric Association, Toronto, Canada.

Vogt, B. A., Finch, D. M., & Olson, C. R. (1992). Functional heterogeneity in cingulate cortex: The anterior executive and posterior evaluative regions. *Cerebral Cortex, 2,* 435–443.

Watt, D. F. (1998). Letter to the Editor: Affect and the limbic system: Some hard problems. *Journal of Neuropsychiatry and Clinical Neuroscience, 10,* 113–116.

Weinberger, D. A. (1990). The construct validity of the repressive coping style. In J. L. Singer (Ed.) *Repression and dissociation: Implications for personality theory, psychopathology and health* (pp. 337–386). Chicago: University of Chicago Press.

Wise, T. N., & Mann, L. S. (1994). The relationship between somatosensory amplification, alexithymia, and neuroticism. *Journal of Psychosomatic Research, 38,* 515–521.

Wise, T. N., Mann, L. S., & Shay, L. (1992). Alexithymia and the five factor model of personality. *Comprehensive Psychiatry, 33,* 147–151.

Wurmser, L. (1974). Psychoanalytic considerations of the etiology of compulsive drug use. *Journal of the American Psychoanalytic Association, 22,* 820–843.

Yehuda, R., Steiner, A., Kahana, B., Binder-Brynes, K., Southwick, S. M., Zemelman, S., & Giller, E. L. (1997). Alexithymia in holocaust survivors with and without PTSD. *Journal of Traumatic Stress, 10,* 93–100.

Yelsma, P. (1996). Affective orientations of perpetrators, victims, and functional spouses. *Journal of Interpersonal Violence, 11,* 141–161.

Zeitlin, S. B., Lane, R. D., O'Leary, D. S., & Schrift, M. J. (1989). Interhemispheric transfer deficit and alexithymia. *American Journal of Psychiatry, 146,* 1434–1439.

CHAPTER FOUR

Emotional Competence

A Developmental Perspective

Carolyn Saarni

In this chapter I describe the construct of emotional competence and subsequently discuss how it differs from the related construct of emotional intelligence. Because I take a developmental perspective, I illustrate emotional competence with the results of research undertaken with children and adolescents. I also think it worthwhile to remind the reader that the subdiscipline within psychology in which each of the contributors to this volume was trained influences the view taken toward such complex concepts as *emotion, intelligence,* or *competence.* For example, the relative weight given to context versus the person is one of the ways in which one's subdiscipline affects the theoretical stance taken. I try to make explicit the assumptions of my theoretical perspective as a developmental psychologist.

DEFINITION OF EMOTIONAL COMPETENCE

My working definition of emotional competence is as follows: emotional competence is the demonstration of self-efficacy in emotion-eliciting social transactions. *Self-efficacy* is used here to mean that the individual believes that he or she has the capacity and skills to achieve a desired outcome. What that particular desired outcome is will reflect cultural values and beliefs, but those values and beliefs will have been transformed by the self into personal meanings. One may think of this as a unique fingerprint that the individual impresses on cultural practices. When the notion of self-efficacy is then applied to emotion-eliciting social transactions, we are describing how people can respond emotionally, yet simultaneously and strategically apply their knowledge about emotions and their emotional expressiveness to relationships with others, such that they can negotiate their way through interpersonal exchanges and regulate their emotional experiences toward desired outcomes or goals. *Desired outcomes or goals* for the emotionally competent individual will, by definition, be integrated with that individual's moral commitments.

Mature emotional competence, as defined here, assumes that moral character and ethical values deeply influence one's emotional responses in ways that promote personal integrity. Mature emotional competence should reflect wisdom, and this wisdom carries with it the significant ethical values of one's culture. Curiously, few psychologists have addressed wisdom, much less how it develops or even how "we know it when we see it." In summary, emotional competence is a broad umbrella-like construct and as such incorporates several contributing processes and yields a variety of consequences. I address these contributing processes and consequences in subsequent sections of this chapter.

CONTRIBUTORS TO EMOTIONAL COMPETENCE

The primary contributors to emotional competence include one's self (or ego identity), one's moral disposition, and one's developmental history. These contributors are themselves complex processes, situated in time and cultural context. The temporal anchor in emotional competence is probably most readily seen in the developmental history of any given individual, yet that history is also deeply contextualized by cultural practices, by societal and individual belief systems, and by the transactional relationships in which individuals have been engaged. The influence of time and context on emotional competence is also noteworthy in that we are all assured of experiencing emotional *in*competence at one time or another, in some situation or another, for which we are unprepared or overextended. We will then experience as a result a sense of diminishment, or stress, or feelings of failure, or perhaps simply confusion. For example, the reader might reminisce—or fantasize—about trying to fathom the "proper" way to express emotions when traveling in a very different cultural setting. Feeling awkward or self-consciously exposed might well be the emotionally toned outcome that one experiences until one has had some time to learn the meaningful and socially appropriate ways to express one's feelings in that different cultural setting.

The Self's Role

The self functions to coordinate and mediate in an adaptive fashion the meaningfulness of the environment for the individual (for example, McAdams, 1996). A critical consequence of the self's role is that values are assigned to the context we are engaged in. When we differentially respond to the particular context facing us because of its relative significance to us, then we are also acting in a goal-directed fashion, and to be goal directed is to function with motives when engaged in a particular context (Lazarus, 1991). It is in this sense that emotions are functional: they serve to goad us into action whereby we initiate, modify, maintain, or terminate our relationship to the particular circumstances we are engaged in (Campos, Mumme, Kermoian, & Campos, 1994). Self-efficacy is clearly served when adaptive goals are attained (Bandura, 1989).

I prefer to think of the self as a system of functions, many of which by adulthood have become automatic. Neisser has developed a readily comprehended taxonomy of the self-system that lends itself well to the construct of emotional competence (Neisser, 1988, 1992; Neisser & Fivush, 1994). His *ecological self* is that feature of the self that is pragmatically engaged with the environment. In adulthood it is probably the least conscious feature of the self-system, yet it is how we bidirectionally interact with our surroundings (social and physical). What happens is a joint function of what we can do with the environment and what the environment provides to us for interaction. Infants and young children spend much of their time exploring and learning about what the environment affords for interaction; in adulthood we often operate on "automatic pilot" until we encounter some aspect of our environment that requires us to seek out its affordant features. Again the example of adapting to a radically different culture fits. As a further, somewhat facetious illustration, some Westerners have never learned to use chopsticks to eat. Such individuals have yet to learn how chopsticks provide an excellent means for eating one's food. A person who has grown up using chopsticks as eating utensils does not have to consciously think about how "to interact" with them.

Neisser's *extended self* allows us to take what we have learned and use it to guide our adaptation to a new context. Essentially our expectations and scripts derive from this sort of learning, and they provide us with a readiness for dealing with similar yet novel situations. In this sense, the extended self allows us to bridge time from the past into the future. We take with us into new interpersonal encounters our social expectancies and beliefs that we have learned directly or vicariously from past encounters and relationships. Obviously, there are frequent occasions when what we import into the new situation does not work well, and we then revise our expectancies as we learn these new features of a novel environment.

The third feature of the self is the *evaluative self;* this aspect emphasizes the feelings and values that people attach to their interactions with the environment. For example, one child grows up with admiration for and fascination with spiders, and another child panics in terror at the sight of one; another example is that some adults love to party, and others would rather stay home curled up with a good book. The significance of the evaluative self is that it refers to the goal-directed nature of the self-system; as we mature we learn to maneuver through our interactions such that we seek out advantages and try to avoid disadvantages. We also apply this approach to our relationships and the perception we have of others' feelings about us. A powerful motivator for much human behavior is to gain or maintain others' approval of oneself, and the evaluative self in conjunction with the extended self internalizes these valenced messages about the self into beliefs and expectancies about oneself. By the time they enter school, children who are developing normally have the capacity for self-evaluation, which is necessary for being able to regulate or monitor the self in relation to others' expectations for appropriate behavior (Harter, 1998; Kopp, 1992), whereas developmentally delayed children often demonstrate a deficit in such self-regulatory capacity (Kopp & Wyer, 1994).

In summary, the concepts of the ecological, extended, and evaluative self permit us to look at functional interactions between individuals and their social and physical environments. This triple concept of self also gives us a conceptual tool to look at how individual differences may manifest themselves, for example, why person A feels self-efficacious in a particular social situation, whereas person B feels overwhelmed in what seems to be the same social situation. The point to be made here is that the ostensibly similar social situation is not experienced transactionally as uniform, with the result that person A's emotional response differs from that of person B. The social situation is a dynamic interaction and varies functionally according to how person A's multifaceted self engages in it, in contrast with how person B's multifaceted self engages in it. Emotional competence then becomes linked to how and when a particular multifaceted self experiences self-efficacy in particular transactions. This is a major source of inconsistency or variability in emotional competence. We may demonstrate emotional competence in 99 different interactions, but in the 100th we may encounter that situation for which we are not prepared or do not have the skills to cope. We may also find that we would rather deceive ourselves about our negative experience altogether rather than deal directly with our emotional incompetence (see also Baumeister's excellent discussion, 1993). Indeed, self-deception has been argued to be a prime mediator between affective disposition (mood states) and subjective well-being (Erez, Johnson, & Judge, 1995) in that individuals discount, ignore, or minimize negative feedback about the self and maintain overly positive views of the self. Harter (1990) has noted that by age four, children in the United States demonstrate this self-favorability bias.

Neisser's model of the tripartite self is one that helps us to look at emotional experience within the individual as it unfolds (1) in a physical and social environment (the ecological self), (2) relative to a temporal framework (the extended self), and (3) in response to the standards and values of the family and societal context (the evaluative self). But how applicable is this model of "self" in other cultures? This is an important issue to consider about emotional competence; recall that the definition given for emotional competence stressed self-efficacy in emotion-eliciting social transactions. If another society did not have the same views as a Western society has about a "self," how would that affect the demonstration of emotional competence in emotion-eliciting social transactions within such societies? I refer the reader to other sources that consider this important question (Kitayama & Markus, 1994; Kitayama, Markus, & Matsumoto, 1995; Markus & Kitayama, 1994; Mesquita & Frijda, 1992; Saarni, 1999; G. M. White, 1994). It is also an issue that confronts the construct of emotional intelligence.

The Role of Moral Disposition

I make the assumption that if we are functioning in an emotionally adaptive and competent fashion, we are invariably also living in accord with our moral disposition but not necessarily, however, with our moral rules. The latter are quite frequently relativistic and change with development and context, but the former is embedded in such concepts as sympathy, self-control, fairness, and a sense of obligation (Campbell & Christopher, 1996; Flanagan, 1991; J. Q. Wilson, 1993). Personal integrity comes with a life lived in accord with one's moral sense or disposition, and concomitantly, such a life reflects emotional competence. Perhaps it is no accident that the individuals studied in Colby and Damon's (1992) case-oriented research on moral action and moral ideals were characterized by their commitment to truth seeking, open-mindedness, compassion for others, flexibility toward change, and a sensitivity to "doing the right thing" in their daily lives and relationships with others. These adults demonstrated the sort of personal integrity that Blasi (1983) had earlier described as characteristic of a moral self or identity, wherein one's self-concept is centrally defined by moral commitment. A moral self, entailing as it must a commitment to moral understanding and action, is synonymous with moral character.

The qualities noted previously by J. Q. Wilson (1993) and others as being essential to moral disposition are not new; they are similar to and overlap with those espoused by Aristotle as constituting virtues (trans. 1985): courage (which was also viewed as necessary for sustaining community), justice (fairness in equity, reciprocity, and impartiality), temperance (or self-control), and wisdom (a felt knowingness of what is a right choice). The philosophers J. Q. Wilson (1993) and MacIntyre (1981) echo Aristotle in their analyses of what is significant about honorable character, and Wilson in particular relies on developmental theory and anthropological findings to buttress his claim that character lies at the heart of a balanced life that is well lived. Walker and Hennig (1997) in their analysis of moral development as part of personality echo a similar theme; indeed, in reviewing their own and others' research on moral development (Haan, 1991; Walker, Pitts, Hennig, & Matsuba, 1995; Walker & Taylor, 1991) they emphasize that moral commitment and personal integrity are inextricable from one's social-emotional experience. I claim as well that such a balanced, well-lived life, characterized by personal integrity, is one that reflects mature emotional competence. I do not see how they can be separated from one another.

The idea that character is embedded in emotional competence also reveals that emotional competence is something we get better at as we mature. Preschool children demonstrate sympathy, some degree of self-control (or compliance), and occasionally a sense of equity in their sharing. Duty, obligation, or conscience require more maturity, and this moral sense becomes evident in school-age children. But it is probably not until adolescence that we see an emerging personal integrity that we call character. I suggest that it is with mature adolescents that we will begin to see well-developed emotional competence. Indeed, when we encounter immature adolescents (that is, for their age, they are acting like younger children), we are apt to hesitate when it comes to having to rely on their personal integrity. In short, their character is still unformed, and I wager our response to their emotional functioning will indicate that we experience them as less than emotionally competent. I think that the well-adjusted school-age child may be a good candidate for emotional competence as well, but because she has not yet gone through the challenges of puberty to her self-definition and emotional experience, I suggest instead that she is well on her way to demonstrating emotional competence, albeit not yet at a mature level.

The Role of Developmental History

As a social constructivist, my view of how developmental history affects emotional competence is one that emphasizes that we *learn* to give meaning to our context-dependent emotional experience via our social exposure to emotion discourse and narrative and our cognitive developmental capacities. In this sense, a social-constructivist approach to emotion is highly individualized: one's emotional experience is contingent on exposure to specific contexts, unique social history, and current cognitive developmental functioning, with this last component permitting us to transform our context by the very fact that we interact with it (Carpendale, 1997). Our unique social history includes our immersion in our culture's beliefs, attitudes, and assumptions (often communicated via narrative and discourse), our observation of important others, and the patterns of reinforcement from those with whom we are significantly involved. All of these factors contribute to our learning what it means to feel something and then do something about it. The concepts we assign to emotional experience are saturated with nuance and context-dependent meaning, including the social roles we occupy, such as gender and age roles.

A social constructivist view of emotional competence emphasizes one's own active creation of emotional experience, integrated as it is with one's cognitive developmental functioning and one's social experience. It is this feature of constructivism that differentiates it from the more commonly encountered term *social construction of emotions* (Armon-Jones, 1986). The latter is related in that it proposes that all emotions are sociocultural products, but it does not allow for the vagaries of human development or the active transformation of context that occurs by virtue of our interaction with it. Indeed, chance encounters *are given meaning* and thus transformed by most Western individuals through attributions such as "as luck would have it" or "little did I know that day would change my life forever" or "I seized the moment" or "fate brought us together" or "bad things happen for a good reason: they make you appreciate life." Social constructivism, then, allows for chance and fortuity in development, whereas constructionism posits a more rigid handing down or internalization of cultural meanings and discourse (see relevant discussions by Bandura, 1998; Gergen, 1998; Krantz, 1998). With emotional competence we can embrace fortuitous events for the possibilities they extend to us; when these random events are destructive and traumatic, the emotionally competent (and thus resilient) response will be to approach one's recovery and subsequent life with an enriched view of our vulnerability to chance, both positive as well as negative. Hopefully, emotional self-efficacy, the final skill of emotional competence described below, is the outcome for those who survive trauma: they can learn to live and feel with greater awareness (Janoff-Bulman, 1998; Janoff-Bulman & Frantz, 1997).

As should be evident by now, central to my view of both developmental history and to the construct of emotional competence is the role played by social experience. For the sake of brevity, I include Table 4.1, adapted from Saarni (1999), which presents in schematic form the major developmental "milestones" for how we learn to connect emotion and social experience meaningfully. I use three broad organizing themes (regulation/coping, expressive behavior, and relationship-building) that capture for me the essence of what is important in emotional development. These organizing themes are also interactive with one another; I think of them as the multidimensional threads that constitute a dynamic fabric's weft and warp, yielding the woven pattern of adaptive emotional functioning. The developmental progression that I illustrate begins with birth and extends through adolescence, but the "fabric of emotional functioning" is indeterminate in length and may even extend its influence across generations. (For readers unfamiliar with developmental research, empirical support for the developmental milestones mentioned in Table 4.1 are reviewed in Harris, 1989; Lewis & Michalson, 1983; Saarni & Harris, 1989; Saarni, Mumme, & Campos, 1998; Thompson, 1990, 1998, among others.)

With this rather lengthy introduction to the theoretical foundations of emotional competence, I turn next to the skills that constitute emotional competence. We learn these skills in social contexts, and as a consequence, the skills listed below should be understood as representing Western cultural beliefs about emotional experience and may have limited generalizability to other cultures. These skills are presented in a sequence, but this sequence is *not* a developmental

Table 4.1. Noteworthy Markers of Emotional Development in Relation to Social Interaction.

Age Period	Regulation/Coping	Expressive Behavior	Relationship Building
Infancy: 0 to 12 months	Self-soothing and learning to modulate reactivity. Regulation of attention in service of coordinated action. Reliance on caregivers for supportive "scaffolding" during stressful circumstances.	Behavior synchrony with others in some expressive channels. Increasing discrimination of others' expressions. Increasing expressive responsiveness to stimuli under contingent control. Increasing coordination of expressive behaviors with emotion-eliciting circumstances.	Social games and turn-taking (e.g., "peek-a-boo"). Social referencing. Socially instrumental signal use (e.g., "fake" crying to get attention).
Toddlerhood: 12 months to 2 years	Emergence of self-awareness and consciousness of own emotional response. Irritability due to constraints and limits imposed on expanding autonomy and exploration needs.	Self-evaluation and self-consciousness evident in expressive behavior accompanying shame, pride, coyness. Increasing verbal comprehension and production of words for expressive behavior and affective states.	Anticipation of different feelings toward different people. Increasing discrimination of others' emotions and their meaningfulness. Early forms of empathy and prosocial action.
Preschool: 2½ to 5 years	Symbolic access facilitates emotion regulation, but symbols can also provoke distress. Communication with others extends child's evaluation of and awareness of own feelings and of emotion-eliciting events.	Adoption of pretend expressive behavior in play and teasing. Pragmatic awareness that false facial expressions can mislead another about one's feelings.	Communication with others elaborates child's understanding of social transactions and expectations for comportment. Sympathetic and prosocial behavior toward peers. Increasing insight into others' emotions.

Table 4.1. Continued.

Age Period	Regulation/Coping	Expressive Behavior	Relationship Building
Early elementary school: 5 to 7 years	Self-conscious emotions (e.g., embarrassment) are targeted for regulation. Seeking support from caregivers still a prominent coping strategy, but increasing reliance on situational problem-solving evident.	Adoption of "cool emotional front" with peers.	Increasing coordination of social skills with one's own and others' emotions. Early understanding of consensually agreed upon emotion "scripts."
Middle childhood: 7 to 10 years	Problem-solving preferred coping strategy if control is at least moderate. Distancing strategies used if control is appraised as minimal.	Appreciation of norms for expressive behavior, whether genuine or dissembled. Use of expressive behavior to modulate relationship dynamics (e.g., smiling while reproaching a friend).	Awareness of multiple emotions toward the same person. Use of multiple time frames and unique personal information about another as aids in the development of close friendships.
Pre-adolescence: 10 to 13 years	Increasing accuracy in appraisal of realistic control in stressful circumstances. Capable of generating multiple solutions and differentiated strategies for dealing with stress.	Distinction made between genuine emotional expression with close friends and managed displays with others.	Increasing social sensitivity and awareness of emotion "scripts" in conjunction with social roles.
Adolescence: 13+ years	Awareness of one's own emotion cycles (e.g., guilt about feeling angry) facilitates insightful coping. Increasing integration of moral character and personal philosophy in dealing with stress and subsequent decisions.	Skillful adoption of self-presentation strategies for impression management.	Awareness of mutual and reciprocal communication of emotions as affecting quality of relationship.

ordering of skills, rather one can observe protodevelopmental manifestations of each skill. It is likely that not until late adolescence would one observe all of the skills being applied effectively and competently. However, given the significance of context, there will inevitably be situations in which we respond with relative emotional incompetence, in spite of our best efforts to cope effectively. Listed below are the skills of emotional competence.

Skills of Emotional Competence

1. Awareness of one's emotional state, including the possibility that one is experiencing multiple emotions, and at even more mature levels, awareness that one might also not be consciously aware of one's feelings because of unconscious dynamics or selective inattention.

2. Skill in discerning others' emotions, based on situational and expressive cues that have some degree of cultural consensus as to their emotional meaning.

3. Skill in using the vocabulary of emotion and expression terms commonly available in one's subculture and, at more mature levels, skill in acquiring cultural scripts that link emotion with social roles.

4. Capacity for empathic and sympathetic involvement in others' emotional experiences.

5. Skill in understanding that inner emotional state need not correspond to outer expression, both in oneself and in others, and at more mature levels, understanding that one's emotional-expressive behavior may impact on another and to take this into account in one's self-presentation strategies.

6. Skill in adaptive coping with aversive or distressing emotions by using self-regulatory strategies (such as "stress hardiness") that ameliorate the intensity or temporal duration of such emotional states.

7. Awareness that the structure or nature of relationships is in part defined by both the degree of emotional immediacy or genuineness of expressive display and by the degree of reciprocity or symmetry within the relationship; as such, mature intimacy is in part defined by mutual or reciprocal sharing of genuine emotions, whereas a parent-child relationship may have asymmetric sharing of genuine emotions.

8. Capacity for emotional self-efficacy: The individual views herself or himself as feeling, overall, the way she or he wants to feel. That is, emotional self-efficacy means that one accepts one's emotional experience, whether unique and eccentric or culturally conventional, and this acceptance is in alignment with the individual's beliefs about what constitutes desirable emotional "balance." In essence, one is living in

accord with one's personal theory of emotion[1] when one demonstrates emotional self-efficacy that is integrated with one's moral sense.

CONSEQUENCES OF EMOTIONAL COMPETENCE

As children acquire these skills of emotional competence in a variety of contexts, they demonstrate in their behavior the consequences of emotional competence. Three such consequences have intrigued me, and all three have a rich empirical research history. The first noteworthy consequence is effective *skill in managing one's emotions*, which is critical to being able to negotiate one's way through interpersonal exchanges. Other important consequences of emotional competence are *a sense of subjective well-being* and adaptive *resilience* in the face of future stressful circumstances. Much of the relevant research supporting both the preceding list of emotional competence skills and these three consequences of emotional competence is available in published reviews (Asher & Rose, 1997; Compas, Worsham, & Ey, 1992; Crick & Dodge, 1994; Denham, 1999; Fox, 1994; Garber, Braafladt, & Zeman, 1991; Parke, Cassidy, Burks, Carson, & Boyum, 1992; Saarni, 1999; Thompson, 1991; Wolchik & Sandler, 1997).

Management of Emotion

Coping Strategies. Critical to the management of emotion are coping strategies, and we know that children learn emotion scripts for socially desirable coping strategies at a relatively young age (six to seven years) and with increasing maturity become more capable of providing more elaborated and contextualized justifications for strategic coping as well as expectations for how one would feel afterward (Saarni, 1997). Similarly, older children take into account dyadic status differences, degree of affiliation, and intensity of felt emotion when considering hypothetical stressful encounters and how they would manage their emotional-expressive behavior in such hypothetical situations (Saarni, 1991). There is now a large body of social cognition research that documents children's script knowledge of how to manage one's emotional-expressive behavior when faced with challenging situations (reviewed by Saarni et al., 1998), and generally speaking, what we have found out is that older children view both genuinely

---

[1] A personal theory of emotion derives from a constructivist position, which assumes that people function according to beliefs and expectations that give meaning to and shape their experience. A personal theory of emotion is one's set of beliefs and explanations for how emotion "works." It may be thought of as an internal working model for emotion (see also the related literature on folk theories of emotion, such as D'Andrade, 1987; Lutz, 1987; Russell, Fernandez-Dols, Manstead, & Wellenkamp, 1996; Saarni, 1999).

expressed emotional behavior as well as dissembled emotional behavior as regulated acts.

Observed Management of Emotional-Expressive Behavior. The number of studies that have collected observational data of children's attempts at managing their emotional-expressive behavior are considerably fewer in number than the preceding social cognition-oriented studies that examine children's script knowledge in hypothetical situations. Here I comment on only two. A recent study by Marion Underwood and colleagues (Underwood, Hurley, Johanson, & Mosley, 1999) examined how children (ages eight to twelve years, $N = 382$) coped with a provoking unfamiliar peer during a rigged computer game. They found unexpectedly that very few expressions of overt anger occurred during these interactions, despite the subject children being mocked and insulted by the confederate peer. Most often, the children remained silent after the confederate's insult, retaining a neutral expression or smiling. Gender differences indicated that girls were more likely to look mildly sad, giggle self-consciously, or make self-deprecating comments. In short, these children managed their emotional-expressive behavior very prudently. They were faced with having to deal with an unknown child, in a university laboratory, and probably realized they were being videotaped. Some children opted to terminate the computer game early, and interestingly, these children were somewhat disproportionately more likely to have been nominated by their classmates as being prone to aggressive behavior (Underwood, 1997). But in this context they were neither aggressive nor expressive of anger. I can imagine that some might have thought to themselves, Who needs this? relative to the onslaught of mild insults being directed at them, and thus they competently asserted their right to terminate the experiment.

The second study was conducted by myself and involved the videotaping of children interacting with an adult confederate, first when she was in a happy, cheerful state and then a week later when she was in a depressed state (Saarni, 1992). The children ($N = 80$) were asked by another adult to try to help cheer her up, and all agreed to do so. In this second session they had to be able to manage their emotional-expressive behavior when dealing with the depressed woman, and compared to the youngest children (six years old), the older children (eleven to twelve years old) demonstrated more composure and talked and smiled more, but they also showed more fidgety, tension-laden behavior. The youngest children were more likely to look distressed and upset, and the middle age group (eight to nine years old), exhibited a curiously emotionally flat profile. I suspect they were just trying to endure the interaction as best they could.

What these two studies suggest is that children's management of their emotional-expressive behavior can be deemed *emotionally competent after the fact.* We can examine their behavior in situation X to see if it served them well under the circumstances. We may not be on such firm ground if we try to predict ahead of time whether a given child will behave in an emotionally competently fashion (Underwood's aggressive children did *not* behave incompetently, as might have been expected by their sociometric ratings; Underwood, 1997). Emotional competence is dynamic; it is a judgment we make about particular behaviors in particular emotion-eliciting circumstances. Yet I also contend that judgments of mature emotional competence will be made when we view individuals as applying their moral principles to the emotion-eliciting circumstances and responding in accord with their moral sense.

Subjective Well-Being

Social psychologists have long examined the components of and contributors to subjective well-being (see Lazarus, 1991, and a recent review by Diener, Suh, Lucas, & Smith, 1999). In an early review of well-being, W. Wilson (1967) had concluded that one would be more likely to be happy if one were also young, educated, relatively affluent, religious, and married. Diener et al. (1999) concluded that the parameters of well-being were construed somewhat differently as the millennium drew to its end: now we more likely feel better if we have a positive temperament, embrace optimism and minimize the negative, and enjoy mutually supportive relationships, and it still helps a great deal if we make adequate money and/or have access to resources so that we can reach our goals. Where does emotional competence fit into subjective well-being? I argue that it is the last skill of emotional competence, the capacity for emotional self-efficacy, that facilitates well-being, for it entails accepting one's emotional experience as justified and worthy. Research with children and adolescents suggests that self-worth mediates both emotional and motivational systems such that positive beliefs about oneself were associated with more positive affect and energetic pursuit of goals important to the self (Harter, 1986, 1999). From this standpoint, high self-esteem may function as an optimism buffer when the individual is feeling badly: one acknowledges that one is feeling quite miserable at the moment, but the aversive emotional experience is given meaning and recognized as appropriate to the specific circumstances. I do not wish to imply that a shallow positive gloss is merely applied to the negative emotional experience, but rather that the negative feelings are *integrated* into one's understanding of oneself such that one emerges as more perceptive and emotionally aware (see Janoff-Bulman & Frantz, 1997).

Research on children's subjective well-being per se is very limited, and comparable constructs to the adult research literature are more often subsumed under self-esteem research or emotion regulation research. Illustrative of the latter is a recent observational study on preschoolers' emotion regulation and social competence (Fabes et al., 1999). The results suggested that young children's skillfulness at focusing their attention and inhibiting inappropriate responses (as rated by their teachers) was related to their being less likely to experience negative emotional arousal when interacting with their peers in high-activity play situations. Children who could access this sort of self-control (referred to by the authors as *effortful control,* an aggregate index) appeared to be able to attenuate some of the escalating emotional dynamic of the play situation (such as yelling, running wildly), avoid aggressive interaction, and respond in more socially competent and constructive ways. Under this research rubric, well-being may be inferred as being present in young children's socially competent behavior and in their successful avoidance of negative emotional arousal in high-intensity social play. What other developmental research appears to confirm is that those children who are capable of self-control are also those who appear to have learned some of the critical and basic skills of emotional competence: awareness of one's own emotions, understanding and empathizing with others' emotions, access to and skill at using an emotion lexicon and emotion scripts, and coping with negative circumstances and negative emotions (Gottman, Katz, & Hooven, 1997; other supporting research reviewed in Saarni, 1999).

Resilience

Resilience is typically defined as the ability to recover rapidly after experiencing some adverse experience. It would make sense that if one behaves with emotional competence across a great many stressful experiences, then one would apparently be demonstrating resilience. However, resilience is hardly a unidimensional construct, and some research docs indicate that repeated debilitating experiences may wear out protective influences and erode competent functioning in some domains (Luthar, Doernberger, & Zigler, 1993). I have found the longitudinal research by Murphy and Moriarty (1976) to be most useful in elaborating on the consequences of emotional competence. Their data showed that if children were exposed to stressors that were *within* their coping capacity and yet they were pushed a little bit to meet the emotional challenge, then those children were more likely to demonstrate improved coping skills when faced with future stressors. A child who behaves emotionally competently is also likely to have the social scaffolding available to her or him such that coping with genuinely difficult and taxing stressors is supported and kept within emotionally manageable boundaries. The child subjected to chronic trauma and who has little or inconsistent social support from attachment figures will show their vulnerability, albeit not necessarily across all domains (see Luthar, et al., 1993, as well as Ackerman, Izard, Schoff, Youngstrom, & Kogos, 1999). In short, resilience is a consequence of emotional competence, but it cannot be divorced from the social relationships that an individual has as resources to draw on.

EMOTIONAL COMPETENCE
VERSUS EMOTIONAL INTELLIGENCE

My final theoretical comments have to do with distinguishing emotional competence from the construct of emotional intelligence. Like emotional competence, the construct of emotional intelligence has also been given a variety of definitions. Surprisingly, it has often been defined without reference to ethical values (with the exception of altruism) or one's ego identity (Goleman, 1995; Mayer & Salovey, 1997), and an individual's developmental history has typically been given scant attention, if any. I include here Mayer and Salovey's (1997) definition of the construct of emotional intelligence: "Emotional intelligence involves the ability to perceive accurately, appraise, and express emotion; the ability to access and/or generate feelings when they facilitate thought; the ability to understand emotion and emotional knowledge; and the ability to regulate emotions to promote emotional and intellectual growth" (p. 10).

The empirical work undertaken to measure these *abilities* that make up emotional intelligence has been largely with adult subjects (but see below), and I have drawn on the recent work by Davies, Stankov, and Roberts (1998) for my comments here. Davies and her colleagues evaluated three large samples of adults (majority male, total sample $N = 530$), giving them rather extensive batteries of tests to determine both the discriminant and the convergent validity of instruments designed to measure emotional intelligence. They included self-report instruments developed by Mayer and others that sought to measure various "abilities" of emotional information processing, and an exploratory instrument designed to directly assess emotional perception and labeling of facial expressions, auditory tones, and colors. In addition, they used a wide variety of other instruments designed to elucidate cognitive aptitudes, verbal ability, social functioning, and personality variables.

After their many analyses, Davies et al. concluded that all that really remained as a somewhat viable, albeit weak, measure of emotional intelligence was the instrument for assessing emotion perception through "correct" identification of facial expressions, and even those results suffered from low reliability. The self-report questionnaires all correlated quite substantively with existing personality tests, and thus discriminating emotional intelligence from personality traits such as extroversion, neuroticism, and agreeableness may be problematic. Verbal ability also correlated with the emotion information processing self-report questionnaires. Davies et al. concluded that perhaps the construct of emotional intelligence is not really a mental aptitude, and they questioned whether it belongs in the traditional psychometric view of intelligence. Their data also clearly demonstrated the difficulties in trying to operationalize emotional intelligence as a distinct construct.

In contrast to Davies et al.'s opinion, recent work by Mayer, Caruso, and Salovey (forthcoming) has focused on establishing the psychometric properties of their proposed construct of emotional intelligence. Their mission was to demonstrate that their composite battery of tests and tasks (the Multifactor Emotional Intelligence Scale [MEIS]) could meet the three traditional classes of criteria for intelligence. Their factor analysis of the MEIS revealed a *general emotional intelligence,* a *perception factor,* an *understanding factor,* and a *managing factor.* The members of their sample ($n = 503$) were mostly young (mean age twenty-three years), mostly female, and relatively educated. Women out-performed men by an average of 0.5 standard deviations; verbal ability correlation with the general factor of emotional intelligence was .36 ($p < .001$), and the correlation of a general self-report empathy measure with this general factor was .33. Their sample of young adults performed a bit better than their sample of adolescents (twelve to 16 years, $n = 229$) with regard to the perception of the facial expression task and the synesthesia task, but the young adults were notably better than the young teens at understanding emotion blends. Verbal ability and empathy correlated positively for the adolescents' general factor of emotional intelligence as well.

Mayer et al. wanted to exclude from their emotional intelligence construct features that detracted from their emphasis on mental ability or information processing aptitude. Culture, context, self-representations (see Harter, 1998), and moral disposition, which are important to emotional competence, would be variables that would "muddy the waters," as it were. Their phrase was very apt: emotional intelligence refers to "a thinker-with-a-heart." These thinkers-with-a-heart apply their mental abilities to perceiving, understanding, and managing social relations, but Mayer et al. declined to make any claims about the goals of these thinkers-with-a-heart, that is, do they apply their talents as con artists or in ways that benefit others? (*Note:* Skillful con artists discern others' emotions rather well, but their seeming empathy is not guided by a felt responsibility to ameliorate another's distress or to behave prosocially.)

We do not know (yet) to what degree these mental abilities would characterize individuals' observed emotional behavior across a variety of emotion-eliciting contexts and across a variety of emotions. In an earlier paper Mayer and Salovey (1997) speculated on the relations between emotional intelligence and prosocial behavior. Mayer et al. will undoubtedly pursue these ramifications of their emotional intelligence construct in productive and thoughtful ways, and I look forward to their continuing programmatic investigations of emotional intelligence.

Others have also sought to operationalize emotional intelligence (Bar-On, 1997; Schutte et al., 1998) and to use the construct as a way of predicting individual differences in life satisfaction and adaptability. The reader is referred to Chapter Seventeen of this volume for further review of measurement approaches to emotional intelligence and an examination of an individual's motivational system as related to effective social and emotional functioning.

As a developmental psychologist, I find myself least comfortable with Mayer et al. and other investigators who persist in wanting to call their assemblage of abilities *intelligence*. Their nesting of different levels of abilities in a hierarchical fashion is reminiscent of the model by Fischer, Shaver, and Carnochan (1990) in which they sought to taxonomize the interlacing of cognitive development with emotion understanding. Interestingly, our Western notion of intelligence is an entity that we locate *inside* the person or as being traitlike in terms of characterizing the person according to some consistent quality. Intelligence is also pragmatically used in our society to indicate relative rankings of individuals: some have "more" and some have "less" intelligence. As a developmental psychologist I am more impressed by the interaction between the person and the situation, and this is what is included in my emphasis on the context that surrounds emotional competence.[2]

Given my emphasis on skills as opposed to "abilities," I also give more weight to learning and development, including the opportunities and exposure to affordant environments for learning about emotion-related processes and emotion scripts (Saarni, 1999). Emotional competence may well prove to be best used to describe a transaction, not necessarily to describe a characteristic of the person. *Competence* also has a history in Western psychology as referring to one's mastery of some skill (R. W. White, 1959), yet one need not necessarily reliably perform the skill because performance depends so heavily on circumstances and incentives. Indeed, in considerable developmental research we find that young children are often capable of some behavior but for a variety of reasons do not reliably perform it, despite their competency at it. Illustrative of this type of research is the series of studies conducted by Dunn and her associates on young children's acquisition of emotion-laden language used in dialogues and conflicts with family members (Brown & Dunn, 1991; Dunn, 1988; Dunn, Bretherton, & Munn, 1987; During & McMahon, 1991). Paradoxically, we also find that young children can perform a behavior but do not yet have the competency for *articulating* that they know what they are doing. Illustrative of this sort of research is a study by Josephs (1993) in which she found that preschoolers could manage their emotional-expressive behavior to some degree when they pretended that sour juice tasted good, yet they could not verbalize their understanding of what it meant to mislead another by dissembling one's facial expression. Along a similar vein, Lewis, Stanger, and Sullivan (1989) found that three-year-olds could expressively deceive an adult about having peeked at a forbidden toy when the adult was absent from the room, yet they would have been unlikely to be able to articulate that expressive dissemblance is part of effective lying.

---

[2] An analogous theoretical position has been taken by Fernandez-Dols (1999), who cautions against attributional biases in explaining causes of emotion. He emphasizes situational (or contextual) influences on emotional responding rather than dispositional "causes."

Lastly, Epstein's construct, constructive thinking, has much in common with the construct of emotional intelligence, and his comments bear repeating here (Epstein, 1998): "If you automatically think constructively, you will exhibit emotional intelligence, and if you don't, you won't" (p. 5). His concern is with individual differences in flexible, problem-solving orientation as assessed by his Constructive Thinking Inventory (CTI). He also locates constructive thinking aptitude in the "experiential mind" rather than in the "rational mind," the former emphasizing associative functioning and the latter logical deduction. He also posits a "personal belief system," which resembles in many ways my thinking about personal and folk theories of emotion (elaborated in Saarni, 1999) and which manifests itself in four basic needs, each accompanied by value-laden expectations for how one's world operates. However, he does not consider cultural influences or context in his model, other than to note that on average, more life experience yields gains in scores on the CTI.

CONCLUSION

From the perspective of a developmental psychologist, I believe we need to acknowledge explicitly the powerful roles played by context and the self in an individual's emotional functioning. Emotional competence, according to how I have defined it, entails taking into account the individual's efficacy motivation for engaging in some emotion-eliciting encounter, the unique sorts of contextual demands and affordances available to that individual, and the values and beliefs the person brings to the emotional experience. Thus, a given measure or instrument could not possibly produce an outcome that said "this person A is more emotionally competent than person B," for this would disregard the transforming aspect of what happens when we interact with an emotionally affordant context: we change the context as a result.

A constructivist perspective suggests considerable fluidity in the moment-to-moment experience of people, and those who are concerned with narrative construction, meaning-making, or the process by which we create "storied selves" (McAdams, 1996) would probably say that emotional competence is much more of an ebb and flow process, not a trait that resides in the person. I suspect that it is something that we conclude after the fact, that we managed to function in an emotionally effective manner relative to our goals; but in the immediate emotion-laden challenge, we engage with a belief in our own emotional resilience. When that belief is fragile (because we are facing an unfamiliar context or emotional challenge) or poorly developed (because our unique social history has encumbered us with liabilities) then our emotional encounters are likely to result more often in ineffectual outcomes relative to our goals. Rest assured that all of us will experience emotional *in*competence at one time or another.

References

Ackerman, B., P., Izard, C., Schoff, K., Youngstrom, E., & Kogos, J. (1999). Contextual risk, caregiver emotionality, and the problem behaviors of six- and seven-year-old children from economically disadvantaged families. *Child Development, 70,* 1415–1427.

Aristotle. (1985). *Nichomachean ethics* (T. Irwin, Trans.). Indianapolis, IN: Hackett.

Armon-Jones, C. (1986). The thesis of constructionism. In R. Harre (Ed.), *The social construction of emotions* (pp. 32–56). Oxford, U.K.: Blackwell.

Asher, S., & Rose, A. (1997). Promoting children's social-emotional adjustment with peers. In P. Salovey & D. Sluyter (Eds.), *Emotional development and emotional intelligence* (pp. 196–224). New York: Basic Books.

Bandura, A. (1989). Human agency in social cognitive theory. *American Psychologist, 44,* 1175–1184.

Bandura, A. (1998). Exploration of fortuitous determinants of life paths. *Psychological Inquiry, 9,* 95–99.

Bar-On, R. (1997). *BarOn Emotional Quotient Inventory (EQ-i): Technical manual.* Toronto, Canada: Multi-Health Systems.

Baumeister, R. F. (1993). Lying to yourself: The enigma of self-deception. In M. Lewis & C. Saarni (Eds.), *Lying and deception in everyday life* (pp. 166–183). New York: Guilford.

Blasi, A. (1983). Moral cognition and moral action: A theoretical perspective. *Developmental Review, 3,* 178–210.

Brown, J. R., & Dunn, J. (1991). "You can cry, Mum": The social and developmental implications and talk about internal states. *British Journal of Developmental Psychology, 9,* 237–256.

Campbell, R. L., & Christopher, J. C. (1996). Moral development theory: A critique of its Kantian presuppositions. *Developmental Review, 16,* 1–47.

Campos, J. J., Mumme, D., Kermoian, R., & Campos, R. G. (1994). A functionalist perspective on the nature of emotion. *The Development of Emotion Regulation: Monographs of the Society for Research in Child Development, 59,* 284–303.

Carpendale, J. (1997). An explication of Piaget's constructivism: Implications for social cognitive development. In S. Hala (Ed.), *The development of social cognition* (pp. 35–64). Hove, East Sussex, U.K.: Psychology Press.

Colby, A., & Damon, W. (1992). *Some do care: Contemporary lives of moral commitment.* New York: Free Press.

Compas, B., Worsham, N., & Ey, S. (1992). Conceptual and developmental issues in children's coping with stress. In A. L. Greca, L. Siegal, J. Wallander, & C. Walker (Eds.), *Stress and coping in child health* (pp. 7–24). New York: Guilford.

Crick, N., & Dodge, K. (1994). A review of social-information processing mechanisms in children's social adjustment. *Psychological Bulletin, 115,* 74–101.

D'Andrade, R. (1987). A folk model of the mind. In D. Holland & N. Quinn (Eds.), *Cultural models in language and thought* (pp. 112–148). New York: Cambridge University Press.

Davies, M., Stankov, L., & Roberts, R. D. (1998). Emotional intelligence: In search of an elusive construct. *Journal of Personality and Social Psychology, 75,* 989–1015.

Denham, S. A. (1999). *Emotional development in young children.* New York: Guilford.

Diener, E., Suh, E., Lucas, R., & Smith, H. L. (1999). Subjective well-being: Three decades of progress. *Psychological Bulletin, 125,* 276–302.

Dunn, J. (1988). *The beginnings of social understanding.* Oxford, U.K.: Basil Blackwell.

Dunn, J., Bretherton, I., & Munn, P. (1987). Conversations about feeling states between mothers and their young children. *Developmental Psychology, 23,* 132–139.

During, S., & McMahon, R. (1991). Recognition of emotional facial expressions by abusive mothers and their children. *Journal of Clinical Child Psychology, 20,* 132–139.

Epstein, S. (1998). *Constructive thinking: The key to emotional intelligence.* Westport, CT: Praeger.

Erez, A., Johnson, D. E., & Judge, T. A. (1995). Self-deception as a mediator of the relationship between dispositions and subjective well-being. *Personality and Individual Differences, 19,* 597–612.

Fabes, R., Eisenberg, N., Jones, S., Smith, M., Guthrie, I., Poulin, R., Shepard, S., & Friedman, J. (1999). Regulation, emotionality, and preschoolers' socially competent peer interactions. *Child Development, 70,* 432–442.

Fernandez-Dols, J. M. (1999). Facial expression and emotion: A situationist view. In P. Philippot, R. S. Feldman, & E. J. Coats (Eds.), *The social context of nonverbal behavior.* (pp. 242–261). Cambridge, U.K.: Cambridge University Press.

Fischer, K. W., Shaver, P., & Carnochan, P. (1990). How emotions develop and how they organize development. *Cognition and Emotion, 4,* 81–127.

Flanagan, O. (1991). *Varieties of moral personality: Ethics and psychological realism.* Cambridge, MA: Harvard University Press.

Fox, N. E. (1994). The development of emotion regulation: Behavioral and biological considerations. *Monographs of the Society for Research in Child Development, 59* (Serial No. 240).

Garber, J., Braafladt, N., & Zeman, J. (1991). The regulation of sad affect: An information processing perspective. In J. Garber & K. Dodge (Eds.), *The development of emotion regulation and dysregulation* (pp. 208–240). New York: Cambridge University Press.

Gergen, K. J. (1998). From control to coconstruction: New narratives for the social sciences. *Psychological Inquiry, 9,* 101–103.

Goleman, D. (1995). *Emotional intelligence.* New York: Bantam.

Gottman, J., Katz, L. F., & Hooven, C. (1997). *Meta-emotion*. Hillsdale, NJ: Erlbaum.

Haan, N. (1991). Moral development and action from a social constructivist perspective. In W. Kurtines & J. Gewirtz (Eds.), *Handbook of moral behavior and development* (Vol. 1, pp. 251 273). Hillsdale, NJ: Erlbaum

Harris, P. L. (1989). *Children and emotion: The development of psychological understanding*. Oxford, U.K.: Basil Blackwell.

Harter, S. (1986). Cognitive-developmental processes in the integration of concepts about emotions and the self. *Social Cognition, 4,* 119–151.

Harter, S. (1990). Developmental differences in the nature of self-representations: Implications for the understanding, assessment, and treatment of maladaptive behavior. *Cognitive Therapy and Research, 14,* 113–142.

Harter, S. (1998). The development of self-representations. In W. Damon & N. Eisenberg (Eds.), *Handbook of child psychology: Vol. 3. Social, emotional, and personality development* (5th ed., pp. 553–617). New York: Wiley.

Harter, S. (1999). *The construction of the self*. New York: Guilford Press.

Janoff-Bulman, R. (1998). From terror to appreciation: Confronting chance after extreme misfortune. *Psychological Inquiry, 9,* 99–101.

Janoff-Bulman, R., & Frantz, C. (1997). The impact of trauma on meaning: From meaningless world to meaningful life. In M. Power & C. Brewer (Eds.), *The transformation of meaning in psychological therapies* (pp. 91–106). London: Wiley.

Josephs, I. E. (1993, March). *The development of display rules: Do you understand what you already do?* Paper presented at the biennial meeting of the Society for Research in Child Development, New Orleans, LA.

Kitayama, S., & Markus, H. (Eds.). (1994). *Emotion and culture*. Washington, DC: American Psychological Association.

Kitayama, S., Markus, H., & Matsumoto, H. (1995). Culture, self and emotion: A cultural perspective on "self-conscious" emotions. In J. Tangney & K. Fischer (Eds.), *Self-conscious emotions: The psychology of shame, guilt, embarrassment, and pride* (pp. 439–464). New York: Guilford.

Kopp, C. (1992). Emotional distress and control in young children. In N. Eisenburg & R. Fabes (Eds.), *Emotion and its regulation in early development* (Vol. 55, pp. 41–56). San Francisco: Jossey-Bass.

Kopp, C., & Wyer, N. (1994). Self-regulation in normal and atypical development. In D. Cicchetti & S. Toth (Eds.), *Disorders and dysfunctions of the self. Rochester symposium on developmental psychopathology* (Vol. 5, pp. 31–56). Rochester, NY: University of Rochester Press.

Krantz, D. L. (1998). Taming chance: Social science and everyday narratives. *Psychological Inquiry, 9,* 87–94.

Lazarus, R. S. (1991). *Emotion and adaptation*. New York: Oxford University Press.

Lewis, M., & Michalson, L. (1983). *Children's emotions and moods: Developmental theory and measurement*. New York: Plenum Press.

Lewis, M., Stanger, C., & Sullivan, M. (1989). Deception in 3-year-olds. *Developmental Psychology, 25,* 439–443.

Luthar, S., Doernberger, C., & Zigler, E. (1993). Resilience is not a unidimensional construct: Insights from a prospective study of inner-city adolescents. *Development and Psychopathology, 5,* 703–717.

Lutz, C. (1987). Goals, events, and understanding in Ifaluk emotion theory. In D. Holland & N. Quinn (Eds.), *Cultural models in language and thought* (pp. 290–312). New York: Cambridge University Press.

MacIntyre, A. (1981). *After virtue: A study in moral theory.* Notre Dame, IN: University of Notre Dame Press.

Markus, H., & Kitayama, S. (1994). *The cultural construction of self and emotion: Implications for social behavior.* Washington, DC: American Psychological Association.

Mayer, J., & Salovey, P. (1997). What is emotional intelligence? In P. Salovey & D. Sluyter (Eds.), *Emotional development and emotional intelligence* (pp. 3–31). New York: Basic Books.

Mayer, J. D., Caruso, D., & Salovey, P. (forthcoming). Emotional intelligence meets traditional standards for an intelligence. *Intelligence.*

McAdams, D. P. (1996). Personality, modernity, and the storied self: A contemporary framework for studying persons. *Psychological Inquiry, 7,* 295–321.

Mesquita, B., & Frijda, N. (1992). Cultural variations in emotions: A review. *Psychological Bulletin, 112,* 179–204.

Murphy, L., & Moriarty, A. (1976). *Vulnerability, coping, and growth.* New Haven, CT: Yale University Press.

Neisser, U. (1988). Five kinds of self-knowledge. *Philosophical Psychology, 1,* 35–59.

Neisser, U. (1992). The development of consciousness and the acquisition of skill. In F. Kessel, P.M. Cole, & D. Johnson (Eds.), *Self and consciousness: Multiple perspectives* (pp. 1–18). Hillsdale, NJ: Erlbaum.

Neisser, U., & Fivush, R. (1994). *The remembering self: Construction and accuracy in the self-narrative.* New York: Cambridge University Press.

Parke, R. D., Cassidy, J., Burks, V., Carson, J., & Boyum, L. (1992). Familial contribution to peer competence among children: The role of interactive and affective processes. In R. Parke & G. Ladd (Eds.), *Family-peer relationships: Modes of linkage* (pp. 107–134). Hillsdale, NJ: Erlbaum.

Russell, J. A., Fernandez-Dols, J. M., Manstead, A., & Wellenkamp, J. (Eds.). (1996). *Everyday conceptions of emotion: An introduction to the psychology, anthropology, and linguistics of emotions.* Hingham, MA: Kluwer.

Saarni, C. (1991, April). *Social context and management of emotional-expressive behavior: Children's expectancies for when to dissemble what they feel.* Paper presented at the the biennial meeting of the Society for Research in Child Development, Seattle, WA.

Saarni, C. (1992). Children's emotional-expressive behaviors as regulators of others' happy and sad states. *New Directions for Child Development, 55,* 91–106.

Saarni, C. (1997). Coping with aversive feelings. *Motivation and Emotion, 21,* 45–63.

Saarni, C. (1999). *The development of emotional competence.* New York: Guilford.

Saarni, C., & Harris, P. L. (Eds.). (1989). *Children's understanding of emotion.* New York: Cambridge University Press.

Saarni, C., Mumme, D., & Campos, J. (1998). Emotional development: Action, communication, and understanding. In W. Damon & N. Eisenberg (Eds.), *Handbook of child psychology: Vol. 3. Social, emotional, and personality development* (5th ed., pp. 237–309). New York: Wiley.

Schutte, N., Malouff, J., Hall, L. E., Haggerty, D., Cooper, J. T., Golden, C. J., & Dornheim, L. (1998). Development and validation of a measure of emotional intelligence. *Personality and Individual Differences, 25,* 167–177.

Thompson, R. A. (1990). Emotion and self-regulation. In R. A. Thompson (Ed.), *Socioemotional development; Nebraska Symposium on Motivation* (Vol. 36, pp. 367–467). Lincoln, NB: University of Nebraska Press.

Thompson, R. A. (1991). Emotional regulation and emotional development. *Educational Psychology Review, 3,* 269–307.

Thompson, R. A. (1998). Early sociopersonality development. In W. Damon & N. Eisenberg (Eds.), *Handbook of child psychology: Vol. 3. Social, emotional, and personality development* (5th ed., pp. 25–104). New York: Wiley.

Underwood, M. K. (1997). Peer social status and children's choices about the expression and control of positive and negative emotions. *Merrill-Palmer Quarterly, 43,* 610–634.

Underwood, M., Hurley, J., Johanson, C., & Mosley, J. (1999). An experimental, observational investigation of children's responses to peer provocation: Developmental and gender differences in middle childhood. *Child Development,* 1428–1446.

Walker, L. J., & Hennig, K. (1997). Moral development in the broader context of personality. In S. Hala (Ed.), *The development of social cognition* (pp. 297–327). East Sussex, U.K.: Psychology Press.

Walker, L. J., Pitts, R., Hennig, K., & Matsuba, M. (1995). Reasoning about morality and real-life moral problems. In M. Killen & D. Hart (Eds.), *Morality in everyday life and developmental perspectives* (pp. 371–407). Cambridge, U.K.: Cambridge University Press.

Walker, L. J., & Taylor, J. H. (1991). Family interactions and the development of moral reasoning. *Child Development, 62,* 264–283.

White, G. M. (1994). Affecting culture: Emotion and morality in everyday life. In S. Kitayama & H. Markus (Eds.), *Emotion and culture* (pp. 219–239). Washington, DC: American Psychological Association.

White, R. W. (1959). Motivation reconsidered: The concept of competence. *Psychological Review, 66,* 297–333.

Wilson, J. Q. (1993). *The moral sense.* New York: Free Press.

Wilson, W. (1967). Correlates of avowed happiness. *Psychological Bulletin, 67,* 294–306.

Wolchik, S. A., & Sandler, I. N. (Eds.). (1997). *Handbook of children's coping: Linking theory and intervention.* New York: Plenum.

CHAPTER FIVE

Emotional Intelligence as Zeitgeist, as Personality, and as a Mental Ability

John D. Mayer, Peter Salovey, and David R. Caruso

*E*motional intelligence and *EQ* were selected as the most useful new words or phrases of 1995 by the American Dialect Society (1995, 1999; Brodie, 1996). And as this volume attests, work on the topic is proliferating. The impetus for this sustained interest in emotional intelligence began with two 1990 articles in academic journals (Mayer, DiPaolo, & Salovey, 1990; Salovey & Mayer, 1990) and follow-up work, much of which was popularized in a best-selling book entitled *Emotional Intelligence* (Goleman, 1995b). From there, the concept of emotional intelligence made it to the cover of *Time* magazine (Gibbs, 1995). Since then, emotional intelligence has been defined and redefined so many times that it would be impossible (or at least, quite a lengthy job) to outline all the ways the phrase has been employed.

It does seem of value, however, to understand the various ways the term *emotional intelligence* is used. In this chapter, we examine three meanings. The first, broadest, meaning is as a designation of a zeitgeist, or cultural trend. The spirit of an age is often referred to as the zeitgeist, an intellectual or passionate trend that characterizes the moment. In a complex world culture there exists not one, but multiple, interwoven, zeitgeists. We suspect emotional intelligence somehow fits into such zeitgeists, and the first meaning of emotional intelligence we

---

Note: The authors wish to acknowledge the help of Tracey Martin, who assisted in important ways with the library research that enriched this chapter.

explore in this chapter is a cultural and political one. A second, generally popular use of the term is to designate a group of personality traits that are believed important to success in life, such as persistence, the drive for achievement, and social skills, as emotional intelligence. The third and final meaning of emotional intelligence, and the one we favor, is found—indeed began—in the scientific literature and designates a set of abilities having to do with processing emotional information.

Our review of emotional intelligence covers both the popular and academic sources. Our purpose is to bring some semblance of order to the various usages of the term *emotional intelligence,* and some consideration of how those different meanings might be confusing if ignored, but contribute to constructive cultural and scientific discussion if attended to. After this introduction, the central section of this chapter examines the three meanings of the term: emotional intelligence as zeitgeist, as personality, and as mental ability. The chapter concludes with a brief discussion.

EMOTIONAL INTELLIGENCE AND THE ZEITGEIST

The popularization of emotional intelligence culminated, perhaps, with 1995 cover stories in *Time* and *USA Today Weekend* magazines on the importance of emotional intelligence to success in school and at work (Gibbs, 1995; Goleman, 1995a). These reports were a mixture of sensationalism and science. The idea was that an overlooked part of personality—one that could be acquired—would greatly improve a person's chances of achieving his or her goals. Still, the attention these articles received was more than a product of their promise of success; more fundamentally, interest in these articles was a consequence of their intersection with two areas of cultural tension. First, was the tension in Western thought between emotion and reason. A term that joined emotion and intelligence could well be considered an oxymoron by some, it was said, because emotions convey the idea of unreasonableness (Salovey & Mayer, 1990, p. 185). Several years earlier, Payne had foreseen an age in which emotion and intelligence would be integrated by teaching emotional responses in schools, and governments would be responsive to the individual's feelings (Payne, 1986, pp. 440–441). The second tension in Western thought was that between egalitarianism and elitism. At about the same time as the popularization of emotional intelligence, Herrnstein and Murray (1994) published *The Bell Curve,* which argued for the importance of IQ in understanding social class in American (and other) societies. When the book *Emotional Intelligence* was published, its author implied it served in some ways as an egalitarian rebuttal to Herrnstein and Murray's arguments, which were widely seen as elitist (Goleman, 1995b, p. 34).

Historical Overview: Stoicism Versus Romanticism

The battle between respecting and denying emotions is a longstanding one in Western thought. The Stoic movement of ancient Greece (approximately 200 BCE to 300 CE) was concerned with the role of emotion in leading a good life. The Stoics viewed moods, impulses, fears, and desires as too individualistic, too unique, and too self-centered to be reliable. Within Stoic philosophy, the wise person admitted no emotion or feeling whatsoever. Rather these were willed away in the process of self-control until all that was left was rationality and logic (Payne, 1986, pp. 17–19). The stoic philosophy became as much religion as philosophy. First, it influenced certain lines of Jewish thought (Guttman, 1964, pp. 21–23), then early Christianity. It finally collapsed after the third century CE, absorbed but still felt in the emerging Christian religion: "Stoicism bequeathed no small part of its disciplines, its dogmas, and its phraseology to the Christianity by which it was ingathered. . . . Stoicism . . . evolved moral and social conceptions that have become an heirloom of Western civilisation, and are embedded in the inmost structure of the Christian state" (quote by Rendall as cited in Payne, 1986, p. 15). The consequence was a strong anti-emotional flavor in much of Western thought.

To be sure, that anti-emotional trend has been punctuated frequently in history. For example, an emotional uprising began in eastern European Jewish circles in the mid eighteenth century. Rabbi Israel ben Eliezer, the Ba'al Shem Tov ("Possessor of the Good Name"), founded the Hassidic movement so as to introduce emotionality and mysticism into what he perceived as the overly intellectualized Jewish traditions of the day. In the later eighteenth century, the European romantic movement stressed how empathic and intuitional thought (which included emotions) could provide insights unobtainable by logic. Writers, painters, and musicians expressed emotional rebellions against the rigid, rational rules of the then-dominant classical movement in the arts. Their emotionality often expressed a feeling of alienation in response to the emerging industrialization of society. To counteract such alienation, expressions of personal love often dominated their poetry, prose, and drama (Upshur et al., 1995, pp. 622–623).

Far closer to the present was the emotional expressiveness of the 1960s in North America and Europe. The 1960s represented a decade-long emotional rebellion against the forces of rationalism. It was also a time that many of the present-day researchers of emotion and intellect came of age. It was a time of energetic political activism that saw the rise of the civil rights movement, of student activism in opposition to the Vietnam War, social movements including hippies and yippies, and the rise of the women's movement. As one participant put it, "there was the promise of universal liberation, there was the profaning of everything holy . . . there was a leap toward equality, there was a degradation of standards, there was disgust with the Pentagon's perversion of reason, there was a flight from the rigors of intellect" (Gitlin, 1993, p. 341). The "flight from the rigors of intellect," included a heady dose of emotionalism. Interestingly, emotionality was closely tied to personal growth.

That decade's chief proponents of humanistic psychology, Gordon Allport, Abraham Maslow, and Carl Rogers, were politically active within psychology and beyond, confronting and contradicting psychological "truths" that had been handed down from earlier in the century—that people were inherently weak, easily manipulated pawns in the family and in society more generally. Instead, they said, people could, indeed must, exercise self-determination (Herman, 1992, p. 90). Humanistic psychology espoused, among other things, that one urgent human need was "to feel good about oneself, experience one's emotions directly, and grow emotionally" (Herman, 1992, p. 88).

In the 1960s, as the inequalities of society were progressively uncovered, unmet emotional needs seemed woven into the very fabric of society. Psychiatrist Alvin Pouissant recalled that southern civil rights workers experienced "acute attacks of rage" in their struggles, requiring many doses of tranquilizers as an antidote (Pouissant, 1970). Implicitly, however, these rebels viewed uncontrollable feelings not as an irrational defect in human nature, but rather as a consequence of, and a message about, a faulty society. When Abraham Maslow (1969, p. 8) posed the rhetorical question, "What shall we think of a well-adjusted slave?" his statement was plainly understood to mean that sometimes angry emotions are a necessary signal of injustice.

Later in the decade, those who were part of the women's movement and the radical psychiatry movement similarly turned to feelings as messages about oppression. "It is imperative . . . that we maintain and deepen our contact with our feelings," wrote one early member of the movement. "Our first concern must not be with whether these feelings are good or bad, but what they are. Feelings are a reality" (Allen, 1973, p. 273). The exploration of feelings was not always part of an organized political movement such as the quest for women's rights. Sometimes feelings were explored, exaggerated, or otherwise altered as a part of the active, often underground, drug culture of the time. Drugs that altered mood, such as marijuana and hashish, were in common use, as were drugs that altered both mood and reality perception, such as the hallucinogen LSD-25.

One of the first mentions we have found of emotional intelligence is in "Emotional Intelligence and Emancipation," which is the translated English title of a German article describing adult women who, apparently because of their low emotional intelligence, rejected their social roles (Leuner, 1966). The author attributed the women's difficulties to being separated too early from their own mothers as infants. In an apotheosis of 1960s culture, the author treated this deficit by administering the hallucinogenic drug LSD-25 to the women during psychotherapy!

Conflict Versus Integration

The relationship between emotion and reason is often viewed as a conflict. Payne (1986) contended that throughout most Western history, those with reason prevailed, whereas the more emotional among us were labeled mentally ill and institutionalized and tortured in (pre-eighteenth-century) mental hospitals, as a means of suppressing emotionality. Those lacking in empathy often ended up as jail keepers and torturers. Payne writes, "Many of us fear uncontrolled emotional expression, such as weeping, with an intensity that rivals our fear of death. Is it any wonder, when we consider the strength of its suppression among our ancestors? Some of us are direct descendants of the people who were locked up and tortured for expression [of] emotion. Others of us are descendants of those who administered the torture" (Payne, 1986, p. 21).

Emotional intelligence, by contrast, can be interpreted as describing societal practices that integrate emotion and thought. As new brain research suggests, the emotional and cognitive systems in the brain are far more integrated than originally believed (Damasio, 1995; LeDoux, 1998).

Many of those writing about emotional intelligence addressed the issue of emotional learning in the schools. For some psychologists and educators, emotional intelligence was viewed as an integrative concept that explained competence in social and emotional skills (Elias et al., 1997, pp. 27–28; Goleman, 1995b) and, perhaps, justified teaching it explicitly. Others went further, however. Payne (1986), for example, believed that emotional intelligence could be fostered in the schools by liberating emotional experience through therapy. Liberating feelings, he wrote, "will be no easy task, politically . . . in terms of the social unrest it will likely create. But we must come to terms with this or continue to raise generations of adults who behave in emotionally ignorant—and, therefore, destructive—ways" (Payne, 1986, p. 441).

Emotional Intelligence as an Equalizer

A second element of the zeitgeist is the conflict between recognizing differences among people and emphasizing people's equality. In 1994, Herrnstein and Murray published the *Bell Curve*—a lengthy tome that combined a review of the intelligence field with public policy on class in the United States. The gist of the book was that people were normally distributed in intelligence, with some people low in intelligence, most in the middle, and some high in intelligence, and that such differences were difficult to change. The authors further added that low intelligence accounted in part for why some people were poor and unemployed, whereas high intelligence accounted for why others were employed and wealthy. Pointing out such nonegalitarian notions in a nation whose founders penned "all men are created equal" in their Declaration of Independence is asking for controversy. Add into that mix (as the authors did), a discussion of intellectual differences among different gender, religious, ethnic, and racial groups, and one can pretty much count on a pitched battle. The book was much commented on in the press and was followed up by other books with such titles as *The Bell Curve Wars* (Fraser, 1995).

The popularization *Emotional Intelligence* was positioned in part as a reply to the *Bell Curve*. Immediately after discussing the *Bell Curve*, Goleman contrasted emotional intelligence to general intelligence by stating that "it can be as powerful, and at times more powerful, than IQ," and that "crucial emotional competencies can indeed be learned" (Goleman, 1995b, p. 34). From this perspective, the cultural spirit of "emotional intelligence"—its zeitgeist value—was egalitarian, for anyone could learn it. For the skeptical, however, it suggested a dumbed-down picture of the future in which reason and critical thinking no longer mattered. The comic strip *Dilbert* is about an engineer facing the irrationalities of postmodern life, and Dogbert, his dog. In one strip, Dogbert announced he was testing his theory that "people get dumber every minute," and clicked his stopwatch on. "It's not so simple," Dilbert replied, "You also have to consider my 'emotional intelligence,' which is defined in a book I haven't read." Dogbert clicks off the stopwatch and announces triumphantly, "Twelve seconds" (Adams, 1997/1998).

Critique

The term *emotional intelligence* conveys some aspects of present-day zeitgeists; it captures something of the many competing interests or spirits of our age. In some contexts, it refers to an integration in the war between emotion and rationality throughout human history. In this sense, an emotionally intelligent society is one that understands how to integrate reason and emotion. In other contexts, emotional intelligence has been suggestive of a kinder, gentler, intelligence—an intelligence anyone can have. In this sense, an emotionally intelligent society is one in which anyone—even those previously thought of as not too bright—can be intelligent. Are these good uses of the term *emotional intelligence*? An answer to the question requires a more detailed understanding of what emotional intelligence is truly about. This scientific understanding may or may not support such descriptions of society.

EMOTIONAL INTELLIGENCE AS PERSONALITY

When we leave the popular realm and enter the scientific realm, we are obliged to employ higher standards in terminology. Those standards include both that terms should be clearly defined and that existing (and new) terms should refer to concepts that are coherently related to one another wherever possible. For example, as psychologists have divided up the mind into its constituent parts, both those parts and their interrelations have been conceived of very carefully (Mayer, 1995b, 1998). These parts include mental mechanisms, structures, functions, and processes. Ideally, labeling a new part of the mind should occur only when a new entity has been discovered; relabeling old parts should occur only when doing so more accurately depicts old concepts or groups of concepts. Personality psychology—the study of an individual's psychological parts, the organization of those parts, and their development—is the most relevant subdiscipline here (Mayer, 1998). In addition, a goal of personality psychology is to connect parts of the mind to life outcomes.

Personality Psychology and the Terminology of Personality

Should the term *emotional intelligence* be used to describe all of personality? That depends on how one thinks of the personality system, but it does not appear to fit with current perspectives on personality psychology (Mayer, 1998; McAdams, 1996; McCrae & Costa, 1999). The difference between personality, on the one hand, and emotional intelligence, on the other, can be made clear from a very brief overview of personality and its parts. This same overview will be of importance to a later discussion of the difference between an intelligence and a nonability trait. To begin with, the terms people sometimes employ when talking about emotional intelligence—*motivation, emotion, cognition,* and *consciousness*—are typically considered in personality psychology as four basic processes that make up personality's near-biological foundation (Mayer, 1995a, 1995b; 1998).

These four processes, and the mechanisms that bring them about, can be arranged from the most inward-looking and biologically based to larger, more outward-looking systems. Basic motivation is inward looking and concerns basic evolutionary needs such as those for food and water, as well as those for basic attachment and safety. The motivation system translates such needs into urges to eat, drink, attach to others, and sometimes to attack or escape from them (among many other needs).

The emotion system involves internal experiences that arise in response to models of external relationships. If a person believes significant others love her, it will make her happy. If she believes they have mistreated her, it will make her angry, and so forth. Although these internal models of relationships mirror the outside world, they are not identical to what is happening externally. We are reminded about the internal nature of models when we encounter someone who tells us that what we thought was going on in our relationship with him or her was not going on at all, and what was really going on was something we would not have dreamed of.

Cognition is the most outward looking of this set of mental mechanisms. True, one of its purposes is to help ensure the satisfaction of motivations and the maintenance of pleasant emotions. True, also, much thought concerns internal planning, including rumination and daydreaming. Nonetheless, cognition is responsible for taking care of daily business in some planned fashion. To do so it must create detailed maps of the world, test them through experimentation and experience, reason effectively, separate truth from fiction, and otherwise process information about the world.

Consciousness is the least well understood of the four basic modes of mind. It is the person's awareness of the rest of the mind. Such consciousness appears to be constantly maintained during waking hours, although it may change its states throughout the day as a result of the influence of fatigue, excitement, and other circumstances. Some believe that consciousness is directed toward creatively changing, interrupting, and redirecting ongoing mental operations when the mind is not solving problems adequately. For example, a person who is speaking at a party may suddenly become conscious of the bored expressions of his listeners and decide to refrain from talking for a while. From this perspective, conscious awareness monitors opportunities for change. The four modes are arranged in the bottom row of Figure 5.1.

These four processes and their associated mechanisms are far from constituting the whole personality, however. Another group of personality parts that has already been mentioned includes the models of one's self and the world, which must be constructed through learning. A chief developmental task of the individual is to create models of the self, the world, and the self in the world. These models incorporate aspects of individual motivations, emotions, cognitions, and conscious states but integrate them together in coherent maps of the self and the world. Thus, a child may develop a mental map of dinosaurs. In so doing, she may read about the gigantasaurus, the largest dinosaur discovered thus far. The child will imagine the aggressive motives of a big, strong dinosaur; she may feel curiosity, fear, and awe about something so big and learn cognitive information such as that gigantasaurus's name refers to "large reptile of the south." Finally, she may become aware of the gigantasaurus at a time when such information is particularly useful (such as when trying to find a good topic for a report in science class). These models draw on motivation, emotion, cognition, and consciousness but can be distinguished from them in that they integrate the modes together, and in that their chief function is to model the internal and external worlds. Examples of such models can be found in the second row of Figure 5.1.

A third aspect of personality—traits or themes—also exists. Such traits emerge when a given motive, emotion, or thought is repeatedly present within models of the self and the world (that is, within learned mental maps). For

	Self-Relevant Traits		General Traits
Level 3: Mental Traits	Examples: self-esteem, self-consciousness, personal intelligence, ego strength		Examples: extroversion, verbal intelligence, conscientiousness, dogmatism, friendliness
Level 2: Mental Maps	Models of the Self Examples: self-concept, ideal self, identity, life story	Models of the Self-in-World Examples: roles, attachments, identifications, rules of conduct	Models of the World Examples: knowing how to spell, expert knowledge of dinosaurs
Level 1: Mental Mechanisms	Basic Motivations Examples: urges to eat, drink, sleep, join others, defend self	Basic Emotions Examples: feeling joy, sadness, anger, and fear, related psychophysiology	Basic Cognitive Operations Examples: learning, remembering, judging, comparing / Basic Consciousness Examples: awareness, attention, stream of consciousness

Figure 5.1. A schematic outline of certain among the major systems of personality (after Mayer, Salovey, & Caruso, 2000, figure 1, and Mayer, 1995b, figure 2).

example, if a child imagines battles with dinosaurs, imagines fights with her dolls, and argues with her parents more than usual, that child may be said to possess the trait of argumentativeness, assertiveness, or, in the extreme, aggression. Or a person's cheerfulness may be evident in his high self-esteem, love of friends, and caring for the world. Finally, a person's intelligence might be evident in her ability to arrange complex personal schedules, solve math problems, understand vocabulary, and perform well in school. These traits differ from simple motives, emotions, or cognitions in that they emerge from interactions between the motives and learned models of the self and world. Examples of such traits can be found in the third row of Figure 5.1.

This is a partial description of personality but it is enough to understand some of the issues of terminology concerning an emotional intelligence. We can see, for example, that emotion covers only one of four foundations of personality, with motivation, cognition, and consciousness distinct from it. Further, we can see that intelligence will involve cognitive problem solving in learned models. One way to view emotional intelligence, which we will discuss in greater detail later, is as a general ability trait (similar to verbal intelligence). In this sense, emotional intelligence employs cognitive and emotional mechanisms in processing the emotional aspects of the self, the world, and the self-in-world, as well as in processing any purely expert knowledge of emotion. To return to personality more generally, it can be seen that some of its parts are more closely related to one another than are other parts. The terms *emotion* and *intelligence* are relatively unrelated to such mechanisms as motivation or to such traits as optimism, sociability, or good relationships.

Mixed-Personality and Socioemotional Definitions of Emotional Intelligence

Emotional intelligence is used by some researchers to refer to a long list of attributes or abilities that appear drawn from a number of aspects of personality. One such interpretation of emotional intelligence comes from the popular book *Emotional Intelligence* (Goleman, 1995b). Therein, emotional intelligence is said to include five parts: knowing emotions, managing emotions, motivating oneself, recognizing emotions in others, and handling relationships (p. 43). Emotional intelligence is redefined and redescribed frequently through that book, each time including a somewhat different set of personality attributes. For example, a later definition retains knowing emotions and managing emotions and adds in "self-awareness, impulse control and delaying gratification, and handling stress and anxiety" (p. 259). The effect of these broad, only partly overlapping definitions is finally to cover almost all of personality. Included are traits based on motivation (motivating oneself), as well as on emotion (such as recognizing emotions in others), and also characterizations of broad areas of behavior (handling relationships) that encompass the entire model of how one operates in the world (see Mayer, 1995a, 1998). It comes as almost no surprise, then, that Goleman pronounces that "there is an old-fashioned word for the body of skills that emotional intelligence represents: character" (p. 285).

It may seem improper to hold up Goleman's (1995b) theory as a scientific one. At first it was presented as a journalistic account of our own theory (Goleman, 1995b, p. 34; Salovey & Mayer, 1990). Nonetheless, many scientists have treated Goleman's work seriously, and Goleman has accepted this blended role, recently writing, for example, "I've also gone back to my professional roots as an academic psychologist, conducting an exhaustive review of the research. . . . And I've performed or commissioned several new scientific analyses of data" (Goleman, 1998, p. 5).

Another definition, by Bar-On (1997, p. 14), characterized emotional intelligence as "an array of noncognitive capabilities, competencies, and skills that influence one's ability to succeed in coping with environmental demands and pressures." He interprets findings from a self-report scale of emotional intelligence that he developed, the EQ-i, as indicating that it is divisible into five broad categories. First is intrapersonal EQ, which further divides into emotional self-awareness, assertiveness, self-regard, self-actualization, and independence. Second is interpersonal EQ, which divides into empathy, interpersonal relationship, and social responsibility. These first two factors are reminiscent of Gardner's (1983/1993) personal intelligences, which are also divided into intrapersonal and interpersonal functions. Third is adaptability EQ, which divides into problem solving, reality testing, and flexibility. Fourth is stress management EQ, which divides into stress tolerance and impulse control. Fifth and last is general mood EQ, which divides into happiness and optimism (Bar-On, 1997, pp. 43–45). Chapter Seventeen presents a revision of Bar-On's (1997) model, in which a number of changes are made, including that the general mood area is viewed as a facilitator of emotional intelligence rather than a part of it. Nonetheless, many of the attributes of the model, such as reality testing, stress management, and impulse control, seem to stretch beyond what is generally meant by emotion or intelligence.

Another definition of emotional intelligence is employed by Goleman in his more recent book, which focused on the workplace (Goleman, 1998). Now the five dimensions of emotional intelligence are broken down into twenty-five different emotional competencies, among them political awareness, service orientation, self-confidence, conscientiousness, and achievement drive (Goleman, 1998, pp. 26–28). Similarly, Cooper's (1996/1997) EQ map begins with emotional self-awareness, emotional awareness of others, interpersonal connections, and the like, but then goes on to include resilience, creativity, compassion, and intuition, among other areas. One begins to wonder what adaptive attributes would *not* be considered emotional intelligence.

Why do we take issue with relabeling all the parts of personality as "emotional intelligence"? If emotional intelligence does not refer exclusively to emotion or intelligence, then it becomes quite unclear to what it does refer. Qualities such as service orientation, interpersonal relationships, intuition, and self-actualization seem to have expanded the concept without any regard to its moorings. Perhaps the larger cost, however, is that labeling personality research as "emotional intelligence"—that is, a new-ish field—directs people away from the relevant research about the new claims being made. This allows a person to create a theory that is disconnected from other, similar theories, and so to be very imaginative—but the process can lead to disappointment once the connection between imagination and reality is reestablished. Empirical studies of the discriminant and convergent validity of scales based on the above approaches have only begun; they will reveal whether these new measures are reinventions of earlier tests or are actually measuring something new. Even with such studies pending, however, there is enough research in personality psychology to indicate what is likely and what is not.

For example, theories that define emotional intelligence as a diverse list of qualities such as political awareness, service orientation, self-confidence, conscientiousness, and achievement drive do not seem to hold up well. For one thing, such groupings bring together quite different parts of personality. Political awareness is a type of consciousness. Service orientation is a role. Self-confidence is a model-of-the-self (or self-schema), and so on (Mayer, 1995b, 1998). We know these separate parts often conflict with one another. For example, a high achievement drive often reduces conscientiousness about completing responsibilities and adhering to rules (McClelland & Koestner, 1992); similarly, high self-confidence can lead to taking advantage of others rather than serving them (Baumeister, 1997). It is highly improbable that any person could meet all twenty-five criteria at any time, let alone meet most or all such criteria over an extended period of time.

The field of personality psychology is largely centered on using groups of variables to predict future life outcomes. Some of the best researchers in the field have spent lifetimes studying groups of personality attributes so as to determine which ones actually lead to success at school and at work. The story, unsurprisingly, is not as simple as the "one variable fits all," approach implied by those who combine lists of traits under the label of *emotional intelligence.* The academic research literature is often excellent (although sometimes not) and well worth examining by those who have become interested in it from the popular literature. Claims by popularizers of emotional intelligence, for example, that it "outpredicts IQ" or is "twice as important as IQ" (Goleman, 1998, p. 34) stand in strong contradiction to such literature. In fact, when those claims have been examined by ourselves and others, they have appeared implausible to begin with, and no serious evidence has yet been offered in support of them (Davies, Stankov, & Roberts, 1998; Epstein, 1998; Mayer & Cobb, 2000; Mayer, Salovey, & Caruso, 2000).

In contrast to popular approaches, scientific research must adhere to carefully developed standards. Chief among those most relevant to the field are that, first, there must be a good correspondence between a given concept (such as emotional intelligence) and any test that is used to measure it. This correspondence is referred to as the test's validity. Second, a new test should measure something above and beyond what prior tests measure. This is called incremental validity and, actually, is a specific form of test validity. An example may suffice to indicate how such issues work.

Schutte et al. (1998) developed a scale of emotional intelligence and then correlated it with several criteria. The scale was based on a self-report in which a person was to agree or disagree with questions such as "I often know how I feel" and others based on the domains of emotional intelligence elaborated in an early ability version of the concept (Salovey & Mayer, 1990). The test's validity was compromised, however, because the test used the self-report approach, which assesses a person's self-perceptions rather than his or her actual abilities. Nonetheless, the authors' used the scale and obtained a fascinating finding: the scale predicted end-of-the-year grade point averages for college students moderately well ($r = .32$). However, the scale was highly correlated with scales known to assess positive mood—an essentially universal characteristic of self-report emotional intelligence scales. The problem is that positive mood alone predicts higher grades (Wessman & Ricks, 1966, p. 123), and vice versa. This raised the following question of incremental validity: was emotional intelligence accounting for higher grades beyond what could be predicted from mood alone? Because mood was not measured independently, the answer is unknown. Such questions of method are essential to the scientist's craft and necessary for addressing the many claims made in the area of emotional intelligence.

Locating the list of proposed traits (including ability traits) within a more general personality framework has a number of other advantages as well. It permits comparison of theories and consequent measures with similar, competing theories and measures. For example, the California Psychological Inventory (CPI) is considered an omnibus inventory of personality. Its scales include Self-Assurance, Interpersonal Effectiveness, Self-Acceptance, Self-Control, Flexibility, Empathy, Dominance, and the like (Cohen, Swerdlik, & Smith, 1992). These scales appear rather similar to some of the scales used to assess emotional intelligence. For example, the EQ-i measures, among other areas, Assertiveness, Interpersonal Effectiveness, Empathy, Impulse Control, Social Responsibility, and Reality Testing (Bar-On, 1997, pp. 45–46; see also Cooper, 1996/1997; Goleman, 1998). To be sure, the CPI includes many scales that the EQ-i does not, and vice versa. The issue is not whether these new tests are identical to earlier ones, or whether they are good or bad. Rather, the two points we wish to make are that first, many of the attributes measured by newer scales of emotional intelligence have been carefully studied before, and second, such overlap as does exist suggests that new scales of emotional intelligence have a breadth of coverage that is not all that different from measures traditionally referred to as omnibus scales of personality. The term *emotional intelligence,* when used to designate tests that are not appreciably different from general scales of personality, may be more of a distraction than a clarification.

EMOTIONAL INTELLIGENCE AS A MENTAL ABILITY

Above, we suggested that the term *emotional intelligence* is better reserved for a more focused portion of personality. Our own suggested use of the term stresses the concept of an intelligence that processes and benefits from emotions. From this perspective, emotional intelligence is composed of mental abilities, skills, or capacities. The central work we have been involved in during the last ten years is to conceptualize the abilities that make up emotional intelligence, to create methods for measuring those abilities, and to determine if emotional intelligence qualifies as a standard intelligence.

We chose to employ the term *emotional intelligence* after a careful review of the intelligence literature convinced us that an emotional intelligence—even more than a social intelligence—could be operationalized and measured as distinct from previously described intelligences (and other parts of personality; Mayer & Salovey, 1993, pp. 433–444). This early work marked the first formal use of the term defined as an intelligence and introduced the first tests that would begin to permit its empirical investigations (Mayer, DiPaolo, & Salovey, 1990; Mayer & Geher, 1996; Salovey & Mayer, 1990).

Intelligence is defined as a group of mental abilities. An ability (of any sort), in turn, is a characteristic of an individual when that individual can "successfully complete (i.e., obtain a specific, desired, outcome on) a task of defined difficulty, when testing conditions are favorable" (Carroll, 1993, pp. 4–8). For example, physical ability might be assessed by asking a person to lift a 100 lb weight; mental ability would involve measuring an individual's performance in recalling seven digits in a row and similar tasks. From this perspective, mental ability is synonymous with mental capacity, similar to mental skill (which specifically connotes something learned), and similar to mental competence, which emphasizes the ability to meet a specific standard.

Mental abilities can be distinguished from other sorts of ability as involving thinking abstractly and solving mental problems. For much of this century, that was sufficient to describe the issue. Since that time, however, there has been a reassessment of what mental abilities are and are not—principally in response to the writings of Howard Gardner (1983/1993), who proposed that, along with widely accepted intelligences such as verbal intelligence and spatial intelligence, there might exist other intelligences such as "physical/bodily intelligence." Gardner (1983/1993) also described "personal intelligences." Scarr (1989) and others have questioned whether such entities as physical/bodily intelligence really exist.

Emotional intelligence has invited this same debate. Researchers who use the term to describe multiple aspects of personality often characterize many mental qualities as *abilities* or *capacities.* For example, Bar-On (1997, p. 14) referred to noncognitive capacities such as assertiveness; Goleman (1998) included initiative and service orientation among such abilities. All those attributes can be of value in their place, but does portraying them in such a fashion constitute a fair use of the mental ability concept? Scarr (1989) has expressed grave concerns about a tradition that "lumps all manner of human virtues under the banner of several intelligences" (p. 76). She views such terminology as a threat to both the area of intelligence research and to other scientific areas:

> There are many human virtues that are not sufficiently rewarded in our society, such as goodness in human relationships, and talents in music, dance, and painting. To call them intelligence does not do justice either to theories of intelligence or to the personality traits and special talents that lie beyond the consensual definition of intelligence. Nor does calling all human virtues intelligence readjust social rewards, the goal toward which I believe such theories are pointed. (p. 78)

Looking at broader personality and all its parts can help answer the question of what an intelligence is and is not (Mayer, 2000). This theoretical perspective makes clear that cognition (and emotion and motivation) saturate all of personality; and that the mere presence of some cognitive mental ability does not constitute an intelligence. Consider the case of artificial intelligence for a moment. We might refer to a "smart" toaster or other device, given that the toaster monitors information about its internal heat levels. Its information processing—which undeniably exists—is so limited, however, that to speak of the toaster as possessing artificial intelligence seems overstated. The term *artificial intelligence* is generally reserved for those devices whose primary focus is problem solving.

Similarly, people who are sociable undeniably process social information as they interact with others. The personality system always works by intertwining motivation, emotion, cognition, and consciousness. Nonetheless, the point of sociability is to interact with others; its point is not social problem solving. In contrast, social intelligence involves understanding how to convince others to do things, how to manage power relationships, how to build group cohesiveness, and the like. Sociability, however, is not social intelligence. More generally, personality traits such as sociability, conscientiousness, or optimism do not, by themselves, indicate an intelligence is present, because none of them centrally concern problem solving. By way of contrast, one might say that social intelligence may determine the sophistication with which sociability is carried out. We view the term *intelligence* as best applied to mental traits whose primary purpose is problem solving in one or another content domains.

Now consider an emotional intelligence. Emotions do convey set meanings, which philosophers have been elucidating for centuries. For example, the experience of anger often designates the presence of a real or perceived injustice or blockage of a desired goal. The experience of sadness indicates a real or perceived loss. In addition, there are evolutionary bases for the meanings of basic emotions (Darwin, 1872/1955; Ekman, 1973). Moreover, emotions develop in predictable patterns that are interrelated with developments in complex social situations. For example, if a person is happy and sad at the same time, only a limited number of events could have brought about such a reaction, and intelligence is necessary to track down the sort of event that brings such feelings (such as a close-by friend finding a much-wanted job in a faraway city). Emotions, in other words, satisfy a complex, coherent, and consistent symbol system that can be puzzled over, understood, and planned for in abstract thought.

An Ability Theory of Emotional Intelligence

Elsewhere we have gone over the intelligence theory of emotional intelligence in greater detail, but it is useful to review some aspects of it briefly here (Mayer, Caruso, & Salovey, 1999; Mayer & Salovey, 1997; Salovey & Mayer, 1990). Theories of intelligence vary, but there is a growing consensus as to the central parts of the intelligence system. This system consists of a capacity for identifying or inputting information, and a capacity for processing information through both immediate symbol manipulation and reference to expert knowledge (Mayer & Mitchell, 1998). Our model views emotional intelligence as operating across both the cognitive and emotional systems. It operates in a mostly unitary fashion but is still subdivisible into four branches (Mayer & Salovey, 1997). The first of these branches, emotional perception and identification, involves recognizing and inputting information from the emotion system. The second and third branches, emotional facilitation of thought and emotional understanding, involve the further processing of emotional information with an eye to problem solving. In general, the emotional facilitation of thought branch involves using emotion to improve cognitive processes, whereas the emotional understanding branch involves cognitive processing of emotion. Our fourth branch, emotion management, concerns emotional self-management and the management of emotions in other people. These four branches are shown arranged in a circle in Figure 5.2.

Partly as a consequence of various popularizations, and partly as a consequence of societal pressures to regulate emotions, many people identify emotional intelligence primarily with its fourth branch, emotional management.

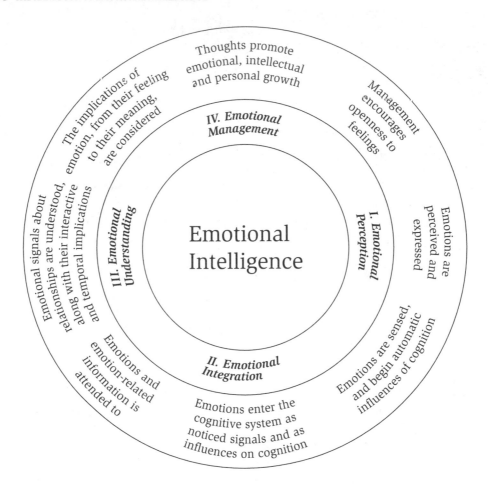

Figure 5.2. A circular depiction of the four-branch model of emotional intelligence (after Mayer & Salovey, 1997, figure 1).

They hope emotional intelligence will be a way of getting rid of troublesome emotions or emotional leakages into human relations and hope to control emotions. Although this is one possible outcome of the fourth branch, optimal levels of emotional regulation may be moderate ones; attempts to minimize or eliminate emotion may stifle emotional intelligence.

Emotional management might be thought of more profitably as beginning with a capacity for openness that allows emotions—both pleasant and unpleasant—to enter into (in other words, to be perceived or identified by) the intelligence system. That is, management encourages emotions to be experienced, although not always expressed. This is because the emotional management branch—to which we will return—works hand-in-hand with the other aspects of emotional intelligence.

The first branch of emotional intelligence begins with the capacity to perceive and to express feelings (Figure 5.2, right). Emotional intelligence cannot begin without the first branch of emotional intelligence. If each time an unpleasant feeling emerged, a person turned his attention away, he would learn nearly nothing about feelings. Emotional perception involves registering, attending to, and deciphering emotional messages as they are expressed in facial expressions, voice tone, objects of art, and other cultural artifacts. A person who sees the fleeting expression of amusement in the face of another understands much more about that other's emotions and thoughts than someone who misses such a signal.

The second branch of emotional intelligence concerns emotional facilitation (Figure 5.2, bottom). Emotions are complex organizations of the physiological, emotional-experiential, cognitive, and conscious aspects of mental life. Emotions enter the cognitive system both as cognized feelings, as is the case when someone thinks, "I am sad now," and as altered cognitions, as when a sad person thinks, "I am no good." When emotions are recognized and labeled, the understanding of emotion (branch 3) is involved, to which we will turn in a moment. The emotional facilitation of thought (branch 2) focuses on how emotion enters the cognitive system and alters cognition to assist thought. Cognition can, of course, be disrupted by anxiety, but emotions can also impose priorities such that the cognitive system attends to what is most important (Easterbrook, 1959; Mandler, 1975; Simon, 1982) and even focuses on what it best does in a given mood (see Palfai & Salovey, 1993). Emotions also change cognitions, making them positive when a person is happy, and negative when a person is sad (Forgas, 1995; Mayer, Gaschke, Braverman, & Evans, 1992; Salovey & Birnbaum, 1989). These changes force the cognitive system to view things from different perspectives, for example, alternating between skeptical and optimistic points of view. The advantage of such alterations to thought are fairly apparent. The shifting of one's point of view between the skeptical and the optimistic encourages the individual to see multiple points of view and, as a consequence, to think about a problem more deeply and perhaps more creatively as well (see Mayer, 1986; Mayer & Hanson, 1995). It is just such an effect that may lead people with mood swings toward greater creativity than those who have stable moods (Goodwin & Jamison, 1990).

Branch 3 involves understanding and reasoning with emotion. As already suggested, emotions form a rich symbol set full of complex relationships that have puzzled and delighted philosophers for centuries (Figure 5.2, left). The person who is able to understand emotions—their meanings, how they blend together, how they progress over time—is truly blessed with the capacity to understand fundamental truths of human nature and of interindividual relationships.

This brief tour of the four branches returns us to the fourth branch (emotion management) shown at the top of Figure 5.2. It is now apparent why management must begin with perception. Only if one has good emotional perception in the first place can one make use of mood changes and understand emotions. And only with such understanding will one have the breadth of knowledge necessary to manage and cope with feelings fully. In fact, the emotionally intelligent individual must regularly cope with states of mood instability, and this requires considerable understanding of moods (Salovey, Bedell, Detweiler, & Mayer, 1999).

How will such an individual manage? Emotions are complex, messy, fuzzy, and contain their own punishments and rewards. A good emotional manager, therefore, must follow some guidelines, but do so with flexibility. For example, openness to feeling is a must, but not all the time. Certainly there will be—for almost anyone—matters too painful to face at times, and emotionality is probably best closed off.

Management also involves how a person understands the emotional progressions in his or her relations with others. These relations can be unpredictable. Thus, management involves the consideration of various different emotional paths and the choosing among them. Is a person angry at his or her spouse? If so, is it best to ignore the difficulty until both partners are more relaxed? Is it possible to forgive without getting angrier next time? Perhaps the person is sufficiently desperate to feel the anger privately for a few hours, days, or even weeks, while weighing against it the pain and sorrow that might ensue after losing the partner. On the other hand, is there some way to deal with the anger-provoking issue directly? Those are at least some of the possibilities that must be addressed.

To accommodate the many emotional reactions possible in situations, emotional management is by necessity plastic: it permits the person to proceed in ways he or she thinks best, on emotional, spiritual, pragmatic, or other grounds. Being emotionally intelligent does not necessarily mean a person will want to, say, stay in a job or save a marriage, just as being intelligent does not mean a person will want to read challenging books all day long. Rather, there are other parts of personality and other situations that must be taken into account to understand what will happen. It is this requirement for plasticity that explains why emotional intelligence, measured as an ability, does not correlate highly with optimism, cheerfulness, friendliness, and other such traits and yet still predicts important life outcomes.

There is a growing body of evidence that emotional intelligence, conceptualized as a mental ability and measured with objective tasks, actually does constitute a unitary intelligence. We review such findings in detail in our companion chapter in this volume (Chapter Fifteen), on ability measures of emotional intelligence. Here, we conclude our consideration of emotional terminology.

CONCLUSION

We have encountered three uses of the term *emotional intelligence*, first, as a zeitgeist, or cultural movement of the times, next as a synonym or near synonym for personality, and finally, as an actual intelligence within personality that is concerned with processing emotions. These three definitions of emotional intelligence are widely different.

The zeitgeist definition refers to a cultural movement. It is unclear whether emotional intelligence is simply a passing fad or could conceivably qualify as some sort of historical movement. It is probably in a class with such historical movements as the stoic, classical, and romantic movements (although it has not yet exhibited the influence and perseverance of any of those movements). From this perspective, emotional intelligence might be said to integrate the stoic and the romantic movements. Still, it remains to be seen whether emotional intelligence has the staying power of, say, stoicism, the influence of which has lasted for more than two thousand years.

Turning to the realm of personality, using the term *emotional intelligence* to refer to broad areas of personality beyond the emotional and cognitive seems unnecessarily vague to us, and even more problematic when such usage is meant to refer to the entirety of personality or character. Much of what is identified in the emotional intelligence literature does not seem to belong there. Traits such as impulse control, self-actualization, zeal, and persistence pertain to motivation; assertiveness and interpersonal relationships involve social skills that include motivations, emotions, and cognitions together, and so on. Suggesting that these are new constellations of traits, in other words, *emotional intelligence*, takes their consideration outside of well-understood aspects of personality psychology. The consequence of separating this new research from the substantial body of personality research that overlaps with it is to ignore the many findings that contradict current claims on behalf of the concept of emotional intelligence. For example, one popular claim made for emotional intelligence is that, unlike other intelligences, it can be learned (see Goleman, 1995b, p. 34), yet a good deal of research into the many personality traits that are listed as a part of emotional intelligence indicates that they can have rather considerable genetic, biological, and early-learning contributions, which, as with other parts of personality, make them difficult, albeit not impossible, to change. (For further critiques of such claims, see Mayer & Cobb, 2000; Mayer, Salovey, & Caruso, 2000.)

A slight change in terminology—to describe an emotionally intelligent constellation of personality traits—might make this definition more palatable. Then, a person's emotional intelligence could be compared with a variety of other personality types with admirable qualities. The *hardy personality* was Kobasa's (1979) description of personalities of people who could overcome hardships to contribute successfully to society. The *constructive thinker* is Epstein's (1998) description of a person who can learn and change for the better and lend a helping hand to surrounding people. *Ego strength* involves the overall ability of the individual to function rationally and self-regulate (see Block & Block, 1980). *Self-actualization* is the view of personality as reaching its potential in all spheres of life. There are other such concepts as well, more or less known, that resemble this emotional intelligence view of personality.

There remain, however, two problems with referring to emotional intelligence as a more-or-less broad constellation of traits. First, because use of the term is no longer constrained by the meanings of the terms *emotion* or *intelligence,* it is difficult to decide what list of traits belongs with the term. Such difficulty is becoming more evident as models by Goleman (1995b, 1998), Cooper (1996/1997), Schutte et al. (1998), Bar-On (1997; this volume), and others increasingly diverge from each other. Second, whatever the list of traits finally chosen, to the extent that they diverge from actual mental ability conceptions, they are unlikely to be integrated into the mental ability approach (see, for example, Chapter Fifteen on our research concerning ability measures).

The ability definition of emotional intelligence, finally, has its own set of competing constructs and concepts. Most closely related are such concepts as emotional competence (Saarni, 1990, 1999) and emotional creativity (Averill & Nunley, 1992). Next, there is a group of additional intelligences that can be called "hot" intelligences because they involve motivational, emotional, or other relations to the self (Mayer & Mitchell, 1998). These include intrapersonal intelligence (Gardner, 1983/1993), which is defined as the ability to accurately understand and assess oneself. It includes social intelligence, which is often defined as the ability to interrelate and manage others (Sternberg & Smith, 1985; Thorndike & Stein, 1937; see also Sternberg, 1988). Should a motivational intelligence exist (which has not yet been determined) it would also presumably need to be tested against that (Mayer & Geher, 1996; Mayer, 2000).

The examination of the three meanings of emotional intelligence covered in this chapter proceeded in order from the most broad and popular to the most focused and (we believe) warranted by the terms *emotion* and *intelligence.* The fact that one term carries three meanings—and there are additional meanings we could review at the cost of overtaxing the reader—creates some problems if one travels among the meanings without indicating one's intentions. It is no secret by now that we believe *emotional intelligence* is a tantalizing term best applied to scientific research and, perhaps, to cultural practices. As we indicate in our companion chapter in this volume (Chapter Fifteen), we believe emotional intelligence as an intelligence is a new concept, and one that may help us better explain how personality, and people, function.

AUTHOR CONTACT INFORMATION

Please address correspondence regarding this chapter to John (Jack) D. Mayer at the Department of Psychology, University of New Hampshire, Durham, NH 03824; or email: jack.mayer@unh.edu.

References

Adams, S. (1998). *Journey to Cubeville.* Kansas City, MO: Andrews McMeel Publishing. (Original comic strip published by United Features Syndicate, February 2, 1997)

Allen, P. (1973). Free space. In A. Koedt, E. Levine, & A. Rapone (Eds.) *Radical feminism,* New York: Quadrangle.

American Dialect Society. (1995). American Dialect Society: E-mail from Allan Metcalf [On-line]. Available: http://www.americandialect.org/excite/collections/adsl/011272.shtml.

American Dialect Society. (1999). American Dialect Society: Words of the Year. Available: http://www.americandialect.org/woty.

Averill, J. R., & Nunley, E. P. (1992). *Voyages of the heart: Living an emotionally creative life.* New York: Free Press.

Bar-On, R. (1997). *BarOn Emotional Quotient Inventory (EQ-i): Technical manual.* Toronto, Canada: Multi-Health Systems.

Baumeister, R. F. (1997). *Evil: Inside human violence and cruelty.* New York: W. H. Freeman.

Block, J., & Block, J. H. (1980). The role of ego-control and ego resiliency in the organization of behavior. In W. A. Collins (Ed.), *The Minnesota symposium on child psychology* (Vol. 13, pp. 33–101). Hillsdale, NJ: Erlbaum.

Brodie, I. (1996, January 5). 'Newtron bomb' fall-out changes slang. *The Times (Overseas News Section).* Times Newspapers Limited.

Carroll, J. B. (1993). *Human cognitive abilities: A survey of factor-analytic studies.* New York: Cambridge University Press.

Cohen, R. J., Swerdlik, M. E., & Smith, D. K. (1992). *Psychological testing and assessment.* Mountain View, CA: Mayfield Publishing.

Cooper, R. K. (1996/1997). *EQ map interpretation guide.* San Francisco: AIT and Essi Systems.

Damasio, A. R. (1995). *Descartes' error: Emotion, reason, and the human brain.* New York: Avon Books.

Darwin, C. (1955). *Expression of the emotions in man and animals.* New York: Philosophical Library. (Original work published 1872)

Davies, M., Stankov, L., & Roberts, R. D. (1998). Emotional Intelligence: In search of an elusive construct. *Journal of Personality and Social Psychology, 75,* 989–1015.

Easterbrook, J. A. (1959). The effects of emotion on cue utilization and the organization of behavior. *Psychological Review, 66,* 183–200.

Ekman, P. (1973). *Darwin and facial expression: A century of research in review.* New York: Academic Press.

Elias, M. J., Zins, J. E., Weissberg, R. P., Frey, K. S., Greenberg, M. T., Haynes, N. M., Kessler, R., Schwab-Stone, M. E., & Shriver, T. P. (1997). *Promoting social and emotional learning: Guidelines for educators.* Alexandria, VA: Association for Supervision and Curriculum Development.

Epstein, S. (1998). *Constructive thinking: The key to emotional intelligence.* Westport, CT: Praeger.

Forgas, J. P. (1995). Mood and judgment: The affect infusion model (AIM). *Psychological Bulletin, 117,* 39–66.

Fraser, S. (Ed.). (1995). *The bell curve wars.* New York: Free Press.

Gardner, H. (1983/1993). *Frames of mind: The theory of multiple intelligences.* New York: Basic Books. (Original work published in 1993)

Gibbs, N. (1995, October 2). The EQ factor. *Time, 146,* 60–68.

Gitlin, T. (1993). *The sixties: Years of hope, days of rage.* New York: Bantam Books.

Goleman, D. (1995a, September 10). Why your emotional intelligence quotient can matter more than IQ. *USA Weekend,* pp. 4–8.

Goleman, D. (1995b). *Emotional intelligence.* New York: Bantam.

Goleman, D. (1998). *Working with emotional intelligence.* New York: Bantam.

Goodwin, F. K., & Jamison, K. R. (1990). *Manic-depressive illness.* New York: Oxford University Press.

Guttman, J. (1964). *Philosophies of Judaism.* New York: Holt, Rinehart, & Winston.

Herman, E. (1992). Being and doing: Humanistic psychology and the spirit of the 1960s. In B. L. Tischler (Ed.), *Sights on the sixties* (pp. 87–101). New Brunswick, NJ: Rutgers University Press.

Herrnstein, R. J., & Murray, C. (1994). *The bell curve: Intelligence and class in American life.* New York: Free Press

Kobasa, S. C. (1979). Stressful life events, personality, and health: An inquiry into hardiness. *Journal of Personality and Social Psychology, 37,* 1–11.

LeDoux, J. (1998). *The emotional brain.* New York: Simon & Schuster.

Leuner, B. (1966). Emotional intelligence and emancipation. *Praxis der Kinderpsychologie und Kinderpsychiatrie, 15,* 196–203.

Mandler, G. (1975). *Mind and emotion.* New York: Wiley.

Maslow, A. (1969). *Toward a psychology of being* (2nd ed.). New York: D. Van Nostrand.

Mayer, J. D. (1986). How mood influences cognition. In N. E. Sharkey (Ed.), *Advances in cognitive science* (pp. 290–314). Chichester, West Sussex, U.K.: Ellis Horwood.

Mayer, J. D. (1995a). The System-Topics Framework and the structural arrangement of systems within and around personality. *Journal of Personality, 63,* 459–493.

Mayer, J. D. (1995b). A framework for the classification of personality components. *Journal of Personality, 63,* 819–877.

Mayer, J. D. (1998). A systems framework for the field of personality. *Psychological Inquiry, 9,* 118–144.

Mayer, J. D. (2000). Spiritual intelligence or spiritual consciousness? *Journal of Psychology and Religion, 10,* 47–56.

Mayer, J. D., Caruso, D., & Salovey, P. (1999). Emotional intelligence meets traditional standards for an intelligence. *Intelligence, 27,* 267–298.

Mayer, J. D., & Cobb, C. D. (2000). Educational policy on emotional intelligence: Does it make sense? *Educational Psychology Review, 12,* 163–183.

Mayer, J. D., DiPaolo, M. T., & Salovey, P. (1990). Perceiving affective content in ambiguous visual stimuli: A component of emotional intelligence. *Journal of Personality Assessment, 54,* 772–781.

Mayer, J. D., Gaschke, Y., Braverman, D. L., & Evans, T. (1992). Mood-congruent judgment is a general effect. *Journal of Personality and Social Psychology, 63,* 119–132.

Mayer, J. D., & Geher, G. (1996). Emotional intelligence and the identification of emotion. *Intelligence, 22,* 89–113.

Mayer, J. D., & Hanson, E. (1995). Mood-congruent judgment over time. *Personality and Social Psychology Bulletin, 21,* 237–244.

Mayer, J. D., & Mitchell, D. C. (1998). Intelligence as a subsystem of personality: From Spearman's *g* to contemporary models of hot-processing. In W. Tomic & J. Kingma (Eds.), *Advances in cognition and educational practice* (Vol. 5, pp. 43–75). Greenwich, CT: JAI Press.

Mayer, J. D., & Salovey, P. (1993). The intelligence of emotional intelligence. *Intelligence, 17,* 433–442.

Mayer, J. D., & Salovey, P. (1997). What is emotional intelligence? In P. Salovey, & D. Sluyter (Eds.), *Emotional development and emotional intelligence: Implications for educators* (pp. 3–31). New York: Basic Books.

Mayer, J. D., Salovey, P., & Caruso, D. (2000). Emotional intelligence. In R. J. Sternberg (Ed.), *Handbook of intelligence* (2nd ed., pp. 396–421). New York: Cambridge University Press.

McAdams, D. P. (1996). Personality, modernity, and the storied self: A contemporary framework for studying persons. *Psychological Inquiry, 7,* 295–321.

McClelland, D. C., & Koestner, R. (1992). The achievement motive. In C. P. Smith (Ed.), *Motivation and personality: Handbook of thematic content analysis* (pp. 143–152). New York: Cambridge.

McCrae, R. R., & Costa, P. T. (1999) A five-factor theory of personality. In L. Pervin & O. P. John (Eds.), *Handbook of personality* (2nd ed., pp. 139–153). New York: Guilford Press.

Palfai, T. P., & Salovey, P. (1993). The influence of depressed and elated mood on deductive and inductive reasoning. *Imagination, Cognition, and Personality, 13,* 57–71.

Payne, W. L. (1986). A study of emotion: Developing emotional intelligence; Self-integration; relating to fear, pain and desire. *Dissertation Abstracts International, 47*(01), 203A. (University Microfilms No. AAC 8605928)

Pouissant, A. F. (1970). A Negro psychiatrist explains the Negro psyche. In R. V. Gutherie (Ed.) *Being Black: Psychological-sociological dilemmas.* San Francisco: Canfield Press.

Saarni, C. (1990). Emotional competence: How emotions and relationships become integrated. In R. A. Thompson (Ed.), *Socioemotional development: Nebraska symposium on motivation* (Vol. 36, pp. 115–182). Lincoln, NE: University of Nebraska Press.

Saarni, C. (1999). *Developing emotional competence.* New York: Guilford Press.

Salovey, P., Bedell, B. T., Detweiler, J. B., & Mayer, J. D. (1999). Coping intelligently: Emotional intelligence and the coping process. In C. R. Snyder (Ed.), *Coping: The psychology of what works* (pp. 141–164). New York: Oxford University Press.

Salovey, P., Bedell, B. T., Detweiler, J. B., & Mayer, J. D. (forthcoming). Current directions in emotional intelligence research. In M. Lewis & J. M. Haviland-Jones (Eds.), *Handbook of emotions* (2nd ed.). New York: Guilford Press.

Salovey, P., & Birnbaum, D. (1989). The influence of mood on health-relevant cognitions. *Journal of Personality and Social Psychology, 57,* 539–551.

Salovey, P., & Mayer, J. D. (1990). Emotional intelligence. *Imagination, Cognition, and Personality, 9,* 185–211.

Scarr, S. (1989). Protecting general intelligence: Constructs and consequences for interventions. In R. L. Linn (Ed.), *Intelligence: Measurement, theory, and public policy.* Urbana, IL: University of Illinois Press.

Schutte, N. S., Malouff, J. M., Hall, L. E., Haggerty, D. J., Copper, J. T., Golden, C. J., & Dornheim, L. (1998). Development and validation of a measure of emotional intelligence. *Personality and Individual Differences, 25,* 167–177.

Simon, H. A. (1982). Comments. In M. S. Clark & S. T. Fiske (Eds.), *Affect and cognition* (pp. 333–342). Hillsdale, NJ: Erlbaum.

Sternberg, R. J. (1988). *The triarchic mind: A new theory of human intelligence.* New York: Penguin.

Sternberg, R. J., & Smith, C. (1985). Social intelligence and decoding skills in nonverbal communication. *Social Cognition, 3,* 168–192.

Thorndike, R. L., & Stein, S. (1937). An evaluation of the attempts to measure social intelligence. *Psychological Bulletin, 34,* 275–284.

Upshur, L. J., Terry, J. J., Holoka, J. P., Goff, R. D., Cassar, G. H., & Lowry, B. (1995). *World history, Volume II, Since 1500: The Age of global integration* (2nd ed.). Minneapolis, MN: West Publishing.

Wessman, A. E., & Ricks, D. E. (1966). *Mood and personality.* New York: Holt, Rinehart, & Winston.

CHAPTER SIX

Psychological Mindedness and Emotional Intelligence

Mary McCallum and William E. Piper

In his comprehensive book on emotional intelligence, Goleman (1995) seemed to make the association between psychological mindedness and emotional intelligence. He stated that "Socrates' injunction 'Know thyself' speaks to [the] keystone of emotional intelligence: awareness of one's own feelings as they occur" (p. 46). Later, he stated that "self-awareness is fundamental to psychological insight; this is the faculty that much of psychotherapy means to strengthen" (p. 54). Hence, self-awareness forms a nexus point for both concepts. Similarly, the term *personal intelligence,* coined by Gardner (1983) has been used interchangeably with both *psychological mindedness* and *emotional intelligence,* suggesting overlap between the concepts.

In this chapter we explore similarities and differences between psychological mindedness and emotional intelligence. Emotional intelligence is a relatively newer concept than psychological mindedness in terms of being the focus of scientific investigation. By discussing issues and difficulties associated with the conceptualization of psychological mindedness, we hope to elucidate issues that are equally pertinent to the continued evolution of the concept of emotional intelligence.

This chapter is organized into two major sections. The first presents the concept of psychological mindedness. The second section compares psychological mindedness and emotional intelligence. The presentation of psychological mindedness begins by exploring how it has been conceptualized. That exploration includes a discussion of its relevance for selecting patients for psychoanalytically oriented, also called psychodynamic, psychotherapies. Following this conceptual discussion is a review of how psychological mindedness has been measured. That review includes a description of our measure, the Psychological Mindedness Assessment Procedure (McCallum & Piper, 1987). We offer a rationale for why we believe the PMAP overcomes problems associated with previous attempts at operationalizing the construct. Following the description of the PMAP, we summarize its psychometric properties. In particular we report its predictive validity with respect to identifying patients who remain in, work with, and benefit from psychodynamic psychotherapy.

The second section, the comparison of psychological mindedness and emotional intelligence, is organized around several issues associated with both constructs. Those issues include applicability, dimensionality, overlap, person-focus, blending of process and outcome, and development. The chapter concludes by inviting the reader to learn from our work with psychological mindedness when approaching the concept of emotional intelligence.

PSYCHOLOGICAL MINDEDNESS

Conceptualization

The concept of psychological mindedness is primarily addressed in the psychotherapy literature, especially by authors affiliated with psychoanalytically oriented psychotherapies. For example, Bachrach and Leaff's (1978) review of the "analyzability" literature (discussions of who makes a suitable candidate for psychoanalysis) revealed that nearly one-quarter of the references concerned psychological mindedness (pp. 900–991). Of the many authors who emphasized psychodynamic concepts when defining psychological mindedness (for example, Appelbaum, 1973; Bloch, 1979; Tyson & Sandler, 1971; Wolitzky & Reuben, 1974), the comprehensive definition offered by Silver (1983) is one of the clearest. Whereas many authors used abstract metapsychological terms, Silver's (1983) definition was stated in a straightforward manner. The capacity for psychological mindedness includes "the patient's desire to learn the possible meanings and causes of his internal and external experiences as well as the patient's ability to look inwards to psychical factors rather than only outwards to environmental factors . . . [and] to potentially conceptualize the relationship between thoughts, feelings, and actions" (p. 516).

Relevance

When viewed as a dimension within a patient, psychological mindedness is generally believed to be important for working within all forms of psychoanalytically oriented psychotherapies. Therefore, it is considered to be an important patient selection criterion. The rationale for this is based on the notion of matching a patient's characteristic with a therapy behavior that is relevant for a successful therapy experience. Theoretically, the achievement of positive outcomes from any psychotherapy depends on the patient's ability to contribute to a therapeutic process that leads to the desired objective. The objective of dynamically oriented therapy is to solve the patient's presenting problems by achieving insight into how his or her difficulties are related to unresolved intrapsychic conflicts and by initiating a process of working through, which will continue between and beyond the treatment sessions (Piper, McCallum, & Azim, 1992).

The dynamically oriented therapist uses an interpretive here-and-now approach that focuses on unconscious conflicts. Specifically, the therapist endeavors to foster insight concerning how the patient's presenting complaints are actually the manifestation of underlying psychic conflicts between unpermissible wishes, anxieties, or fears to which these wishes give rise and (partially effective) defense mechanisms that are mobilized to cope with the anxiety and maintain the repression of the wish. This insight is fostered by interpreting or hypothesizing a link between the patient's current pattern of behavior, feelings, and cognitions with this unconscious process. In addition, the psychodynamic therapist hypothesizes a link between the patient's patterns of past relationships, current relationships, and his or her interaction with the therapist (transference).

The relevant behaviors required for success in psychodynamic therapy include an ability to work with interpretations. Working with interpretations requires that the patient has an "ability to see relationships among thoughts, feelings, and actions, with the goal of learning the meanings and causes of his experiences and behavior" (Appelbaum, 1973, p.36). Although this definition identifies an ability that is requisite for working with interpretations, it was intended by Appelbaum as a definition of psychological mindedness. Hence, psychological mindedness represents a patient dimension that is conceptually related to desired dynamic therapy behavior.

Measurement

Eighteen years ago, we began exploring psychological mindedness as a formal selection criterion for psychodynamic therapy. At that time, there were few studies that operationalized psychological mindedness and investigated its relationship with therapy process and outcome. The results of the studies were inconsistent and inconclusive (Abramowitz & Abramowitz, 1974; Kernberg et al., 1972; Piper, Debbane, Bienvenu, & Garant, 1984). The paucity of research seemed to reflect ambiguities associated with the definition and measurement of psychological mindedness.

The term *psychological mindedness* is at times used interchangeably with terms for other concepts such as *insight, introspection,* and *self-awareness* (Appelbaum, 1973; Bloch, 1979; Tyson & Sandler, 1971; Wolitzky & Reuben,

1974). It is also associated with constructs such as alexithymia (Taylor, 1994), personal intelligence (Park, Imboden, Park, Hulse, & Unger, 1992), and private self-consciousness (Fenigstein, Scheier, & Buss, 1975). Psychological mindedness has been conceptualized in numerous ways: as an ability, an interest, and a motive (Hall, 1992). Finally, approaches to its measurement have involved questionnaires (Conte et al., 1990; Gough, 1957; Tolor & Reznikoff, 1960), clinical appraisals (Piper et al., 1984; Ryan & Cicchetti, 1985), and the combination of related measures (Kernberg et al., 1972; Horowitz, Rosenberg, & Kalehzan, 1992; Luborsky et al., 1980). Each approach has been associated with certain problems; for example, there has been overlap with other concepts, rater inference, and indirect measurement. Clearly there is a need for a reliable and valid measure of psychological mindedness.

Psychological Mindedness Assessment Procedure

Informed by previous attempts, we endeavored to construct a reliable and valid measure of psychological mindedness. We chose to define psychological mindedness as one's ability to identify dynamic (intrapsychic) components and to relate them to one's difficulties. Our approach was influenced by our experience using a process analysis system that identifies therapist interpretations. That system, the Therapist Intervention Rating System (Piper, Debbane, Bienvenu, & de Carufel, 1987), defines interpretations as therapist interventions that identify one or more components of an intrapsychic conflict, such as wishing, anxiety, or defensiveness. We used the system to rate individual therapy sessions from a comparative study of four forms of psychodynamic psychotherapy (Piper et. al, 1984). Differences were noticed among patients' responses to interpretations. Some patients struggled, seemingly perplexed, whereas others worked with them, often formulating elegant interpretations of their own and others' dynamics. These latter patients seemed to be receptive to the therapists' hypotheses that their current difficulties were linked to unconscious conflicts between wishes, fears, and defenses. It was as if they entered therapy "speaking the same language" as the therapist. We postulated that these were highly psychologically minded patients. We proceeded to develop scoring criteria that would reflect these patients' ability to identify dynamic (intrapsychic) components and to relate them to difficulties.

We constructed a test stimulus by scripting and videotaping two simulated patient-therapist interactions. Each interaction begins with a patient describing a recent event to her therapist. After viewing each interaction, the person being assessed is asked, "What seems to be troubling this woman?" The person's responses are scored according to how well they reflect basic assumptions of psychodynamic theory. Whereas there remain debates among psychodynamic clinicians from the various theoretical schools of thought (for example, object relations theory versus drive theory) concerning aspects of the theories, all psychodynamic therapists agree on certain basic assumptions regarding the etiology of problems and the workings of the psyche. These commonly held assumptions include psychic determinism whereby all conscious experience is thought to be at least partially determined by intrapsychic processes; intrapsychic conflict whereby tension and anxiety arise from conflictual unconscious forces of unpermissible wishes and fears; and the use of defense mechanisms whereby the person minimizes, distorts, or avoids some part of his or her experience in order to alleviate fears and maintain the repression of threatening impulses.

Rationale for the PMAP's Approach

The videotape and manual for applying the scoring criteria became the Psychological Mindedness Assessment Procedure (PMAP) (McCallum & Piper, 1987). The PMAP is individually administered, and it takes approximately fifteen minutes to complete the assessment and determine the score. Our approach differed from past attempts to operationalize the variable. First, by emphasizing analytic concepts, we attempted to distinguish the construct from other specific and nonspecific therapeutic factors rather than incorporating related concepts into the assessment of psychological mindedness, for example, motivation. Second, by constructing the PMAP to use objective, clearly defined behavioral referents, we attempted to enhance reliability. Third, consistent with the current era's preference for video stimuli, the PMAP is a videotape measure. Developing a videotape measure helped protect our assessment of psychological mindedness from the possible confounds of education and intelligence. Specifically, we did not want to bias the performance of those individuals, especially those with limited formal education, who were often very astute about others' dynamics but quite apprehensive about forms or "tests." Finally, using a standardized video and interview format to assess psychological mindedness decreases threats to validity, such as halo effects.

Psychometric Properties of the PMAP

The psychometric properties of the PMAP were investigated with five separate populations. We first investigated the measure's construct validity with a nonclinical population of thirty adult volunteers (McCallum, 1989). Our second sample involved a controlled clinical trial of patients in short-term, analytically oriented group psychotherapy. The PMAP was used to investigate the suitability of 154 pathologically bereaved patients for this treatment modality (McCallum, 1989; Piper et al., 1992). Our third sample involved a clinical trial of an intensive day treatment program. The PMAP was investigated as a selection criterion for 165 day treatment patients with serious long-term disorders, mainly affective and personality disorders (Piper, Rosie, Azim, & Joyce, 1993; Piper, Rosie, Joyce, & Azim, 1996). Our fourth sample involved using the PMAP to predict the response of 190 patients with serious long-term disorders, mainly affective and personality disorders, who were admitted to an evening treatment program (McCallum, Piper, & O'Kelly, 1997). Our fifth sample involved a comparative trial of two forms of short-term, time-limited individual therapy. The PMAP was investigated as a therapy-matching variable for 171 outpatients presenting with problems with depression, anxiety, low self-esteem, and interpersonal conflict who were randomly assigned to either an interpretive or supportive form of individual psychotherapy (Piper, Joyce, McCallum, & Azim, 1998).

The results of these studies supported the manner in which the PMAP operationalized psychological mindedness. The rater reliability was consistently found to be strong, with intraclass correlation coefficients ranging from .88 to .96 in the clinical trials. Concerning its construct validity, psychological mindedness was consistently independent of several demographic characteristics, psychiatric symptomatology, psychological distress, medication use, and diagnosis. The statistical associations were low and nonsignificant. Concerning convergent validity, the PMAP was found to be significantly and moderately related to other measures of psychological mindedness.

Predictive Validity of the PMAP

Concerning predictive validity, in the three clinical trials of group therapy, psychological mindedness was related to "working" in dynamically oriented group therapy. Psychological mindedness was predictive of remaining in short-term loss groups but not of remaining in the two partial hospitalization (day and evening treatment) programs or in individual therapy. With regard to outcome, psychological mindedness predicted positive outcome in both forms of individual therapy and in day treatment but not in the other two clinical trials. We believe that our differential findings reflect the influence of other patient and therapy variables on attrition and outcome. In terms of selecting patients who will work in dynamically oriented therapy, we believe the PMAP is a useful clinical tool. It is efficient, easily administered, and reliably scored. Psychological mindedness is independent of potentially confounding variables such as intelligence and psychopathology. Moreover, patients seem to enjoy the break from the usual self-report battery of tests. By using a measure of psychological mindedness to match patients with the most appropriate therapy, we hope to ultimately reduce emotional and financial costs associated with inappropriate treatment.

PSYCHOLOGICAL MINDEDNESS AND EMOTIONAL INTELLIGENCE

Applicability

Emotional intelligence is considered to be a general construct encompassing emotional, personal, and social abilities that influence one's overall capability to effectively cope with environmental demands and pressures (see Chapter Seventeen).

Conversely, as reviewed in the first part of this chapter, psychological mindedness has usually been considered to be a concept specifically relevant for identifying suitable candidates for psychotherapy. Therefore, a major difference between emotional intelligence and psychological mindedness is the scope of its applicability, with that of psychological mindedness being comparatively narrower. Perhaps these two different applications partially explain why any association between the two concepts has not as yet been explored. However, some authors have discussed the merits of psychological mindedness in more general terms.

Specifically, there has been debate over whether psychological mindedness (and concepts related to it) facilitate or hinder effective living. There is no comparable debate regarding emotional intelligence. Whereas there have been disagreements regarding the adaptive versus maladaptive aspects of emotion, emotional intelligence is consistently presented as an exclusively positive attribute (Goleman, 1995; Salovey & Mayer, 1990).

Most clinicians, especially those who follow the psychodynamic theoretical approach, value psychological mindedness in their patients and their colleagues. Similarly, most authors believe that psychological mindedness is more associated with positive events than negative ones. Farber (1989; Farber & Golden, 1997) summarized many of the advantages associated with high levels of psychological mindedness. The advantages included feeling special and having an increased tolerance for the complexities of people, which can lead to becoming a more sensitive, compassionate, and genuinely forgiving person. Psychological mindedness can also be used pleasurably and playfully to understand and appreciate cultural, historical, artistic, and personal events. Finally, psychological mindedness can help people know themselves better, thereby freeing them from the tyranny of unconscious impulses.

Disadvantages associated with high levels of psychological mindedness have also been documented. Psychological mindedness has been found to exacerbate anxiety, depression, and paranoia, and has been associated with lower self-esteem (Farber, 1989; Farber & Golden, 1997; Fenigstein, 1984, 1994; Park et al., 1992). Other disadvantages include the inability to allow people and things to be simple; loneliness and disappointment with the superficiality of nonpsychologically minded people; and self-imposed isolation so as not to unwittingly intrude or eavesdrop on someone's unconscious (Farber & Golden, 1997).

Whereas some authors believe that psychological mindedness can be detrimental to the person (for example, Fenigstein & Vanable, 1992), most consider it a mixed blessing. Farber and Golden (1997) advocated the merits of self-knowledge while warning of the dangers associated with it. In their words, the highly psychologically minded person is "wiser but sadder." Empirical support for this latter idea was provided by Conte and her colleagues who found that psychological mindedness facilitated behavioral adjustment but intensified subjective distress (Conte et al., 1990).

We believe that psychological mindedness helps a person make sense out of a seemingly random world. However, the insights that are gleaned may be quite ambivalently held. As one falls in love, one dreads losing the other; as one celebrates life, one fears its fragility; as one becomes aware of one's strengths, one becomes simultaneously aware of one's weaknesses. By integrating all aspects of the psyche, the petty and flawed aspects as well as the generous and courageous aspects, we believe that an individual can find a self-acceptance that comes from self-knowledge.

Dimensionality of the Concepts

The most striking aspect of the emotional intelligence literature is the breadth, variety, and differences among authors regarding which abilities emotional intelligence is thought to entail (Goleman, 1995; Mayer & Salovey, 1993). The model proposed by Reuven Bar-On (see Chapter Seventeen) is perhaps the clearest and the most comprehensive to date. He conceptualized the emotional intelligence abilities to reflect the following factors: intrapersonal, interpersonal, stress management, motivational and general mood, and adaptability (see Chapter Seventeen). Whereas emotional intelligence may be discussed as a general factor, it is clearly considered by its advocates as a multidimensional construct. There is no such consensus concerning psychological mindedness. Some authors consider it to be multidimensional, whereas others consider it to be unidimensional. We believe that some dimensions included in a multidimensional conceptualization of psychological mindedness are actually independent constructs, for example, motivation. Furthermore, we believe that their inclusion in the definition dilutes and possibly confounds the psychological mindedness construct.

As an example, let us consider the concept of personal intelligence, which is related to both psychological mindedness and emotional intelligence. Park and Park (1997) operationalized personal intelligence such that items on their scale encompass two types of personal intelligence (intrapersonal and interpersonal), as well as concepts believed to be associated with them. Accordingly, items are included to attempt to detect perceptual competence, preoccupation with using this competence, empathy, and low-level grandiosity. It is not clear whether these additional concepts are considered to be a reflection of personal intelligence or independent concepts that may be associated with it. In either case the concept of interest becomes diffused and complex. Some models of emotional intelligence may be at risk for the same type of diffusion and complexity.

In our own attempts to predict patients' response to psychodynamic psychotherapies, we have conceptualized psychological mindedness as only one of many important predictor and process variables that interact to determine whether a patient will remain in, work in, and benefit from therapy. Consequently, we chose to operationalize psychological mindedness as a narrowly defined construct. Our scale, the PMAP, consists of a hierarchy whose scoring criteria reflect basic assumptions of psychodynamic theory. The scale's higher levels incorporate criteria from the lower levels, such that each level becomes more comprehensive and complex in its focus. However, it is possible that the levels may represent separate variables. We are currently planning an empirical investigation of this possibility.

As our own work attests, sometimes what was initially conceived as a unitary concept changes as a function of research findings. Similarly, Fenigstein (1997) consistently indicated that the supposed global concept of self-consciousness—a concept similar to psychological mindedness—was actually composed of two distinct components called private and public self-consciousness. Hence, what began as a unidimensional concept evolved into a multidimensional concept as dictated by the data.

Further complications arise when principal components analyses are applied to various scales of psychological mindedness. This was the case with each of two questionnaire measures of psychological mindedness, the Psychological Mindedness Scale (Conte & Ratto, 1997) and the Toronto Alexithymia Scale (considered to measure the obverse of psychological mindedness) (Bagby, Parker, & Taylor, 1991; Bagby, Taylor, & Parker, 1994). Both scales were reported to have high internal reliability coefficients. Such high alpha coefficients often are interpreted to mean that a scale's items are homogeneous, that is, highly intracorrelated, and that the items represent one concept or factor, for example, are unidimensional. Nevertheless, factor analyses conducted on the scales' items yielded a number of factors. Those results suggested that different items reflect different constructs or that the concept being assessed is multidimensional. This fairly common state of affairs creates difficulty in understanding and conceptualizing concepts such as psychological mindedness (Briggs & Cheek, 1986). With respect to emotional intelligence, it is an empirical question whether the various emotional intelligence abilities coalesce within one construct. It is possible that the various abilities are distinct and independent of each other.

Overlap of the Concepts

With respect to the actual abilities each concept is thought to entail, the strongest overlap involves intrapersonal factors. Abilities related to the intrapersonal factors of emotional intelligence include (1) the ability to be aware of, accurately understand, accept, and respect oneself, (2) the ability to recognize and understand one's feelings, and (3) the ability to express feelings, beliefs, and thoughts (see Chapter Seventeen). These abilities are consistent with the theoretical definitions of psychological mindedness that are presented in the first part of this chapter.

Emotional intelligence is also conceptualized as involving interpersonal factors. As noted in Chapter Seventeen, the interpersonal factors include the ability to be aware of, understand, and appreciate the feelings of others, the ability to demonstrate oneself as a cooperative, contributing, and constructive member of one's social group, and the ability to establish and maintain mutually satisfying interpersonal relationships that are characterized by emotional closeness and intimacy and by giving and receiving affection.

Psychological mindedness has been linked to certain interpersonal abilities, specifically, the ability to be aware of, understand, and appreciate the feelings of others. However, the other aspects of interpersonal abilities that are related to emotional intelligence—parts (2) and (3) mentioned above—seem to refer to the outcome of understanding the emotions of oneself and others. There are two issues here that relate to how psychological mindedness and emotional intelligence are conceptualized. The first relates to the person focus of the concepts: the self versus another. The second relates to whether each construct is seen as a means to an end or an end in itself. Next we discuss these issues in terms of how they relate to psychological mindedness.

The Person Focus

Conceivably, psychologically minded patients achieve self-knowledge when they focus that skill on themselves. Therefore, a pretherapy assessment of psychological mindedness toward the self (as opposed to another) would probably be a good predictor of response to therapy. However, there is a significant problem associated with assessing psychological mindedness directed toward the self. Assessments of the person's own issues tend to be influenced by defense mechanisms and the unconscious (Menna & Cohen, 1997; Park & Park, 1997). Similarly, Hatcher and Hatcher (1997; Hatcher, Hatcher, Berlin, Okla, & Richards, 1990) warned of problems with confounds due to differences among patients regarding the relevance of stimuli. Relevance refers to the similarity between the conflict depicted in the stimuli and the person's own intrapsychic conflicts. Some patients may experience difficulty responding to stimuli that they find irrelevant, whereas other patients may experience difficulty responding to stimuli that are all too relevant or "too close to home." This confound can occur whether the stimuli specifically depict the self or another.

There are differences among measures of psychological mindedness (and concepts similar to it) concerning their person focus. Some measures focus solely on the self (Bagby et al., 1994; Fenigstein et al., 1975). Some focus solely on others (Dollinger, 1985; McCallum & Piper, 1987). Some focus on both the self and others (Conte et al., 1990; Hatcher et al., 1990; Menna & Cohen, 1997; Park & Park, 1997). Finally, some do not differentiate between psychological mindedness with respect to the self and others (Farber & Golden, 1997). Whether the assessment of psychological mindedness focuses on the self or others, it is important to know whether this ability generalizes to an ability to understand the self within the therapy situation. Our findings that psychological mindedness (as assessed by the PMAP) was positively related to working in three different forms of group therapy indicates that psychological mindedness toward another generalizes to the therapy situation.

With respect to emotional intelligence, it would be important to know whether emotional intelligence toward the self requires the same skills as emotional intelligence directed toward another. If these were found to be somewhat independent abilities, it would be interesting to know which is more important in terms of adjustment. Of course, adjustment is considered a part of emotional intelligence. Included in the definition of emotional intelligence is the person's ability to function in an adaptive manner. Therefore, not only is emotional intelligence conceptualized as the person's ability to read the emotions of him or herself and another, it is also conceptualized as the consequences of that ability. Hence, as stated above, interpersonal factors include the ability to demonstrate oneself as a cooperative, contributing, and constructive member of one's social group, and the ability to establish and maintain mutually satisfying interpersonal relationships. Moreover, emotional intelligence is conceptualized as including stress management factors, motivational and general mood factors, and adaptability factors. This blending of process and outcome is also seen with the concept of psychological mindedness. We discuss this issue in the next section.

A Means or an End

To address this blending of process and outcome, one might alternatively ask whether psychological mindedness is a path or a goal. Although the definitions of psychological mindedness use different terms, they all convey the idea that an attribute, capacity, or ability leads, through discussion, to an understanding or insight. Therefore, psychological mindedness is repeatedly conceptualized as a means to an end versus an end in itself. Because we consider adjustment, rather than psychological mindedness, as a therapeutic goal or an end, psychological mindedness is not regarded as an index of adjustment. Our repeated finding that psychological mindedness, as assessed by the PMAP, is not significantly associated with (pretherapy) measures of psychiatric symptomatology or psychological distress supports the independence of psychological mindedness and mental health. Even the most psychologically minded person can be profoundly disturbed. Rather than representing a treatment goal (or outcome criterion), we contend that psychological mindedness should be viewed as a useful tool by which one can engage in a psychodynamically oriented therapeutic process to arrive at a beneficial outcome.

Let us consider some analogous examples that involve other approaches to therapy. Whereas recording incremental fear responses to phobic stimuli is a method by which one engages in behavior therapy, record keeping is not an indicator of mental health in and of itself. Whereas free association is a method by which one engages in psychoanalysis, free association is not an indicator of mental health. Similarly, whereas psychological mindedness facilitates a method by which one engages in psychodynamic psychotherapy, it is not an indicator of mental health. For that matter, neither is insight an indicator of mental health. However, insight can lead to behavior change and therefore behavior that may be healthier. For example, suppose a psychologically minded man derives the insight that he feels angry and abandoned when his wife is out of town. Such insight might lead him to question why he wants to go to a single's bar with his younger coworkers. By being aware of his unconscious wish for revenge, he may resist the temptation to act it out sexually. Rather than acting out, he may channel the impulse for revenge verbally and consciously by calling his wife and expressing his hurt to her directly.

Whereas we believe that psychological mindedness is distinct from adjustment, it remains an empirical question as to whether this is true for emotional intelligence. It is possible that the ability to read the emotions of oneself and another does not immediately translate into healthier adjustment. There may be mediating variables that determine whether those intrapersonal and interpersonal abilities are used for health or pathology.

For example, many authors have found that despite heightened capabilities in the area of complex social cognition, patients with borderline personality disorder experience remarkably dysfunctional relationships (Cohen, Kershner, & Wehrspann, 1985; Menna & Cohen, 1997; Westen, Lohr, Silk, Gold, & Kerber, 1990). Westen et al. (1990) interpreted this discrepancy as reflecting an interference from motivational and defensive processes. It would be interesting to explore whether the same phenomenon occurred for some people scoring high on subtests of emotional intelligence; in other words, despite being able to read the emotions of themselves and others, they are unable to effectively cope with the world.

Development of Psychological Mindedness

Goleman (1995) devoted Chapter Sixteen of his book to presenting his persuasive argument that the world would be a less violent place and have happier people if emotional intelligence were encouraged, especially in children. Given that psychological mindedness is a mixed blessing, one could question whether psychological mindedness should be encouraged in children. Menna and Cohen (1997) believed that an increase in "social perspective taking" would improve behavior and adjustment. Social perspective taking is another concept that is similar to psychological mindedness. It refers to the ability to free oneself of one's own view and to recognize and understand the thoughts, feelings, and motives of the self and others (Shantz, 1983). Menna and Cohen's (1997) rationale for associating social perspective taking and better adjustment was based on two findings. First, social perspective taking has been found to be associated with forming and maintaining friendships (Selman, 1981). Second, the presence of a social support network has been found to positively influence a person's ability to cope with stress, particularly loss. Therefore, increasing children's social perspective taking would indeed be a helpful pursuit.

In contrast is the work of Park (1992; Park & Park, 1997) with personal intelligence. Park and Park contended that children with high personal intelligence can be perceived as threatening by their parents, especially narcissistic mothers. They believed that this interaction is fertile ground for parental abuse and the development of borderline personality disorder in the children.

As we stated above, we have an optimistic view of psychological mindedness and believe that it should be encouraged in children. Our view is consistent with those who postulate an evolutionary advantage to psychological mindedness. Its evolutionary advantage is based on the ability of the highly psychological minded person to develop an empathic altruistic response to others, which elicits reciprocity and ensures survival.

Considering psychological mindedness as an evolutionary next step, and therefore genetically predetermined, begs a more basic question than whether psychological mindedness should be encouraged. The question is *can* psychological mindedness be encouraged? Developing psychological mindedness may be analogous to learning a language. By observing others and the self, the child begins to develop a theory of the mind, in other words, a theory of how others organize their conscious and unconscious mental activities that feel, perceive, will, and especially reason (Mish, 1983). The child fits new information into that developing theory and continually revises the theory. Just as with language, if this process of developing a theory of the mind is disrupted or compromised, the effect may be irreversible.

This irreversibility speaks to the stability of the construct. Most authors consider psychological mindedness to be relatively stable after a person reaches adulthood (Conte & Ratto, 1997; Dollinger, 1997; Taylor & Taylor, 1997). Results of our investigations also suggested that psychological mindedness tends to be a stable characteristic. Although manifestations of the ability can be influenced by motivational factors, psychological mindedness has remained relatively stable even after participation in intensive psychodynamic psychotherapies. For example, over a one-month period the test-retest reliability for a nonclinical population was $r(13) = .76, p < .001$. After participating in the intensive evening treatment program, the correlation coefficient yielded by a Pearson correlation between patients' pretreatment and posttreatment psychological mindedness scores was $r(152) = .40, p < .001$. Although the latter coefficient is smaller than for the nonclinical population, it attests to the relative stability of the construct despite the possible interference of a lessened motivation among patients at the posttreatment assessment.

However, the psychological mindedness of children seems to be more susceptible to influence. Most authors conceptualize psychological mindedness as developing in childhood. It is as if there is a critical period for its development. If the opportunity is missed, it is forever lost. Kennedy (1979) postulated that psychological mindedness is a two-part process involving the cognitive capacity for understanding oneself and others and the ability to tolerate painful feelings. These two lines of development are interrelated: the child's increased capacity to tolerate feelings both contributes to and is aided by an increased understanding of the meaning and nature of those feelings. Interestingly, Kennedy's (1979) process integrates emotional intelligence and psychological mindedness.

Empirical support for a developmental model of psychological mindedness is reflected in studies of developmental delays. In cases of developmental delays, children from progressively older age groups gave responses that reflected a progression through the same stages and in the same sequence as the responses of younger children without developmental delays. Further evidence is provided by data indicating that children's performance improves as they grow older and develop more of the cognitive and emotional abilities involved in psychological mindedness (Dollinger, 1997; Menna & Cohen, 1997).

Despite genetic structures that may permit the development of psychological mindedness, most authors agree, therefore, that its development is influenced by, if not contingent on, cultural and caretaker factors. We believe that environmental factors may disrupt, pervert, delay, or even accelerate the social, emotional, and psychological development of children. We believe that psychotherapy can redress and diminish the effects of negative environmental experiences, and that psychological mindedness is the language of psychotherapy.

CONCLUSION

In this chapter, we reviewed the concept of psychological mindedness. We believe that it is a valuable construct for selecting patients for psychotherapy. We explored its overlap with emotional intelligence. Emotional intelligence is a general construct encompassing a broad array of abilities that influence one's overall capability to effectively cope. We reviewed the differences in applicability and dimensionality of the two constructs. Despite the differences, there are commonalities between them. Although neither construct is particularly new, both have suffered from conceptual ambiguity, research scarcity, and flawed attempts at operationalization. We are familiar with the issues that arise in conceptualizing and operationalizing psychological mindedness. Some of these issues include whether it is a good thing, whether it is a means or an end, whether it can be developed, and whether it focuses on the self or another. The ambiguities and difficulties that have affected the concept of psychological mindedness may also affect the concept of emotional intelligence. By understanding the various issues associated with conceptualizing psychological mindedness, we hope that the reader may productively use them in conceptualizing emotional intelligence.

References

Abramowitz, S. I., & Abramowitz, C. V. (1974). Psychological-mindedness and benefit from insight-oriented group therapy. *Archives of General Psychiatry, 30,* 610–615.

Appelbaum, S. A. (1973). Psychological mindedness: Word, concept, and essence. *International Journal of Psycho-Analysis, 54,* 35–46.

Bachrach, H. M., & Leaff, L. A. (1978). "Analyzability": A systematic review of the clinical and quantitative literature. *Journal of the American Psychoanalytic Association, 26,* 881–920.

Bagby, R. M., Parker, J. D. A., & Taylor, G. J. (1991). Reassessing the reliability and validity of the MMPI Alexithymia Scale. *Journal of Personality Assessment, 56,* 238–253.

Bagby, R. M., Taylor, G. J., & Parker, J. D. A. (1994). The Twenty-Item Toronto Alexithymia Scale: II, Convergent, discriminant, and concurrent validity. *Journal of Psychosomatic Research, 38,* 33–40

Bloch, S. (1979). Assessment of patients for psychotherapy. *British Journal of Psychiatry, 135,* 193–208.

Briggs, S. R., & Cheek, J. M. (1986). The role of factor analysis in the development and evaluation of personality scales. *Journal of Personality, 54,* 106–148.

Cohen, N. J., Kershner, J., & Wehrspann, W. (1985). Characteristics of social cognition in children with different symptom patterns. *Journal of Applied Developmental Psychology, 6,* 277–290.

Conte, H. R., Plutchik, R., Jung, B. B., Picard, S., Karasu, T. B., & Lotterman, A. (1990). Psychological mindedness as a predictor of psychotherapy outcome: A preliminary report. *Comprehensive Psychiatry, 31,* 426–431.

Conte, H. R., & Ratto, R. (1997). Self-report measures of psychological mindedness. In M. McCallum & W. E. Piper (Eds.), *Psychological mindedness: A contemporary understanding* (pp. 1–26). Mahwah, NJ: Erlbaum.

Dollinger, S. J. (1985). Sagacious judgment via word association. *Journal of Personality and Social Psychology, 49,* 1738–1752.

Dollinger, S. J. (1997). Psychological mindedness as "reading between the lines." In M. McCallum & W. E. Piper (Eds.), *Psychological mindedness: A contemporary understanding* (pp. 169–188). Mahwah, NJ: Erlbaum.

Farber, B. A. (1989). Psychological-mindedness: Can there be too much of a good thing. *Psychotherapy, 26,* 210–217.

Farber, B. A., & Golden, V. (1997). Psychological mindedness in psychotherapists. In M. McCallum & W. E. Piper (Eds.), *Psychological mindedness: A contemporary understanding* (pp. 211–236). Mahwah, NJ: Erlbaum.

Fenigstein, A. (1984). Self-consciousness and the overperception of self as a target. *Journal of Personality and Social Psychology, 47,* 860–870.

Fenigstein, A. (1994). Paranoia. In V. S. Ramachandran (Ed.), *Encyclopedia of human behavior.* San Diego, CA: Academic Press.

Fenigstein, A. (1997). Self-consciousness and its relation to psychological mindedness. In M. McCallum & W. E. Piper (Eds.), *Psychological mindedness: A contemporary understanding* (pp. 105–132). Mahwah, NJ: Erlbaum.

Fenigstein, A., Scheier, M. F., & Buss, A. H. (1975). Public and private self-consciousness: Assessment and theory. *Journal of Consulting and Clinical Psychology, 43,* 522–527.

Fenigstein, A., & Vanable, P. A. (1992). Paranoia and self-consciousness. *Journal of Personality and Social Psychology, 62,* 129–138.

Gardner, H. (1983). *Frames of mind: The theory of multiple intelligences.* New York: Basic Books.

Goleman, D. (1995). *Emotional intelligence.* New York: Bantam Books.

Gough, H. G. (1957). *California psychological inventory.* Palo Alto, CA: Consulting Psychological Press.

Hall, J. A. (1992). Psychological-Mindedness: A conceptual model. *American Journal of Psychotherapy, 46,* 131–140.

Hatcher, R. L., & Hatcher, S. L. (1997). Assessing the psychological mindedness of children and adolescents. In M. McCallum & W. E. Piper (Eds.), *Psychological mindedness: A contemporary understanding* (pp. 59–76). Mahwah, NJ: Erlbaum.

Hatcher, R., Hatcher, S., Berlin, M., Okla, K., & Richards, J. (1990). Psychological mindedness and abstract reasoning in late childhood and adolescence: An exploration using new instruments. *Journal of Youth and Adolescence, 19,* 307–326.

Horowitz, L. M., Rosenberg, S. E., & Kalehzan, B. M. (1992). The capacity to describe other people clearly: A predictor of interpersonal problems in brief dynamic psychotherapy. *Psychotherapy Research, 2,* 37–51.

Kennedy, H. (1979). The role of insight in child analysis: A developmental viewpoint. *Journal of the American Psychoanalytic Association, 27 (Suppl.),* 9–28.

Kernberg, O., Burstein, E., Coyne, L., Appelbaum, H., Horwitz, L., & Voth, H. (1972). Psychotherapy and psychoanalysis: Final report of the Menninger Foundation's psychotherapy research project. *Bulletin of the Menninger Clinic, 36,* 1–275.

Luborsky, L., Mintz, J., Auerbach, A., Christoph, P., Bachrach, H., Todd, T., Johnson, M., Cohen, M., & O'Brien, P. (1980). Predicting the outcome of psychotherapy: Findings of the Penn Psychotherapy Project. *Archives of General Psychiatry, 37,* 471–481.

Mayer, J. D., & Salovey, P. (1993). The intelligence of emotional intelligence. *Intelligence, 17,* 433–442.

McCallum, M. (1989). *A controlled study of effectiveness and patient suita bility for short-term group psychotherapy.* Unpublished doctoral dissertation, McGill University, Montreal, Quebec, Canada.

McCallum, M., & Piper, W. E. (1987). *The psychological mindedness assessment procedure.* Unpublished manual and videotape.

McCallum, M., Piper, W. E., & O'Kelly, J. (1997). Predicting patient benefit from a group oriented, evening treatment program. *International Journal of Group Psychotherapy, 47,* 291–314.

Menna, R., & Cohen, N. J. (1997). Social perspective taking. In M. McCallum & W. E. Piper (Eds.), *Psychological mindedness: A contemporary understanding* (pp. 189–210). Mahwah, NJ: Erlbaum.

Mish, F. C. (Ed.) (1983). *Webster's Ninth New Collegiate Dictionary.* Markham, Ontario: Thomas Allen & Son.

Park, L. C., Imboden, J. B., Park, T. J., Hulse, S. H., & Unger, H. T. (1992). Giftedness and psychological abuse in borderline personality disorder: Their relevance to genesis and treatment. *Journal of Personality Disorders, 6,* 226–240.

Park, L. C., & Park, T. J. (1997). Personal intelligence. In M. McCallum & W. E. Piper (Eds.), *Psychological mindedness: A contemporary understanding* (pp. 133–167). Mahwah, NJ: Erlbaum.

Piper, W. E., Debbane, E. G., Bienvenu, J. P., & de Carufel, F. L. (1987). A system for differentiating therapist interpretations and other interventions. *Bulletin of the Menninger Clinic, 51,* 532–550.

Piper, W. E., Debbane, E. G., Bienvenu, J. P., & Garant, J. (1984). A comparative study of four forms of psychotherapy. *Journal of Consulting and Clinical Psychology, 52,* 268–279.

Piper, W. E., Joyce, A. S., McCallum, M., & Azim, H.F.A. (1998). Interpretive and supportive forms of psychotherapy and patient personality variables. *Journal of Consulting and Clinical Psychology, 66,* 558–567.

Piper, W. E., McCallum, M., & Azim, H.F.A. (1992). *Adaptation to loss through short-term group psychotherapy.* New York: Guilford Press.

Piper, W. E., Rosie, J. S., Azim, H.F.A., & Joyce, A. S. (1993). A randomized trial of psychiatric day treatment for patients with affective and personality disorders. *Hospital and Community Psychiatry, 44,* 757–763.

Piper, W. E., Rosie, J. S., Joyce, A. S., & Azim, H.F.A. (1996). *Time-limited day treatment for personality disorders: Integration of research and practice in a group program.* Washington, DC: American Psychological Association.

Ryan, E. R., & Cicchetti, D. V. (1985). Predicting quality of alliance in the initial psychotherapy interview. *Journal of Nervous and Mental Disease, 173,* 717–725.

Salovey, P., & Mayer, J. D. (1990). Emotional intelligence. *Imagination, Cognition and Personality, 9,* 185–211.

Selman, R. L. (1981). The development of interpersonal competence: The role of understanding in conduct. *Developmental Review, 1,* 401–422.

Shantz, C. (1983). Social cognition. In P. H. Mussen (Ed.), *Handbook of Child Psychology; Cognitive development* (Vol. 3, pp. 495–555). New York: Wiley.

Silver, D. (1983). Psychotherapy of the characterologically difficult patient. *Canadian Journal of Psychiatry, 28,* 513–521.

Taylor, G. J. (1994). The alexithymia construct: Conceptualization, validation, and relationship with basic dimensions of personality. *New Trends in Experimental and Clinical Psychiatry, 10,* 61–74.

Taylor, G. J., & Taylor, H. L. (1997). Alexithymia. In M. McCallum & W. E. Piper (Eds.), *Psychological mindedness: A contemporary understanding* (pp. 77–104). Mahwah, NJ: Erlbaum.

Tolor, A., & Reznikoff, M. (1960). A new approach to insight: A preliminary report. *Journal of Nervous and Mental Disease, 130,* 286–296.

Tyson, R. L., & Sandler, J. (1971). Problems in the selection of patients for psycho-analysis: Comments on the application of the concepts of "indications," "suitability" and "analysability." *British Journal of Medical Psychology, 44,* 211–228.

Westen, D., Lohr, N., Silk, K., Gold, L., & Kerber, K. (1990). Object relations and social cognition in borderlines, major depressives, and normals: A TAT analysis. *Psychological Assessment: A Journal of Consulting and Clinical Psychology, 2,* 355–364.

Wolitzky, D. L., & Reuben, R. (1974). Psychological-mindedness. *Journal of Clinical Psychology, 30,* 26–30.

CHAPTER SEVEN

Too Many Intelligences?

Integrating Social, Emotional, and Practical Intelligence

Jennifer Hedlund and Robert J. Sternberg

Emotional, social, practical intelligence, and the like have been called the *nonacademic* intelligences (Sternberg, 1985, 1997), the *noncognitive* intelligences (Bar-On, 1997), and the *nonintellective* intelligences (Wechsler, 1940). Aside from sometimes creating oxymorons, these terms represent attempts to distinguish several less traditional views of intelligence from the more widely recognized and researched abstract, or academic, intelligence, at the core of which is sometimes alleged to be *g* (general ability), which typically is measured by IQ-type tests. The legitimacy of these alternative forms of intelligence depends on the answers to two primary questions. First, are the various factors that researchers have classified as social, emotional, or practical intelligence appropriately characterized as cognitive abilities? Second, can reliable and valid measures of these "nontraditional" intelligences be developed? Assuming these two questions are answered satisfactorily, uncertainty remains regarding the independence of these constructs. In other words, are social, emotional, and practical intelligence distinct or overlapping constructs? In this chapter, we explore these issues through a review of research on social, emotional, and

Note: Preparation of this chapter was supported by the U.S. Army Research Institute (contract MDA903–92-K) and the Javitz Act program (Grant #R206R00001) as administered by the Office of Educational Research and Improvement, U.S. Department of Education. Although we are grateful to these agencies for their support, the ideas expressed in this chapter are solely those of the authors and do not represent any official position or policy on the part of these agencies.

practical intelligence. We conclude with a proposition for using tacit knowledge as an integrated approach for understanding social, emotional, and practical intelligence.

FROM IQ TO EQ?

The idea that there is more to intelligence than just the types of abilities valued in school is not a novel one. Researchers as early as E. L. Thorndike (1920) suggested that social ability was an important component of intelligence. Thorndike defined social intelligence as comprising the abilities to understand others and to act or behave wisely in relation to others. Thorndike distinguished this form of intelligence from abstract and mechanical forms of intelligence. Almost 80 years later, researchers found themselves with little agreement concerning the conceptual or operational definition of the construct. Additionally, during this time a number of alternative conceptualizations of nonacademic intelligence have emerged, including practical, emotional, kinesthetic, and even moral intelligence.

From 1920 through the 1990s, research interest in social intelligence has fluctuated and has been characterized by diverse approaches. Definitions of social intelligence have included the ability to deal with other people (Hunt, 1928; Moss & Hunt, 1927; Wechsler, 1958), interpersonal knowledge (Strang, 1930), insights into the states and traits of others (Vernon, 1933), the ability to judge correctly the feelings, moods, and motivations of others (Wedeck, 1947), effective social functioning (Keating, 1978; Ford & Tisak, 1983), skill at decoding nonverbal cues (Barnes & Sternberg, 1989; Sternberg & Smith, 1985), and empathy (Marlowe, 1986). The proliferation of conceptual definitions has been accompanied by a comparable number of operational definitions, few of which have met with success. Many researchers became discouraged by repeated failures to distinguish adequately social from academic intelligence and moved on to new endeavors. A number of researchers, however, were not ready to abandon the notion that intelligence comprises more than IQ. Among these researchers was Neisser (1976), who suggested that the distinction between academic and practical abilities lay in the types of tasks associated with school and real-world settings.

Academic problems tend to be (1) formulated by others, (2) well defined, (3) complete in the information they provide, (4) characterized by having only one correct answer, (5) characterized by having only one method of obtaining the correct answer, (6) disembedded from ordinary experience, and (7) of little or no intrinsic interest. These are the types of tasks commonly found in school and on IQ tests. These features do not necessarily characterize the types of problems people face every day.

Practical, everyday problems tend to be (1) unformulated or in need of reformulation, (2) of personal interest, (3) lacking in information necessary for solution, (4) related to everyday experience, (5) poorly defined, (6) characterized by multiple "correct" solutions, each with liabilities as well as assets, and (7) characterized by multiple methods for picking a problem solution. Given the differences in the nature of academic and practical problems, it is no surprise that people who are adept at solving one kind of problem may well not be adept at solving problems of the other kind (Wagner & Sternberg, 1986).

The concept of practical intelligence is a key component of Sternberg's (1985, 1997) theory of *successful intelligence.* Successfully intelligent people are those who recognize their strengths and weaknesses and who capitalize on their strengths while at the same time compensating for or correcting their weaknesses. These strengths and weaknesses can be identified in relation to three broad kinds of abilities: analytic, creative, and practical. *Practical intelligence,* as a component of successful intelligence, is the ability to accomplish personally valued goals by adapting to the environment, shaping (or changing) the environment, or selecting a new environment. Research by Sternberg and his colleagues (Sternberg, Wagner, & Okagaki, 1993; Sternberg, Wagner, Williams, & Horvath, 1995; Sternberg et al., 2000) has shown that practical intelligence is distinct from academic intelligence and can explain individual differences in performance beyond IQ.

During this same general time period, other theories challenging traditional IQ-based views of intelligence emerged, including most notably Gardner's (1983, 1993, 1999a) theory of *multiple intelligences.* In his theory, Gardner acknowledges the role of social, or what he calls *interpersonal,* intelligence and defines it as understanding others and acting on that understanding. Some recent approaches to understanding social intelligence focus on its application to the solution of everyday life problems (Cantor & Kihlstrom, 1987; Kihlstrom & Cantor, 2000). *Intrapersonal* intelligence, in Gardner's theory, is the ability to understand oneself—to know how one feels about things, to understand one's range of emotions, to have insights about why one acts the way one does, and to behave in ways that are appropriate to one's needs, goals, and abilities. Interest in the concept of intrapersonal intelligence is seen in emerging research on *emotional intelligence* (for example, Bar-On, 1997; Salovey & Mayer, 1990; Mayer, Salovey, & Caruso, 2000). This research also covers some aspects of interpersonal intelligence.

Empirical support for each of these nonacademic intelligences varies. Of course, research on practical and emotional intelligence has a shorter history than does research on social intelligence. Enough work has been done, however, for researchers to begin to draw some conclusions about the potential for describing both emotional and social intelligence as distinct constructs and about the possible interrelationships between them. We review the empirical support for each of these nonacademic intelligences and then present an integrative framework that addresses some of the limitations of existing approaches.

MEASUREMENT OF SOCIAL INTELLIGENCE

The primary question addressed by research on social intelligence is whether it is distinct from academic intelligence. Researchers have long viewed social intelligence as a multidimensional construct consisting of both cognitive elements (the ability to understand others) and behavioral elements (the ability to act or behave wisely in relation to others) (for example, E. L. Thorndike, 1920). But researchers generally have had more difficulty distinguishing traditional cognitive ability tests from those cognitively oriented measures that assess dimensions such as social judgment and social insight (for example, R. L. Thorndike, 1936) than from behaviorally oriented measures that assess effectiveness in social interactions (for example, Ford & Tisak, 1983). Some researchers attributed the failures of cognitive approaches to reliance on self-report and verbal measures of social intelligence (for example, Sternberg & Smith, 1985). Using nonverbal measures of social perception, these investigators had some success distinguishing social from abstract academic intelligence. To date, however, there is no resolution, regardless of the approach, of the question of whether social intelligence can be separated psychometrically from abstract, academic intelligence.

Forerunners of Social Intelligence Testing

One of the earliest formal tests of social intelligence was the George Washington Social Intelligence Test (GWSIT) (Moss, Hunt, Omwake, & Woodward, 1955). This test consists of a number of subtests that assess judgment in social situations, recognition of the mental states behind messages and facial expressions, memory for names and faces, observation of human behavior, and sense of humor. A number of early studies found the GWSIT to correlate significantly with and load on the same factor as measures of abstract intelligence (Hunt, 1928; R. L. Thorndike, 1936; R. L. Thorndike & Stein, 1937). A review by Cronbach (1960) reported that there was no empirical evidence of a distinction between social intelligence as measured by the GWSIT and general verbal ability.

Another early social intelligence test was the Vineland Social Maturity Scale (Doll, 1935, 1965). The original Vineland was developed in the 1930s to assess the relationship between social competence and mental deficiency (Doll, 1935). The test relies on third parties (for example, parents, teachers) to provide assessment of the individual's social competence in domains such as communication and socialization. More recently, a revised version of Doll's instrument, the Vineland Adaptive Behavior Scales (Sparrow, Balla, & Cicchetti, 1984), was developed for use in diagnosis and treatment planning and evaluation.

During the same time period, Chapin (1942, 1967) developed the Social Insight Test, which presents brief descriptions of social situations and asks respondents to select, from among four possible alternatives, the statement that best characterizes the situation. Little research was done using Chapin's test, however, until the mid 1960s. H. G. Gough (1965) found somewhat lower correlations (.24 to .40) between the Social Insight Test and tests of abstract intelligence than were found for the GWSIT, but the significance of these correlations still raised questions regarding the psychological distinctiveness of social intelligence.

After a twenty-year period during which little progress was made in the area of social intelligence testing, a set of new measures emerged based on Guilford's (1967) Structure of Intellect model, including most notably the Six Factor Tests of Social Intelligence (O'Sullivan, Guilford, & deMille, 1965). The tests measure abilities such as understanding facial expressions, understanding social relationships, and drawing implications from a social situation. For example, one set of questions presents cartoons and asks respondents to select among four alternatives for completing the cartoon strip. Another set asks respondents to indicate the thought or feeling depicted in drawings of facial expressions and hand gestures. All but one of the six subtests are nonverbal measures of social intelligence.

Hoepfner and O'Sullivan (1968) reported an average correlation of .34 with verbal intelligence as measured by the Henmon-Nelson Test. Further, they showed that although high IQ was associated with high social intelligence, many individuals with low IQ also had high social intelligence. Some subsequent studies have found the Six Factor Test of Social Intelligence to load on a separate factor from abstract intelligence tests (for example, Wong, Day, Maxwell, & Meara, 1995), but most have found that the test correlates modestly, yet significantly, with abstract intelligence (for example, Jones & Day, 1997; Riggio, Messamer, & Throckmorton, 1991; Shanley, Walker, & Foley, 1971; Wong et al., 1995).

Although the initial work on social intelligence was less than encouraging, researchers found strong support for the concept of social intelligence in people's implicit theories of intelligence (Bruner, Shapiro, & Tagiuri, 1958; Cantor, 1978). Sternberg, Conway, Ketron, and Bernstein (1981), for example, asked samples of laypersons and academic researchers who study intelligence to provide and rate the importance and frequency of characteristics of intelligent individuals. Factor analyses of the frequency ratings showed three major aspects of people's conceptions of intelligence: the ability to solve practical problems (such as balancing a checkbook), verbal ability (such as writing and speaking well), and social competence (such as getting along with other people).

Multimethod-Multitrait Approaches to Studying Social Intelligence

Research from the late 1970s on was characterized by the application of more rigorous methodologies, particularly multimethod-multitrait approaches, to understanding social intelligence. Keating (1978), for example, administered

Chapin's (1967) Social Insight Test, along with a measure of moral reasoning (the Defining Issues Test) (Rest, 1975), and a measure of effective social functioning (Social Maturity Index) (H. G. Gough, 1966). He also obtained three measures of academic intelligence: the Concept Mastery Test (Terman, 1950), the Standard Progressive Matrices (Raven, 1960), and the Remote Associates Test (Mednick & Mednick, 1967). Keating found that the Social Intelligence Test and the Concept Mastery Test loaded on one factor, whereas the remaining measures loaded on a second factor. Using the Social Maturity Index as a criterion, he found that the best predictors of effective social functioning were the three academic intelligence tests.

Similar findings were obtained by Riggio et al. (1991) using a different set of measures. They administered O'Sullivan and Guilford's (1976) Factor Tests of Social Intelligence, plus a measure of social communication skills (the Social Skills Inventory) (Riggio, 1986, 1989), and a social etiquette/tacit knowledge test. The Shipley-Hartford Institute of Living Scale (Shipley, 1940) and the Wechsler Adult Intelligence Scale-Revised (WAIS-R) (Wechsler, 1981) were given to assess academic intelligence. Through an exploratory factor analysis, Riggio et al. identified two factors, one that represented "abstract reasoning intelligence" and one that represented "verbal intelligence," with measures of social and academic intelligence loading on both.

Marlowe (1985) proposed a model of social intelligence consisting of four domains: social interest (concern for others), social self-efficacy, empathy skills (the ability to cognitively and affectively understand another), and social performance skills (observable social behaviors). In order to test his model, Marlowe (1986) administered eight different measures of social intelligence, which were found to represent five factors: prosocial attitude, social skills, empathy skills, social anxiety, and emotionality. These five factors further loaded on factors separate from the Shipley-Hartford measures of verbal and abstract intelligence. All of the social intelligence measures in Marlowe's study were self-reported, which may have contributed to their distinction from the more objective tests used to measure verbal and abstract intelligence.

One method used to distinguish social intelligence tests from academic intelligence tests was to control for the tendency of both types of tests to tap verbal ability. Several researchers developed tests to assess nonverbal decoding skills (Archer, 1980; Archer & Akert, 1980; Barnes & Sternberg, 1989; Halberstadt & Hall, 1980; Rosenthal, 1979; Rosenthal, Hall, DiMatteo, Rogers, & Archer, 1979; Sternberg & Smith, 1985). Sternberg and Smith (1985), for example, presented participants with two types of photographs. In one type, a man and woman were shown posing as if they were in a close relationship, and participants were asked to judge if the photograph depicted a real or a fake couple. In the second type, the picture showed a supervisor and his or her supervisee, and participants were asked to judge who of the two individuals was the supervisor. Participants were rated in terms of their accuracy in judging the picture correctly.

Sternberg and Smith's nonverbal decoding task did not correlate significantly with other tests of social intelligence such as the George Washington Social Intelligence Test (Moss et al., 1955) and the Social Insight Test (Chapin, 1967) and correlated significantly only with performance on the Embedded Figures Test (Oltman, Raskin, & Witkin, 1971).

A subsequent study by Barnes and Sternberg (1989), however, found significant correlations between accuracy at nonverbal decoding in the couples' task and measures of social competence, such as Hogan's (1969) Empathy Scale and Snyder's (1974) Self-Monitoring Scale. Furthermore, decoding accuracy did not correlate with the Henmon-Nelson Test of Mental Ability (Nelson & Lamke, 1973), which is a measure of abstract, cognitive intelligence.

Behaviorally Based Measures of Social Intelligence

A number of researchers have pursued more behaviorally oriented measures of social intelligence (Brown & Anthony, 1990; Ford & Tisak, 1983; Frederiksen, Carlson, & Ward, 1984; Stricker & Rock, 1990). Using self, peer, and teacher ratings of behavioral effectiveness, Ford and Tisak found that all but teacher ratings loaded on a social factor that was distinct from measures of academic intelligence. Additionally, the social intelligence measures accounted for more variance in ratings of social-behavioral effectiveness based on an interview than did the academic intelligence measures. Ford and Tisak suggested that "the degree of overlap one finds between social and academic intelligence may depend greatly on the criteria one uses to evaluate social competence" (1983, p. 204).

Similar results have been found using ratings of interview skills displayed by fourth-year medical school students (Frederiksen et al., 1984) and self and peer ratings of college students' functioning in various social roles (Brown & Anthony, 1990). Brown and Anthony further found that both social-personality ratings and grade point average predicted social-behavioral effectiveness, suggesting some overlap between school performance and social intelligence.

Stricker and Rock (1990), however, found little evidence of convergent or discriminant validity using a behavioral situational-judgment test, the Interpersonal Competence Instrument (ICI), to assess social intelligence. The ICI measures effectiveness in dealing with people by asking the examinee to play the role of a superior dealing with a subordinate in a video. Examinees are rated on the effectiveness and originality of their responses and their accuracy in judging key characteristics of the subordinate in the video. Similar to the measures of Riggio et al. (1991), the measures of social and academic intelligence used by Stricker and Rock appeared to tap either verbal ability or general reasoning ability. The only test to emerge as distinct was a measure of nonverbal decoding skills (Communication of Affect Receiving Ability Test) (Buck, 1976).

Using a fairly rigorous methodology, Wong et al. (1995) explored the relationships between cognitive and behavioral measures of social intelligence and academic intelligence. They obtained both verbal and nonverbal as well as both self-reported and other-reported data for each variable. Using confirmatory factor analysis, they found that the model that best fit the data consisted of three separate factors: social perception, effectiveness in heterosexual interaction, and academic intelligence. These three factors, however, correlated significantly with one another, with the highest correlation between social perception and academic intelligence ($r = .67, p < .05$) and the lowest between effectiveness in heterosexual interaction and academic intelligence ($r = .33, p < .05$).

In a second study, Wong et al. sought to distinguish three cognitive aspects of social intelligence: social knowledge (knowledge of etiquette rules), social perception (the ability to understand the emotional states of others), and social insight (the ability to comprehend behavior observed in a social context). The best-fitting model, using confirmatory factor analysis, consisted of three factors: academic intelligence, a combined social perception–social insight factor, and social knowledge. The social perception–social insight factor correlated significantly with the academic intelligence factor ($r = .47, p < .05$), but the social knowledge factor exhibited a nonsignificant correlation with academic intelligence ($r = .13$, ns).

Legree, Pifer, and Grafton (1996) measured social intelligence using three knowledge-based tests: the U.S. Army Situational Judgment Test, a measure of dinner-related knowledge, and a measure of knowledge of alcohol abuse indicators. He found that the three social intelligence tests loaded on a single factor, which he labeled social insight, and were distinct from factors representing general cognitive abilities (verbal, quantitative, speed, and technical ability) as measured by the Armed Services Vocational Aptitude Battery (ASVAB) (Bayroff & Fuchs, 1970). The social-insight factor, however, did correlate significantly with the four ASVAB factors, suggesting some overlap between social and general abstract intelligence.

Jones and Day (1997) differentiated the cognitive aspects of social intelligence into two dimensions: crystallized social knowledge (declarative and procedural knowledge about familiar social events) and social-cognitive flexibility (the ability to apply social knowledge to relatively novel problems). They obtained self and teacher ratings as well as objective test scores for crystallized social knowledge, social-cognitive flexibility, and academic problem solving. Confirmatory factor analyses suggested that social-cognitive flexibility was distinct from both crystallized social knowledge and academic problem solving, but that the latter two were not distinct from one another. The relationship between crystallized social knowledge and academic problem solving may have been attributable to common method variance, because both measures involved items with one correct answer (Jones & Day, 1997).

A Nonpsychometric Approach
to Understanding Social Intelligence

Social knowledge and its flexible application are the cornerstones of theory and research by Cantor and Kihlstrom and their colleagues (Cantor & Harlow, 1994; Cantor & Kihlstrom, 1987; Kihlstrom & Cantor, 2000) on social intelligence. Cantor and Kihlstrom (1987) initially proposed that social intelligence forms the cognitive basis of personality. That is, social intelligence characterizes the cognitive processes that distinguish individual approaches to solving problems of everyday life. Cantor and Harlow (1994) added that intelligent behavior involves attunement to the consequences of one's actions, the implications of those consequences for other goals, and the goal-fulfilling potentials of different situations. Attunement allows for flexibility in terms of what tasks to pursue, where and when opportunities are present to work on various tasks, and how to pursue the tasks. Therefore, attunement and flexibility are critical aspects of personality and intelligence, allowing individuals to successfully pursue goals and solve problems.

Social intelligence is viewed as a distinct repertoire of knowledge that is tapped in solving social problems (Cantor & Kihlstrom, 1987; Kihlstrom & Cantor, 2000). It consists of both declarative knowledge (such as abstract social concepts and memory for specific social events) and procedural knowledge (such as rules, skills, and strategies for applying social knowledge). Cantor and her colleagues provided various arguments against psychometric approaches to studying social intelligence, including (1) individual variation in the types of problems that tap social intelligence, (2) difficulty identifying the specific knowledge that is tapped in solving social problems, (3) inappropriate treatment of social intelligence as a trait on which individuals can be compared, and (4) an overemphasis in measurement on how much social intelligence a person has rather than on what social intelligence the person possesses. As we discuss later in this chapter, some of these limitations have been addressed by the approach used by Sternberg and his colleagues (Sternberg et al., 1993, 1995) to study tacit knowledge.

Rather than developing instruments to assess individual differences in social intelligence, Cantor and her colleagues (Kihlstrom & Cantor, 2000) have chosen to study the application of social intelligence to life tasks. Life tasks represent the problems that provide meaning in individuals' lives and serve to organize daily activities. Life tasks include things such as making friends, finding a spouse, establishing a career, and getting good grades. Studying these life tasks and the strategies employed in pursuing goals related to these tasks provides insight about the behaviors that are indicative of social intelligence. For example, socially intelligent people develop specific action plans, monitor their progress, and evaluate the outcomes of their actions. They also exhibit flexibility in altering their plans when obstacles emerge in the pursuit of their goals (Kihlstrom & Cantor, 2000).

Based on even a brief review of the literature, it is clear that researchers have not determined definitively whether social intelligence is distinct from academic intelligence. The inconsistencies throughout this literature are likely attributable to, in part, the variety of ways social intelligence has been defined and measured. Social intelligence has been characterized as social perception, social knowledge, social insight, empathy, social memory, social adaptation, and social-behavioral effectiveness. It has been measured using more than thirty different instruments. Yet, unlike Cantor and her colleagues, we do not consider the failure to establish consistent evidence that social intelligence is a unique construct to imply that psychometric approaches to understanding nonacademic intelligences are inappropriate. It is apparent from the growing number of tests of emotional and practical intelligence that other researchers agree.

EMOTIONAL INTELLIGENCE

The concept of emotional intelligence has gained popularity through the publication of a number of commercially successful books (Goleman, 1995, 1998). Research explicitly targeted at the construct of emotional intelligence is fairly recent and more limited than research on social intelligence. However, a number of tests purported to measure social intelligence or social competence assessed skills (for example, perceiving affective information, interpreting nonverbal cues) that since have been subsumed under the label of emotional intelligence. See, for example, the Communication of Affect Receiving Ability Test (Buck, 1976), the Profile of Nonverbal Sensitivity (Rosenthal et al., 1979), and the Social Interpretation Task (Archer & Akert, 1980). In addition, almost twenty-five years ago the Beth Israel Psychosomatic Questionnaire (Sifneos, 1973) was developed to measure alexithymia, which refers to a difficulty with verbal expressions of emotions (Apfel & Sifneos, 1979; Lesser, 1981). The concept of alexithymia is related to the concepts of emotional self-awareness and emotional expression, which are represented in current frameworks of emotional intelligence (Bar-On, 1997; Mayer et al., 2000).

Initially, researchers were optimistic that emotional intelligence, compared with social intelligence, would be distinguished more clearly from academic intelligence (Mayer & Salovey, 1993). The issue of whether emotional intelligence is distinct from academic intelligence has taken somewhat of a backseat to another issue. Some researchers have questioned whether emotional intelligence is anything more than a set of personality variables for which adequate measures already exist (Davies, Stankov, & Roberts, 1998).

Two opposing views have emerged. One view is that emotional intelligence includes almost everything related to success that is not measured by IQ (Bar-On, 1997; Goleman, 1995, 1998), whereas the other argues for a more restrictive view of emotional intelligence as the ability to perceive and understand emotional information (Mayer et al., 2000). A recent study by Davies et al. (1998) even suggested that emotional intelligence may represent a very limited construct once one has accounted for personality and general cognitive ability factors.

Emotional Intelligence as Almost Everything but IQ

One of the more prominent spokespersons for emotional intelligence is Daniel Goleman (1995, 1998). His best-selling book, *Emotional Intelligence,* brought widespread, popular attention to the concept. He argued, as have other researchers (Gardner, 1983; Sternberg, 1997), that part of the roughly 80 percent of the variance among people in various forms of success that is unaccounted for by IQ tests and similar tests can be explained by other characteristics that Goleman argues constitute emotional intelligence. He has defined emotional intelligence as including "abilities such as being able to motivate oneself and persist in the face of frustrations; to control impulses and delay gratification; to regulate one's moods and keep distress from swamping the ability to think; to empathize and to hope" (1995, p. 34), and more recently, in *Working with Emotional Intelligence,* as "the capacity for recognizing our own feelings and those of others, for motivating ourselves, and for managing emotions well in ourselves and in our relationships" (1998, p. 317).

A limitation of Goleman's use of the term *emotional intelligence* is that he attempts to capture almost everything but IQ. His framework includes emotional awareness, accurate self-assessment, self-confidence, self-control, trustworthiness, conscientiousness, adaptability, innovation, achievement drive, commitment, initiative, optimism, understanding others, influence, communication, cooperation, and so on (1998, pp. 26–27). This framework arguably stretches the definition of intelligence way beyond acceptable limits (Gardner, 1999b; Sternberg, 1999). Under his definition, it is likely that much of the residual variance beyond IQ would be accounted for by emotional intelligence, because by his definition it seems to capture all of the residual factors within the individual (personality traits, motivation, and so forth).

Although Goleman (1995, 1998) does cite some empirical support for his claims and, along with Richard Boyatzis, has developed the Emotional Competence Inventory (see Chapter Sixteen), he has yet to offer any hard validity evidence that what he has defined as emotional intelligence does indeed account for any of the variance in educational or job performance beyond IQ. Goleman bases his work primarily on anecdotal evidence and questionable extrapolations from past research. There is validity evidence, however, for other measures of emotional intelligence.

Like Goleman's, Bar-On's (1997) definition of emotional intelligence incorporates a broad array of factors. Bar-On (1997) proposed a model of noncognitive intelligences that includes five broad areas of skills or competencies, and within each, more specific skills that appear to contribute to success. These include intrapersonal skills (emotional self-awareness, assertiveness, self-regard, self-actualization, independence), interpersonal skills (interpersonal relationships, social responsibility, empathy), adaptability (problem solving, reality testing, flexibility), stress management (stress tolerance, impulse, control), and general mood (happiness, optimism).

Bar-On developed the Emotional Quotient Inventory (EQ-i) (Bar-On, 1997) based on his model of noncognitive skills and cites research conducted over a twelve-year period with more than 6,300 respondents to assess the reliability and validity of the EQ-i. The fifteen subscales have fairly high internal consistency (the average α ranging from .69 to .86 across samples). It is not known whether the overall EQ-i exhibits the same level of internal consistency. Given how many factors compose the EQ-i, this information would be valuable to know. In other words, are all of these factors adequately represented under the same general construct? Results of exploratory and confirmatory factor analyses indicate that a fifteen-factor solution provides a good fit to the EQ-i, and the results are generally supportive of Bar-On's model.

The EQ-i has been validated in relation to more than fifteen different measures (primarily personality inventories) (Bar-On, 1997, and Chapter 17). There is a need, however, for this research to be published in available peer-reviewed scientific journals. On the whole, the pattern of correlations of EQ-i scales with these other measures is as expected. For example, self-regard correlates positively with measures of ego strength, self-satisfaction, self-fulfillment, self-esteem, and self-confidence and correlates negatively with measures of depression and hopelessness. Empathy correlates positively with measures of interpersonal warmth and sensitivity, and negatively with measures of need for privacy, antisocial attitudes, and aggression. A number of these correlations are of a fairly high magnitude ($r > .70$), suggesting that some of the EQ-i scales may be redundant with existing measures. The correlations may also be augmented by shared variance because of the use of self-report forms of measurement. Given the breadth of Bar-On's model, it would be rather surprising if the EQ-i scales failed to correlate with these measures. The high number of significant correlations with existing measures and the method of assessment (such as self-report) together may suggest that the EQ-i is best characterized as a kind of personality inventory, with the attendant difficulties of such inventories, such as social-desirability effects and susceptibilty to faking.

It is clear that Bar-On has engaged in extensive efforts to develop and validate his measure of emotional intelligence. Because Bar-On considers it virtually impossible to separate the various forms of "noncognitive" intelligence, he has chosen to develop a measure that encompasses almost all of them, including factors that have been studied under the realms of social and practical intelligence (such as interpersonal skills, problem solving, and flexibility). Mayer et al. (2000) referred to models such as Bar-On's as *mixed models* because they combine skills that can be characterized as mental abilities (such as problem solving) and others that can be considered personality traits (such as optimism). Mayer and his colleagues argued for a more restrictive view of emotional intelligence.

Emotional Intelligence as a Cognitive Ability

Salovey, Mayer, and their colleagues (Mayer & Salovey, 1993, 1997; Mayer et al., 2000; Salovey & Mayer, 1990) have gradually shifted from a more all-encompassing model of emotional intelligence to a more restrictive model. Initial theorizing by Salovey and Mayer (1990) related emotional intelligence to personality factors such as warmth and outgoingness. But in the time since, they have argued that emotional intelligence should be distinguished from personality variables and defined more strictly as an ability, specifically the ability to recognize the meanings of emotions and to use that knowledge to reason and solve problems. These investigators have proposed a framework of emotional intelligence to organize the various abilities involved in the adaptive processing of emotionally relevant information. These abilities pertain to (1) accurate appraisal and expression of emotions in oneself and in others, (2) assimilation of emotional experience into cognition, (3) recognition, understanding, and reasoning about emotions, and (4) adaptive regulation of emotions in oneself and in others (Mayer et al., 2000; Salovey & Mayer, 1994).

Mayer, Salovey, and their colleagues have developed a test of emotional intelligence, called the Mutifactor Emotional Intelligence Scale (MEIS) (Mayer, Salovey, & Caruso, 1997). The MEIS consists of twelve ability measures that fall into the four classes of abilities identified above: perception, assimilation, understanding, and managing emotions. Mayer, Caruso, and Salovey (forthcoming) validated the MEIS with 503 adults and 229 adolescents. A factor analysis of the MEIS suggested three primary factors corresponding to perception, understanding, and managing emotion, and a higher order, general factor of emotional intelligence (Mayer, Caruso, & Salovey, forthcoming). The general emotional intelligence factor correlated significantly with a measure of verbal intelligence (Army Alpha Vocabulary Scale) (Yerkes, 1921) and with a measure of self-reported empathy (Caruso & Mayer, 1997). Of the three factor scores, understanding correlated most highly with verbal intelligence, followed by managing emotions and then perception. They also found that the emotional intelligence of adults was higher than that of adolescents, suggesting age-related changes. Mayer et al. (1997) concluded that emotional intelligence can be characterized appropriately as a mental ability because their results follow the patterns of other well-established measures of intelligence. The specific abilities in the MEIS are intercorrelated, scores on the MEIS develop with age as do scores on other standard intelligence tests, and emotional intelligence overlaps, to some extent, with traditional intelligence.

Schutte et al. (1998) developed their own measure of emotional intelligence based on an earlier version of Salovey and Mayer's (1990) model. Their thirty-three-item self-report measure correlated significantly with eight theoretically related constructs including awareness of emotion, outlook on life, depressed mood, ability to regulate emotions, and impulsivity. They also showed differences on their measure with groups expected to differ in emotional intelligence (for example, psychotherapists and prisoners, men and women). They further showed that scores on indices of emotional intelligence were predictive of end-of-year grade point averages of college freshman but were unrelated to SAT or ACT scores. Finally, they found that of the big five personality traits, emotional intelligence related significantly only to openness to experience.

Davies et al. (1998) took the position that in order for emotional intelligence to be considered in the tradition of other cognitive abilities, it should be distinct from both personality variables and traditional intelligence. Over three separate studies, they administered various tests of emotional intelligence, personality, and general cognitive ability. They found that self-report measures of emotional intelligence tended to load on factors along with personality variables (such as neuroticism, extraversion, and agreeableness) or measures of verbal ability. Measures of social intelligence, which were also included in the first study, loaded primarily on an extroversion factor, suggesting that social intelligence may not be clearly distinguished from personality. The only factor that emerged as distinct from personality and cognitive abilities factors was an emotion perception factor. These findings led Davies et al. to suggest a more restrictive definition of emotional intelligence as "the ability to perceive emotional information in visual and auditory stimuli" (1998, p. 1001).

PRACTICAL INTELLIGENCE

Practical intelligence, like social and emotional intelligence, has been conceptualized as distinct from academic intelligence. It is sometimes conceived of as interchangeable with social intelligence (Ford, 1986; Kihlstrom & Cantor, 1989; Mercer, Gomez-Palacio, & Padilla, 1986), but as we discuss later, practical intelligence is not limited to use in solving problems of a social nature. A number of researchers have distinguished the ability to solve practical problems from the ability to solve academic problems (Neisser, 1976; Sternberg, 1985, 1997;

Wagner & Sternberg, 1986). Practical problems are the types of problems encountered in everyday life, which may not be clearly defined and for which solutions may not be readily available or easily derived. Academic problems, on the other hand, tend to be more clearly defined and have more readily available and identifiable solutions.

Practical intelligence is used to characterize the intellectual skills that individuals exhibit in solving practical problems. Sternberg (1985, 1997) has defined practical intelligence more formally as intelligence that serves to find a more optimal fit between the individual and the demands of the individual's environment, by adapting to the environment, changing (or shaping) the environment, or selecting a different environment. Research on practical intelligence can be classified into two primary tracks: one addressing practical problem-solving skills and the other addressing practical, tacit knowledge.

Practical Problem Solving

Of the three nonacademic intelligences addressed in this chapter, practical intelligence, or practical problem-solving ability, arguably has received the most attention by contemporary researchers (Berg, 2000; Sternberg et al., 2000; Wagner, 2000). Initially, the examination of practical intelligence issued from a concern that the intelligence of adults functioning largely outside the academic environment was evaluated primarily by traditional tests of intelligence constructed to predict academic success. Research on implicit theories of intelligence also indicated that individuals considered practical, or everyday, intelligence to be distinct from academic intelligence (Sternberg, 1985; Sternberg et al., 1981).

The concept of practical intelligence, like the concepts of social and emotional intelligence, has been characterized in different ways. Some researchers define everyday intelligence as a specific expression of conventional abilities that permit adaptive behavior within a distinct class of everyday-life situations (Willis & Schaie, 1986), whereas others view practical intelligence as a distinct set of abilities (Neisser, 1976; Wagner, 1987). Most studies of practical abilities focus on solving problems that concern poorly defined goals and solutions, and that are frequently encountered in daily life at home, at work, and in dealing with people (Cornelius & Caspi, 1987; Denney, 1989).

A number of studies have shown that the abilities measured in school or on IQ-type tests do not necessarily transfer to real-world settings. We briefly provide some examples here. For other reviews see work by Berg (2000), Ceci and Roazzi (1994), Rogoff and Lave (1984), Scribner and Cole (1981), Sternberg and Wagner (1986, 1994), and Wagner (2000).

Several studies have shown that individuals who are able to accurately solve everyday math problems do not necessarily do well on abstract mathematical tests or IQ tests (Ceci & Liker, 1986, 1988; Lave, Murtaugh, & de la Roche, 1984;

Murtaugh, 1985; Scribner, 1984, 1986). For example, Ceci and Liker (1986) found that expert racetrack handicappers applied complex algorithms for predicting post time odds, but that this ability was unrelated to their IQ scores. Scribner (1984, 1986) similarly observed that assemblers in a milk-processing plant used complex strategies to fill orders of differing quantities, but that the use of these strategies was unrelated to school performance, math test scores, or IQ.

Similar relationships between academic and practical abilities have been observed in children. For example, researchers found that school children in Brazil performed better on mathematics and reasoning problems when the problems were presented in an academic form (such as $2 + ? = 4$), whereas children who worked as street vendors performed better on the same problems presented in the context of vending (for example, if an orange costs 76 cruzeiros and a passion fruit costs 50, how much do the two cost together?) (Carraher, Carraher, & Schliemann, 1985; see also Nuñes, 1994; Nuñes, Schliemann, & Carraher, 1993; Roazzi, 1987).

Age-related patterns of intellectual development also suggest a distinction between practical and academic abilities. Age-related changes in intellectual performance are commonly described in relation to the distinction between fluid and crystallized abilities (Horn, 1994; Horn & Cattell, 1966). *Fluid* abilities are those required to deal with novelty (such as discovering the pattern in a sequence of numbers). *Crystallized* abilities represent accumulated knowledge (such as correctly identifying the synonym of a low-frequency word). A number of studies have shown that fluid abilities are more susceptible to age-related decline than are crystallized abilities (Cornelius & Caspi, 1987; Denney & Palmer, 1981; Dixon & Baltes, 1986; Horn, 1982; Labouvie-Vief, 1982; Schaie, 1977/1978). Denny and Palmer (1981), for example, compared performance of adults (ages twenty to seventy-nine) on traditional analytical reasoning problems (such as the "twenty questions" task) and a practical problem-solving task ("If you were traveling by car and got stranded out on an interstate highway during a blizzard, what would you do?"). They found that performance on the traditional task declined almost linearly from age twenty on, but that performance on the practical task increased to a peak in the forty- to fifty-year-olds and declined thereafter. Cornelius and Caspi (1987) found that performance on measures of fluid ability (for example, letter series completion) increased from age twenty to age thirty, leveled off between ages thirty and fifty, and then declined. Performance on measures of crystallized ability (verbal meanings) and of everyday problem solving (for example, dealing with a landlord who won't make repairs, filling out a complicated form) increased through age seventy.

As indicated by Cornelius and Caspi's findings, performance on real-life problem-solving tasks has been found to remain relatively stable or to increase with age, up to a certain point (see Berg & Klaczynski, 1996, for a review).

Baltes and his colleagues have characterized these different developmental paths in terms of the mechanics and pragmatics of intelligence (Baltes, 1987; Baltes, Smith, & Staudinger, 1992). *Mechanics* refer to basic cognitive skills and resources involved in information processing and tend to decline with age. *Pragmatics* refer to the applications of these processes to cognitive performance and environmental adaptation and tend to remain stable throughout adulthood (Baltes, Sowarka, & Kliegl, 1989).

Research on emotional intelligence also shows similar age-related patterns. Bar-On (1997) found a steady increase in EQ-i scores from age sixteen to forty-nine, with a slight decrease after age fifty. The most consistently significant increase occurred among respondents in age groups twenty to twenty-nine and thirty to thirty-nine. Mayer et al. (forthcoming) compared the MEIS scores of a sample of adults (mean age of twenty-three) with a sample of adolescents (mean age of thirteen). They found that scores for adults were higher than those for adolescents, suggesting that emotional intelligence increases with age.

Approaches to Studying Practical Intelligence

A number of researchers (Berg, 1989; Berg & Calderone, 1994; Denney & Pearce, 1989; Sansone & Berg, 1993) have taken an approach similar to that employed by Cantor and her colleagues in studying social intelligence. These investigators aim to understand practical intelligence by studying the everyday problems experienced by individuals at different life stages. Researchers have found that the nature of salient problems varies as a function of age: the problems of preschool children center on family and home life, those of school-aged children center on school, friends, and extracurricular activities, and those of adults center on family and health issues (Berg & Calderone, 1994). Furthermore, the perceived effectiveness of various problem-solving strategies (such as seeking more information, changing one's perception of the problem, adapting to the problem) differs depending on the context in which the problem occurs (for example, school versus home) (Berg, 1989; see also Ceci & Bronfenbrenner, 1985; Cornelius & Caspi, 1987).

Sternberg and his colleagues (Sternberg et al., 1993, 1995, 2000) have employed a psychometric approach to studying practical intelligence. One of their efforts involved developing a measure of practical ability as part of a broader triarchic theory of intelligence. The Sternberg Triarchic Abilities Test (STAT) (Sternberg, 1993) measures three domains of mental processing (analytical, creative, and practical) by means of multiple-choice and essay questions. Practical questions address the ability to solve real-world, everyday problems and include questions such as what to do about a friend who seems to have a substance abuse problem, how to make chocolate chip cookies, using a map or diagram to plan a route efficiently, and how to solve a practical problem in one's own life.

In a study of the effectiveness of matching instruction to students' abilities, Sternberg and his colleagues (Sternberg, Ferrari, Clinkenbeard, & Grigorenko, 1996; Sternberg, Grigorenko, Ferrari, & Clinkenbeard, 1999) used STAT scores to classify students into one of five ability groupings: high analytical, high creative, high practical, high balanced (high in all three abilities), or low balanced (low in all three abilities). Students were then assigned to different sections of an introductory psychology class based on their classification. The instructional section emphasized either memory, analytical, creative, or practical thinking. For example, in the memory condition, students were asked to describe the main tenets of a major theory of depression. In the practical condition, they were asked how they could use what they had learned about depression to help a friend who was depressed. Sternberg et al. (1996) found that all three ability tests—analytical, creative, and practical—significantly predicted course performance. More importantly, there was an aptitude-treatment interaction whereby students who were placed in instructional conditions that better matched their pattern of abilities outperformed students who were mismatched. For example, students high in practical ability who were taught in a way that emphasized practical thinking performed better than did those taught for memory, analytical, or creative thinking.

More recently, alternative measures of analytic, creative, and practical intelligence were obtained for an adult population in a large industrial city in Russia (Grigorenko & Sternberg, forthcoming). Grigorenko and Sternberg administered the series and the matrices subtests of the Test of *g: Culture Fair, Level II* (Cattell, 1940; Cattell & Cattell, 1973) to measure fluid abilities, and Russian versions of analogy and synonym/antonym tests to measure crystallized abilities. Practical intelligence was assessed by asking participants to report their practical skills in the social domain (such as effective and successful communication with other people), in the family domain (such as how to fix household items, how to run the family budget), and in the domain of effective resolution of sudden problems (such as organizing something that has become chaotic). The participants were also asked to respond to four vignettes based on themes of (1) how to maintain the value of one's savings, (2) what to do when one makes a purchase and discovers that the item one has purchased is broken, (3) how to locate medical assistance in a time of need, and (4) how to manage a salary bonus one has received for outstanding work. Participants were asked to select the best option among the five presented for each vignette. The most frequently chosen option was used as the keyed answer. Self-report measures of physical and mental health were used to assess successful adaptation. Participants also completed the Beck Anxiety Scale (Beck, Epstein, Brown, & Steer, 1988) and the Beck Depression Inventory (Beck, Ward, Mendelson, Mock, & Erbaugh, 1961), as well as five items that measured their self-efficacy for adaptation.

Grigorenko and Sternberg found that practical intelligence consistently predicted self-reported adaptive functioning on all indicators, with higher practical intelligence associated with better physical and mental health. Analytical intelligence was associated with lower anxiety and higher self-efficacy on two items. The results suggested that both analytical and practical intelligence have a positive effect on adaptive functioning.

Practical, Tacit Knowledge

In addition to the STAT and other triarchic ability measures, Sternberg and his colleagues have developed measures targeted specifically at practical intelligence (Sternberg et al., 1993, 1995; Wagner & Sternberg, 1985). These measures address one particularly important aspect of practical intelligence—tacit knowledge—the procedural knowledge one learns in one's everyday life that usually is not taught and that often is not even verbalized. Knowledge identified as tacit typically has three characteristic features. It is generally acquired on one's own with little support from the environment (through personal experience rather than through instruction), it is procedural in nature (associated with particular uses in particular situations), and it has value in pursuing one's personal goals.

Sternberg and his colleagues have studied tacit knowledge in populations as diverse as business managers, military leaders, university professors, elementary-school teachers, salespeople, and U.S. and rural Kenyan children. Tacit-knowledge tests present a set of problem situations, often based on actual situations encountered by individuals in the respective position, and ask respondents to rate the quality or appropriateness of a number of possible responses to those situations.

For example, a hypothetical situation describes a second-year assistant psychology professor whose primary goals are to become a top person in her field and get tenure in her department. She has published two unrelated articles in top journals, has obtained good teaching evaluations, has one graduate student working with her, has no external funding, and has yet to serve on a university committee. The respondent is asked to rate several options (usually on a 1 = low to 9 = high scale) in terms of their value in reaching the defined goals. Examples of responses include improve the quality of your teaching, write a grant proposal, begin long-term research that may lead to a major theoretical article, and volunteer to be chairperson of the undergraduate curriculum committee.

The set of ratings the individual generates for all the situations is used to assess the individual's tacit knowledge for that domain. Tacit-knowledge tests have been scored in one of three ways: by correlating participants' responses with an index of group membership (expert, intermediate, novice), by judging the degree to which participants' responses conform to professional "rules of thumb," or by computing the difference between participants' responses and an expert prototype.

Tacit-knowledge tests have been found to have trivial and nonsignificant to significant but modest correlations with tests of academic intelligence. Scores on tacit-knowledge tests for academic psychologists and managers correlated nonsignificantly ($-.04$ to $.16$) with verbal reasoning in undergraduate samples (Wagner, 1987; Wagner & Sternberg, 1985). Scores on the tacit-knowledge inventory for managers also exhibited nonsignificant correlations with measures of academic intelligence for a sample of business executives (Wagner & Sternberg, 1990) and a sample of air force recruits (Eddy, 1988). Similar findings were obtained with a test of tacit knowledge for sales in samples of undergraduates and salespeople (Wagner, Rashotte and Sternberg, 1994; see also Wagner, Sujan, Sujan, Rashotte, & Sternberg, 1999). Scores on tacit-knowledge tests for military leaders exhibited nonsignificant as well as significant correlations ($.02$ to $.25$) with a measure of verbal reasoning ability (Hedlund et al., 1998). The more important finding of this research was that tacit-knowledge test scores explained variance in leadership effectiveness beyond verbal ability scores. In other words, tacit knowledge accounted for variance in performance not accounted for by a traditional test of academic intelligence.

Recent evidence suggests that tacit knowledge may exhibit a significantly negative association with academic intelligence. In a study in a rural village in Kenya, Sternberg et al. (forthcoming) developed a test to measure children's tacit knowledge for herbal medicines used to treat various illnesses, knowledge that is not acquired in the classroom, but rather in the community from family members and healers. The tacit-knowledge test was administered, along with several measures of academic intelligence, to eighty-five children ages twelve to fifteen. The tests of academic intelligence were all significantly and positively correlated with each other. Scores on the tacit-knowledge test correlated in a negative direction with all of the academic intelligence tests and showed a significant negative correlation with vocabulary test scores and English achievement. Sternberg et al. concluded that practical intelligence, as manifested in tacit knowledge relevant to adaptation in daily life, may be distinct from the kind of academic intelligence associated with school success. The negative correlations obtained further suggest that expertise developed in one environment (for example, school) may have limited application in other environments (for example, home or community life).

In addition to exhibiting distinctions from academic intelligence, tacit knowledge appears to be distinct from personality variables. In a study with business executives, Wagner and Sternberg (1990) obtained data on several personality-type tests, including the California Psychological Inventory (H. D. Gough, 1986), the Myers-Briggs Type Indicator (Myers, 1962), and the Fundamental Interpersonal Relations Orientation-Behavior (FIRO-B) (Schutz, 1989). Tacit-knowledge scores generally exhibited nonsignificant correlations with all of the personality measures, with the exception of the social presence factor of the California

Psychological Inventory and the control expressed factor of the FIRO-B ($r = .29$ and .25, respectively).

One of the limitations of existing research on social and emotional intelligence is that few researchers have attempted to establish the incremental validity of their measures relative to other existing measures in the prediction of performance criteria. A major accomplishment of the tacit-knowledge research has been to show not only that practical intelligence can be distinguished from academic intelligence, but that it contributes to our understanding of individual differences in performance. Across the various domains, Sternberg and his colleagues have found tacit-knowledge to correlate generally in the range of .2 to .5 with a number of criteria of success.

In studies with business managers, tacit-knowledge scores correlated in the range of .2 to .4 with criteria such as salary, years of management experience, and whether the manager worked for a company at the top of the Fortune 500 list (Wagner, 1987; Wagner & Sternberg, 1985). Wagner and Sternberg (1990) obtained a correlation of .61 between tacit knowledge and performance on a managerial simulation and found that tacit-knowledge scores explained additional variance beyond IQ and other personality and ability measures. In a study with bank branch managers, Wagner and Sternberg (1985) obtained significant correlations between tacit-knowledge scores and average percentage of merit-based salary increase ($r = .48, p < .05$) and average performance rating for the category of generating new business for the bank ($r = .56, p < .05$). Williams and Sternberg (as cited in Sternberg et al., 1995) further found that tacit knowledge was related to several indicators of managerial success, including compensation, age-controlled compensation, level of position, and job satisfaction, with correlations ranging from .23 to .39.

Although much of the tacit-knowledge research has involved business managers, there is evidence that tacit knowledge explains performance in other domains. In the field of academic psychology, correlations in the .4 to .5 range were found between tacit-knowledge scores and criterion measures such as citation rate, number of publications, and quality of department (Wagner, 1987; Wagner & Sternberg, 1985). In studies with salespeople, Wagner et al. (1994) found correlations in the .3 to .4 range between tacit knowledge and criteria such as sales volume and sales awards received. In research with military leaders at three organizational levels, tacit-knowledge scores correlated significantly with ratings of leadership effectiveness made by subordinates, peers, or superiors, with correlations ranging from .14 to .42 (Hedlund et al., 1998). Tacit-knowledge scores also explained variance in leadership effectiveness above and beyond scores on a verbal reasoning test and a tacit-knowledge test for managers.

INTEGRATING SOCIAL, EMOTIONAL, AND PRACTICAL INTELLIGENCE WITHIN A TACIT-KNOWLEDGE FRAMEWORK

Although constructs such as social and emotional intelligence have gained widespread popularity, there is limited empirical support or, at best, mixed support for the validity of these nonacademic intelligences. Research progress is perhaps impeded by a lack of consistency in how these constructs are conceptualized and operationalized. Definitions of social and emotional intelligence range from specific, cognitive factors (such as social judgment, emotion perception) to all-encompassing models that include personality (such as extroversion), motivational (such as achievement orientation), and cognitive ability (such as problem solving) factors. Adding confusion to the issue is the overlap in some approaches to measuring social and emotional intelligence (such as decoding nonverbal information, interpreting affective information). We are inclined to agree with critiques (Davies et al., 1998; Gardner, 1999b) that conclude that many of the conceptualizations of these nontraditional intelligences exceed the boundaries of a reasonable definition of intelligence. The empirical support for practical intelligence has been more promising, attributable in part to a more focused definition and measurement approach. The question of the status of these intelligences, however, is still fully open.

Jones and Day (1997) noted that practical, social, and emotional intelligence share a focus on declarative and procedural knowledge, flexible knowledge-retrieval capabilities, and problem solving that involves more than one correct interpretation or solution. We add that the main difference among these concepts lies in terms of content of the knowledge and the types of problems emphasized.

Knowledge plays a focal role in research on practical intelligence by Sternberg and his colleagues. The emphasis in this research has been on a type of knowledge that has particular relevance to practical everyday problems, that is, tacit knowledge. Unlike many approaches to studying social or emotional intelligence, the tacit-knowledge approach is more focused in its attempt to understand practical intelligence. As such, it limits the definition of practical intelligence to cognitive ability (such as knowledge acquisition) rather than encompassing an array of individual difference variables. A further advantage of the tacit-knowledge approach is that it is not limited to a particular domain of performance. Tacit knowledge is relevant to understanding problems of a task-related, social, or emotional nature.

Many of the distinctions raised between social and emotional intelligence overlap with three different categories of tacit knowledge: managing self, managing others, and managing tasks (Wagner & Sternberg 1985, 1986). Tacit knowledge about managing oneself refers to knowledge about self-motivational and self-organizational aspects of performing everyday tasks. It may include knowledge of one's emotions and how to manage them effectively. For example, important tacit knowledge for military leaders pertains to how to handle stress and manage one's emotions. Military leaders need to know how to keep their composure in the face of anger toward a subordinate. They also need to know how to manage the stress of long hours and sleep deprivation during field missions.

Tacit knowledge about managing others refers to knowledge about how to manage one's interpersonal relationships, both in work and nonwork settings. It includes knowing how to function effectively in social interactions as well as understanding verbal and nonverbal social information. A major part of a manager's role is managing interpersonal relations. Accordingly, much of the tacit knowledge pertaining to management is about how to effectively manage these relations. For example, imagine that you are a manager of a department that has not switched to flextime scheduling, although many other departments in your organization have. You oppose flextime scheduling because your department must communicate often with outside organizations during regular business hours (8 to 5). Some of your subordinates are very angry with you, to the point of being rude, and morale in your department has suffered. The tacit knowledge relevant to this situation pertains to how to address subordinate anger and how to improve morale. Clearly this problem requires knowledge of a social nature (how to communicate one's position) and emotional nature (how to address employee anger).

Tacit knowledge about managing tasks refers to knowledge about how to perform specific tasks, including how to plan one's activities, how to monitor one's progress, and how to evaluate one's outcomes. For example, a salesperson needs to know what strategies to employ in order to increase sales for a slow-moving product. College students need to know what activities have the most value in obtaining a high grade. These processes are consistent with those identified by Cantor and her colleagues in their study of life tasks (Cantor & Kihlstrom, 1987; Kihlstrom & Cantor, 2000).

The ability to acquire knowledge, whether it pertains to managing oneself, managing others, or managing tasks, can be characterized appropriately as an aspect of intelligence. It requires cognitive processes such as encoding essential information from the environment and recognizing associations between new information and existing knowledge. The decision to call this aspect of intelligence social, emotional, or practical intelligence will depend on one's perspective and one's purpose. Ultimately, it will be important to assess empirically the relations among these constructs and integrate them into a unified model in order to avoid a run-away proliferation of "intelligences." Should the proliferation continue, the field will risk the inevitable backlash of those who long for a return to the "good old days" of *g*. The field would then risk the loss of much of the progress that has been made.

NOTES

Send correspondence to Jennifer Hedlund, Department of Psychology, Yale University, P.O. Box 208205, New Haven, CT 06520–8205.

References

Apfel, R. J., & Sifneos, P. E. (1979). Alexithymia: Concept and measurement. *Psychotherapy and Psychosomatics, 32,* 180–190.

Archer, D. (1980). *How to expand your social intelligence quotient.* New York: M. Evans.

Archer, D., & Akert, R. M. (1980). The encoding of meaning: A test of three theories of social interaction. *Sociological Inquiry, 50,* 393–419.

Baltes, P. B. (1987). Theoretical propositions of life-span developmental psychology: On the dynamics between growth and decline. *Developmental Psychology, 23,* 611–626.

Baltes, P. B., Smith, J., & Staudinger, U. (1992). Wisdom and successful aging. In T. B. Sonderegger (Ed.), *Psychology and aging* (pp. 123–167). Lincoln, Nebraska: University of Nebraska Press.

Baltes, P. B., Sowarka, D., & Kliegl, R. (1989). Cognitive training research on fluid intelligence in old age: What can older adults achieve by themselves? *Psychology and Aging, 4,* 217–221.

Barnes, M. L., & Sternberg, R. J. (1989) Social intelligence and decoding of nonverbal clues. *Intelligence, 13,* 263–287.

Bar-On, R. (1997). *BarOn Emotional Quotient Inventory (EQ-i): Technical Manual.* Toronto, Canada: Multi-Health Systems.

Bayroff, A. G., & Fuchs, E. F. (1970). *The Armed Services Vocational Aptitude Battery.* Arlington, VA: U.S. Army Behavior and Systems Research Laboratory.

Beck, A. T., Epstein, N., Brown, G., & Steer, R.A. (1988). An inventory for measuring clinical anxiety: Psychometric properties. *Journal of Consulting and Clinical Psychology, 56,* 893–897.

Beck, A. T., Ward, C. H., Mendelson, M., Mock, J., & Erbaugh, J. (1961). An inventory for measuring depression. *Archives of General Psychiatry, 4,* 561–571.

Berg, C. A. (1989). Knowledge of strategies for dealing with everyday problems from childhood through adolescence. *Developmental Psychology, 25,* 607–618.

Berg, C. A. (2000). The intellectual development in adulthood. In R. J. Sternberg (Ed.), *Handbook of intelligence* (2nd ed., pp. 117–137). New York: Cambridge University Press.

Berg, C. A., & Calderone, K. (1994). The role of problem interpretations in understanding the development of everyday problem solving. In R. J. Sternberg & R. K. Wagner (Eds.), *Mind in context* (pp. 105–132). New York: Cambridge University Press.

Berg, C. A., Klaczynski, P. (1996). Practical intelligence and problem solving: Searching for perspective. In F. Blanchard-Fields & T. M. Hess (Eds.), *Perspectives on cognition in adulthood and aging* (pp. 323–357). New York: McGraw-Hill.

Brown, L. T., & Anthony, R. G. (1990). Continuing the search for social intelligence. *Personality and Individual Differences, 11,* 463–470.

Bruner, J. S., Shapiro, D., & Tagiuri, R. (1958). The meaning of traits in isolation and in combination. In R. Tagiuri & I. Petrollo (Eds.), *Person perception and interpersonal behavior* (pp. 277–288). Stanford, CA: Stanford University Press.

Buck, R. (1976). A test of nonverbal receiving ability: Preliminary studies. *Human Communications Research, 2,* 162–171.

Cantor, N. (1978). *Prototypicality and personality judgments.* Unpublished doctoral dissertation, Stanford University, Palo Alto, CA.

Cantor, N., & Harlow, R. (1994). Social intelligence and personality: Flexible life-task pursuit. In R.J. Sternberg & P. Ruzgis (Eds.), *Personality and intelligence* (pp. 137–168). Cambridge, U.K.: Cambridge University Press.

Cantor, N., & Kihlstrom, J. F. (1987). *Personality and social intelligence.* Englewood Cliffs, NJ: Prentice Hall.

Carraher, T. N., Carraher, D., & Schliemann, A. D. (1985). Mathematics in the streets and in schools. *British Journal of Developmental Psychology, 3,* 21–29.

Caruso, D. R., & Mayer, J. D. (1997). *A quick scale of empathy.* Unpublished manuscript.

Cattell, R. B. (1940). A culture free intelligence test: Part I, *Journal of Educational Psychology, 31,* 161–180.

Cattell, R. B., & Cattell, H.E.P. (1973). *Measuring intelligence with the Culture Fair Tests.* Champaign, IL: Institute for Personality and Ability Testing.

Ceci, S. J., & Bronfenbrenner, U. (1985). Don't forget to take the cupcakes out of the oven: Strategic time-monitoring, prospective memory and context. *Child Development, 56,* 175–190.

Ceci, S. J., & Liker, J. (1986). Academic and nonacademic intelligence: An experimental separation. In R. J. Sternberg & R. K. Wagner (Eds.), *Practical intelligence: Nature and origins of competence in the everyday world* (pp. 119–142). New York: Cambridge University Press.

Ceci, S. J., & Liker, J. (1988). Stalking the IQ-expertise relationship: When the critics go fishing. *Journal of Experimental Psychology: General, 117,* 96–100.

Ceci, S. J. & Roazzi, A. (1994). The effects of context on cognition: Postcards from Brazil. In R. J. Sternberg & R. K. Wagner (Eds.), *Mind in context: Interactionist perspectives on human intelligence* (pp. 74–101). New York: Cambridge University Press.

Chapin, F. S. (1942). Preliminary standardization of a social impact scale. *American Sociological Review, 7,* 214–225.

Chapin, F. S. (1967). *The Social Insight Test.* Palo Alto, CA: Consulting Psychologists Press.

Cornelius, S. W., & Caspi, A. (1987). Everyday problem solving in adulthood and old age. *Psychology and Aging, 2,* 144–153.

Cronbach, L. J. (1960). *Essentials of psychological testing* (2nd ed.). New York: Harper & Row.

Davies, M., Stankov, L., & Roberts, R. D. (1998). Emotional intelligence: In search of an elusive construct. *Journal of Personality and Social Psychology, 75,* 989–1015.

Denney, N. W. (1989). Everyday problem solving: Methodological issues, research findings, and a model. In I. W. Poon, D. C. Rubin, & B. A. Wilson (Eds.), *Everyday cognition in adulthood and late life* (pp. 330–351). New York: Cambridge University Press.

Denney, N. W., & Palmer, A. M. (1981). Adult age differences on traditional and practical problem-solving measures. *Journal of Gerontology, 36,* 323–328.

Denney, N. W., & Pearce, K. A. (1989). A developmental study of practical problem solving in adults. *Psychology and Aging, 4,* 438–442.

Dixon, R. A., & Baltes, P. B. (1986). Toward life-span research on the functions and pragmatics of intelligence. In R. J. Sternberg & R. K. Wagner (Eds.), *Practical intelligence: Nature and origins of competence in the everyday world* (pp. 203–235). New York: Cambridge University Press.

Doll, E. A. (1935). A genetic scale of social maturity. *The American Journal of Orthopsychiatry, 5,* 180–188.

Doll, E. A. (1965). *Vineland Social Maturity Scale.* Circle Pines, MN: American Guidance Service.

Eddy, A. S. (1988). *The relationship between the Tacit Knowledge Inventory for Mangers and the Armed Services Vocational Aptitude Battery.* Unpublished master's thesis, St. Mary's University, San Antonio, TX.

Ford, M. E. (1986). For all practical purposes: Criteria for defining and evaluating practical intelligence. In R. J. Sternberg & R. K. Wagner (Eds.), *Practical intelligence: Nature and origins of competence in the everyday world* (pp. 183–200). New York: Cambridge University Press.

Ford, M. E., & Tisak, M. S. (1983). A further search for social intelligence. *Journal of Educational Psychology, 75,* 196–206.

Frederiksen, N., Carlson, S., & Ward, W. C. (1984). The place of social intelligence in a taxonomy of cognitive abilities. *Intelligence, 8,* 315–337.

Gardner, H. (1983). *Frames of mind: The theory of multiple intelligences.* New York: Basic Books.

Gardner, H. (1993). *Multiple intelligences: The theory in practice.* New York: Basic Books.

Gardner, H. (1999a). Are there additional intelligences? The case for naturalist, spiritual, and existential intelligences. In J. Kane (Ed.), *Education, information, and transformation* (pp. 111–131). Upper Saddle River, NJ: Prentice-Hall.

Gardner, H. (1999b). Who owns intelligence? *The Atlantic Monthly, 283,* 67–76.

Goleman, D. (1995). *Emotional intelligence.* New York: Bantam Books.

Goleman, D. (1998). *Working with emotional intelligence.* NewYork: Bantam Books.

Gough, H. D. (1986). *California Psychological Inventory.* Palo Alto, CA: Consulting Psychologists Press.

Gough, H. G. (1965). A validation study of the Chapin Social Insight Test. *Psychological Reports, 17,* 355–368.

Gough, H. G. (1966). Appraisal of social maturity by means of the CPI. *Journal of Abnormal Psychology, 71,* 189–195.

Grigorenko, E. L., & Sternberg, R. J. (forthcoming). Analytical, creative, and practical intelligence as predictors of self-reported adaptive functioning: A case study in Russia. *Intelligence.*

Guilford, J. P. (1967). *The nature of human intelligence.* New York: McGraw-Hill.

Halberstadt, A. G., & Hall, J. A. (1980). Who's getting the message?: Children's nonverbal skills and their evaluation by teachers. *Developmental Psychology, 16,* 564–573.

Hedlund, J., Horvath, J. A., Forsythe, G. B., Snook, S., Williams, W. M., Bullis, R. C., Dennis, M., & Sternberg, R. J. (1998). *Tacit knowledge for military leadership: Evidence of construct validity* (Tech. Rep. No. 1080). Alexandria, VA: U.S. Army Research Institute for the Behavioral and Social Sciences.

Hoepfner, R., & O'Sullivan, M. (1968). Social intelligence and IQ. *Educational and Psychological Measurement, 28,* 339–344.

Hogan, R. (1969). Development of an empathy scale. *Journal of Consulting & Clinical Psychology, 33,* 307–316.

Horn, J. L. (1982). The theory of fluid and crystallized intelligence in relation to concepts of cognitive psychology and aging in adulthood. In F.I.M. Craik & A. Trehum (Eds.), *Aging and cognitive processes* (pp. 237–278). New York: Plenum.

Horn, J. L. (1994). Theory of fluid and crystallized intelligence. In R. J. Sternberg (Ed.), *The encyclopedia of human intelligence* (Vol. 1, pp. 443–451). New York: Macmillan.

Horn, J. L., & Cattell, R. B. (1966). Refinement and test of the theory of fluid and crystallized intelligence. *Journal of Educational Psychology, 57,* 253–270.

Hunt, T. (1928). The measurement of social intelligence. *Journal of Applied Psychology, 12,* 317–334.

Jones, K. & Day, J. D. (1997). Discrimination of two aspects of cognitive-social intelligence from academic intelligence. *Journal of Education Psychology, 89,* 486–497.

Keating, D. K. (1978). A search for social intelligence. *Journal of Educational Psychology, 70,* 218–233.

Kihlstrom, J. F., & Cantor, N. (1989). Social intelligence and personality: There's room for growth. In R. S. Wyer, & T. K. Srull (Eds.), *Advances in social cognition* (pp. 197–214). Hillsdale, NJ: Erlbaum.

Kihlstrom, J. F., & Cantor, N. (2000). Social intelligence. In R. J. Sternberg (Ed.), *Handbook of intelligence* (2nd ed., pp. 359–379). New York: Cambridge University Press.

Labouvie-Vief, G. (1982). Dynamic development and mature autonomy. *Human Development, 25,* 161–191.

Lave, J., Murtaugh, M., & de la Roche, O. (1984). The dialectic of arithmetic in grocery shopping. In B. Rogoff & J. Lace (Eds.), *Everyday cognition: Its development in social context* (pp. 67–94). Cambridge, MA: Harvard University Press.

Legree, P. J., Pifer, M. E., & Grafton, F. C. (1996). Correlations among cognitive abilities are lower for higher ability groups. *Intelligence, 23,* 45–57.

Lesser, I. M. (1981). A review of the alexithymia concept. *Psychosomatic Medicine, 43,* 531–543.

Marlowe, H. A. (1985). Competence: A social intelligence approach. In H. A. Marlowe, & R. B. Wienberg (Eds.), *Competence development: Theory and practice in special populations* (pp. 50–52). Springfield, IL: Charles C. Thomas.

Marlowe, H. A. (1986). Social intelligence: Evidence for multidimensionality and construct independence. *Journal of Educational Psychology, 78,* 52–58.

Mayer, J. D., Caruso, D., & Salovey, P. (forthcoming). Emotional intelligence meets traditional standards for an intelligence test. *Intelligence.*

Mayer, J. D., & Salovey, P. (1993). The intelligence of emotional intelligence. *Intelligence, 17,* 433–442.

Mayer, J. D., & Salovey, P. (1997). What is emotional intelligence? In P. Salovey & D. Sluyter (Eds.), *Emotional development and emotional intelligence: Implications for educators* (pp. 3–31). New York: Basic Books.

Mayer, J. D., Salovey, P., & Caruso, D. (1997). *Emotional IQ test* [CD ROM]. Needham, MA: Virtual Knowledge.

Mayer, J. D., Salovey, P., & Caruso, D. (2000). Emotional intelligence. In R. J. Sternberg (Ed.), *Handbook of intelligence* (2nd ed., pp. 396–421). New York: Cambridge University Press.

Mednick, S. A., & Mednick, M. T. (1967). *Manual for the Remote Associates Test.* Boston: Houghton-Mifflin.

Mercer, J. R., Gomez-Palacio, M., & Padilla, E. (1986). The development of practical intelligence in cross-cultural perspective. In R. J. Sternberg & R. K. Wagner (Eds.), *Practical intelligence: Nature and origins of competence in the everyday world* (pp. 183–200). New York: Cambridge University Press.

Moss, F. A., & Hunt, T. (1927) Are you socially intelligent? *Scientific American, 137,* 108–110.

Moss, F. A., Hunt, T., Omwake, K. T., & Woodward, L. G. (1955). *Manual for the George Washington University Series Social Intelligence Test.* Washington, DC: Center for Psychological Services.

Murtaugh, M. (1985). The practice of arithmetic by American grocery shoppers. *Anthropology and Education Quarterly, 16,* 186–192.

Myers, I. B. (1962). *The Myers-Briggs type indicator.* Palo Alto, CA: Consulting Psychologists Press.

Neisser, U. (1976). General, academic, and artificial intelligence. In L. Resnick (Ed.), *Human intelligence: Perspectives on its theory and measurement* (pp. 179–189). Norwood, NJ: Ablex.

Nelson, M. J., & Lamke, T. A. (1973). *The Henmon-Nelson test of mental ability.* Boston: Houghton Mifflin.

Nuñes, T. (1994). Street intelligence. In R. J. Sternberg (Ed.), *Encyclopedia of Human Intelligence* (pp. 1045–1049). New York: Macmillan.

Nuñes, T., Schliemann, A. D., & Carraher, D. W. (1993). *Street mathematics and school mathematics.* New York: Cambridge University Press.

Oltman, P. K., Raskin, F., & Witkin, H. A. (1971). *Group Embedded Figures Test.* Palo Alto, CA: Consulting Psychologists Press.

O'Sullivan, M., & Guilford, J. P. (1976). *Four factor tests of social intelligence (behavioral cognition): Manual of instructions and interpretations.* Orange, CA: Sheridan Psychological Services.

O'Sullivan, M., Guilford, J. P., & deMille, R. (1965). *The measurement of social intelligence.* (Psychological Laboratory Rep. No. 34). Los Angeles: University of Southern California.

Raven, J. C. (1960). *Guide to the Standard Progressive Matrices.* London: H. K. Lewis.

Rest, J. (1975). Longitudinal study of the Defining Issues Test of moral judgement: A strategy for analyzing developmental change. *Developmental Psychology, 11,* 738–748.

Riggio, R. E. (1986). Assessment of basic social skills. *Journal of Personality and Social Psychology, 51,* 649–660.

Riggio, R. E. (1989). *Manual for the Social Skills Inventory.* Palo Alto, CA: Consulting Psychologists Press.

Riggio, R. E., Messamer, J., & Throckmorton, B. (1991). Social and academic intelligence: Conceptually distinct but overlapping constructs. *Personality and Individual Differences, 12,* 695–702.

Roazzi, A. (1987). Effects of context on cognitive development. In J. F. Cruz & R. A. Goncalves (Eds.), *Psicologia e Educao: Investigacao e intervencao.* Porto, Portugal: Associacao dos Piscologos Portugueses.

Rogoff, B. & Lave, J. (Eds.). (1984). *Everyday cognition: its development in social context.* Cambridge, MA: Harvard University Press.

Rosenthal, R. (Ed.) (1979). *Skill in nonverbal communication: Individual differences.* Cambridge, MA: Oelgeschlager, Gunn, & Hain.

Rosenthal, R., Hall, J. A., DiMatteo, M. R., Rogers, P. L., & Archer, D. (1979). *Sensitivity to nonverbal communication: The PONS test.* Baltimore: Johns Hopkins University Press.

Salovey, P., & Mayer, J. D. (1990). Emotional intelligence. *Imagination, Cognition, and Personality, 9,* 185–211.

Salovey, P., & Mayer, J. D. (1994). Some final thoughts about personality and intelligence. In R. J. Sternberg, & P. Ruzgis (Eds.), *Personality and intelligence* (pp. 303–318). Cambridge, U.K.: Cambridge University Press.

Sansone, C., & Berg, C. A. (1993). Adapting to the environment across the life span: Different process or different inputs? *International Journal of Behavioral Development, 16,* 215–241.

Schaie, K. W. (1977/1978). Toward a stage theory of adult cognitive development. *International Journal of Aging and Human Development, 8,* 129–138.

Schutte, N. S., Malouff, J. M., Hall, L. E., Haggerty, D. J., Cooper, J. T., Golden, C. J., & Dornheim, L. (1998). Development and validation of a measure of emotional intelligence. *Personality and Individual Differences, 25,* 167–177.

Schutz, W. (1989). *FIRO-B.* Palo Alto, CA: Consulting Psychologists Press.

Scribner, S. (1984). Studying working intelligence. In B. Rogoff & J. Lave (Eds.), *Everyday cognition: Its development in social context* (pp. 9–40). Cambridge, MA: Harvard University Press.

Scribner, S. (1986). Thinking in action: Some characteristics of practical thought. In R. J. Sternberg & R. K. Wagner (Eds.), *Practical intelligence: Nature and origins of competence in the everyday world* (pp. 13–30). New York: Cambridge University Press.

Scribner, S., & Cole, M. (1981). *The psychology of literacy.* Cambridge, MA: Harvard University Press.

Shanley, L. A., Walker, R. E., & Foley, J. M. (1971). Social intelligence: A concept in search of data. *Psychological Reports, 29,* 1123–1132.

Shipley, W. C. (1940). A self-administering scale for measuring intellectual impairment and deterioration. *Journal of Psychology, 9,* 371–377.

Sifneos, P. E. (1973). The prevalence of "alexithymic" characteristics in psychosomatic patients. *Psychotherapy and Psychosomatics, 22,* 255–262.

Snyder, M. (1974). Self-monitoring of expressive behavior. *Journal of Personality and Social Psychology, 30,* 526–537.

Sparrow, S. S., Balla, D. A., & Cicchetti, D. V. (1984). *Vineland Adaptive Behavior Scales.* Circle Pines, MN: American Guidance Service.

Sternberg, R. J. (1985). *Beyond IQ: A triarchic theory of human intelligence.* New York: Cambridge University Press.

Sternberg, R. J. (1993). *Sternberg Triarchic Abilities Test.* Unpublished manuscript.

Sternberg, R. J. (1997). *Successful intelligence.* New York: Plume.

Sternberg, R. J. (1999). [Review of D. Goleman's book *Working with Emotional Intelligence*]. *Personnel Psychology, 52,* 780–783.

Sternberg, R. J., Conway, B. E., Ketron, J. L., & Bernstein, M. (1981). People's conceptions of intelligence. *Journal of Personality and Social Psychology, 41,* 37–55.

Sternberg, R. J., Ferrari, M., Clinkenbeard, P. R., & Grigorenko, E. L. (1996). Identification, instruction, and assessment of gifted children: A construct validation of a triarchic model. *Gifted Child Quarterly, 40(3),* 129–137.

Sternberg, R. J., Forsythe, G. B., Hedlund, J., Horvath, J. A., Wagner, R. K., Williams, W. M., Snook, S., & Grigorenko, E. L. (2000). *Practical intelligence in everyday life.* New York: Cambridge University Press.

Sternberg, R. J., Grigorenko, E. L., Ferrari, M., & Clinkenbeard, P. (1999). A triarchic analysis of an aptitude-treatment interaction. *European Journal of Psychological Assessment, 15(1),* 1–11.

Sternberg, R. J., Nokes, K., Geissler, P. W., Prince, R., Okatcha, F., Bundy, D. A., & Grigorendo, E. L. (forthcoming). The relationship between academic and practical intelligence: A case study in Kenya. *Intelligence.*

Sternberg, R. J., & Smith, C. (1985). Social intelligence and decoding skills in nonverbal communication. *Social Cognition, 3,* 168–192.

Sternberg, R. J., & Wagner, R. K. (Eds.). (1986). *Practical intelligence: Nature and origins of competence in the everyday world.* New York: Cambridge University Press.

Sternberg, R. J., & Wagner, R. K. (Eds.). (1994). *Mind in context.* New York: Cambridge University Press.

Sternberg, R. J., & Wagner, R. K., & Okagaki, L. (1993). Practical intelligence: The nature and role of tacit knowledge in work and at school. In H. Reese & J. Puckett (Eds.), *Advances in lifespan development* (pp. 205–227). Hillsdale, NJ: Erlbaum.

Sternberg, R. J., Wagner, R. K., Williams, W. M., & Horvath, J. A. (1995). Testing common sense. *American Psychologist, 50,* 912–927.

Strang, R. (1930). Measures of social intelligence. *American Journal of Sociology, 36,* 263–269.

Stricker, L. J., & Rock, D. A. (1990). Interpersonal competence, social intelligence, and general ability. *Personality and Individual Differences, 11,* 833–839.

Terman, L. M. (1950). *Concept Mastery Test.* New York: Psychological Corporation.

Thorndike, E. L. (1920). Intelligence and its use. *Harper's Magazine, 140,* 227–235.

Thorndike, R. L. (1936). Factor analysis of social and abstract intelligence. *Journal of Educational Psychology, 27,* 231–233.

Thorndike, R. L., & Stein, S. (1937). An evaluation of the attempts to measure social intelligence. *Psychological Bulletin, 34,* 275–285.

Vernon, P. E. (1933). Some characteristics of the good judge of personality. *Journal of Social Psychology, 4,* 42–57.

Wagner, R. K. (1987). Tacit knowledge in everyday intelligent behavior. *Journal of Personality and Social Psychology, 52,* 1236–1247.

Wagner, R. K. (2000). Practical intelligence. In R. J. Sternberg (Ed.), *Handbook of intelligence* (2nd ed. pp. 380–395). New York: Cambridge University Press.

Wagner, R. K., Rashotte, C. A., & Sternberg, R. J. (1994). *Tacit Knowledge in sales: Rules of thumb for selling anything to anyone.* Paper presented at the annual meeting of the American Educational Research Association, Washington, DC.

Wagner, R. K., & Sternberg, R. J. (1985). Practical intelligence in real-world pursuits: The role of tacit knowledge. *Journal of Personality and Social Psychology, 49,* 436–458.

Wagner, R. K., & Sternberg, R. J. (1986). Tacit knowledge and intelligence in the everyday world. In R. J. Sternberg & R. K. Wagner (Eds.), *Practical intelligence: Nature and origins of competence in the everyday world* (pp. 51–83). New York: Cambridge University Press.

Wagner, R. K., & Sternberg, R. J. (1989). *Tacit Knowledge Inventory for Sales: Written.* Unpublished manuscript.

Wagner, R. K., & Sternberg, R. J. (1990). Street smarts. In K. E. Clark & M. B. Clark (Eds.), *Measures of leadership* (pp. 493–504). West Orange, NJ: Leadership Library of America.

Wagner, R. K., Sujan, H., Sujan, M., Rashotte, C. A., & Sternberg, R. J. (1999). Tacit knowledge in sales. In R. J. Sternberg & J. A. Horvath (Eds.), *Tacit knowledge in professional practice* (pp. 155–182). Mahwah, NJ: Erlbaum.

Wechsler, D. (1940). Nonintellective factors in general intelligence. *Psychological Bulletin, 37,* 444–445.

Wechsler, D. (1958). *The measurement and appraisal of adult intelligence* (4th ed.). Baltimore: Williams & Wilkins.

Wechsler, D. (1981). *Wechsler Adult Intelligence Scale-Revised.* New York: Psychological Corporation.

Wedeck, J. (1947). The relationship between personality and psychological ability. *British Journal of Psychology, 36,* 133–151.

Willis, S. L., & Schaie, K. W. (1986). Practical intelligence in later adulthood. In R. J. Sternberg & R. Wagner (Eds.), *Practical intelligence* (pp. 236–270). New York: Cambridge University Press.

Wong, C. T., Day, J. D., Maxwell, S. E., & Meara, N. M. (1995). A multitrait-multimethod study of academic and social intelligence in college students. *Journal of Educational Psychology, 87,* 117–133.

Yerkes, R. M. (1921). Psychological examining in the United States Army. *Memoirs of the National Academy of Sciences: Vol. 15.* Washington, D.C.: U.S. Government Printing Office.

PART TWO

NORMAL AND ABNORMAL DEVELOPMENT OF EMOTIONAL INTELLIGENCE

CHAPTER EIGHT

Levels of Emotional Awareness

Neurological, Psychological, and Social Perspectives

Richard D. Lane

The concept of levels of emotional awareness (Lane and Schwartz, 1987) was articulated shortly before the first article on emotional intelligence was published (Salovey & Mayer, 1990). Although awareness of one's own emotions is thought to be one component of emotional intelligence, it may be a particularly important or primary component in the sense that it may be the foundation for the successful implementation of the other components of emotional intelligence. In this chapter I explore the links between emotional awareness and emotional intelligence and then discuss the psychological, neurobiological, and social dimensions of emotional awareness.

Emotional intelligence may be broadly defined as the ability to use emotional information in a constructive and adaptive manner. Emotional information consists of one's own subjective emotional responses as well as the information conveyed by the emotional responses of others. This definition of emotional intelligence is consistent with that of the creators of the construct, who view emotional intelligence as a set of mental abilities (Mayer & Salovey, 1997; Mayer, Salovey, & Caruso, 2000). These include the ability to perceive emotions, access and generate emotion to assist thought, understand and reason about emotion, and reflectively regulate emotions to promote emotional and intellectual growth. All involve the ability to consciously process emotional information.

Note: Supported by Research Scientist Development Award MH00972 from the National Institute of Mental Health to RDL.

Another, broader view of emotional intelligence is one that links these basic abilities to aspects of overt behavior in social contexts, including impulse control, persistence, zeal and self-motivation, empathy, and social deftness (Goleman, 1995). Although this broader conception of emotional intelligence goes beyond the concept of mental abilities, the behaviors in question may also be based on the capacity to be consciously aware of emotional information. These other components of emotional intelligence may be conceptualized as the enhancement or suppression of approach or avoidance behavior based on an awareness of the current or anticipated subjective emotional state of the self or others.

For example, impulse control involves not taking a particular action aimed at short-term gratification in order to avoid possible negative long-term consequences. To not act on an impulse requires that a mental representation of possible future consequences influence the behavioral expression of the impulse before it occurs. Thus, impulse control involves recognition of an incipient approach behavior and the ability to anticipate the negative consequences of that course of action, which may include a representation of how the self and/or the other would feel if the action were taken. Impulse control thus involves suppression of approach behavior.

In contrast, persistence requires the ability to overcome one's negative emotional reactions in the face of obstacles or adversity in order to continue to pursue one's goals. Persistence typically involves being aware of one's negative reactions sufficiently to recognize them and not act on them. Persistence therefore involves the suppression of avoidance responses.

Zeal and self-motivation, on the other hand, reflect the ability to create positive affect to enhance motivation and achieve one's personal goals. Zeal and self-motivation thus involve the enhancement of approach behavior. Creating positive affect requires the ability to recognize its absence and requires self-monitoring to maintain the positive state.

Finally, social deftness involves the ability to successfully negotiate social interactions in order to achieve one's goals in a social context. To interact effectively with other people requires the capacity to monitor one's own interests and concerns and those of other people and to integrate them for effective action. Social deftness thus requires accurate monitoring of both the self and others. A particularly important aspect of social deftness may involve actively avoiding the creation of negative responses in others, which involves enhancement of one's own avoidance responses in certain key areas, that is, not doing the wrong thing. Of course, social deftness also involves the capacity to enhance positive responses in others.

The ability to accurately anticipate whether a given course of action will evoke positive or negative responses in others requires the capacity for accurate empathy. One way of conceptualizing empathy is that it consists of putting oneself in the place of another person and imagining how one would feel if one were that person. As such, awareness of one's own emotions is a prerequisite for empathy. One corollary of this is that one's ability to empathize cannot exceed one's ability to monitor one's own emotional states.

Given the importance of the ability to be aware of one's own emotions for emotional intelligence, it would be useful to have a conceptual framework for understanding individual differences in this area and a method for measuring these individual differences. Below I review the theoretical background and empirical data supporting a cognitive-developmental approach to these individual differences. Next, I review neuroimaging findings from studies of emotional awareness and attention to emotional experience that differentially implicate subregions of the anterior cingulate cortex and medial prefrontal cortex. I then discuss the observation that the medial prefrontal cortex plays a preferential role in the representation of the mental state of other people. The prefrontal areas that participate in the representation of mental states of the self and others are then linked to the emotional awareness model, which in turn is applied to emotional behavior in a social context.

LEVELS OF EMOTIONAL AWARENESS

In 1987 Gary Schwartz and I (Lane & Schwartz, 1987) proposed that an individual's ability to recognize and describe emotion in oneself and others, called emotional awareness, is a cognitive skill that undergoes a developmental process similar to that which Piaget described for cognition in general. A fundamental tenet of this model is that individual differences in emotional awareness reflect variations in the degree of differentiation and integration of the schemata used to process emotional information, whether that information comes from the external world or the internal world through introspection. To the extent that awareness of emotional information is adaptive, it follows that the more information one has about one's emotional state, the greater the potential to use this information in achieving adaptational success.

Gary Schwartz and I (1987) posited five levels of emotional awareness that share the structural characteristics of Piaget's stages of cognitive development. The five levels of emotional awareness in ascending order are physical sensations, action tendencies, single emotions, blends of emotion, and blends of blends of emotional experience (the capacity to appreciate complexity in the experiences of the self and others).

These levels describe the organization of experience. They describe traits, although they may also be used to describe states. The levels are hierarchically related in that functioning at each level adds to and modifies the function of previous levels but does not eliminate them. For example, level 4 experiences should be associated with more differentiated somatic sensations (level 1) than level 2 experiences. A given emotional experience can be thought of as a construction consisting of each of the levels of experience up to and including the highest level attained.

The development of schemata is driven by the words or other representation mode used to describe emotion. This perspective draws on the work on symbol formation by Werner and Kaplan (1963), who maintained that things in the world become known to an observer by virtue of the way in which they are represented symbolically. Thus, the nature of conscious emotional experience, and the ability to appreciate complexity in one's own experience and that of others, is influenced by what one knows about emotion, which itself is based on how emotion has been represented in the past.

This position is also consistent with that of successors to Piaget, such as Karmiloff-Smith (1992), who hold that cognitive development in different domains of knowledge proceeds through a process called *representational redescription*. In essence, cognitive development from this theoretical perspective consists of the transformation of knowledge from implicit (procedural, sensorimotor) to explicit (conscious thought) representations through use of language or another representation mode, which renders thought more flexible, adaptable, and creative. This viewpoint is consistent with the theory that the way language is used to describe emotion modifies what one knows about emotion and how emotion is consciously experienced.

Levels of Emotional Awareness Scale: Psychometric Findings

The Levels of Emotional Awareness Scale (LEAS) is a written performance measure that asks the subject to describe his or her anticipated feelings and those of another person in each of twenty scenes described in two to four sentences (Lane, Quinlan, Schwartz, Walker, & Zeitlin, 1990). Scoring is based on specific structural criteria aimed at determining the degree of differentiation in the use of emotion words (the degree of specificity in the terms used and the range of emotions described) and the differentiation of self from other. The scoring involves essentially no inference by raters. Because the scoring system evaluates the structure of experience and not its content, subjects cannot modify their responses to enhance their score, as is the case with some self-report instruments. A glossary of words at each level was created to guide scoring.

Each of the twenty scenes receives a score of 0 to 5 corresponding to the cognitive-developmental theory of emotional awareness that underlies the LEAS (Lane & Schwartz, 1987). A score of 0 is assigned when nonaffective words are used, or when the word *feel* is used to describe a thought rather than a feeling. A score of 1 is assigned when words indicating physiological cues are used in the description of feelings (for example, "I'd feel tired"). A score of 2 is assigned when words are used that convey relatively undifferentiated emotion (for example, "I'd feel bad"), or when the word *feel* is used to convey an action tendency (for example, "I'd feel like punching the wall"). A score of 3 is assigned when one word conveying a typical, differentiated emotion is used (happy, sad, angry, and so forth). A score of 4 is assigned when two or more level 3 words are used in a way that conveys greater emotional differentiation than would either word alone. Respondents receive a separate score for the "self" response and for the "other" response ranging from 0 to 4. In addition, a total LEAS score is given to each scene equal to the higher of the self and other scores. A score of 5 is assigned to the total when self and other each receive a score of 4 and are differentiated from one another; thus, a maximum total LEAS score of 100 is possible. An example of a scene from the LEAS and responses that are scored at each level is provided in the appendix at the end of this chapter.

To date, eight separate psychometric studies have been conducted with the LEAS. The first study, with Yale undergraduates ($n = 94$) enabled us to examine the reliability of the LEAS and its correlation with other psychological tests (Lane et al., 1990). The second study involved students at the Chicago Medical School ($n = 57$) and focused on the correlation with the Levy Chimeric Faces Test (Lane, Kevley, DuBois, Shamasundara, & Schwartz, 1995). The third study in Arizona and Minnesota ($n = 385$) established norms for the scale (Lane et al., 1996). A fourth study with University of Arizona undergraduates ($n = 215$) involved additional psychometric and psychophysiologic assessments. The fifth and sixth studies have been conducted in collaboration with Dr. Lisa Feldman Barrett at Boston College. In addition, two international studies have been conducted: a study of 331 German students (Wrana et al., 1998) and a Canadian study of 30 subjects with borderline personality disorder and 40 control subjects (Levine, Marziali, & Hood, 1997). The findings from these studies are selectively reviewed below.

The LEAS has consistently been shown to have high interrater reliability and internal consistency (Lane, Reiman, et al., 1998). An adequate assessment of test-retest reliability of the LEAS in the general population has not been undertaken. Norms for age, sex, and socioeconomic status have been established based on the study completed in Arizona and Minnesota.

In the Yale study we administered two instruments that, like the LEAS, are cognitive-developmental measures based on Piaget's model: the Sentence Completion Test of Ego Development (Loevinger & Wessler, 1970; Loevinger, Wessler, & Redmore, 1970) and the cognitive complexity of the description of parents (Blatt, Wein, Chevron, & Quinlan, 1979). The LEAS correlated moderately ($r = .37$ and $r = .36$, respectively) and significantly ($p < .01$) in the predicted direction in both cases. These results support the claim that the LEAS is measuring a cognitive-developmental continuum and that the LEAS is not identical to these other measures.

A key question is whether the LEAS is simply another measure of verbal ability. In the Yale sample the LEAS correlated .38 ($p < .001$) with the vocabulary subtest of the Wechsler Adult Intelligence Scale—Revised (WAIS-R) (Wechsler, 1981). In the study at the Chicago Medical School the LEAS correlated .17 (not significant) with the Shipley Institute of Living Scale (Shipley, 1940), a multiple choice measure of verbal ability. These data suggest that verbal ability may contribute to LEAS performance. However, several studies have now been conducted demonstrating that when verbal ability is controlled, significant effects are still observed. For example, LEAS scores in men and women could be compared in all eight studies. In three of these studies, measures of verbal ability, including the WAIS vocabulary subtest and the Shipley Institute of Living Scale, were also obtained. In each study women scored higher than men on the LEAS ($p < .01$), even when controlling for verbal ability ($p < .05$) (Barrett, Lane, Sechrest, & Schwartz, forthcoming). Thus, the finding that women score higher than men on the LEAS is a highly stable and generalizable finding.

Lisa Feldman Barrett administered the LEAS and the Weinberger Adjustment Inventory to sixty-three subjects at Penn State and fifty-five subjects at Boston College (Barrett et al., forthcoming). In both samples the LEAS correlated significantly ($p < .05$, two-tailed) with self-restraint, one of three superordinate dimensions of the scale. The LEAS also correlated significantly with impulse control (.35, $p < .01$, two-tailed and .30, $p < .05$, two-tailed), a component of self-restraint that involves the tendency to think before acting. Self-restraint refers directly to suppression of egoistic desires in the interest of long-term goals and relations with others. This replication in independent samples indicates that greater emotional awareness is associated with greater self-reported impulse control, a key component of emotional intelligence according to Goleman, and is consistent with the theory that functioning at higher levels of emotional awareness (levels 3 through 5) modulates function at lower levels (actions and action tendencies at level 2).

Evidence for the discriminant validity of the LEAS is provided by data from the study in which norms were established and the Arizona undergraduate study. In both studies ($n = 385$ and $n = 215$, respectively) the Affect Intensity Measure (Larsen & Diener, 1987), a trait measure of the tendency to experience emotions intensely, did not correlate significantly with the LEAS despite the large sample sizes. Thus, inadequate statistical power cannot explain the lack of correlation. The LEAS also does not correlate significantly with measures of negative affect, such as the Taylor Manifest Anxiety Scale (Bendig, 1956) and the Beck Depression Inventory (Beck, Ward, Mendelson, Mock, & Erbaugh, 1961). These results are consistent with the view that the LEAS measures the structure or complexity and not the intensity of affective experience.

Behavioral Findings with the LEAS

A key assumption in this work on emotional awareness is that language promotes the development of schemata for the processing of emotional information, whether that information comes from the internal or external world. Once the schemata are established they should affect the processing of emotional information whether the information is verbal or nonverbal. Thus, the LEAS should correlate with the ability to recognize and categorize external emotional stimuli. Furthermore, this correlation should hold whether the external stimulus and the response are purely verbal or purely nonverbal.

These hypotheses were tested in the Norms study by use of the Perception of Affect Task (PAT), a set of four emotion recognition tasks (thirty-five items each) developed by Jim Rau and Alfred Kaszniak at the University of Arizona (Rau, 1993). The first subtask consists of stimuli describing an emotional situation without the use of emotion words. For example, "The man looked at the photograph of his recently departed wife." The response involves choosing one from an array of seven terms (happy, sad, angry, afraid, disgust, neutral, surprise) to identify how the person in question was feeling. The fourth subtask is purely nonverbal. The stimuli consist of photographs of faces developed by Ekman (1982), each of which depicts an individual emotion. The response consists of selecting one from an array of seven photographs depicting emotional scenes without faces (like two people standing arm-in-arm by a grave with their backs to the camera). The other two subtasks involve a verbal stimulus (sentence) and a nonverbal response (from an array of seven faces), and a nonverbal stimulus (face) and a verbal response (from an array of seven words).

Across the entire scale, the correlation between the LEAS and the PAT was highly significant (.43, $n = 385$, $p < .001$), accounting for about 18 percent of the variance. Furthermore, significant correlations were observed between the LEAS and each of the PAT subtasks. When dividing the sample into upper (high), middle, and lower thirds on the LEAS, the high-scoring LEAS subjects scored higher on each of the PAT subtasks than the low-scoring LEAS subjects. Thus, high LEAS scores were associated with better emotion recognition no matter whether the task was purely verbal or purely nonverbal (Lane et al., 1996). Furthermore, when combining results for each of the seven emotion categories across the four subtasks (there were five stimuli of each emotion type in each subtask), the same findings for high-, moderate-, and low-scoring LEAS subjects were observed (Lane, Shapiro, Sechrest, & Riedel, 1998). These findings support the claim that the LEAS is (1) a measure of the schemata used to process emotional information, whether the information is verbal or nonverbal; (2) a measure of the complexity of experience; and (3) not simply a measure of verbal ability.

NEURAL CORRELATES OF EMOTIONAL AWARENESS

To explore the underlying functional neuroanatomy of emotional awareness, we administered the LEAS to subjects participating in a positron emission tomography (PET) study of emotion (Lane, Reiman, et al., 1998). Subjects included twelve right-handed female volunteers who were free of medical, neurological, or psychiatric abnormalities. The LEAS and other psychometric instruments were completed prior to PET imaging. Happiness, sadness, disgust, and three neutral control conditions were induced by film and recall of personal experiences (twelve conditions). Twelve PET images of blood flow were obtained in each subject using the ECAT 951/31 scanner (Siemens, Knoxville, Tenn.), 40 mCi intravenous bolus injections of ^{15}O-water, a fifteen second uptake period, sixty second scans, and an interscan interval of ten minutes.

To examine neural activity attributable to emotion generally, rather than to specific emotions, one can subtract the three neutral conditions from the three emotion conditions in a given stimulus modality (film or recall). This difference, which can be calculated separately for the six film and six recall conditions, identifies regions of the brain where blood flow changes specifically attributable to emotion occur. These blood flow changes, which are indicative of neural activity in that region, can then be correlated with LEAS scores to identify regions of the brain that are associated with emotional awareness during emotional arousal.

Findings from this covariate analysis revealed one cluster for film-induced emotion, with a maximum located in the right midcingulate cortex (BA 23; coordinates of maximum = [16, −18, 32]; $Z = 3.40$; $p < .001$, uncorrected). For recall-induced emotion, the most statistically significant cluster was located in the right anterior cingulate cortex (BA 24; coordinates of maximum = [16, 6, 30]; $Z = 2.82$; $p < .005$, uncorrected). A conjunction analysis was performed next to identify areas of significant overlap between the two covariance analyses. With a height threshold of $Z = 3.09$, $p < .001$, and an extent threshold of five voxels, a single cluster was observed in the right anterior cingulate cortex (BA 24) maximal at [14, 6, 30] $Z = 3.74$, $p < .001$ ($p = 9.2 \times 10^{-5}$), uncorrected. As can be observed in Figure 8.1, the point of maximum change is located in white matter adjacent to the anterior cingulate cortex.

Given that blood flow changes in white matter are unlikely, the imprecision in anatomical localization associated with image normalization, the extension of the area of significant change into the anterior cingulate cortex, and the absence of other gray matter structures in the immediate vicinity, the likeliest location of this cluster is the anterior cingulate cortex (Lane, Reiman, et al., 1998).

Traditionally the anterior cingulate cortex was thought to have a primarily affective function (Papez, 1937; Vogt, Finch, & Olson, 1992). However, in addition to its role in emotion, it is now recognized to play important roles in attention, pain, response selection, maternal behavior, vocalization, skeletomotor function, and autonomic control (Vogt & Gabriel, 1993). The multiple functions of the anterior cingulate cortex no doubt contribute to the significant changes in activation that have been observed in a variety of studies. How can these different functions be reconciled with the present findings involving emotional awareness?

Sagittal   Coronal

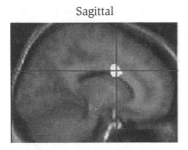 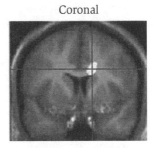

Figure 8.1. Results of the conjunction analysis demonstrating overlap of the separate associations during film and recall-induced emotion between LEAS and cerebral blood flow in the dorsal anterior cingulate cortex. The cluster depicted contains sixty-six voxels with a maximum activation at coordinates [14, 6, 30], = 3.74, p < .001. These results are displayed in the sagittal and coronal planes superimposed on the average structural magnetic resonance image of the twelve female subjects.

One answer might be that these various functions of the anterior cingulate cortex may reflect its superordinate role in executive control of attention and motor responses (Lane, Reiman, et al., 1998). According to this view, emotion, pain, or other salient exteroceptive or interoceptive stimuli provide moment-to-moment guidance regarding the most suitable allocation of attentional resources for the purpose of optimizing motor responses in interaction with the environment. The conscious experience of emotion could occur concomitantly and automatically as attention is redirected by emotion. As such, a role of the anterior cingulate cortex in the conscious experience of emotion fits well with its other functions but suggests that this role is not exclusive to emotion. To the extent that people who are more emotionally aware attend more to internal and external emotion cues, the cognitive processing of this information can contribute to ongoing emotional development.

Subsequent to the study just described, we examined the pattern of neural activation associated with attending to one's own emotional experience (Lane, Fink, Chua, & Dolan, 1997). To confirm that subjects were allocating their attention as we instructed, we had them indicate on a keypad how each emotion-evoking picture made them feel. In essence, we were examining an aspect of conscious experience involving commentary on that experience (Weiskrantz, 1997).

We studied ten healthy men as they viewed twelve picture sets, each consisting of pleasant, unpleasant, and neutral pictures from the International Affective Picture System (Lang, Bradley, & Cuthbert, 1995). Pictures were presented for 500 msec every 3.0 seconds. Twelve PET-derived measures of cerebral blood flow were obtained in each subject, one for each picture set. During half the scans subjects attended to their emotional experience (indicating on a keypad whether the picture evoked a pleasant, unpleasant, or neutral feeling); during the other half they attended to spatial location (indicating whether the scene depicted was indoors, outdoors, or indeterminate). Across subjects, picture sets were counterbalanced across the two attention conditions.

During attention to subjective emotional responses, increased neural activity was elicited in rostral anterior cingulate cortex (BA32) and medial prefrontal cortex (coordinates: 0, 50, 16; $Z = 6.74$, $p < .001$, corrected) (Figure 8.2), and right temporal pole, insula, and ventral cingulate cortex (all $p < .001$, corrected).

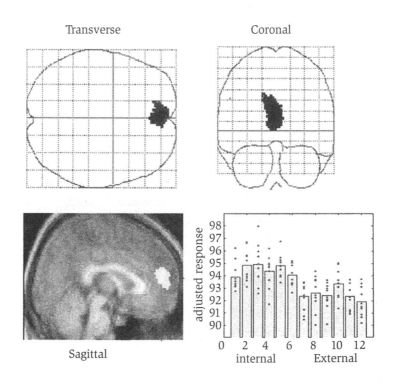

Figure 8.2. A statistical parametric map (SPM) showing significant cerebral blood flow increases in anterior cingulate cortex (BA32)–medial prefrontal cortex (BA9) during selective attention to subjective emotional responses (minus activations specific to the external condition). The figures in the upper left and upper right are projection images in the transverse and coronal planes, respectively. The sagittal view in the lower left depicts the spatial distribution of the activation in the internal focus condition ($Z = 6.87$, $p < .001$, corrected) superimposed on the average structural magnetic resonance image of the ten male subjects. The figure in the lower right demonstrates blood flow values in each condition (internal: 1–6; external: 7–12).

Under the same stimulus conditions, when subjects attended to spatial aspects of the picture sets, activation was observed in parieto-occipital cortex bilaterally ($Z = 5.71$, $p < .001$, corrected), a region known to participate in the evaluation of spatial relationships.

Our interpretation of these findings is that the rostral anterior cingulate–medial prefrontal activation may be where a representation of one's own emotional state is established. Several lines of evidence support this view. (1) *Anatomical connections:* This region is densely connected with the amygdala, orbitofrontal cortex, other sectors of the anterior cingulate cortex, and other paralimbic structures such as the insula (Price, Carmichael, & Drevets, 1996). Thus, emotional information is transmitted to it. (2) *Lesion studies:* Follow-up studies of patients with prefrontal leukotomy, which most commonly targeted the medial prefrontal area through a transorbital approach, revealed significant deficits in the capacity to experience emotion (Hoffman, 1949). (3) *Function of neighboring regions:* The adjacent dorsolateral prefrontal cortex is known to participate in working memory (Goldman-Rakic, 1987); perhaps the medial prefrontal cortex serves a similar function with regard to emotion, that is, holding emotional information on-line for use in cognitive operations (Lane, 1999).

The findings from this study can therefore be interpreted as follows. When attending to one's own emotional state, several brain areas are activated including those involved in (1) establishing a representation of the emotional state (rostral anterior cingulate–medial prefrontal cortex); (2) processing visceral information (anterior insula) (Augustine, 1996); (3) performing complex visual discrimination, possibly including retrieval of emotion-laden episodic memories (right temporal pole) (Fink et al., 1996); and (4) regulating autonomic responses (ventral cingulate) (Vogt et al., 1992).

The rostral anterior cingulate–medial prefrontal cortex is hypothesized to participate in the representation of emotional experience. This structure may be essential for knowing how one is feeling, a function that is critical in the control of emotional behavior. We have discussed above the critical importance of representations in creating knowledge and their critical role in emotional intelligence. The influence of representations on phenomenal experience may at least in part be mediated by the tight anatomical linkage (Price et al., 1996) between the rostral and dorsal anterior cingulate cortices. The dynamic interaction between phenomenal experience, establishing a representation of it, elaborating that representation (for example, identifying the source of the emotional response), and integrating it with other cognitive processes are the fundamental processes involved in the cognitive elaboration of emotion addressed by the levels of emotional awareness model.

Much work remains to be done to confirm these hypotheses. However, doing so could serve an integrative function. Stuss (1991a, 1991b) has discussed how the prefrontal cortex serves a self-monitoring and regulatory function. Damasio

(1994) has discussed how the sense of self may derive in part from the so-matovisceral sensations associated with emotion that are integrated with the higher cognitive functions of prefrontal cortex. It will be important to explore in the years ahead the extent to which the rostral anterior cingulate cortex–medial prefrontal cortex serves an exclusively emotional function or, like the dorsal anterior cingulate, may serve a superordinate function that may be greatly influenced by but not necessarily exclusively dedicated to emotion.

DEVELOPMENTAL ORIGINS OF AWARENESS OF SELF AND OTHER

Healthy individuals spontaneously model and respond to the mental states of other people (their knowledge, intentions, beliefs, and desires) to guide their own interpersonal behavior. This ability to make inferences about what is going on in another person's mind is a cognitive skill called *theory of mind*. This ability to make mentalistic inferences enables more accurate predictions of another person's future behavior than is possible solely on the basis of the other person's manifest behavior.

A growing body of evidence suggests that the fundamental problem in autism is a deficit in theory of mind. Experimental approaches have been developed to measure the theory of mind function. Autistic individuals do well on many cognitive tasks, but have difficulty making mentalistic inferences on theory of mind tasks. The evidence suggesting that a discrete cognitive deficit exists in autism has contributed to the search for the neural substrates of this cognitive skill. One of the strategies for identifying the neural substrates in question is to have healthy volunteers perform a theory of mind task in the context of functional neuroimaging.

Several neuroimaging studies (Figure 8.3) revealed that an area of medial prefrontal cortex very close to that identified in our attention to emotional experience study has been implicated during the performance of theory of mind tasks (Happé et al., 1996; Goel, Grafman, Sadato, & Hallett, 1995; Mazoyer et al., 1993).

Given the results cited above, these findings suggest that the neural substrates of the mental representation of one's own and others' mental states are closely related.

In the human infant, organized emotional behavior is present at birth, whereas the capacity for mental representation, the ability to think about things or experiences, does not typically emerge during ontogenesis until some time in the third year (Cowan, 1978). Thus, the perception of emotional signals is probably the earliest theory of mind task. Given that such perception must occur in

Sagittal

Coronal

Transverse

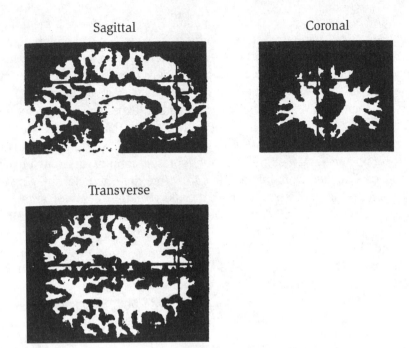

Figure 8.3. The location of peak activation in medial prefrontal cortex during response to stories requiring a theory of mind compared to physical stories. Regions of significantly increased activity as measured by PET are shown superimposed on a standard magnetic resonance image of the six healthy volunteers. Sagittal, coronal, and horizontal views depict a significant activation on the border between Brodmann areas 8 and 9 in prefrontal cortex at coordinates [−12, 36, 36], $Z = 4.1, p < .001$.

infancy before there is a clear mental representation of the self, the perception of emotional signals arising externally and the perception of emotional signals arising internally (the subjective experience of emotion) are likely to be undifferentiated and commingled.

Over time the young child comes to know what it is experiencing emotionally by virtue of the emotional responses of caregivers and others in the environment (Stern, 1985). The complex process by which this occurs is not understood but may be related to the intensity and timing of the caregiver's responses (Gergeley & Watson, 1996). It is interesting to consider how facial and vocal expressions of attunement in a caregiver must differ from those of spontaneous emotional expressions of the caregiver in order for the infant to begin to differentiate the two.

Teasdale has shown in a neuroimaging study in adults that the medial pre-frontal cortex is preferentially activated during the cognitive generation of affect (the appraisal of environmental stimuli leading to the generation of an emotional response) (Teasdale et al., 1999). Given the findings in our study of attention to emotional experience, it is possible that in adults, closely related structures par-ticipate in generating an emotional response and in experiencing the emotions associated with it. If so, it is consistent with the hypothesis derived from the developmental considerations just discussed that the perception and evaluation of exteroceptive emotional stimuli and the representation of one's own experi-ence are closely linked from infancy onward. Note that the neuroimaging evi-dence just cited is consistent with that aspect of the levels of emotional awareness model that states that the same schemata are used for processing inter-oceptive and exteroceptive information.

As noted above, the capacity for accurate empathy consists of putting one-self in the place of another person and imagining how one would feel if one were that person. The evidence just cited is consistent with the hypothesis that this occurs in neighboring or overlapping regions of prefrontal cortex.

The prefrontal cortex is known to process and integrate interoceptive and exteroceptive emotional information in the service of generating goal-directed behavior. The above considerations suggest that subregions of medial prefrontal cortex play key roles in the staging of this integration.

In our original model of emotional awareness we proposed that the repre-sentations of self and other become progressively differentiated from one another as one's level of emotional awareness increases. In patients with severe psychopathology, such as borderline personality disorder, the representations of states associated with self and other are more fluid and permeable, for exam-ple, there is confusion as to who is feeling what. Borderline personality disor-der has been associated with lower levels of emotional awareness (Levine et al., 1997). This finding provides clinical evidence for the concept that lower levels of development are associated with a lower degree of differentiation between the representations of the emotional states of the self and others.

Thus, the neural substrates of the representations of the mental state of oth-ers and the emotional state of the self are closely related anatomically. We spec-ulate that early in development the representations of the emotional states of the self and others are indistinguishable. The ability to be aware of one's own emotions probably derives from input from others such as caregivers. Over time the representations of the experiences of the self and others become progres-sively differentiated from one another. With development, the ability to be accu-rately attuned to the emotional state of others is probably a function of the ability to draw on one's own emotional experience, which itself is a function of how these emotional experiences were represented and communicated to oth-ers in the past.

ROLE OF EMOTIONAL AWARENESS IN SOCIAL COGNITION DURING SOCIAL INTERACTIONS

Baddeley and colleagues (Baddeley, Della Sala, Papagno, & Spinnler, 1997) demonstrated that despite equivalent performance on traditional tests of frontal lobe function such as verbal fluency, patients with frontal lobe lesions and socially disrupted behavior were more impaired in their performance in a dual task paradigm than were patients with frontal lobe lesions but no behavioral impairment. Baddeley and colleagues argue that successful social adaptation requires the "dual task" ability to stay in touch with the needs of others while paying due attention to one's own needs.

This formulation fits well with the description of level 5 on the levels of emotional awareness continuum. Optimal social adaptation requires the ability to appreciate the differentiated feelings of the self and others and integrate this information into a plan of action that permits attainment of personal goals in a manner that also fits with the social context. To the extent that one is operating at a level lower than level 5, information about the self or others will be left out that may lead to a less harmonious fit with the social context.

An important question that has not yet been addressed in empirical research is the extent to which one's level of emotional awareness corresponds to actual interpersonal behavior. One of the ways that emotional awareness can influence social interaction is through the modulation of emotional expressions. Because such expressions are influenced both by learned display rules and by the demands of the situation, emotional expressions can be executed with differential accuracy and efficiency (Buck, Miller, & Caul, 1974; Buck, Savin, Miller, & Caul, 1972). Coordinating emotional expressions to the complex and changing demands of the social context implies a considerable degree of differentiation and complexity in expressive behavior. The ability to know what one is feeling, monitor and modulate how that might be expressed outwardly, and anticipate how a given display will be experienced by others all may influence the nature of emotional expression. In this regard, it may be predicted that the higher level of emotional awareness, the greater the appropriateness of emotional expression in social contexts.

Another possible behavioral correlate of emotional awareness is the level of interpersonal negotiation strategy, as described by Selman (1981). Using a cognitive-developmental approach, Selman argued that the degree to which the other person is construed as an independent person with his or her own thoughts and feelings will determine the nature of one's interpersonal transactions. The five levels of interpersonal negotiation strategy in ascending order are negotiation through physical force (level 0), implicit power (threat or will power) (level 1), psychological power (persuasion) (level 2), interpersonal collaboration (level 3), and integration and synthesis (level 4). At each successive level there is an increase in the degree to which the other person is viewed as separate, autonomous, and yet interdependent, with needs, feelings, and rights that are as legitimate as one's own.

As noted above, emotion, like other areas of cognition, is broadly transformed from implicit into explicit processes during the course of development. Clyman (1991) has also discussed how explicit emotional reactions can become routinized so that they become automatic, implicit behaviors that are not associated with conscious emotional experience. Repetitive maladaptive behavior patterns, the kind that can be considered to reflect a relative lack of emotional intelligence, can be conceptualized in this way. Bringing to conscious awareness the emotional experiences associated with such behavior patterns makes it possible to identify the motivational origins of the behavior and use conscious cognitive mechanisms to alter the behavior patterns. The ability to use conscious emotional experiences in this way and to improve the social adaptability of one's behavior is likely to be greater the greater one's level of emotional awareness.

Finally, a growing amount of literature suggests that social support buffers the impact of psychological stress and is associated with better health outcomes (House, Landis, & Umberson, 1988). To the extent that one's success in social adaptation varies as a function of emotional awareness, it may be predicted that higher levels of emotional awareness are associated with greater degrees of social support and better health outcomes.

CONCLUSION

The ability to be aware of one's own emotional states is a skill that may be fundamental to some of the key features of emotional intelligence, including impulse control, persistence, zeal and self-motivation, empathy, and social deftness. Emotional awareness is conceptualized as a domain of cognitive development that unfolds in a manner parallel to that of intelligence in the usual cognitive sense. Emotional experience becomes more differentiated and integrated with development, transforming the representations of emotional states from implicit to explicit forms. Inherent in the theory is the progressive development of the capacity to maintain awareness of the differentiated feelings of both the self and others during social interactions and integrate them in the service of goal-directed activity. The degree of differentiation and integration of the schemata used to process information from the internal world of emotion and the external interpersonal world may have an important bearing on how emotion is expressed in a social context and how interpersonal transactions are negotiated. An important area of future research is to determine how development of these representations occurs in healthy subjects or fails to occur in those with maladaptive behavior patterns.

The body of work reviewed in this chapter may potentially provide a conceptual framework for integrating neurobiological, psychological, and social aspects of emotional intelligence. This chapter reviewed the theory of levels of emotional awareness and its implications for emotional intelligence and social cognition. Empirical support for the theory was presented including psychometric, behavioral, and neuroimaging data. The neural substrates of the representation of the mental states of the self and others were reviewed. Current data suggest that representations of the self and others are established in neighboring or overlapping subregions of medial prefrontal cortex. An important area of future investigation is to determine the extent to which these areas overlap and the extent to which the neural activation patterns in question change during the course of psychological development and are associated with corresponding changes in social behavior.

APPENDIX

You and your best friend are in the same line of work. There is a prize given annually to the best performance of the year. The two of you work hard to win the prize. One night the winner is announced: your friend. How would you feel? How would your friend feel?

Examples of responses at each level:

0   I don't work hard to win "prizes." My friend would probably feel that the judges knew what they were doing.

1   I'd feel sick about it. It's hard for me to say what my friend would feel—it would all depend on what our relationship was like and what the prize meant to her.

2   I'd probably feel bad about it for a few days and try to figure out what went wrong. I'm sure my friend would be feeling really good.

3   We would both feel happy. Hey, you can't win 'em all!

4   I would feel depressed—the friend in this light is just like any other competitor. I would also begrudgingly feel happy for my friend and rationalize that the judges had erred. My friend would feel very gratified but would take the prize in stride to save the friendship.

5   I'd feel disappointed that I didn't win but glad that if someone else did, that person was my friend. My friend probably deserved it! My friend would feel happy and proud but slightly worried that my feelings might be hurt.

NOTES

Address correspondence to: Richard D. Lane, M.D., Ph.D., Department of Psychiatry; P.O. Box 245002; Tucson, AZ 85724-5002. Fax: 520-626-2004; voice: 520-626-2154; e-mail: lane@u.arizona.edu

References

Augustine, J. R. (1996). Circuitry and functional aspects of the insular lobe in primates including humans. *Brain Research Reviews, 22,* 229-244.

Baddeley, A., Della Sala, S., Papagno, C., & Spinnler, H. (1997). Dual-task performance in dysexecutive and nondysexecutive patients with a frontal lesion. *Neuropsychology, 11,* 187-194.

Barrett, L. F., Lane, R. D., Sechrest, L., & Schwartz, G. E. (forthcoming). Sex differences in emotional awareness. *Personality and Social Psychology Bulletin.*

Beck, A. T., Ward, C. H., Mendelson, M., Mock, J. E., & Erbaugh, J. K. (1961). An inventory for measuring depression. *Archives of General Psychiatry, 4,* 561-571.

Bendig, A. (1956). The development of a short form of the Manifest Anxiety Scale. *Journal of Consulting Psychology, 20,* 384.

Blatt, S. J., Wein, S. J., Chevron, E., & Quinlan, D. M. (1979). Parental representations and depression in normal young adults. *Journal of Abnormal Psychology, 88,* 388-397.

Buck, R., Miller, R. E., & Caul, W. F. (1974). Sex, personality, and physiological variables in the communication of affect via facial expression. *Journal of Personality and Social Psychology, 30,* 587-596.

Buck, R., Savin, V. J., Miller, R. E., & Caul, W. F. (1972). Communication of affect through facial expressions in humans. *Journal of Personality and Social Psychology, 23,* 362-371.

Clyman, R. B. (1991). The procedural organization of emotions: A contribution from cognitive science to the psychoanalytic theory of therapeutic action. *Journal of the American Psychoanalytic Association, 39,* 349-382.

Cowan, P. A. (1978). *Piaget: With feeling. Cognitive, social, and emotional dimensions.* New York: Holt, Rinehart and Winston.

Damasio, A. R. (1994). *Descartes' Error: Emotion, Reason, and the Human Brain.* New York: G. P. Putnam's Sons.

Ekman, P. (1982). *Emotion in the human face* (2nd ed.). New York: Cambridge University Press.

Fink, G. R., Markowitsch, H. J., Reinkemeier, M., Bruckbauer, T., Kessler, J., & Heiss, W. D. (1996). Cerebral representation of one's own past: Neural networks involved in autobiographical memory. *Journal of Neuroscience, 16,* 4275-4282.

Gergely, G., & Watson, J. S. (1996). The social biofeedback theory of parental affect-mirroring: The development of emotional self-awareness and self-control in infancy. *International Journal of Psycho-Analysis, 77,* 1181–1212.

Goel, V., Grafman, 'J., Sadato, N., & Hallett, M. (1995). Modeling other minds. *Neuroreport, 6,* 1741–1746.

Goldman-Rakic, P. S. (1987). Circuitry of the primate prefrontal cortex and regulation of behavior by representational memory. In F. Plum (Ed.), *Handbook of physiology: Vol. 5. The nervous system* (pp. 373–417). Bethesda, MD: American Physiological Society.

Goleman, D. (1995). *Emotional intelligence.* New York: Bantam Books.

Happé, F., Ehlers, S., Fletcher, P., Frith, U., Johansson, M., Gillberg, C., Dolan, R., Frackowiak, R., & Frith, C. (1996). "Theory of mind" in the brain. Evidence from a PET scan study of Asperger syndrome. *Neuroreport, 8,* 197–201.

Hoffman, J. L. (1949). Clinical observations concerning schizophrenic patients treated by prefrontal leukotomy. *New England Journal of Medicine, 241,* 233–236.

House, J. S., Landis, K. R., Umberson, D. (1988). Social relationships and health. *Science, 241,* 540–545.

Karmiloff-Smith, A. (1992). *Beyond modularity: A developmental perspective on cognitive science.* Cambridge, MA: MIT Press.

Lane, R. D. (1999). Neural correlates of conscious emotional experience. In R. Lane, L. Nadel, G. Ahern, J. Allen, A. Kaszniak, S. Rapscak, & G. E. Schwartz (Eds.), *Cognitive neuroscience of emotion* (pp. 345–370). New York: Oxford University Press.

Lane, R. D., Fink, G. R., Chua, P.M.L., & Dolan, R. J. (1997). Neural activation during selective attention to subjective emotional responses. *Neuroreport, 8,* 3969–3972.

Lane, R. D., Kevley, L. S., DuBois, M. A., Shamasundara, P., & Schwartz, G. E. (1995). Levels of emotional awareness and the degree of right hemispheric dominance in the perception of facial emotion. *Neuropsychologia, 33,* 525–528.

Lane, R. D., Quinlan, D. M., Schwartz, G. E., Walker, P. A., & Zeitlin, S. B. (1990). The Levels of Emotional Awareness Scale: A cognitive-developmental measure of emotion. *Journal of Personality Assessment, 55,* 124–134.

Lane, R. D., Reiman, E. M., Axelrod, B., Yun, L. S., Holmes, A., & Schwartz, G. E. (1998). Neural correlates of levels of emotional awareness: Evidence of an interaction between emotion and attention in the anterior cingulate cortex. *Journal of Cognitive Neuroscience, 10,* 525–535.

Lane, R. D., & Schwartz, G. E. (1987). Levels of emotional awareness: A cognitive-developmental theory and its application to psychopathology. *American Journal of Psychiatry, 144,* 133–143.

Lane, R. D., Sechrest, L., Reidel, R., Weldon, V., Kaszniak, A., & Schwartz, G. E. (1996). Impaired verbal and nonverbal emotion recognition in alexithymia. *Psychosomatic Medicine, 58,* 203–210.

Lane, R. D., Shapiro, D. E., Sechrest, L., & Riedel, R. (1998). Pervasive emotion recognition deficit common to alexithymia and repression. *Psychosomatic Medicine, 60,* 92.

Lang, P. J., Bradley, M. M., & Cuthbert, B. N. (1995). *The International Affective Picture System (IAPS): Photographic slides.* Gainsville, FL: University of Florida Center for Research in Psychophysiology.

Larsen, R. J., & Diener, E. (1987). Affect intensity as an individual difference characteristic: A review. *Journal of Research in Personality, 21,* 1–39.

Levine, D., Marziali, E., & Hood, J. (1997). Emotion processing in borderline personality disorders. *Journal of Nervous and Mental Disease, 185,* 240–246.

Loevinger, J., & Wessler, R. (1970). *Measuring ego development, Vol. 1. Construction and use of a sentence completion test.* San Francisco: Jossey-Bass.

Loevinger, J., Wessler, R., & Redmore, C. (1970). *Measuring ego development, Vol. 2. Scoring manual for women and girls.* San Francisco: Jossey-Bass.

Mayer, J. D., & Salovey, P. (1997). What is emotional intelligence? In P. Salovey & D. J. Sluyter (Eds.), *Emotional development and emotional intelligence* (pp. 3–31). New York: Basic Books.

Mayer, J. D., Salovey, P., & Caruso, D. (2000). Emotional intelligence. In R. J. Sternberg (Ed.), *Handbook of intelligence* (2nd ed., pp. 396–421). New York: Cambridge University Press.

Mazoyer B. M., Tzourio N., Frak V., Syrota A., Murayama, N., Levrier, D., Salamon, G., Dehaene, S., Cohen, L., & Mehler, J. (1993). The cortical representation of speech. *Journal of Cognitive Neuroscience, 5,* 467–469.

Papez, J. W. (1937). A proposed mechanism of emotion. *Archives of Neurology and Psychiatry, 38,* 725–734.

Price, J. L., Carmichael, S. T., & Drevets, W. C. (1996). Networks related to the orbital and medial prefrontal cortex; a substrate for emotional behavior? *Progress in Brain Research, 107,* 523–536.

Rau, J. C. (1993). Perception of verbal and nonverbal affective stimuli in complex partial seizure disorder. *Dissertation Abstracts International [B], 54,* 506B.

Salovey, P., & Mayer, J. D. (1990). Emotional intelligence. *Imagination, Cognition and Personality, 9,* 185–211.

Selman, R. L. (1981). The development of interpersonal competence: The role of understanding conduct. *Developmental Review, 1,* 401–422.

Shipley, W. (1940). A self-administering scale for measuring intellectual impairment and deterioration. *Journal of Psychology, 9,* 371–377.

Stern, D. N. (1985). *The interpersonal world of the infant: A view of psychoanalysis and developmental psychology.* New York: Basic Books.

Stuss, D. T. (1991a). Self, awareness, and the frontal lobes: A neuropsychological perspective. In J. Strauss & G. R. Goethals (Eds.), *The self: Interdisciplinary approaches* (pp. 255–278). New York: Springer-Verlag.

Stuss, D. T. (1991b). Disturbance of self-awareness after frontal system damage. In G. P. Prigatano & D. L. Schacter (Eds.), *Awareness of deficit after brain injury: Clinical and theoretical issues* (pp. 63–83). New York: Oxford University Press.

Teasdale, J. D., Howard, R. J., Cox, S. G., Ha, Y., Brammer, M. J., Williams, S.C.R., & Checkley, S. A. (1999). Functional MRI study of the cognitive generation of affect. *American Journal of Psychiatry, 156,* 209–215.

Vogt, B. A., Finch, D. M., & Olson, C. R. (1992). Functional heterogeneity in cingulate cortex: The anterior executive and posterior evaluative regions. *Cerebral Cortex, 2,* 435–443.

Vogt, B. A., & Gabriel, M. (1993). *Neurobiology of Cingulate Cortex and Limbic Thalamus.* Boston: Birkhauser.

Wechsler, D. (1981). *Manual for the Wechsler Adult Intelligence Scale—Revised (WAIS-R).* San Antonio, TX: Psychological Corporation.

Weiskrantz, L. (1997). *Consciousness lost and found: A neuropsychological exploration.* Oxford: Oxford University Press.

Werner, H., & Kaplan, B. (1963). *Symbol formation: An organismic-developmental approach to language and the expression of thought.* New York: John Wiley & Sons.

Wrana, C., Thomas, W., Heindichs, G., Huber, M., Obliers, R., Koerfer, A., & Köhle, K. (Leipzig, March 1998). Levels of Emotional Awareness Scale (LEAS): Ein Beitrag zur empirischen Überprüfung von Validität und Reliabilität einer deutschen Fassung [Contribution to the empirical study of the validity and reliability of a German version]. Postervortrag bei der 47 Arbeitstagung des Deutschen Kollegiums für Psychosomatische Medizin.

CHAPTER NINE

Poor Judgment in Spite of High Intellect

Neurological Evidence for Emotional Intelligence

Antoine Bechara, Daniel Tranel, and Antonio R. Damasio

There is no question that emotion plays a major role in influencing many of our everyday cognitive and behavioral functions, including memory and decision making. The importance of emotion in human affairs is obvious. Disorders of emotion plague patients with many neurological and psychiatric conditions. Despite the fundamental role that emotion plays in many cognitive, neurological, and psychiatric disorders, scientific study of the neural correlates of emotion and emotion's influence on thought and cognition has been largely ignored. Indeed, the study of emotion by researchers in cognitive science, neuroscience, and artificial intelligence has lagged behind the study of nearly all other major aspects of mind and brain. Given emotion's importance in the understanding of human suffering, its value in the management of disease, its role in social interactions, and its relevance to fundamental neuroscience and cognitive science, a comprehensive understanding of human cognition requires far greater knowledge of the neurobiology of emotion. In this chapter, we outline recent progress in understanding the role of emotion in cognition.

Over the past few years, we have begun to characterize the neurobiological basis of the decision-making impairment of patients with bilateral lesions of the ventromedial prefrontal cortex. This work is predicated on the availability of a theoretical framework, the somatic marker hypothesis (Damasio, 1994), which outlines a neural explanation for this decision-making impairment. One of the most intriguing conclusions from this work is that decision making is a process that depends on emotional signals, which we define as the bioregulatory responses that are aimed at maintaining homeostasis and ensuring survival. In fact, we have found that too little emotion has profoundly deleterious effects on decision making and may perhaps be just as bad as excessive emotion has long been considered to be.

One of the first and most famous cases of the so-called frontal lobe syndrome was the patient Phineas Gage, described by Harlow (Harlow, 1848, 1868). Phineas Gage was a dynamite worker and survived an explosion that blasted an iron tamping bar through the front of his head. Before the accident, Gage was a man of normal intelligence and energetic and persistent in executing all his plans of operation. He was responsible, sociable, and popular among peers and friends. After the accident, his medical recovery was remarkable. He survived the accident with normal intelligence, memory, speech, sensation, and movement. However, his behavior changed completely. He became irresponsible, untrustworthy, and impatient of restraint or advice when it conflicted with his desires.

Using modern neuroimaging techniques, Damasio and colleagues have recently reconstituted the accident by relying on measurements taken from Gage's skull (Damasio, Grabowski, Frank, Galburda, & Damasio, 1994). The key finding of this neuroimaging study was that the most likely placement of Gage's lesion was the bilateral ventromedial region of the prefrontal cortex. Interestingly, the case of Phineas Gage, and similar cases that were described after him, received little attention for many years. The revival of interest in this case and in various aspects of the "frontal lobe syndrome" came in studies by several investigators of patients like Phineas Gage (Benton, 1991; Eslinger & Damasio, 1985; Stuss, Gow, & Hetherington, 1992). The modern counterpart to Phineas Gage is the patient described by Eslinger and Damasio (Eslinger & Damasio, 1985). Over the years, we have studied numerous patients with ventromedial prefrontal lesions. Such patients develop severe impairments in personal and social decision making, in spite of otherwise largely preserved intellectual abilities. These patients were intelligent and creative before their brain damage. After the damage, they had difficulties planning their workday and future, and difficulties in choosing friends, partners, and activities. The actions they elect to pursue, often lead to losses of diverse order, for example, financial losses, losses in social standing, and losses of family and friends. The choices they make are no longer advantageous and are remarkably different from the kinds of choices they were known to make before their brain injuries. These patients often decide against their best interests. They are unable to learn from previous mistakes, as reflected by repeated engagement in decisions that lead to negative consequences. In striking contrast to this real-life decision-making impairment, the patients perform normally in most laboratory tests of problem solving. Their intellect remains normal, as measured by conventional clinical neuropsychological tests.

STATEMENT OF THE PROBLEM

The class of patients with ventromedial prefrontal cortex lesions presents a puzzling defect. It is difficult to explain their disturbance in terms of defects in knowledge pertinent to the situation or in terms of deficient general intellectual ability. The disturbance also cannot be explained in terms of impaired language comprehension or expression, working memory, or attention. For many years, the condition of these patients has posed a double challenge. First, although the decision-making impairment is obvious in the real-world behavior of these patients, there has been no effective laboratory probe to detect and measure this impairment. Second, there has been no satisfactory theoretical account of the neural and cognitive mechanisms underlying the impairment. Over the past few years, we have begun to overcome these challenges. We have developed the "gambling task," which enabled us to detect these patients' elusive impairment in the laboratory, measure it, and investigate its possible causes (Bechara, Damasio, Damasio, & Anderson, 1994). We have also made progress in understanding the nature of this impairment at the behavioral, psychophysiological, and cognitive levels. Why was the gambling task successful in detecting the decision-making impairment in these patients, and why is it important for the study of the neurology of decision making? Perhaps because the gambling task mimics real-life decisions so closely. The task is carried out in real time, and it resembles real-world contingencies. It factors reward and punishment (winning and losing money) in such a way that creates a conflict between an immediate, luring reward and a delayed, probabilistic punishment. Therefore, the task engages the subject in a quest to make advantageous choices. As in real-life choices, the task offers choices that may be risky, and there is no obvious explanation of how, when, or what to choose. Each choice is full of uncertainty because a precise calculation or prediction of the outcome of a given choice is not possible. The way that one can do well on this task is to follow one's "hunches" and "gut feelings."

BACKGROUND

We have been using a theoretical framework known as the *somatic marker hypothesis* to investigate the neural basis of decision making (Damasio, 1994). The somatic marker hypothesis posits that the neural basis of the decision-making impairment characteristic of patients with ventromedial prefrontal lobe damage is defective activation of somatic states (emotional signals) that attach value to given options and scenarios, which function as covert, or overt, biases for guiding decisions. Deprived of such somatic states, patients must rely on slow cost-benefit analyses of various conflicting options. These options may be too numerous, and their analysis may be too lengthy to permit rapid, on-line decisions to take place appropriately. Patients may resort to decisions based on the immediate reward of an option, or they may fail to decide altogether if many options have the same basic value. The failure to enact somatic states, and consequently to decide advantageously, results from dysfunction in a neural system in which the ventromedial prefrontal cortex is a critical component. Other neural regions, including the amygdala and somatosensory cortices (SI, SII, and insula), are also components of this same neural system (Figure 9.1), although the different regions may provide different contributions to the overall process of decision making (Bechara, Damasio, Damasio, & Lee, 1999).

Mechanisms of arousal, attention, and memory are also necessary to evoke and display the representations of various options and scenarios when contemplating a decision. However, another mechanism is necessary for weighing these various options and for selecting the most advantageous response. This mechanism for selecting good from bad is what we call decision making, and the physiological changes occurring in association with the behavioral selection are part of what we call somatic states. In this chapter, we outline studies aimed at addressing these main questions: (1) What is the evidence that emotion is a crucial ingredient in the process of decision making? (2) What brain lesions are associated with impairments in decision making? (3) The disruption of what aspect of the emotional process causes impairments in decision making?

BIASES GUIDE DECISIONS

Situations involving personal and social matters are strongly associated with positive and negative emotions. Reward or punishment, pleasure or pain, happiness or sadness all produce changes in body states, and these changes are expressed as emotions. We believe that such prior emotional experiences often come into play when we are deliberating a decision. Whether these emotions remain unconscious or are perceived consciously in the form of feelings, they provide the go, stop, and turn signals needed for making advantageous decisions. In other words, the activation of these somatic states provides "biasing" signals that covertly or overtly mark various options and scenarios with a value. Accordingly, these biases assist in the selection of advantageous responses from among an array of available options. Deprived of these biases or somatic markers, response options become more or less equalized, and decisions become dependent on a slow, reasoned cost-benefit analysis of numerous and often conflicting options. At the end, the result is an inadequate selection of a response. In the following sections, we describe studies that support the idea that decision making is a process guided by emotions.

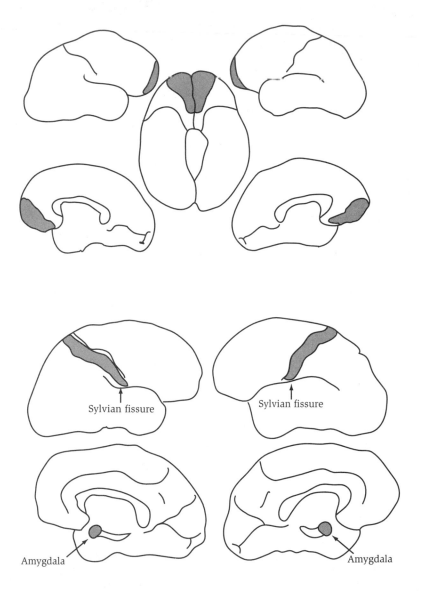

Figure 9.1. *Top panel:* The shaded areas represent the ventromedial prefrontal cortex. The top two schematics show external (lateral) views of the brain. The lower two schematics show the brain spilt in half and exposing the internal (medial) views of the brain. The center schematic provides a view of the brain from below. *Lower panel:* Schematics of lateral and medial views of the brain. The dark circles represent the position of the amygdala. The elongated structures attached to the amygdala (dark circles) mark the position of the hippocampus. The shaded areas cover the primary somatosensory cortices (SI). Other somatosensory areas, namely SII and the insula, are buried inside the Sylvian fissure and cannot be seen unless the lateral surface of the brain is removed.

The Gambling Task

A detailed account of the gambling task can be found elsewhere (Bechara et al., 1994, 1999). Briefly the task involves four decks of cards named A, B, C, and D. The goal in the task is to maximize profit on a loan of play money. Subjects are required to make a series of 100 card selections. However, they are not told ahead of time how many card selections they must make. Subjects can select one card at a time from any deck they choose, and they are free to switch from one deck to any another at any time, and as often as they wish. However, the subject's decision to select from one deck versus another is largely influenced by various schedules of immediate reward and future punishment. These schedules are preprogrammed and known to the examiner, but not to the subject, and they entail the following principles.

Every time the subject selects a card from deck A or deck B, the subject gets $100. Every time the subject selects a card from deck C or deck D, the subject gets $50. However, in each of the four decks, subjects encounter unpredictable punishments (money loss). The punishment is set to be higher in the high-paying decks (A and B), and lower in the low-paying decks (C and D). For example, if ten cards were picked from deck A, one would earn $1,000. However, in those ten picks, five unpredictable punishments would be encountered, ranging from $150 to $350, resulting in a total cost of $1,250. Deck B is similar: every ten cards that are picked from deck B would earn $1,000; however, these ten picks would encounter one high punishment of $1,250. On the other hand, every ten cards from deck C or D earn only $500, but only cost $250 in punishment. Hence, decks A and B are disadvantageous because they cost more in the long run: one loses $250 every ten cards. Decks C and D are advantageous because they result in an overall gain in the long run: one wins $250 every ten cards. We have recently devised a computerized version of the task with slightly different schedules of reward and punishment; however, the basic principles of the task remain unchanged.

We investigated the performance of this task by normal controls and patients with ventromedial prefrontal cortex lesions. Normal subjects avoided the bad decks (A and B) and preferred the good decks (C and D). In sharp contrast, the patients with ventromedial lesions did not avoid the bad decks (A and B); indeed, they preferred them (Figure 9.2). From these results, we suggested that the patients' performance profile is comparable to their real-life inability to decide advantageously. This is especially true in personal and social matters, a domain for which in life, as in the task, an exact calculation of the future outcomes is not possible and choices must be based on hunches and gut feelings.

Anticipatory Psychophysiological Responses as Indices of Emotional Signals (Biases)

In light of the finding that the gambling task is laboratory instrument that detects the decision-making impairment of patients with ventromedial lesions,

Normal Control
(*n* = 13)

Ventromedial Prefrontal (VM)
(*n* = 6)

▲ Disadvantageous Decks (A & B)

─○─ Advantageous Decks (C & D)

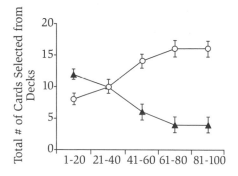
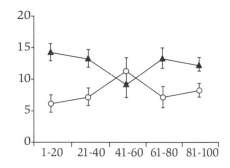

Order of Card Selection from the 1st to the 100th Trial

Figure 9.2. Card selection on the gambling task as a function of group (normal control, ventromedial prefrontal), deck type (disadvantageous versus advantageous), and trial block. Normal control subjects shifted their selection of cards toward the advantageous decks. The patients with ventromedial prefrontal cortex lesions did not make a reliable shift and opted for the disadvantageous decks.

we went on to address the question of whether the impairment is linked to a failure in somatic signaling (Bechara, Tranel, Damasio, & Damasio, 1996).

To address this question we added a physiological measure to the gambling task. The goal was to assess somatic state activation while subjects were making decisions during the gambling task. We studied two groups: normal subjects and patients with ventromedial lesions. We had them perform the gambling task while we recorded their electrodermal activity in the form of skin conductance responses (SCRs). As the body begins to change as a result of a thought, and as a given emotion begins to be enacted, the autonomic nervous system begins to increase the activity in the skin's sweat glands. Although this sweating activity is relatively small and not observable by the naked eye, it can be amplified and recorded by a polygraph as a wave. The amplitude of this wave can be measured and thus provide an indirect measure of the emotion experienced by the subject.

Both normal subjects and the patients with ventromedial lesions generated SCRs after they had picked a card and were told that they won or lost money. The most important difference, however, was that normal subjects, as they became experienced with the task, began to generate SCRs *prior* to the selection of any cards (such as during the time when they were pondering from which deck to choose). These anticipatory SCRs were more pronounced before picking a card from the risky decks (A and B) compared to the safe decks (C and D). In other words, these anticipatory SCRs were like "gut feelings" that warned the subject against picking from the bad decks. Frontal patients failed to generate such SCRs before picking a card. This failure to generate SCRs *before* picking cards from the bad decks correlates with their failure to avoid these bad decks and choose advantageously in this task (Figure 9.3). These results provide strong support for the notion that decision making is guided by emotional signals (gut feelings) that are generated in anticipation of future events.

Biases Do Not Need to Be Conscious

Further experiments revealed that the biasing somatic signals (gut feelings) do not need to be perceived consciously. We carried out an experiment similar to the previous one, in which we tested normal subjects and patients with ventromedial lesions on the gambling task while recording their SCRs. However, every time the subject picked ten cards from the decks, we stopped the game briefly and asked the subject to declare whatever he or she knew about what was going on in the game (Bechara, Damasio, Tranel, & Damasio, 1997). From

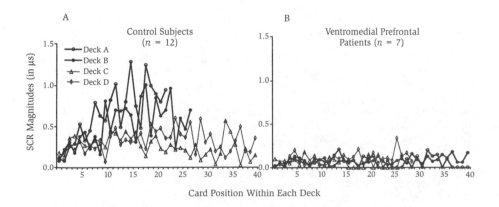

Figure 9.3. Magnitudes of anticipatory skin conductance responses (SCRs) as a function of deck and card position within each deck. Data from controls are shown in (A); data from patients with ventromedial prefrontal cortex lesions are shown in (B). Note that control subjects gradually began to generate high-amplitude SCRs to the disadvantageous decks. The patients with ventromedial prefrontal lesions failed to do so.

the answers to the questions, we were able to distinguish four periods as subjects went from the first to the last trial in the task. The first was a prepunishment period during which subjects sampled the decks and before they had yet encountered any punishment. The second was a prehunch period in which subjects began to encounter punishment, but when asked about what was going on in the game, they did not know. The third was a hunch period during which subjects began to express a hunch about which decks were riskier, but they were not sure. The fourth was a conceptual period during which subjects knew very well the contingencies in the task, which decks were good, which decks were bad, and why this was so (Figure 9.4).

When examining the anticipatory SCRs from each period, we found that there was no significant activity during the prepunishment period. These were expected results because, at this stage, the subjects were picking cards and gaining money and had not yet encountered losses. There was a substantial rise in anticipatory responses for the control subjects during the prehunch period (for example, after encountering some money losses, but still before the subject knew what was going on in the game). This SCR activity was sustained for the remaining periods (during the hunch and then during the conceptual period). When

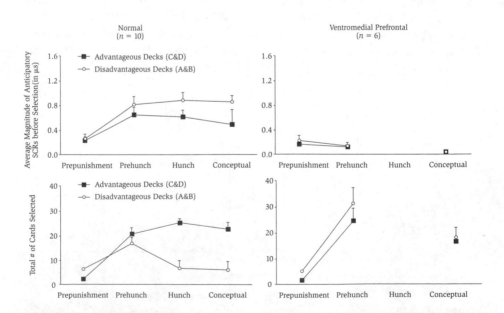

Figure 9.4. Anticipatory skin conductance responses (SCRs) and behavioral responses (card selection) as a function of four periods (prepunishment, prehunch, hunch, and conceptual) from normal control subjects and patients with ventromedial prefrontal lesions.

examining the behavior during each period, we found that there was a preference of control subjects for the high-paying decks (A and B) during the prepunishment period, although there was the beginning of a shift in the pattern of card selection, away from the bad decks, even in the prehunch period. This shift in preference for the good decks became more pronounced during the hunch and conceptual periods. The patients with ventromedial lesions, on the other hand, never reported a hunch about which decks were good or bad. Furthermore, they never developed anticipatory SCRs, and they continued to choose more cards from the bad decks (A and B) relative to the good decks (C and D).

An especially intriguing observation was that not all the normal control subjects were able to figure out the task, explicitly, in the sense that they did not reach the conceptual period. Only 70 percent of them were able to do so. Although 30 percent of controls did not reach the conceptual period, they still performed advantageously. On the other hand, 50 percent of the patients with ventromedial lesions were able to reach the conceptual period and state explicitly which decks were good and which ones were bad and why. Although 50 percent of the patients did reach the conceptual period, they still performed disadvantageously. After the experiment, when these patients were asked why they continued to pick from the decks they thought were bad, they offered excuses such as "I was trying to figure out would happen if I kept playing the $100 decks," or "I wanted to recover my losses fast, and the $50 decks are too slow."

These results show that the patients with ventromedial lesions continued to choose disadvantageously in the gambling task, even after realizing explicitly the consequences of their action. This suggests that the anticipatory SCRs represent unconscious biases derived from prior experiences with reward and punishment. These biases (or gut feelings) help deter the normal subjects from pursuing a course of action that is disadvantageous in the future. This occurs even before the subjects become aware of the goodness or badness of the choice they are about to make. Without these biases, the knowledge of what is right and what is wrong may still become available. However, by itself, this knowledge is not sufficient to ensure an advantageous behavior. Therefore, although the patient with a ventromedial lesion may manifest declarative knowledge of what is right and what is wrong, he or she fails to act accordingly. Thus, they may "say" the right thing, but they "do" the wrong thing.

A NEURAL SYSTEM FOR DECISION MAKING

A detailed account of the somatic marker hypothesis is found elsewhere (Damasio, 1994). Based on neuroanatomy from nonhuman primates, the ventromedial prefrontal cortex receives projections from all sensory modalities, directly or indirectly. In addition, the ventromedial cortex has extensive bidirectional connections with the amygdala, an almond-shaped structure that is important for emotion. Also, it has extensive bidirectional connections with the somatosensory (SI and SII) and insular cortices. When a person is confronted with a decision and the ventromedial prefrontal cortex is activated, one or both of the following chains of physiological events take place (Figure 9.5).

In one chain, an appropriate emotional (somatic) state is actually reenacted, and signals from its activation are then relayed back to subcortical and cortical somatosensory processing structures, especially in the somatosensory (SI and SII) and insular cortices. This anatomical system is described as the *body loop*. The enacted somatic state can then act consciously or nonconsciously on the neural processes that enable the person to do or to avoid doing a certain action.

After emotions have been expressed and experienced at least once, one can form representations of these emotional experiences in the somatosensory/insular cortices. Therefore, after emotions are learned, one possible chain of physiological events is to bypass the body altogether, activate the insular/somatosensory cortices directly, and create a fainter image of an emotional body state than if the emotion were actually expressed in the body. This anatomical system is described as the *as if body loop*.

Thus, the neural network mediating the activation of emotional (somatic) states involves numerous neural regions. The ventromedial prefrontal cortex is one critical region. However, there are other critical components in this neural network. The following are investigations pertaining to two critical structures.

The Amygdala

Central autonomic structures, such as the amygdala, can activate somatic responses in the viscera, vascular bed, endocrine system, and nonspecific neurotransmitter systems. Furthermore, the amygdala plays an important role in emotion, as demonstrated repeatedly in various lesion and functional neuroimaging studies (Davidson & Irwin, 1999). Therefore, we tested the hypothesis that the amygdala plays a role in decision making. Using the gambling task as a tool for measuring decision making, we investigated a group of patients with bilateral amygdala lesions, and a group of demographically and educationally matched normal subjects. We monitored the SCR activity of these subjects during their performance of the gambling task. The results showed that normal controls selected more cards from the advantageous decks C and D (low immediate gain, but larger future yield), and fewer cards from the disadvantageous decks A and B (high immediate gain, but larger future loss). Similar to the patients with bilateral lesions of the ventromedial prefrontal cortex, the patients with amygdala lesions did the opposite and selected more cards from the disadvantageous decks as compared to the advantageous decks.

When examining the anticipatory SCRs, the patients with amygdala lesions were similar to the patients with ventromedial lesions in that they also failed

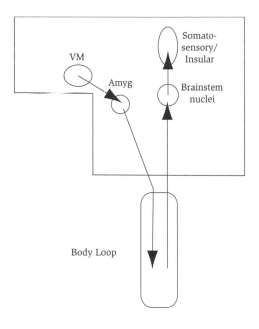

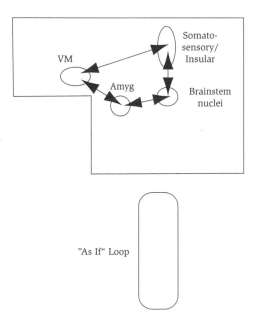

Figure 9.5. Simple diagrams illustrating the *body loop* and *as if loop* chains of physiological events. In both panels, the brain is represented by the top black perimeter and the body by the bottom one. VM, ventromedial prefrontal cortex; Amyg, amygdala.

to generate anticipatory SCRs before the selection of a card (Bechara et al., 1999). The results support the hypothesis that the amygdala is a critical component of a system involved in decision making. However, as we explain later, the underlying mechanism responsible for the decision-making impairment in patients with amygdala lesions may be different from patients with ventromedial lesions.

The Somatosensory/Insular Cortices

The somatosensory and insular cortices receive signals from the soma (the body). Furthermore, based on studies from patients with lesions in the right somatosensory/insular cortices, it has been proposed that these areas may hold representations of the body states such as those occurring during the experience of an emotion (Damasio, 1994). Indeed, anosognosia is a neurological condition resulting from dysfunction of the right hemisphere (damage to somatosensory cortices) in which the patient is paralyzed on the left side of the body. The anosognosic patient cannot move the left hand and arm, or the left leg and foot. The left half of the face may also be immobile, and the patient is unable to stand or walk. Yet, this same patient is oblivious to the entire problem, reporting that nothing is wrong, and it is only when confronted with his or her blatant problem that the patient begins to admit that something may be wrong. In other words, these patients are unable to sense the defect automatically, rapidly, and internally through the body sensory system. Not only this, those with anosognosia are unable to make appropriate decisions on personal and social matters, just as in the case of patients with ventromedial lesions, except that this defect is less noticeable. The reason is that patients with ventromedial lesions appear neurologically normal and thus can engage in a variety of social interactions that can easily expose their impaired judgment and decision making. On the other hand, patients with anosognosia are considered sick because of their motor and sensory impairments and are thus limited in the range of social interactions in which they can engage. In other words, their opportunity to place themselves in situations that lead to negative consequences is reduced. On the basis of these clinical observations, we hypothesized that these somatosensory structures are critical for decision making and somatic state activation. We administered the gambling task to a group of patients with right- or left-sided lesions in the somatosensory/insular cortices, and to a demographically and educationally matched group of normal subjects. We monitored the SCR activity of these subjects during their performance of the gambling task (Bechara, Tranel, Damasio, & Damasio, 1997). Patients with left lesions performed like normal subjects on the gambling task. By contrast, patients with right lesions did the opposite and selected more cards from the disadvantageous decks as compared to the advantageous decks. As in the case of the patients with ventromedial and amygdala lesions, those with right (but not left) somatosensory/insular lesions failed to generate anticipatory SCRs before the selection of a card. This supports the hypothesis that the right somatosensory/insular cortices are critical components of a system involved in decision making. However, as we explain later, the underlying mechanism responsible for this decision-making impairment is perhaps different from that in the amygdala or the ventromedial prefrontal cortex.

Different Lesions Disrupt Different Aspects of the Emotional Process

It is apparent that emotion is not a unitary process, and various studies have shown that it consists of several dissectable components (Davidson & Irwin, 1999; LeDoux, 1996). There are many different aspects of emotion. One aspect includes the ability to perceive or recognize emotions in facial expressions. In the social realm, when seeing the face of an angry person, it is important to recognize and interpret the intention of that person from the facial expression of the emotion and then behave accordingly. Another aspect of emotional processing is the ability to attach emotional significance to events that are otherwise neutral (conditioning). As an example, going to a fast food restaurant on a given night of the week may be a neutral routine event. However, one night while a person was eating, an argument between two individuals led to a fight at the restaurant, guns were used, and a stray bullet hit that person in the arm. If that person passes by that restaurant again (a previously neutral place), he or she may experience intense fear. Imagine that this person could not form an association between that particular restaurant and fear. The person may decide to go back again to that restaurant and be subjected to another harmful experience. A third aspect of emotional processing that is important for decision making is the ability to experience emotions from recalling previous emotional events. Suppose that a few months later the same person is at a different restaurant and two patrons begin to fight. Recalling the previous restaurant experience may evoke a feeling of fear, which may influence the decision to finish the meal or leave the restaurant. If recalling that previous experience does not evoke fear, the person may ignore the fight, continue to eat, and risk more harm.

These are simple examples that illustrate how different aspects of emotional processing can influence decision making. In everyday life decisions, the emotion need not be fear induced by a gunshot; it can be sadness from the loss of a large sum of money, happiness from winning a prestigious award, or satisfaction from a smile from a content boss. Similarly, the decision need not be about entering or leaving a particular restaurant; it can be about accepting a new job, pursuing new goals, or helping to elect an official. In all these instances, positive or negative emotions may be evoked. If one mechanism of emotional processing is defective, then the process of somatic state activation becomes altered, and the quality of decision making becomes compromised. In the following studies, we sought to link the decision-making impairment of patients with different brain lesions to deficits in different aspects of the emotional process.

The Recognition of Emotions in Facial Expressions. In these experiments, three groups of target patients were used. The patients had lesions in one of the following areas: (1) bilateral lesions of the ventromedial cortex, (2) bilateral lesions of the amygdala, or (3) lesions of the right somatosensory/insular cortices. These patients were shown pictures of emotional facial expressions, and they were asked to rate how intense the emotion was in each picture. The results indicate that patients with ventromedial lesions are not impaired in this capacity (R. Adolphs, personal communication, 1998, but see Rolls, 1999, for an exception). However, the amygdala has been shown to be essential for the recognition of emotions in facial expressions, especially fear (Adolphs, Tranel, Damasio, & Damasio, 1995), and in judging the trustworthiness of a given individual (Adolphs, Tranel, & Damasio, 1998). Similarly, the right somatosensory/insular cortices have been shown to play a role in the recognition of emotions in facial expressions (Adolphs, Damasio, Tranel, & Damasio, 1996).

These results suggest that the amygdala and right somatosensory/insular cortices are important for this aspect of emotional processing (the recognition of emotions in facial expressions). Although these experiments do not directly address the question of whether an inability to recognize and interpret the emotion in a facial expression results in an impairment in decision making on the gambling task, such results indicate that the neural substrates subserving these aspects of emotional processing and decision making overlap. In short, a defect in emotional processing can have adverse consequences on social decision making. Indeed, the recognition of emotions in faces is crucial for the ability to read and interpret the emotions of others, which is very essential for making social decisions.

Emotional Conditioning. We used a fear-conditioning paradigm to test whether impaired decision making associated with a given brain lesion is due to a defect in the ability to attach emotional significance to certain events (emotional conditioning). The paradigm consisted of the use of four different colors of monochrome slides as conditioned stimuli (CS), and a startlingly loud sound (100 db) as the unconditioned stimulus (US). SCR activity served as an index of emotional response (Bechara et al., 1995). In this procedure, the different color slides were presented to the subjects in random order. Initially, none of these slides evoked SCRs, because they were neutral. However, every time one of the colors (blue) appeared on the screen, the loud sound followed the presentation of the slide. Hearing the loud sound inevitably caused the subject to startle, and a large SCR was evoked. After the blue slide was paired with the US (the loud sound) a few times, the blue slide was no longer neutral. Subsequently, in normal individuals when the blue slide was shown alone (without being followed by the loud sound), it began to evoke SCRs. In other words, the blue slide acquired new emotional attributes from being paired with the loud sound.

Using this emotional conditioning procedure, we tested three groups of target patients with lesions in one of the following areas: (1) bilateral lesions of the ventromedial cortex, (2) bilateral lesions of the amygdala, or (3) lesions of the right somatosensory/insular cortices. The results showed that patients with bilateral ventromedial prefrontal cortex lesions did acquire the conditioning, and so did the patients with right somatosensory/insular cortex lesions. In other words, these patients began to evoke SCRs when seeing the CS, the blue slide. The only group that did not acquire the conditioning was the one with bilateral amygdala lesions. These patients evoked large SCRs when they heard the loud sound itself. However, they failed to evoke SCRs when they saw the blue slide. When asked questions about which slide was associated with the loud sound, which slides were not, and what color the slides were, the patients could remember perfectly these facts from the experiment. In other words, these patients were able to remember the facts, but they failed to attach an emotional attribute to the blue slide. This finding suggests that the amygdala is a crucial structure for this aspect of emotional processing, that is, emotional conditioning. Consequently, it is reasonable to assume that the failure of these patients to acquire anticipatory SCRs in the gambling task, and their decision-making impairment in real life, is the indirect result of this failure to acquire conditioned emotional responses.

The Experience of Emotions. We used emotional imagery to test whether impaired decision making associated with a given brain lesion is due to a defect in the ability to evoke an emotion from recalling a previous emotional experience. In this emotional imagery procedure, the subjects were asked to think about a situation in their life in which they felt each of the following emotions: happiness, sadness, fear, and anger. After a brief description of each story was obtained, the subjects were then put to a physiological test. They were asked to image and reexperience each emotional scenario; while doing this, SCR activity was monitored to obtain some objective measure of the emotion they were experiencing. As a control condition, the same subjects were asked to recall and image a nonemotional experience, such as getting up in the morning, showering, dressing, having breakfast, and then going to work. At the end of the imagery of the emotional situation, the subjects were asked to rate how much they "felt" the target emotion (on a scale of 0 to 4).

Using this procedure, we tested the same three groups of target patients with lesions in one of the following areas: (1) bilateral lesions of the ventromedial prefrontal cortex, (2) bilateral lesions of the amygdala, or (3) lesions of the right somatosensory/insular cortices. The patients with ventromedial and amygdala lesions were able to retrieve previous emotional experiences. They gave high subjective ratings and generated high SCR activity during the imagery of the angry relative to the neutral situations. Although all the patients with ventro-medial and amygdala lesions reliably experienced anger, the reexperience of fear was less reliable. Some could not reexperience fear at all, and those who could did so with a less intense response (when the response was compared to the angry emotion). The patients with ventromedial lesions had difficulties conjur-ing up the emotions of happy and sad situations, whereas some of the patients with amygdala lesions were able to conjure up happy and sad emotions. These findings suggest that damage to either the ventromedial prefrontal cortex or the amygdala weakens the ability to reexperience an emotion from the recall of a previous emotional event. This weakness can contribute to the failure of these patients to activate appropriate somatic states and implement advantageous deci-sions. However, the fact that these patients are not completely emotionless, and that they can recall and reexperience emotions to some degree, suggests that this weakness is not the sole factor responsible for the impaired decision making.

In contrast, the patients with lesions in the right somatosensory/insular cor-tices were able to recall emotional situations that occurred before their brain lesion (such as weddings, funerals, or car accidents). However, they had diffi-culties reexperiencing the emotion associated with that situation (Damasio, Bechara, Tranel, & Damasio, 1997; Tranel, Bechara, Damasio, & Damasio, 1998). None of these patients was able to evoke changes in their SCR activity when recalling any of the target emotions. Consequently, these patients gave low sub-jective ratings of the imagery of these emotions. This suggests that the right somatosensory/insular cortices are critical for this aspect of emotional pro-cessing, that is, evoking emotions from an imagined scenario. Consequently, it is reasonable to assume that the failure of right insular/somatosensory cortex patients to acquire anticipatory SCRs in the gambling task, and their decision-making impairment, is the indirect result of this failure to conjure up the somatic state of a previous emotional situation.

Nature of the Decision-Making Deficit in Frontal Patients

Our studies suggest that the decision-making impairment associated with amyg-dala damage may result from the failure to acquire conditioned emotional responses. The decision-making impairment associated with damage of right somatosensory/insular cortices may result from a failure to reexperience the emotion of a previous emotional event. On the other hand, the decision-making impairment associated with ventromedial prefrontal cortex damage remains unspecified. Here we consider some possible mechanisms.

Impulsiveness and Response Inhibition. *Impulsiveness* is a poorly defined term, but it is often linked to the function of the prefrontal cortex (Fuster, 1996; Miller, 1992), and it usually means the lack of response inhibition. The behavior of patients with ventromedial lesions on the gambling task, and in real life, can be viewed as similar to the impulsive behavior of a child who sees a candy on the table but has been told by the parent "No, you must eat dinner first, or you will be punished." The child understands the information and may deliberate for a short while, but after two minutes, he can no longer resist the temptation, delay the gratification, and inhibit his response to reach for the candy. The child gets up and reaches for the candy. Similarly, when the patients with ventromedial lesions are presented with a deck of cards with a large immediate reward, but which may have a large future loss, the patients seek the reward. This is also true of the real-life behavior of these patients. They seem unable to delay the gratification of the reward for very long, as indicated by their tendency to return quickly and more often to the decks that yield high immediate reward, but an even larger future loss. However, the unanswered question in this context is the following: what is the nature of the mechanism that decides when to suppress, or not to suppress, a certain response, such as the seeking of a large immediate reward? We argue that the nature of this mechanism is a somatic state, in other words, an emotional signal.

Using the impulsive behavior of the child with the candy as an illustrative example, one can see the conflict created by the decision to reach, or not reach, for the candy. On the one hand, there are positive somatic states generated by the immediate and available reward (the candy). On the other hand, there are negative somatic states generated by the delayed and absent punishment posed by the parent. If the threat of punishment is severe enough, then the evoked negative somatic states from the threat of punishment will counteract the positive somatic states produced by the immediate reward. The choice to seek the reward would thus be marked with a negative value, and the response to reach for the immediate reward may be inhibited. However, if the situation is that of a mild punishment, which would let the immediate reward outweigh the future punishment, the negative somatic states triggered by the possible punishment might not be sufficiently strong to counteract the positive states triggered by the immediate reward. In this case, the choice would be marked with a positive value, and the response should not be inhibited. This example illustrates two different readings of the same situation involving an immediate reward and a future punishment. In one, the inhibition of the action to seek the reward should be inhibited, whereas in the other, there is a good reason to seek the reward. The construct of impulsiveness by itself does not explain when to inhibit, or not to inhibit, a given response. However, the activation of somatic states provides the important signals that help decide whether to inhibit, or not to inhibit, the response under consideration. Therefore, although one might be able to say that the decision-making impairment in patients with ventromedial lesions may be due to their impulsiveness, the unanswered question remains: why do they fail to activate somatic states, that is, to generate anticipatory SCRs? High-order conditioning is one possible explanation.

High-Order Conditioning. Studies have shown consistently that monkeys with lesions of the amygdala have an increased tendency to approach objects such as snakes (Aggleton, 1992), as if the object of fear can no longer evoke a state of fear. Using a parallel line of reasoning, it is conceivable and even likely that humans learn throughout development to associate the idea of winning and losing money with items that represent actual, innate, and immediate (or *primary*) reward and punishment, such as food, shelter, sex, pain, and so forth. When the amygdala is damaged, such items can no longer evoke the appropriate somatic states of reward and punishment, just like an object of fear can no longer elicit the state of fear in an amygdalatomized monkey. Consequently, the concepts of winning and losing money can no longer elicit the appropriate somatic states. On the other hand, when the ventromedial cortex is damaged, we believe that the concepts of winning and losing money can still evoke appropriate somatic states. However, if new exteroceptive information is associated with a punishment such as losing money, which is abstract, learned, and remote (or *secondary*), then these patients begin to show impairments. In other words, they fail to couple exteroceptive information (the bad decks) with the somatic state of a secondary punishment (money loss).

To test this idea, we studied a group of patients with bilateral amygdala but not ventromedial prefrontal cortex damage, and a group of patients with bilateral lesions of the ventromedial prefrontal cortex but not amygdala damage. We used the gambling task to measure decision-making performance and SCR activity as an index of somatic state activation (Bechara et al., 1999). Consistent with our hypothesis, we found that patients with amygdala lesions failed to generate SCRs when they won or lost money in the gambling task. Such a failure to evoke somatic states when winning and losing money precluded the development of the anticipatory SCRs necessary for learning to choose advantageously in the gambling task. By contrast, patients with ventromedial lesions did generate SCRs when they won or lost money. However, the problem was in the development of anticipatory SCRs. Normal subjects formed associations between new stimuli (decks of cards) and the somatic states evoked by a secondary punishment (losing money). Consequently, normal subjects began to generate somatic states whenever they contemplated selection of cards from the decks associated with large money loss (they generated anticipatory SCRs), and they also learned to avoid such decks. By contrast, patients with ventromedial lesions failed to generate anticipatory SCRs when selecting from a losing deck, and consequently they continued to select cards from the losing decks.

These results suggest that the amygdala and ventromedial prefrontal cortex are both essential for the coupling of exteroceptive information with interoceptive information concerning somatic states. These somatic states serve to bias the decision-making process toward an advantageous course of action. The difference, however, between the amygdala and the ventromedial prefrontal cortex is the following: in the case of the amygdala, the defect is in coupling the exteroceptive information with somatic states generated by a *primary* punishment; in the case of the ventromedial prefrontal cortex, the defect is in coupling exteroceptive information with somatic states evoked by a *secondary* punishment.

The proposal that the ventromedial prefrontal cortex couples exteroceptive information with the somatic state of abstract, learned, and remote punishment as opposed to the amygdala, which couples exteroceptive information with the somatic state of actual, innate, and immediate punishment, is significant. This distinction may reflect two types of decision-making deficit observable in the behaviors of real-life activities of these patients. The decision-making impairments of patients with ventromedial cortex lesions have remote consequences and usually do not cause bodily harm. For instance, patients with these lesions make choices that lead to long-term financial losses, or to the loss of friend and family relationships, but rarely engage in actions that may lead to physical harm for themselves or others. In other words, the type of decision impairment that they exhibit in real life is related to secondary as opposed to primary reward and punishment. On the other hand, although patients with bilateral amygdala lesions do exhibit decision-making impairments in the social realm similar to those of the patients with ventromedial lesions, they tend to pursue actions that eventually lead to physical harm to themselves and others. Several of the patients with amygdala lesions who participated in our studies live under supervised care and are unable to function alone in society. In some cases, some of these patients have pursued actions that endangered themselves and others.

CONCLUSION

Although studies of emotional intelligence are relatively new, several competing models of emotional intelligence already exist (for example, Mayer, Salovey & Caruso, 2000). Our studies of neurological patients cannot speak in favor of one model of emotional intelligence over another. However, our research does provide strong support for the main concept of emotional intelligence, which may be viewed as a collection of emotional abilities that constitute a form of intelligence that is different from cognitive intelligence or IQ. This emotional intelligence enables the individual to be more socially effective than other individuals in certain aspects of social life. Indeed, the patients with ventromedial prefrontal cortex lesions whom we described in this chapter provide a clear illustration of how good knowledge and high IQ alone are not sufficient for implementing advantageous decisions in real life. These patients suffer from a specific deficit in their ability to process emotional signals. The consequences are a severe compromise in the ability to cope effectively with environmental and social demands. This provides strong support for the idea that emotions are the ingredients for a distinct form of ability that is critical for overall intelligence in social life.

It is important to draw a distinction between the research approach we took with neurological patients, and the approach taken in many other studies of emotional intelligence. Our research focused on isolating defects in simpler mechanisms of emotion, such as those we outlined in this chapter. Emotional intelligence research has focused on much more sophisticated, complex, and psychological forms of emotionality. Good examples of these complex forms of emotionality are those described by Bar-On (Chapter Seventeen), such as (1) the ability to be aware, to understand, and to express one's self; (2) the ability to be aware, to understand, and to accept the feelings and emotions of others; (3) the ability to resist and delay gratification; (4) the ability to generate positive feelings; and (5) the ability to adapt and change one's emotions to changing external demands and contingencies. However, we believe that defects in the simple mechanisms of emotions we identified can be manifested at a higher level as defects in the emotional factors that Bar-On outlines. For example, the first factor outlined by Bar-On is reminiscent of the defect of anosognosic patients who do not sense their severe body defect automatically, rapidly, and internally through the body sensory system and therefore do not realize that there is something wrong with them. The patients with ventromedial prefrontal cortex are similar to those with anosognosia in this respect: they are usually indifferent to their health status and seem to have an unusual tolerance for pain. Bar-On's second factor can be explained by the findings that many of our patients have defects in their ability to recognize emotions in facial expressions. A defect in such a mechanism inevitably translates into a poor ability to understand and interpret the emotions of others. The mechanisms of impulsiveness and response inhibition that we discussed are relevant to the third factor outlined by Bar-On. The defects in the ability to generate emotions from mental imagery perhaps speak directly to the fourth factor outlined by Bar-On. Finally, the mechanisms of emotional conditioning and acquisition of anticipatory emotional responses (SCRs) in the gambling task are closely relevant to the fifth factor outlined by Bar-On. Overall, it appears that the neural network involved in the activation of somatic states provides a substrate for what is known as emotional intelligence. Although none of our patients has been formally tested on any of the developed emotional intelligence scales, it seems likely that many of these patients would be found to be quite deficient on the emotional scale, but entirely normal on the standard IQ scale. It would be interesting to see whether one can find brain lesions that provide opposite dissociation, in other words, low IQ, but high emotional intelligence, and to see if this matches their performance in real life. Through this research approach, one may eventually be able to provide a neurobiological substrate for emotional intelligence and dissect the relative contributions of emotional intelligence and IQ to overall intelligence.

References

Adolphs, R., Damasio, H., Tranel, D., & Damasio, A. R. (1996). Cortical systems for the recognition of emotion in facial expressions. *Journal of Neuroscience, 16,* 7678–7687.

Adolphs, R., Tranel, D., & Damasio, A. R. (1998). The human amygdala in social judgement. *Nature, 393,* 470–474.

Adolphs, R., Tranel, D., Damasio, H., & Damasio, A. R. (1995). Fear and the human amygdala. *Journal of Neuroscience, 15,* 5879–5892.

Aggleton, J. P. (1992). The functional effects of amygdala lesions in humans: A comparison with findings from monkeys. In J. P. Aggleton (Ed.), *The amygdala: Neurobiological aspects of emotion, memory, and mental dysfunction,* (pp. 485–504). New York: Wiley-Liss.

Bechara, A., Damasio, A. R., Damasio, H., & Anderson, S. W. (1994). Insensitivity to future consequences following damage to human prefrontal cortex. *Cognition, 50,* 7–15.

Bechara, A., Damasio, H., Damasio, A. R., & Lee, G. P. (1999). Different contributions of the human amygdala and ventromedial prefrontal cortex to decision-making. *Journal of Neuroscience, 19,* 5473–5481.

Bechara, A., Damasio, H., Tranel, D., & Damasio, A. R. (1997). Deciding advantageously before knowing the advantageous strategy. *Science, 275,* 1293–1295.

Bechara, A., Tranel, D., Damasio, H., Adolphs, R., Rockland, C., & Damasio, A. R. (1995). Double dissociation of conditioning and declarative knowledge relative to the amygdala and hippocampus in humans. *Science, 269,* 1115–1118.

Bechara, A., Tranel, D., Damasio, H., & Damasio, A. R. (1996). Failure to respond autonomically to anticipated future outcomes following damage to prefrontal cortex. *Cerebral Cortex, 6,* 215–225.

Bechara, A., Tranel, D., Damasio, H., & Damasio, A. R. (1997). An anatomical system subserving decision-making. *Society for Neuroscience Abstracts, 23,* 495.

Benton, A. L. (1991). The prefrontal region: its early history. In H. Levin, H. Eisenberg, & A. Benton (Eds.), *Frontal lobe function and dysfunction.,* (pp. 3–12). New York: Oxford University Press.

Damasio, A. R. (1994). *Descartes' error: Emotion, reason, and the human brain.* New York: Grosset/Putnam.

Damasio, H., Bechara, A., Tranel, D., & Damasio, A. R. (1997). Double dissociation of emotional conditioning and emotional imagery relative to the amygdala and right somatosensory cortex. *Society For Neuroscience Abstracts, 23,* 1318.

Damasio, H., Grabowski, T., Frank, R., Galburda, A. M., & Damasio, A. R. (1994). The return of Phineas Gage: Clues about the brain from the skull of a famous patient. *Science, 264,* 1102–1104.

Davidson, R. J., & Irwin, W. (1999). The functional neuroanatomy of emotion and affective style. *Trends in Cognitive Sciences, 3,* 11–21.

Eslinger, P. J., & Damasio, A. R. (1985). Severe disturbance of higher cognition after bilateral frontal lobe ablation: Patient EVR. *Neurology, 35,* 1731–1741.

Fuster, J. M. (1996). *The prefrontal cortex: Anatomy, physiology, and neuropsychology of the frontal lobe* (3rd ed.). New York: Raven Press.

Harlow, J. M. (1848). Passage of an iron bar through the head. *Boston Medical and Surgical Journal, 39,* 389–393.

Harlow, J. M. (1868). Recovery from the passage of an iron bar through the head. *Publications of the Massachusetts Medical Society, 2,* 327–347.

LeDoux, J. (1996). *The emotional brain: The mysterious underpinnings of emotional life.* New York: Simon and Schuster.

Mayer, J. D., Salovey, P., & Caruso, D. R. (2000). Emotional intelligence. In R. J. Sternberg (Ed.), *Handbook of intelligence* (2nd ed., pp. 396–421). New York: Cambridge University Press.

Miller, L. A. (1992). Impulsivity, risk-taking, and the ability to synthesize fragmented information after frontal lobectomy. *Neuropsychologia, 30,* 69–79.

Rolls, E. T. (1999). *The brain and emotion.* Oxford: Oxford University Press.

Stuss, D. T., Gow, C. A., & Hetherington, C. R. (1992). "No longer Gage": frontal lobe dysfunction and emotional changes. *Journal of Consulting and Clinical Psychology, 60,* 349–359.

Tranel, D., Bechara, A., Damasio, H., & Damasio, A. R. (1998). Neural correlates of emotional imagery. *International Journal of Psychophysiology, 30,* 107.

CHAPTER TEN

Practical Intelligence and Its Development

Robert J. Sternberg and Elena L. Grigorenko

Studies of intelligence and its development during childhood have tended to focus on intelligence as it is traditionally defined (Ferrari & Sternberg, 1998; Sternberg & Berg, 1992; Sternberg & Powell, 1983). In contrast, studies of intelligence and its development during adulthood have tended in recent years to focus more on the practical aspects of intelligence (Sternberg, 2000). In this chapter, we review the literature on practical intelligence and its development. In particular we argue, as have others (Baltes, 1997; Berg, 2000), that the development of conventional "academic" intelligence and of practical intelligence show rather distinct trajectories.

By *academic intelligence,* we mean intelligence as it is typically defined by conventional definitions and tests, comprising so-called general ability and related abilities. In terms of our own theorizing, it comprises primarily memory and analytical skills (Sternberg, 1997). By *practical intelligence,* we mean intelligence as it applies in everyday life in adaptation to, shaping of, and selection of environments (Sternberg, 1985, 1997, 1999). A number of different terms have been used for practical intelligence, and they are used here interchangeably.

Note: Preparation of this article was supported under the Javits Act Program (Grant No. R206R950001) as administered by the Office of Educational Research and Improvement, U.S. Department of Education. Grantees undertaking such projects are encouraged to express freely their professional judgment. This article, therefore, does not necessarily represent the position or policies of the Office of Educational Research and Improvement or the U.S. Department of Education, and no official endorsement should be inferred.

215

Thus, we include within the domain of practical intelligence *practical problem solving, pragmatic intelligence,* and *everyday intelligence.*

Practical intelligence involves a number of skills as applied to adaptation to, shaping of, and selection of environments. These skills include, among others, (1) recognizing problems, (2) defining problems, (3) allocating resources to solving problems, (4) mentally representing problems, (5) formulating strategies for solving problems, (6) monitoring solution of problems, and (7) evaluating solutions of problems.

If we are to distinguish between academic and practical intelligence, we need some grounds at the outset for distinguishing between them and for asserting their relative independence. One ground is theoretical (see Chapter Seven). For example, the triarchic theory of human intelligence views these two kinds of intelligence as distinct (Sternberg, 1985), as do other theories of intelligence to be discussed. Empirical data also support this distinction. For example, two empirical studies of a test for high school students measuring academic-analytical as well as creative and practical intelligence have shown through confirmatory factor analysis the distinctiveness of academic and practical intelligence (Sternberg, Grigorenko, Ferrari, & Clinkenbeard, 1999; Sternberg, Castejón, Prieto, Hautakami, & Grigorenko, forthcoming). Yet another study has shown that that elementary and middle school students taught triarchically (for practical as well as academic intelligence) outperform students taught either in conventional ways, emphasizing memory, or in ways emphasizing academic-analytical thinking (Sternberg, Torff, & Grigorenko, 1998a, 1998b). Thus, we believe that there is good empirical as well as theoretical evidence for making a distinction at the outset between academic and practical intelligence.

Before we even consider theoretical issues, we deal with a metatheoretical one. Why consider practical intelligence an intelligence at all? Our basis for doing so is threefold:

1. *Theoretical basis.* An ability is posited by a psychological theory as an intelligence.

2. *Internal validity.* The ability is more or less homogeneous with respect to itself: one kind of measure of the ability tends to correlate with others measures of the ability. At the same time, the ability is more or less heterogeneous with respect to other abilities: the correlations of measures of this ability with other abilities are low, and in particular, lower than the correlations of the measures of this ability with itself.

3. *External validity.* The ability predicts behavior in the real world that is indicative of adaptation to, shaping of, or selection of environments. Note that our criteria involve both theoretical basis and validity as revealed by empirical operations. It is insufficient to have just theory or just data. One needs both.

DEVELOPMENTAL TRAJECTORIES OF ACADEMIC VERSUS PRACTICAL INTELLIGENCE

The idea that practical versus academic-analytical abilities might have different developmental trajectories has been supported in a number of studies (see Berg & Klaczynski, 1996, for a review). Denney and Palmer (1981) were among the first research teams to demonstrate this discrepancy. They compared the performance of adults (ages twenty through seventy-nine) on traditional analytical reasoning problems (for example, a "twenty questions" task) and a problem-solving task involving real-life situations (such as "If you were traveling by car and got stranded out on an interstate highway during a blizzard, what would you do?"). One of the many interesting results obtained in this study was a difference in the shape of the developmental function for performance on the two types of problems. Performance on the traditional problem-solving task or cognitive measure declined almost linearly from age twenty, onward. Performance on the practical problem-solving task increased to a peak in the forty- and fifty-year-old groups, declining thereafter (see also Chapter Seventeen). Expanding on this line of research, Smith and colleagues (Smith, Staudinger, & Baltes, 1994) compared responses to life-planning dilemmas in a group of younger (mean age thirty-two) and older (mean age seventy) adults. Unlike the results of studies of aging and academic abilities, which demonstrated the superior performance of younger adults over the elderly, in this study, young and older adults did not differ. In addition, each age-cohort group received the highest ratings when responding to a dilemma matched to its own life phase.

Similar results were obtained in a study by Cornelius and Caspi (1987). They studied adults between the ages of twenty and seventy-eight. These researchers examined relationships between performance on tasks measuring fluid intelligence (letter series), crystallized intelligence (verbal meanings), and everyday problem solving (for example, dealing with a landlord who won't make repairs, filling out a complicated form, responding to criticism from a parent or child). Performance on the measure of fluid ability increased from ages twenty to thirty, remained stable from ages thirty to fifty, and then declined. Performance on the everyday problem-solving task and the measures of crystallized ability increased through age seventy.

Likewise, the neofunctionalist position, advanced by Baltes and his associates (Baltes, 1987; Baltes, Smith, & Staudinger, 1992; Baltes, Dittmann-Kohli, & Dixon, 1984; Dittmann-Kohli & Baltes, 1990), suggests that although some aspects of intellectual functioning estimated via traditional tests may decline with age, stability and growth also exist, if to a lesser extent. The approach of Baltes and his colleagues also uses the constructs of fluid and crystallized intelligence, although a different emphasis is placed on the relative roles and meanings of these two kinds of intelligence. Here, both aspects of intelligence are considered as coequals in defining the developmental course of intelligence. In general, Baltes argues that crystallized intelligence has been too narrowly defined and that its importance increases as one moves into adulthood and old age. In this sense, it may be inappropriate to associate a decrease in fluid intelligence with an average decline in intellectual competence.

Baltes and his associates see adult cognitive competence in terms of a dual-process model. The first process, called the *mechanics* of intelligence, is concerned with developmental change in basic information processing that is genetically driven and assumed to be knowledge free. With aging, there is a biologically based reduction in reserve capacity (Baltes, 1987; Baltes et al., 1992). The second process, *pragmatic* intelligence, relates the basic cognitive skills and resources of the first process to everyday cognitive performance and adaptation. It seems to be equivalent to what others call *practical intelligence*. Measures of pragmatic intelligence within select domains are viewed as tapping abilities more characteristic of adult intellectual life than are traditional psychometric measures of cognitive abilities. Similar to empirical findings on the distinction between fluid and crystallized intelligence, Baltes, Sowarka, and Kliegl (1989) showed that the mechanics of intelligence tend to decline with age almost linearly, whereas the pragmatics of intelligence tend to maintain relative stability throughout adulthood. For example, whereas linear declines were found in the speed of comparing information in short-term memory (aspects of intellectual mechanics), no age differences were registered for measures of reasoning about life planning (aspects of intellectual pragmatics).

Cognitive abilities are assumed to operate on content domains involving factual and procedural knowledge; they are regulated by higher-level, transsituational, procedural skills and by higher-order reflective thinking (metacognition), all of which define the "action space" in which problem solving occurs within a given individual. According to this approach, successful aging entails limiting one's tasks and avoiding excessive demands. Baltes and Baltes (1990) used the concept of selection to refer to a self-imposed restriction in one's life to fewer domains of functioning as a means to adapt to age-related losses. It is assumed that by concentrating on high-priority domains and devising new operational strategies, individuals can optimize their general reserves (Baltes, 1993). By relating adult intelligence to successful cognitive performance in one's environment, this position acknowledges that not all tasks are equally relevant for measuring intelligence at different ages (Baltes et al., 1984, 1992).

Specific manifestations of pragmatic intelligence are said to differ from person to person as people proceed through selection, optimization, or compensation (Dittmann-Kohli & Baltes, 1990). Selection refers simply to diminishing the scope of one's activities to things that one is still able to accomplish well, despite a diminution in reserve capacity. Optimization refers to the fact that older people can maintain high levels of performance in some domains by practice, greater effort, and the development of new bodies of knowledge. Compensation comes into play when one requires a level of capacity beyond remaining performance potential. For example, Salthouse (1984) was able to show that older typists, although slower on several simple speeded reaction-time tasks, were able to compensate for this deficit and maintain their speed by reading further ahead in the text and planning ahead. According to Salthouse and Somberg (1982), age-related decrements at the "molecular" level (such as speed of execution of the elementary components of typing skill) produce no observable effects at the "molar" level (such as the speed and accuracy with which work is completed).

Charness (1981) showed similar effects with older chess players, who exhibited poorer recall in general, but were better able to plan ahead than younger, less experienced players. In related studies, older adults have been found to compensate for declines in memory by relying more on external memory aids than do younger adults (Loewen, Shaw, & Craik, 1990). Older adults must often transfer the emphasis of a particular task to abilities that have not declined in order to compensate for those that have (see Bäckman & Dixon, 1992, for a review of these issues). In other words, when a task depends heavily on knowledge, and speed of processing is not a significant constraint, peak performance may not be constrained in early-to-middle adulthood (Charness & Bieman-Copland, 1994). As an example, consider chess competitions by correspondence. In these "chess-by-mail" competitions, players are permitted three days to deliberate each move. The mean age of the first-time winners of one postal world championship is forty-six. In contrast, the peak age for tournament chess, where deliberation averages three minutes per move, is about thirty (Charness & Bosman, 1995). A series of studies on the relationship between aging and cognitive efficiency in skilled performers has attested to the compensatory and stabilizing role of practical intelligence (Baltes & Smith, 1990; Charness & Bosman, 1990; Colonia-Willner, 1998; Hartley, 1989; Willis, 1989).

The developmental trajectory of practical, or everyday, intelligence has been examined by a number of researchers (see Berg, 2000; Berg & Klaczynski, 1996, for reviews). The summary of the field today is that the pattern of age differences in practical intelligence differs dramatically depending on how problems to be solved are defined and what criteria are used for optimal problem solving. For example, Berg, Klaczynski, Calderone, and Strough (1994), studying participants' own ratings of how effective they were in solving their own everyday problems, did not find any age differences. Denney and her colleagues (Denney & Palmer, 1981; Denney & Pearce, 1989) used the number of "safe and effective solutions" as the criterion of optimal problem solving and found that the highest number of such solutions was generated by middle-aged adults, with both younger and older adults offering fewer solutions. Cornelius and Caspi

(1987), using the closeness between participants' ratings of strategy effectiveness and "prototype" of the optimal everyday problem solver as the criterion, found an increase in everyday problem-solving ability with adult age.

A number of studies have examined everyday problem solving with a neo-Piagetian approach to intellectual development in adulthood (Labouvie-Vief, 1992). According to this paradigm, in middle and late adulthood, the formal-operational reasoning of late adolescents and young adults, with its focus on logic, is replaced by more sophisticated mental structures distinguished by relativistic reasoning based on synthesizing the irrational, emotive, and personal. Specifically, Blanchard-Fields (1986, 1994; Blanchard-Fields & Norris, 1994) stated that, when dealing with social dilemmas, older adults are superior to younger adults in their integrative attributional reasoning (reasoning based on the integration of dispositional and situational components).

To conclude, there is reason to believe that the developmental trajectories of abilities used to solve strictly academic problems do not coincide with the trajectories of abilities used to solve problems of a practical nature.

WHAT DEVELOPS?

The evidence supporting the supposition that practical intelligence has a different developmental trajectory than academic-analytical intelligence supports the relative independence of practical and academic abilities but is only one of many research advances revealing the developmental mechanisms of practical intelligence. Developmental research on practical abilities is still in its early stages. However, data available at this point shed some light on what Sinnott (1989) called the chaotically complex reality of practical problem solving; evidence supports the existence of different developmental trajectories (maintenance, improvement, and decline) across the life span without a pronounced preference for any single one.

There is no formal theory of the stages of the development of practical intelligence (Berg et al., 1994), unlike for academic intelligence (Piaget, 1972). Some results, however, suggest that differences in performance on practical versus analytical tasks are observed rather early (for example, Freeman, Lewis, & Doherty, 1991).

RESEARCH ON PRACTICAL INTELLIGENCE IN ADULTHOOD

Research on practical intelligence is becoming more and more central to mainstream psychology (see Berg & Klaczynski, 1996, for a review). Initially, the examination of practical intelligence issued from a concern that the intelligence of adults functioning largely outside the academic environment from the moment they obtained their academic degrees and virtually for the rest of their lives was evaluated primarily by traditional tests of intelligence constructed to predict academic, not practical, success.

Various aspects of the meaning of the concept of practical intelligence are expressed in a number of diverse constructs. Some researchers define everyday intelligence as a specific expression of conventional abilities that permit adaptive behavior within a distinct class of everyday-life situations (for example, Willis & Schaie, 1986), whereas others stress the unique nature of practical abilities (for example, Neisser, 1976; Wagner, 1987). Most psychological studies of practical abilities focus on solving problems that are ill structured in their goals and solutions and are frequently encountered in daily life (at home, work, and in dealing with people) (for example, Cornelius & Caspi, 1987; Denney, 1989).

A number of studies have addressed the relation between practical and academic-analytical intelligence. These studies have been carried out in a wide range of settings, using a variety of tasks, and with diverse populations. We review some examples of research on problem solving and reasoning. For other reviews see Ceci and Roazzi (1994), Rogoff and Lave (1984), Scribner and Cole (1981), Sternberg, Forsythe, et al. (2000), Sternberg and Wagner (1986, 1994), Voss, Perkins, and Segal (1991), and Wagner (2000). Taken together, these studies show that ability measured in one setting (for example, school) does not necessarily transfer to another setting (for example, a real-world task).

Empirical Investigations: Practical Problem Solving

Several studies have compared performance on mathematical types of problems across different contexts. Scribner (1984, 1986) studied the strategies used by milk processing plant workers to fill orders. Workers who assemble orders for cases of various quantities (like gallons, quarts, or pints) and products (like whole milk, two percent milk, or buttermilk) are called assemblers. Rather than employing typical mathematical algorithms learned in the classroom, Scribner found that experienced assemblers used complex strategies for combining partially filled cases in a manner that minimized the number of moves required to complete an order. Although the assemblers were the least educated workers in the plant, they were able to calculate in their heads quantities expressed in different base number systems, and they routinely outperformed the more highly educated white collar workers who substituted when assemblers were absent. Scribner found that the order-filling performance of the assemblers was unrelated to measures of school performance, including intelligence test scores, arithmetic test scores, and grades.

Another series of studies of everyday mathematics involved shoppers in California grocery stores who sought to buy at the cheapest cost when the same products were available in different-sized containers (Lave, Murtaugh, & de la

Roche, 1984; Murtaugh, 1985). (These studies were performed before cost per unit quantity information was routinely posted.) For example, oatmeal may come in two sizes, ten ounces for $.98 and twenty-four ounces for $2.29. One might adopt the strategy of always buying the largest size, assuming that the larger size is always the most economical. However, the researchers (and savvy shoppers) learned that the larger size did not represent the least cost per unit quantity for about one-third of the items purchased. The findings of these studies were that effective shoppers used mental shortcuts to get an easily obtained answer, accurate enough to determine which size to buy. A common strategy, for example, was to mentally change the size and price of an item to make it more comparable with the other size available. For example, one might mentally double the smaller size, thereby comparing twenty ounces at $1.96 versus twenty-four ounces at $2.29. The difference of four ounces is about 35 cents, or about 9 cents per ounce, which seems to favor the twenty-four-ounce size, given that the smaller size of ten ounces for $.98 is about ten cents per ounce. These mathematical shortcuts yield approximations that are as useful as the actual values of 9.80 and 9.33 cents per ounce for the smaller and larger sizes, respectively, and are much more easily computed in the absence of a calculator. When the shoppers were given a mental-arithmetic test, no relation was found between test performance and accuracy in picking the best values (Lave et al., 1984; Murtaugh, 1985).

Ceci and colleagues (Ceci & Liker, 1986, 1988; see also Ceci & Ruiz, 1991) studied expert racetrack handicappers. Ceci and Liker (1986) found that expert handicappers used a highly complex algorithm for predicting post-time odds that involved interactions among seven kinds of information. By applying the complex algorithm, handicappers adjusted times posted for each quarter mile on a previous outing by factors such as whether the horse was attempting to pass other horses and, if so, the speed of the other horses passed and where the attempted passes took place. By adjusting posted times for these factors, a better measure of a horse's speed is obtained. It could be argued that the use of complex interactions to predict a horse's speed would require considerable cognitive ability (at least as it is traditionally measured). However, Ceci and Liker reported that the successful use of these interactions by handicappers was unrelated to their IQ.

A subsequent study attempted to relate performance at the racetrack to making stock-market predictions in which the same algorithm was involved. Ceci and Ruiz (1991) asked racetrack handicappers to solve a stock-market-prediction task that was structured similarly to the racetrack problem. After 611 trials on the stock-market task, the handicappers performed no better than chance, and there was no difference in performance as a function of IQ. Ceci and Roazzi (1994) attribute this lack of transfer to the low correlation between performance on problems and their isomorphs. *Problem isomorphs* is a term that refers to two or more problems that involve the same cognitive processes but that use different terminology or take place in different contexts.

Additional research has shown that the use of complex reasoning strategies does not necessarily correlate with IQ. Dörner and colleagues (Dörner & Kreuzig, 1983; Dörner, Kreuzig, Reither, & Staudel, 1983) studied adults who were asked to play the role of city managers for the computer-simulated city of Lohhausen. A variety of problems were presented to these individuals, such as how best to raise revenue to build roads. The simulation involved more than one thousand variables. Performance was quantified in terms of a hierarchy of strategies, ranging from the simplest (trial and error) to the most complex (hypothesis testing with multiple feedback loops). No relation was found between IQ and complexity of strategies used. A second problem was created to cross-validate these results. This problem, called the Sahara problem, required participants to determine the number of camels that could be kept alive by a small oasis. Once again, no relation was found between IQ and complexity of strategies employed.

The above studies indicate that demonstrated abilities do not necessarily correspond between everyday tasks (such as price-comparison shopping) and traditional academic tasks (such as math achievement tests). In other words, some people are able to solve concrete, ill-defined problems better than well-defined, abstract problems that have little relevance to their personal lives, and vice versa. Few of these researchers would claim, however, that IQ is totally irrelevant to performance in these various contexts. There is evidence that conventional tests of intelligence predict both school performance and job performance (Barrett & Depinet, 1991; Schmidt & Hunter, 1998; Wigdor & Garner, 1982). What these studies do suggest is that there are other aspects of intelligence that may be independent of IQ and that are important to performance, but that have been largely neglected in the measurement of intelligence. We also observe this incongruity between conventional notions of ability and real-world abilities in research on age-related changes in intellectual ability.

Research on practical intelligence and its development is moving in a number of directions, each of which might help us to detect the internal mechanisms of its development. Most of the work is centered on specific characteristics of practical tasks. The assumption here is that if we understand the differences in the ways these tasks are formulated and solved at different stages of development, we will be closer to understanding the developmental dynamics of practical intelligence. The distinction made earlier between academic and practical tasks suggests five main directions of research: (1) studies of developmentally variable contexts of practical problem solving, (2) studies of developmental changes in the content of practical problems encountered at different stages of development, (3) studies of the developmental diversity of the goals of practical problem solving, (4) studies of differential strategies used in practical problem solving at different periods of development, and (5) studies on developmental variation in problem interpretation and definition.

Context of Practical Problem Solving

There is virtually unanimous agreement on the centrality of context for understanding practical problem solving. This view, which holds that practical problem solving cannot be separated from the context in which it unfolds, is referred to as the contextual perspective (Dixon, 1994; Wertsch & Kanner, 1994). In general, the metaphor used to describe the contextual approach is that of trying to follow forever-changing events (that is, the life course is represented as being a series of changing events, activities, and contexts). When applied to studies of practical problem solving, this perspective assumes that (1) the demands posed by these contexts vary across development; (2) strategies accomplishing adaptation differ across contexts; (3) these strategies also differ across individuals; and finally, (4) the effectiveness of everyday problem solving is determined by the interaction of individual and context (Berg & Calderone, 1994).

One of the most interesting developments in studies on context and practical problem solving concerns the effect of compensation; this is the phenomenon in which gains in (mostly) practical intelligence balance out age-related decrements in other areas. Researchers argue that compensation—considered in terms of the dynamic relationship between the individual's changing cognitive skills and expectations of performance, on the one hand, and shifting contextual demands, on the other hand—should be viewed as central to cognitive aging (Dixon, 1994). One example of practical intelligence compensating for declines in g-based intellectual performance is older adults' effective use of external aids. One common source of external cognitive aid is other people. For example, Dixon and his colleagues (Dixon, 1994) explored the extent to which older and younger adults use same-age collaborators in solving memory problems and found that older adults use previously unknown collaborators to boost their performance levels to a much greater extent than do younger adults.

Two other important characteristics of the context in which practical problem solving occurs, which might explain some aspects of the observed development variability in practical intelligence, are the complexity and familiarity of the context.

As for the complexity of the environment in which practical intelligence unfolds, one variable that has been pointed out as extremely important for shaping the development of practical abilities in adulthood is that of the immediate conditions and demands of work (see Schooler, forthcoming, for a review). For example, Kohn and Schooler (1983), examining a group of men between the ages of twenty-four and sixty-four, longitudinally studied the link between the extent to which one's work-related activities involve independent thought and judgment and workers' creative flexibility in dealing with complex intellectual demands. They found that the more the substantive complexity of one's job, the greater the incremental gains in intellectual performance over a ten-year period. Even more astounding, a similar relationship between job complexity and intellectual performance was revealed for women doing complex housework (Schooler, 1984). Moreover, Miller and Kohn (1983) found that individuals with higher flexibility in dealing with complex intellectual activities tended to engage in more stimulating and demanding intellectual activities (for example, reading books versus watching television).

The major criticism of this nonexperimental evidence of the intellectual effects of doing complex work (whether in the work place or the household) is that these designs are unable to conclusively rule out the possibility that individuals who maintain their intellectual functioning are more capable of following and staying in challenging work environments. Yet, even though the causal path is difficult to infer among individuals, the evidence that among individuals more intellectually complex work leads to enriched intellectual functioning deserves attention and more thorough investigation.

Regarding familiarity or experience with the domain in which practical problem solving is carried out, studies have demonstrated that intellectual performance is greater for both younger and older adults when individuals are given either familiar materials (Smith & Baltes, 1990) or a chance to practice prior to assessment (Berg, Hertzog, & Hunt, 1982). Yet, results are ambiguous as to whether differential familiarity is a factor that can help to explain age differences in practical problem solving (Denney & Pearce, 1989).

Researchers reported, for example, that older adults perceived traditional intelligence tests as less familiar than did young adults (Cornelius, 1984). Therefore, when younger and older adults are compared on conventional intelligence tests, older adults might perform worse because these tests are less familiar to them and they may have forgotten how to evoke specific strategies relevant to situations of traditional intellectual assessment.

To explore the importance of the familiarity factor, several studies have been carried out in which younger and older adults were asked to solve problems that were constructed to be more familiar or more normative for one age group or the other. For example, Denney and colleagues (Denney, Pearce, & Palmer, 1982) showed that, in adults, the more normative for their age group everyday problems are, the better their performance is. Similarly, Smith and Baltes (1990) found that adults perform best when the problems are more normative for their age group. As Berg (2000) pointed out, memory research using tasks with familiar materials (for example, remembering words that were in frequent use during their adulthood years versus contemporary equivalents) is consistent in showing that older adults tend to perform better with materials more familiar to them (Barrett & Watkins, 1986; Worden & Sherman-Brown, 1983).

Content of Practical Problem Solving

The main hypothesis underlying this line of research is that the content of practical intelligence or problem solving differs at different stages of development. The literature concerning this hypothesis contains heterogeneous evidence; some is supportive (Aldwin, Sutton, Chiara, & Spiro, 1996) and some is not supportive (Folkman, Lazarus, Pimley, & Novacek, 1987) of the assertion that individuals of different ages experience different everyday problems.

Berg and colleagues (Berg & Calderone, 1994; Sansone & Berg, 1993) asked preschoolers, teenagers, college students, and adults to describe a recent problem (hassle, conflict, challenge, and so on) that they had experienced and to describe the problem in as much detail as possible. The intent was to investigate whether the types of domains of problems remain constant across development or whether different types of problems would appear for different age groups. The researchers found significant variation in the content of everyday problems across development. The everyday problem-solving content for five- and six-year-olds consisted predominantly of problems dealing with family (for example, disagreements with family members) and assigned responsibilities (such as home chores). For eleven- and twelve-year-olds, everyday life problems centered on school and after-school activities and environments. No single content area dominated the everyday life of college students, and their salient problems had to do with free time, work, friends, family, and romantic relationships. Finally, the everyday problem solving of the older adults centered on the family context and health.

Barker (1978) suggested that the content of practical problem solving is determined by the ecological characteristics of a given developmental period. Specifically, it has been shown that (1) college students' tasks are primarily aimed at succeeding academically, forming social networks, developing an identity, and separating from family (Cantor, Norem, Neidenthal, Langston, & Brower, 1987); (2) adults focus on a variety of tasks, ranging from starting a family and a career in young adulthood, through the pragmatic tasks of middle adulthood, to adapting to impairments of health and adjusting to retirement during old and advanced old age (Baltes et al., 1984; Havinghurst, 1972; Neugarten Moore, & Lowe, 1968).

Goals of Practical Problem Solving

The goal-directedness (Goodnow, 1986; Scribner, 1986; Wertsch, 1985) of practical problem solving is one of the most often cited characteristics of practical intelligence in application. Therefore, the second line of research concerns the developmental trajectories of goals of practical problem solving.

Strough, Berg, and Sansone (1996) showed that there is developmental variation in the types of goals underlying everyday problem solving. The profile of this developmental variation reflects developmental life tasks (Cantor, 1990).

Specifically, preadolescents reported more goals for task improvement, and a large portion of their problems involved the school context. Interpersonal goals appeared to be more salient to middle-aged adults than to preadolescents. Preadolescents, however, reported more other-focused assistance-recruiting goals than did adults. Older and middle-aged adults reported more physical goals than did younger individuals, and the adult group as a whole reported more affective goals than did preadolescents.

Belief in the plasticity and fluidity of human developmental goals throughout the life span is also reflected by the notion that there is no single outcome or endpoint to intellectual development in general, or to the development of practical intelligence in particular (Rogoff, 1982). The implication of this line of reasoning is that the individual and his or her context form a complex systemic unit; changes in the unit shape the content, dynamics, and adaptability of the individual's intellectual functioning in specific contexts. Thus, there is no "ideal" trajectory of intellectual development, and there is no optimal instrument for the assessment of intellectual functioning equally well at all periods of the life span.

Practical Problem-Solving Strategies

One of the main focuses of research in the field of practical intelligence is strategies used in problem solving. Among the central characteristics of strategies discussed in the research literature of the past twenty years (Belmont & Butterfield, 1969; Berg, 1989; Brown, 1975; Flavell, 1970; Naus & Ornstein, 1983; Pressley, Forrest-Pressley, Elliot-Faust, & Miller, 1985) are selectivity, goal-directedness, and intentionality. Many developmental researchers have been especially interested in strategy selection both as an individual indicator and as a developmental indicator of everyday problem-solving performance (Frederiksen, 1986; Frederiksen, Jensen, & Beaton, 1972; Lazarus & Folkman, 1984).

Most of the early developmental work on everyday problem solving has been carried out under the assumption that individuals' chosen strategies can be compared irrespective of the developmental variation in the goals motivating these strategies (Band & Weisz, 1988; Berg, 1989; Cornelius & Caspi, 1987; Folkman et al., 1987). The major theoretical hypothesis dominating the field is that greater experience with everyday problems leads to better problem solving (Baltes et al., 1984; Denney, 1982). This claim assumes that a particular type of strategy—for example, primary control reflected in independent coping and problem-focused action—is a more effective way of dealing with various problems than is some other strategy—for example, secondary control reflected in reliance on others and emotion-focused action (Denney, 1989; Folkman et al., 1987). Self-action was the strategy most frequently mentioned across all ages in a study of reported everyday problems (Berg, Calderone, Sansone, Strough, & Weir, 1998). Problem-focused action was most frequently mentioned for hypothetical problems (Blanchard-Fields, Jahnke, & Camp, 1995). Developmental differences have been encountered, suggesting that secondary control strategies, emotion-focused strategies, and dependence on others increase across early childhood (Band & Weisz, 1988), with further elevation in later adulthood (Brandtstaedter & Greve, 1994; Denney & Palmer, 1981; Folkman et al., 1987; Heckhausen & Schultz, 1995).

The empirical literature, however, does not uniformly support the claim that more experience equals better problem solving (Baltes, 1997; Berg, 1989; Cornelius & Caspi, 1987). Recent research suggests that strategies are differentially effective depending on the context of the everyday problem (Berg, 1989; Ceci & Bronfenbrenner, 1985; Cornelius & Caspi, 1987; Scribner, 1986). Thus, Cornelius and Caspi (1987) showed that different types of strategies (problem-focused action, cognitive problem analysis, passive-dependent behavior, and avoidant thinking and denial) were viewed as differentially effective in different contexts.

Findings regarding the localization of age differences are also somewhat contradictory. The often-cited trend in the literature is that older adults tend to use more secondary control (Heckhausen & Schulz, 1995) and less problem-focused action or primary control (Folkman et al., 1987) when compared with younger adults. Blanchard-Fields et al. (1995) found minimal age differences in problem-focused action. Furthermore, Berg et al. (1998) reported age differences for older adults only, with older people using relatively less cognitive regulation and more self-action than either college students or middle-aged adults. The situation has become even less transparent, with Aldwin et al. (1996) showing that for the most part, age differences existed among adults only when individuals' strategies were assessed through a checklist; these distinctions were greatly reduced when individuals' strategies were elicited through open-ended interviews.

One of the possible explanations for the heterogeneity of these findings is that what develops over time is sensitivity to specific contexts. In other words, the repertoire of dealing with everyday problems is rather broad, and different modules of problem solving are used in different situations; in many ways, consistency across situations may be maladaptive (Mischel, 1984). Some researchers argue that successful everyday problem solving will involve carefully fitting strategies to the specific demands of a problem and modifying these strategies in response to changes in the problem (Berg & Sternberg, 1985; Rogoff, Gauvain, & Gardner, 1987; Scribner, 1986). And sensitivity to the contextual features of a problem is characteristic of a developmental factor (Mischel, 1984; Rogoff et al., 1987). Others, on the contrary, suggest that these strategies become less context-dependent with age (Kreitler & Kreitler, 1987).

Yet another, although not contradictory possibility, is that the lesson derived from experience with everyday problems is how to avoid getting into everyday problems (Berg, 1989). Thus, it is plausible that no simple relation between kind of experience and everyday problem-solving ability is likely to exist. Moreover, researchers have presented evidence demonstrating that so-called effective-across-all-context (or primary) strategies fail in situations in which so-called ineffective strategies (such as relinquishing) work (Berg, Calderone, & Gunderson as cited in Berg & Calderone, 1994). Certain kinds of experience may be differentially related to success at solving particular kinds of everyday problems, and development might be better construed as individuals becoming increasingly capable of modifying their strategies or avoiding potentially problematic situations (Berg, 1989; Rogoff et al., 1987).

Another line of research focuses on studying individual differences that appear to lead to more optimal problem-solving performance (Ceci & Liker, 1986; Denney, 1989; Willis & Schaie, 1986). Many factors (such as conventional intellectual abilities, personality traits, social skills, and achievement motivation) have been shown to impact the use of strategies in everyday problem solving (Ceci & Liker, 1986; Charness, 1981; Kuhn, Pennington, & Leadbeater, 1983), but no specific constellations of these factors were found to be better predictors of effective problem solving.

Problem Interpretation and Definition

In an attempt to systematize the literature on the development of everyday problem solving, Berg and colleagues have introduced the concepts of *problem interpretation* (Berg & Calderone, 1994; Sansone & Berg, 1993) and *problem definition* (Berg et al., 1998). Problem interpretation arises at the intersection of the context and the individual and, in essence, is the transaction of the individual with his or her context. Problem interpretation derives from features of both the individual and the context, but it might selectively engage all or only some features. Berg and her colleagues argued that such individual and contextual features may have different weights and may be differentially combined at different stages of development; thus, the search for developmental variation in everyday problem solving should focus on the development of problem interpretation (Berg & Calderone, 1994).

Because it is interactive in nature, problem definition reflects those aspects of the self and context that are activated with respect to a specific problem unfolding at a specific moment in time. Problem definition is a complex, psychological, subjective reality, which, according to Berg et al. (1998), reflects the individual's goals and expectations (Bandura, 1986), determines the strategies to be used to meet these expectations and accomplish subjective goals (Vallacher & Wegner, 1987), affects the outcome attribution and meaning interpretation (Dodge, Pettit, McClaskey, & Brown, 1986), and induces the affective representation of the problem (Fleeson & Cantor, 1995).

A number of studies provide supportive evidence for the transactional approach to everyday problem solving. Sinnott (1989) showed that older adults' interpretations of Piagetian logical-combination problems, especially those experienced in real life (for example, assigning relatives to sleeping locations), vary to a greater degree than do the interpretations of younger adults. Specifically, older adults tend to be more sensitive to social and interpersonal facets of the problem when compared with younger adults, who concentrate on the problem's logical aspects. Similarly, Laipple (1992) showed that older adults were less likely to interpret the situation of solving logical problems with the meaning intended by the experimenter; older adults tended to leave the logical confines of the problem and inject into the experimental situation more personal experience than did the younger adults. Chi and Ceci (1987) suggested that many types of problem solving appear to be directly influenced by the mental context the child brings to the task.

In their own work, Berg and colleagues (Berg & Calderone, 1994) registered a number of developmental characteristics of problem definition. First, they showed that, with age, there was a decrease in the frequency of task-oriented interpretations of problems and an increase in interpersonal, self, and mixed (task and self) interpretations. In their interpretation, researchers suggested that these findings correspond to the literature on the development of the self system, according to which changes of the self system involve movement away from a concrete and specific system to one that incorporates more abstract and interrelated psychological constructs (Harter, 1983). Second, Berg et al. (1998) studied the link between the problem definition and the selection of strategies for problem solving. In general, problem definition appears to be a more precise predictor of strategy use than does problem context. Specifically, individuals who defined a problem in terms of interpersonal concerns alone were more likely to report using strategies involving regulating or including others. In contrast, individuals who defined a problem solely in terms of competence concerns were more likely to use strategies that included independent action and that were less likely to engage others. Finally, the links between problem definition and strategy selection were not found to vary as a function of age.

Problem definition is very important to practical intelligence. For example, a key difference between the results of Berg et al. (1998) and those of previous research is the importance that individuals placed on the social aspects of practical problem solving. Berg and colleagues found that the majority of individual problem definitions in any age group (preadolescents, college students, and adults) involved interpersonal concerns. These problem definitions, in turn, determined the selection of strategies that involved regulating or including others. Note that this interpretation differs significantly from the argument used in previous research. Earlier work typically assumed that reliance on others reflected ineffective problem solving because individuals exhibited dependence on others (Cornelius & Caspi, 1987; Denney & Palmer, 1981; Folkman et al.,

1987). However, the reinterpretation of the role of social-dependent strategies suggests that using others to deal with everyday problems is a strategy rather well suited to particular problems (Baltes, 1997; Meacham & Emont, 1989).

DEVELOPMENT OF TACIT KNOWLEDGE

Our own program of research has been based on the notion that there is more to successful prediction of a person's performance than just measuring the so-called general factor from conventional psychometric tests of intelligence (Sternberg, Nokes, et al., forthcoming; Sternberg & Wagner, 1993; Sternberg, Wagner, Williams, & Horvath, 1995). We propose that tacit knowledge, as an aspect of practical intelligence, is a key ingredient of success in any domain. Tacit knowledge is the procedural knowledge one needs to function effectively in everyday environments but that is not explicitly taught and often is not even verbalized. Of course, there are those who disagree with our position (Jensen, 1993; Ree & Earles, 1993; Schmidt & Hunter, 1993, 1998), believing that individual differences in performance are explained primarily by general cognitive ability. Some proponents of using general cognitive ability tests have argued further that the value of these tests are that they are applicable for all jobs, have the lowest cost to develop and administer, and have the highest validity (Schmidt & Hunter, 1998). But even Schmidt and Hunter acknowledged that alternative measures such as work sample tests and job knowledge tests have comparable and perhaps even higher validities than do general ability tests, and provide incremental prediction above such tests.

A program of research by Sternberg and his colleagues has examined tacit knowledge research with business managers, college professors, elementary school teachers, sales people, college students, and general populations. This important aspect of practical intelligence, in study after study, has been found generally to be uncorrelated with academic intelligence as measured by conventional tests, in a variety of populations and occupations and at a variety of age levels (Sternberg, Forsythe, et al., 2000; Sternberg, Wagner, & Okagaki, 1993; Sternberg et al., 1995; Wagner, 1987; Wagner & Sternberg, 1985). A major task of this tacit-knowledge research has been to identify the content of tacit knowledge and develop ways to measure the possession of tacit knowledge. Tacit-knowledge tests present a set of problem situations and ask respondents to rate the quality or appropriateness of a number of possible responses to those situations.

Next we consider four main issues: (a) the relationship of tacit knowledge to experience, (b) the relationship of tacit knowledge to general intelligence, (c) tacit knowledge as a general construct, and (d) the relationship of tacit knowledge to performance.

Tacit Knowledge and Experience

In most of our studies, tacit knowledge was found to relate to experience, indicated either by group membership (expert versus novice) or the number of years in one's current position.

In several studies, Sternberg and his colleagues showed that individuals with less experience in a given domain tend to exhibit lower tacit-knowledge scores (Sternberg et al., 1993; Wagner, 1987; Wagner & Sternberg, 1985). Wagner and Sternberg (1985), for example, found group differences among business managers, business graduate students, and undergraduates on thirty-nine of the response-item ratings on a tacit-knowledge test for managers, with a binomial test of the probability of finding this many significant differences by chance yielding $p < .001$. Comparable results were obtained with Yale undergraduates, psychology graduate students, and psychology faculty on a tacit-knowledge test for academic psychologists.

In addition, Wagner (1987) found that business managers obtained the highest tacit-knowledge scores, followed by business graduate students and undergraduates, with comparable results obtained in a study of psychology professors, psychology graduate students, and undergraduates. Wagner, Rashotte, & Sternberg (1994) also found that scores on a tacit-knowledge test for salespeople correlated significantly with number of years of sales experience.

Williams and Sternberg (cited in Sternberg et al., 1995), however, did not find significant correlations between several experience-based measures, including age, years of management experience, and years in current position, and tacit-knowledge scores. But they did find that the importance of specific pieces of tacit knowledge varied across organizational level. Their findings suggest that it may not simply be the amount of experience but what a manager learns from experience that matters to success.

Tacit Knowledge and General Intelligence

In proposing a new approach to measuring intelligence, it is important to show that one has not accidentally reinvented the concept of "g," or so-called general ability, as measured by traditional intelligence tests. We do not dispute the relevance of general cognitive ability to performance. Schmidt and Hunter (1998) have shown that g predicts performance in a number of domains. Our aim is to show that tacit-knowledge tests measure something in addition to g. In all the above studies in which participants were given a traditional measure of cognitive ability, tacit-knowledge test scores correlated insignificantly with g (see also Chapter Seventeen).

The most consistently used measure of g in the above studies was the verbal reasoning subtest of the Differential Aptitudes Test. The absolute values of the correlations between tacit knowledge and verbal reasoning ranged from .04 to

.16 with undergraduate samples (Wagner, 1987; Wagner & Sternberg, 1985) and were .14 with a sample of business executives (Wagner & Sternberg, 1990).

One potential limitation of these findings is that they were obtained with restricted samples (such as Yale undergraduates and business managers). However, similar support for the relationship between tacit knowledge and g was found in a more general sample of air force recruits studied by Eddy (1988). The correlations between scores on the Tactic Knowledge Inventory for Managers (TKIM; Wagner & Steinberg, 1985) and the Armed Services Vocational Aptitude Battery (ASVAB; U.S. Department of Defense, 1984) scales were modest, and none of the four ASVAB factors correlated significantly with the tacit-knowledge score.

Tacit-knowledge tests may also be a better predictor of managerial success than are measures of personality, cognitive style, and interpersonal orientation, as suggested by the findings from the Center for Creative Leadership study (Wagner & Sternberg, 1990). Sternberg et al. (1999) recently developed a test of common sense for the workplace (for example, how to handle oneself in a job interview) that predicts self-ratings of common sense but not self-ratings of various kinds of academic abilities. The test also predicts supervisory ratings at a correlational level of about .40.

Tacit Knowledge as a General Construct

Although the kinds of informal procedural knowledge measured by tacit-knowledge tests do not correlate with traditional psychometric intelligence, tacit-knowledge test scores do correlate across domains. Furthermore, the structure of tacit knowledge appears to be represented best by a single, general factor.

Wagner (1987) examined the structure of tacit knowledge inventory for managers. He performed two kinds of factor analyses on the tacit-knowledge scores of these business managers in his study. First, a principal-components analysis yielded a first principal component that accounted for 44 percent of the total variance, and 76 percent of the total variance after the correlations among scores were disattenuated for unreliability. The 40 percent variance accounted for by the first principal component is typical of analyses carried out on traditional cognitive-ability subtests. Second, results of a confirmatory factor analysis suggested that a model consisting of a single general factor provided the best fit to the data. The results of both factor analyses suggested a general factor of tacit knowledge.

Similar analyses were performed on a measure of tacit knowledge for academic psychologists. Consistent with the managers' study, the factor-analytic results suggested a single factor of tacit knowledge within the domain of academic psychology. Wagner (1987) also examined the generalizability of tacit-knowledge across domains by administering both tacit-knowledge measures (for business managers and academic psychologists) to undergraduates in his study. He obtained a significant correlation of .58 between the two scores, suggesting that in addition to the existence of a general factor of tacit knowledge within a domain, individual differences in tacit knowledge generalize across domains. These findings lend support for a common factor underlying tacit knowledge—a factor that is considered to be an aspect of practical intelligence.

Tacit Knowledge and Performance

Finally, we have shown that tacit-knowledge measures are predictive of performance in a number of domains, correlating between .2 and .5 with measures such as rated prestige of business or institution, salary, simulation performance, and number of publications. These correlations, uncorrected for attenuation or restriction of range, compare favorably with those obtained for IQ within the range of abilities we have tested.

In studies with business managers, tacit-knowledge scores correlated in the range of .2 to .4 with criteria such as salary, years of management experience, and whether the manager worked for a company at the top of the Fortune 500 list (Wagner, 1987; Wagner & Sternberg, 1985). Wagner and Sternberg (1990) obtained a correlation of .61 between tacit knowledge and performance on a managerial simulation and found that tacit-knowledge scores explained additional variance beyond IQ and other personality and ability measures. In a study with bank branch managers, Wagner and Sternberg (1985) obtained significant correlations between tacit-knowledge scores and average percentage of merit-based salary increase (.48, $p < .05$) and average performance rating for the category of generating new business for the bank (.56, $p < .05$).

Williams and Sternberg (cited in Sternberg et al., 1995) also found that tacit knowledge was related to several indicators of managerial success, including compensation, age-controlled compensation, level of position, and job satisfaction, with correlations ranging from .23 to .39.

Although much of the tacit-knowledge research has involved business mangers, there is evidence that tacit knowledge explains performance in other domains. In the field of academic psychology, correlations in the .4 to .5 range were found between tacit-knowledge scores and criterion measures such as citation rate, number of publications, and quality of department (Wagner, 1987; Wagner & Sternberg, 1985). In studies with salespeople, Wagner et al. (1994) found correlations in the .3 to .4 range between tacit knowledge and criteria such as sales volume and sales awards received. Finally, tacit knowledge for college students was found to correlate with indices of academic performance and adjustment to college (Williams & Sternberg cited in Sternberg et al., 1993).

CONCLUSION

In summary, the program of tacit-knowledge research we have reviewed shows that, generally, tacit knowledge increases with experience but is not simply a proxy for experience; that tacit-knowledge tests measure a distinct construct from that measured by traditional, abstract intelligence tests; that scores on tacit-knowledge tests represent a general factor, which appears to correlate across domains; and finally, that tacit-knowledge tests are predictive of performance in a number of domains and compare favorably with those obtained for IQ within the range of abilities we have tested.

More generally, the total body of research shows that practical intelligence is distinct from but complementary to academic intelligence. Both kinds of intelligence matter for success in everyday life. Fortunately, many researchers in the field of intelligence, recognizing this fact, are moving from exclusive emphasis on the traditional academic aspect of intelligence to a broader emphasis that encompasses the practical as well as the academic aspect of intelligence.

NOTES

Requests for reprints should be sent to Robert J. Sternberg, Department of Psychology, Yale University, P.O. Box 208205, New Haven, CT 06520–8205 USA.

References

Aldwin, C. M., Sutton, K. J., Chiara, G., & Spiro, A. (1996). Age differences in stress, coping, and appraisal: Findings from the normative aging study. *Journal of Gerontology: Psychological Sciences, 51B,* 178–188.

Bäckman, L., & Dixon, R. A. (1992). Psychological compensation: A theoretical framework. *Psychological Bulletin, 112,* 259–283.

Baltes, P. B. (1987). Theoretical propositions of life-span developmental psychology: On the dynamics between growth and decline. *Developmental Psychology, 23,* 611–626.

Baltes, P. B. (1993). The aging mind: Potentials and limits. *The Gerontologist, 33,* 580–594.

Baltes, P. B. (1997). On the incomplete architecture of human ontogeny: Selection, optimization, and compensation as foundation of developmental theory. *American Psychologist, 52,* 366–380.

Baltes, P. B., & Baltes, M. M. (1990). Psychological perspectives on successful aging: A model of selective optimization with compensation. In P. B. Baltes & M. M. Baltes (Eds.), *Successful aging: Perspectives from the behavioral sciences* (pp. 1–34) Cambridge, U.K.: Cambridge University Press.

Baltes, P. B., Dittmann-Kohli, F., & Dixon, R. A. (1984). New perspectives on the development of intelligence in adulthood: Toward a dual-process conception and a model of selective optimization with compensation. In P. B. Baltes & O. G. Brim (Eds.), *Life-span development and behavior* (Vol 6., pp. 33–76). New York: Academic Press.

Baltes, P. B., & Smith, J. (1990). Toward a psychology of wisdom and its ontogenesis. In R. J. Sternberg (Ed.), *Wisdom: Its nature, origins, and development* (pp. 87–120). New York: Cambridge University Press.

Baltes, P. B., Smith, J., & Staudinger, U. (1992). Wisdom and successful aging. In T. B. Sonderegger (Ed.), *Psychology and aging* (pp. 123–167). Lincoln, NE: University of Nebraska Press.

Baltes, P. B., Sowarka, D., & Kliegl, R. (1989). Cognitive training research on fluid intelligence in old age: What can older adults achieve by themselves? *Psychology and Aging, 4,* 217–221.

Band, E. B., & Weisz, J. R. (1988). How to feel better when it feels bad: Children's perspective on coping with everyday stress. *Developmental Psychology, 24,* 247–253.

Bandura, A. (1986). *Social foundations of thought and action.* Englewood Cliffs, NJ: Prentice Hall.

Barker, R. G. (Ed.) (1978). *Habitats, environments, and human behavior.* San Francisco: Jossey-Bass.

Barrett, G. V., & Depinet, R. L. (1991). A reconsideration of testing for competence rather than for intelligence. *American Psychologist, 46,* 1012–1024.

Barrett, G. V., & Watkins, S. K. (1986). Word familiarity and cardiovascular health as determinants of age-related recall differences. *Journal of Gerontology, 41,* 222–224.

Belmont, J. N., & Butterfield, E. C. (1969). The relations of short-term memory to development and intelligence. In L. Lipsitt & H. Reese (Eds.), *Advances in child development and behavior* (Vol. 4, pp. 30–83). New York: Academic Press.

Berg, C. A. (1989). Knowledge of strategies for dealing with everyday problems from childhood through adolescence. *Developmental Psychology, 25,* 607–618.

Berg, C. A. (2000). The intellectual development in adulthood. In R. J. Sternberg (Ed.), *Handbook of intelligence* (2nd ed., pp. 117–137). New York: Cambridge University Press.

Berg, C. A., & Calderone, K. (1994). The role of problem interpretations in understanding the development of everyday problem solving. In R. J. Sternberg & R. K. Wagner (Eds.), *Mind in context* (pp. 105–132). New York: Cambridge University Press.

Berg, C. A., Calderone, K., Sansone, C., Strough, J., & Weir, C. (1998). The role of problem definitions in understanding age and context effects on strategies for solving everyday problems. *Psychology and Aging, 13,* 29–44.

Berg, C. A., Hertzog, C., & Hunt, E. (1982). Age differences in the speed of mental rotation. *Developmental Psychology, 18,* 95–107.

Berg, C. A., & Klaczynski, P. (1996). Practical intelligence and problem solving: Searching for perspective. In F. Blanchard-Fields & T. M. Hess (Eds.), *Perspectives on cognition in adulthood and aging* (pp. 323–357). New York: McGraw-Hill.

Berg, C. A., Klaczynski, P., Calderone, K. S., & Strough, J. (1994). Adult age differences in cognitive strategies: Adaptive or deficient. In J. Sinnott (Ed.), *Interdisciplinary handbook of adult lifespan learning* (pp. 371–388). Westport, CT: Greenwood Press.

Berg, C. A., & Sternberg, R. J. (1985). A triarchic theory of intellectual development during adulthood. *Developmental Review, 5,* 334–370.

Blanchard-Fields, F. (1986). Reasoning and social dilemmas varying in emotional saliency: An adult developmental perspective. *Psychology and Aging, 1,* 325–333.

Blanchard-Fields, F. (1994). Age differences in causal attributions from an adult developmental perspective. *Journal of Gerontology: Psychological Sciences, 49,* 43–51.

Blanchard-Fields, F., Jahnke, H. C., & Camp, C. (1995). Age differences in problem-solving style: The role of emotional salience. *Psychology & Aging, 10,* 173–180.

Blanchard-Fields, F., & Norris, L. (1994). Causal attributions from adolescence through adulthood: Age differences, ego level, and generalized response style. *Aging Neuropsychology & Cognition, 1,* 67–86.

Brandtstaedter, J., & Greve, W. (1994). The aging self: Stabilizing and protective processes. *Developmental Review, 14,* 52–80.

Brown, A. L. (1975). The development of memory: Knowing, knowing about knowing, and knowing how to know. In H. W. Reese (Ed.), *Advances in child development and behavior* (Vol. 10, pp. 103–152). New York: Academic Press

Cantor, N. (1990). From thought to behavior: "Having" and "doing" in the study of personality and cognition. *American Psychologist, 45,* 735–750.

Cantor, N., Norem, J. K., Niedenthal, P. M., Langston, C. A., & Brower, A. M. (1987). Life tasks, self-concept ideals, and cognitive strategies in a life transition. *Journal of Personality and Social Psychology, 53,* 1178–1191.

Ceci, S. J., & Brofenbrenner, U. (1985). Don't forget to take the cupcakes out of the oven: Strategic time-monitoring, prospective memory and context. *Child Development, 56,* 175–190.

Ceci, S. J., & Liker, J. (1986). Academic and nonacademic intelligence: An experimental separation. In R. J. Sternberg & R. K. Wagner (Eds.), *Practical intelligence: Nature and origins of competence in the everyday world* (pp. 119–142). New York: Cambridge University Press.

Ceci, S. J., & Liker, J. (1988). Stalking the IQ-expertise relationship: When the critics go fishing. *Journal of Experimental Psychology: General, 117,* 96–100.

Ceci, S. J., & Roazzi, A. (1994). The effects of context on cognition: Postcards from Brazil. In R. J. Sternberg & R. K. Wagner (Eds.), *Mind in context: Interactionist perspectives on human intelligence* (pp. 74–101). New York: Cambridge University Press.

Ceci, S. J., & Ruiz, A. (1991). Cognitive complexity and generality: A case study. In R. Hoffman (Ed.), *The psychology of expertise.* New York: Springer-Verlag.

Charness, N. (1981). Search in chess: Age and skill differences. *Journal of Experimental Psychology: Human Perception and Performance, 7,* 467–476.

Charness, N., & Bieman-Coplan, S. (1994). The learning prospective: Adulthood. In R. J. Sternberg & C. A. Berg (Eds.), *Intellectual development* (pp. 301–327). New York: Cambridge University Press.

Charness, N., & Bosman, E. A. (1990). Expertise and aging: Life in the lab. In T. M. Hess (Ed.), *Aging and cognition: Knowledge organization and utilization* (pp. 343–385). Amsterdam: Elsevier Science.

Charness, N., & Bosman, E. A. (1995). Compensation through environmental modification. In R. A. Dixon & L. Baeckman (Eds.), *Compensating for psychological deficits and declines: Managing losses and promoting gains.* (pp. 147–168). Mahwah, NJ: Erlbaum.

Chi, M.T.H., & Ceci, S. J. (1987). Content knowledge: Its role, representation, and restructuring in memory development. In H. W. Reese (Ed.), *Advances in child development and behavior* (Vol. 20, pp. 91–142). Orlando, FL: Academic Press.

Colonia-Willner, R. (1998). Practical intelligence at work: Relationship between aging and cognitive efficiency among managers in a bank environment. *Psychology and Aging, 13,* 45–57.

Cornelius, S. W. (1984). Classic pattern of intellectual aging: Test familiarity, difficulty, and performance. *Journal of Gerontology, 39,* 201–206.

Cornelius, S. W., & Caspi, A. (1987). Everyday problem solving in adulthood and old age. *Psychology and Aging, 2,* 144–153.

Denney, N. W. (1982). Aging and cognitive changes. In B. B. Wolman (Ed.), *Handbook of developmental psychology* (pp. 807–827). Englewood Cliffs, NJ: Prentice Hall.

Denney, N. W. (1989). Everyday problem solving: Methodological issues, research findings, and a model. In I. W. Poon, D. C. Rubin, & B. A. Wilson (Eds.), *Everyday cognition in adulthood and late life* (pp. 330–351). New York: Cambridge University Press.

Denney, N. W., & Palmer, A. M. (1981). Adult age differences on traditional and practical problem-solving measures. *Journal of Gerontology, 36,* 323–328.

Denney, N. W., & Pearce, K. A. (1989). A developmental study of practical problem solving in adults. *Psychology and Aging, 4,* 438–442.

Denney, N. W., Pearce, K. A., & Palmer, A. M. (1982). A developmental study of adults' performance on traditional and practical problem-solving tasks. *Experimental Aging Research, 8,* 115–118.

Dittmann-Kohli, F., & Baltes, P. B. (1990). Towards a neofunctionalist conception of adult intellectual development: Wisdom as a prototypical case of intellectual growth. In C. N. Alexander & E. J. Langer (Eds.), *Higher stages of human development: Perspectives on adult growth* (pp. 54–78). New York: Oxford University Press.

Dixon, R. A. (1994). Contextual approaches to adult intellectual development. In R. J. Sternberg & C. A. Berg (Eds.), *Intellectual development* (pp. 350–380). New York: Cambridge University Press.

Dodge, K. A., Pettit, G. S., McClaskey, C. L., & Brown, M. M. (1986). Social competence in children. *Monographs of the Society for Research in Child Development, 51,* 1–85.

Dörner, D., & Kreuzig, H. (1983). Problemlosefahigkeit und intelligenz [Problem solving ability and intelligence]. *Psychologische Rundschaus, 34,* 185–192.

Dörner, D., Kreuzig, H., Reither, F., & Staudel, T. (1983). *Lohhausen: Vom Umgang mit Unbestimmtheir und Komplexitat* [Lohhausen: On dealing with uncertainty and complexity]. Bern: Huber.

Eddy, A. S. (1988). *The relationship between the Tacit Knowledge Inventory for Mangers and the Armed Services Vocational Aptitude Battery.* Unpublished master's thesis, St. Mary's University, San Antonio, TX.

Ferrari, M., & Sternberg, R. J. (Eds.) (1998). *Self-awareness: Its nature and development.* New York: Guilford Press.

Flavell, J. H. (1970). Developmental studies of mediated memory. In H. W. Reese & L. P. Lipsitt (Eds.), *Advances in child development and child behavior* (Vol 5., pp. 181–211). New York: Academic Press.

Fleeson, W., & Cantor, N. (1995). Goal relevance and the affective experience of daily life: Ruling out situation explanation. *Motivation and Emotion, 19,* 25–57.

Folkman, S., Lazarus, R. S., Pimley, S., & Novacek, J. (1987). Age differences in stress and coping processes. *Psychology and Aging, 2,* 171–184.

Frederiksen, N. (1986). Toward a broader conception of human intelligence. *American Psychology, 41,* 445–452.

Frederiksen, N., Jensen, O., & Beaton, A. E. (1972). *Prediction of organizational behavior.* New York: Pergamon Press.

Freeman, N. H., Lewis, C., & Doherty, M. J. (1991). Preschoolers' grasp of a desire for knowledge in false-belief prediction: Practical intelligence and verbal report. *British Journal of Developmental Psychology, 9,* 139–157.

Goodnow, J. J. (1986). Some lifelong everyday forms of intelligence behavior: Organizing and reorganizing. In R. J. Sternberg & R. K. Wagner (Eds.), *Practical intelligence* (pp. 31–50). New York: Cambridge University Press.

Harter, S. (1983). Developmental prospectives on the self-system. In P. H. Mussen (Ed.), *Handbook of child psychology* (Vol. 4, pp. 275–385). New York: Wiley.

Hartley, A. A. (1989). The cognitive etiology of problem solving. In L. W. Poon, D. C. Rubin, &. B. A. Wilson (Eds.), *Everyday cognition in adulthood and late life* (pp. 300–329). New York: Cambridge University Press.

Havinghurst, R. (1972). *Developmental tasks and education.* New York: Van Nostrand.

Heckhausen, J., & Schulz, R. (1995). A life-span theory of control. *Psychological Review, 102,* 284–304.

Jensen, A. R. (1993). Test validity: g versus "tacit knowledge." *Current Directions in Psychological Science, 1,* 9–10.

Kohn, M. L., & Schooler, C. (Eds.) (1983). *Work and personality.* Norwood, NJ: Ablex.

Kreitler, S., & Kreitler, H. (1987). Conceptions and processes of planning: The developmental perspective. In S. L. Friedman & E. K. Scholnick (Eds.), *Blueprints for thinking: The role of planning in cognitive development* (pp. 205–272). Cambridge, U.K.: Cambridge University Press.

Kuhn, D., Pennington, N., & Leadbeater, B. (1983). Adult thinking in developmental perspective. In P. B. Baltes & O. G. Brim (Eds.), *Life-span development and behavior* (Vol. 5, pp. 158–195). New York: Academic Press.

Labouvie-Vief, G. (1992). A neo-Piagetian perspective on adult cognitive development. In R. J. Sternberg & C. A. Berg (Eds.), *Intellectual development* (pp. 197–228). New York: Cambridge University Press.

Laipple, J. S. (1992). Problem-solving in young and old adulthood: The role of task interpretation. *Dissertation Abstracts International, 53*(1-B), 582.

Lave, J., Murtaugh, M., & de la Roche, O. (1984). The dialectic of arithmetic in grocery shopping. In B. Rogoff & J. Lace (Eds.), *Everyday cognition: Its development in social context* (pp. 67–94). Cambridge, MA: Harvard University Press.

Lazarus, R. S., & Folkman, S. (1984). *Stress, appraisal, and coping.* New York: Springer.

Loewen, E. R., Shaw, J. R., & Craik, F.I.M. (1990). Age differences in components of metamemory. *Experimental Aging Research, 16,* 43–48.

Meacham, J. A., & Emont, N. C. (1989). The interpersonal basis of everyday problem solving. In J. D. Sinnott (Ed.), *Everyday problem solving* (pp. 7–23). New York: Praeger.

Miller, K. A., & Kohn, M. L. (1983). The reciprocal effects on job conditions and the intellectuality of leisure time activities. In M. L. Kohn & C. Schooler (Eds.), *Work and personality* (pp. 217–241). Norwood, NJ: Ablex.

Mischel, W. (1984). Convergences and challenges in the search for consistency. *American Psychologist, 39,* 351–364.

Murtaugh, M. (1985). The practice of arithmetic by American grocery shoppers. *Anthropology and Education Quarterly, 16,* 186–192.

Naus, M. J., & Ornstein, P. A. (1983). Development of memory strategies: Analysis, questions and issues. In M.T.M. Chi (Ed.), *Trends in memory development research: Contributions to human development* (Vol. 9, pp. 1–30). Basel, Switzerland: S. Karger.

Neisser, U. (1976). General, academic, and artificial intelligence. In L. Resnick (Ed.), *Human intelligence: Perspectives on its theory and measurement* (pp. 179–189). Norwood, NJ: Ablex.

Neugarten, B. L., Moore, J. W., & Lowe, J. C. (1968). Age norms, age constraints, and adult socialization. In B. L. Neugarten (Ed.), *Middle age and aging* (pp. 22–28). Chicago: University of Chicago Press.

Piaget, J. (1972). *The psychology of intelligence.* Totowa, NJ: Littlefield Adams.

Pressley, M., Forrest-Pressley, D. L., Elliot-Faust, D., & Miller, G. (1985). Children's use of cognitive strategies: How to teach strategies, and what to do if they can't be taught. In M. Pressley & C. J. Brainers (Eds.), *Cognitive learning and memory in children: Progress in cognitive development research* (pp. 1–47). New York: Springer.

Ree, M. J., & Earles, J. A. (1993). *g* is to psychology what carbon is to chemistry: A reply to Sternberg and Wagner, McClelland, and Calfee. *Current Directions in Psychological Science, 1,* 11–12.

Rogoff, B. (1982). Integrating context and cognitive development. In M. E. Lamb & A. L. Brown (Eds.), *Advances in development psychology* (Vol. 2, pp. 125–169). Hillsdale, NJ: Erlbaum.

Rogoff, B., Gauvain, M., & Gardner, W. (1987). Children's adjustment of plans to circumstances. In S. L. Friedman, E. K., Scholnick, & R. R. Cocking (Eds.), *Blueprints for thinking* (pp. 303–320). New York: Cambridge University Press.

Rogoff, B., & Lave, J. (Eds.). (1984). *Everyday cognition: its development in social context.* Cambridge, MA: Harvard University Press.

Salthouse, T. A. (1984). Effects of age and skill in typing. *Journal of Experimental Psychology: General, 113,* 345–371.

Salthouse, T. A., & Somberg, B. L. (1982). Skilled performance: The effects of adult age and experience on elementary processes. *Journal of Experimental Psychology: General, 111,* 176–207.

Sansone, C., & Berg, C. A. (1993). Adapting to the environment across the life span: Different process or different inputs? *International Journal of Behavioral Development, 16,* 215–241.

Schaie, K. W. (1996). *Intellectual development in adulthood: The Seattle Longitudinal Study.* New York: Cambridge University Press.

Schmidt, F. L., & Hunter, J. E. (1993). Tacit knowledge, practical intelligence, general mental ability, and job knowledge. *Current Directions in Psychological Science, 1,* 8–9.

Schmidt, F. L, & Hunter, J. E. (1998). The validity and utility of selection methods in personnel psychology: Practical and theoretical implications of 85 years of research findings. *Psychological Bulletin, 124,* 262–274.

Schooler, C. (1984). Psychological effects of complex environments during the life span: A review and theory. *Intelligence, 8,* 259–281.

Schooler, C. (forthcoming). The intellectual effects of the demands of the work environment. In R. S. Sternberg & E. L. Grigorenko (Eds.), *Environmental effects on intellectual functioning.* Hillsdale, NJ: Erlbaum.

Scribner, S. (1984). Studying working intelligence. In B. Rogoff & J. Lave (Eds.), *Everyday cognition: Its development in social context* (pp. 9–40). Cambridge, MA: Harvard University Press.

Scribner, S. (1986). Thinking in action: Some characteristics of practical thought. In R. J. Sternberg & R. K. Wagner (Eds.), *Practical intelligence: Nature and origins of competence in the everyday world* (pp. 13–30). New York: Cambridge University Press.

Scribner, S., & Cole, M. (1981). *The psychology of literacy.* Cambridge, MA: Harvard University Press.

Sinnott, J. D. (1989). A model for solution of ill-structured problems: Implications for everyday and abstract problem solving. In J. D. Sinnott (Ed.), *Everyday problem solving: Theory and applications* (pp. 72–99). New York: Praeger.

Smith, J., & Baltes, P. B. (1990). Wisdom-related knowledge: Age/cohort differences in response to life-planning problems. *Developmental Psychology, 26,* 494–505.

Smith, J., Staudinger, U. M., & Baltes, P. B. (1994). Occupational settings facilitating wisdom-related knowledge: the sample case of clinical psychologists. *Journal of Consulting and Clinical Psychology, 62,* 989–999.

Sternberg, R. J. (1985). *Beyond IQ: A triarchic theory of human abilities.* New York: Cambridge University Press.

Sternberg, R. J. (1997). *Successful intelligence.* New York: Plume.

Sternberg, R. J. (1999). The theory of successful intelligence. *Review of General Psychology, 3,* 292–316.

Sternberg, R. J. (Ed.). (2000). *Handbook of intelligence.* New York: Cambridge University Press.

Sternberg, R. J., & Berg, C. A. (1992). *Intellectual development.* New York: Cambridge University Press.

Sternberg, R. J., Castejón, J. L., Prieto, M. D., Hautakami, J., & Grigorenko, E. L. (forthcoming). Confirmatory factor analysis of the Sternberg Triarchic Abilities Test (multiple-choice items) in three international samples: An empirical test of the triarchic theory of intelligence. *European Journal of Psychological Assessment.*

Sternberg, R. J., Forsythe, G. B., Hedlund, J., Horvath, J., Snook, S., Williams, W. M., Wagner, R. K., & Grigorenko, E. L. (2000). *Practical intelligence in everyday life.* New York: Cambridge University Press.

Sternberg, R. J., Grigorenko, E. L., Ferrari, M., & Clinkenbeard, P. (1999). A triarchic analysis of an aptitude-treatment interaction. *European Journal of Psychological Assessment, 15,* 1–11.

Sternberg, R. J., Nokes, K., Geissler, P. W., Prince, R., Okatcha, F., Bundy, D. A., & Grigorenko, E. L. (forthcoming). The relationship between academic and practical intelligence: A case study in Kenya. *Intelligence.*

Sternberg, R. J., & Powell, J. S. (1983). The development of intelligence. In J. Flavell & E. Markman (Eds.), *Handbook of child psychology* (Vol. 3, 3rd ed., pp. 341–419). New York: Wiley.

Sternberg, R. J., Torff, B., & Grigorenko, E. L. (1998a). Teaching for successful intelligence raises school achievement. *Phi Delta Kappan, 79,* 667–669.

Sternberg, R. J., Torff, B., & Grigorenko, E. L. (1998b). Teaching triarchically improves school achievement. *Journal of Educational Psychology, 90,* 374–384.

Sternberg, R. J., & Wagner, R. K. (Eds.). (1986). *Practical intelligence: Nature and origins of competence in the everyday world.* New York: Cambridge University Press.

Sternberg, R. J., & Wagner, R. K. (1993). The geocentric view of intelligence and job performance is wrong. *Current Directions in Psychological Science, 2,* 1–5.

Sternberg, R. J., & Wagner, R. K. (Eds.). (1994). *Mind in context.* New York: Cambridge University Press.

Sternberg, R. J., & Wagner, R. K., & Okagaki, L. (1993). Practical intelligence: The nature and role of tacit knowledge in work and at school. In H. Reese & J. Puckett (Eds.), *Advances in lifespan development* (pp. 205–227). Hillsdale, NJ: Erlbaum.

Sternberg, R. J., Wagner, R. K., Williams, W. M., & Horvath, J. A. (1995). Testing common sense. *American Psychologist, 50,* 912–927.

Strough, J., Berg, C., & Sansone, C. (1996). Goals for solving everyday problems across the life span: age and gender differences in the salience of interpersonal concerns. *Developmental Psychology, 32,* 1106–1115.

U.S. Department of Defense. (1994). *Test Manual for the Armed Services Vocational Aptitude Battery.* North Chicago, IL: U.S. Military Entrance Processing Command.

Vallacher, R. R., & Wegner, D. M. (1987). What do people think they're doing? Action identification and human behavior. *Psychological Review, 94,* 3–15.

Voss, J. F., Perkins, D. N., & Segal, J. W. (Eds.). (1991). *Informal reasoning and education.* Hillsdale, NJ: Erlbaum.

Wagner, R. K. (1987). Tacit knowledge in everyday intelligent behavior. *Journal of Personality and Social Psychology, 52,* 1236–1247.

Wagner, R. K. (2000). Practical intelligence. In R. J. Sternberg (Ed.), *Handbook of intelligence* (2nd ed., pp. 380–395). New York: Cambridge University Press.

Wagner, R. K., Rashotte, C. A., & Sternberg, R. J. (1994, May). *Tacit Knowledge in sales: Rules of thumb for selling anything to anyone.* Paper presented at the Annual Meeting of the American Educational Research Association, Washington, DC.

Wagner, R. K., & Sternberg, R. J. (1985). Practical intelligence in real-world pursuits: The role of tacit knowledge. *Journal of Personality and Social Psychology, 49,* 436–458.

Wagner, R. K., & Sternberg, R. J. (1990). Street smarts. In K. E. Clark & M. B. Clark (Eds.), *Measures of leadership* (pp. 493–504). West Orange, NJ: Leadership Library of America.

Wertsch, J. V. (1985). *Vygotsky and the social formation of mind.* Cambridge, MA: Harvard University Press.

Wertsch, J., & Kanner, B. G. (1994). A sociocultural approach to intellectual development. In R. J. Sternberg & C. A. Berg (Eds.), *Intellectual development* (pp. 328–349). New York: Cambridge University Press.

Wigdor, A. K., & Garner, W. R. (Eds.) (1982). *Ability testing: Uses, consequences, and controversies.* Washington, DC: National Academy Press.

Willis, S. L. (1989). Improvement with cognitive training: Which dogs learn what tricks? In L. W. Poon, D. C. Rubin, & B. A. Wilson (Eds.), *Everyday cognition in adulthood and late life* (pp. 300–329). New York: Cambridge University Press.

Willis, S. L., & Schaie, K. W. (1986). Practical intelligence in later adulthood. In R. J. Sternberg & R. Wagner (Eds.), *Practical Intelligence* (pp. 236–270). New York: Cambridge University Press.

Worden, P. E., & Sherman-Brown, S. (1983). A word-frequency cohort effect in young versus elderly adults' memory for words. *Developmental Psychology, 19,* 521–530.

CHAPTER ELEVEN

Development of Emotional Expression, Understanding, and Regulation in Infants and Young Children

Elaine Scharfe

The Cat only grinned when it saw Alice. It looked good-natured,
she thought: still it had VERY long claws and a great many teeth,
so she felt that it ought to be treated with respect. "Cheshire Puss," she began,
rather timidly, as she did not at all know whether it would like the name:
however, it only grinned a little wider. "Come, it's pleased so far," thought Alice,
and she went on. "Would you tell me, please, which way I ought to go from here?"
—Lewis Carroll, *Alice's Adventures in Wonderland*

Learning to accurately express, recognize, and understand emotional expressions is an important developmental task for infants and children. Children use emotional knowledge to guide them through the social world, just as Alice uses the facial expression of the Cheshire cat to judge whether he will be helpful in her quest to find a way out of Wonderland. Although, Alice seems to comprehend the emotional world, readers sympathize with her struggle to understand the ambiguous expressions of the Cheshire cat. Alice's eventual success in finding her way can be attributed, at least in part, to her ability to accurately judge emotions.

Recently, researchers from clinical, social, educational, and developmental psychology have independently proposed theories to explain the development of emotional or social intelligence (Bar-On, 1997; Gardner, 1983; Goleman, 1995; Mayer & Salovey, 1993, 1997; Saarni, 1990; Taylor, Bagby, & Parker, 1997). For the most part, researchers agree that emotionally intelligent individuals are able to regulate, as well as accurately perceive and generate, emotional expressions, and that this ability develops across the life span. With the noted exception of Carolyn Saarni (see Saarni, 1990, for theory of development of emotional competence), few developmental researchers have specifically addressed the development of emotional intelligence. There is, however, a substantial body of developmental research detailing how infants and children learn to accurately express, understand, and regulate their emotions, and researchers are becoming increasingly aware of the developmental sequence underlying emotional development. Children learn to express, understand, and regulate their emotions in interactions with their parents, siblings, and peers. Due to the vast diversity of social worlds and individual potential, some children learn to skillfully master emotions of themselves and others, whereas for others, their skills in interpreting emotions are insufficient to achieve success in the social world. Not surprisingly, there is some support for the proposal that consideration of individual differences contributes to understanding of emotional development, in particular the superior emotional abilities of some individuals (Denham, 1986; Fox, 1989; Malatesta, Culver, Tesman, & Shepard, 1989). In this chapter, I summarize recent developmental literature examining the development of expression, understanding, and regulation of emotions in infants and young children and briefly outline how competence in the emotional world of children is associated with superior social skills and acceptance by peers.

EXPRESSION OF EMOTIONS

Researchers propose that humans have an innate capacity to express the emotions of joy, fear, anger, sadness, surprise, and disgust (Izard, 1971; Izard et al., 1995). Although infants seem to spontaneously produce expressions of happiness, sadness, and anger (Malatesta et. al., 1989), it is much less clear when children can deliberately produce facial expressions to communicate their felt emotions. Field, Woodson, Greenberg, & Cohen (1982) demonstrated that infants could imitate adults' facial expressions during the first few days of life. Furthermore, observers accurately judged the infants' imitated expressions of surprise (76 percent accuracy), happiness (58 percent accuracy), and sadness (59 percent accuracy). However, it is unclear whether the infants felt the emotions that they imitated or were merely imitating caregivers' facial expressions.

In a comprehensive examination of the development of emotional expression during the first three years of life, Malatesta and her colleagues explored the ability of infants to spontaneously generate emotional expressions, the stability of individual differences of expression, and the association between expressive behavior and several mother and infant variables (Malatesta et al., 1989; Malatesta-Magai et al., 1994). To assess infants' expressivity, researchers videotaped mother-infant play and separation-reunion sessions at two and one-half, five, seven and one-half, and twenty-two months. Mother-child play, as well as play with an unfamiliar peer, was also videotaped when the children were thirty-four months old. The researchers reported that infants as young as two and one-half months displayed an extensive array of facial expressions. Furthermore, they demonstrated that several variables influenced the development of individual differences in infant expression. First, maternal expressive behavior in reaction to infants' behavior predicted infant expressivity. In particular, the researchers reported benefits for infants of mothers who displayed moderate contingency in response to changes in infant facial expressions. Low levels of maternal contingency were associated with neutral affect for both mothers and infants in the third year. High levels of maternal contingency, which may be perceived as aversive by infants, were associated with increased levels of negative affect in the third year. Furthermore, maternal interest in response to early emotional expressions was associated with positive expressivity in infants. When mothers ignored expressions such as pain and sadness, their infants expressed more sadness and anger during the separation-reunion episode at two years. Second, inconsistent with expectations, birth status was associated with negative outcomes. Preterm infants displayed higher levels of negative affect during play sessions, and three-year-old preterm infants and their mothers were likely to develop an engaged and conflictual relationship. Third, insecure children were more likely to display seemingly positive expressions during times of stress in a probable attempt to suppress negative expressions. For example, during the thirty-four-month follow-up, insecure children displayed an increased tendency to bite their lip during the laboratory play sessions. This behavior was presumed to indicate anxiety felt by the insecure children during the play session with the unfamiliar peer. In summary, Malatesta and her colleagues demonstrated that infants have the capacity to display expressions early in life and that the infants' birth status and maternal care characteristics influence this capacity.

In an attempt to determine if maternal affect would influence infants' tendency to express certain emotions, Pickens and Field (1993) compared the facial expressions of three-month-old infants and their mothers during face-to-face play. Mothers were categorized as nondepressed, depressed, or low scoring[1] on the Beck Depression Inventory (BDI). As expected, infants of nondepressed mothers showed significantly less sadness and anger, and significantly more interest than infants of depressed and low-scoring mothers. Nondepressed mothers also showed less negative affect during the face-to-face play session than the depressed and low-scoring mothers. Although the results supported that infants of depressed mothers were likely to exhibit negative affect, it was difficult to determine, as pointed out by Pickens and Field (1993), whether infants were mimicking their mothers' specific negative expressions or exhibiting general negative affect.

The difficulty in determining whether infants differ in their expressivity or their ability to mimic facial expressions has lead some researchers to examine

---

[1] In a previous study, Field and her colleagues (Field et al., 1991) found that mothers who scored zero on the BDI acted more depressed with their infants than nondepressed mothers with higher BDI scores.

physiological predictors of emotional expressivity. Fox and his colleagues found that expressive infants and preschoolers tend to have higher heart rate variability and higher vagal tone than inexpressive infants and preschoolers (Cole, Zahn-Waxler, Fox, Usher, & Welsh, 1996; Fox, 1989; Stifter & Fox, 1990). Furthermore, in several studies Davidson and Fox found that emotional inhibition of infants was associated with greater relative frontal lobe activation. Infants with greater right lobe activation at baseline tended to be more reactive to maternal separation (Davidson & Fox, 1989). Increased left frontal lobe activation in infants was observed when infants were attempting to approach a caregiver (Fox and Davidson, 1987, 1988). Finally, increased relative right frontal lobe activation was observed in infants who were distressed during maternal separation (Fox and Davidson, 1987). The results from these studies have lead researchers to propose an association between individual differences in emotional expressivity and brain activation.

Researchers examining expression and identification in older children report more conclusive evidence that children can accurately produce and identify emotions. For example, Field and Waldon (1982) demonstrated that three- to five-year-olds could produce facial expressions when given a photograph to be imitated. Furthermore, with the photograph to guide their imitation attempts, children could successfully imitate emotions with or without a mirror or an emotional label (for example, children were told the name of the emotion in the picture and asked to imitate that emotion). Adults accurately judged these posed expressions and the expressions were somewhat less accurately judged by the children. Children's productions from labels only were less accurately judged by others than children's productions when the children were given additional information to model their facial expressions. Furthermore, the production of socially undesirable expressions such as anger and fear were less accurate. The researchers also reported individual differences in the expression and identification of expressions. Field and Waldon (1982) reported that children who produced "easy to judge" expressions tended to judge their own expressions accurately. They proposed that the processes of encoding and decoding emotional information may be related and distinguishable at an early age.

Several studies have also demonstrated that gender is associated with infant expressivity and the expressivity of caregivers. In a study exploring the development of expressions from three months to six months, Malatesta and Haviland (1982) reported similar rates of all facial expressions except for interest; female infants displayed significantly more expressions of interest than male infants. Furthermore, although mothers tended to smile more often at their daughters, they found that from three to six months, mothers tended to increase contingency in response to smiles of male infants and decrease contingency in responding to female infants. In their longitudinal study, Malatesta and her colleagues (Malatesta et al., 1989; Malatesta-Magai et al., 1994) also found gender differences in the way mothers responded to their infants. In particular, mothers showed greater expressivity to girls than boys, and when children were three years old, mothers displayed more positive affect with girls and more negative vocals with boys. Again, with one exception, girls and boys did not differ on the rates of expressions displayed. The exception was that girls and boys displayed similar levels of anger during play, but girls displayed more anger during the second reunion episode of the Strange Situation.[2]

There is much evidence that expressivity is associated with subsequent personality development. For example, Malatesta and her colleagues reported that expressive, outgoing infants tended to grow up into secure, socially competent children (Malatesta et al. 1989; Malatesta-Magai et al., 1994). However, expressivity may also influence other areas of emotional development. For example, perhaps, infants who have higher rates of expressivity are more proficient at communicating their feelings and understanding emotional displays of others. Research presented by Denham and her colleagues (see page 252) provides some support for this hypothesis. Nevertheless, in order for infant expressivity to influence later emotional development, emotional expressiveness of infants and young children must be stable across time and context. Several researchers have reported stability of expressivity across time. For example, Fox (1989) reported stability of expressivity between five and fourteen months. In a somewhat more representative sample, Malatesta et al. (1989) reported moderate consistency between two and one-half and twenty-two months. In a study examining expression in four- to five-year-olds, LaFreniere and Sroufe (1985) reported stability across time and contexts. Specifically, they reported that with the exception of physical assertiveness, expressive behavior was moderate to highly consistent in small and large group interactions throughout the school year. In conclusion, although there are individual differences in expressivity for infants and young children, these individual differences tend to be stable across time and contexts and therefore may influence other aspects of social and personality development.

In summary, researchers have found that infants spontaneously produce expressions of happiness, sadness, and anger within the first few days of life. During the first year, infants acquire the ability to spontaneously generate facial expressions, and within three years, individual differences in expressivity are observed. Researchers have illustrated that both maternal expressivity and

---

[2] The Strange Situation is a twenty-minute separation-reunion episode that includes an infant, a caregiver, and a female stranger. This laboratory procedure was designed by Mary Ainsworth to assess infant attachment (Ainsworth, Blehar, Waters, & Wall, 1978). Infants' attachment status is determined by their reactions to the female stranger and separations and reunions with their caregiver.

gender of the child are associated with individual differences in expressivity, and that these individual differences are stable over time.

UNDERSTANDING OF EMOTIONS

Mayer and Salovey (1993, 1997) and Saarni (1990) proposed that one of the primary characteristics of individuals with high emotional intelligence was their ability to accurately identify emotions and judge the integrity of emotional expressions. Infants may have the ability to discriminate and imitate emotions in the first few days of life (Field et al., 1982), but this seemingly innate ability to perceive and compare facial expressions is rudimentary in comparison to the capacity to accurately identify the meaning of emotional expressions. Early studies exploring emotional development of infants demonstrated that understanding of facial expressions develops in sequence; understanding of happiness and sadness develops first followed by understanding of expressions such as anger and surprise (Izard, 1971). This developmental sequence is well established, and recently researchers have sought to examine individual difference factors that influence this sequence of development.

Researchers have demonstrated that infants can discriminate between happy, sad, and surprised facial expressions of the same adult during the first few days of life (Field et al., 1982); happy, sad, and angry expressions of their mother at ten weeks (Haviland & Lelwica, 1987); and happy and surprised expressions of different adults by thirty weeks (Caron, Caron, & Myers, 1982). To determine whether infants are discriminating among facial expressions because of their perception of changing features or because of a more sophisticated understanding of emotions, researchers have examined infants' fixations on different parts of the face. Field et al. (1982) reported that infants tended to look at the mouth more than eyes when imitating happy and sad expressions and alternated their visual fixations on the mouth and eyes when imitating surprised expressions. Caron et al. (1982) proposed that infants younger than thirty weeks could detect a change in the person but not the expression. However, Haviland and Lelwica (1987) found that infants were not merely reacting to changes in facial features, but they were reacting to the intended emotion. For example, after repeated presentations of maternal joy, Haviland and Lelwica reported that infants gradually changed from imitating maternal expressions of joy to increased expressions of interest or excitement. This change in emotional state supports that the infants are not merely imitating features but recognizing the emotions of others.

In a recent paper, Dondi, Simion, and Caltran (1999) provided additional evidence that newborn infants can distinguish between their own and another infant's expressed emotion. They conducted two experiments to determine if infants could discriminate their own cry and the cry of another infant; in the first experiment infants were in an alert state and in the second experiment infants were in an asleep state. In both experiments, infants were put into one of three groups: infants who heard their own cry, infants who heard the cry of one of the infants in the first group, and a control group of infants. To determine if the infants could distinguish their own cry from that of other infants, researchers recorded infants' facial expressions and nonnutritive sucking in response to cry stimuli. They demonstrated that infants who heard another infants' cry responded with increased expressions of distress when compared to infants who heard their own cry and infants in the control group. Infants who heard the cry of another infant were also observed to have decreased rates of nonnutritive sucking as compared to the rates of infants in the other two groups. Overall, the results demonstrated that infants could discriminate between their own and another infants' cry. Furthermore, the cry of others was effective in inducing negative affect, which supports the belief that vicarious arousal, which is necessary but not sufficient for feelings of empathy, may be evident in newborns (see also Campos, Campos, & Barrett, 1989; Fabes, Eisenberg, & Eisenbud, 1993; Zahn-Waxler, Kochanska, Krupnick, & McKnew, 1990).

It is well known that infants and children tend to look toward a trusted caregiver before deciding whether to approach or avoid an ambiguous toy, situation, or stranger. This tendency to engage in social referencing relies on accurate identification of emotional expressions to be effective. Sorce, Emde, Campos and Klinnert (1985) examined social referencing of twelve-month-old infants using the visual cliff paradigm. The visual cliff is an apparatus used to study infants' perception of depth. Two sides of the visual cliff ("shallow" and "deep" sides) are covered with a glass platform. Infants are judged to perceive depth if they show a preference for the shallow side and refusal to cross the deep side. Sorce et al. (1985) found that maternal expressions of happiness and interest persuaded children to cross the visual cliff, whereas maternal expressions of fear, anger, and sadness were associated with retreat. Several researchers have criticized the validity of the visual cliff and explored children's tendency to use social referencing in relatively social contexts. For example, Dickstein and Parke (1988) examined social referencing behavior of eleven-month-old infants with mothers and fathers when in the company of a female stranger. They found that infants referenced equally to both parents in this ambiguous situation. Interestingly, social referencing to fathers was positively associated with fathers' reported marital satisfaction. Several researchers have reported consistent results in similarly ambiguous social situations (Feinman & Lewis, 1983; Waldon & Baxter, 1989).

Repacholi (1998) expanded the standard social referencing paradigm to include two choices to determine if infants' exploratory behavior could be differentially influenced by distinct emotional messages. Experimenters showed two sets of two boxes to fourteen- and eighteen-month-old infants. In one condition, the experimenter looked in the boxes at a hidden toy and expressed either happiness or disgust. In another condition, the experimenter touched the hidden object and expressed either happiness or disgust. She found that a significant proportion of infants who searched for the hidden object opened the happy box first and were more likely to insert their hands into the happy box than the disgust box. Repacholi (1998) concluded that infants as young as fourteen months were able to accurately identify the experimenter's emotion as well as the target of the emotion.

In the first and second year, children are able use emotional information to make choices; however, their choices are limited to deciding, for example, whether to approach or avoid particular stimuli. Sophisticated understanding of the multiplicity of emotions and complexity of facial expressions develops in toddler and preschool years. In particular, researchers have examined the process of understanding specific features of emotional expressions. Using pictures of facial expressions, Waldon and Field (1982) varied features of expressions of happiness, sadness, surprise, and anger to determine if children could match a target emotion with five drawings. The five stimulus drawings had either the same matching features, the same mouth, eyes, or hair, or no matching features. They demonstrated that three- to five-year-old children were more accurate when identifying expressions of happiness and sadness than surprise and anger, and overall, older children made fewer errors than younger children. Furthermore, they reported that type of error was dependent on type of emotion. In particular, children were more likely to make an error for happiness or anger if an alternative choice had the same eyes as the target picture. For errors on sadness and surprise, children tended to choose pictures with one similar feature (either eyes or mouth). In summary, during preschool years, children gradually acquire an understanding that facial expressions are combinations of several facial features, which results in increased accuracy of emotion identification.

Inability to identify emotions accurately may contribute to inferior social relationships. For example, Kropp and Haynes (1987) proposed that the inappropriate reactions of abusive parents may be due to their limited ability to accurately identify emotions. Consistent with these expectations, they found that abusive mothers were less likely than nonabusive mothers to correctly identify emotions of infants. The authors postulated that because abusive parents are unable to accurately identify their children's emotions, they therefore react inappropriately to their children's behavior. However, using pictures of children rather than infants, Camras et al. (1988) found that abusive mothers were not inferior at recognizing emotions, but their children performed worse than nonabused children at posing and recognizing emotions. All children's ability to recognize emotions was significantly and positively associated with their mother's ability to pose facial expressions. In other words, children who were given clear, nonambiguous emotional messages from their mothers seemed to have developed a greater understanding of emotional expressions than children who received incorrect or ambiguous messages.

Denham and her colleagues (Denham, 1986; Denham, McKinley, Couchoud, & Holt, 1990) studied the influence of emotional understanding on peer relationships. They assessed emotional understanding using puppets to act out several emotion-ladened vignettes. Some vignettes conveyed emotions that were consistent with emotions most people would feel if in that situation, and some vignettes displayed emotions that were inconsistent with emotions that mothers reported their participating child would feel if in that situation. Overall, gender differences indicated that girls were more prosocial and better liked (Denham et al., 1990) than boys. Controlling for gender differences, the researchers found that, although there was much variation among participants, children as young as two years could accurately identify emotions (Denham, 1986), and understanding emotions was significantly associated with higher ratings of peer "likability" (Denham et al., 1990). Consistent with previous research, there was some support for the hypothesis that happiness and anger are easier to understand than sadness (Denham, 1986). Interestingly, identification errors that confused happiness with sadness or anger were negatively associated with likability. Furthermore, during free-play sessions, children responded differently to different emotions. Denham (1986) found that children often matched or reinforced happy peer expressions, responded prosocially to expressions of hurt, and responded to expressions of sadness or anger by leaving the interaction or ignoring the peer. Furthermore, children who tended to exhibit higher levels of happiness and lower levels of anger during free play were also more likely to respond prosocially to peers (Denham, 1986; Denham et al., 1990) and subsequently received higher ratings of likability from peers (Denham et al., 1990). These findings provide some support for the belief that individuals' expressivity and understanding of emotions may be linked.

In summary, newborn infants seem to have an innate ability to discriminate emotional expressions, and their understanding of facial expressions develops in sequences from happiness to sadness to anger to surprise. Children as young as ten months have developed the ability to use emotional expressions of others to make choices about ambiguous situations. Finally, researchers have demonstrated that emotional understanding is associated with maternal expressiveness and influences later peer relationships.

REGULATION OF EMOTIONS

Infants' early behaviors to regulate emotions are restricted to gaze aversion, and their early abilities to calm anxious feelings are restricted to soothing attempts by their caregivers (Haviland & Lelwica, 1987). For infants, the development of emotional regulation includes acquiring a relatively sophisticated repertoire of behaviors to regulate negative emotions (Malatesta et al., 1989). For example, Malatesta and her colleagues have observed that by two and one-half months, some infants displayed facial behaviors such as a knit brow, presumably in an attempt to control or suppress negative emotions. Over the next few months, infants added to this repertoire of self-regulatory behavior. By five months, some infants were observed to display compressed lips, and by twenty-two months some infants were observed to display lip biting (Malatesta et al., 1989). Malatesta proposed that the gradual appearance and relative sophistication of these behaviors in twenty-two-month-old infants as compared to two-and-one-half-month-old infants demonstrated that the ability to regulate emotions develops in the first years of life. In summary, the researchers found that the younger infants were not able to regulate their emotions. Although many infants younger than five months had acquired some regulatory behaviors, five-month-old infants could not successfully regulate their negative emotions. The older children, however, were more skilled and more likely to be able to hide their true (negative) feelings.

The ability to regulate emotions becomes more sophisticated during the preschool and early childhood years. Saarni (1984) proposed that there were three plausible determinants necessary for the developmental progression of emotional regulation. Specifically, to regulate expressions, children need to have the ability to regulate emotion, knowledge of appropriate action, and motivation to regulate emotions.

The ability to spontaneously control expressions of negative emotion when mildly disappointed and in the presence of another is evident in children as young as three years (Cole, 1986; Harris, Donnelly, Guz, & Pitt-Watson, 1986); however, the normative age for the majority of children, in particular boys, is ten years (Gnepp & Hess, 1986; Saarni, 1984; Zeman & Garber, 1996). Saarni (1984) found that ten-year-olds were able to reliably hide their negative feelings after receiving a disappointing gift and to cite reasons why it was desirable to hide true feelings. Younger children (six years old) displayed more negative affect after receiving a disappointing gift, and youngest boys displayed the highest frequency of negative behavior and lowest frequency of positive behavior. Cole (1986) found similar gender differences but did not replicate data demonstrating age differences.

Several studies have demonstrated that girls tend to be better at masking emotions (Cole, 1986; Saarni, 1984). Cole (1986) found that girls smiled more than boys when presented with a disappointing prize and that this smile was exaggerated. She also demonstrated that girls were more likely to be sensitive to the social context; girls tended to smile in the social context and to not smile in the nonsocial context.

Although girls tend to regulate expressions better than boys, few researchers have explored the factors that affect children's motivation to regulate emotions.

Davis (1995) explored the hypothesis that girls have more motivation than boys to regulate their emotional expressions. Using a standard paradigm,[3] Davis (1995) rewarded children with a preferred prize and then a nonpreferred prize for helping with two related experimental tasks. Consistent with previous work, girls, as compared to boys, displayed lower levels of negative emotion in general after receiving both gifts and higher levels of positive emotion after receiving the nonpreferred prize. Next, to determine if motivation was associated with ability to mask emotions, she asked children to participate in a game in which it was necessary to mask that they did not want a least favorite prize to win a favored prize. Although the findings supported that both girls and boys seemed to be motivated to hide their disappointment with the least preferred prize, girls' ability to mask negative emotions in this situation was superior.

Zeman and Garber (1996) expanded the work of Saarni (1984) and others by exploring whether persons present influenced children's regulation of negative expressions. They explored emotion regulation in seven-, nine-, and eleven-year-olds in response to sad, angry, or painful situations in the presence of peers, mothers, or fathers, or when they were alone. Unlike previous studies in which researchers observed children's response to receiving a disappointing gift, the experimental procedure consisted of children's reports of emotional regulation in response to one of twelve hypothetical stories. Children, regardless of age or audience condition, most frequently reported that they would expect negative interpersonal consequences in response to an expressed negative emotion. Consistent with expectations, Zeman and Garber (1996) found that younger children reported that they would express sadness and anger more often than older children, and girls reported that they would express sadness and pain more often than boys. The consideration of audience proved to be important to understand the findings. Children, regardless of age and gender, reported that they would be more likely to control negative emotion expressions with a peer than when they were alone or with their mother or father. Mothers and fathers were perceived to be more accepting of expressions of pain and mothers were perceived to be more accepting of sadness. Older children perceived that fathers would be less accepting of emotional displays than younger children (see also Zeman and Shipman, 1996).

The ability to regulate emotions is proposed to be one of the defining features of emotional intelligence (Mayer & Salovey, 1993; Saarni, 1990). Despite

---

[3] Children's ability to mask negative emotions (such as disappointment) with positive emotions (such as happiness) is assessed by first asking children to help with tasks, for which they are given rewards. When each task is finished, children are given either a preferred prize or a nonpreferred prize. Children's responses to each prize are compared to determine if they masked their disappointment when receiving the nonpreferred prize.

the plethora of research examining children's development of emotional regulation, to date, developmental psychologists have not explored the association between children's ability to regulate emotions and their later emotional and intellectual growth. However, psychologists have explored the association between the ability to control desires and later intellectual potential, and this research provides some support for the hypothesis that emotional regulation would be positively associated with emotional and intellectual growth. During the 1960s, Stanford psychologist Walter Mischel and his colleagues began a series of studies exploring children's self-control or delay of gratification (see Mischel, Shoda, & Rodriguez, 1989 for a review). The research paradigm included a situation where the child was given the choice to end a wait of undetermined amount of time for a less preferred object (like one marshmallow) or to wait for the researcher to return for a more preferred object (like two marshmallows). The researchers found that strategies such as hiding the treats, encouraging the child to imagine the treats as pictures, and encouraging the children to think fun thoughts while waiting for the treats improved children's ability to delay gratification (Mischel & Ebbesen, 1970; Mischel, Ebbesen, & Raskoff-Zeiss, 1972). Furthermore, many children were observed to spontaneously generate their own diversions. Mischel and his colleagues examined the long-term outcome of children's ability to generate effective self-control strategies in several longitudinal studies. For example, Shoda, Mischel, and Peake (1990) compared adolescent outcomes in children who had been tested in one of four versions of the delay of gratification task. Variations of the delay of gratification task included combinations of exposing or obscuring rewards and spontaneous versus suggested ideation. The follow-up assessment included 185 of the original 653 children tested. They found that the only condition that was predictive of later adjustment was the condition in which rewards were exposed and ideation was spontaneous. In this condition, preschoolers who were able to delay gratification for longer periods of time were later judged as adolescents to have higher levels of self-control, concentration, and motivation, and higher Scholastic Aptitude Test scores than participants who as preschoolers were not able to delay gratification.

In summary, recent work on the development of emotion regulation has demonstrated that infants acquire simple regulatory behaviors within the first year of life and children's regulatory skills become more sophisticated over the first few years of life. During the early school years, children couple their ability to regulate emotions with the knowledge of when to hide negative emotions (such as in social situations) and the motivation to do so. Finally, Mischel's work on delay of gratification provides some evidence that ability to successfully regulate emotions may be associated with superior intellectual ability.

INDIVIDUAL DIFFERENCES IN EMOTIONAL DEVELOPMENT

Despite the plethora of research examining the development of emotions, many researchers have restricted their explorations to normative development, and only recently have researchers begun to explore individual differences in emotional development. Furthermore, although researchers have discussed age, gender, and family differences that influence the normative emotional development, only a handful of researchers have examined the prospective outcome of early individual differences of expressivity, understanding, or regulation of emotions. Previously, researchers who reported variability within samples rarely reassessed samples to determine if early individual differences were associated with increased understanding of emotions at a later age. For example, Field et al. (1982) found great variability in the number of trials before habituation in three-day-old infants when determining if infants could distinguish between happy, sad, and surprised expressions. However, to date, no studies have examined whether this variability in newborns differentially predicts later emotional development. Previous work has demonstrated that infants' performance in traditional habituation-dishabituation tasks was associated with childhood intelligence (Colombo, 1995; McCall & Carriger, 1993; Rose & Feldman, 1995; Slater, 1995). Future work using this paradigm to predict emotional intelligence may be productive. For example, in a recent study Axia, Bonichini, and Benini (1999) reported that infants who looked at visual stimuli (such as checkerboards, faces, and inverted faces) for shorter periods of time were also likely to quickly regulate distress after vaccinations. The researchers found that the duration of pain-distress response and all indices of visual attention decreased with age. The authors propose that "short-lookers" may have a superior neural system that influences both their cognitive and emotional abilities (Axia et al., 1999).

EMOTIONS IN THE SOCIAL CONTEXT

Developmental psychologists examining emotional development from the functional or attachment perspective have proposed that emotional expression, understanding, and regulation develops in a social context (Bowlby, 1988; Campos et al., 1989). These researchers assume that expressiveness in families influences ability to recognize emotions. In other words, children from families in which both positive and negative emotions are openly expressed are more likely to learn to accurately recognize emotional expressions. Several researchers have examined expressiveness of positive and negative emotions within the family, and the subsequent socioemotional development of infants and children. For example, Malatesta and Haviland (1982) found that the degree of correspondence of expressivity within mother-infant dyads increased from three months to six months of age. Dunn and her colleagues (Dunn, Brown, & Maguire, 1995) concluded that emotion-related experiences with mothers and siblings were associated with children's understanding of others' feelings. Considering the strong association between caregivers' expressiveness (for example, sensitivity) and their children's attachment status, it is not surprising that several researchers have extended the exploration of rates of expressiveness in the family and emotional development to examinations of associations among expressiveness in the family and children's emotional understanding and attachment security.

Researchers examining family expressiveness have found some support for the proposed association between emotional development and attachment in children. Malatesta et al. (1989) reported that infants who developed a secure relationship with their mother at twenty-two months tended to display a pattern of increased smiling from two and one-half months to seven months. Infants who later developed an insecure relationship tended to display a pattern of decreased smiling during face-to-face play. Dickstein, Thompson, Estes, Malkin, and Lamb (1984) found that insecure resistant children engaged in social referencing (for example, tendency to look toward a trusted caregiver before deciding whether to approach or avoid an ambiguous toy, situation, or stranger) most frequently and persistently early in the Strange Situation episode. Although secure children engaged in social referencing during the Strange Situation, their attempts seemed to be much more efficient than those of the insecure resistant children. In an adult sample, Bell (1998) found that expressiveness in families was associated with adult patterns of attachment. In particular, individuals who reported low expressiveness reported insecure-avoidant attachment, and individuals who reported high levels of negative expressiveness reported insecure-preoccupied attachment. In summary, parents who respond to their children with positive, sensitive, emotional responses tend to have children who develop a good understanding of their own and others emotions, as well as secure attachment.

The influence of emotional development can be seen in the peer group as well as the family. In particular, researchers have explored whether understanding of emotion influence children's success in their peer group. According to Denham et al. (1990), by three and one-half years, children who do not respond prosocially to peers and/or have not mastered basic happy-sad differentiation tend to be at risk for peer difficulties. They conclude that popular children tend to be more adept in understanding emotional situations and are more prosocial. Interesting, Cassidy, Parke, Butkovsky, & Braungart (1992) found that understanding of emotions in five- and six-year-olds was not associated with family expressiveness but was associated with peer acceptance. Although, they did not find a direct association between family expressiveness and emotional understanding, there was limited support for the proposal that emotional understanding may indirectly influence the effect of family expressiveness and peer acceptance.

CONCLUSION

In this chapter, I outlined developmental research to support the notion that individuals gradually develop a more sophisticated understanding of emotions. Furthermore, I demonstrated that (1) researchers have reported individual differences in emotional development of infants and children and (2) individual differences in emotions were associated with differences in attachment status and peer acceptance. I reported results from several studies in which researchers found that securely attached children tended to be emotionally expressive, have superior understanding of emotions, and have superior abilities to regulate emotions than insecure children. Future work is necessary to determine the association between attachment security and emotional intelligence. Perhaps, a relatively high level of emotional intelligence is one characteristic of securely attached individuals, or alternatively, attachment security may be necessary, but not sufficient, to acquire emotional intelligence. With respect to the developmental literature, I do not summarize work examining the development of higher-order emotions, such as shame, guilt, or empathy. I would expect that individual differences in the development of higher-order emotions would further contrast the importance of individual differences to understanding the development of emotional intelligence. Furthermore, this chapter summarized research in infancy and early childhood and therefore did not address life-span development. Researchers have become increasingly interested in the continuing development of emotional understanding and regulation in adulthood. Labouvie-Vief, DeVoe, and Bulka (1989) observed improved emotional understanding from preadolescence to midadulthood; this improvement was also associated with individuals' ego level. They concluded that individuals with high verbal ability and ego level described their emotional experiences in a more mature fashion and advocated for a life-span perspective for researchers interested in emotional understanding. Moreover, in a recent article, Carstensen, Isaacowitz, and Charles (1999) proposed a theory to understand the development of emotional regulation in adulthood. They suggested that emotional and social goals become more salient during adulthood, and thus adults improve their ability to regulate emotions. It may be, however, that enhanced attention to emotional goals is characteristic of emotionally intelligent individuals at all ages.

References

Ainsworth, M.D.S., Blehar, M. C., Waters, E., & Wall, S. (1978). *Patterns of attachment: A psychological study of the strange situation.* Hillsdale, NJ: Erlbaum.

Axia, G., Bonichini, S., & Benini, F. (1999). Attention and reaction to distress in infancy: A longitudinal study. *Developmental Psychology, 35,* 500–504.

Bar-On, R. (1997). *BarOn Emotional Quotient Inventory (EQ-i): Technical Manual.* Toronto, Canada: Multi-Health Systems.

Bell, K. L. (1998). Family expressiveness and attachment. *Social Development, 7,* 37–53.

Bowlby, J. (1988). *A secure base: Parent-child attachment and healthy human development.* New York: Basic.

Campos, J. J., Campos, R. G., & Barrett, K. C. (1989). Emergent themes in the study of emotional development and emotion regulation. *Developmental Psychology, 25,* 394–402.

Camras, L. A., Ribordy, S., Hill, J., Martino, S., Spaccarelli, S., & Stefani, R. (1988). Recognition and posing of emotional expressions by abused children and their mothers. *Developmental Psychology, 24,* 776–781.

Caron, R. F., Caron, A. J., & Myers, R. S. (1982). Abstraction of invariant face expressions in infancy. *Child Development, 53,* 1008–1015.

Carstensen, L. L., Isaacowitz, D. M., & Charles, S. T. (1999). Taking time seriously: A theory of socioemotional selectivity. *American Psychologist, 54,* 165–181.

Cassidy, J. Parke, R. D., Butkovsky, L. & Braungart, J. M. (1992). Family-peer connections: The roles of emotional expressiveness within the family and children's understanding of emotions. *Child Development, 63,* 603–618.

Cole, P. M. (1986). Children's spontaneous control of facial expression. *Child Development, 57,* 1309–1321.

Cole, P. M., Zahn-Waxler, C., Fox, N. A., Usher, B. A., & Welsh, J. D. (1996). Individual differences in emotion regulation and behavior problems in preschool children. *Journal of Abnormal Psychology, 103,* 518–529.

Colombo, J. (1995). On the neural mechanisms underlying developmental and individual differences in visual fixation in infancy: Two hypotheses. *Developmental Review, 15,* 97–135.

Davidson, R. J., & Fox, N. A. (1989). Frontal brain asymmetry predicts infants' response to maternal separation. *Journal of Abnormal Psychology, 98,* 127–131.

Davis, T. L. (1995). Gender differences in masking negative emotions: Ability or motivation? *Developmental Psychology, 31,* 660–667.

Denham, S. A. (1986). Social cognition, prosocial behavior, and emotion in preschoolers: Contextual validation. *Child Development, 57,* 194–201.

Denham, S. A., McKinley, M., Couchoud, E. A., & Holt, R. (1990). Emotional and behavioral predictors of preschool peer ratings. *Child Development, 61,* 1145–1152.

Dickstein, S., & Parke, R. D. (1988). Social referencing in infancy: A glance at fathers and marriage. *Child Development, 59,* 506–511.

Dickstein, S., Thompson, R. A., Estes, D., Malkin, C., & Lamb, M. E. (1984). Social referencing and the security of attachment. *Infant Behavior and Development, 7,* 507–516.

Dondi, M., Simion, F., & Caltran, G. (1999). Can newborns discriminate between their own cry and the cry of another newborn infant? *Developmental Psychology, 35,* 418–426.

Dunn, J., Brown, J. R., & Maguire, M. (1995). The development of children's moral sensibility: Individual differences and emotion understanding. *Developmental Psychology, 31,* 649–659.

Fabes, R. A. Eisenberg, N., & Eisenbud, L. (1993). Behavioral and physiological correlates of children's reactions to others in distress. *Developmental Psychology, 29,* 655–663.

Feinman, S., & Lewis, M. (1983). Social referencing at ten months: A second-order effect on infants' responses to strangers. *Child Development, 54,* 878–887.

Field, T. M., Morrow, C. J., Healy, B. T., Foster, T., Adlestein, D., & Goldstein, S. (1991). Mothers with zero Beck Depression scores act more "depressed" with their infants. *Development and Psychopathology, 3,* 253–262.

Field, T. M., & Waldon, T. A. (1982). Production and discrimination of facial expressions by preschool children. *Child Development, 53,* 1299–1311.

Field, T. M., Woodson, R., Greenberg, R., & Cohen, D. (1982). Discrimination and imitation of facial expressions by neonates. *Science, 218,* 179–181.

Fox, N. A. (1989). Psychophysiological correlates of emotional reactivity during the first year of life. *Developmental Psychology, 25,* 364–372.

Fox, N. A., & Davidson, R. J. (1987). Electrocephalogram asymmetry in response to the approach of a stranger and maternal separation in 10-month-old infants. *Developmental Psychology, 23,* 233–240.

Fox, N. A., & Davidson, R. J. (1988). Patterns of brain electrical activity during facial signs of emotion in 10-month-old infants. *Developmental Psychology, 24,* 230–236.

Gardner, H. (1983). *Frames of mind: The theory of multiple intelligences.* New York: Bantam Books.

Gnepp, J., & Hess, D.L.R. (1986). Children's understanding of display rules for expressive behavior. *Developmental Psychology, 22,* 103–108.

Goleman, D. (1995). *Emotional Intelligence.* New York: Bantam Books.

Harris, P. L., Donnelly, K., Guz, G. R., & Pitt-Watson, R. (1986). Children's understanding of the distinction between real and apparent emotion. *Child Development, 57,* 895–909.

Haviland, J. M., & Lelwica, M. (1987). The induced affect response: 10-week-old infants' responses to three emotional expressions. *Developmental Psychology, 23,* 97–104.

Izard, C. E. (1971). *The face of emotion.* New York: Appleton-Century-Crofts.

Izard, C. E., Fantauzzo, C. A., Castle, J. M., Haynes, O. M., Rayias, M. F., & Putman, P. H. (1995). The ontogeny and significance of infants' facial expressions in the first 9 months of life. *Developmental Psychology, 31,* 997–1013.

Kropp, J. P., & Haynes, O. M. (1987). Abusive and nonabusive mothers' ability to identify general and specific emotion signals of infants, *Child Development, 58,* 187–190.

Labouvie-Vief, G., DeVoe, M., & Bulka D. (1989). Speaking about feelings: Conceptions of emotion across the life span. *Psychology and Aging, 4,* 425–437.

LaFreniere, P. J., & Sroufe, L. A. (1985). Profiles of peer competence in the preschool: Interrelations between measures, influence of social ecology, and relation to attachment history. *Developmental Psychology, 21,* 56–69.

Malatesta, C. Z., Culver, C., Tesman, J. R., & Shepard, B. (1989). The development of emotion expression during the first two years of life. *Monographs of the Society for Research in Child Development, 54,* 1–103.

Malatesta, C. Z., & Haviland, J. M. (1982). Learning display rules: The socialization of emotion expression in infancy. *Child Development, 53,* 991–1003.

Malatesta-Magai, C., Leak, S., Tesman, J., Shepard, B., Culver, C., & Smaggia, B. (1994). Profiles of emotional development: Individual differences in facial and vocal expression of emotion during the second and third years of life. *International Journal of Behavioral Development, 17,* 239–269.

Mayer, J. D., & Salovey, P. (1993). The intelligence of emotional intelligence. *Intelligence, 17,* 433–442.

Mayer, J. D., & Salovey, P. (1997). What is emotional intelligence? In P. Salovey & D. J. Sluyter (Eds.), *Emotional development and emotional intelligence: Educational implications* (pp. 3–31). New York: Basic Books.

McCall, R. B., & Carriger, M. S. (1993). A meta-analysis of infant habituation and recognition memory performance as predictors of later IQ. *Child Development, 64,* 57–69.

Mischel, W., & Ebbesen, E. B. (1970). Attention in delay of gratification. *Journal of Personality and Social Psychology, 16,* 329–337.

Mischel, W., Ebbesen, E. B., & Raskoff-Zeiss, A. (1972). Cognitive and attentional mechanisms in delay of gratification. *Journal of Personality and Social Psychology, 21,* 204–218.

Mischel, W., Shoda, Y., & Rodriguez, M. L. (1989). Delay of gratification in children. *Science, 26,* 933–938.

Pickens, J., & Field, T. M. (1993). Facial expressivity in infants of depressed mothers. *Developmental Psychology, 29,* 986–988.

Repacholi, B. M. (1998). Infants' use of attentional cues to identify the referent of another person's emotional expression. *Developmental Psychology, 34,* 1017–1025.

Rose, S. A., & Feldman, J. F. (1995). Prediction of IQ and specific cognitive abilities at 11 years from infancy measures. *Developmental Psychology, 31,* 685–696.

Saarni, C. (1984). An observational study of children's attempts to monitor their expressive behavior. *Child Development, 55,* 1504–1513.

Saarni, C. (1990). Emotional competence: How emotions and relationships become integrated. In R. A. Thompson (Ed.), *Nebraska Symposium on Motivation: Volume 36, Socioemotional development* (pp. 115–161). Lincoln: University of Nebraska Press.

Shoda, Y., Mischel, W., & Peake, P. K., (1990). Predicting adolescent cognitive and self-regulatory competencies from preschool delay of gratification: Identifying diagnostic conditions. *Developmental Psychology, 26,* 978–986.

Slater, A. (1995). Individual differences in infancy and later IQ. *Journal of Child Psychology and Psychiatry, 36,* 69–112.

Sorce, J. F., Emde, R. N., Campos, J., & Klinnert, M. D. (1985). Maternal emotional signalling: Its effect of the visual cliff behavior of 1 year olds. *Developmental Psychology, 21,* 195–200.

Stifter, C., & Fox, N. A. (1990). Preschoolers' ability to identify and label emotions. *Journal of Nonverbal Behavior, 10,* 255–266.

Taylor, G. J., Bagby, R. M., & Parker, J.D.A. (1997). *Disorders of affect regulation: Alexithymia in medical and psychiatric illness.* New York: Cambridge University Press.

Waldon, T. A., & Baxter, A. (1989). The effect of context and age on social referencing. *Child Development, 60,* 1511–1518.

Waldon, T. A., & Field, T. M. (1982). Discrimination of facial expressions by preschool children. *Child Development, 53,* 1312–1319.

Zahn-Waxler, C., Kochanska, G., Krupnick, J., & McKnew, D. (1990). Patterns of guilt in children of depressed and well mothers. *Developmental Psychology, 26,* 51–59.

Zeman, J., & Garber, J. (1996). Display rules for anger, sadness, and pain: It depends on who is watching. *Child Development, 67,* 957–973.

Zeman, J., & Shipman, K. (1996). Children's expression of negative affect: Reasons and methods. *Developmental Psychology, 32,* 842–849.

CHAPTER TWELVE

Emotional Intelligence from the Perspective of the Five-Factor Model of Personality

Robert R. McCrae

The idea of emotional intelligence—originally denoting a domain of abilities specifically linked to the perception and utilization of emotions (Salovey & Mayer, 1989–90)—has proven to be immensely appealing to psychologists, journalists, and entrepreneurs. Indeed, many writers (Bar-On, 1997; Goleman, 1995) have been so pleased with the construct that they have broadened it to include desirable motivational, interpersonal, and intrapsychic attributes that resemble personality traits more than traditional abilities. An evaluation of the construct might well begin with this broader conception, because there is a huge body of research on personality traits on which to draw. Most of the traits identified as parts of emotional intelligence can be located within a comprehensive taxonomy of personality traits, the five-factor model (FFM) (Digman, 1990; McCrae & John, 1992). The specific traits that appear most relevant to the original ability conception appear to be related to one of the five factors: openness to experience (McCrae & Costa, 1997). In this chapter I attempt to describe the personality profile of the hypothetical emotionally intelligent person from the perspective of the FFM, and to draw some implications about the emotional intelligence construct from established knowledge about personality traits.

MIXED MODELS OF EMOTIONAL INTELLIGENCE

Peter Salovey and Jack Mayer are both the originators of the term *emotional intelligence* (Mayer, DiPaolo, & Salovey, 1990; Salovey & Mayer, 1989–90) and are some of the most articulate critics of the construct (Mayer, Salovey, &

264 THE HANDBOOK OF EMOTIONAL INTELLIGENCE

Caruso, 2000). In their original article they argued boldly and creatively for broader notions of "intelligence," pointing to the adaptive values of flexible planning, social adroitness, and interpersonal considerateness. Structurally, they claimed that emotional intelligence need not fit within the classic hierarchical models of intellect, that is, that the components of emotional intelligence "need not intercorrelate" (p. 201) and "may or may not correlate with other types of intelligence" (p. 187).

The theoretical license they granted to the construct was promptly exploited by Goleman (1995) and others, who in effect argued that any beneficial noncognitive trait might be construed as emotional intelligence. From this, the construct was inflated to include group or corporate emotional intelligence, manifested in organizational policies that boost morale (Hatfield, 1998–99). Emotional intelligence soon became a panacea, promising profitability, cleanliness, and better immune responses (Hatfield, 1998–99; Toms, 1998–99).

Mayer, Salovey, and Caruso (2000), apparently alarmed by some of the claims made on behalf of their construct, began to distinguish between *ability models* and *mixed models* of emotional intelligence. They focused their research on the development and validation of measures of emotional ability (Mayer, Caruso, & Salovey, 1999) and warned that models that mixed abilities with a variety of desirable traits and attitudes lacked internal consistency and were correspondingly difficult to evaluate.

One way to evaluate mixed models is by a systematic analysis of their components, and the comprehensive taxonomy of the FFM offers one basis for such an analysis. Table 12.1 lists the thirty traits measured by the Revised NEO Personality Inventory (NEO-PI-R) (Costa & McCrae, 1992), a widely used operationalization of the FFM. Also given in the table are aspects of emotional intelligence proposed by Bar-On and Goleman (as summarized in Mayer et al., 2000); corresponding concepts are given in the same row of the table. Some of these correspondences are probably very close (for example, assertiveness in the NEO-PI-R and in Bar-On's scheme); others are rougher (such as openness to values and independence). A few of the features of emotional intelligence (such as marshaling emotions in the service of a goal, in Goleman, 1995) do not have clear counterparts in the NEO-PI-R system. Overall, however, it does appear that there is substantial overlap, and there is some empirical data in support of this interpretation (Bar-On, 1997; Schutte et al., 1998). Overlap is exactly what personality psychologists would expect. The NEO-PI-R was designed to assess important traits in the FFM, and the FFM is supposed to be a comprehensive classification of personality traits. If emotional intelligence consists of personality traits, then it should map onto the FFM.

Conversely, if features of emotional intelligence map onto the FFM, then they are presumably personality traits. That seems somewhat clearer in Bar-On's version of emotional intelligence (see Chapter Seventeen), which was derived from

Table 12.1. Conceptual Correspondences Between NEO-PI-R Facets and Proposed Aspects of Emotional Intelligence.

Costa and McCrae (1992)	Bar-On (1997)	Goleman (1995)
Neuroticism		
N1: Anxiety		Ability to shake off anxiety (R)
N2: Angry hostility		
N3: Depression	Happiness (R)	
N4: Self-consciousness	Self-regard (R)	
N5: Impulsiveness	Impulse control (R)	Stifling impulsiveness (R)
N6: Vulnerability	Stress tolerance (R)	
Extraversion		
E1: Warmth		
E2: Gregariousness		
E3: Assertiveness	Assertiveness	
E4: Activity		
E5: Excitement seeking		
E6: Positive emotions	Optimism	
Openness to Experience		
O1: Fantasy		
O2: Aesthetics		
O3: Feelings	Emotional self-awareness	Monitoring feelings
O4: Actions	Flexibility	
O5: Ideas	Reality testing	
O6: Values	Independence	
Agreeableness		
A1: Trust	Interpersonal relationships	
A2: Straightforwardness		
A3: Altruism		Attunement to what others need or want
A4: Compliance		Interacting smoothly with others
A5: Modesty		
A6: Tender-mindedness	Empathy	Empathic awareness
Conscientiousness		
C1: Competence	Problem solving	
C2: Order		
C3: Dutifulness	Social responsibility	
C4: Achievement striving		Zeal and persistence
C5: Self-discipline		Ability to motivate oneself
C6: Deliberation		

Note: Features marked "(R)" correspond to the NEO-PI-R facet if reverse scored.

a review of personality characteristics related to life success, than in Goleman's version, which was based more directly on the emotional ability conceptualization of Salovey and Mayer (1989–90). Although they differ somewhat in the specific facets involved (Table 12.1), these conceptualizations suggest that emotional intelligence should be associated with low scores for neuroticism and high scores for extraversion, openness, agreeableness, and conscientiousness. Mixed models of emotional intelligence seem to combine the evaluatively positive poles of each of the five factors (Paulhus, Bruce, & Trapnell, 1995); presumably this is why they sound so appealing.

If emotional intelligence consists of a particular combination of familiar personality traits, then it is possible to say a great deal about it from decades of research on personality. First, we know that the component traits do not covary to form a unitary construct. People who are able to shake off anxiety may or may not be prone to monitoring their feelings and may or may not show zeal and persistence: emotional stability (or low a low level of neuroticism), openness, and conscientiousness are separate factors. A few individuals score low for neuroticism and high for openness and conscientiousness, and corporate managers might want to identify and select such people as employees. But in order to identify them they would need to use valid measures of neuroticism, openness, and conscientiousness instead of relying on a single, global measure of emotional intelligence.

Second, we know a good deal about the origins and development of personality traits. Traits from all five factors are strongly influenced by genes (Riemann, Angleitner, & Strelau, 1997) and are extraordinarily persistent in adulthood (Costa & McCrae, 1997). This is likely to be unwelcome news to proponents of emotional intelligence, who have sometimes contrasted a supposed malleability of emotional intelligence with the relative fixity of traditional IQ. Goleman, for example, was quoted as saying that "people can change from being pessimists to being optimists in a matter of weeks" (Toms, 1998–99, p. 15)—a claim that most psychotherapists and personality psychologists would dispute. It is possible to change specific attitudes, behaviors, and institutional policies, but deep, pervasive, and lasting changes in personality are far more difficult (Costa & McCrae, 1986). And because the effects of personality are pervasive and enduring, superficial changes in attitudes and behaviors may not solve problems for long. Employees who score high for neuroticism are probably going to find something to complain about no matter how enlightened the management.

Third, we know about the developmental trajectory of personality traits. Although individual differences are strongly preserved over most of the adult life span, there are maturational trends that affect everyone. Between late adolescence and age thirty, neuroticism, extraversion, and openness decline, whereas agreeableness and conscientiousness increase (McCrae et al., 1999). After age thirty, changes are much slower but apparently continue in the same direction. The fact that neuroticism decreases while agreeableness and conscientiousness increase suggests that emotional intelligence should increase with age. On the other hand, extraversion and openness to experience decline with age (Sapolsky, 1998), suggesting a decrease in emotional intelligence. Perhaps the two trends cancel out, and one could say that there is no net relation of age to emotional intelligence. But surely it would be more informative to say, for example, that young adults are better than older adults at monitoring their feelings and being optimistic, but worse at persistence and stifling impulsiveness. This is a nice illustration of the value of preserving the distinction between different traits instead of combining them into a single, undifferentiated construct (Briggs & Cheek, 1986).

Finally, we know a good deal about how to assess personality traits, using both self-reports and observer ratings (McCrae, 1994a). If one wished to assess the features described in Table 12.1, it might make more sense to combine relevant scales on the NEO-PI-R or other established measures of the FFM (John, Donahue, & Kentle, 1991; Wiggins, Trapnell, & Phillips, 1988) than to try to create measures of emotional intelligence from scratch. Certainly part of the process of validating any measure of emotional intelligence would be to demonstrate that the new scale has incremental validity over that afforded by established measures of familiar constructs.

ABILITY MODEL OF EMOTIONAL INTELLIGENCE

In their more recent work, Mayer and colleagues have focused on a narrower, ability model of emotional intelligence (Mayer et al., 2000). Just as individuals may show intelligence in their understanding and use of numbers or words or geometric shapes, so people may be more or less intelligent in dealing with emotions. Mayer and colleagues distinguish several conceptually related abilities, including facility in identifying emotions, in understanding the causes and consequences of emotions, and in managing emotions in the self and others. The distinction between these abilities and personality traits is sometimes subtle, but it can be drawn. For example, one can be optimistic simply because one has a cheerful disposition (which requires no intelligence of any kind); or one may understand that one can create an optimistic assessment by deliberately calling to mind the chances of success or by summoning social support from others. This process of manipulating one's own emotional state requires a certain degree of psychological mindedness that Mayer and colleagues deem a form of intelligence.

From this perspective, the criteria by which measures of emotional intelligence should be evaluated shift radically and come to resemble those by which verbal or quantitative intelligence measures would be evaluated. Mayer and colleagues have begun to develop a battery of tests (the Multifactor Emotional

Intelligence Scale [MEIS]) (Mayer et al., 2000) to assess abilities to identify the mood portrayed by a piece of music, to analyze complex emotions into more basic components, to predict temporal sequences of emotional reactions, to choose effective strategies for influencing others' feelings, and so on. They showed that scores on such tests covary to define a general factor that is related, albeit modestly, to both verbal IQ and self-reported empathy. They also showed that adults score higher on average than adolescents, suggesting a developmental progression.

These promising findings stand in contrast to another evaluation of emotional intelligence. Davies, Stankov, and Roberts (1998) used both self-report scales and objective tests (including identification of emotion in faces, colors, and music). They reported that many of these measures had low internal consistency, that the self-report scales measured traits redundant with established personality dimensions, and that only a narrow emotion perception factor could be identified among the objective tests. But Davies and colleagues (1998) used measures developed prior to 1990; the new MEIS shows substantially higher reliabilities. It seems reasonable to conclude that considerably more research is needed before the status of emotional intelligence as an ability is well understood.

OPENNESS TO EXPERIENCE AND INTELLIGENCE

The peculiar status of emotional intelligence as a variable on the boundary between personality and cognition is shared in some respects by one of the five basic personality factors: openness to experience (McCrae & Costa, 1997). It therefore seems worthwhile to consider in some detail research relating openness to both dispositions and abilities. At one level, the history of this research may offer some lessons for future research on emotional intelligence. At another level, it seems likely that many of the features attributed to emotional intelligence are substantively related to openness. If so, then measures of openness should be routinely included in studies of emotional intelligence in order to provide information on convergent, discriminant, and incremental validity.

Openness is manifested most directly in an intense interest in novelty, variety, and experience for its own sake: open people are imaginative, sensitive, flexible, curious, and independent, whereas closed people are down-to-earth, businesslike, and traditional. Although regarded by humanistic psychologists as a means to self-actualization, openness to experience is not an unmixed blessing. The emotional sensitivity that open men and women possess means that they feel distress as well as joy more keenly than others (McCrae & Costa, 1991). They are more prone to nightmares (Hartmann, Russ, Oldfield, Sivan, & Cooper, 1987) and depression (Wolfenstein & Trull, 1997). In contrast to closed individuals who deny inner conflicts (Frenkel-Brunswik, 1950/1969) and avoid noxious stimuli (Druschel & Sherman, 1999), open people are in some respects emotionally vulnerable.

The psychological literature is studded with constructs related to openness versus closedness, including authoritarianism (Adorno, Frenkel-Brunswik, Levinson, & Sanford, 1950/1969), absorption (Tellegen & Atkinson, 1974), thin boundaries (Hartmann, 1991), and need for closure (Kruglanski & Webster, 1996). During the 1980s it became clear that all these constructs were aligned with the fifth lexical factor—culture or intellect (Goldberg, 1981)— that defines an exceptionally broad but robust personality factor (McCrae, 1994b).

The term *intellect* has sometimes been used to designate the openness factor because the English language contains a wealth of trait-descriptive adjectives designating aspects of intellect, such as *intelligent, perceptive, analytical,* and *introspective,* but relatively few describing aesthetic sensitivity, need for variety, or breadth of interests (McCrae, 1990). Researchers who began from a consideration of natural language trait terms were thus led to the conclusion that intellect, or even intelligence, is a major personality factor. Under this interpretation, other traits related to openness might be seen as correlates or consequences of cognitive ability. For example, when explaining what they meant by *intelligence,* laypersons pointed to such characteristics as "keeps an open mind," "tries new things," and "displays curiosity" (Sternberg, Conway, Ketron, & Bernstein, 1981).

The problem with this conclusion is that measures of self-reported (or observer rated) intellect correlate quite modestly (.20 to .30) with psychometric tests of mental ability (McCrae & Costa, 1985; Sternberg et al., 1981). Instead, they are more strongly related to other personality characteristics, such as sensation seeking, Jungian intuition, and global measures of openness (McCrae, 1994b). Self-perceptions of intelligence are thus more a matter of personality than of IQ (Paulhus, Lysy, & Yik, 1998).

Other researchers have proposed that openness may be related to intelligence in ways that are not tapped by IQ tests. Ability tests assess maximal performance, what the individual is capable of when highly motivated. But in everyday circumstances people may choose to use more or less of this capacity; the tendency to use it often, to apply one's intellect to the world, has been called *typical intellectual engagement.* As assessed by self-report, this tendency is strongly correlated with NEO-PI-R openness (.65) (Goff & Ackerman, 1992).

A related construct is the need for cognition, which is the "tendency to engage in and enjoy effortful cognitive activity" (Cacioppo, Petty, Feinstein, & Jarvis, 1996, p. 197). Beginning in 1997, participants in the Baltimore Longitudinal Study of Aging (BLSA) (Shock et al., 1984) completed the short form of a Need for Cognition measure. (The BLSA is an interdisciplinary study of men and women that has gathered biomedical and psychosocial data from adults for more than forty years.) At some time within the past ten years, most of the participants had also completed the NEO-PI-R (mean intertest interval was 3.5 years), and about half of them had been given the WAIS-R vocabulary subtest (Matarazzo, 1972). Table 12.2 reports correlations of the Need for Cognition test and the WAIS-R vocabulary subtest with NEO-PI-R factors and openness facets. The first column of the table shows that Need for Cognition scores are related chiefly to levels of openness to experience, and secondarily to levels of conscientiousness. Regarding the openness facet scales, correlation is highest with the ideas facet—indeed, given the long retest interval and the less-than-perfect reliability of the two measures, these constructs appear to be virtually identical. But Need for Cognition scores are also significantly related to each of the other facets of openness, suggesting a disposition broader than mere intellectual engagement (Berzonsky & Sullivan, 1992).

Does this mean that openness in such areas as fantasy, aesthetics, and feelings should be interpreted as forms or consequences of some cognitive disposition? Certainly they require some mental activity, but not, apparently, what is conventionally called intelligence. The second column of Table 12.2 reports correlations between WAIS-R vocabulary scores and personality measures. Although

Table 12.2 Correlations of Need for Cognition and Intelligence with Revised NEO Personality Inventory Factors and Facets.

	Need for Cognition	WAIS-R Vocabulary
NEO-PI-R Factors		
Neuroticism	$-.15^*$	$-.05$
Extraversion	.01	$-.11$
Openness factor	$.55^{***}$	$.19^*$
Agreeableness	$-.01$	.12
Conscientiousness	$.33^{***}$	.10
Openness Facets		
O1: Fantasy	$.21^{**}$	.05
O2: Aesthetics	$.29^{***}$	.08
O3: Feelings	$.24^{***}$	$.19^*$
O4: Actions	$.36^{***}$	.10
O5: Ideas	$.68^{***}$	$.22^{**}$
O6: Values	$.13^*$	$-.04$

Note: N = 97 men, 145 women (N = 133 for vocabulary).
*p < .05. **p < .01. ***p < .001.

the correlation between openness and vocabulary is significant, it is quite small; most of the facets of openness are not significantly related to IQ. The correlation between Need for Cognition scores and vocabulary scores is only .32.

Perhaps most important from an interpretive point of view is the fact that cognition alone cannot account for the emergence of an openness factor. If both Need for Cognition and WAIS-R vocabulary scores are partialled out of the inter-correlations among the thirty NEO-PI-R facet scales, varimax rotation of five principal components from the resulting partial correlation matrix yields the familiar five factors—including a clear openness factor. These data suggest that the preference for intellectual activity and intellectual ability itself are correlates rather than sufficient causes of openness.

Verbal intelligence may be a correlate of openness because intelligence facilitates the processing of experience, or conversely, because inquisitive people tend to develop larger vocabularies. But openness has also been associated with other cognitive or quasi-cognitive variables, including moral reasoning (Lonky, Kaus, & Roodin, 1984), cognitive complexity (Tetlock, Peterson, & Berry, 1993), and wisdom (Staudinger, Maciel, Smith, & Baltes, 1998). Of particular interest are studies showing that openness is related to divergent thinking abilities (McCrae, 1987) as well as lifetime creative achievement (Helson, 1999). All these findings lend plausibility to the hypothesis that openness may be especially relevant to emotional intelligence, whether construed as an ability or as a disposition.

OPENNESS AND EMOTIONAL INTELLIGENCE

One of the lessons to be drawn from the history of research on openness is that this dimension of personality is broader than mere intellect. A focus on its non-intellective aspects shows a close resemblance to some elements of emotional intelligence. Certainly the most directly relevant facet of openness is feelings, which is defined as "receptivity to one's own inner feelings and emotions and the evaluation of emotion as an important part of life" (Costa & McCrae, 1992, p. 17). Mayer and colleagues (2000) assert that emotionally intelligent people are empathic, and one of the NEO-PI-R feelings subtest items states "I find it easy to empathize with others—to feel myself what others are feeling." Gardner's (1983) intrapersonal intelligence (a concept closely related to emotional intelligence) "allows one to detect and to symbolize complex and highly differentiated sets of feelings" (p. 239), and respondents who scored high in openness to feeling claim that they "experience a wide range of emotions or feelings." Aesthetics is another facet of openness in the NEO-PI-R, and Salovey and Mayer (1989–90) noted that "aesthetic appreciation may involve special qualities of emotional perception and awareness" (p. 197).

Because there are no well-established measures of emotional intelligence, there is no clear empirical evidence regarding these hypothesized links; but data with existing instruments is at least partially supportive. Davies and colleagues (1998) found that NEO-PI openness scores were unrelated to performance on a facial emotion recognition task but were strongly related (.57) to the Trait Meta-Mood Scale, a measure of emotional attention, repair, and clarity (Salovey, Mayer, Goldman, Turvey, & Palfai, 1995). Schutte and colleagues (1998) reported a substantial correlation between their self-report measure of emotional intelligence and openness (.54). However, two unpublished studies, among adolescents and university students, found little association between openness and the scales of the Bar-On Emotional Quotient Inventory (personal communication, R. Bar-On, July 12, 1999). Instead, emotional intelligence as measured by this instrument was related to extraversion, agreeableness, conscientiousness, and low levels of neuroticism, as analyses of the mixed model of emotional intelligence had predicted. To date, there has been no study relating openness to experience to a full battery of tests of emotional intelligence abilities. If past attempts to relate openness to other abilities are any guide, then such studies are likely to find significant but small correlations. If so, then instead of debating whether emotional intelligence is a disposition or an ability, it may be wiser to say that the processing of emotional experience involves both specific abilities and particular personality traits. Either of these, or perhaps a combination of the two, may best predict the real life outcomes—self-regulation, effective management, flexible planning—for which emotional intelligence has been promoted.

CONCLUSION

The concept of emotional intelligence as a set of abilities in dealing with emotions in self and others clearly merits continued attention. Current batteries of tests are promising; further development of such tools will facilitate research on the relations between emotional abilities and personality traits, especially openness.

Prospects for the effective use of the mixed model of emotional intelligence are more dubious. It is unlikely that any psychological characteristic will be advantageous in every circumstance. Sympathy befits a grief counselor more than a prosecuting attorney, and if ignorance is bliss, then emotional stupidity must sometimes be a blessing. It is doubtless true that educators, politicians, and managers should recognize that individuals differ in more than verbal and spatial ability, but instead of adopting an undifferentiated construct operationalized by untested measures, they might be wiser to focus on the well-known dimensions of the five-factor model.

References

Adorno, T. W., Frenkel-Brunswik, E., Levinson, D. J., & Sanford, R. N. (1969). *The authoritarian personality.* New York: Norton. (Original work published 1950)

Bar-On, R. (1997). *BarOn Emotional Quotient Inventory (EQ-i): Technical manual.* Toronto, Canada: Multi-Health Systems.

Berzonsky, M. D., & Sullivan, C. (1992). Social-cognitive aspects of identity style: Need for cognition, experiential openness, and introspection. *Journal of Adolescent Research, 7,* 140–155.

Briggs, S. R., & Cheek, J. M. (1986). The role of factor analysis in the development and evaluation of personality scales. *Journal of Personality, 54,* 106–148.

Cacioppo, J. T., Petty, R. E., Feinstein, J. A., & Jarvis, W.B.G. (1996). Dispositional differences in cognitive motivation: The life and times of individuals differing in the need for cognition. *Psychological Bulletin, 119,* 197–253.

Costa, P. T., Jr., & McCrae, R. R. (1986). Personality stability and its implications for clinical psychology. *Clinical Psychology Review, 6,* 407–423.

Costa, P. T., Jr., & McCrae, R. R. (1992). *Revised NEO Personality Inventory (NEO-PI-R) and NEO Five-Factor Inventory (NEO-FFI) professional manual.* Odessa, FL: Psychological Assessment Resources.

Costa, P. T., Jr., & McCrae, R. R. (1997). Longitudinal stability of adult personality. In R. Hogan, J. A. Johnson, & S. R. Briggs (Eds.), *Handbook of personality psychology* (pp. 269–290). New York: Academic Press.

Davies, M., Stankov, L., & Roberts, R. D. (1998). Emotional intelligence: In search of an elusive construct. *Journal of Personality and Social Psychology, 75,* 989–1015.

Digman, J. M. (1990). Personality structure: Emergence of the Five-Factor Model. *Annual Review of Psychology, 41,* 417–440.

Druschel, B. A., & Sherman, M. F. (1999). Disgust sensitivity as a function of the Big Five and gender. *Personality and Individual Differences, 26,* 739–748.

Frenkel-Brunswik, E. (1969). Dynamic and cognitive personality organization as seen through the interviews. In T. W. Adorno, E. Frenkel-Brunswik, D. J. Levinson, & R. N. Sanford (Eds.), *The authoritarian personality* (pp. 442–467). New York: Norton. (Original work published 1950)

Gardner, H. (1983). *Frames of mind.* New York: Basic Books.

Goff, M., & Ackerman, P. L. (1992). Personality-intelligence relations: Assessment of typical intellectual engagement. *Journal of Educational Psychology, 84,* 537–552.

Goldberg, L. R. (1981). Language and individual differences: The search for universals in personality lexicons. In L. Wheeler (Ed.), *Review of personality and social psychology* (Vol. 2, pp. 141–165). Beverly Hills, CA: Sage.

Goleman, D. (1995). *Emotional intelligence.* New York: Bantam Books.

Hartmann, E. (1991). *Boundaries in the mind: A new psychology of personality differences.* New York: Basic Books.

Hartmann, E., Russ, D., Oldfield, M., Sivan, I., & Cooper, S. (1987). Who has night-mares? The personality of the lifelong nightmare sufferer. *Archives of General Psychiatry, 44,* 49–56.

Hatfield, D. (1998–99, December-January). Gallup Organization: New research links emotional intelligence with profitability. *The Inner Edge,* 5–8.

Helson, R. (1999). A longitudinal study of creative personality in women. *Creativity Research Journal, 12,* 89–101.

John, O. P., Donahue, E. M., & Kentle, R. L. (1991). *The "Big Five" Inventory—Versions 4a and 54.* Berkeley: University of California, Berkeley, Institute of Personality and Social Research.

Kruglanski, A. W., & Webster, D. M. (1996). Motivated closing of the mind: "Seizing" and "freezing." *Psychological Review, 103,* 263–283.

Lonky, E., Kaus, C. R., & Roodin, P. A. (1984). Life experience and mode of coping: Relation to moral judgment in adulthood. *Developmental Psychology, 20,* 1159–1167.

Matarazzo, J. D. (1972). *Wechsler's measurements and appraisal of adult intelligence.* Baltimore: Williams and Wilkins.

Mayer, J. D., Caruso, D. R., & Salovey, P. (1999). Emotional intelligence meets traditional standards for an intelligence. *Intelligence, 27,* 267–298.

Mayer, J. D., DiPaolo, M., & Salovey, P. (1990). Perceiving affective content in ambiguous visual stimuli: A component of emotional intelligence. *Journal of Personality Assessment, 54,* 772–781.

Mayer, J. D., Salovey, P., & Caruso, D. R. (2000). Emotional intelligence. In R. J. Sternberg (Ed.), *Handbook of intelligence* (2nd ed., pp. 396–420). New York: Cambridge University Press.

McCrae, R. R. (1987). Creativity, divergent thinking, and openness to experience. *Journal of Personality and Social Psychology, 52,* 1258–1265.

McCrae, R. R. (1990). Traits and trait names: How well is Openness represented in natural languages? *European Journal of Personality, 4,* 119–129.

McCrae, R. R. (1994a). The counterpoint of personality assessment: Self-reports and observer ratings. *Assessment, 1,* 159–172.

McCrae, R. R. (1994b). Openness to Experience: Expanding the boundaries of Factor V. *European Journal of Personality, 8,* 251–272.

McCrae, R. R., & Costa, P. T., Jr. (1985). Updating Norman's "adequate taxonomy": Intelligence and personality dimensions in natural language and in questionnaires. *Journal of Personality and Social Psychology, 49,* 710–721.

McCrae, R. R., & Costa, P. T., Jr. (1991). Adding *Liebe und Arbeit:* The full five-factor model and well-being. *Personality and Social Psychology Bulletin, 17,* 227–232.

McCrae, R. R., & Costa, P. T., Jr. (1997). Conceptions and correlates of Openness to Experience. In R. Hogan, J. A. Johnson, & S. R. Briggs (Eds.), *Handbook of personality psychology* (pp. 269–290). Orlando, FL: Academic Press.

McCrae, R. R., Costa, P. T., Jr., Lima, M. P. de., Simões, A., Ostendorf, F., Angleitner, A., Marui, I., Bratko, D., Caprara, G. V., Barbaranelli, C., Chae, J. H., & Piedmont, R. L. (1999). Age differences in personality across the adult life span: Parallels in five cultures. *Developmental Psychology, 35,* 466–477.

McCrae, R. R., & John, O. P. (1992). An introduction to the Five-Factor Model and its applications. *Journal of Personality, 60,* 175–215.

Paulhus, D. L., Bruce, M. N., & Trapnell, P. D. (1995). Effects of self-presentation strategies on personality profiles and their structure. *Personality and Social Psychology Bulletin, 21,* 100–108.

Paulhus, D. L., Lysy, D.C., & Yik, M. S. M. (1998). Self-report measures of intelligence: Are they useful as proxy IQ tests? *Journal of Personality, 66,* 525–554.

Riemann, R., Angleitner, A., & Strelau, J. (1997). Genetic and environmental influences on personality: A study of twins reared together using the self- and peer report NEO-FFI scales. *Journal of Personality, 65,* 449–475.

Salovey, P., & Mayer, J. D. (1989–90). Emotional intelligence. *Imagination, Cognition and Personality, 9,* 185–211.

Salovey, P., Mayer, J. D., Goldman, S. L., Turvey, C., & Palfai, T. P. (1995). Emotional attention, clarity, and repair: Exploring emotional intelligence using the Trait Meta-Mood Scale. In J. W. Pennebaker (Ed.), *Emotion, disclosure, and health* (pp. 125–154). Washington, DC: American Psychological Association.

Sapolsky, R. M. (1998, March 30). Open season: When do we lose our taste for the new? *New Yorker,* 57–58, 71–72.

Schutte, N. S., Malouff, J. M., Hall, L. E., Haggerty, D. J., Cooper, J. T., Golden, C. J., & Dornheim, L. (1998). Development and validation of a measure of emotional intelligence. *Personality and Individual Differences, 25,* 167–177.

Shock, N. W., Greulich, R. C., Andres, R., Arenberg, D., Costa, P. T., Jr., Lakatta, E. G., & Tobin, J. D. (1984). *Normal human aging: The Baltimore Longitudinal Study of Aging (NIH Publication No. 84–2450).* Bethesda, MD: National Institutes of Health.

Staudinger, U. M., Maciel, A. G., Smith, J., & Baltes, P. B. (1998), What predicts wisdom-related performance? A first look at personality, intelligence, and facilitative experiential contexts. *European Journal of Personality, 12,* 1–17.

Sternberg, R. J., Conway, B. E., Ketron, J. L., & Bernstein, M. (1981). People's conceptions of intelligence. *Journal of Personality and Social Psychology, 41,* 37–55.

Tellegen, A., & Atkinson, G. (1974). Openness to absorbing and self-altering experiences ("absorption"), a trait related to hypnotic susceptibility. *Journal of Abnormal Psychology, 83,* 268–277.

Tetlock, P. E., Peterson, R. S., & Berry, J. M. (1993). Flattering and unflattering personality portraits of integratively simple and complex managers. *Journal of Personality and Social Psychology, 64,* 500–511.

Toms, M. (1998–99, December-January). Emotional intelligence in the workplace: An interview with Daniel Goleman. *The Inner Edge,* 14–17.

Wiggins, J. S., Trapnell, P., & Phillips, N. (1988). Psychometric and geometric characteristics of the Revised Interpersonal Adjective Scales (IAS-R). *Multivariate Behavioral Research, 23,* 119–134.

Wolfenstein, M., & Trull, T. J. (1997). Depression and Openness to Experience. *Journal of Personality, 69,* 614–632.

CHAPTER THIRTEEN

Intelligence, Emotion, and Creativity

From Trichotomy to Trinity

James R. Averill

In ordinary language, the concept of intelligence encompasses a broad spectrum of abilities, including, in the words of Neisser (1979), "verbal fluency, logical ability, and wide general knowledge but common sense, wit, creativity, lack of bias, sensitivity to one's own limitations, intellectual independence, openness to experience, and the like" (p. 186) (see also Sternberg, 1985). Scientific progress depends, in part, on making everyday concepts more precise, thereby eliminating part of their meaning in ordinary language. That has happened with the concept of intelligence. With the advent of intelligence testing, the original purpose of which was to predict success in school, the concept of intelligence has become restricted to the capacity for abstract reasoning. Obviously, much of what characterizes intelligence, as ordinarily conceived, has been left out.

This poses a dilemma. Should we follow scientific precedent and restrict the concept of intelligence to those aspects measured (however imperfectly) by IQ tests, thus ignoring other abilities that are important for success in life—including academic life? Or should we retain the breadth of our everyday concept, but at the expense of scientific precision? Ordinarily, the solution to this dilemma would be obvious; in science, precision takes precedence over breadth. This solution is made difficult, however, by the fact that intelligence is highly valued; we are loath to admit that some individuals are blessed with more of it than are others. Extending the concept of intelligence to a broad range of abilities allows more of us to bask in the glow of its positive connotation. But there are also disadvantages to such a strategy, namely, it tends to reinforce the very tendency—an overvaluation of intelligence as measured by IQ tests—that it is intended to combat. It would be better, I believe, to restrict the concept of intelligence to the capacity for abstract reasoning, but to recognize that a high degree of intelligence in this sense is not necessary, and certainly not sufficient, for a full and successful life.

Limiting the concept of intelligence to the capacity for abstract reasoning has an advantage other than precision. We can then ask, What is the relation of intelligence to other important human abilities? The abilities of most concern in this chapter are those related to emotions and creativity. The central thesis of the chapter is that emotions are not only related to intelligence, but are also subject to creative change. In other words, behind the trichotomy of intelligence, emotion, and creativity, there lies a unity, such that each shares features with the others.

RELATIONS BETWEEN INTELLIGENCE, EMOTION, AND CREATIVITY

In developing the above thesis, I begin by considering separately each pair in the trichotomy, that is, intelligence and emotion, intelligence and creativity, and emotion and creativity. In subsequent sections, I review the theoretical rationale and empirical evidence for creativity in the domain of emotion.

Intelligence and Emotion

In discussions of emotional intelligence, it is sometimes unclear whether the focus is on the intelligent use of emotions, or on emotions as a form of intelligence. Theoretically, these are different concepts, although in practice they may be difficult to distinguish. The first (the intelligent use of emotions) leaves intact the traditional view of emotions as primitive, relatively automatic responses. To use an overdrawn analogy, a wild animal may be domesticated and put to intelligent use by its trainer, without thereby making the animal any more intelligent. The second concept (emotions as a form of intelligence) is more radical. It presumes that emotions are determined by some of the same processes that help account for other forms of intelligent behavior.

In order to avoid terminological confusion in subsequent discussion, I use *intelligence* in the narrow sense described earlier, that is, to refer to the capacity for abstract reasoning as measured more or less accurately by IQ tests; I use *ability* to refer to any of the panoply of human talents, of which intelligence is only one; and I use *cognition* to refer to the processes (perception, memory, thinking, and so forth) that help mediate both intellectual and emotional behavior. These distinctions are illustrated in Figure 13.1.

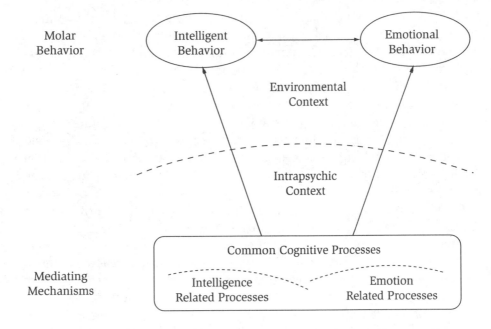

Figure 13.1. Common and specific cognitive processes that help mediate intelligent and emotional behavior.

The top portion of Figure 13.1 represents the interaction between intelligence and emotion, as they are manifested in molar behavior, that is, a meaningful pattern of responses. It is at this level that one can speak of the intelligent use of emotion and, conversely, the facilitation or inhibition of intelligence by emotion. The more interesting question is whether, on a deeper level, different kinds of cognitive processes mediate intelligent and emotional behavior. Although there is no simple answer to this question, the following observations are relevant. The human brain (which necessarily mediates cognitive processes, however conceived) is an exceedingly complex organ that has evolved over many millions of years. Past adaptations are seldom discarded, but rather, are maintained and incorporated into newer systems; thus, different types of cognitive processes undoubtedly exist. Some of these processes (such as concept formation) may be more relevant to intelligent behavior, whereas others (such as sensitivity to interpersonal cues) may be more relevant to emotion. However, intelligence and emotion are concepts that apply to molar behavior; they may be extended only metaphorically to underlying processes. There is no reason to assume a one-to-one relation between one set of processes and intelligent behavior, on the one hand, and a different set of processes and emotional behavior, on the other.

Humans are both the most intelligent and the most emotional of animal species; no infrahuman animal has the range or subtlety of emotions that human beings have. The most parsimonious explanation for this fact is that many of the same processes that mediate intelligence on one occasion may mediate emotion on another occasion. Parsimony, however, is the eye of the beholder. Consider the following observations by Zajonc (1998): "At the basic level we share emotions with lower animals. Except for trivial features, cognitions are probably uniquely human . . . There are 'cognitive virtuosos'—mathematical prodigies, mnemonists, geniuses—but there are no 'emotional prodigies.' We can speak of an 'intellectual giant' but an 'emotional giant' is an absurdity" (p. 597).

Is an "emotional giant" really such an absurdity? Zajonc mentions Gauss and Pascal as examples of cognitive virtuosos. Dante and Meister Eckhart might be mentioned as their equals in the emotional domain. But Dante and Meister Eckhart were also highly intelligent. This raises the following question: Is there a relation between intelligence and emotion within the human species, as there is between humans and infrahuman animals? Because of the restriction of range and many possible confounding variables, any within-species relation would necessarily be small. Nevertheless, it is not unreasonable to assume that the more intelligent a person, the greater the range and subtlety of his or her emotions. Emotions, after all, presume an ability to discriminate among complex and often conflicting situational cues; a knowledge of social norms and standards regarding the appropriate occasions for, and expression of, emotions; and the foresight to anticipate the consequences of one's behavior. Samuel Johnson remarked with respect to happiness, "A peasant and a philosopher may be equally *satisfied*, but not equally *happy*. Happiness consists in the multiplicity of agreeable consciousness. A peasant has not capacity of having equal happiness with a philosopher" (cited by Boswell, 1791/1934, p. 9).

Johnson was perhaps too generous to philosophers and not generous enough to peasants, but his point should be well taken: happiness is more than feeling satisfied, and that "more" is related to the cognitive processes that help mediate intelligent as well as emotional behavior. Similarly, fear is more than fright at an immediate danger, anger is more than lashing out in frustration, love is more than sexual infatuation, grief is more than depression over loss, and so forth for the myriad of other emotions recognized in ordinary language, even those often considered the most basic.

Intelligence and Creativity

People of equal intelligence (or other ability, depending on the domain) may vary greatly in creativity. For a response to be considered creative—not simply intelligent—three criteria must be met: novelty, effectiveness, and authenticity.

Novelty. Novelty is perhaps the most frequently mentioned criterion for creativity. However, as Kaufmann (1993) has pointed out, novelty (together with effectiveness, which is discussed below) is not sufficient to distinguish creativity from intelligence, for the latter also implies the ability to find novel solutions to difficult problems. Kaufmann therefore suggests that a creative solution should also be unconventional, or even anticonventional.

Unconventionality may characterize what Richards (1990) calls eminent as opposed to everyday creativity. Eminent creativity refers to solutions of socially significant problems; everyday creativity, by contrast, is meaningful primarily to the originator—a new way to do household chores, for example. We can state this difference in a more general fashion. A response may be novel in comparison to typical behavior in the society as a whole, or it may be novel in comparison to an individual's own past behavior. Responses novel to the group tend to be unconventional and, if they solve significant problems, eminent. However, creativity is not limited to a few individuals who achieve eminence. All learning and development involves the acquisition of novel behavior (from the individual's perspective) and hence some degree of creativity.

Effectiveness. Not all novel responses are creative; some are simply bizarre or eccentric. To be considered creative, a response must be of potential benefit. As in the case of novelty, effectiveness may be evaluated either from a group or individual perspective. A response that is beneficial for a group may be detrimental to the welfare of the individual (for example, heroism and death in battle), and vice versa. To complicate matters further, a temporal dimension must be taken into account. A response that is beneficial in the short term may be detrimental in the long term, and vice versa. Not surprisingly, then, the determination of a response as effective is always subject to reevaluation. Creativity, it might be said, depends as much on hindsight as on foresight.

Authenticity. Imagine a highly talented art student who copies the painting of an old master in every detail. Because the two paintings are exactly the same, they are equally distinct (novel) in comparison to other paintings, and they are equally aesthetic (effective). Yet only the original is considered truly creative; the copy lacks authenticity. Arnheim (1966) speaks of creativity as involving the "pregnant sight of reality" (p. 299). Pursuing this metaphor, we might say that a copy is stillborn; cut off from the self, its creator, it lacks the possibility for further growth. By contrast, stemming from the self, a creative product is alive with new possibilities.

Authenticity is as important to science as it is to art. Like young artists who often copy the works of past masters in order to develop their own techniques, aspiring scientists may replicate classic experiments, thus internalizing the paradigm of their science (Kuhn, 1970). Creativity comes later, as the scientist expands on and perhaps overthrows the paradigm.

Emotions, too, can be either authentic (stemming from the self) or inauthentic (mere copies of social expectations), a tact captured by the hackneyed phrase, "get in touch with your true feelings." But where were the feelings before one got in touch? Getting in touch with one's feelings is less an act of discovery than it is an act of creation (Morgan & Averill, 1992).

Emotion and Creativity

Emotions can either facilitate or hinder creativity; and conversely, success or failure in emotional endeavors can be a source of intense emotions, from exhilaration to despair (Russ, 1999; Shaw & Runco, 1994). But emotions and creativity may interact in yet another way, namely, emotions may be creative products in their own right. This is not a novel idea. The Renaissance scholar Erasmus (1511/1941) concluded his satirical work, *The Praise of Folly*, with the following paean to the ecstasies of Christian mystics:

> They say things that are not quite coherent, and this not in the ordinary way of men, but they make a sound without meaning, and suddenly they change the whole aspect of their faces; now cheerful, now downcast, they will weep, then laugh, and then sigh; in brief, they are truly outside themselves. When presently they return to themselves they say that they do not know where they have been, whether in the body or out of it, waking or sleeping; they do not remember what they have heard, seen, spoken or done; and yet through a cloud, or as in a dream, they know one thing, that they were at their happiest while they were thus out of their wits. (p. 124)

A similar description might be applied *mutatis mutandis* to highly creative emotional experiences of all types, not just mystical ecstasies. The following is a description by a young woman, a student in a course on human stress and emotion, of her reactions at her sister's wedding:

> I felt so many emotions in such an intense manner that it is very difficult to differentiate and describe them separately. I felt such pride in and for her, that I could not stop smiling. I felt such a sense of loss and grieving, that my stomach tightened and ached. Lastly I felt an emotion similar to, but beyond, happiness. I was genuinely smiling with tears streaming down my face throughout the ceremony. This particular combination of emotions continued throughout the day and most of the night. My thoughts tended to be with others. I was wondering how others were feeling and projecting their feelings onto myself. I was also imagining what I would be experiencing if it was my wedding. Combining these feelings with those I was already experiencing was a little overwhelming.

Such a combination of emotions (pride, hope, grief) is understandable within the context; nevertheless, it was a novel experience for the student. Moreover, she believed the combination to be effective in communicating her feelings to others, and it was certainly authentic.

Numerous other examples of emotionally creative experiences by people from all walks of life were presented in Averill and Nunley (1992). It is difficult, however, to convey the nature of such experiences in words. When we use ordinary language to describe an experience we tend to "normalize" the experience—to make it appear more ordinary and compartmentalized than it actually may have been.

Nor need an experience be as extreme as the above examples in order to be considered creative. Three levels of emotional creativity can be distinguished, depending on the extent to which a standard emotion is transformed. To illustrate the first, or simplest, level with a nonemotional example, consider an artist who uses a preexisting object (a piece of driftwood, say) to achieve an aesthetic effect, without altering the characteristics or form of the object in any fundamental way. Analogously, an emotionally creative response at this level might involve the particularly effective and authentic application of a preexisting emotion, without the emotion itself undergoing fundamental change. Returning now to the example of an artist working with a piece of driftwood, the artist might carve the wood to alter its form, while still conforming to accepted cultural standards (for example, producing a statue or figurine). Analogously, an emotionally creative response might involve the refinement ("sculpting") of a standard emotion to better meet the needs of the individual or group. At the furthermost level of transformation, an artist might break with tradition and develop a new form of expression, one that appears at first strange or "unnatural" within the cultural context. Correspondingly, emotional creativity at this level might involve the development of a new way of responding, one not easily identifiable in ordinary language.

These three levels represent points along a continuum, reflecting the extent to which the object is transformed. They do not necessarily reflect the degree of creativity involved; that is, at each level the creative response may be considered eminent (achieve wide recognition), everyday (of importance primarily to the individual), or even trivial (of little consequence to anyone). Our concern in the following discussion is primarily with emotional creativity at the third, or transformational, level—whether eminent or everyday—for that level is theoretically the most interesting and problematic.

THEORETICAL BACKGROUND

How is emotional creativity possible theoretically? And how can it be demonstrated empirically? These two questions are treated separately in this and the next section; the answers are not, however, independent. Theoretical assumptions dictate how we interpret empirical data—indeed, what we even recognize as data. Conversely, empirical data help determine our theories. This interdependence of fact and theory has provided much grist for postmodern philosophers debating the nature and limits of knowledge. Greenwood (1994) provided a good introduction to this debate as it applies to emotion. For our purposes, it is only important to note that ostensibly empirical conflicts can often be traced to differences in theoretical assumptions.

The idea of emotional creativity is based on a social-constructionist view of emotion as extended to individual development and change (Averill, 1980, 1984, 1990; Averill & Nunley, 1992; Averill & Thomas-Knowles, 1991). A social constructionist view has a particular "range of convenience," that is, type of emotional experience to which it is most applicable. In both everyday discourse and the psychological literature, the term *emotional* is often used to refer to a general matrix of experience in which behavior is embedded. A depressed mood is a good example of such a state. Considerable research has been devoted to the influence of mood on creative activity (Vosburg & Kaufman, 1999). However, moods themselves are not creative products as here conceived, and hence this research falls outside the purview of the present analysis. Another type of emotional experience involves short-term, relatively automatic reactions to events of biological significance. Sudden fright to an immediate danger is paradigmatic of this category. Such reactions are also not open to innovation and change, but neither are they representative of the broad range of human emotions. The third—and broadest—category of emotion consists of those states recognized in ordinary language as love, anger, grief, jealousy, and so forth. These are the primary concern of this chapter.

To see how emotions of this third type are subject to creative change, further distinctions must be introduced, namely, between emotional syndromes, schemas, states, and responses.

Emotional Syndrome

The notion of a syndrome is familiar from its use in medicine. Measles, mumps, polio, and whooping cough are disease syndromes. A disease syndrome describes a coordinated set of reactions that can be related to a specific etiology or cause, and that develops in a particular manner over time (its prognosis). Emotional syndromes (such as anger, fear, grief) can be defined in a similar manner, except that the "symptoms" are more behavioral than physiological, and the etiology of an emotion is not some microbe or injury, but rather the way a person appraises the situation. For example, in anger, the person perceives some unjustified affront; in fear, some potential danger; in grief, the loss of a loved one; and so forth.

Put differently, emotional syndromes are the folk equivalent of the theoretical constructs found in science. This means, among other things, that although emotional syndromes are manifested *by* individuals, they are not localized *in* individuals. Pursuing the disease analogy, one can speak of small pox as a syndrome even though no one is actually afflicted with the disease (because the small pox virus has been eradicated, except for a few samples retained for research purposes). Similarly, emotional syndromes can exist in the abstract, independent of any particular responding individual.

As folk theoretical constructs, emotional syndromes play a role in our everyday explanation of behavior similar to the role played by disease syndromes in the more formal theories of physiology and medicine. That is, the meaning of emotion qua syndrome depends on a matrix of culturally specific beliefs (implicit theories) about the nature of emotion, just as the meaning of disease syndromes depends on beliefs about microbes, immunity, homeostasis, and the like.

Two types of beliefs are relevant to emotional syndromes: existential beliefs and social rules. As the term implies, existential beliefs concern what is, what exists. Not all existential beliefs are true; some are mythical. For example, it is true that people in love want to be together, but it is a myth that love is made in heaven, that there is only one "true" love, and so forth. Unfortunately, the dividing line between true beliefs and myths is not as clear as these examples might suggest, because myths about behavior—if believed as true—have a way of becoming self-fulfilling. And even when a mythical belief is recognized as such, it can still influence the way we think, feel, and respond when emotional.

Whereas existential beliefs describe what *is,* whether in truth or myth, social rules prescribe what *should be.* Scientists strive to make scientific theories be objective, free of value judgments, to the extent that is ever possible. That is not the case with respect to folk theories of emotion, which are infused with value judgments. In American culture, for example, it is considered highly gauche to laugh at a funeral; at a good Irish wake, the rules are somewhat different.

All theorists recognize that social rules help regulate the display of emotion, such as laughing at a funeral. Less frequently recognized is the fact that many rules of emotions have a constitutive as well as regulative function. To illustrate the difference between the regulative and constitutive functions of rules, consider the grammar of a language: grammatical rules not only regulate how a person speaks, they help constitute the language that is spoken. Thus, without an English grammar, there would be no English language. The same is true with respect to the rules of emotion. Without the rules of anger, there would be not anger, but some other emotion, or perhaps only inarticulate expressions of rage or frustration.

Emotional Schemas

As stated above, emotional syndromes are objective phenomena; they exist "out there" as folk theoretical constructs, independent of how anyone actually responds. In order to get from the outside in, that is, to the thoughts, feelings, and behavior of individuals, the relevant beliefs and rules must be internalized. Those internalized beliefs and rules constitute emotional schemas, as illustrated in Figure 13.2.

Internalization is never complete, of course. Because of individual differences in temperament, socialization, and position in society, only a subset of beliefs and rules that constitute an emotional syndrome may be internalized by an individual, and then with varying degrees of fidelity. Because of this, no two individuals will experience an emotional syndrome in exactly the same way: the

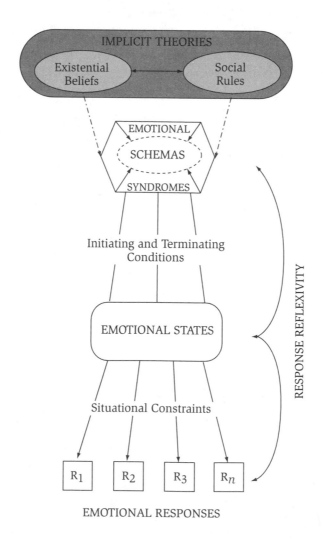

Figure 13.2. Relation of emotional syndromes and schemas to emotional states and responses.

way you experience love is different from the way I experience love, yet both are manifestations of love as a syndrome.

Emotional States

An emotional state is a temporary (episodic) disposition to respond in a manner consistent with an emotional syndrome, as that syndrome is understood by the individual. The notion of a disposition is subject to misunderstanding, especially as applied to emotional states (as opposed to temperamental traits). Dispositions can be transitory as well as relatively enduring properties of an object. Magnetism, for example, is a dispositional property of some materials. In a reversible magnet, the dispositional property (the ability to attract metal objects) lasts only a long as the magnet is turned on. Similarly, when in an emotional state, a person is disposed to respond, but only as long as he or she is "turned on."

A person is in an emotional state when relevant emotional schemas are activated. This does not mean that cognitive schemas exist fully formed in the mind (or brain) of the individual, just waiting to be triggered by appropriate initiating conditions. Some emotional schemas may be stored and recalled as such; however, when the situation is unusual or in flux, emotional schemas may be constructed "on-line" as an episode develops.

Emotional Responses

Emotional responses are what a person thinks, feels, and does when in an emotional state. Instrumental acts (hitting, running, and so forth) are one kind of response. Physiological changes (such as increased heart rate) and expressive reactions (smiling, frowning, and so on) are other common emotional responses. As with any other kind of judgment, the appraisals that persons make when emotional (for example, that an event is dangerous, in the case of fear) are also responses. And so, too, are feelings—the subjective experience of emotion. It is not usual to think of feelings as a kind of response. But even simple perceptual experiences, such as seeing red or hearing voices, can be treated as responses. This is particularly evident in hallucinations, in which the perceptual response occurs in the absence of an adequate stimulus. Emotional feelings are more complex than simple perceptions, but similar considerations apply (Averill, 1993).

Some emotional responses are under genetic control. For example, emotions that involve aggressive intent, such as anger or jealousy, may frequently—but not invariably—be accompanied by biologically based facial expressions that also indicate aggressive intent. However, we must be careful not to mistake a part for the whole.

It is not just isolated responses, such as a facial grimace, that are under genetic control. The ways responses—learned as well as innate—are organized into complex wholes or syndromes are also influenced by our biological heritage. Some patterns of response are simply easier to acquire than are others. But again, a caveat must be added; namely, the same is true of responses in the intellectual as in the emotional domain. For example, it is easier to form some mathematical concepts (integers, say, or two-dimensional spaces) than others (complex numbers, or ten-dimensional spaces). In other words, biology alone is not sufficient to distinguish emotional from nonemotional behavior. The social beliefs and rules that help constitute emotional syndromes are fundamental in this regard.

A reflexive or bidirectional relation exists among emotional responses, states, and schemas/syndromes, as illustrated by the curved arrows at the right of Figure 13.2. Moving down the hierarchy in the figure depicts how emotional syndromes help organize and lend meaning to the responses a person makes when in an emotional state. Even responses that are relatively automatic are experienced as emotional only to the extent that they are interpreted within the framework of an emotional syndrome; for example, it is this reflexivity that transforms mere arousal (from climbing the stairs, say) into emotional arousal (an angry episode). Conversely, as one moves up the hierarchy, an emotional state remains incomplete or dispassionate in the absence of responses.

Pathways to Change

The above analysis suggests that emotional creativity can start from the top (emotional syndromes) and "trickle down," or it can start from the bottom (emotional responses) and "bubble up." A trickle-down approach is common during psychotherapy, where attempts are often made to alter the beliefs and rules that constitute maladaptive emotional syndromes (Nunley & Averill, 1996). Bubble-up approaches are typical in early emotional development, during which the cognitive capacities of the child are limited (Averill, 1984). Under ordinary circumstances, of course, top-down and bottom-up approaches occur in tandem, each reinforcing the other. As the philosopher and historian, R. G. Collingwood (1938/1967) observed, "Until a man has expressed his emotions, he does not yet know what emotion it is. The act of expressing it is therefore an exploration of his own emotions" (p. 111).

Whether from the top down or the bottom up, emotional change does not come easily. Emotional innovations, like biological mutations, often have detrimental effects. Selection mechanisms are therefore necessary in order to weed out the bad from the good. Emotions literally embody the values of a society, and they are fundamental to a person's own sense of self. Selection mechanisms may thus take the form of public opinion and censure, on the social level, and feelings of shame and guilt, on the individual level. Difficulties arise when selection is either too strong or too weak: when too strong, the result is an inability to adapt to changing situations; when too weak, the result is a kind of emotional anarchy.

EMPIRICAL DATA

Three kinds of research support the validity of emotional creativity as a theoretical construct: (1) social or cultural difference in emotional syndromes, (2) individual differences in the ability to be emotionally creative, and (3) rhetorical analyses of emotional episodes.

Cultural Differences in Emotional Syndromes

As mentioned earlier, the idea of emotional creativity is based on a social-constructionist view of emotion as extended to individual development. Hence, data relevant to a social-constructionist thesis, especially historical and cross-cultural differences in emotion, are also relevant to emotional creativity. Because the social-constructionist literature on emotion has been extensively reviewed elsewhere (for example, Harre, 1986; Harre & Parrott, 1996), I do not discuss it further here except for one common objection that deserves brief discussion.

No one doubts that large differences exist across cultures in the way emotions are experienced and expressed. Thus, the question is not whether such variations exist, but what they mean. Is there some underlying condition—the "real" emotion—that is manifested differently depending on cultural "display" rules? Or are the variations themselves distinct emotions that bear only a family resemblance to one another?

This dispute is more conceptual than empirical. I illustrate this point here with reference to anger, often considered one of the most basic and universal of human emotions. The concept of anger may be applied in two ways: first, in a generic sense to cover a wide range of related emotional syndromes, for example, envy, jealousy, fury, frustration, annoyance, and contempt in our own culture, not to mention related syndromes in other cultures; and, second, in a specific sense to refer to one kind of emotion on a par with other emotions in the same general category (such as anger versus envy). Linguistically, when a single term is used to refer to phenomena at two different levels of generality, the term so used is referred to as a synecdoche. "Anger" (and many other emotional terms, especially those referring to so-called basic emotions) is often used as a synecdoche, both in everyday speech and in psychological theory.

It is important to distinguish the generic and specific uses of a concept such as anger, for what is true of a category at one level of generality need not be true at another (higher or lower) level. To conflate levels of generality is to commit what Ryle (1949) called a "category mistake." Category mistakes are particularly common when synecdoches are involved, because the use of the one term makes it easy to traverse between levels of generality without realizing that a shift in meaning has occurred.

Consider, for example, the meaning of anger in a generic sense. What do envy, jealousy, and fury—as well as anger as a specific emotion—have in common?

On some occasions, at least, all are associated with aggressive behavior. In its generic sense, then, anger may be used to refer to almost any aggressive emotional response. Angry aggression in this sense is typically contrasted with instrumental aggression, that is, aggression deliberately used as a means for achieving some extrinsic reward (as in a robbery).

Now consider anger as a specific emotion. How does anger in a narrow sense differ from other members of the general category of angerlike emotions such as envy, jealousy, and fury? As a specific emotion, anger involves an attribution of blame for wrongdoing and a desire for reparation. Only rarely is anger in this sense accompanied by aggression, at least by physical aggression. The main objective of anger is not to harm the instigator, but to correct the perceived wrong and prevent recurrence.

Is anger universal? Only if we interpret "anger" in a generic sense. As a specific emotion, anger is culturally relative. (See Averill, 1982, for cross-cultural comparisons.) What is true of anger is true of other emotions as well.

With few exceptions (such as sudden fright, attacking a source of pain), specific emotions are not immutable, as is evidenced by wide variations across cultures. This point is important, for although we may think and theorize abstractly (on a generic level), we feel and respond concretely (in terms of specific emotions); and on the concrete level, there is ample room for emotional innovation and change.

Individual Differences in Emotional Creativity

If it were not for innovations on the individual level, and their subsequent diffusion through society, there would be no cross-cultural differences in emotion. However, not all members of a society are equally creative—emotionally any more than intellectually or artistically. One way, then, to explore emotional creativity is through individual differences in the ability to produce innovative yet adaptive emotional responses.

Individual differences in the ability to be emotionally creative can be assessed by applying the three criteria for creativity (novelty, effectiveness, authenticity) to a person's past behavior—assuming that the past predicts the future. Degree of preparation is another potential indicator of individual differences in creative potential. Expertise (practical knowledge and understanding) is necessary before an individual is capable of truly creative accomplishments within a given domain (Hayes, 1981; Weisberg, 1986).

Based on the above considerations, a thirty-item Emotional Creativity Inventory (ECI) has been constructed (Averill, 1999). Seven of the items refer to emotional preparation (for example, "I think about and try to understand my emotional reactions"), fourteen refer to the novelty of emotional experiences (such as "My emotional reactions are different and unique"), five refer to effectiveness (such as "My emotions help me achieve my goals in life"), and four refer to authenticity (for example, "I try to be honest about my emotional reactions, even when it causes me problems").

The ECI has high internal consistency ($\alpha = .90$, $n = 489$) and three-month test-retest reliability ($r = .91$, $n = 45$). Construct validity is indicated by the fact that people who score high on the ECI are better able to express their emotions creatively in both writing and drawings (Gutbezahl & Averill, 1996), and they are rated by their peers as more emotionally creative (Averill, 1999).

A principal components factor analysis suggests that the ECI is basically unidimensional—all items have loadings of .30 or greater on the first unrotated factor. Upon oblique rotation, however, three more homogeneous facets or subdimensions are clearly identifiable. The first facet represents emotional preparation; the second, the ability to respond in a novel fashion; and the third, a combination of effectiveness and authenticity. The relation of the ECI to other variables differs somewhat depending on the facet under consideration. For example, women score higher than men on the preparation and effectiveness/authenticity facets, but not on the novelty facet. For most purposes, however, the total score is the most meaningful index of individual differences in emotional creativity.

Relations between the ECI and other variables are presented in detail elsewhere (Averill, 1999); the following is a brief overview of some of the more salient findings. As would be expected, ECI total scores are associated ($r = .58$, $df = 147$, $p < .001$) with openness to experience (also referred to as *culture* or *intellect*), one of the "big five" personality traits measured by the NEO-PI (Costa & McCrae, 1985). Persons who score high on the ECI are also more likely to have had experiences that transcend the usual boundaries between self and other, space and time, as measured by the nonreligious dimension of Hood's (1975) Mysticism Scale ($r = .39$, $df = 89$, $p < .001$).

Creativity in any domain requires self-confidence and a willingness to question established procedures. Not surprisingly, therefore, scores on the ECI are positively related to Rosenberg's (1965) measure of self-esteem ($r = .26$, $df = 89$, $p < .05$), and (to about the same degree) with several measures of nonauthoritarian and inquiring attitudes.

People who score high on the ECI also report having had more traumatic experiences during childhood and adolescence (for example, death or divorce of their parents). The direction of causality cannot be determined from these data: early trauma, if successfully overcome, may facilitate creativity in meeting subsequent challenges; alternatively, emotionally creative people may be more prone to think about and report early trauma. These two alternatives are not mutually exclusive, of course. But whatever the case, preparedness—as might be afforded by prior experience—is important for creativity in any domain.

With regard to recent stressful events (within the prior month), emotionally creative people are flexible in their choice of coping strategies, as measured by the Ways of Coping Questionnaire (Folkman & Lazarus, 1988). Flexibility, however, does not preclude preferences. The strategies most associated with emotional creativity tend to emphasize control over one's own behavior and the situation, whether through individual or collective action.

What the ECI is *not* related to is as informative as what it is related to. For example, total scores on the ECI are unrelated to extraversion and emotional lability (neuroticism), two personality traits often associated with positive and negative emotionality, respectively. This supports the notion that emotional creativity is less a matter of emotional reactivity than it is an ability to be innovative and adaptive in response.

To take a final example, the ECI is *negatively* associated with alexithymia ($r = -.34$, $df = 87$, $p < .01$), as assessed by the Twenty-Item Toronto Alexithymia Scale (TAS-20) total score (Bagby, Parker, & Taylor, 1994). Alexithymia involves an inability to identify and describe one's own emotional experiences. Emotional creativity, too, involves experiences that are difficult to describe in ordinary language, and hence there is overlap between the two constructs. However, people can have difficulty identifying and describing their emotions for different reasons. In the case of those with alexithymia, the difficulty is due to the vagueness and shallowness of experience, and an impoverished fantasy life; in the case of emotionally creative persons, it is due to the complexity and originality of experience.

Findings such as the above support the notion of emotional creativity as a theoretical construct. They do not, however, address some of the more interesting questions concerning individual differences in the ability to be emotionally creative. Consider, for example, the lack of relation between ECI total scores and the introversion-extraversion dimension. Does this mean that emotionally creative introverts respond in the same way as emotionally creative extraverts? That seems unlikely. In the intellectual domain, introverts and extraverts of equal ability differ in the way they express their creativity; for example, introverts tend to prefer more theoretically oriented disciplines, such as mathematics, whereas extraverts tend to prefer more empirically oriented disciplines, such as zoology, where direct observation of the external world is important (Kretschmer, 1948). An analogous division might apply to emotional creativity, with introverts conforming more to the still-waters-run-deep stereotype, and extraverts, more to the happy-go-lucky stereotype.

Similar issues arise with respect to other personal characteristics. For example, are there differences between older and younger persons in the way emotional creativity is manifested? This question is of particular interest considering the aging of the population and the numerous challenges (retirement, loss of income, failing health, bereavement) faced by older people. Contrary to common stereotype, Carstensen and her colleagues (for example, Carstensen & Charles, 1998) have found that emotional well-being does not decline and may actually increase as people grow older—at least until near the very end of life. Specifically, there appears to be little change in the amount of positive emotions experienced with age, but there is a decrease in, or better regulation of, negative affect. This does not represent a simplification of the emotions among the elderly, as though a positive but bland plateau were reached. On the contrary, the emotions of older adults also tend to be more complex and differentiated than those of younger adults, as when joy becomes laced with sadness. According to Carstensen and Charles (1998), "people approaching the end of life appear to place more value on emotion, choosing social partners along affective lines and processing emotionally salient information more deeply" (p. 146). Of course, not all elderly people live emotionally rich lives. In addition to favorable circumstances (for example, adequate financial resources), creativity also seems to play a role. In a middle-class Swedish sample, Smith and van der Meer (1997) found elderly people with creative interests to be emotionally more vibrant—and physically more healthy—than their less creative cohorts.

Rhetorical Analyses of Emotional Episodes

The fact that people differ in their ability to be emotionally creative tells us little about the nature of emotionally creative responses or how they are produced on a given occasion. For that, we must turn to a different kind of analysis. As mentioned earlier, emotional schemas may be constructed on-line, during the course of an episode. In the construction process, the person has recourse to a large database of experience stored in memory, as well as general beliefs about the emotion and its consequences. Depending on the situation and the person's motives and goals, only a subset of this store of information may be accessed in any given episode.

Parkinson (1995) has compared the on-line construction of an emotional episode to a conversation. What is said and done during a conversation (including nonverbal expressions) varies as a function of the intended message, the audience, and the setting. Moreover, the same message can be conveyed in very different words, sometimes with triteness and banality, but sometimes with grace and style. And so it is with the emotions. Rather than being automatic and highly stereotyped, emotional behavior during an episode is flexible and often creative.

And what is communicated during the course of an emotional episode? That depends, of course, on the emotion: anger conveys a different message than does love or fear. In general, however, emotions convey, in an emphatic way, how a situation is being evaluated, and what, if anything, might be done about it. For example, love communicates the desire for a warm and close relationship, and anger communicates the desire to correct a perceived wrong.

Few investigators have taken the effort to analyze the on-line construction of emotional episodes. The reason, I believe, is based on a misconception of what is required for such an analysis. Parkinson (1995) cites Peery's assertion that the true nature of many emotional episodes is only evident after a frame-by-frame analysis of a videotape. But perhaps the task is not as formidable as Peery suggests. What is needed is not an "affective microscope" (Peery's term), which focuses on modes of expression, but an "affective rhetoric," which focuses on the message being conveyed.

The application of rhetorical analyses to emotion is as old as Aristotle. In his *Rhetoric*, Aristotle (1941) was concerned with the use of emotions to augment a persuasive message. Our concern is different, namely, the use of rhetoric to characterize and, ultimately, to transform an emotional episode.

Averill and Rodis (1998) described three rhetorical strategies to effect change during an ongoing emotional episode. One strategy involves *hedonic transformation*. An experience that is hedonically neutral—neither pleasurable nor painful—hardly deserves to be called emotional. But pleasure and pain are not static qualities, unalterable and mutually exclusive. If the hedonic quality of an emotion is changed during the course of an episode (for example, by pointing out positive aspects of an otherwise negative situation), the emotion itself may be transformed. A second rhetorical strategy involves *ethical-ideological discourse*. As described earlier, emotions are constituted, in part, by social rules and existential beliefs. Consequently, one device for emotional change is to challenge the ethical and ideological assumptions on which those rules and beliefs are based. The result may be a creative emotional experience. The third strategy (which may incorporate the first two) involves the use of *narrative* to construct a "reality" different from the reality made salient by the occurrent emotion. The ability to imagine a new and different reality is one of the major precursors to emotional creativity. Thus, by imagining new realities, new emotions may be created.

Sternberg (1996) also illustrates the utility of a narrative approach to the analysis of emotional episodes. Sternberg has identified twenty-four different love stories or plots that couples create (for example, love as addiction, as art, as business, as mystery, as war) in the course of a relationship. Change the plot and you change the emotion. Sternberg's approach is especially relevant to emotions, such as love, that develop over extended periods of time. But even short-term emotions, such as anger, have a narrative structure; the general plot may be scripted by society, but ample opportunity exists for improvisation on the individual level (Averill, 1982, 1993).

Another approach to the analysis of emotional episodes—especially the creation of novel emotions—is through art and literature. Oatley (1992), for example, has used Homer's *Iliad* and George Eliot's *Middlemarch* to explore not only how emotions are transmitted culturally, but also how they may be transformed in the process. In George Eliot's own words, "But my writing is simply a set of experiments in life—an endeavor to see what our thought and emotion may be capable of—what stories of motive, actual or hinted as possible, give promise of a better [*sic*] after which we may strive." (Letter of January 25, 1876, quoted by Oatley, 1992, p. 347). In short, the on-line construction of emotional episodes provides the opportunity for creative change in behavior. A rhetorical approach helps clarify how such change can be brought about. And, as explained earlier, changes in behavior can "bubble-up," producing corresponding changes in an individual's emotional schemas. If the individual has sufficient social influence, the changes may, in turn, be incorporated into the network of beliefs and rules (implicit theory) that help constitute emotional syndromes within the society.

CONCLUSION

Intelligence, emotion, and creativity form a triunity. To fully appreciate that triunity, we must think about emotions in a new way—as social and individual constructions that develop over time, not simply as automatic reactions distinct from "higher" thought processes. But the relevance of the triunity is more than theoretical. Otto Rank (1936/1978) was among the first to suggest that many neurotic syndromes (such as conversion reactions) can be considered instances of creativity gone awry. In terms of the three criteria for creativity outlined earlier in this chapter, neurotic behavior lacks novelty, either because it is overly conforming to social standards or, when it deviates from accepted standards (as it often does), because it has a rigid, compulsive quality that prevents the individual from behaving in new (for him or her) and more adaptive ways. Almost by definition, neurotic syndromes lack effectiveness, either because they disrupt interpersonal relationships or because they are stressful to the individual. Finally, neurotic syndromes often lack authenticity—a disjunct exists between the person's behavior and his or her fundamental beliefs and values ("true feelings"). To the extent that psychotherapy helps to overcome such deficiencies, it can be considered an exercise in emotional creativity (Averill & Nunley, 1992; Nunley & Averill, 1996).

The practical implications of emotional creativity are not limited to individuals. Many of the problems that face contemporary societies (for example, sexually transmitted diseases, ethnic prejudices and strife, unprecedented increases in the life span, overpopulation, degradation of the environment) require changes in the way we respond emotionally. As discussed earlier, however, emotional innovations may call into question the fundamental values of a society and hence are often met with strong resistance. A healthy society, like a healthy individual, is one in one in which the beliefs and rules that help constitute emotional syndromes are sufficiently flexible to allow new forms of emotion to emerge, while still being sufficiently restrictive to eliminate potentially harmful variants.

References

Aristotle. (1941). *Rhetoric* (W. Rhys Roberts, Trans.). In R. McKeon (Ed.), *The basic works of Aristotle* (pp. 1318–1451). New York: Random House.

Arnheim, R. (1966). *Toward a psychology of art.* Berkeley, CA: University of California Press.

Averill, J. R. (1980). A constructivist view of emotion. In R. Plutchik and H. Kellerman (Eds.), *Emotion: Theory, research and experience: Vol. I. Theories of emotion* (pp. 305–339). New York: Academic Press.

Averill, J. R. (1982). *Anger and aggression: An essay on emotion.* New York: Springer-Verlag.

Averill, J. R. (1984). The acquisition of emotions during adulthood. In C. Z. Malatesta & C. Izard (Eds.), *Affective processes in adult development* (pp. 23–43). Beverly Hills, CA: Sage.

Averill, J. R. (1990). Inner feelings, works of the flesh, the beast within, diseases of the mind, driving force, and putting on a show: Six metaphors of emotion and their theoretical extensions. In D. E. Leary (Ed.), *Metaphors in the history of psychology* (pp. 104–132). New York: Cambridge University Press.

Averill, J. R. (1993). Illusions of anger. In R. B. Felson & J. T. Tedeschi (Eds.), *Aggression and violence: Social interactionist perspectives* (pp. 171–192). Washington, DC: American Psychological Association.

Averill, J. R. (1999). Individual differences in emotional creativity: Structure and correlates. *Journal of Personality, 67,* 331–371.

Averill, J. R., & Nunley, E. P. (1992). *Voyages of the heart: Living an emotionally creative life.* New York: The Free Press.

Averill, J. R., & Rodis, P. (1998). Le rôle du langage dans les transformations émotionnelles [The role of language in emotional transformation]. In J. M. Barbier & O. Galatanu (Eds.), *Action Affects et Transformation de Soi.* Paris: Presses Universitaires de France.

Averill, J. R., & Thomas-Knowles, C. (1991). Emotional creativity. In K. T. Strongman (Ed.), *International review of studies on emotion* (Vol. 1, pp. 269–299). London: Wiley.

Bagby, R. M., Parker, J.D.A., & Taylor, G. J. (1994). The twenty-item Toronto Alexithymia Scale: I, Item selection and cross-validation of the factor structure. *Journal of Psychosomatic Research, 38,* 23–32.

Boswell, J. (1934). *The life of Johnson* (Vol. 2). (L. F. Powell, Ed.). Oxford, U.K.: Clarendon Press. (Original work published 1791)

Carstensen, L. L., & Charles, S. T. (1998). Emotion in the second half of life. *Current Directions in Psychological Science, 7,* 144–149.

Collingwood, R. G. (1967). *The principles of art.* Oxford, U.K.: Clarendon Press. (Original work published 1938)

Costa, P. T., Jr., & McCrae, R. R. (1985). *The NEO Personality Inventory manual.* Odessa, FL: Psychological Assessment Resources.

Erasmus, D. (1941). *The praise of folly* (H. H. Hudson, Trans.). Princeton, NJ: Princeton University Press. (Original work published 1511)

Folkman, S., & Lazarus, R. S. (1988). *Ways of coping questionnaire.* Palo Alto, CA: Consulting Psychologists Press.

Greenwood, J. D. (1994). *Realism, identity and emotion.* Thousand Oaks, CA: Sage.

Gutbezahl, J., & Averill, J. R. (1996). Individual differences in emotional creativity as manifested in words and pictures. *Creativity Research Journal, 9,* 327–337.

Harre, R. (Ed.) (1986). *The social construction of emotions.* Oxford, U.K.: Basil Blackwell.

Harre, R., & Parrott, W. G. (Eds.) (1996). *The emotions: Social, cultural and biological dimensions.* Thousand Oaks, CA: Sage.

Hayes, J. R. (1981). *The complete problem solver.* Philadelphia: Franklin Institute Press.

Hood, R. W., Jr., (1975). The construction and preliminary validation of a measure of reported mystical experience. *Journal for the Scientific Study of Religion, 14,* 29–41.

Kaufmann, G. (1993). The structure and content of creativity concepts: An inquiry into the conceptual foundations of creativity research. In S. G. Isaksen, M. C. Murdock, R. L. Firestein, & D. J. Treffinger (Eds.), *Understanding and recognizing creativity: The emergence of a discipline* (pp. 141–157). Norwood, NJ: Ablex.

Kretschmer, E. (1948). *Geniale Menschen* (4th ed.). Berlin: Springer.

Kuhn, T. (1970). *The structure of scientific revolutions* (2nd ed.). Chicago: University of Chicago Press.

Morgan, C., & Averill, J. R. (1992). True feelings, the self, and authenticity: A psychosocial perspective. In D. D. Franks & V. Gecas (Eds.), *Social perspectives on emotion* (Vol. 1, pp. 95–124). Greenwich, CT: JAI Press.

Neisser, U. (1979). The concept of intelligence. In R. J. Sternberg & D. K. Detterman (Eds.), *Human intelligence: Perspectives on its theory and measurement.* Norwood, NJ: Ablex.

Nunley, E. P., & Averill, J. R. (1996). Emotional creativity: Theoretical and applied aspects. In K. T. Kuehlwein & H. Rosen (Ed.), *Constructing realities: Meaning-making perspectives for psychotherapists* (pp. 223–251). San Francisco: Jossey-Bass.

Oatley, K. (1992). *Best laid schemes: The psychology of emotions.* New York: Cambridge University Press.

Parkinson, B. (1995). *Ideas and realities of emotion.* London: Routledge

Rank, O. (1978). *Truth and reality.* New York: W. W. Norton and Co. (Original work published 1936)

Rosenberg, M. (1965). *Society and the adolescent self-image.* Princeton, NJ: Princeton University Press.

Richards, R. (1990). Everyday creativity, eminent creativity, and health. *Creativity Research Journal, 3,* 300–326.

Russ, S. W. (Ed.). (1999). *Affect, creative experience and psychological adjustment.* Philadelphia: Brunner/Mazel.

Ryle, G. (1949). *The concept of mind.* London: Hutchinson.

Smith, G.J.W., & van der Meer, G. (1997). Creativity in old age. In M. A. Runco & R. Richards (Eds.), *Eminent creativity, everyday creativity, and health* (pp. 333–353). Greenwich, CT: Ablex.

Sternberg, R. (1985). Implicit theories of intelligence, creativity, and wisdom. *Journal of Personality and Social Psychology, 49,* 607–627.

Sternberg, R. (1996). Love stories. *Personal Relationships, 3,* 59–79.

Shaw, M. P., & Runco, M. A. (Eds.). (1994). *Creativity and affect.* Norwood, NJ: Ablex.

Vosburg, S., & Kaufman, G. (1999). Mood and creativity research. In S. W. Russ (Ed.), *Affect, creative experience, and psychological adjustment.* Philadelphia: Brunner/Mazel.

Weisberg, R. W. (1986). *Creativity: Genius and other myths.* New York: W. H. Freeman.

Zajonc, R. B. (1998). Emotions. In D. T. Gilbert, S. T. Fiske, & G. Lindzey (Eds.), *Handbook of social psychology* (Vol. 1, pp. 591–632). Boston, MA: McGraw-Hill.

PART THREE

ASSESSMENT METHODS
AND ISSUES

CHAPTER FOURTEEN

Assessment of Alexithymia
Self-Report and Observer-Rated Measures

Graeme J. Taylor, R. Michael Bagby, and Olivier Luminet

Since the formulation of the alexithymia construct in the mid-1970s (Nemiah, Freyberger, & Sifneos, 1976), there has been controversy over its measurement. Several measures have been developed, including observer-rated questionnaires, self-report scales, projective techniques, and a Q-sort (Block, 1961/1978). Some of the self-report scales, such as the Schalling-Sifneos Personality Scales (Apfel & Sifneos, 1979; Sifneos, 1986) and the MMPI Alexithymia Scale (Kleiger & Kinsman, 1980), were constructed hastily and with little concern for standard methods of test construction. Not surprisingly, subsequent investigations found that these scales lack adequate reliability and validity (Taylor, Bagby, & Parker, 1997). Although several investigators have used the Rorschach and/or the Thematic Apperception Test to assess various facets of the alexithymia construct, there is little empirical support for the reliability and validity of these methods.

Because most of the measures of alexithymia have been reviewed previously (Linden, Wen, & Paulhus, 1995; Taylor & Bagby, 1988; Taylor et al., 1997), we focus this chapter on the self-report Twenty-Item Toronto Alexithymia Scale (Bagby, Parker, & Taylor, 1994), which has become the most widely used measure of the construct. Recognizing the need for a multimethod approach for assessing a construct, we also describe the observer-rated Beth Israel Hospital Psychosomatic Questionnaire (Sifneos, 1973) and a recently developed modified version. We conclude the chapter with a description of two new measures—

the self-report Bermond-Vorst Alexithymia Questionnaire (Bermond & Vorst, 1998) and the self- and observer-rated California Q-Set Alexithymia Prototype (Haviland & Reise, 1996a)—which were not included in previous review articles. Given the strong overlap of the alexithymia construct and the emotional intelligence construct (which we discussed in Chapter Three), some of the measures of alexithymia reviewed in this chapter can also be considered potential methods for identifying individuals with low emotional intelligence.

TWENTY-ITEM TORONTO ALEXITHYMIA SCALE

The Twenty-Item Toronto Alexithymia Scale (TAS-20) was developed by Bagby, Parker, and Taylor (1994) and is a revised version of the earlier twenty-six-item Toronto Alexithymia Scale (TAS-26) (Taylor, Ryan, & Bagby, 1985). The TAS-20 has demonstrated good internal consistency and test-retest reliability. In the initial validational study, exploratory factor analysis of the TAS-20 with a student sample yielded a three-factor structure congruent with the theoretical construct of alexithymia: (F1) difficulty identifying feelings and distinguishing between feelings and the bodily sensations of emotional arousal, (F2) difficulty describing feelings to others, and (F3) externally oriented thinking. Despite the absence of items on the TAS-20 directly assessing daydreaming and other imaginal activity, which were included on the TAS-26, the third factor together with the second factor seem to reflect the *pensée opératoire* (operatory thinking) component of the alexithymia construct, that is, a cognitive style that shows a preference for the external details of everyday life rather than thought content related to feelings, fantasies, and other aspects of a person's inner experience (Marty & de M'Uzan, 1963; Nemiah et al., 1976). Subsequent research showed that the externally oriented thinking factor correlates significantly and negatively ($r = -.45, p < .01$) with the fantasy subscale of the openness to experience dimension in the NEO Personality Inventory (Bagby, Taylor, & Parker, 1994). Given that high scores on the fantasy subscale reflect a vivid imagination and capacity to create an interesting inner world, this finding indicates that the externally oriented thinking factor of the TAS-20 adequately assesses the constricted imaginal processes facet of the alexithymia construct.

Replicability of the Factor Structure

The replicability of the three-factor structure of the TAS-20 has been demonstrated with both clinical and nonclinical populations by the use of confirmatory factor analysis (Bagby, Parker, & Taylor, 1994; Parker, Bagby, Taylor, Endler, & Schmitz, 1993). Although the first two factors correlated highly, a three-factor model provided a better fit to the data obtained from several different samples than either a one- or two-factor model. The TAS-20 has also been translated into many languages using the method of back translation to establish cross-language equivalence. The validity of the three-factor structure has been demonstrated in these translated versions by confirmatory factor analyses for the following languages: German (Bach, Bach, de Zwaan, Serim, & Böhmer, 1996; Parker et al., 1993), Hindi (Pandey, Mandal, Taylor, & Parker, 1996), Italian (Bressi et al., 1996), Korean (Lce, Rim, & Lee, 1996), Lithuanian (Beresnevaite, Taylor, Parker, & Andziulis, 1998), Portuguese (Prazeres, Parker, & Taylor, forthcoming), Spanish (Páez et al., 1999), and Swedish (Simonsson-Sarnecki et al., forthcoming).

Notwithstanding the evidence for the replicability of the three-factor structure of the TAS-20, and the considerable empirical and theoretical justifications that have produced the scale, some clinicians and researchers still question the suitability and usefulness of its three-factor-derived scales (for example, Deary, Scott, & Wilson, 1997; Erni, Lötscher, & Modestin, 1997; Haviland & Reise, 1996a; Sifneos, 1996). Loas, Otmani, Verrier, Fremaux, & Marchand (1996), for example, conducted principal components analysis on data collected from students at a French university and obtained a two-factor solution; the items assessing difficulty identifying feelings and difficulty describing feelings constituted a single factor, and the items assessing externally oriented thinking comprised a second factor. It must be remembered, however, that exploratory factor analyses are theory weak compared to confirmatory factor analyses, because they generate different factor solutions from which the researcher selects the most sensible, rather than evaluating a priori models (Kline, 1991). When confirmatory factor analysis was applied to the same French data, the original three-factor structure of the scale was found to provide a better fit than a two-factor solution (Loas, Parker, Otmani, Verrier, & Fremaux, 1997).

Haviland and Reise (1996b) conducted confirmatory factor analyses on data sets from medical students and from inpatients who were dependent on psychoactive substances and reported that the three-factor solution provided a poor fit to the data in both samples. In addition, in the sample of inpatients who were substance dependent, the correlations between factors one and three, and between factors two and three, were nonsignificant. Examination of the results for the medical student sample, however, reveals that one of the goodness of fit indices met its criterion standard and two other indices were just below their criteria standards. Furthermore, the patients with substance dependence constituted an extremely unstable population for a factor analytic study because they were recently abstinent from alcohol or psychoactive drugs and completed the TAS-20 within their first week of hospitalization (Haviland, Hendryx, Shaw, & Henry, 1994).

Given that the results of factor analysis of a scale can be influenced by the type of subjects selected (Nunnally, 1978) and that the original derivation sample in the construction of the TAS-20 was a homogeneous group of undergraduate university students, although cross-validated with a clinical sample, it is possible that a different factor solution might emerge with a more heterogeneous population. Moreover, some investigators have found TAS-20 scores to be associated with male gender and age (Lane, Sechrest, & Riedel, 1998; Salminen, Saarijärvi, Äärelä, Toikka, & Kauhanen, 1999). As Nunnally (1978) points out, such variables also might influence the factor structure of a scale.

These issues were addressed in a recent study by Parker, Taylor, and Bagby (1999), who administered the TAS-20 to a community sample of almost 2000 adults. The results of confirmatory factor analyses replicated the three-factor model of the TAS-20, and the three-factor model provided a better fit to the data than both a one-factor model and a two-factor model. Multisample confirmatory factor analyses showed that the three-factor model of the TAS-20 fit well for both men and women, and equivalent models were obtained when the sample was divided at the median age of thirty-two years into younger and older respondents.[1]

Validity of the TAS-20 Factors

Some researchers have criticized the TAS-20 (or the earlier twenty-six-item TAS) on the grounds that the factor scales do not always show similar relationships with other constructs (for example, Deary et al., 1997; Haviland et al., 1994; Hendryx, Haviland, & Shaw, 1991; Kirmayer & Robbins, 1993; Lane et al., 1998). When evaluating the convergent validity of a measure of a multifaceted construct, however, one can expect the full scale and its factors to be related in similar ways only to measures of closely related constructs (Carver, 1989). Some facets are likely to relate to other constructs better than the broad construct, and some may even be unrelated to other constructs.

As we summarized in Chapter Three, strong support for the convergent validity of the TAS-20 and for each of its three factors was provided by the findings of significant negative correlations with the overlapping constructs of psychological mindedness, need for cognition, and affective orientation, as well as with the openness to experience dimension in the five factor model of personality (Bagby, Taylor, & Parker, 1994; Taylor et al., 1997). In addition, the TAS-20 and its three factors were shown to correlate significantly and negatively not only with the total score on the BarOn Emotional Quotient Inventory (EQ-i) (Bar-On, 1997), but also with the four second-order factors assessing intrapersonal intelligence, interpersonal intelligence, adaptability skills, and stress management skills.

Other studies have examined relationships between the TAS-20 and measures of *less* closely related constructs. Not surprisingly, the patterns of correlations that emerge for the three factors depend on the nature of the other construct.

---

[1] Copyright on the TAS-20 is held by G. J. Taylor, R. M. Bagby, and J.D.A. Parker. Information for ordering the scale may be found at www.gtaylorpsychiatry.org.

For example, on theoretical grounds, one would expect factors one and two of the TAS-20 to be associated with constructs related to emotional experience or expression, and factor three to be associated with creative interests and imaginal and analytical capacities. This discriminability among the factors has been demonstrated in studies examining the relationship between alexithymia and the five factor model of personality. In a university student sample, for example, only factors one and two correlated positively with the neuroticism dimension of the NEO Personality Inventory (Bagby, Taylor, & Parker, 1994). All three factors correlated negatively with the positive emotions subscale of the extraversion dimension, but only factors one and two correlated negatively with the full dimension of extraversion. Although all three TAS-20 factors correlated negatively with the receptivity to feelings subscale of the openness to experience dimension, only factor three correlated negatively with the openness to aesthetics and openness to ideas subscales. None of the TAS-20 factors were related significantly to the agreeableness and conscientiousness dimensions.

Given their difficulty in identifying feelings and distinguishing between feelings and the bodily sensations that accompany states of emotional arousal, individuals with alexithymia are considered prone to functional somatic symptoms (Taylor et al., 1997). This tendency, however, is most likely assessed by factor one of the TAS-20 and to some extent by factor two, with minimal contribution from the externally oriented thinking factor. This was demonstrated in a student sample by Martínez-Sánchez (1996), who found that the full-scale TAS-20 and factors one and two correlated positively with the Pennebaker Inventory of Limbic Languidness (a checklist of fifty-four common physical symptoms and bodily sensations) (Pennebaker & Skelton, 1978), whereas factor three did not. In a mixed clinical and nonclinical sample, Deary et al. (1997) also found that factors one and two of the TAS-20 correlated positively with a checklist of medically unexplained symptoms, whereas factor three did not. However, such findings are not always consistent across studies. Bach, Bach, & de Zwaan (1996), for example, found that factor two of the TAS-20 does not always correlate significantly with functional somatic symptoms, and factor three may sometimes show a significant positive correlation.

TAS-20 as a Measure of Emotional Intelligence. The finding of strong negative correlations between the TAS-20 and the EQ-i suggests that the TAS-20 could be used in the assessment of emotional intelligence, at least as a brief screening device for identifying individuals with low emotional intelligence. To further support this recommendation, we summarize some additional findings from a study by Parker, Taylor, and Bagby (forthcoming) in which they constructed latent models to examine the relationship between the alexithymia construct (represented by TAS-20 scores) and Bar-On's (1997) broad concept of emotional intelligence (represented by EQ-i scores). Given that some researchers

(Deary et al., 1997) have questioned whether the three factors of the TAS-20, as a whole, best represent the alexithymia construct, the same model was tested separately for each of the three factors from the TAS-20. It was predicted that the TAS-20 total score and the scores for each of its three factors would be independent of, but strongly and inversely associated with, the total score of the EQ-i.

For each of the models tested, all of the goodness-of-fit indices met preestablished criteria standards. The parameter estimates between the EQ-i and the TAS-20 and its factors were $-.94$ ($p < .001$) for the total TAS-20, $-.78$ ($p < .001$) for factor one (difficulty identifying feelings), $-.70$ ($p < .001$) for factor two (difficulty describing feelings), and $-.55$ ($p < .001$) for factor three (externally oriented thinking). As with the Pearson correlations between the TAS-20 and the EQ-i (see Chapter Three), the strength of these parameter estimates indicates considerable overlap of the two constructs and suggests that the TAS-20 could be a useful measure in the assessment of emotional intelligence. For each of the latent models tested, however, a two-factor solution was superior to a one-factor solution, indicating that the construct measured by the TAS-20 is also independent of the construct measured by the EQ-i. As Mayer, Salovey, and Caruso (2000) point out, the EQ-i is based on a model of emotional intelligence that combines mental abilities concerned with understanding emotions and a diverse set of personality characteristics that Bar-On (1997) related to the potential to succeed in life. Although the TAS-20 may correlate with many of these personality characteristics, they are not part of the definition of the alexithymia construct, nor are they included in the models of emotional intelligence proposed by Salovey and Mayer (1989/1990) and Mayer, Salovey, and Caruso (2000). Future research might investigate the relationship between the TAS-20 and measures of emotional intelligence that restrict themselves to mental abilities concerning the awareness and cognitive processing of emotion.

State Effects Versus Trait Stability

One of the more challenging problems in the assessment of a personality trait that is hypothesized to be a vulnerability or risk factor for certain medical or psychiatric illnesses is to ensure that its measurement is not confounded by the state effects of the illness. Some investigators have argued that the presence of alexithymia may merely reflect a concomitant state reaction to an illness, which may be predicted by state anxiety, a depressed mood, or lowered quality of life, and lessens over time as the illness improves (Haviland et al., 1994; Keltikangas-Järvinen, 1987; Wise, Mann, Mitchell, Hryvniak, & Hill, 1990). However, several longitudinal studies have yielded strong support for alexithymia being a stable trait that is independent of psychological distress or other effects of a medical or psychiatric illness. Salminen, Saarijärvi, Äärelä, and Tamminen (1994), for example, followed a group of patients with anxiety and depressive disorders and found that the mean TAS score was unchanged after one year, even though there was a significant decrease in the mean score on a measure of psychological distress. In a study of newly abstinent alcoholic patients, Haviland, Shaw, Cummings, and MacMurray (1988) found no significant change in the mean TAS score over a three-week treatment period despite a significant drop in the mean score on the Beck Depression Inventory (BDI). Similar findings were reported by Pinard, Negrete, Annable, and Audet (1996), who administered the TAS-20 and the BDI to a group of substance-dependent patients before and after a four- to six-week period of treatment, and by Porcelli, Leoci, Guerra, Taylor, and Bagby (1996), who had a group of patients with inflammatory bowel disease complete the TAS-20 and the Hospital Anxiety and Depression Scale before and after six months of treatment. In a group of university students in Spain, Martínez-Sánchez, Ato-García, Córcoles, Adam, Huedo Medina, and Selva España (1998) demonstrated stability of TAS-20 scores despite fluctuations in measures of psychological and somatic distress during and after university examinations.

Notwithstanding the positive findings from these longitudinal studies, none have examined the distinction between absolute and relative stability, an important concept in trait psychology. Absolute stability refers to the extent to which personality scores change over time, whereas relative stability indicates the extent to which the relative differences among individuals remain the same over time (Santor, Bagby, & Joffe, 1997). Evidence of relative stability in the context of change in symptomatology for a personality construct such as alexithymia confers the assumption of individual vulnerability to any given disorder or disease.

Treatment studies represent an ideal way to test for relative stability because profound changes are expected. In a recent study, Luminet, Bagby, and Taylor (1999) evaluated the absolute and relative stability of alexithymia in a sample of patients who entered a treatment program for major depression. Depression was used as the "disease" state on which to examine the stability of alexithymia because several studies with clinical or nonclinical populations have reported positive and significant relationships between the TAS-20 and measures of depression. It was hypothesized that depression and alexithymia would be correlated at both treatment initiation (baseline) and at follow-up (treatment completion), and that both constructs would show significant reductions from baseline to treatment completion. However, it was also hypothesized that alexithymia scores at baseline and treatment completion would be highly correlated, and that alexithymia assessed at baseline would still predict alexithymia assessed at treatment completion even after controlling for the effects of depression. Such a finding would demonstrate that change in alexithymia from baseline to treatment completion cannot be attributed entirely to the severity of depressive symptoms.

In a sample of forty-six outpatients who met DSM-IV criteria for major depressive disorder and were treated with antidepressant medication for fourteen weeks, there was no significant correlation between the measures of alexithymia and depression at treatment initiation (.09); at treatment completion, however, the two measures did correlate significantly (.38, $p < .01$). As expected, there was a significant and substantial reduction in depressive symptoms over fourteen weeks of treatment: mean change score $= -11.31$, $t(45) = 10.54$, $p < .0001$, as measured by the Hamilton Rating Scale for Depression (HRSD). There was also a smaller but still significant change in alexithymia as measured by the TAS-20: mean change score $= -5.11$, $t(45) = 2.61$, $p < .01$. Despite this large reduction in depression severity, the relative stability of alexithymia was demonstrated by a positive and significant correlation between TAS-20 scores at baseline and treatment completion (.64, $p < .001$).

To demonstrate further evidence of the relative stability of the alexithymia construct, Luminet et al. (1999) used a hierarchical regression analysis with TAS-20 scores at treatment completion as the criterion variable. TAS-20 scores at baseline and HRSD scores at baseline and treatment completion served as the predictor variables. HRSD scores were forced into the model first and accounted for approximately 14 percent of the variance [$F(1, 44) = 7.31$, $p < .01$]. TAS-20 scores at baseline were then entered into the model and accounted for an additional 34 percent of the variance [$F(2, 43) = 26.41$, $p < .001$]. These results indicate that although alexithymia scores may change in the context of a marked reduction in depression, there is strong evidence for the relative stability of alexithymia despite such changes. Such findings, together with results from the various longitudinal studies, support the view that the TAS-20 is measuring a stable trait, independent of depression.

BETH ISRAEL HOSPITAL PSYCHOSOMATIC QUESTIONNAIRE

The Beth Israel Hospital Psychosomatic Questionnaire (BIQ) was developed by Sifneos (1973) in an attempt to quantify differences he had observed in the cognitive-affective style between psychoneurotic patients and patients with "classical" psychosomatic diseases. It is a seventeen-item, forced choice questionnaire (1 = presence; 0 = absence) completed by an interviewer or observer. Of these seventeen questions, Sifneos (1973) selected eight "key" items that best assess alexithymic characteristics; higher scores on these items indicate higher degrees of alexithymia. The method of interviewing, as outlined by Nemiah et al. (1976), involves an initial period of unstructured conversation followed by repeated exploration of the patient's ability to describe feelings and to report fantasies and dreams.

Studies evaluating the psychometric properties of the BIQ have been reviewed elsewhere (Linden et al., 1995; Taylor et al., 1997), so here we summarize only the essential findings and then describe the development and preliminary testing of a modified version of the questionnaire. Factor analysis of the BIQ and correlations with total word count in response to the Thematic Apperception Test or Rotter Sentence Completion Test (as indices of the capacity to fantasize) have provided partial support for the construct validity of the BIQ (Gardos, Schniebolk, Mirin, Wolk, & Rosenthal, 1984; Lesser, Ford, & Friedmann, 1979; Sriram, Chaturvedi, Gopinath, & Shanmugam, 1987). In addition, the BIQ has demonstrated concurrent validity with the twenty-six-item TAS in both clinical and nonclinical populations, with the magnitude of the correlations ranging from .39 to .77 ($p < .01$) (Fukunishi, Saito, & Ozaki, 1992; Jimerson, Wolfe, Franko, Covino, & Sifneos, 1994; Kauhanen, Julkunen, & Salonen, 1992; Sriram, Pratap, & Shanmugam, 1988). There is less support, however, for the reliability of the scale. Although Sriram et al. (1988) demonstrated adequate internal consistency and test-retest reliability, there is evidence that interrater reliability is influenced by the experience, bias, and style of the interviewer (Taylor & Bagby, 1988). Moreover, studies that used independently rated audiotapes or videotapes of a single interview have reported high interrater reliability of the BIQ, whereas unacceptably low interrater reliabilities have been reported in studies that used separate interviews to rate the same patients (Taylor et al., 1997).

Notwithstanding these limitations, Linden et al. (1995) concluded that the BIQ shows potential for becoming a useful observer-rated measure of the alexithymia construct. In an attempt to improve the reliability and validity of the BIQ, some researchers have recommended several modifications to the questionnaire. These include revising the item content, using dimensional rating scales, and developing a standardized method of interviewing as well as guidelines for rating responses. An important step in this direction was initiated by Sriram et al. (1988), who proposed a set of guidelines and probes for rating the eight key items of the BIQ.

Modified BIQ

Following Sriram et al. (1988), Bagby, Taylor, and Parker (1994) developed a modified version of the BIQ by adding four new items for rating alexithymia and eliminating nine of the original seventeen items that are less relevant to the construct. In addition, the rating scale was changed from a dichotomous format to a seven-point Likert-type format to enhance the reliability. The resulting twelve-item questionnaire comprises six items pertaining to the ability to identify and verbally communicate feelings (affect awareness), and six items pertaining to imaginal activity and externally oriented thinking (operatory thinking).[2]

Even without probe questions and rating guidelines, Bagby, Taylor, and Parker (1994) obtained statistically significant interrater agreement among three clinicians who interviewed thirty-nine outpatients referred to a behavioral medicine clinic ($\kappa = .51$). Evidence of the concurrent validity of the modified BIQ

[2] The modified BIQ is published as an appendix in Taylor et al., 1997.

was demonstrated by significant positive correlations with the TAS-20 (.53, p < .01) and its three factor scales. The BIQ subscale assessing affect awareness correlated with factor one (.43, p < .01) and factor two (.52, p < .01) of the TAS-20; and the BIQ subscale assessing operatory thinking correlated with factor two (.58, p < .01) and factor three of the TAS-20 (.30, p < .05) (Bagby, Taylor, & Parker, 1994).

Because several other measures were completed by the same group of behavioral medicine outpatients, it was possible to examine the relationships of the modified BIQ and its subscales with general intelligence and with neurotic psychopathology. General intellectual functioning was assessed with the Shipley Institute of Living Scale (SILS) (Zachary, 1986), which provides subscores for vocabulary and abstract concept formation. Neurotic psychopathology was measured with the Crown-Crisp Experiential Index (CCEI) (Crown & Crisp, 1979). The modified BIQ and its two subscales were unrelated to the total score and vocabulary score on the SILS; however, the subscale assessing affect awareness was significantly and negatively related to the abstract thinking score ($r = -.32$, p < .05). The modified BIQ and its two subscales were unrelated to the total score on the CCEI; this result is consistent with findings from a study of patients with anorexia nervosa in which the twenty-six-item TAS also was unrelated to the CCEI (Bourke, Taylor, Parker, & Bagby, 1992).

The psychometric properties of the modified BIQ were subsequently evaluated in Japan by Fukunishi, Nakagawa, Nakamura, Kikuchi, and Takubo (1997) in samples of college students and psychiatric outpatients. Principal components factor analysis yielded a two-factor solution, which accounted for approximately 41 percent of the total variance in both samples and corresponded to the two subscales identified by Bagby, Taylor, & Parker (1994). In addition, and in both samples, the modified BIQ and its two subscales demonstrated adequate internal consistency (Cronbach α coefficients ranged from .72 to .85) and test-retest reliability over a three-month interval ($r = .71$ for college students and .51 for psychiatric outpatients, p < .05).

The level of agreement between observer ratings on the modified BIQ and self-report TAS-20 scores was evaluated by Martínez-Sánchez (1996) in a group of university students in Spain. In this study, the modified BIQ and its two subscales correlated positively and significantly with the TAS-20 total score; the magnitude of the correlations ranged from .47 to .51, p < .001). Significant positive correlations were also obtained with the three factors of the TAS-20, except for the correlation between the affect awareness subscale of the BIQ and the externally oriented thinking factor of the TAS-20, which was nonsignificant.

Although further studies are needed to evaluate the reliability and construct validity of the modifed BIQ, the preliminary findings are promising. Investigators who use the modified version are advised to employ a semistructured form of interview, as outlined by Nemiah et al. (1976). Interrater reliability should be established by using different raters who interview separately the same group of subjects. Alternatively, different clinicians/researchers could interview and rate different subjects if they are randomly assigned to conduct the actual interview while the other clinicians/researchers observe and rate the live interview.

BERMOND-VORST ALEXITHYMIA QUESTIONNAIRE

Recently, Dutch investigators introduced a new self-report measure of alexithymia: the Bermond-Vorst Alexithymia Questionnaire (BVAQ). Bermond and colleagues (Bermond, Vorst, Gerritsen, & Vingerhoets, 1994; Bermond, Vorst, Vingerhoets, & Gerritsen, 1999; Vingerhoets, Van Heck, Grim, & Bermond, 1995) initially developed a twenty-item scale (the Amsterdam Alexithymia Scale), which was subsequently extended into the forty-item BVAQ with the purpose of having two parallel versions. Items were written to assess five elements of alexithymia, which were confirmed by exploratory factor analysis of data collected from samples of university students (Bermond & Vorst, 1998). The factors were defined as identifying, verbalizing, analyzing, fantasizing, and emotionalizing. Whereas the first three factors assess facets of the alexithymia construct that correspond to those assessed by the three TAS-20 factors, the fantasizing factor attempts to assess directly the facet involving constricted imaginal processes, and the emotionalizing factor assesses the degree to which a person can be emotionally aroused by emotion-inducing events (Bermond & Vorst, 1998). Each factor of the BVAQ comprises eight items that are rated on five-point Likert scales; half the items are negatively keyed. High scores are indicative of higher degrees of alexithymia. Originally developed in Dutch, the BVAQ has been translated into several languages including English and French. Acceptable levels of internal consistency have been demonstrated for the Dutch version and the English and French translations (Vorst & Bermond, 1999; Zech, Luminet, Rimé, & Wagner, 1999), but estimates of test-retest reliability have not yet been reported.

The replicability of the factor structure of the BVAQ was evaluated recently by Zech et al. (1999) for both English and French versions by means of confirmatory factor analysis. These investigators found that although the parameter estimates of all items of the forty-item BVAQ in both language versions loaded significantly on each of the a priori factors ($p < .001$ for all), most of the indices of goodness of fit were just below the standard criteria. Examining the two parallel versions of the questionnaire separately, however, the second twenty-item version (BVAQ-20B) yielded much better indices of fit for both the English and the French versions. Although the first four factors of the BVAQ correspond to the four salient features in Nemiah et al.'s (1976) definition of the alexithymia construct, and also to the four factors of the original TAS, emotionalizing is not part of the original definition of the construct and should be considered a correlate of alexithymia.

The concurrent validity of the BVAQ-20B was demonstrated by positive correlations with the TAS-20 total score for both the English version (.62, p < .001) and the French version (.61, p < .001). Bermond and Vorst (1998) found a similar correlation between the TAS-20 and the Dutch version of the forty-item BVAQ (.64). The moderate magnitude of these correlations might be due to the presence in the BVAQ of two factors that are not shared with the TAS-20, namely, fantasizing and emotionalizing. This was confirmed when Zech et al. (1999) computed correlations between total TAS-20 scores and BVAQ-20B scores excluding these two factors. The correlation coefficients were .82 for the English translations of both scales and .79 for the French translations.

There is also evidence that the three conceptually similar factors in the TAS-20 and the two twenty-item versions of the BVAQ correlate positively and strongly (Zech et al., 1999). Although all three factors of the TAS-20 correlate positively with the total score on the BVAQ-20B (magnitude of the correlations range from .42 to .65, p < .01), in agreement with their conceptual specificity, the factors assessing fantasizing and emotionalizing within the BVAQ-20B remained statistically uncorrelated with the total TAS-20 and showed low or nonsignificant correlations with the three TAS-20 factor scales. Moreover, the emotionalizing and fantasizing factors showed nonsignificant or low-magnitude correlations with the other factors of the BVAQ-20B. Although the results of preliminary tests of reliability and validity of the BVAQ are encouraging, further research is needed to determine whether responses to items on the fantasizing factor of the BVAQ are influenced by social desirability, as was found during the development of the TAS-20. Additional tests of convergent validity are needed also and will help determine whether the emotionalizing factor should be retained within the BVAQ.

CALIFORNIA Q-SET ALEXITHYMIA PROTOTYPE

Haviland and Reise (1996b) developed a new self- and observer-rated measure of alexithymia using the Q-sort method (Block, 1961/1978). In contrast to the development of most self-report scales in which items are written to compare one person to another person on a variety of attributes, the Q-sort method is a person-centered approach in which attributes are compared to other attributes within the same person. The goal in developing such an instrument was to come up with a prototype of alexithymia based on expert judges' categorization of cognitions and behaviors highly representative of the construct. Haviland and Reise (1996b) asked seventeen experts in the field of alexithymia to sort 100 personality statements from the California Q-Set (CAQ) into a forced, nine-category, quasi-normal distribution ranging from most uncharacteristic of alexithymia to most characteristic of alexithymia. Usable sorts were returned by thirteen judges, who gave each CAQ item a score ranging from 1 to 9. Individual items were then ranked and converted to a normal nine-points score distribution. The average interjudge correlation was satisfactory (.58), and the judge-prototype correlation was high (.77). The normal distribution of the 100 items led to 13 "most characteristic" and 13 "most uncharacteristic" attributes of alexithymia.

The items representing the "most characteristic" attributes of alexithymia included difficulties experiencing and expressing emotion, lack of imagination, lack of insight, being literal and utilitarian, being humorless, and experiencing meaninglessness. This description is reasonably consistent with Nemiah et al.'s (1976) definition of the alexithymia construct. The items representing the "most uncharacteristic" attributes of alexithymia included engaging in personal fantasy and daydreams, having insight into one's own motives and behaviors, being warm and compassionate, having the capacity for close relationships, being introspective and concerned with self as an object, and enjoying aesthetic impressions.

To date, there are only sparse data on the validity of the CAQ–Alexithymia Prototype (CAQ-AP). In the development of the measure, Haviland and Reise (1996b) found that high scores correlated moderately and positively with a Q-sort prototype for ego control, and strongly and negatively with a Q-sort prototype for ego resiliency. In a subsequent study with a college student sample, Haviland (1998) correlated Q-sorts similarity scores given by observers with self-ratings on measures of depression, anxiety, emotional expression, and dimensions of personality. The CAQ-AP similarity score evidenced significant positive correlations with neuroticism (.27), depression (.38), and anxiety (.17), and significant negative correlations with extraversion (−.38), openness (−.17), and emotional expression (−.34). In contrast to studies using the TAS-20, however, a significant negative correlation was found with agreeableness (−.24).

Although the preliminary validity data for the CAQ-AP are consistent with theoretical assumptions about the alexithymia construct, there are several uncertainties about the measure. First, there are no data available on concurrent validity; because the CAQ-AP is claimed to be both a self- and observer-rated measure of the alexithymia construct, future studies should investigate its relationship with the TAS-20 and the modified version of the BIQ. Second, completing the 100 items of the CAQ-AP can be a tedious task, especially if judges have to rate several people. Finally, one can question whether the CAQ-AP can represent equally the most characteristic and most uncharacteristic attributes of alexithymia. The alexithymia construct is relatively specific in contrast to the broad focus of the CAQ, which was designed to cover a large domain of personality. Consequently, whereas the most characteristic attributes of alexithymia selected by the judges are likely to be very characteristic of the construct, it may be argued that the most uncharacteristic attributes of alexithymia in the CAQ can be more heterogeneous with respect to their conceptual distance from the alexithymia construct.

CONCLUSION

The TAS-20 is currently the best-validated measure of the alexithymia construct and can be recommended for both clinical and research purposes. Results from various studies that use the TAS-20 as a dependent variable are directly comparable to one another; and investigators using the scale to determine "alexithymic" and "nonalexithymic" subjects in between-group experimental designs can be assured that their designation is similar to that used in other studies. Although alexithymia is considered a dimensional construct, upper and lower cutoff scores have been established empirically for the TAS-20, which allows for comparisons of rates of alexithymia across studies (Taylor et al., 1997).

Although some researchers have criticized the use of self-report measures to assess alexithymia and/or emotional intelligence (Lane, Ahern, Schwartz, & Kaszniak, 1997; Lane et al. 1998; Mayer, Salovey, & Caruso, 2000), the findings of consensual agreement between TAS-20 scores and observer ratings on the modified BIQ in two different cultures suggest that even when used as a sole measure, the TAS-20 can assess the construct adequately. Nonetheless, if researchers are able to include the modified BIQ in their studies, empirical research is always enhanced by the use of a multimethod assessment approach. In clinical situations, when in-depth evaluations of patients may be required, we have found it useful to administer not only the TAS-20 and the modified BIQ, but also the EQ-i (Bar-On, 1997) and the Revised NEO Personality Inventory (Costa & McCrae, 1992). The EQ-i provides a more comprehensive assessment of intrapersonal and interpersonal intelligence, and alexithymic individuals generally score in the low range on the openness to fantasy and the receptivity to feelings facets of the openness dimension of personality.

References

Apfel, R. J., & Sifneos, P. E. (1979). Alexithymia: Concept and measurement. *Psychotherapy and Psychosomatics, 32,* 180–190.

Bach, M., Bach, D., & de Zwaan, M. (1996). Independency of alexithymia and somatization. *Psychosomatics, 37,* 451–458.

Bach, M., Bach, D., de Zwaan, M., Serim, M., & Böhmer, F. (1996). Validierung der deutschen version der 20-item Toronto-Alexithymie-Skala bei normalpersonen und psychiatrischen patienten. *Psychotherapie, Psychosomatik Medizinische, Psychologie, 46,* 23–28.

Bagby, R. M., Parker, J.D.A., & Taylor, G. J. (1994). The Twenty-Item Toronto Alex-ithymia Scale: I, Item selection and cross-validation of the factor structure. *Journal of Psychosomatic Research, 38,* 23–32.

Bagby, R. M., Taylor, G. J., & Parker, J.D.A. (1994). The Twenty-Item Toronto Alex-ithymia Scale: II, Convergent, discriminant, and concurrent validity. *Journal of Psychosomatic Research, 38,* 33–40.

Bar-On, R. (1997). *BarOn Emotional Quotient Inventory (EQ-i): Technical manual.* Toronto, Canada: Multi-Health Systems.

Beresnevaite, M., Taylor, G. J., Parker, J.D.A., & Andziulis, A. (1998). Cross validation of the factor structure of the 20-item Toronto Alexithymia Scale. *Acta Medica Litu-anica, 5,* 146–149.

Bermond, B., & Vorst, H. C. (1998). *Validity and reliability of the Bermond-Vorst Alex-ithymia Questionnaire.* Unpublished manuscript, University of Amsterdam, The Netherlands.

Bermond, B., Vorst, H. C., Gerritsen, W., & Vingerhoets, A. J. (1994). *Psychometric properties of the Amsterdam Alexithymia Scale.* Unpublished manuscript, Univer-sity of Amsterdam, The Netherlands.

Bermond, B., Vorst, H.C.M., Vingerhoets, A. J., & Gerritsen, W. (1999).The Amsterdam Alexithymia scale: Its psychometric values and correlations with other personality traits. *Psychotherapy and Psychosomatics, 68,* 241–251.

Block, J. (1978). *The Q-sort method in personality assessment and psychiatric research* (reprint edition). Palo Alto, CA: Consulting Psychologist's Press. (Original work published 1961.)

Bourke, M. P., Taylor, G. J., Parker, J.D.A., & Bagby, R. M. (1992). Alexithymia in women with anorexia nervosa. *British Journal of Psychiatry, 161,* 240–243.

Bressi, C., Taylor, G., Parker, J., Bressi, S., Brambilla, V., Aguglia, E., Allegranti, I., Bongiorno, A., Giberti, F., Bucca, M., Todarello, O., Callegari, C., Vender, S., Gala, C., Invernizzi, G. (1996). Cross validation of the factor structure of the 20-item Toronto Alexithymia Scale: An Italian multicenter study. *Journal of Psychosomatic Research, 41,* 551–559.

Carver, C. S. (1989). How should multifaceted personality constructs be tested? Issues illustrated by self-monitoring, attributional style, and hardiness. *Journal of Person-ality and Social Psychology, 56,* 577–585.

Costa, P. T. Jr., & McCrae, R. R. (1992). *Revised NEO Personality Inventory (NEO-PI-R) and NEO Five-Factor Inventory (NEO-FFI) professional manual.* Odessa, FL: Psy-chological Assessment Ressources.

Crown, S., & Crisp, A. H. (1979). *Manual of the Crown-Crisp Experiential Index.* Lon-don: Hodder & Stoughton.

Deary, I. J., Scott, S., & Wilson, J. A. (1997). Neuroticism, alexithymia and medically unexplained symptoms. *Personality and Individual Differences, 22,* 551–564.

Erni, T., Lötscher, K., & Modestin, J. (1997). Two-factor solution of the 20-Item Toronto Alexithymia Scale confirmed. *Psychopathology, 30,* 335–340.

Fukunishi, I., Nakagawa, T., Nakamura, H., Kikuchi, M., & Takubo, M. (1997). Is alexithymia a culture-bound construct? Validity and reliability of the Japaneses versions of the 20-item Toronto Alexithymia Scale and modified Beth Israel Hospital Psychosomatic Questionnaire. *Psychological Reports, 80,* 787–799.

Fukunishi, I., Saito, S., & Ozaki, S. (1992). The influence of defense mechanisms on secondary alexithymia in hemodialysis patients. *Psychotherapy and Psychosomatics, 57,* 50–56.

Gardos, G., Schniebolk, S., Mirin, S. M., Wolk, P. C., & Rosenthal, K. (1984). Alexithymia: Towards validation and measurement. *Comprehensive Psychiatry, 25,* 278–282.

Haviland, M. G. (1998). The validity of the California Q-set alexithymia prototype. *Psychosomatics, 39,* 536–539.

Haviland, M. G., Hendryx, M. S., Shaw, D. G., & Henry, J. P. (1994). Alexithymia in women and men hospitalized for psychoactive substance dependence. *Comprehensive Psychiatry, 35,* 124–128.

Haviland, M. G., & Reise, S. P. (1996a). A California Q-set alexithymia prototype and its relationship to ego-control and ego-resiliency. *Journal of Psychosomatic Research, 41,* 597–608.

Haviland, M. G., & Reise, S. P. (1996b). Structure of the Twenty-Item Toronto Alexithymia Scale. *Journal of Personality Assessment, 66,* 116–125.

Haviland, M. G., Shaw, D. G., Cummings, M. A., & MacMurray, J. P. (1988). Alexithymia: Subscales and relationship to depression. *Psychotherapy and Psychosomatics, 50,* 164–170.

Hendryx, M. S., Haviland, M. G., & Shaw, D. G. (1991). Dimensions of alexithymia and their relationships to anxiety and depression. *Journal of Personality Assessment, 56,* 227–237.

Jimerson, D. C., Wolfe, B. E., Franko, D. L., Covino, N. A., & Sifneos, P. E. (1994). Alexithymia ratings in bulimia nervosa: Clinical correlates. *Psychosomatic Medicine, 56,* 90–93.

Kauhanen, J., Julkunen, J., & Salonen, J. T. (1992). Validity and reliability of the Toronto Alexithymia Scale (TAS) in a population study. *Journal of Psychosomatic Research, 36,* 687–694.

Keltikangas-Järvinen, L. (1987). Concept of alexithymia: II, The consistency of alexithymia. *Psychotherapy and Psychosomatics, 47,* 113–120.

Kirmayer, L. J., & Robbins, J. M. (1993). Cognitive and social correlates of the Toronto Alexithymia Scale. *Psychosomatics, 34,* 41–52.

Kleiger, J. H., & Kinsman, R. A. (1980). The development of an MMPI alexithymia scale. *Psychotherapy and Psychosomatics, 34,* 17–24.

Kline, R. B. (1991). Latent variable path analysis in clinical research: A beginner's tour guide. *Journal of Clinical Psychology, 47,* 471–484.

Lane, R. D., Ahern, G. L., Schwartz, G. E., & Kaszniak, A. W. (1997). Is alexithymia the emotional equivalent of blindsight? *Biological Psychiatry, 42,* 834–844.

Lane, R. D., Sechrest, L., & Riedel, R. (1998). Sociodemographic correlates of alexithymia. *Comprehensive Psychiatry, 39,* 377–385.

Lee, Y-H., Rim, H-D. & Lee, J-Y. (1996). Development and validation of a Korean version of the 20-item Toronto Alexithymia Scale (TAS-20K). *Journal of the Korean Neuropsychiatric Association, 35,* 888–899.

Lesser, I. M., Ford, C. V., & Friedmann, C.T.H. (1979). Alexithymia in somatizing patients. *General Hospital Psychiatry, 1,* 256–261.

Linden, W., Wen, F., & Paulhus, D. L. (1995). Measuring alexithymia: Reliability, validity, and prevalence. *Advances in Personality Assessment, 10,* 51–95.

Loas, G., Otmani, O., Verrier, A., Fremaux, D., & Marchand, M. P. (1996). Factor analysis of the French version of the 20-Item Alexithymia scale (TAS-20). *Psychopathology, 29,* 139–144.

Loas, G., Parker, J.D.A., Otmani, O., Verrier, A., & Fremaux, D. (1997). Confirmatory factor analysis of the French translation of the 20-item Toronto Alexithymia Scale. *Perceptual and Motor Skills, 83,* 1018.

Luminet, O., Bagby, R. M., & Taylor, G. J. (1999). *An evaluation of the absolute and relative stability of alexithymia in patients with major depression.* Unpublished manuscript.

Martínez-Sánchez, F. (1996). The Spanish version of the Toronto Alexithymia Scale (TAS-20). *Clinica y Salud, 7,* 19–32.

Martínez-Sánchez, F., Ato-García, M., Córcoles, Adam, E., Huedo Medina, T. B., and Selva España, J. J. (1998). Stability in alexithymia levels: A longitudinal analysis on various emotional answers. *Personality and Individual Differences, 24,* 767–772.

Marty, P., & de M'Uzan, M. (1963). La "pensée opératoire." *Revue Francaise de Psychanalyse, 27* (Suppl.), 1345–1356.

Mayer, J. D., Salovey, P., & Caruso, D. R. (2000). Emotional intelligence. In R. J. Sternberg (Ed.), *Handbook of intelligence* (2nd ed., pp. 396–420). New York: Cambridge University Press.

Nemiah, J. C., Freyberger, H., & Sifneos, P. E. (1976). Alexithymia: A view of the psychosomatic process. In O. W. Hill (Ed.), *Modern trends in psychosomatic medicine* (Vol. 3, pp. 430–439). London: Butterworths.

Nunnally, J. C. (1978). *Psychometric Theory.* New York: McGraw-Hill.

Páez, D., Martínez-Sánchez, F., Velasco, C., Mayordomo, S., Fernández, I., & Blanco, A. (1999). Validez psicométrica de la Escala de Alexitimia de Toronto: Un estudio transcultural. *Boletín de Psicología, 63,* 55–76.

Pandey, R., Mandal, M. K., Taylor, G. J., & Parker, J.D.A. (1996). Cross-cultural alexithymia: Development and validation of a Hindi translation of the Twenty-Item Toronto Alexithymia Scale. *Journal of Clinical Psychology, 142,* 1150–1155.

Parker, J.D.A., Bagby, R. M., Taylor, G. J., Endler, N. S., & Schmitz, P. (1993). Factorial validity of the 20-item Toronto Alexithymia Scale. *European Journal of Personality, 7,* 221–232.

Parker, J.D.A., Taylor, G. J., & Bagby, R. M (1999). *The factorial validity and convergent validity of the Twenty-Item Toronto Alexithymia Scale.* Unpublished manuscript.

Parker, J.D.A., Taylor, G. J., & Bagby, R. M. (forthcoming). The relationship between alexithymia and emotional intelligence. *Personality and Individual Differences.*

Pennebaker, J., & Skelton, J. (1978). Psychological parameters of physical symptoms. *Personality and Social Psychology Bulletin, 4,* 524–530.

Pinard, L., Negrete, J. C., Annable, L., & Audet, N. (1996). Alexithymia in substance abusers: Persistence and correlates of variance. *American Journal on Addictions, 5,* 32–39.

Porcelli, P., Leoci, C., Guerra, V., Taylor, G. J., & Bagby, R. M. (1996). A longitudinal study of alexithymia and psychological distress in inflammatory bowel disease. *Journal of Psychosomatic Research, 41,* 569–573.

Prazeres, N., Parker, J.D.A., & Taylor, G. J. (forthcoming). Portuguese adaptation of the 20-item Toronto Alexithymia Scale (TAS-20). *Revista IberoAmericana de Diagnóstico y Evaliación.*

Salminen, J. K., Saarijärvi, S., Äärelä, E., & Tamminen, T. (1994). Alexithymia—state or trait? One-year followup study of general hospital psychiatric consultation outpatients. *Journal of Psychosomatic Research, 38,* 681–685.

Salminen, J. K., Saarijärvi, S., Äärelä, E., Toikka, T., & Kauhanen, J. (1999). Prevalence of alexithymia and its association with sociodemographic variables in the general population of Finland. *Journal of Psychosomatic Research, 46,* 75–82.

Salovey, P., & Mayer, J. D. (1989/1990). Emotional intelligence. *Imagination, Cognition, and Personality, 9,* 185–211.

Santor, D. A., Bagby, R. M., & Joffe, R. T. (1997). Evaluating stability and change in personality and depression. *Journal of Personality and Social Psychology, 73,* 1354–1362.

Sifneos, P. E. (1973). The prevalence of "alexithymic" characteristics in psychosomatic patients. *Psychotherapy and Psychosomatics, 22,* 255–262.

Sifneos, P.E. (1986). The Schalling-Sifneos Personality Scale-Revised. *Psychotherapy and Psychosomatics, 45,* 161–165.

Sifneos, P.E. (1996). Alexithymia: Past and present. *American Journal of Psychiatry, 153,* 137–142.

Simonsson-Sarnecki, M., Lundh, L. G., Torestad, B., Bagby, R. M., Taylor, G. J., & Parker, J.D.A. (forthcoming). A Swedish translation of the 20-item Toronto Alexithymia Scale: Cross-validation of the factor structure. *Scandinavian Journal of Psychology, 41,* 25–30.

Sriram, T. G., Chaturvedi, S. K., Gopinath, P. S., & Shanmugam, V. (1987). Controlled study of alexithymic characteristics in patients with psychogenic pain. *Psychotherapy and Psychosomatics, 47,* 11–17.

Sriram, T. G., Pratap. L., & Shanmugam, V. (1988). Towards enhancing the utility of the Beth Israel Hospital Psychosomatic Questionnaire. *Psychotherapy and Psychosomatics, 49,* 205–211.

Taylor, G. J., & Bagby, R. M. (1988). Measurement of alexithymia: Recommendations for clinical practice and future research. *Psychiatric Clinics of North America, 11,* 351–366.

Taylor, G. J., Bagby, R. M., & Parker, J.D.A. (1997). *Disorders of Affect Regulation: Alexithymia in Medical and Psychiatric Illness.* Cambridge, U.K.: Cambridge University Press.

Taylor, G. J., Ryan, D. P., & Bagby, R. M. (1985). Toward the development of a new self-report alexithymia scale. *Psychotherapy and Psychosomatics, 44,* 191–199.

Vingerhoets, J.J.M., Van Heck, G. L., Grim, R., & Bermond, B. (1995). Alexithymia: A further exploration of its nomological network. *Psychotherapy and Psychosomatics, 64,* 32–42.

Vorst, H.C.M., & Bermond, B. (1999, June). *Validity and reliability of the Bermond-Vorst Alexithymia Questionnaire.* Paper presented at the Second International Conference on the (Non)Expression of Emotions in Health and Disease. Tilburg University, Tilburg, The Netherlands.

Wise, T. N., Mann, L. S., Mitchell, J. D., Hryvniak, M., & Hill, B. (1990). Secondary alexithymia: An empirical validation. *Comprehensive Psychiatry, 31,* 284–288.

Zachary, R. A. (1986). *Shipley Institute of Living Scale. Revised Manual.* Los Angeles: Western Psychological Services.

Zech, E., Luminet, O., Rimé, B., & Wagner, H. (1999). Alexithymia and its measurement: Confirmatory factor analyses of the twenty-item Toronto Alexithymia Scale and the Bermond-Vorst alexithymia questionnaire. *European Journal of Personality, 13,* 511–532.

CHAPTER FIFTEEN

Selecting a Measure of Emotional Intelligence

The Case for Ability Scales

John D. Mayer, David R. Caruso, and Peter Salovey

The development of theoretical models of emotional intelligence has been paralleled by the development of tests to measure the concept. Since 1990, when the first scale measuring an aspect of emotional intelligence was reported in a scientific journal (Mayer, DiPaolo, & Salovey, 1990), there has been an explosion of measures of emotional intelligence. These include a number of nonscientific self-report scales that appeared in newspapers, magazines, and World Wide Web sites (for example, *USA Today,* the *Utne Reader*), and also a wide variety of serious endeavors (Bar-On, 1997; Boyatzis, Goleman, & Hay/McBer, 1999; Cooper, 1996/1997; Mayer & Geher, 1996; Mayer, Salovey, & Caruso, 1997, 1999a).

With so many tests available, it would be helpful to have an overview of the existing scales of measurement, and we provide that at the beginning of this chapter. Here, we examine the content coverage of available scales and these tests' methods of measurement. Our own focus is on ability measures of emotional intelligence because we view these instruments as most promising. In the latter parts of this chapter we examine our current scales for assessing emotional intelligence, and finally, the correlates of emotional intelligence, defined as an intelligence.

GENERAL MEASUREMENT ISSUES IN SELECTING A SCALE

What Do Emotional Intelligence Tests Measure? The Problem of Content Validity

The first consideration in evaluating a measure of emotional intelligence is the aspect of mental life it measures. The match between what a test says it measures and the content of its items is known as content validity. The content of emotional intelligence tests varies greatly due to the fact that interpretations of the meaning of the term *emotional intelligence* vary widely (see our Chapter Five). Table 15.1 provides a comparison of such scales, which are arranged into three groups: ability, self-report, and observer-rating measures. These distinctions are discussed further below. For now, however, we focus on the content of each scale.

The ability scale represented is the Multifactor Emotional Intelligence Scale (MEIS). This scale measures emotional intelligence according to the theory that emotional intelligence is an intelligence per se, in that it relates to processing information (Mayer & Salovey, 1997; Salovey, Bedell, Detweiler, & Mayer, 2000). It is divided into four components. The first, *emotional perception,* involves such abilities as identifying emotions in faces, music, and stories. The second, *emotional facilitation of thought,* involves abilities such as relating emotions to other mental sensations such as taste and color (relations that might be employed in artwork), and using emotion in reasoning and problem solving. The third area, *emotional understanding,* involves solving emotional problems such as knowing which emotions are similar, or opposites, and what relations they convey. The fourth area, *emotional management,* involves understanding the implications of social acts on emotions and the regulation of emotion in the self and others.

Next, we move to two self-report scales. The BarOn EQ-i is intended to measure "an array of noncognitive capabilities, competencies, and skills that influence one's ability to succeed in coping with environmental demands and pressures" (Bar-On, 1997, p. 14). The EQ-i is divided into five sections. The first, *intrapersonal,* includes measures of self-awareness, the ability to assert oneself, and the ability to view oneself positively. The second, *interpersonal,* includes such skills as empathy and social responsibility. The third, *stress management,* includes skills such as problem solving and reality testing. The fourth, *adaptability,* includes stress tolerance and impulse control. Finally, *general mood* includes happiness and optimism. (See Chapter Seventeen for an updated view of the EQ-i that indicates general mood to be a facilitator of emotional intelligence, rather than a part of it.)

A second self-report scale, the EQ-Map (Cooper, 1996/1997), also divides emotional intelligence into five attributes. The first, *current environment,* measures life pressures and life satisfactions. The second, *emotional literacy,* includes measures of emotional self-awareness, emotional expression, and emotional

Table 15.1. Emotional Intelligence and Personality Tests, Using Ability, Self-Report, and Informant Approaches to Measurement.

Ability	Self-Report		Informant
Multifactor Emotional Intelligence Scale (MEIS) (Mayer, Salovey, & Caruso, 1997/1999)	*BarOn EQ-i* (Bar-On, 1997)	*EQ-Map* (Cooper, 1996/1997)	*Emotional Competence Inventory* (ECI) (Boyatzis, Goleman, & Hay/McBer, 1999)
Emotional Perception Identifying emotions in faces, emotions in designs, emotions in music, emotions in stories	*Intrapersonal* Emotional self-awareness, assertiveness, self-regard, self-actualization, independence	*Current Environment* Life pressures, life satisfactions	*Self-Awareness* Emotional self-awareness, accurate self-assessment, self-confidence
Emotional Facilitation Translating feelings (Synesthesia), Using emotions to make judgments (Feeling Biases)	*Interpersonal* Empathy, interpersonal relationship, social responsibility	*Emotional Literacy* Emotional self-awareness, emotional expression, emotional awareness of others	*Social Awareness* Empathy, organizational awareness, service orientation
Emotional Understanding Defining emotions, complex emotional blends, emotional transitions, emotional perspectives	*Stress Management* Problem solving, reality testing, flexibility	*EQ Competencies* Intentionality, creativity, resilience, interpersonal connections, constructive discontent	*Self-Management* Self-control, trustworthiness, conscientiousness, adaptability, achievement orientation, initiative
Emotional Management Managing own emotions, managing other's emotions	*Adaptability* Stress tolerance, impulse control	*EQ Values & Attitudes* Outlook, compassion, intuition, trust radius, personal power, integrated self	*Social Skills* Developing others, leadership, influence, communication, change catalyst, conflict management, building bonds, teamwork
	(General Mood) Happiness, optimism	*EQ Outcomes* General health, quality of life, relationship quotient, optimal performance	

awareness of others. The third, *EQ competencies,* includes intentionality, creativity, resilience, interpersonal connections, and constructive discontent. The fourth, *EQ values and attitudes,* includes outlook, compassion, intuition, trust radius, personal power, and integrated self. Finally, the *outcomes* area of the EQ-Map measures explicit outcomes of emotional intelligence: general health, quality of life, relationship quotient, and optimal performance.

Moving next to a joint self-report/observer rating scale, the Emotional Competence Inventory (ECI) defines emotional intelligence as the "capacity for recognizing our own feelings and those of others, for motivating ourselves, and for managing emotions well in ourselves and in our relationships" (Boyatzis et al., 1999, p. 1). The ECI measures four aspects of emotional intelligence. The first, *self-awareness,* includes measures of emotional self-awareness, accurate self-assessment, and self-confidence. The second, *self-management,* measures self-control, trustworthiness, conscientiousness, adaptability, achievement orientation, and initiative. The third, *social awareness,* consists of empathy, organizational awareness, and service orientation. The fourth, *social skills,* includes measures of developing others, leadership, influence, communication, change catalyst, conflict management, building bonds, and teamwork and collaboration. These competencies are measured by asking informants to rate the target person, as well as by having the target evaluate himself or herself via self-report.

Which test content best represents the concept of emotional intelligence? To help evaluate the content of emotional intelligence measures, one needs to define emotion and intelligence. Emotion is an organized response system that coordinates physiological, perceptual, experiential, cognitive, and other changes into coherent experiences of moods and feelings, such as happiness, anger, sadness, and surprise (Smith & Lazarus, 1990, p. 610). Emotions typically arise in response to changes in relationships. Intelligence has many different definitions, but the central ones always place a primary emphasis on abstract reasoning and may, secondarily, refer to adaptation. Terman (1921, p. 128) stated that "an individual is intelligent in proportion as he is able to carry on abstract thinking."

Elsewhere, we have argued that a great number of models under the rubric of "emotional intelligence" reflect personality more broadly (Mayer, Salovey, & Caruso, 2000). Personality involves all the major parts of the person's psychology—the mechanisms, processes, structures, and so forth—how those parts are organized, and how those parts develop (Mayer, 1998). For example, a widely used measure of personality is the California Personality Inventory (CPI) (Gough, 1994). That scale measures four broad aspects of personality. The first, *interpersonal style,* contains measures of dominance, capacity for status, sociability, social presence, self-acceptance, independence, and empathy. The second, *normative social behavior,* measures responsibility, socialization, self-control, good impression, communality, well-being, and tolerance. The third, *cognitive functioning-achievement,* includes the measurement of achievement via conformance, achievement via independence, and intellectual efficiency. The final *qualitative aspects of thinking* scales include psychological mindedness, flexibility, and femininity/masculinity. In comparison to a personality scale such as the CPI, it seems to us, a measure of emotional intelligence should be differentiated by its focus on the idea that one thinks intelligently with one's emotions and, conversely, that emotions enhance intelligence. This analysis indicates that some of the scales of emotional intelligence reviewed earlier appear to have considerable overlap with standard measures of personality, such as the CPI.

This is not merely a semantic argument. It reflects fundamental issues of content validity—what a test measures—and incremental validity—what a test adds to our understanding beyond what we already know or can already measure, with existing tests. In fact, the overlap between self-report measures of emotional intelligence and personality inventories recently led a group of researchers to conclude that "as presently postulated, little remains of emotional intelligence that is unique and psychometrically sound. Thus, [self-report] questionnaire measures are too closely related to 'established' personality traits [to be considered anything new]" (Davies, Stankov, & Roberts, 1998, p. 1013).

Although we think the above quote represents an extreme position, the degree of overlap between self-report scales of emotional intelligence and already-existing personality scales is a matter of legitimate concern. Given the investment many people are placing in emotional intelligence, one would want to ensure there is something new about it.

Measurement Approaches

We now turn to the second dimension on which to evaluate emotional intelligence tests: the method by which the test gathers information. As shown in Table 15.1, these tests use self-report, informant, or performance approaches.

Self-Report. Self-report measures ask people to endorse a series of descriptive statements, indicating to what extent these describe or do not describe themselves. For example, one can ask questions of the sort, "Are you generally clear about your feelings or confused about them?" (Mayer & Gaschke, 1988; Salovey, Mayer, Goldman, Turvey, & Palfai, 1995). Self-reported abilities and traits rely on the individual's self-understanding. If a person's self-concept is accurate, then these sorts of measures can often serve as an accurate measure of the actual ability or trait. If the person's self-concept is inaccurate, which is often the case (Taylor & Brown, 1988), then self-report measures yield information concerning only the person's self-concept, rather than the actual ability or trait. People are notoriously inaccurate reporters in several areas of functioning, including the self-assessment of ability: self-reported intelligence correlates only modestly with actual measured intelligence—below .30 or so (Paulhus, Lysy, & Yik, 1998). Such associations indicate that people's self-reports of their mental abilities are quite independent of their actual abilities. Although self-beliefs are important (Bandura, 1977, 1997), we are interested in measuring emotional intelligence itself. In contrast to self-report, ability measures tap facets of the person's actual intelligence.

Informants. Informants are the second method used to measure a trait. The use of informants yields information about how a person is perceived by others and employs questions such as "Indicate the level (very high, high, average, low, very low) the person has attained for each of the following: stays open to ideas; readily adapts to changes; is a good listener."

This alternative has obvious advantages over self-report measures—or does it? The informant approach essentially measures a person's reputation. That reputation is influenced by many things, such as how well the person treats those around him or her, and the informant's beliefs about how personality operates (Funder, 1995). The advantage of using informants is that one obtains a very good idea of a person's reputation—and reputations are important (for example, Hogan & Shelton, 1998). A person's reputation may even be more important than his or her actual abilities for some purposes (for example, running in an election), but reputation is also different from abilities. In addition, some aspects of a reputation are fairly visible and appear to be judged accurately. These include talkativeness, and sociability. More internal cognitive styles and capacities, however, are judged much less accurately (Funder & Dobroth, 1987). What an informant perceives, therefore, remains a step removed from actual abilities.

A related approach enlists observers who directly code specific behaviors (the observer rating approach). Although we are aware of no test of emotional intelligence that employs this method, it would be appropriate only for observable behaviors, not for mental abilities with no fixed behavioral consequences.

Ability or Performance Measures. The third method to measure a trait is to use a performance measure. With this method, to determine how smart a person is, that individual is asked to solve problems such as "How much is thirteen multiplied by three?"; "What does the word 'analyze' mean?"; or, "What city is the capital of France?" Ability testing is the gold standard in intelligence research because intelligence corresponds to the actual capacity to perform well at mental tasks, not just one's beliefs about those capacities (Carroll, 1993; Mayer & Salovey, 1993; Neisser et al., 1996; Scarr, 1989). If one wants to understand how well people perceive emotion, one can show them a sad face, for example, and see if they recognize the facial expression. Or, if one wants to understand how well they reason about emotions, one can provide an emotional problem and assess the quality of their reasoning in response.

THE ABILITY APPROACH
TO ASSESSING EMOTIONAL INTELLIGENCE

This brief review indicates that the available tests of emotional intelligence vary widely both in their content and method of assessment. Different tests are valid for different purposes. We have pursued an ability approach to the assessment of emotional intelligence, in part because of our commitment to an intelligence model of emotional intelligence, and in part because of the advantages inherent in this approach. For further reviews of self-report scales we recommend additional chapters in this handbook (see also Salovey, Woolery, & Mayer, forthcoming). In the remainder of this chapter we focus on ability measures of emotional intelligence and their predictions.

Measurement Issues Specific to Ability Testing

Many issues related to ability testing of emotional intelligence have been dealt with in thoughtful ways in research literatures closely related to emotional intelligence. Interested readers may wish to examine reviews of nonverbal communication (Buck, 1984), empathic accuracy (Ickes, 1997), emotional perception (Lane et al., 1996), social intelligence (Legree, 1995; Sternberg & Smith, 1985; Thorndike & Stein, 1937; Wong, Day, Maxwell, & Meara, 1995), and several other intelligences related to emotional intelligence (see Mayer, Salovey, & Caruso, 2000, for a more complete review).

The Problem of the Correct Answer. The first issue concerning the measurement of emotional intelligence as an intelligence is determining the correct answer to a given problem. Say we want to know how much happy emotion is suggested by an abstract painting. What should we accept as the right answer? People often say there is no right way to feel, and they would extend this philosophy to the present situation by remarking, "Whatever you think, is right," meaning that whatever response a person has to a piece of art is a true response, or at the very least is a personal affair. We are sympathetic to such points of view; they recognize the legitimate differences in perception from one person to the next and represent a practical reality in many areas of life. At the same time, we believe there are limits to legitimate interpretations—that is, illegitimate interpretation is possible as well.

We argue that there is some basis for claiming "right answers" on emotional intelligence test items because there are both evolutionary and cultural foundations for the consistency of emotionally signaled information. Biologically speaking, there is an emotional body language across species, such that we freely recognize emotional states such as contentedness in the cat or anger in the dog. The evolution of emotion was discussed at considerable length by Darwin (1872/1965), who argued for a consistent emotional "language" across many species, and universal facial expressions of emotion among humans—a position strongly supported one hundred years later (Ekman, 1973).

Culturally speaking, cultural memes—ideas that replicate themselves across books, recordings, articles, and the Word Wide Web—can be thought of as analogous to biological genes. Emotional ideas are disseminated and reproduced as popular ideas according to the degree to which people within a culture find them useful. This cultural transmission further perpetuates the joint biological and cultural evolution of emotional understanding (Ball, 1984).

If we wish to impose a criterion of correctness for emotional intelligence test items—which we must, if we are to use an ability approach—we have at least three alternatives for designating a correct answer: target criteria, expert criteria, or consensus criteria. The target criteria can be illustrated with the following example. Say we take a poll around the office and ask a variety of people how their coworker, Todd, is feeling. Some people say he is fine, others say he is sad, and still others, say he is angry. If we match people's guesses against what Todd tells us he is honestly feeling (such as "a little sad"), that would be a target criterion; that is, those who guessed "sad" met the criterion of correctness. In our actual research, we have asked people to write down what they are doing and thinking and, also, how they are feeling. That written description then becomes an item on an ability task. The test taker guesses how the target was feeling at the time by referring to multiple emotion rating scales.

Expert criteria, by contrast, are established in the same case by asking experts in emotions (such as clinical psychologists, emotions researchers) to read the target's story and, using their best judgment, to determine how the target was feeling at the time. The test taker receives credit if his or her ratings correspond to those of the experts. Consensus, the third method, pools the judgments of hundreds of people. The test taker receives credit for endorsing emotions that the group endorses.

The correlations among the above three criteria are generally positive. For instance, the correlations between target and consensus scores over twelve emotional intelligence ability tests ranged from a low positive correlation of .22 to a very high positive correlation of .81 (Mayer, Caruso, & Salovey, 1999). These findings indicate that target and consensus scoring are often rather similar. One important aspect of these three scoring methods is that the similarity among scoring methods enables us to view some answers as more plausible than others. In our own research, we find that the consensus criterion is the best single means of determining a correct answer for two reasons. First, targets appear to minimize their own negative feelings when asked about them (Mayer & Geher, 1996). Second, large numbers of people, when their observations are pooled, seem to become reliable forecasters (Legree, 1995; Mayer & Geher, 1996; Mayer, Caruso, & Salovey, 1999). In addition, if one subscribes to the idea that emotional signals evolve, either biologically or culturally, then a wide, representative, sample of observers is probably a good judge of correctness under at least some circumstances.

How Do You Measure Whether People Can Recognize Their Own Feelings?

Up to now, we have been discussing one person's accuracy in judging another person's emotions. Is there any way to determine how accurately a person judges his or her *own* feelings? One can certainly ask the person directly, but such self-report measures are often highly correlated with present mood: happy people say they understand their feelings, and unhappy people report being confused about them (Mayer & Gaschke, 1988). Fortunately, there are other approaches. For example, one can assess physiological signs of emotions (localized brain activity, increased heart rate, systolic blood pressure, skin conductance, and so forth) and compare them to a person's self-report (Davidson & Irwin, 1998; Gross, 1998). Such procedures require a great deal of equipment, not to mention expertise. Fortunately, it may not be necessary to assess people psychophysiologically to discover how good they are at reading their own moods. In carefully controlled laboratory settings, Zuckerman, Rosenthal, and colleagues have found that the perception of emotion within oneself is significantly correlated to the ability to assess it in others (Zuckerman, Lipets, Koivumaki, & Rosenthal, 1975; Zuckerman, Hall, DeFrank, & Rosenthal, 1976). For that reason, tasks typically included in ability scales of emotional intelligence that measure a person's ability to perceive emotion—in the faces of people around them, their responses to artwork, and so forth—can be expected to indicate introspective capacity as well.

The Problem of Reliability. One further concern raised about ability measures of emotional intelligence is whether they are sufficiently reliable (that is, measure an ability consistently). For example, Davies et al., (1998) found that early "objective measures of emotional intelligence suffer from poor reliability" (p. 1013). Scales of nonverbal perception (which include some measures of emotional perception) suffered from problems of low reliability (Buck, 1984; Mayer et al., 1990). Indeed, early tasks designed to measure emotional intelligence possessed only modest test reliability, in the $r = .50$ range. Although we viewed these reliabilities as acceptable for experimental research in the early 1990s, our newer ability scales have demonstrated higher internal consistencies. The next section describes the development of such scales and what they measure.

OUR APPROACH TO EMOTIONAL INTELLIGENCE

Mayer and Salovey's ability model of emotional intelligence was based on a line of theoretical work aimed at taking a general notion of an emotional intelligence and rendering it so that it could be operationalized (Mayer & Salovey, 1993, 1995, 1997; Salovey & Mayer, 1990). According to that framework, emotional intelligence involves the capacity to reason with and about emotions, including "[1] the ability to perceive accurately, appraise, and express emotions; [2] the ability to access and/or generate feelings when they facilitate thought; [3] the ability to understand emotion and emotional knowledge; and [4] the ability to regulate emotions to promote emotional and intellectual growth" (Mayer & Salovey, 1997, p. 10, *numbering added here*).

The ability scales discussed below measure each of these four areas of abilities: perception, facilitation, understanding, and management.

MULTIPLE-TASK MEASURES OF EMOTIONAL INTELLIGENCE

Advent of Multiple-Task Ability Measures

The early 1990s saw the development and study of initial measures of aspects of emotional intelligence, for example, individual measures of emotional perception, or emotional understanding (Mayer et al., 1990; Mayer & Geher, 1996; for a review, see Mayer, Salovey, & Caruso, 2000). The more comprehensive study of emotional intelligence, however, awaited the examination of multiple tasks together. This was necessary because an intelligence is classically defined as a group of mental abilities that rise and fall more or less together. In the case of emotional intelligence, we began construction of a series of multitask ability tests in the middle 1990s, developing first the Multifactor Emotional Intelligence Scale (MEIS), a twelve-subscale ability test, and then the Mayer, Salovey, and Caruso Emotional Intelligence Test (MSCEIT) (Mayer et al., 1999a). We focus here on the MSCEIT, the newer of our scales (see Mayer, Caruso, & Salovey, 1999, for a description of the MEIS).

Mayer, Salovey, Caruso Emotional Intelligence Test

The MSCEIT is an ability measure of emotional intelligence designed to yield an overall emotional intelligence score, as well as subscale scores for perception, facilitation, understanding, and management. Each branch includes several subtests, some of which are described below.

Branch 1: Perception of Emotion. The MSCEIT contains three subtests measuring the perception of emotion: in faces, in landscapes, and in abstract designs. A sample design of the sort employed in the MSCEIT is shown in Figure 15.1. In this subscale, the person views the design (or face, or landscape) and must then report the amount of emotional content in it, judging, for example, how much happiness, how much sadness, how much fear, and so on. For each emotion, the participant responds using a five-point scale. For example, in the design shown in Figure 15.1, the swirling yellow, blue, and other colors may suggest happiness, so the participant might be expected to indicate that happiness is present. Moreover, the soft colors and shapes also suggest an absence of anger, so the participant might be expected to indicate that anger is mostly absent.

Figure 15.1. Sample design and landscape from the MSCEIT.

The branch 1 tasks on the MSCEIT are designed to be as uncontaminated with verbal content as possible. For that reason, the response alternatives for a given item on the landscape and designs tasks are anchored by faces expressing varying degrees of each emotion (verbal labels are used as well to clarify any ambiguity in the drawings). The faces task uses a numerical scale, however, so there is no interference between the faces being judged and the faces that make up the response scales.

Branch 2: Emotional Facilitation. The MSCEIT contains several subscales assessing whether people use emotion to facilitate cognitive activities. Most central to this measurement is the synesthesia subscale. The synesthesia task asks participants to judge the similarity between an emotional feeling, such as love, and other internal experiences, such as temperatures and tastes. The idea is that such internal comparisons indicate that emotions are not only sensed and perceived, but also processed in some meaningful, initial way. A participant might be asked to "imagine feeling *love* toward a friend, who has been very kind and supportive of you. How much is that love like each of the following sensations?"

	Not Alike				Very Much Alike
Hot	1	2	3	4	5
Slow	1	2	3	4	5

Other branch 2 tasks on the MSCEIT examine facilitation in other ways.

Branch 3: Understanding Emotion. The third group of MSCEIT tasks examines the understanding of emotion. These tasks include blends, wherein a person tries to match a set of emotions, such as joy and acceptance, to another, single, emotion that is closest to it. Responses are in a multiple choice format. One item might ask which alternative combines "joy and acceptance: (a) guilt, (b) challenge, (c) mania, (d) love, or (e) desire." Also included is a transitions task, in which the test taker is asked what happens as an emotion intensifies or changes. For example, a problem might ask, "Jamie felt happier and happier, joyful, and excited; if this feeling intensified it would be closest to (a) challenge, (b) admiration, (c) pride, (d) peacefulness, (e) ecstasy." A similar, progressions, task asks participants to identify a change of relationship that might bring about a specific mood change. For example, participants might choose an alternative such as "a piece of music he liked came on the radio" to explain why a person's happiness might rise slightly. Other tasks measure this branch as well.

Branch 4: Managing Emotion. The managing emotion tasks concern the best way to regulate emotions in oneself and other people. Each item of the managing emotion cluster of items describes a person with a goal of changing or maintaining a feeling, such as staying happy, or feeling better. The test taker must choose a given alternative that describes a course of action that might satisfy the goal. For example, if a sad person wanted to cheer up, the alternatives might involve "talking to some friends," "seeing a violent movie," "eating a big meal," or "taking a walk alone." Some alternatives are more likely to lead to cheering the person up than others, and those are scored more highly according to a consensus criterion. The managing emotion in situations subscale is similar, except that more complex social situations are described and the actions more often involve interpersonal interactions.

GENERAL PROPERTIES OF ABILITY MEASURES OF EMOTIONAL INTELLIGENCE

Results from the MSCEIT and its precursor, the MEIS, are providing increasing information about the measurement of emotional intelligence as an ability and what it predicts. In this section, we look at the evidence for considering whether emotional intelligence is indeed a form of intelligence. For an intelligence to be considered a standard intelligence, it must meet certain criteria. It must be reliable, of course. Beyond that, tasks that are believed to measure the intelligence must be correlated with one another. In addition, the candidate for an intelligence must be related to, but also independent of, other existing intelligences. Finally, the intelligence must develop with age.

Reliability of Ability Measures of Emotional Intelligence

Earlier, we indicated that early tasks measuring emotional perception suffered from low reliability. Our newer multiple-scale measures of emotional intelligence, the MEIS and MSCEIT, indicated that this mental ability can be reliably measured. The four MEIS branch scores (perception, facilitation, understanding, and management) had coefficient alphas ranging from .81 to .96, with a full-scale internal consistency of .96. The initial, research version of the MSCEIT had branch score alphas from .59 to .87 (based on 277 participants). These levels will rise as poorly performing test items are dropped during revision of the test (Mayer, Salovey, & Caruso, 1999b). The internal consistencies of the MEIS and MSCEIT are comparable to many standard tests of intelligence.

There are also a number of individual tasks on the MEIS (or item clusters on the MSCEIT) that are internally consistent. For example, the four MEIS emotional perception subscales' alphas ranged from $\alpha = .85$ to .94 (identifying emotions in faces, $\alpha = .94$; music, $\alpha = .90$; designs, $\alpha = .85$; stories, $\alpha = .89$). The MEIS subscales with the lowest alphas, $\alpha = .49$ and .51, had only eight items each. Because reliability is a direct function of length (other factors held constant), these alphas can be drastically improved by adding items. The low reliabilities found by Davies et al. (1998) were comparable, albeit somewhat lower, than those we have found with our early (and rather short) scales. We expect that if Davies et al. evaluate our present scales, they will find them of adequate reliability. In fact, an independent study using the MEIS indicated that its overall internal consistency is $\alpha = .90$ (Ciarrochi, Chan, & Caputi, 2000).

Structure of the MEIS

The structure of emotional intelligence can be inferred from a study of the intercorrelations among the twelve MEIS tasks (preliminary results from the MSCEIT provide a similar picture). If all the ability tasks rise and fall in lock-step across people, they are assumed to measure one thing. If there are several clusters of tasks, each of which rises and falls independently, then the scale is said to measure several different intelligences. Factor analyses indicate that emotional intelligence can be represented as a two-level hierarchy. At the top of the hierarchy is an overall emotional intelligence factor that represents a fairly cohesive group of skills. Although all of the ability tasks rise and fall together, emotional intelligence can be broken down further into four subsidiary factors representing emotional perception, emotional facilitation, emotional understanding, and emotional management. Findings with the MEIS are supportive of the four-branch model of emotional intelligence (Mayer & Salovey, 1997), that is, that there is an overall emotional intelligence that can be broken down into several subsidiary groups of skills (Mayer, Caruso, & Salovey, 1999, study 1).

Emotional Intelligence and Other Intelligences

The MEIS is somewhat related to—but still reasonably independent of—verbal intelligence. The correlation between the MEIS, in a sample of 503 adults, and a vocabulary measure was $r = .36$ ($p < .01$), and it was $r = .45$ ($p < .01$) in a sample of about 200 adolescents (Mayer, Caruso, & Salovey, 1999). However, the MEIS may not be related to other, nonverbal, types of intelligences. For instance, Ciarrochi et al., (2000) found that the MEIS was unrelated to their measure of IQ, the Raven Progressive Matrices ($r = .05$, n.s.). The Raven is generally considered to be a measure of performance or spatial intelligence, as opposed to verbal intelligence. Such findings indicate that emotional intelligence may be related to other specific intelligences to varying degrees. These correlations indicate that the MEIS measures different things than do these other intelligence tests, although there is some relationship between them. Typically, intelligence tests correlate with each other between $r = .50$ and $.80$ (see, for instance, Matarazzo, 1972).

Emotional Intelligence and Development

In absolute terms, adults outperform adolescents in detecting consensus answers on the MEIS (Mayer, Caruso, & Salovey, 1999, study 2). Age differences in an ability measure of emotional intelligence that was based on the MEIS (the Emotional Intelligence Scale for Children [EISC]) were also obtained for a sample of 100 children (Sullivan, 1999).

WHAT DOES EMOTIONAL INTELLIGENCE PREDICT?

As the previous section demonstrates, emotional intelligence, defined as an ability, can be measured reliably. Moreover, multiple tasks of emotional intelligence are correlated, forming a single, emotional intelligence factor. As we indicated earlier, one of the criticisms of self-report measures of emotional intelligence is that these tasks measure the same thing as do self-report scales of general personality. We next examine to what degree emotional intelligence overlaps with other aspects of personality, and whether it predicts behavioral outcomes.

Emotional Intelligence and Personality

Relationship Between Ability and Self-Report Emotional Intelligence. In work comparing the MSCEIT scores with those of the BarOn EQ-i, a self-report measure of emotional intelligence (Bar-On, 1997), the overall test-to-test correlation in a subsample of 137 was $r = .36$, which indicates the two tests share about 10 percent of their variance in common.

Empathy. Emotional intelligence (measured by the MEIS) correlates with self-reported empathy ($r = .33$, $p < .01$, Mayer, Caruso, & Salovey, 1999; $r = .43$, $p < .01$, Ciarrochi et al., 2000). Sullivan (1999) found that the EISC ability measure correlated about .35 with children's self-reported empathy. Rubin (1999) administered an adolescent version of the MEIS (the AMEIS) to fifty-two seventh and eighth grade students in an urban school district. She found a significant association between emotional intelligence and empathy ($r = .28$, $p < .05$).

Parental Warmth. Studies with the MEIS indicate that emotional intelligence is significantly related to self-reported parental warmth ($r = .23$, $p < .01$, Mayer, Caruso, & Salovey, 1999; $r = .18$, $p < .05$; Ciarrochi et al., 2000). These findings are important because of the large emphasis we and others have placed on developmental antecedents of emotional intelligence (Mayer & Salovey, 1995; Salovey & Sluyter, 1997).

Life Satisfaction Measures. Ciarrochi et al. (2000) found that people scoring higher on the MEIS had higher levels of life satisfaction ($r = .28$, $p < .05$), and of self-reported relationship quality ($r = .19$, $p < .05$).

Broader Aspects of Personality. Ciarrochi et al. (2000) found that the MEIS correlated at low to moderate levels with tests of extroversion ($r = .26$, $p < .05$), openness to feelings ($r = .24$, $p < .05$), and self-esteem ($r = .31$, $p < .05$). Similarly, a series of studies in our own laboratory shows that the MEIS is relatively independent of many of the self-report trait scales of personality as measured by the omnibus personality measure, the 16 PF (Mayer, Caruso, Salovey,

Formica, & Woolery, 2000). In 186 college students, we found that the MEIS full-scale score correlated as follows with each of the 16 PF scales: .13, n.s., with Warmth; .19, $p < .05$ with Reasoning; .09, n.s., with Emotional Stability; .05, n.s. with Dominance; .12, n.s., with Liveliness; .02, n.s., with Rule-Consciousness; $-.02$, n.s., with Social Boldness; $.22, p < .01$ with Sensitivity; $-.17, p < .05$ with Vigilance; $-.01$, n.s., with Abstractedness; $-.10$, n.s., with Privateness; .09, n.s., with Apprehension; $.14, p = .05$ with Openness to Change; $-.21, p < .01$ with Self-Reliance; -11, n.s., with Perfectionism; and .01, n.s., with Tension. Importantly, the MEIS correlated .01 with the Impression Management Scale of the 16 PF. Likewise, the scales of the MSCEIT are, encouragingly, almost entirely unrelated to the Positive Impression scale of the EQ-i (.16, n.s.).

The individuals in our recent study also completed the Fundamental Interpersonal Orientation Scale-Behavior (FIRO-B; Schutz, 1978), a self-report measure of social skills and needs. The full-scale MEIS correlated .14, n.s., with expressed Inclusion (which measures how much the subject expresses interest in people in general), $r = .22, p < .01$ with wanted Inclusion (how much a subject desires to be with people), $r = .05$, n.s. with expressed Affection (a measure of how warm a person is toward others), $r = .19, p < .01$ with wanted Affection (how much closeness a person desires with others), $r = -.09$, n.s. with expressed Control (the amount of responsibility and decision making in which the person engages), and $r = -.05$, n.s. with wanted Control (how much structure or direction the person desires). A brief mood scale administered to these respondents correlated $r = -.09$, n.s. with total MEIS scores.

Emotional Intelligence and Behavior

We have stated that emotional intelligence, as a mental capacity or set of abilities, is best measured with a performance measure. However, any intelligence is usually of interest because of its relationship with observable, and important, outcomes. In this section, we examine the preliminary evidence that relates emotional intelligence to outcomes and behaviors.

Emotional Intelligence and Reductions in Behavior Problems and Violence.
The studies in our laboratory (Mayer, Caruso, et al., 2000) also employed measures of participants' life space—a person's description of his or her activities, behaviors, and surrounding environment (Mayer, Carlsmith, & Chabot, 1998). These investigations indicated, tantalizingly, that the MEIS may be associated with lower self-reports of violent and trouble-prone behavior among college students, with correlations of test to life space in the $r = .40$ range. This relation remained significant even after measures of analytic intelligence and empathy were partialed out. Such findings indicate that emotional intelligence is measuring unique variance.

In another study, Rubin (1999) collected teacher and peer ratings of aggression and prosocial behavior. The peer ratings included a measure of direct, overt aggression (such as hitting a child or insulting a child) and relational aggression (such as excluding a child). Teacher-rated aggression was not significantly related to total AMEIS scores ($r = -.21$), although the association was in the appropriate direction, and the stories subtest was significantly correlated ($-.37, p < .01$). However, peer-nominated direct aggression ($r = -.39, p < .01$), peer-nominated relational aggression ($r = -.37, p < .01$), and peer-nominated combined aggression ($r = -.48, p < .001$) were all significantly related to AMEIS scores.

Prosocial behavior, as measured by teacher ratings, was also highly related to emotional intelligence ($r = .49, < .001$), but overall AMEIS scores were not significantly related to peer-nominated prosocial behavior ($r = .26$, n.s.), although the correlation was in the appropriate direction, and specific subtests were significantly related (stories and managing emotions).

Observer Ratings of Emotional Intelligence. Sullivan's EISC had modest correlations with teacher ratings of children's combined emotional Recognition and Response ($r = .23, p < .05$), and with combined teacher and parent ratings ($r = .35, p < .01$), although not with the parents' ratings alone (Sullivan, 1999).

Emotional Intelligence and Team Performance. Rice (1999) suggests that emotional intelligence plays a role in certain aspects of effective team leadership and team performance. She administered a short form of the MEIS to 164 employees of an insurance company, who staffed twenty-six customer claims teams, as well as to eleven of their team leaders. One of the two department managers rated her teams and her team leaders on five variables: customer service, accuracy of claims processing, productivity, commitment to continuous improvement, and team leader overall performance. The MEIS scores of the eleven team leaders correlated $r = .51$ with the department manager's ranking of those leaders' effectiveness. The emotional intelligence of the twenty-six teams, as measured by the average MEIS score across team members, was significantly related to the department manager's ratings of the team performance for customer service ($r = .46$). In other areas, emotional intelligence did not seem to help and may have even hurt some teams. For example, higher team leader emotional intelligence, as measured by the MEIS, was negatively related to the team's accuracy ($r = -.35$) and productivity ($r = -.40$) in handling customer complaints.

APPLICATIONS OF ABILITY MEASURES OF EMOTIONAL INTELLIGENCE

Our enthusiasm for an ability approach to emotional intelligence is due to several factors. The first is that we believe that these scales are measuring a set of abilities, an actual intelligence. Second, as such, these scales are measuring something that is new and unique: we are not simply measuring "people skills," extraversion, or emotional stability. Third, ability measures are less susceptible to response bias, socially desirable responding, or "faking" than are self-report or informant approaches to measurement. Although we are just at the beginning of the learning curve in this area, we do believe that enough data exist for us to encourage researchers and practitioners to consider an ability measure of emotional intelligence in their work.

Clinical Assessment

Clinicians regularly employ standard measures of general intelligence and broad-based personality traits. An ability measure of emotional intelligence may yield new information about a client's potential functioning. The MEIS or MSCEIT can provide information on clients' emotional resources: what do they know about emotions; are they able to identify their own and other's emotions accurately; are effective emotion management strategies available to them? We envision a time when clinicians will be able to enhance their prediction of clients' therapeutic progress, based in part on their emotional intelligence abilities.

Education

Ability measures of emotional intelligence appear to predict prosocial behavior and the absence of negative behavior among adolescents and young adults. If these emotional intelligence abilities play a role in such important areas of functioning, then it is good news for educators and parents. An ability approach to emotional intelligence can focus on skill development or knowledge acquisition, as opposed to the enhancement of personality. Such an ability focus seems to be more clearly connected with education (Salovey & Sluyter, 1997).

Workplace

Leading and managing people require technical skills as well as emotional skills. One difficulty for workplace settings is to create tests that employees and managers are willing to take. We have found in our field work with managers that they respond positively to an ability approach to emotional intelligence; they recognize that the ability to "read" people is an important ingredient in their management effectiveness. When they are asked to take the MEIS and identify the facial expressions of people, they connect this to their day-to-day work. (See Caruso, Mayer, & Salovey, forthcoming, for a discussion of emotional intelligence and leadership.) Team effectiveness research and training will also likely benefit from an ability approach to emotional intelligence. Although personality traits, such as agreeableness, have been examined, emotional knowledge and skills may provide new information on high-performance teams. As the study by Rice (1999) indicated, this relationship is likely a complex and interesting one.

CONCLUSION

There are a number of scales of emotional intelligence. These can be distinguished according to the way they define emotional intelligence and the measurement approach they employ. We view emotional intelligence as a form of intelligence that combines emotions and thinking. Tests of emotional intelligence that examine outcomes (such as leadership or teamwork) or noncognitive traits (such as assertiveness or impulse control) seem to tap a dimension of personality that is different from the idea of an intelligence. Such content may be more similar to existing personality models or scales.

We believe that an intelligence is best measured with performance, or ability, measures. This is the approach we have taken in the development of our scales of emotional intelligence. Our theory of emotional intelligence divides emotional intelligence into four areas of abilities: emotional perception, emotional facilitation, emotional understanding, and emotional management (Mayer & Salovey, 1997).

Our ability tests—the MEIS and MSCEIT—measure each of these four areas. Although some early ability scales of emotional intelligence lacked internal consistency, our more recent scales measure emotional intelligence at an adequate level of internal consistency and reliability. Research with these scales indicates that emotional intelligence—defined and measured as an ability—is related to, but mostly independent from, other intelligences. Emotional intelligence is also independent of many of the personality traits that we and others have studied, such as dominance and neuroticism.

The exploration of what emotional intelligence, modeled and measured as an ability, predicts has just begun. Nonetheless, the MEIS and MSCEIT have interesting and important relationships with behaviors and other outcomes. For example, emotional intelligence scores correlate with teacher-parent evaluations of children's abilities to recognize and respond emotionally. Emotional intelligence may play an interesting role in team effectiveness and customer service. Finally, preliminary evidence suggests that emotional intelligence appears to be associated with reductions in violent and related problem behavior.

Plainly, much more research will be needed to understand the ability approach to emotional intelligence's contribution to personality development and growth. Investigators have just begun to examine cross-cultural issues, the development of emotional intelligence, and the application of emotional intelligence in clinical, educational, and workplace settings. As we continue to explore emotional intelligence, we hope that our preliminary studies will continue to be successful. But to be successful, further studies must insure that the scale of measurement is not an afterthought, but part of a well-conceptualized and well-designed research program. If emotional intelligence is an intriguing set of mental abilities, then we believe that it must be measured as an intelligence, and that the way to achieve this goal is with ability measures.

NOTES

All correspondence regarding this chapter may be addressed to John (Jack) D. Mayer, Department of Psychology, University of New Hampshire, Durham, NH 08324. Electronic mail may be sent to jack.mayer@unh.edu.

References

Ball, J. A. (1984). Memes as replicators. *Ethology and Sociobiology, 5,* 141–161.

Bandura, A. (1977). Self-efficacy: Toward a unifying theory of behavioral change. *Psychological Review, 84,* 191–215.

Bandura, A. (1997). *Self-efficacy: The exercise of control.* New York: Freeman.

Bar-On, R. (1997). *BarOn Emotional Quotient Inventory (EQ-i): Technical manual.* Toronto, Canada: Multi-Health Systems.

Boyatzis, R. E., Goleman, D., & Hay/McBer. (1999). *Emotional competence inventory.* Boston: HayGroup.

Buck, R. (1984). *The communication of emotion.* New York: Guilford Press.

Carroll, J. B. (1993). *Human cognitive abilities: A survey of factor-analytic studies.* New York: Cambridge University Press.

Caruso, D. R., Mayer, J. D., & Salovey, P. (forthcoming). Emotional intelligence and emotional leadership. In R. Riggio & S. Murphy (Eds.), *Multiple intelligences and leadership.* Mahwah, NJ: Erlbaum.

Ciarrochi, J. V., Chan, A.Y.C., & Caputi, P. (2000). A critical evaluation of the emotional intelligence construct. *Personality and Individual Differences, 28,* 539–561.

Cooper, R. K. (1996/1997). *EQ Map.* San Francisco: AIT and Essi Systems.

Darwin, C. (1965). *The expression of emotions in man and animals.* Chicago: University of Chicago Press. (Original work published 1872)

Davidson, R. J., Irwin, W. (1998). The functional neuroanatomy of emotion and affective style. *Trends in Cognitive Science, 3,* 11–21.

Davies, M., Stankov, L., & Roberts, R. D. (1998). Emotional Intelligence: In search of an elusive construct. *Journal of Personality and Social Psychology, 75,* 989–1015.

Ekman, P. (1973). *Darwin and facial expression: A century of research in review.* New York: Academic Press.

Funder, D. C. (1995). On the accuracy of personality judgment: A realistic approach. *Psychological Review, 102,* 652–670.

Funder, D. C., & Dobroth, K. M. (1987). Differences between traits: Properties associated with inter-judge agreement. *Journal of Personality and Social Psychology, 52,* 409–418.

Gough, H. G. (1994). *California Psychological Inventory.* Palo Alto, CA: Consulting Psychologists Press.

Gross, J. J. (1998). Antecedent- and response-focused emotion regulation: Divergent consequences for experience, expression, and physiology. *Journal of Personality and Social Psychology, 74,* 224–237.

Hogan, R., & Shelton, D. (1998). A socioanalytic perspective on job performance. *Human Performance, 11,* 129–144.

Ickes, W. (Ed.). (1997). *Empathic accuracy.* New York: Guilford Press.

Lane, R. D., Sechrest, L., Reidel, R., Weldon, V., Weldon, V., Kaszniak, A., & Schwartz, G. E. (1996). Impaired verbal and nonverbal emotion recognition in alexithymia. *Psychosomatic Medicine, 58,* 203–210.

Legree, P. J. (1995). Evidence for an oblique social intelligence factor established with a based-based testing procedure. *Intelligence, 21,* 247–266.

Matarazzo, J. D. (1972). *Wechsler's measurement and appraisal of adult intelligence* (5th ed.). New York: Oxford University Press.

Mayer, J. D. (1998). A systems framework for the field of personality. *Psychological Inquiry, 9,* 118–144.

Mayer, J. D., Carlsmith, K. M., & Chabot, H. F. (1998). Describing the person's external environment: Conceptualizing and measuring the life space. *Journal of Research in Personality, 32,* 253–296.

Mayer, J. D., Caruso, D., & Salovey, P. (1999). Emotional intelligence meets traditional standards for an intelligence. *Intelligence, 27,* 267–298.

Mayer, J. D., Caruso, D. R., Salovey, P., Formica, S. A., & Woolery, A. (2000). [A correlation of MEIS scores with data on the life space.] Unpublished raw data.

Mayer, J. D., DiPaolo, M. T., & Salovey, P. (1990). Perceiving affective content in ambiguous visual stimuli: A component of emotional intelligence. *Journal of Personality Assessment, 54,* 772–781.

Mayer, J. D., & Gaschke, Y. N. (1988). The experience and meta-experience of mood. *Journal of Personality and Social Psychology, 55,* 102–111.

Mayer, J. D., & Geher, G. (1996). Emotional intelligence and the identification of emotion. *Intelligence, 22,* 89–113.

Mayer, J. D., & Salovey, P. (1993). The intelligence of emotional intelligence. *Intelligence, 17,* 433–442.

Mayer, J. D., & Salovey, P. (1995). Emotional intelligence and the construction and regulation of feelings. *Applied and Preventive Psychology, 4,* 197–208.

Mayer, J. D., & Salovey, P. (1997). What is emotional intelligence? In P. Salovey & D. Sluyter (Eds.), *Emotional development and emotional intelligence: implications for educators* (pp. 3–31). New York: Basic Books.

Mayer, J. D., Salovey, P., & Caruso, D. R. (1997). *The Emotional IQ Test* [CD-Rom]. Needham, MA: Virtual Knowledge.

Mayer, J. D., Salovey, P., & Caruso, D. R. (1999a). *MSCEIT Item Booklet (Research Version 1.1.)* Toronto, Canada: Multi-Health Systems.

Mayer, J. D., Salovey, P., & Caruso, D. R. (1999b). *Working Manual for the MSCEIT Research Version 1.1.* Manuscript in preparation, available from Multi-Health Systems, Toronto, Canada.

Mayer, J. D., Salovey, P., & Caruso, D. R. (2000). Emotional intelligence. In R. J. Sternberg (Ed.), *Handbook of intelligence* (2nd ed., pp. 396–420). New York: Cambridge University Press.

Neisser, U., Boodoo, G., Bouchard, T. J., Boykin, A. W., Brody, N., Ceci, S. J., Halpern, D. F., Loehlin, J. C., Perloff, R., Sternberg, R. J., & Urbina, S. (1996). Intelligence: Knowns and unknowns. *American Psychologist, 51,* 77–101.

Paulhus, D. L., Lysy, D. C., & Yik, M.S.M. (1998). Self-report measures of intelligence: Are they useful as proxy IQ tests? *Journal of Personality, 66,* 525–554.

Rice, C. L. (1999). *A quantitative study of emotional intelligence and its impact on team performance.* Unpublished master's thesis, Pepperdine University, Malibu, CA.

Rubin, M. M. (1999). *Emotional intelligence and its role in mitigating aggression: A correlational study of the relationship between emotional intelligence and aggression in urban adolescents.* Unpublished manuscript, Immaculata College, Immaculata, PA.

Salovey, P., Bedell, B. T, Detweiler, J. B, & Mayer, J. D. (2000).Current directions in emotional intelligence research. In M. Lewis & J. M. Haviland-Jones (Eds.), *Handbook of emotions* (2nd ed., pp. 504–520). New York: Guilford Press.

Salovey, P., & Mayer, J. D. (1990). Emotional intelligence. *Imagination, Cognition, and Personality, 9,* 185–211.

Salovey, P., Mayer, J. D., Goldman, S., Turvey, C., & Palfai, T. (1995). Emotional attention, clarity, and repair: Exploring emotional intelligence using the Trait Meta-Mood Scale. In J. W. Pennebaker (Ed.), *Emotion, disclosure, and health* (pp. 125–154). Washington, DC: American Psychological Association.

Salovey, P. & Sluyter, D. (Eds.). (1997). *Emotional development and emotional intelligence: Implications for educators.* New York: Basic Books.

Salovey, P., Woolery, A., & Mayer, J. D. (forthcoming). Emotional intelligence: Conceptualization and measurement. In G. Fletcher & M. Clark (Eds.), *The Blackwell handbook of social psychology.* London: Blackwell.

Scarr, S. (1989). Protecting general intelligence: Constructs and consequences for intervention. In R. L. Linn (Ed.), *Intelligence: Measurement, theory, and public policy* (pp. 74–118). Urbana, IL: University of Illinois Press.

Schutz, W. (1978). FIRO Awareness Scales manual. Palo Alto, CA: Consulting Psychologists Press.

Smith, C. A., & Lazarus, R. S. (1990). Emotion and adaptation. In L. A. Pervin (Ed.), *Handbook of personality* (pp. 609–637). New York: Guilford Press.

Sternberg, R. J., & Smith, C. (1985). Social intelligence and decoding skills in nonverbal communication. *Social Cognition, 3,* 168–192.

Sullivan, A. K. (1999). *The emotional intelligence scale for children.* Unpublished doctoral dissertation, University of Virginia, Charlottesville, VA.

Taylor, S. F., & Brown, J. D. (1988). Illusion and well-being: A social psychological perspective on mental health. *Psychological Bulletin, 103,* 193–210.

Terman, L. M. (1921). Intelligence and its measurement: A symposium (II.). *Journal of Educational Psychology, 12,* 127–133.

Thorndike, R. L., & Stein, S. (1937). An evaluation of the attempts to measure social intelligence. *Psychological Bulletin, 34,* 275–284.

Wong, C. T., Day, J. D., Maxwell, S. E., & Meara, N. M. (1995). A multitrait-multimethod study of academic and social intelligence in college students. *Journal of Educational Psychology, 87,* 117–133

Zuckerman, M., Hall, J. A., DeFrank, R. S., & Rosenthal, R. (1976). Encoding and decoding of spontaneous and posed facial expressions. *Journal of Personality and Social Psychology, 34,* 966–977.

Zuckerman, M., Lipets, M. S., Koivumaki, J. H., & Rosenthal, R. (1975). Encoding and decoding nonverbal cues of emotion. *Journal of Personality and Social Psychology, 32,* 1068–1076.

CHAPTER SIXTEEN

Clustering Competence in Emotional Intelligence

Insights from the Emotional Competence Inventory

Richard E. Boyatzis, Daniel Goleman, and Kenneth S. Rhee

In this chapter, we briefly describe a model of emotional intelligence based on the competencies that enable people to demonstrate intelligent use of their emotions in managing themselves and working effectively with others. The history and development, as well as preliminary statistical results, of a new test based on this model, the Emotional Competence Inventory (ECI), are reported. The implications for a theory of performance in work settings and an integrated personality theory are mentioned in emphasizing the importance of clusters of competencies in predicting performance and making links to all levels of the human psyche.

Emotional intelligence is a convenient phrase with which to focus attention on human talent. Even though it is a simple phrase, it incorporates the complexity of a person's capability. Although the earliest psychologist to explore this arena of "social intelligence" (Thorndike in the 1920s and 1930s, see Goleman, 1995) offered the idea as a single concept, more recent psychologists have appreciated its complexity and described it in terms of multiple capabilities (Bar-On, 1997; Goleman, 1998; Saarni, 1988). Gardner (1983) conceptualized this arena as constituting intrapersonal and interpersonal intelligence. Salovey and Mayer (1990) first used the expression *emotional intelligence* and described it in terms of four domains involving knowing and handling one's own and others' emotions. Other conceptualizations have labels such as *practical intelligence* and *successful intelligence* (Sternberg, 1996), which often blend the capabilities described by the other psychologists with cognitive abilities and anchor the concepts around the consequence of the person's behavior, notably success or effectiveness.

A closely related stream of research has focused on explaining and predicting the outcome of effectiveness in various occupations, often with a primary emphasis on managers and leaders (Boyatzis, 1982; Bray, Campbell, & Grant, 1974; Kotter, 1982; Luthans, Hodgetts, & Rosenkrantz, 1988; McClelland, 1973; McClelland, Baldwin, Bronfenbrenner, & Strodbeck, 1958; Spencer & Spencer, 1993; Thornton & Byham, 1982). In this "competency" approach, specific capabilities were identified and validated against effectiveness measures, or often inductively discovered and then articulated as competencies.

An integrated concept of emotional intelligence offers more than a convenient framework for describing human dispositions; it offers a theoretical structure for the organization of personality and the linking of emotional intelligence to a theory of action and job performance (Goleman, 1995). Goleman (1998) defined an "emotional competence" as a "learned capability based on emotional intelligence that results in outstanding performance at work." Integrating the work of Goleman (1995, 1998) and Boyatzis (1982), we offer the following descriptive definition: emotional intelligence is observed when a person demonstrates the competencies that constitute self-awareness, self-management, social awareness, and social skills at appropriate times and ways in sufficient frequency to be effective in the situation.

If defined as a single construct, the term *emotional intelligence* might be deceptive and suggest an association with cognitive capability (traditionally defined intelligence or what psychologists often call *g*, referring to general cognitive ability) (Ackerman & Heggestad, 1997; Davies, Stankov, & Roberts, 1998). Although this association has not been substantiated when empirically studied, the tendency to believe that more effective people have the vital ingredients for success invites the attribution of a halo effect. For example, person A is effective, therefore she has all of the right stuff, such as brains, savvy, and style. Like the issue of finding the best "focal point" with which to look at something, the dilemma of finding the best level of detail in defining constructs with which to build a personality theory maybe an issue of which focal point is chosen. Photographers appreciate the difficulty and complexity of choosing appropriate focal point, because every scene can be viewed in many ways, each with its own perspectives and detriments to understanding. With regard to emotional intelligence, we believe the most helpful focal point allows for the description and study of a variety specific competencies, or capabilities, that can be empirically, causally related to effectiveness *and* describe the clusters within which these competencies are organized. But we must start with the competencies.

DEVELOPMENT OF THE EMOTIONAL INTELLIGENCE MODEL AND THE EMOTIONAL COMPETENCE INVENTORY

Building on and integrating a great deal of research, Goleman (1998) presented a model of emotional intelligence with twenty-five competencies arrayed in five clusters (Boyatzis, 1982; Jacobs, 1997 [as cited in Goleman, 1998]; Spencer & Spencer, 1993): (1) the Self-Awareness cluster included Emotional Awareness, Accurate Self-Assessment, and Self-Confidence; (2) the Self-Regulation cluster included Self-Control, Trustworthiness, Conscientiousness, Adaptability, and Innovation; (3) the Motivation cluster included Achievement Drive, Commitment, Initiative, and Optimism; (4) the Empathy cluster included Understanding Others, Developing Others, Service Orientation, Leveraging Diversity, and Political Awareness; and (5) the Social Skills cluster included Influence, Communication, Conflict Management, Leadership, Change Catalyst, Building Bonds, Collaboration and Cooperation, and Team Capabilities.

Although numerous methods were available to assess these competencies behaviorally through behavioral event interviews (Boyatzis, 1982; Spencer & Spencer, 1993), simulations, and assessment centers (Thornton & Byham, 1982), a questionnaire form was desirable for ease of use (that is, amenable to 360-degree applications [collecting information about a person's behavior from his or her coworkers]), comprehensiveness (to insure that all of the competencies in this theory could be measured within one instrument), and validity (capturing others' views of a person's behavior easily). Starting with a competency assessment questionnaire developed by Boyatzis in 1991 (Boyatzis, 1994; Boyatzis, Cowen, & Kolb, 1995; Boyatzis, Leonard, Rhee, & Wheeler, 1996; Boyatzis, Murphy, & Wheeler, 1997) called the Self-Assessment Questionnaire, Boyatzis and Goleman rewrote items for the noncognitive competencies. Additional items were created for competencies not addressed in Boyatzis's model. (Because that model focused on managers, executives, and leaders, there was a desire to develop an instrument with broader applicability across all occupations and life settings.) About 40 percent of the new instrument, the Emotional Competence Inventory, (ECI) was from the earlier questionnaire. The earlier instrument was a useful starting point because it had been developed from competencies validated against performance in hundreds of competency studies of managers, executives, and leaders in North America (Boyatzis, 1982; Spencer & Spencer, 1993). The specific questionnaire had also been validated against performance for a variety of job families in dozens of industrial organizations in Italy and one large financial institution in Brazil (Boyatzis & Berlinger, 1992; Valenca, 1996; Vitale, 1998; Boyatzis, Wheeler, and Wright, forthcoming). Reliability and construct validation had been established against other questionnaire measures as well as behavioral measures coded from videotapes and audiotapes, and numerous longitudinal studies of competency development (Boyatzis et al., forthcoming).

In the summer and fall of 1998, data was collected with the ECI from 596 people; this group was composed of samples of managers and salespeople from several industrial corporations, and graduate students in master's programs in management, engineering, and social work. Based on analysis of the reliabilities and intercorrelation of items, the scales of the ECI were revised in December of 1998. In January and February 1999, the ECI was rewritten again with Ruth Jacobs, Ron Garonzik, Patricia Marshall, and Signe Spencer (several of the research staff of McBer and Company, a unit of the Hay/McBer Group), using their database of competency assessment information from hundreds of companies. At this time, the items were arranged and constructed to reflect the developmental scaling characteristic of the current McBer instruments (see McClelland, 1998, and Spencer & Spencer, 1993, for a description of the developmental scaling and some of its implications). Although the developmental scaling will be empirically determined, for the early applications of the ECI the developmental scaling assumptions were based on expert opinion from previous studies (McClelland, 1998; Spencer & Spencer, 1993).

A preliminary sample was collected with the revised ECI from the managers and professionals in several industrial and professional service companies. Scale reliabilities are shown in Table 16.1 for the earlier instrument and both versions of the ECI, as well as the average item score method of composing the scales, and the developmental weighting method of composing the scales (Boyatzis & Burckle, 1999). The reliabilities of the earlier Self-Assessment Questionnaire (SAQ) were based on a sample of 180 people with master's degrees in business administration (average age twenty-seven, 32 percent female, 19 percent nonnative English speakers). This earlier instrument included scales assessing a number of cognitive competencies or abilities: Use of Concepts, $\alpha = .896$; Systems Thinking, $\alpha = .857$; Pattern Recognition, $\alpha = .838$; Theory Building, $\alpha = .881$; Use of Technology, $\alpha = .882$; Quantitative Analysis, $\alpha = .891$; and Written Communication, $\alpha = .881$.

The SAQ and its 360-degree version, the External Assessment Questionnaire (EAQ), as well as both versions of the ECI, have similar response categories based on frequency of demonstration or observation. An optional answer of "I don't know" or "I have not had the opportunity to observe the person in an appropriate setting" is read into the data as blank. The current version of the ECI asks the respondent to describe himself or herself or another person on each item on a scale of 1 to 7. Each step is progressively labeled starting from "the behavior is only slightly characteristic of the individual (the individual behaves this way only sporadically)" to the highest response indicating "the behavior is very characteristic of this individual (the individual behaves this way in most or all situations where it is appropriate)."

Table 16.1a. Scale Reliabilities (Cronbach's Alpha) for Average Item Scores.

Competency	Self-Assessment Quest. (180)	ECI:1	ECI:2 Self-Assessment	Others' Assessment
Emotional Self-Awareness	na[b]	.761 (585)	.629 (668)	.798 (427)
Accurate Self-Assessment	na	.706 (584)	.715 (663)	.886 (427)
Self-Confidence	.825	.684 (595)	.825 (660)	.909 (428)
Self-Control	.735	.710 (575)	.808 (668)	.906 (427)
Trustworthiness	na	.543 (584)	.667 (667)	.814 (427)
Conscientiousness[a]	.774	.751 (596)	.816 (664)	.911 (428)
Adaptability[a]	.819	.721 (561)	.618 (664)	.834 (428)
Achievement Orientation[a]	.700	.751 (553)	.835 (660)	.921 (428)
Initiative	.769	.789 (571)	.754 (663)	.897 (427)
Empathy	.838	.715 (567)	.837 (657)	.948 (425)
Organizational Awareness	na	.721 (558)	.786 (660)	.913 (426)
Developing Others	.904	.769 (523)	.818 (653)	.927 (426)
Service Orientation	na	.707 (509)	.854 (628)	.938 (426)
Leadership[a]	.824	.801 (521)	.658 (649)	.824 (427)
Influence[a]	.824	.739 (541)	.767 (637)	.881 (425)
Communication[a]	.848	.695 (557)	.789 (654)	.910 (427)
Change Catalyst	na	.799 (535)	.866 (637)	.935 (426)
Conflict Management[a]	.902	.773 (529)	.778 (660)	.894 (426)
Building Bonds[a]	.822	.600 (565)	.773 (670)	.882 (427)
Teamwork and Collaboration[a]	.909	.785 (522)	.842 (645)	.943 (426)

Note: The number of subjects is shown in parentheses following the instrument; for the ECI II, due to missing item and scale data the *n* is shown for each scale separately. Table from Boyatzis & Burckle (1999).

[a] In the Self-Assessment Questionnaire: Conscientiousness = Attention to Detail; Adaptability = Flexibility; Achievement Orientation = Efficiency Orientation; Leadership = Persuasiveness; Influence = Persuasiveness; Communication = Oral Communication; Conflict Management = Negotiation; Building Bonds = Networking; Teamwork & Collaboration = Group Management.
[b] na, not available.

On the basis of factor, cluster, and reliability analyses of the data on the first version of the ECI, a number of competency scales were reconsidered and reclassified from Goleman's (1998) earlier model. Innovation behaviors were integrated into the Initiative scale. The Optimism scale was highly correlated with the Achievement Drive scale, so it was integrated into the newly named Achievement Orientation scale. The Leveraging Diversity items were highly correlated with the Understanding Others scale, so they were integrated into the newly

Table 16.1b. Scale Reliabilities (Cronbach's Alpha)
for Developmental Scores (Sample Size in Parentheses).

	Self-Assessment	Composite Others' Assessment
Emotional Self-Awareness	.609 (668)	.732 (427)
Accurate Self-Assessment	.677 (663)	.847 (427)
Self-Confidence	.778 (660)	.870 (428)
Self-Control	.780 (668)	.866 (427)
Trustworthiness	.587 (667)	.743 (427)
Conscientiousness	.817 (664)	.878 (428)
Adaptability	.546 (664)	.779 (428)
Achievement Orientation	.761 (660)	.864 (428)
Initiative	.721 (663)	.858 (427)
Empathy	.774 (657)	.905 (425)
Organizational Awareness	.734 (660)	.856 (426)
Developing Others	.750 (653)	.870 (426)
Service Orientation	.811 (628)	.896 (426)
Leadership	.660 (649)	.795 (427)
Influence	.761 (637)	.856 (425)
Communication	.747 (654)	.873 (427)
Change Catalyst	.807 (637)	.890 (426)
Conflict Management	.747 (660)	.856 (426)
Building Bonds	.705 (670)	.822 (427)
Teamwork and Collaboration	.760 (645)	.892 (426)

named Empathy scale. A number of the original Leveraging Diversity items formed the highest developmental levels of the Empathy scale consistent with other empirical evidence from the McBer database and the Boyatzis SAQ scale relationships. The Commitment items were highly correlated with the Leadership scale; they all addressed commitment to "group" goals, values, and vision, which was a set of the themes in the Leadership scale, so they were integrated into the Leadership scale. The Collaboration items were highly correlated with the Team Capabilities scale, so they were integrated into the newly named Teamwork and Collaboration scale. Two other minor name changes included changing Political Awareness to Organizational Awareness, and Emotional Awareness to Emotional Self-Awareness.

Clustering of Competencies

The clustering, or organizing, of several of the competencies into larger categories for the purpose of analysis or application offers two choices: (1) Do we organize the characteristics theoretically (using an a priori framework) or empirically?; (2) Do we organize them in the context of the other competencies that may affect each other most closely, independently (treating each as if the human organism has that ability independent of the others), or developmentally (arranged in a framework of inferred causality)?

Clusters are behavioral groups of the desired competencies. They are often linked conceptually and defined by a "theory" as a convenient way to describe which competencies are associated with others. Clustering provides parsimony. The competencies within such a cluster may be linked empirically. That is, statistical analysis may allow us to discover how the human organism demonstrates these desired competencies in various settings, answering the question, "Which of the desired competencies are demonstrated together or associated with each other?"

Within a cluster, various competencies may have one of four types of relationships. First, they may be parts of a whole and complement each other in functional behavior (such as Adaptability and Conscientiousness). A person can demonstrate flexibility in adapting to situations. His demonstration of reliability and consistency (such as Conscientiousness) would not interfere with the demonstration of Adaptability, but if the person can use both competencies his effectiveness would increase in many situations. For example, if the situation changed but a reliable response was still needed, the use of Adaptability and Conscientiousness would allow for continued appropriate behavior even in the new situation.

Second, they may be alternate manifestations, in which case the specific competency used would vary by setting or stimulus. Which competencies are noted as being used depends on whether the competencies have been defined broadly or narrowly. Alternate manifestations are often found in competency models with highly behaviorally specific definitions of the competencies. If the competencies are defined as a more broad capability, the behavioral indicators of the competency are alternate manifestations. This reduces the likelihood that the cluster may have competencies within it that have this relationship.

Third, the competencies within the cluster may be compensatory. That is, using one competency makes up for using less of another (such as Achievement Orientation and Initiative). A person can demonstrate a great deal of concern about doing better, contemplating and acting on cost-benefit utility analysis, and so forth (such as Achievement Orientation). This may drive a degree of innovation and discovery of new and better ways to accomplish things. At the same time, someone else in the same situation may find new and better ways to accomplish things because she is starting things before anyone has thought of them, seeking information in distinctive ways, and so forth (such as demonstrating Initiative). Although the outcomes are the same, the specific behavior used and the intention underlying the behavior are different.

Fourth, the competencies within the cluster may be antagonistic. Frequent use of one "crowds" out the ease or possible use of another (for example, Self-Control versus Initiative). If someone demonstrates a great deal of Self-Control and thereby inhibits his impulses and actions, he would have an increasingly difficult time demonstrating Initiative and starting things before anyone asks.

Clusters Within a Model

Clusters within a competency model should be related in some way and not be just a list. They maybe related as being parts of a whole. In other words, the clusters might complement each other (such as Goal and Action Management, Social Skills, or People Management). Demonstrating the competencies in one of these clusters does not preclude nor arouse the competencies in the other cluster, but when both are demonstrated, the person is typically more effective in professional and management positions.

The clusters within a model may have a developmental relationship. For example, the Self-Awareness cluster of competencies is needed for sustainable Self-Management, or more specifically for the competencies in the Self-Management cluster to be demonstrated in sustained ways. Another example is that the Social Awareness cluster is needed for sustainable demonstration and use of the Social Skills cluster.

The clusters within a model may have compensatory relationships. For example, the Analytic Reasoning cluster and the Goal and Action Management or Self-Management cluster can occasionally compensate for the demonstration of the other. Using more Initiative, Achievement Orientation, and Adaptability competencies may compensate for System Thinking—or vice versa. In other words, using the competencies in the Self-Management cluster may allow a person to want to think about and organize what is needed to solve a problem. Using the competencies in the Analytic Reasoning cluster, in particular Systems Thinking and Pattern Recognition, could also result in a framework or model being constructed that organizes the issues and needs in the situation. Competencies in either cluster, in such a situation, could provide ideas for what to do next to solve the problem.

The dilemma facing the scholar or researcher is that the a priori clustering seems to make more sense—it comes out of our mental and theoretical models. On the other hand, the actual appearance of the competencies and clusters may be different, suggesting the importance of an empirical method of determining the clusters. There are dramatic differences. The clustering shown in Table 16.2 reflects both theoretical and empirical clustering from two sets of studies reported by Boyatzis (1982) and Boyatzis, Cowen, and Kolb (1995) regarding generic competency models of management and leadership.

Although the a priori clusters appear conceptually meaningful, and the empirical clusters seem to be a confused assortment, the empirically determined

Table 16.2. Theoretical and Empirical Clustering of Generic Models of Management and Leadership.

From Boyatzis (1982)

Theoretical Clusters	**Empirical Clustering (via Cluster Analysis)[a]**

Entrepreneurial Cluster
  Efficiency Orientation
  Initiative
	Goal and Action Management Cluster
	  Efficiency Orientation
	  Initiative (i.e., Proactivity)
	  Diagnostic Use of Concepts
	  Concern with Impact

Interpersonal Cluster
  Concern with Impact
  Use of Unilateral Power
  Developing Others
  Managing Group Process
  Use of Socialized Power
  Oral Presentations
	Directing Subordinates Cluster
	  Developing Others
	  Use of Unilateral Power
	  Spontaneity

Intellectual Reasoning Cluster
  Diagnostic Use of Concepts
  Logical Thought
  Conceptualization
	Human Resource Management Cluster
	  Managing Group Process
	  Use of Socialized Power
	  Accurate Self-Assessment
	  Logical Thought

Socio-Emotional Maturity Cluster
  Stamina/Adaptability
  Accurate Self-Assessment
  Perceptual Objectivity
  Spontaneity
  Self-Control
	Focus on Others Cluster
	  Stamina/Adaptability (i.e., Flexibility)
	  Perceptual Objectivity
	  Self-Control

	Leadership Cluster
	  Self-Confidence
	  Conceptualization
	  Oral Presentations

From Boyatzis, Cowen, and Kolb (1995)

Theoretical Clusters	**Empirical Clustering (via Factor Analysis)[b]**

Goal and Action Management Cluster
  Efficiency Orientation
  Planning
  Initiative
  Self-Control
  Attention to Detail
  Flexibility
	Goal and Action Management Cluster
	  Efficiency Orientation
	  Planning
	  Initiative
	  Self-Confidence
	  Persuasiveness
	  Written Communication
	  Oral Communication
	  Flexibility

Table 16.2. (continued)

Theoretical Clusters	Empirical Clustering (via Factor Analysis)[b]
People Management Cluster	*People Management Cluster*
Empathy	Empathy
Persuasiveness	Networking
Networking	Negotiating
Negotiating	Group Management
Self-Confidence	Developing Others
Group Management	Social Objectivity
Developing Others	Self-Control
Oral Communication	
	Analytic Reasoning Cluster
Analytic Reasoning Cluster	Use of Concepts
Use of Concepts	Systems Thinking
Systems Thinking	Pattern Recognition
Pattern Recognition	Use of Technology
Theory Building	Quantitative Analysis
Use of Technology	
Quantitative Analysis	
Social Objectivity	
Written Communication	

[a] Cluster analysis of 253 managers, predominantly male. Alverno College study of 103 female managers revealed similar empirical structure with the exception of Accurate Self-Assessment associated with the Goal and Action Management cluster instead of Concern with Impact; Stamina/Adaptability clustered with Concern with Impact and Use of Socialized Power; Positive Regard clustered with Developing Others and Managing Group Process.

[b] Integration of four factor analyses via Learning Skills Profile (self-report card sort, $n = 724$), Self-Assessment Questionnaire (self-report, $n = 454$), behaviorally coded critical incident interview (audiotaped, $n = 497$), behaviorally coded Group Discussion Exercise (videotaped, $n = 482$); all master's in business administration students, average age 27, about one-third female.

clusters showed greater validity against performance data (Boyatzis, 1982). They also "made sense" to executives and human resource professionals when presented and discussed at various professional meetings. For example, the Goal and Action Management cluster does not include only entrepreneurial competencies; it appears to reflect a person's orientation to his environment. The empirical cluster could be said to represent how the person asserts herself in various settings. The finding from the research conducted at Alverno College (Mentkowski, McEachern, O'Brien, & Fowler, 1982) on an exclusively female managerial sample showed the fascinating substitution of Accurate

Self-Assessment for the Concern with Impact competency in this cluster, as noted in Figure 16.1. The researchers' interpretation was that women in middle-level management positions had to be far more self-monitoring than their male counterparts to "make it" in the private sector in 1982.

Other shifts shown in Figure 16.1 include the observation that cognitive abilities or competencies do not cluster together for this management sample. The analytic or cognitive competencies sort themselves into clusters of functional behavior with other competencies that are often used along with the specific cognitive ones. For example, Conceptualization, which was later renamed Pattern Recognition, loaded on the Leadership cluster. In studies of executives and chief executive officers, it has often been found that Pattern Recognition, the ability to see themes and patterns in seemingly unrelated data, is crucial in "reading" the internal organizational climate, trends in the market, and concerns of customers, stakeholders, and so on (Dalziel, 1998 [as cited in Goleman, 1998]; Goleman, 1998). The competency would be expected to fit more closely with Self-Confidence and within the Leadership cluster than to be clustered with other cognitive abilities.

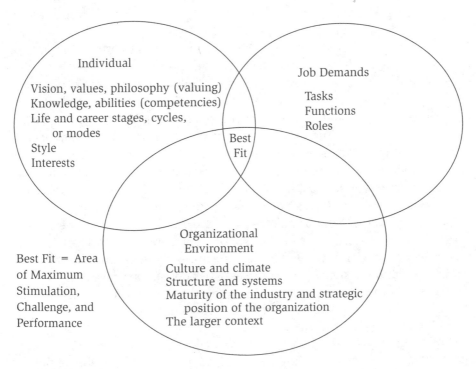

Figure 16.1. Contingency theory of action and job performance (Boyatzis, 1982).

In the 1995 and later samples (Boyatzis, Baker, Leonard, Rhee, & Thompson, 1995; Boyatzis et al., 1996, 1997), the clustering appears different. The Analytic Reasoning or cognitive competencies cluster with each other. This is probably a function of the samples; the 1995 and later samples were from students pursuing a master's degree in business administration and who come from and seek a wide variety of occupations including sales, financial analyst, human resources, and managerial positions. In this sample, the assertiveness on the environment aspect of the Goal and Action Management cluster appears even stronger. Persuasiveness and the Oral and Written Communication competencies load within this cluster, as well as Self-Confidence. It appears closely related to the Self-Management cluster within the Emotional Intelligence Model from the ECI analysis, as shown in Table 16.3.

On the basis of preliminary factor analysis and cluster analysis of the ECI with the 596 subjects, three clusters emerged: (1) Self-Awareness, which included Emotional Self-Awareness, Accurate Self-Assessment, and Conscientiousness; (2) Self-Management, which included Self-Confidence, Adaptability, Achievement Orientation, Initiative, Change Catalyst, and Self-Control; and (3) Social Skills, which included Empathy, Service Orientation, Developing Others, Communication, Organizational Awareness, Building Bonds, Collaboration, Trustworthiness, Leadership, Influence, and Team Capability. The comparison is shown in Figure 16.2.

Recent findings by Boyatzis (1999b) illustrate the differential impact of demonstration of the competencies in each of these clusters. He found that experienced partners at a large consulting firm contributed significantly more profit to the firm from their accounts if they had demonstrated a significant number of the competencies from that cluster above the tipping point. The tipping point analysis determined the frequency of demonstration that appears sufficient to "tip" a person into effectiveness and superior performance (McClelland, 1998); in complexity theory terms, this is the "trigger" point precipitating the discontinuous break into effectiveness. In his study, McClelland (1998) found that this tipping point could be identified where the line describing the frequency of demonstration of a competency by "superior" performers crosses the line describing the frequency of demonstration of that competency by "average" performers. He showed that this significantly differentiated bonuses paid to divisional top executives at a food and beverage company; the bonuses paid to the executives were a function of the division's financial performance. The results comparing the four clusters in this firm's competency model of partners are shown in Table 16.4.

The table shows that experienced partners demonstrating a significant number of the competencies within the Self-Regulation cluster above the tipping point contributed the highest differential profit to the firm per year compared with those demonstrating competencies below the tipping point. The Social

Table 16.3. Theoretical and Empirical Clustering
of Competencies in the Emotional Intelligence Model.

From Goleman (1998) **Theoretical Clustering**	ECI Original Version **Empirical Clustering**	ECI Current Version **Current Clustering**
Self-Awareness Cluster	*Self-Awareness Cluster*	*Self-Awareness Cluster*
Emotional Self-Awareness Accurate Self-Assessment Self-Confidence	Emotional Self-Awareness Accurate Self-Assessment Conscientiousness	Emotional Self-Awareness Accurate Self-Assessment Self-Confidence
Self-Regulation Cluster	*Self-Management Cluster*	*Self-Management Cluster*
Self-Control Trustworthiness Conscientiousness Adaptability Innovation	Self-Control Self-Confidence Adaptability Change Catalyst	Self-Control Trustworthiness Conscientiousness Adaptability
Self-Motivation Cluster		
Achievement Orientation Commitment Initiative Optimism	Achievement Orientation Initiative	Achievement Orientation Initiative
Empathy Cluster	*Social Skills Cluster*	*Social Awareness Cluster*
Empathy Organizational Awareness Service Orientation Developing Others Leveraging Diversity	Empathy Organizational Awareness Service Orientation Developing Others	Empathy Organizational Awareness Service Orientation
Social Skills		*Social Skills*

Leadership
Communication
Influence
Change Catalyst
Conflict Management
Building Bonds
Collaboration and
  Cooperation
Team Capabilities
	Leadership
	Communication
	Influence
	Trustworthiness
	Conflict Management
	Building Bonds
	Teamwork and
	  Collaboration
		Leadership
		Communication
		Influence
		Change Catalyst
		Conflict Management
		Building Bonds
		Teamwork and
		  Collaboration
		Developing Others

Table 16.4a. A Comparison of the Impact of the Number of Competencies
Above/Below the Tipping Point by Cluster (000s).

Cluster	Above TP Acct. Rev.	Below TP Acct. Rev.	Above TP Acct.Margin	Below TP Acct.Marg
Self-Management	$2,942	$1,803	59%	54%
Self-Regulation	$2,969	$896	62%	42%
Social Skills	$2,819	$1,797	63%	47%
Analytic Reasoning	$2,545	$2,164	60%	47%

Table 16.4b. A Profit Contribution Comparison of the Impact of the Number
of Competencies Above/Below the Tipping Point by Cluster.

Cluster	Incremental Profit per Year per Partner
Self-Management	$762,000 per year = 78% more/experienced partner
Self-Regulation	$1,465,000 per year = 390% more/experienced partner
Social Skills	$931,000 per year = 110% more/experienced partner
Analytic Reasoning	$510,000 per year = 50% more/experienced partner

Skills and Self-Management clusters followed in size of contribution. It is worth noting that frequently demonstrating the competencies in all of the clusters was linked to substantial increased profit contribution to the firm. Using the same type of tipping point analysis, Boyatzis (1999b) showed that demonstrating three or four of the clusters with the sufficient number of competencies in each above the tipping point was sufficient to trigger effectiveness.

IMPLICATIONS FOR A THEORY OF ACTION AND PERSONALITY

Clusters Help in Building a Theory of Action

Boyatzis (1982) used a contingency model of management effectiveness that postulated that the degree of overlap, or "best fit," between the individual, his or her job demands, and the organizational environment would predict effectiveness, as shown in Figure 16.1. He claimed that seeking one-to-one correspondence between the competencies and job functions or tasks was a futile exercise. Similarly, the search for connections between specific competencies and elements of the organizational climate, culture, structure, systems, or strategy would be a reductionistic nightmare. To try to link elements of specific job demands or the organizational environment to one of the competencies such as

Building Bonds forces the connections to be stretched. For example, one examines the function of "championing a specific change project" and determines that it would require Building Bonds, but that this competency cannot be used alone. It would need to be used with other competencies such as Change Catalyst, Conflict Management, and Teamwork and Collaboration. To see the connections easily, one must expand the competency to a cluster of competencies, such as Social Skills.

Similarly, connecting a component of the organizational culture to a competency cluster seems easier than connecting to a single competency. To ask that a person "fit into" an entrepreneurial culture in a fast-growing company is asking that person to frequently demonstrate Achievement Orientation *and* Initiative *and* Adaptability, to name a few competencies in the Goal and Action Management or Self-Management cluster. Merely showing Achievement Orientation frequently could lead to a fascination with cost-cutting and risk moderation, which might work against the cultural norms of taking advantage of opportunities, if not making your own opportunities.

This confusion about searching for links at the competency or cluster level has often been the source of mistakes in linking the needed competencies from individuals with the "core competence" of the organization. If engineering excellence is the core competence of a company, we would predict that the Goal and Action Management cluster (or the Self-Management Cluster in the Emotional Intelligence Model) would need to be the most frequently observed cluster to create and sustain this culture and strategy. If an increasing number of the executives had this as their third most frequent competency, we would predict increasingly confusing messages within the organization as to priorities and a shift from utilizing core engineering excellence as a distinguishing feature in their strategy, customer service, and product innovation.

Clusters Offer Hope in Building a Theory of Personality

One of the major benefits of the conceptualization of emotional intelligence is the potential for establishing causal connections among the various levels of a person's psyche. Boyatzis (1982) followed an often-described causal link between the unconscious motive and trait level of personality to the social role and self-image level to the behavioral level, as evident in competencies. The effort resulted in attempts to make the links for each competency. The result was intriguing to some but had the conceptual elegance of a hardware manual.

The clusters of competency, on the other hand, offer an appropriate focal point from which to identify, predict, and establish the multiple levels of causal connections, as suggested in Figure 16.2. Neurological and hormonal characteristics predispose or arouse certain motives or traits, which in turn predispose, arouse, or drive competencies within the context of certain philosophical orientations (Boyatzis, 1982; Goleman, 1995, 1998). Our contention is that these

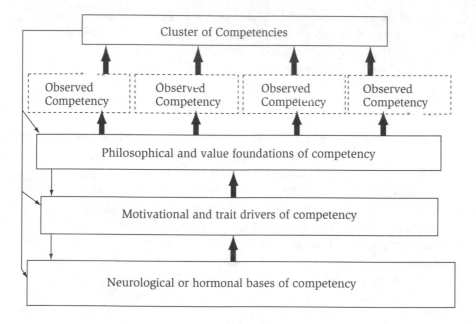

Figure 16.2. Levels within the personality structure.

connections or causal paths are easier to identify for clusters of competencies than for separate competencies. For example, research has begun to establish a link between high resting levels of epinephrine secretion and high Need for Power motives (McClelland, 1985) and other such links among hormonal levels and unconscious motives (Schultheiss, 1999a, 1999b). We also know that high Need for Power predicts frequency of demonstration of influence behaviors, such as those evident in the competencies of the Social Skills cluster.

In the literature, the links between unconscious motives and traits and behaviorally observed competencies are the most clearly established of these links. Need for Power drives Teamwork and Collaboration, Influence, Building Bonds, Leadership, and so forth (McClelland, 1985; McClelland & Boyatzis, 1982; Winter, 1973). Need for Affiliation drives Empathy (Boyatzis & Burruss, 1977; Burruss & Boyatzis, 1981). Need for Achievement drives Achievement Orientation (McClelland, 1961, 1985). A sense of Self-Efficacy and Self-definition drives Initiative (Boyatzis, 1982; Stewart, 1978). In a similar way, cognitive complexity drives Systems Thinking and Pattern Recognition, as analytic competencies.

We can also conjecture relationships among the "big five" traits and competencies (McCrae & Costa, 1990). For example, extroversion probably drives Building Bonds, Influence, Leadership, Communication, and so forth—the Social

Skills cluster. Openness and conscientiousness probably both drive the Goal and Action Management or Self-Management cluster, although they probably have different sets of competencies within the cluster. Agreeableness probably drives the Social Awareness cluster. There appears no direct link to the Self-Awareness cluster of competencies.

Philosophical orientations, such as pragmatism, rationalism, and humanism, offer a conceptualization that provides a closer link to the underlying traits, such as learning style, while at the same time a closer link to the frequency of demonstrated behaviors of specific competencies (Boyatzis, Murphy, & Wheeler, 2000). Boyatzis et al. (1996) reported evidence from multiple samples showing a stronger association between a person's operating philosophy (or philosophical orientation) and clusters of the competencies, than with specific competencies.

These causal links do not imply determinism but forms of association and disposition. For more specific causality, we must conduct further research with comprehensive multimethod, multitrait, and multilevel designs. Complexity theory suggests that fractals do exist. We predict they exist within the structure of human personality and that competency clusters are a necessary level of variable needed to find and see the fractals. At the same time, prior research suggests that arousal or activation of any of the motive, trait, philosophical, and/or behavioral levels through competencies affects and arouses the hormonal, motive, trait, and other levels within the personality, as suggested by the feedback loops indicated in Figure 16.2.

CONCLUSION

The need for more research into the construction of personality and determinants and consequences of our behavior is more than a perpetual plea of scholars; it is an expression of our commitment to the benefits that accrue from our drive to satisfy our curiosity about being human. We seek to understand characteristics that predict better performance because we wish to be more effective. We seek to understand characteristics that predict more fulfilling lives because we see injustice and suffering and know that many of our lives are "out of balance." Although cynics can point to hundreds or even thousands of irrelevant if not misleading studies that have been published during the past one hundred years, few would contradict the observation that our understanding of individual personality and behavior has advanced tremendously during this century. Research has contributed to this advancement. More research is needed to understand how our emotions and capabilities affect our lives and work. In this chapter, we have offered a number of observations and emerging theoretical frameworks that we hope will stimulate curiosity and more research.

References

Ackerman, P. L., & Heggestad, E. D. (1997). Intelligence, personality, and interests: Evidence for overlapping traits. *Psychological Bulletin, 121,* 219–245.

Bar-On, R. (1997). *BarOn Emotional Quotient Inventory (EQ-i): Technical manual.* Toronto, Canada: Multi-Health Systems.

Boyatzis, R. E. (1982). *The competent manager: A model for effective performance.* New York:Wiley.

Boyatzis, R. E. (1994). Stimulating self-directed change: A required MBA course called Managerial Assessment and Development. *Journal of Management Education, 18,* 304–323.

Boyatzis, R. E. (1999a). Self-directed change and learning as a necessary meta-competency for success and effectiveness in the 21st century. In R. Sims & J. G. Veres (Eds.), *Keys to employee success in the coming decades* (pp. 15–32). Westport, CT: Greenwood.

Boyatzis, R. E. (1999b). *The financial impact of competencies in leadership and management of consulting firms* (Working Paper). Cleveland, OH: Case Western Reserve University, Department of Organizational Behavior.

Boyatzis, R. E., Baker, A., Leonard, D., Rhee, K., and Thompson, L. (1995). Will it make a difference?: Assessing a value-based, outcome oriented, competency-based professional program. In R. E. Boyatzis, S. S. Cowen, & D. A. Kolb (Eds.) *Innovating in professional education: Steps on a journey from teaching to learning.* San Francisco: Jossey-Bass.

Boyatzis, R. E., & Berlinger, L. (1992). *Report to CORUM on managerial competencies of cooperatives in Northern Italy.* Modena, Italy: CORUM S.r.l.

Boyatzis, R. E., & Burckle, M. (1999). *Psychometric properties of the ECI: Technical Note.* Boston: Hay/McBer Group.

Boyatzis, R. E., & Burruss, J. A. (1977). *Validation of a competency model for alcoholism counselors in the Navy* (Report to the U.S. Navy on Contract Number N00123–77-C-0499). Boston: McBer and Company.

Boyatzis, R. E., Cowen, S. S., & Kolb, D. A. (Eds.). (1995). *Innovation in professional education: Steps on a journey from teaching to learning.* San Francisco: Jossey-Bass.

Boyatzis, R. E., Leonard, D., Rhee, K., & Wheeler, J. V. (1996). Competencies can be developed, but not the way we thought. *Capability, 2,* 25–41.

Boyatzis, R. E., Murphy, A. J., & Wheeler, J. V. (1997). Philosophy as the missing link between values and behavior. Working paper 97–3(3a) of the Department of Organizational Behavior. Cleveland: Case Western Reserve University.

Boyatzis, R. E., Murphy, A. J., & Wheeler, J. V. (2000). Philosophy as the missing link between values and behavior. *Psychological Reports, 86,* 47–64.

Boyatzis, R. E., Wheeler, J., & Wright, R. (forthcoming). Competency development in graduate education: A longitudinal perspective. In *Proceedings of the First World Conference on Self-Directed Learning*, Montreal: GIRAT.

Bray, D. W., Campbell, R. J., & Grant, D. L. (1974). *Formative years in business: A long term AT&T study of managerial lives.* New York: Wiley.

Burruss, J. A., & Boyatzis, R. E. (1981). *Continued validation of a competency model of alcoholism counselors in the Navy* (Report to the U.S. Navy on contract number N002-44-80-C0521). Boston: McBer and Company.

Davies, M., Stankov, L., & Roberts, R. D. (1998). Emotional intelligence: In search of an elusive construct. *Journal of Personality and Social Psychology, 75,* 989–1015.

Gardner, H. (1983). *Frames of mind: The theory of multiple intelligences.* New York: Basic Books.

Goleman, D. (1995). *Emotional intelligence.* New York: Bantam.

Goleman, D. (1998). *Working with emotional intelligence.* New York: Bantam.

Kotter, J. P. (1982). *The general managers.* New York: Free Press.

Luthans, F., Hodgetts, R. M., & Rosenkrantz, S. A. (1988). *Real managers.* Cambridge, MA: Ballinger Press.

McClelland, D. C. (1961). *The achieving society.* New York: D. Van Nostrand.

McClelland, D. C. (1973). Testing for competence rather than intelligence. *American Psychologist, 28,* 1–14.

McClelland, D. C. (1985). *Human motivation.* Glenview, IL: Scott, Foresman & Co.

McClelland, D. C. (1998). Identifying competencies with behavioral-event interviews. *Psychological Reports, 9,* 331–339.

McClelland, D. C., Baldwin, A. L., Bronfenbrenner, U., & Strodbeck, F. L. (1958). *Talent and society: New perspectives in the identification of talent.* Princeton, NJ: D. Van Nostrand.

McClelland, D. C., & Boyatzis, R. E. (1982). Leadership motive pattern and long term success in management. *Journal of Applied Psychology, 67,* 737–743.

McCrae, R. R., & Costa, P. T., Jr. (1990). *Personality in adulthood.* New York: Guilford Press.

Mentkowski, M., McEachern, W., O'Brien, K., & Fowler, D. (1982). *Developing a professional competence model for management education* (Final Report to the National Institutes of Education from Alverno College). Milwaukee, WI: Alverno College.

Saarni, C. (1988). Emotional competence: How emotions and relationships become integrated. In R. A. Thompson (Ed.), *Nebraska Symposium on Motivation* (Vol. 36, pp. 115–182). Lincoln: University of Nebraska Press.

Salovey, P., & Mayer, J. D. (1990). Emotional intelligence. *Imagination, Cognition, and Personality, 9,* 185–211.

Schultheiss, O. C. (1999a, August). *Psychophysiological and health correlates of implicit motives.* Paper presented at the 107th American Psychological Association Annual Meeting, Boston.

Schultheiss, O. C. (1999b, August). *A neurobiological perspective on implicit power motivation, testosterone, and learning.* Paper presented at the 107th American Psychological Association Annual Meeting, Boston.

Spencer, L. M. Jr., & Spencer, S. M. (1993). *Competence at work: Models for superior performance.* New York: Wiley.

Sternberg, R. J. (1996). *Successful intelligence: How practical and creative intelligence determine success in life.* New York: Simon and Shuster.

Stewart, A. J. (1978). A longitudinal study of coping styles in self-defining and socially defined women. *Journal of Consulting and Clinical Psychology, 46,* 1079–1084.

Thornton, G. C. III, & Byham, W. C. (1982). *Assessment centers and managerial performance.* New York: Academic Press.

Valenca, A. C. (1996). *Competency analysis of managers in a bank in Pernambuco.* Recife, Brazil: Valenca and Associates.

Vitale, P. (1998, June). *Competency analysis of executives, managers, and technical professionals in the companies of ENI Gruppo, S.p.A.* Paper presented at the Third International Conference on Competencies and Human Capital, Castelgondolfo, Italy.

Winter, D. G. (1973). *The power motive.* New York: Free Press.

CHAPTER SEVENTEEN

Emotional and Social Intelligence

Insights from the Emotional Quotient Inventory

Reuven Bar-On

In the era of the EQ (Bar-On, 1996), ushered in by the enigmatic popularity of emotional intelligence following the publication of a bestseller by the same name (Goleman, 1995), lay people and psychologists alike are trying to learn more about this construct. Since the publication of Goleman's book, we have witnessed renewed attempts to define, measure, and apply what is popularly referred to as *emotional intelligence,* in spite of the fact that serious scientific work has been conducted in this area from the early part of the twentieth century onward (Thorndike, 1920). In that there is a great deal of overlap between many of the concepts involved, I prefer to generically refer to this wider area as *emotional and social intelligence.*

The purpose of this chapter is to share with the reader insights about emotional and social intelligence that have been gained by applying the Emotional Quotient Inventory (EQ-i) in a number of studies conducted around the world during the past seventeen years. The EQ-i was originally constructed as an experimental instrument designed to examine a concept of emotional and social functioning that I began developing in the early 1980s (Bar-On, 1985, 1988). It was reasoned that the results gained from applying such an instrument on diverse population samples in various settings would tell us more about emotionally and socially competent behavior and, eventually, about the underlying construct of emotional and social intelligence. This instrument was eventually published in 1997 (Bar-On, 1997a) and reviewed by the Buros Institute for Mental Measurement in 1999 and described in the *Supplement to the Thirteenth Mental*

Measurement Yearbook (Plake & Impara, 1999). A description of the EQ-i will also appear in the *Fourteenth Mental Measurement Yearbook,* to be published in 2001.

Although the EQ-i is the first test of emotional intelligence to be published by a psychological test publisher, it may more accurately be described as a self-report measure of emotionally and socially competent behavior that provides an estimate of one's emotional and social intelligence. It is important to stress that the EQ-i was developed to measure this particular construct and not personality traits or cognitive capacity (Dawda & Hart, 2000; Derksen, Kramer, & Katzko, 1999; Parker, Taylor, & Bagby, forthcoming).

After a brief description of the EQ-i and the way it was developed, I go on to discuss what we have learned about emotional and social intelligence based on its general psychometric properties and validation over the years. I conclude with a brief summary of what we presently know about emotional and social intelligence from the EQ-i and then recommend an approach for the continued exploration of this domain.

DESCRIPTION OF THE EQ-i AND ITS DEVELOPMENT

The development of the EQ-i began in 1983 in order to examine various factors thought to be key components of effective emotional and social functioning that lead to psychological well-being (Bar-On, 1988). The general approach involved four basic phases: (1) identifying key factors related to effective emotional and social functioning, (2) defining these factors as clearly as possible, (3) constructing a psychometric instrument (the original version of the EQ-i) designed to examine the factors involved, and (4) norming and validating the instrument across cultures. A more detailed discussion of the instrument's development is found elsewhere (Bar-On, 1997b).

The instrument has been translated into twenty-two languages, normative data have been collected in more than fifteen countries, and numerous reliability and validity studies have been conducted to date. A youth version (EQ-i:YV) (Bar-On & Parker, 2000) for children from six to twelve years of age and for adolescents from thirteen to seventeen years of age, has recently been normed in North America on approximately 9,500 individuals. A semistructured interview (the EQ-Interview) and a multirater instrument (the EQ-360) have also been developed and are presently being normed and validated. All of these measures are based on the Bar-On model of emotional and social intelligence, which will be described below. The information in this chapter relates primarily to the adult version of the EQ-i, which was normed in North America and published in 1997 (Bar-On, 1997a; for a review in the *Buros Mental Measurement Yearbook,* see Plake & Impara, 1999).

The published version of the EQ-i comprises 133 brief items and employs a five-point Likert scale ranging from "very seldom or not true of me" to "very often true of me or true of me." Based on the Flesch formula of readability (Flesch, 1948), the reading level in English has been assessed at the North American sixth grade level (Bar-On, 1997b). The EQ-i is suitable for individuals seventeen years of age and older, based on the age breakdown of the normative sample. It takes approximately forty minutes to complete the inventory.

The EQ-i renders a total EQ score and the following five EQ composite scale scores comprising fifteen subscale scores: (1) Intrapersonal EQ (comprising self-regard, emotional self-awareness, assertiveness, independence, and self-actualization), (2) Interpersonal EQ (comprising empathy, social responsibility, and interpersonal relationship), (3) Stress Management EQ (comprising stress tolerance and impulse control), (4) Adaptability EQ (comprising reality testing, flexibility, and problem solving), and (5) General Mood EQ (comprising optimism and happiness). The inventory includes the following four validity indicators: Omission Rate (the number of omitted responses), Inconsistency Index (the degree of inconsistency between similar types of items), Positive Impression (the tendency to give an exaggerated positive response), and Negative Impression (the tendency to give an exaggerated negative response). The EQ-i has a built-in correction factor that automatically adjusts the scale scores based on the Positive Impression and Negative Impression Scale scores. This is an important feature for self-report measures in that it reduces the distorting effects of social response bias, thereby, increasing the accuracy of the results obtained. A list of the inventory's items are included in the EQ-i technical manual (Bar-On, 1997b).

The fifteen subscales on the EQ-i are defined as follows: self-regard (SR) is the ability to be aware of, understand, accept, and respect oneself; emotional self-awareness (ES) is the ability to recognize and understand one's emotions; assertiveness (AS) is the ability to express feelings, beliefs, and thoughts, and to defend one's rights in a nondestructive manner; independence (IN) is the ability to be self-directed and self-controlled in one's thinking and actions and to be free of emotional dependency; self-actualization (SA) is the ability to realize one's potential and to do what one wants to do, enjoys doing, and can do; empathy (EM) is the ability to be aware of, understand, and appreciate the feelings of others; social responsibility (RE) is the ability to demonstrate oneself as a cooperative, contributing, and constructive member of one's social group; interpersonal relationship (IR) is the ability to establish and maintain mutually satisfying relationships that are characterized by emotional closeness, intimacy, and by giving and receiving affection; stress tolerance (ST) is the ability to withstand adverse events, stressful situations, and strong emotions without "falling apart" by actively and positively coping with stress; impulse control (IC) is the ability to resist or delay an impulse, drive, or temptation to act, and to control one's emotions;

reality testing (RT) is the ability to assess the correspondence between what is internally and subjectively experienced and what externally and objectively exists; flexibility (FL) is the ability to adjust one's feelings, thoughts, and behavior to changing situations and conditions; problem solving (PS) is the ability to identify and define personal and social problems as well as to generate and implement potentially effective solutions; optimism (OP) is the ability "to look at the brighter side of life" and to maintain a positive attitude, even in the face of adversity; happiness (HA) is the ability to feel satisfied with one's life, to enjoy oneself and others, and to have fun and express positive emotions.

The scores are computer generated, and the results are displayed in numeric, verbal, and graphic fashion followed by a textual report. Raw scores are automatically tabulated and converted to standard scores based on a mean of 100 and standard deviations of 15. This scoring structure resembles that of various cognitive intelligence (IQ) measures; hence, the term *EQ* (emotional quotient) was coined by me in the early 1980s to describe this parallel approach (Bar-On, 1985). Average to above average scores on the EQ-i suggest an individual who is potentially effective in emotional and social functioning (that is, one who is most likely emotionally and socially intelligent). The higher the scores, the more positive the prediction for effective functioning in meeting environmental demands and pressures. On the other hand, an inability to succeed in life and the possible existence of emotional, social, or behavioral problems are suggested by low scores. Low scores on the following subscales are considered more problematic for coping with one's environment: stress tolerance, impulse control, reality testing, and problem solving (Bar-On, 1997b).

The published version of the EQ-i was normed on a large and representative sample of the North American population including nearly 4,000 participants in the United States and Canada. Earlier versions of the inventory were completed by close to 3,000 individuals in six countries (Argentina, Germany, India, Israel, Nigeria, and South Africa). In addition to providing cross-cultural data for the inventory, this preliminary piloting of the EQ-i was important for item selection and alteration, continued scale development and validation, and establishing the final nature of the response format. In addition to being one of the largest normative samples, the North American sample is also the most diverse regarding age, ethnic, socioeconomic, educational, and occupational breakdown. Moreover, the sample is geographically representative of North America. The gender and age composition of the sample comprised 49 percent males and 51 percent females from seventeen years of age. The sample was composed of 79 percent white, 8 percent Asian American, 7 percent African American, 3 percent Hispanic, 1 percent Native American, 2 percent other participants. For more detailed demographic information, including the educational and occupational backgrounds of the members of the normative sample, the reader is referred to other work by Bar-On (1997b).

PSYCHOMETRIC PROPERTIES OF THE EQ-i

Age, Gender, and Ethnic Differences

Analysis of variance was employed to examine the effect of age and gender on EQ-i scores (Bar-On, 1997b). Although the results indicated numerous significant differences among the age groups that were compared (Bar-On, 1997b), these differences are relatively small. In brief, the older groups scored significantly higher than the younger groups on most of the EQ-i scale scores; respondents in their late forties and early fifties received the highest mean scores. A similar increase in emotional and social intelligence with age is observed in children and adolescents, based on a study conducted by Bar-On and Parker (2000). These findings are interesting when one takes into account that cognitive (or academic) intelligence increases significantly up until about seventeen years of age and then begins to mildly decrease between the second and third decade of life (Wechsler, 1958). The age effects suggest that emotional and social intelligence increases with age, at least up until the fifth decade of life; similar findings have been reported by others (Denney & Palmer, 1981; Goleman, 1998).

With respect to gender, no differences appeared between males and females regarding overall emotional and social competence. Significant gender differences, however, do exist for a few factorial components of this construct, but the effects are small for the most part. Based on the normative sample studied, females appear to have stronger interpersonal skills than males, but the latter have a higher intrapersonal capacity, are better at stress management, and are more adaptable. More specifically, women are more aware of emotions, demonstrate more empathy, relate better interpersonally, and act more socially responsible than men; on the other hand, men appear to have better self-regard, are more independent, cope better with stress, are more flexible, solve problems better, and are more optimistic than women. Similar significant differences related to social responsibility, interpersonal relationship, and stress tolerance between males and females have been observed in almost every other population sample that has been examined with the EQ-i around the world to date. Men's deficiencies in interpersonal skills, especially in the realm of empathy and social responsibility, could possibly explain why psychopathy is observed much more frequently in men than in women (American Psychiatric Association, 1994). On the other hand, significantly lower stress tolerance among women may possibly explain why they suffer more from anxiety-related disturbances than men (American Psychiatric Association, 1994).

Lastly, an examination of the North American sample did not reveal significant differences on emotional and social intelligence between the various ethnic groups that were compared. This is an interesting finding when compared with some of the controversial conclusions that have been presented over the years suggesting significant differences in cognitive intelligence between various ethnic groups (see, for example, Suzuki & Valencia, 1997).

Interscale Correlations

The EQ-i subscales were examined for the degree of intercorrelation. This was done to examine the level of correlation between the Positive Impression Scale and the other inventory subscales in order to assess the level of social desirability response bias, as well as to examine the intercorrelations among the subscales themselves.

The overall intercorrelation among the subscales and the Positive Impression Scale proved to be .19, indicating that the subscales are not strongly socially biased. It can, thus, be concluded that the subscales and the inventory as a whole are relatively independent from a social desirability factor, meaning that they are contributing unique information (Jackson, 1974).

The average intercorrelation of the fifteen subscales is .50; this indicates a fairly high intercorrelation among factors, which was expected. The optimism subscale demonstrated the highest degree of intercorrelation with the other factors (an average of .61). Other interesting high correlations among the subscales are worthy of comment. For example, the highest intercorrelation was observed between the social responsibility and the empathy subscales (.80). This may mean that responsible behavior is highly dependent on one's ability to be aware of and appreciate the feelings of others; and a lack of empathy may help to better explain psychopathic behavior. Especially high intercorrelations also appeared between assertiveness and independence (.60) and between self-regard and self-actualization (.67), optimism (.75) and happiness (.71). These specific intercorrelations are discussed later when we more closely examine the basic factorial structure of the Bar-On model and measure of emotional and social intelligence. Finally, the high correlation between optimism and stress tolerance (.76) suggests that optimism most likely is a significant factor in one's ability to cope with stress and could very well be an important facilitator of this important component of emotional intelligence.

Internal Consistency

The internal consistency of the EQ-i scales was examined on several population samples around the world. The average Cronbach alpha coefficients are high for all of the subscales, ranging from a low of .69 (social responsibility) to a high of .86 (self-regard), with an overall average internal consistency coefficient of .76 for the seven countries examined in the EQ-i technical manual (Bar-On, 1997b). Additional studies have produced similar internal consistency results on large population samples (for example, approximately 9,500 children and adolescents in the United States and Canada, 5,000 late adolescents and young adults in Israel, and 1,700 adults in the Netherlands); the results are presently being summarized and prepared for publication by the researchers involved in each of these studies. These results indicate very good reliability, especially when one considers that internal consistency procedures tend to underestimate actual reliability (Guilford & Fruchter, 1978).

Stability Reliability

An Israeli sample of forty adults was retested on the EQ-i after a period of three months. The preliminary results indicate that the overall stability coefficient is .66 for this sample (Dayan, 2000). These results are similar to those presented in the EQ-i technical manual, which revealed a stability coefficient of .73 for a sample of thirty-nine young adults who were retested after a period of four months in South Africa (Bar-On, 1997b).

FACTORIAL STRUCTURE OF THE EQ-i

Factor analysis was used to examine the structure of the EQ-i to empirically assess the extent to which it is theoretically justified. Moreover, this statistical procedure was employed to examine the results of logically clustering the major factors thought to be related to emotional and social intelligence as was previously described (that is, to see the extent to which the factorial components of the Bar-On model of emotional and social intelligence structurally exist). The analysis was performed on the data from the normative sample described above ($n = 3,831$), progressing from exploratory to confirmatory factor analysis.

Exploratory Factor Analysis

A principal component factor analysis was applied to 117 items of the 133-item EQ-i after the fifteen validity scale items were omitted as well as item 133 (which is not scored on any of the scales). An eigenvalue greater than one was used to determine the appropriate number of factors for the factor analysis solution together with a scree plot examination. The number of factor solutions examined was twelve, thirteen, fourteen, and fifteen. The thirteen-factor solution with a varimax rotation afforded the most meaningful interpretation theoretically. The process employed to identify and label the factors that emerged was based on examining the derivation of the highest loading items on each factor (factor loadings of .40 and higher across and within factors).

The names chosen for the empirical factors, which were matched with the theoretical factors, closely paralleled the scale structure of the EQ-i (Bar-On, 1997b). The thirteen empirical factors that emerged are as follows (together with their EQ-i subscale composition in parentheses): (1) self-contentment (primarily self-regard with some self-actualization, optimism, and happiness), (2) social responsibility (social responsibility), (3) impulse control (primarily impulse control), (4) problem solving (problem solving), (5) emotional self-awareness (emotional self-awareness), (6) assertiveness/independence (assertiveness and independence), (7) flexibility (flexibility), (8) anger control (some impulse control), (9) stress tolerance (stress tolerance), (10) enjoyment (some self-actualization and happiness), (11) interpersonal relationship (interpersonal relationship), (12) empathy (empathy), and (13) reality testing (reality testing).

The results of the exploratory factor analysis provided a reasonable match with the scale structure of the EQ-i. Nonetheless, the thirteen-factor empirical structure raised an important question that had to be addressed: can the fifteen-factor model used in the current EQ-i still be justified in light of the findings, which suggested a thirteen-factor structure? The essential differences that were identified between theoretical structure and that which had surfaced as a result of exploratory factor analysis were as follows: (1) two factors (factor 3 and factor 8) emerged from the original impulse control items (one single factor); (2) self-regard, self-actualization, optimism, and happiness were treated as (four) separate factors, but most of these items loaded on two factors (factor 1 and factor 10); (3) although assertiveness and independence are considered to be two separate factors on the EQ-i, items from both factors loaded on one factor (factor 6); (4) although two separate experimental factors emerged based on two individual EQ-i subscales (empathy and social responsibility), they turned out to be the highest correlating factors (.80) partly because four items are scored on both subscales, which tap a very similar domain.

Confirmatory Factor Analysis

An initial confirmatory factor analysis was applied to resolve the above-mentioned differences between the fifteen-factor structure of the EQ-i and the thirteen factors that emerged from the exploratory factor analysis. Although this initial analysis clearly indicated a fifteen-factor structure that fits the theoretical basis of the EQ-i (Bar-On, 1997b), an additional confirmatory factor analysis was subsequently applied to the same sample ($n = 3,831$), in an attempt to explain an alternative factorial structure that appears to be equally acceptable. The items from the above-mentioned problematic subscales/factors (independence, self-actualization, optimism, happiness, and social responsibility) were excluded from the second confirmatory factor analysis; and the results are presented in Table 17.1. Self-actualization, optimism, and happiness were excluded from this analysis because a number of their items loaded on factor 1 with self-regard whereas others loaded on factor 10; moreover, these three factors appear in the literature more as facilitators of emotional and social intelligence rather than actual components of this construct; David Wechsler referred to them as *conative factors* more than half a century ago (Wechsler, 1940, 1943). Independence was excluded from the analysis because its items loaded heavily on assertiveness and also because it does not appear in the literature as a component of emotional and social intelligence; however, assertiveness (the ability to express one's emotions, ideas, needs, and desires) does appear in the literature as part of this construct. For similar empirical and theoretical reasons, it was

Table 17.1. The Factorial Structure of Key Compenents of Emotional Intelligence.

Factor	Item	Loading	Factor	Item	Loading
1. Self-regard	11	.37	6. Flexibility	14	.40
	24	.48		28	.52
	40	.53		43	.58
	56	.64		59	.46
	70	.64		74	.53
	85	.62		87	.57
	100	.74		103	.70
	114	.75		131	.43
	129	.61	7. Reality testing	8	.39
2. Interpersonal	31	.54		38	.65
relationship	39	.69		53	.46
	62	.63		68	.52
	69	.48		83	.68
	99	.42		97	.42
	113	.67	8. Stress tolerance	4	.58
	128	.38		20	.57
3. Impulse control	13	.73		33	.64
	73	.51		49	.59
	86	.35		64	.42
	117	.76		78	.52
	130	.75		108	.54
4. Problem solving	1	.58		122	.35
	15	.72	9. Assertiveness	37	.57
	29	.66		67	.67
	45	.63		82	.57
	60	.73		96	.54
	89	.67		111	.54
5. Emotional	7	.76		126	.59
self-awareness	9	.58	10. Empathy	61	.50
	23	.76		72	.68
	35	.35		98	.64
	52	.74		119	.68
	116	.64		124	.59

decided to exclude social responsibility and retain empathy; moreover, these two subscales proved to be the highest correlating (.80) components of the EQ-i (Bar-On, 1997b), meaning that they are tapping very similar constructs.

The results presented in Table 17.1 clearly suggest a ten-factor structure that is both empirically feasible and theoretically acceptable as an alternative to the above-mentioned fifteen-factor structure. In the order of their extraction, the ten factors that emerged are (1) self-regard, (2) interpersonal relationship, (3) impulse control, (4) problem solving, (5) emotional self-awareness, (6) flexibility, (7) reality testing, (8) stress tolerance, (9) assertiveness, and (10) empathy. The percentage of variance of these ten factors is as follows: 23.6, 5.2, 4.7, 3.9, 3.2, 2.6, 2.3, 2.2, 2.0, and 1.8 percent. The high degree of variance accounted for by the first factor (23.6 percent) indicates the importance of self-regard (accurate self-appraisal) within the Bar-On conceptual model of emotional and social intelligence. These ten factors appear to be the key components of emotional and social intelligence. The five factors that were excluded from the confirmatory factor analysis (optimism, self-actualization, happiness, independence, and social responsibility), for the above-mentioned reasons, appear to be important correlates and facilitators of this construct. The ten key components and five facilitators together describe and predict emotionally and socially competent behavior, as is seen below.

VALIDATION OF THE EQ-i

In addition to factor analysis, other methods of validating the EQ-i have been applied to examine how well it describes what it was intended to describe (namely, the key components of emotional and social intelligence). The reader is referred to the EQ-i technical manual (Bar-On, 1997b) and the supplement to the thirteenth edition of the *Buros Mental Measurement Yearbook* (Plake & Impara, 1999) for a review of these validity studies. In this chapter, I summarize, primarily, the construct validation of the Bar-On model and measure of emotional and social intelligence.

Instruments upon which the EQ-i's construct validity was examined include the following: Attributional Style Questionnaire (Seligman, Abramson, Semmel, & von Baeyer, 1979); Beck Depression Inventory (Beck & Steer, 1987); Coping Inventory for Stressful Situations (Endler & Parker, 1990); Emotional Stroop Task (MacLeod, 1991); Eysenck Personality Questionnaire (EPQ) (Eysenck & Eysenck, 1975); Kobasa Hardiness Scale (Kobasa, 1979, 1982); Mayer-Salovey-Caruso Emotional Intelligence Test (MSCEIT) (Mayer, Caruso, & Salovey, forthcoming-a); Minnesota Multiphasic Personality Inventory (MMPI-2) (Butcher, Dahlstrom, Graham, Tellegen, & Kaemmer, 1989); NEO Five Factor Inventory (Costa & McCrae, 1991); Ninety Symptom Check List (SCL-90) (Derogatis, 1973); Personality Assessment Inventory (PAI) (Morey, 1991); Personality Orientation Inventory (POI) (Shostrom, 1964); Short Acculturation Scale (Marin, Sabogal, Marin, Otero-Sabogal, & Perez-Stable, 1987); Sixteen Personality Factor Questionnaire (16PF) (Cattell, Eber, & Tatsuoka, 1970); Structured Interview for Alexithymia (SIFA) (Dawda, 1997); Toronto Alexithymia Scale (TAS-20) (Bagby, Taylor, & Parker, 1994); Trait

Meta-Mood Scale (TMMS) (Salovey, Mayer, Goldman, Turvey, & Palfai, 1995); Zung Self-Rating Depression Scale (Zung, 1965).

The above measures were concomitantly administered with the EQ-i to diverse population samples in various settings around the world from 1983 onward. The most theoretically relevant results are summarized below for each component of the EQ-i. The discussion first focuses on the total EQ scale followed by the ten major components of emotional and social intelligence, and then concludes with the five facilitators of this construct.

Emotional and Social Intelligence

The findings obtained to date suggest that the EQ-i is measuring emotional and social intelligence based on the way the total EQ scale score correlates with various other measures that are thought to tap this construct or very closely related aspects of it. More specifically, the EQ-i is tapping the ability to be aware of, understand, control, and express emotions: r was $+.36$ with an Emotional Stroop Task (Parker, 1999), $-.72$ with the TAS-20 total score (Parker et al., forthcoming), $-.44$ with the SIFA total score (Dawda & Hart, 2000), $+.58$ with the TMMS total score (Henner, 1998), and $+.46$ with the MSCEIT total score (Mayer, Caruso, & Salovey, forthcoming-b). These specific abilities may be considered the *essence,* or *core components,* of emotional and social intelligence.

However, the emotional and social intelligence construct is complex and comprises additional emotional, personal, and interpersonal abilities that interact with one another to influence one's overall ability to effectively cope with daily demands and pressures. This overall ability is seen in the way the EQ-i total EQ scale correlates with various psychological tests that measure effectiveness in coping with daily demands and pressures. More succinctly, the EQ scale shares a common domain with other scales that measure the ability to actively cope with such demands: r was $+.72$ with the 16PF factor C (Bar-On, 1997b), $-.55$ with the 16PF factor O (Bar-On, 1997b), $-.44$ with the 16PF factor Q4 (Bar-On, 1997b), and $+.54$ with the Kobasa Commitment Scale (Fund, 2000). Furthermore, the EQ scale correlates significantly with additional indicators of general emotional and social functioning such as the SCL-90 GSI Scale $(-.85)$, the EPQ Neuroticism-Stability Scale $(-.36)$, and the Beck Depression Inventory $(-.56)$ (Bar-On, 1997b). Moreover, high negative correlations were obtained with the PAI Anxiety $(-.71)$, Depression $(-.76)$, Borderline Features $(-.77)$, and Schizophrenia $(-.54)$ (Bar-On, 1997b) Scales. All of these scales are indicators of psychopathology, which is manifested when normal emotional functioning and the overall ability to cope with daily demands break down. The above findings support the notion that emotional and social intelligence, as conceptualized by the Bar-On model, is an array of emotional, personal, and social abilities that effect one's overall ability to effectively cope with daily demands and pressures; this ability is apparently based on a core capacity to be aware of, understand, control, and express emotions effectively.

Major Components of Emotional and Social Intelligence

Self-Regard (Measured by the EQ-i SR Subscale). A high negative correlation ($-.74$) was obtained between the EQ-i self-regard subscale and the PAI Borderline Features Scale (Bar-On, 1997b), suggesting that people who receive low scores on the SR subscale have a weak sense of identity, which is symptomatic of borderline personality disturbance. This finding indicates that knowing who one is plays an important part of self-regard as defined within the Bar-On model. Knowing who one is encompasses, inter alia, a knowledge of the way one generally feels, thinks, and behaves in certain situations. This assumption is supported by other findings. Knowing who one is requires a general awareness of emotions [r was $+.49$ with an Emotional Stroop Task (Parker, 1999)]; an ability to identify them [r was $-.47$ with the TAS-20 IF Scale (Parker et al., forthcoming)]; an ability to distinguish between and describe emotions [r was $-.38$ with the TAS-20 DF Scale (Dawda & Hart, 2000)]; and to understand them [r was $+.40$ with the TMMS Clarity of Feelings Scale (Henner, 1998)].

These are important findings in that they suggest a fairly strong connection between self-regard and emotional intelligence. Moreover, it is logical to assume that self-regard (the ability to be aware of oneself and accurately appraise one's self) is a *prerequisite* of emotional self-awareness (the ability to be aware of our emotions) and empathy (the ability to be aware of others' emotions). This specific relationship between accurate self-appraisal and emotional intelligence has not been fully addressed in the literature. In addition to this logical connection between accurate self-appraisal and emotional intelligence, it has been demonstrated that self-regard is directly related to inner strength [r was $+.64$ on the 16PF Factor C (Bar-On, 1997b) and r was $+.41$ on the Kobasa Control Scale (Fund, 2000)]. Self-regard is also related to self-confidence and feelings of adequacy [r was $-.56$ with the 16PF Factor O (Bar-On, 1997b)], feeling satisfied with oneself [r was $-.60$ with the NEO N Factor (Dawda & Hart, 2000)], and feeling fulfilled [r was $-.34$ with the 16PF Factor Q4 (Bar-On, 1997b)].

Lastly, it is important to note that not only did self-regard emerge structurally as the most important component of the Bar-On model with strong construct validity, but it surfaces again and again as one of the most powerful predictors of competent behavior based on a number of validity studies that have been conducted (Bar-On, 1997b).

Emotional Self-Awareness (Measured by the EQ-i ES Subscale). A moderate but significant correlation ($+.33$) was obtained between the ES subscale and an Emotional Stroop Task (Parker, 1999), suggesting that this scale taps emotional awareness in general. A closer examination of the findings reveals that the ES subscale is, indeed, describing what it was intended to describe. More specifically, this construct apparently describes the ability to be aware of and identify emotions: r was $-.46$ with TAS-20 IF in one study (Parker et al., forthcoming), $-.44$ in another study (Dawda & Hart, 2000), $-.44$ with the SIFA IF Scale (Dawda & Hart, 2000), and $+.41$ with the TMMS Attention to Feelings Scale (Henner, 1998). Furthermore, emotional self-awareness also describes the ability to understand and distinguish between emotions in addition to being aware of them: r was $-.72$ with the TAS-20 DF Scale in one study (Parker et al., forthcoming), $-.73$ in another study (Dawda & Hart, 2000), as well as $+.41$ with the TMMS Clarity of Feelings Scale (Henner, 1998). This empirical verification of the definition is encouraging in that emotional self-awareness represents an extremely important foundation stone of conceptual models of emotional and social intelligence put forth in the past 80 years. It can be said that emotional self-awareness is the minimal component required by any model that attempts to define emotional intelligence.

Lastly, it is interesting to note that the ES subscale correlated highly with the Treatment Rejection Scale $(-.63)$ of the PAI (Bar-On, 1997b). This finding is logical, because it is very difficult for people who are deficient in emotional self-awareness to make serious progress in therapy (see Chapter Twenty-Two). This key component of emotional intelligence, together with an average or higher cognitive capacity and motivation for treatment could be considered as minimal criteria for predicting positive outcome in therapy.

Assertiveness (Measured by the EQ-i AS Subscale). The ability to express oneself and one's emotions is another very important component required in conceptual models that attempt to describe emotional intelligence and closely related concepts. It is, therefore, encouraging to note a fairly high correlation $(+.60)$ between the EQ-i AS subscale and the 16PF Factor E (Bar-On, 1997b), confirming that the AS subscale is tapping the ability to be assertive and express oneself in general. An important part of assertiveness apparently depends on one's ability to understand emotions: r was $+.60$ with the TMMS Clarity of Feelings Scale (Henner, 1998) and $-.51$ with the TAS-20 DF Scale (Parker et al., forthcoming).

Furthermore, the ability to be assertive appears to depend on not being too overcontrolled, submissive, or shy: r was $-.68$ with the Si, $-.54$ with the Si2, $-.68$ with the SOD, and $-.64$ with the SOD2 Scales on the MMPI-2 (Dupertuis, 1996); it also correlated $-.76$ with the SCL-90 Phobia Scale (Bar-On, 1997b). Additional qualities associated with assertiveness and self-expression are being guided by one's own principles, being bold, and being able to affirm oneself: r was $+.44$ with the POI I Scale (Bar-On, 1997b), $+.54$ with the 16PF Factor H (Bar-On, 1997b), $+.40$ with the POI Sr Scale (Bar-On, 1997b), and $+.49$ with the POI S Scale (Bar-On, 1997b). With respect to these findings, it is interesting to note that the AS subscale correlated significantly (−.46) with the NEO N Factor (Dawda & Hart, 2000); this raises the possibility that those with neurosis may have difficulty in more freely expressing their emotions, perhaps because they feel ashamed of doing so or are fearful of the reaction that they will receive from others (for example, rejection). Moreover, the fairly high correlation (−.52) obtained between the AS subscale and the PAI Depression Scale (Bar-On, 1997b) is logical because depressed people find it difficult to mobilize the emotional energy required to be assertive and express themselves. Lastly, the significant correlation (−.36) with the PAI Somatic Complaints Scale (Bar-On, 1997b) suggests what can happen when people are unable to assert themselves and express their emotions openly and adequately (they run the risk of having their deficiencies in self-expression converted into psychosomatic disturbance at the tissue level).

Empathy (Measured by the EQ-i EM Subscale). Another extremely important component that has surfaced in most conceptual models that have attempted to describe emotional and social intelligence over the years is empathy (the ability to be aware of and understand the feelings and needs of others). From the onset, it is logical to assume that our ability to be aware of and understand others is dependent on our ability to be aware of and understand ourselves, as was previously mentioned: r was −.46 with the TAS-20 total score (Parker et al., forthcoming), +.33 with the TMMS Attention to Feelings Scale (Henner, 1998), and +.42 with the TMMS Clarity of Feelings Scale (Henner, 1998). The EQ-i EM subscale also correlated significantly (+.39) with Factor A on the NEO (Dawda & Hart, 2000), which is an important finding because this factor assesses one's ability to be empathic, considerate, and concerned about others and their feelings (Costa & McCrae, 1991). Moreover, the EM subscale also demonstrated a low but significant correlation (+.31) with Factor A on the 16PF (Bar-On, 1997b), which measures the expression of warmth toward others (Cattell et al., 1970). Although these correlations are moderate in magnitude, they help to define the EM subscale and match fairly closely with the way the underlying construct (empathy) was conceptualized within an emotional and social intelligence framework.

Lastly, it is interesting to note that the EM subscale demonstrated a moderately high correlation with the Antisocial Features (−.52) and Aggression (−.45) Scales on the PAI (Bar-On, 1997b). These findings suggest that the lack of empathy may be an important factor in aggressive antisocial behavior, which may prove to have both diagnostic and remedial applicability.

Interpersonal Relationship (Measured by the EQ-i IR Subscale). The EQ-i IR subscale taps a wide area often referred to as *social skills,* considered by many to represent an important component of emotional and social intelligence (see Chapters One, Two, Eleven, Eighteen, and Nineteen). The IR subscale correlated significantly (+.44) with an Emotional Stroop Task (Parker, 1999), suggesting a connection between the ability to be aware of emotions and the ability to create and maintain interpersonal relationships. This connection is probably related to the specific way in which the construct was defined (the ability to form and maintain relations characterized by the capacity for giving and receiving emotional closeness). The ability to give and receive emotional closeness in relations is not only dependent on the ability to be aware of emotions, but also on the ability to understand feelings and emotions within those relations. The IR subscale correlated +.48 with the TMMS Clarity of Feelings Scale (Henner, 1998), −.50 with the TAS-20 DF Scale in one study (Parker et al., forthcoming) and −.48 in another study (Dawda & Hart, 2000). This point is further supported by a moderately high correlation (+.44) that was obtained between the EQ-i IR subscale and the MSCEIT Emotions in Relationships Scale (Mayer et al., forthcoming-b). The IR subscale also correlated significantly (+.66) with Factor E on the NEO (Dawda & Hart, 2000), further indicating that the IR subscale is tapping the ability to express warmth, affection, and intimacy in interpersonal relations.

The IR subscale also correlated well with a number of other scales that measure various aspects of interpersonal relationships. For example, in one study (Bar-On, 1997b) it correlated significantly with Factor H on the 16PF (+.56) and with the SCL-90 Interpersonal Sensitivity Scale (−.85). These results demonstrate that interpersonal relationship is related to being sensitive to others, a desire to establish relations, having positive expectations concerning interpersonal behavior, and feeling at ease with relations in general. The IR subscale also correlated well with a number of MMPI-2 scales that measure a variety of interpersonal skills (Dupertuis, 1996): Si (−.77), CYN (−.69), and SOD (−.79). This indicates that people who score low on the IR subscale are most likely shy, introverted, uneasy around others, and prone to avoiding social contact.

Lastly, it is interesting to note that the IR subscale demonstrated a high negative correlation (−.64) with the Borderline Features Scale on the PAI (Bar-On, 1997b). This finding is understandable, in that individuals who are diagnosed as having a borderline personality disorder have great difficulty in establishing and maintaining intimate contact (American Psychiatric Association, 1994), most likely because they lack a basic ability to express warmth (r = +.73 with the correlation with the PAI Warmth Scale) (Bar-On, 1997b).

Stress Tolerance (Measured by the EQ-i ST Subscale). The results from a number of studies clearly indicate that the EQ-i ST subscale assesses one's ability to effectively manage stress and anxiety-provoking conditions. The importance of stress management for emotional intelligence can be seen in the way it is related to identifying feelings [r was −.47 with the TAS-20 IF Scale (Parker et al., forthcoming)], understanding emotions [+.62 with the TMMS Clarity of Feelings Scale (Henner, 1998)], and in controlling moods [+.52 with the TMMS

Mood Repair Scale (Henner, 1998)]. Moreover, this factor has to do with an ability to deal with environmental demands, to influence stressful events [r was +.43 with the Kobasa Control Scale (Fund, 2000)], and to actively do something to improve the immediate situation (+.45 with the Kobasa Commitment Scale (Fund, 2000)], and an inability to cope with stress will most likely lead to anxiety. This last point is well demonstrated by a significant negative correlation (−.52) between the EQ-i ST subscale and the NEO N Factor (Dawda & Hart, 2000), which measures general anxiety, apprehension, and tension. The ST subscale also correlated highly with the following 16PF factors (Bar-On, 1997b) that are thought to predict anxiety: Factor C (+.67), Factor O (−.60), and Factor Q4 (−.39). This is further confirmed by significant correlations with the EPQ N Scale (−.35, Bar-On, 1997b) and with the SCL-90 Anxiety Scale (−.51, Bar-On, 1997b).

The ST subscale also demonstrated a moderate to high correlation (−.49) with the SCL-90 PHY Scale (Dawda & Hart, 2000), which taps a tendency to develop somatic symptoms under stress. Lastly, the ST subscale also demonstrated a fairly high negative correlation with the following MMPI-2 anxiety scales (Dupertuis, 1996): ANX (−.50), ANG (−.49), OBS (−.52), and A (−.60). These scales measure basic symptoms of anxiety such as irritability, tension, a tendency to worry and ruminate, poor concentration, difficulty in making decisions, and somatic complaints such as disturbances in various bodily functions and assorted aches and pains. The ST subscale also correlated negatively with the MMPI-2 DEP (−.49) and TRT (−.50) Scales (Dupertuis, 1996), which gauge poor stress management tactics such as surrendering to feelings of hopelessness and helplessness rather than facing problems. These particular findings are important because anxiety results when this component of emotional intelligence is not functioning adequately.

Impulse Control (Measured by the EQ-i IC Subscale). To the extent that the TMMS taps emotional intelligence, impulse control as defined in the Bar-On model shares a common domain with this construct as conceptualized by Salovey and Mayer (Salovey, Mayer, Goldman, Turvey, & Palfai, 1995). More specifically, the nature of this overlap has to do primarily with understanding emotions [r was +.50 with the TMMS Clarity of Feelings Scale (Henner, 1998)], as well as controlling them [r was +.39 with the TMMS Mood Repair Scale (Henner, 1998)]. This specific contribution of impulse control to emotionally intelligent behavior can also be seen from the way the IC subscale significantly correlated with the POI A Scale [r was −.42 (Bar-On, 1997b)], as well as with Factor E (+.38), Factor Q3 (+.44) and Factor Q4 (−.51) on the 16PF (Bar-On, 1997b); it also correlated fairly highly (−.59) with the SCL-90 Hostility Scale (Bar-On, 1997b). These findings demonstrate that the IC subscale measures acceptance of one's aggression and the ability to be composed and to control aggression and hostile, aggressive, and irresponsible behavior. Furthermore, the

IC subscale correlates highly (−.54) with the PAI Aggression Scale (Bar-On, 1997b) and with the following MMPI-2 scales (Dupertuis, 1996): Pd (−.49), Ma (−.53), ANG (−.77), and TPA (−.76). These scales measure a tendency toward impulsiveness, low frustration tolerance, abusiveness, unpredictable behavior, anger control problems, loss of self-control, and explosive behavior.

Reality Testing (Measured by the EQ-i RT Subscale). The correlation between the EQ-i RT subscale and the following measures indicates that this scale measures what it was designed to measure: 16PF Factor C was +.58, SCL-90 Psychoticism was −.51, SCL-90 Paranoia was −.41, PAI Paranoia was −.55, and PAI Schizophrenia was −.56 (Bar-On, 1997b). This suggests that the RT subscale shares a common domain with these particular measures that tap disturbances in perception, affect, and cognition (characterized by an impaired ability to validate that which one is perceiving, feeling, or thinking). Secondly, to the extent that the TMMS and the TAS-20 are tapping what they were designed to tap, the relatively high correlations between these scales and the EQ-i RT subscale demonstrate that reality testing is, indeed, an important component of emotional intelligence. More specifically, the ability to accurately identify [r was −.60 with the TAS-20 IF Scale and −.56 with the total score (Parker et al., forthcoming)] and understand feelings [r was +.56 with the TMMS Clarity of Feelings Scale (Henner, 1998)] is clearly related to reality testing (the ability to accurately and realistically assess the immediate situation). This suggests that the ability to accurately identify and understand feelings is dependent on accurate reality testing (and vice versa). This could also mean that reality testing plays an important role in the cognitive processing of emotions, a point that has not yet been fully addressed in the emotional intelligence literature. Reality testing possibly acts as a "rudder" in keeping the cognitive processing of emotions on track; this also might explain what happens in psychotic behavior.

Flexibility (Measured by the EQ-i FL Subscale). The EQ-i Flexibility subscale correlated moderately with the POI Ex (+.35) and the Sy (+.35) Scales (Bar-On, 1997b), suggesting that this factor is measuring flexibility at least to some extent. Furthermore, the FL subscale demonstrated a low moderate correlation (+.33) with the Short Acculturation Scale (Bar-On, 1997b), which taps the ability to adjust to a different social environment (Marin et al., 1987). On the other hand, high negative correlations with the SCL-90 Obsessive-Compulsive (−.70) and Paranoia (−.85) Scales (Bar-On, 1997b) suggests that people who score low on the FL subscale most likely exhibit rigidity in their thinking and behavior, which is characteristic of both disturbances (American Psychiatric Association, 1994). This scale also correlated significantly (−.37) with the NEO N Factor (Dawda & Hart, 2000); rigidity is a very common symptom, if not pathognomic, of neurotic behavior (a tendency to react the same way irrespective of the situation and condition). In addition to thinking and behaving in rigid patterns, those with neurosis exhibit rigidity in the way they emotionally react to certain events. Lastly, a fairly high negative correlation was found with the PAI Treatment Rejection Scale [r was −.57 (Bar-On, 1997b)] and with the MMPI-2 TRT Scale [r was −.51 (Dupertuis, 1996)]. This finding could mean that people who receive a low score on the FL subscale resist change in general and in themselves in particular.

Problem Solving (Measured by the EQ-i PS Subscale). The EQ-i PS subscale correlated significantly with the TMMS, suggesting a relationship between problem solving and emotional intelligence. More specifically, a correlation (+.41) with the TMMS Clarity of Feelings Scale (Henner, 1998) may mean that it is important to understand emotions in order to solve problems or, at least, problems of a more emotional nature (for example, problem solving with specific emotional or affective content is most likely facilitated by possessing knowledge of one's and others' feelings). In an effort to better understand problem solving within this context, it is important to examine additional findings related to this dimension. For example, the correlation (+.36) with the 16PF Factor G (Bar-On, 1997b) suggests that problem solving may involve a persistent, persevering, and disciplined approach in dealing with problematic situations. Furthermore, the PS subscale correlated significantly (+.43 for males and +.61 for females) with the Coping Inventory for Stressful Situations Task Scale (Bar-On, 1997b), which measures task-oriented behavior aimed at solving problems (Endler & Parker, 1990). The PS subscale's ability to tap this aspect of problem solving is strengthened by the way it correlated (+.37) with the Kobasa Commitment Scale (Fund, 2000), which measures one's commitment to actively cope with problematic situations in order to improve them.

The PS subscale also correlated (+.32) with the POI S Scale (Bar-On, 1997b), which may also suggest a need for spontaneity in the problem-solving process (as observed in "brainstorming" potential solutions). This assumption is supported with the high negative correlation (−.85) that was obtained with the SCL-90 O-C Scale (Bar-On, 1997b), indicating that rigidity hinders this process. On the other hand, the positive correlation (+.37) with the NEO C Factor (Dawda & Hart, 2000) suggests the importance of a more organized and disciplined approach in another aspect of problem solving (as often observed in planning, organizing, and carrying out prospective solutions). According to McCrae, problem solving in the Bar-On model was expected to share a common domain with this factor (see Chapter Twelve). Interestingly, the PS subscale demonstrated a negative correlation (−.54) with the SCL-90 Psychoticism Scale (Bar-On, 1997b), which measures thought disturbances that interfere with reasoning, decision making, and problem solving. Impairment in problem solving is also observed in anxiety and depression, which is confirmed by the fairly high correlations obtained between the PS subscale and the PAI Anxiety (−.49) and

Depression ($-.51$) Scales (Bar-On, 1997b). This last point is further supported by the significant correlation ($-.57$) that was obtained between the PS subscale and the DEP4 Scale on the MMPI-2 (Dupertuis, 1996). This finding demonstrates that typical symptoms of depression such as impaired concentration interfere with problem solving, which is also observed clinically (American Psychiatric Association, 1994). Additional empirical evidence of the connection between depression and impaired problem solving is demonstrated by the fairly high correlations between the PS subscale and the Beck Depression Inventory [r was $-.57$ (Bar-On, 1997b)] and the Zung Self-Rating Depression Scale [r was $-.52$ (Bar-On, 1997b)].

Key Facilitators of Emotional and Social Intelligence

Optimism (Measured by the EQ-i OP Subscale). In one study, the EQ-i OP subscale demonstrated a significant correlation with the Attributional Style Questionnaire (Bar-On, 1997b), although the magnitude of the correlation was not high ($+.31$). This finding is important in that this instrument was specifically designed to measure optimism. The OP subscale correlated much higher ($-.68$) with a questionnaire that was especially constructed to tap pessimism in a study conducted by Luria (1999). A moderately high correlation was also obtained between the OP subscale and the NEO N Factor [r was $-.55$ (Dawda & Hart, 2000)] and Factor E [r was $+.48$ (Dawda & Hart, 2000)]. The fairly high negative correlation with the N Factor is probably related to its depression subcomponent (N3), which measures closely related characteristics of depression such as hopelessness, whereas the positive correlation with the E Factor is most likely caused by an overlap with its positive emotions subcomponent (E6).

These findings are strengthened by the fact that the OP subscale demonstrated moderate to high correlations with the Beck Depression Inventory [r was $-.52$ (Dawda & Hart, 2000)], the PAI Depression Scale [r was $-.69$ (Bar-On, 1997b)], and Suicidal Ideation Scale [r was $-.63$ (Bar-On, 1997b)]. These findings are both interesting and important in that pessimism is a key symptom in patients with depression and suicidal ideation (American Psychiatric Association, 1994). Moreover, the relatively high correlation ($-.68$) with the PAI Treatment Rejection Scale (Bar-On, 1997b) is logical in that optimism is thought to play an important part in psychotherapy, probably because people who are pessimistic tend to submit to passivity more than actively commit themselves to doing something about their general condition. This assumption is supported by a significant correlation ($+.42$) that was obtained between the OP subscale and the Kobasa Commitment Scale (Fund, 2000). These findings support what was earlier suggested regarding the potential contribution of emotional self-awareness in assessing therapy outcome together with cognitive capacity and motivation for treatment. Lastly, it is important to note that the EQ-i OP subscale correlated fairly highly ($+.55$) with the TMMS Mood Repair Scale (Henner, 1998).

In addition to explaining a very general conceptual domain related to emotional intelligence shared by both scales, much of this overlap is probably directly related to the specific nature of the TMMS Mood Repair Scale, which clearly comprises a very high percentage of items that tap optimism. Although optimism is related to emotional intelligence, it is most likely a facilitator rather than an actual factorial component of it. With respect to this assumption, it is important to recall that Wechsler considered optimism (together with drive and positive mood) to be part of the conative factors that he thought facilitated intelligent behavior. These factors were considered to be motivational in nature rather an integral part of intelligence itself (Wechsler, 1940, 1943).

Self-Actualization (Measured by the EQ-i SA Subscale). Based on the way self-actualization is defined within the Bar-On model, and based on the research findings obtained to date, this factor is apparently tapping what has been referred to as *achievement drive*. As mentioned above, this is one of the key conative factors considered by Wechsler to play an important role in facilitating intelligent behavior, probably by supplying emotional energy, which helps motivate the individual to do his or her best. To better understand the nature of this construct, it is important to note that the EQ-i SA subscale correlates well (+.44) with factor C on the NEO (Dawda & Hart, 2000), most likely sharing a common domain with its achievement striving subcomponent (C4). This suggests that self-actualization, within the Bar-On conceptual framework, comprises a general achievement drive, as well as a sense of direction in life and a desire to work toward personal goals. Additionally, a significant correlation (+.45) with the Kobasa Commitment Scale (Fund, 2000) confirms that aspect of self-actualization related to being committed to and involved with activities that actively attempt to improve the individual. At the other end of the continuum, the SA subscale correlated negatively (−.33) with the EPQ N Scale (Bar-On, 1997b), which is interesting in that this scale taps neurotic behavior, a sense of general frustration, and difficulty in doing things that one wants to do and can do. Furthermore, people who receive low scores on the SA subscale may not know what they want to achieve because they are confused about themselves in general and what they want to do in life [the correlation with the PAI Borderline Features Scale was −.61 (Bar-On, 1997b)], or they may know what they want to accomplish in life but are unable to realize their potential for various reasons [the correlation with the PAI Depression Scale was −.70 (Bar-On, 1997b)].

With respect to this assumption, the SA subscale correlated negatively (−.45) with the Beck Depression Inventory (Bar-On, 1997b) as well as (−.52) with the Zung Self-Rating Depression Scale (Bar-On, 1997b). Moreover, the SA subscale correlated highly (−.83) with the SCL-90 Depression Scale (Bar-On, 1997b), which measures typical symptoms of depression such as withdrawal from one's interests. A negative correlation (−.51) with the MMPI-2 TRT Scale (Dupertuis,

1996) indicates that people who receive low scores on the SA subscale do not try to improve themselves. Additional negative correlations with other scales on the MMPI-2 indicate that this tendency may stem from low motivation [TRT1 was −.54 (Dupertuis, 1996)] and a lack of drive [DEP1 was −.51 (Dupertuis, 1996)]. These findings emphasize that the curtailment of personal pursuits is one of the key symptoms of depression. Evidently, the ability to actualize one-self requires drive and emotional energy.

Happiness (Measured by the EQ-i HA Subscale). A third conative component measured by the EQ-i is happiness. In addition to the motivational value of opti-mism and achievement drive, described above, happiness is also "barometric" in nature (it both monitors one's overall well-being and interjects positive mood into the way one copes with daily demands). In a way, it helps us do what we want to do and then tells us how well we are doing. It is this positive mood that fuels the emotional energy required to increase one's motivational level to get things done. In an effort to better understand this, it is important to note that the EQ-i HA subscale demonstrated a significant correlation (+.50) with the 16PF factor F (Bar-On, 1997b), which directly taps happiness and enthusiasm (Cattell et al., 1970). The HA subscale also correlated highly with Factors E (+.61) and N (−.59) on the NEO (Dawda & Hart, 2000). The overlap with Factor E is likely because of its positive emotions subcomponent (E6), which assess the tendency to experience positive emotions such as happiness and excitement. The shared domain with Factor N is probably with its depression subcomponent (N3), which is thought to measure the tendency to experience depressive affect such as sad-ness and hopelessness. In support of these findings, the HA subscale also corre-lated with the Beck Depression Inventory [r was −.52 (Dawda & Hart, 2000)], the SCL-90 Depression Scale [r was −.77 (Bar-On, 1997b)], the Zung Self-Rating Depression Scale [r was −.54 (Bar-On, 1997b)], the PAI Depression Scale [r was −.74 (Bar-On, 1997b)], and with the MMPI-2 D Scale [r was −.51 (Dupertuis, 1996)]. These correlations strongly suggest that a person who receives a markedly low score on the HA subscale may possess typical symptoms of depres-sion, such as a tendency to worry, sadness, uncertainty about the future, with-drawal from one's immediate environment, lack of drive, depressive thoughts, guilt, dissatisfaction with one's life, and possible suicidal thoughts.

Independence (Measured by the EQ-i IN Subscale). The EQ-i IN subscale cor-related moderately well (+.44) with the 16PF Factor E (Bar-On, 1997b), suggest-ing that it taps what it was designed to tap (independence). The construct validity of the IN subscale is further strengthened by the way it correlated with the 16PF Factor C [r was +.46 (Bar-On, 1997b)] and with the POI I Scale [r was +.36 (Bar-On, 1997b)], which also tap various aspects of self-directive thinking and behav-ior. Furthermore, the ability to be independent is apparently dependent on one's degree of self-confidence [r was $-.47$ with the 16PF Factor O (Bar-On, 1997b)], inner strength [r was $+.38$ with POI Sr Scale (Bar-On, 1997b)], as well as a desire to meet expectations and obligations without becoming a slave to them [r was $+.36$ with the POI C Scale (Bar-On, 1997b)]. Moreover, it can also be seen that the EQ-i IN subscale correlated ($+.36$) with the Kobasa Control Scale (Fund, 2000), which taps the feeling that one is in control and can influence difficult situations. Lastly, it is important to reiterate that independence and self-directiveness in one's thinking and ability to relate with others correlates with emotionally and socially intelligent behavior but is not a factorial component of this construct. This can be seen in the relatively high correlations between independence and various factorial components of emotional and social intelligence—assertiveness ($+.60$), stress tolerance ($+.58$), reality testing ($+.51$), and problem solving ($+.50$)—based on sources cited by Bar-On (1997b).

Social Responsibility (Measured by the EQ-i RE Subscale). In an effort to bring the nature of social responsibility into sharper focus, it is worth noting that this subscale correlates moderately highly ($r = -.45$) with the TAS-20 total score (Parker et al., forthcoming) and with the TMMS Clarity of Feelings Scale [r was $+.48$ (Henner, 1998)], suggesting that the factor that the RE subscale is measuring is related to identifying and understanding feelings in addition to being aware of emotions. More precisely, the underlying construct appears to be related to being sensitive [r was $-.60$ with the SCL-90 Interpersonal Sensitivity Scale (Bar-On, 1997b)], considerate and concerned about others and their feelings [r was $+.40$ with the NEO A Factor (Dawda & Hart, 2000)], as well as demonstrating responsibility [r was $+.40$ with the 16PF Factor G (Bar-On, 1997b)], and being cooperative and willing to contribute to the group [r was $-.33$ with the SCL-90 Hostility Scale (Bar-On, 1997b)].

In a massive survey conducted in thirty-six countries around the world, social responsibility surfaced as one of the most important factors determining effectiveness at work. Approximately 100,000 managers and staff members from hundreds of private companies and government organizations were asked what they considered to be the most important characteristics of effective and successful employees. A number of the more recurring answers clearly focused attention on a strong group orientation and social responsibility component described as "respect and consideration for others," "loyalty toward the people and goals of the organization," "cooperation with others," and "responsibility for both the success and failure of the organization." The results were similar in all of the countries surveyed over a ten-year period from 1988 until 1998. The results were clustered into eleven key characteristics describing what it takes to be a good employee, or *employeeship,* as it is referred to (Møller, 1992): commitment, responsibility, loyalty, initiative, productivity, relations, work quality, professional competence, flexibility, implementation, and energy. These results have been outlined in more detail by Møller and Bar-On (2000).

Divergent Validity

Divergent validity can be considered a way of evaluating the degree to which something *is not* in an effort to establishing what it might be. This type of validity brings convergent, construct, discriminant, and predictive validity into sharper focus. In an effort to examine the divergent validity of the Bar-On model and measure of emotional and social intelligence, the EQ-i (EQ) was concomitantly administered with various measures of cognitive intelligence (IQ) in four studies. The results suggest that the two types of intelligence are not significantly related. The total EQ score on the EQ-i correlated .12 with the full IQ score on the Wechsler Adult Intelligent Scale (WAIS; Wechsler, 1958) in a study conducted on forty adults in the United States (Pallazza & Bar-On, 1995), .08 with the General Ability Measure for Adults (GAMA; Haglieri & Bardos, 1997) in a study conducted on 873 adults in the Netherlands (Derksen et al., 1999), .01 with the Raven Standard Progressive Matrices in one study conducted on 100 adults in the Philippines (Hee-Woo, 1998), and .01 in another study conducted on 2,670 late adolescents and young adults in Israel (Fund, 2000).

CONCLUSION

I have examined a comprehensive model and measure of emotional and social intelligence. The findings presented suggest that emotional and social intelligence is a multifactorial array of interrelated emotional, personal, and social abilities that influence our overall ability to actively and effectively cope with daily demands and pressures. The factorial structure of this construct is composed of the following ten components: (1) self-regard (accurate self-appraisal), (2) emotional self-awareness (the ability to be aware of and understand one's emotions), (3) assertiveness (the ability to express one's emotions and oneself), (4) empathy (the ability to be aware of and understand others' emotions), (5) interpersonal relationship (the ability to form and maintain intimate relationships), (6) stress tolerance (the ability to manage emotions), (7) impulse control (self-control), (8) reality testing (the ability to validate one's thinking and feelings), (9) flexibility (the ability to change), and (10) problem-solving (the ability to effectively and constructively solve problems of a personal and social nature). In addition to these key factorial components, five facilitators of emotionally and socially intelligent behavior were described in detail (optimism, self-actualization, happiness, independence, and social responsibility). Not only do these factors correlate significantly high with emotional and social intelligence, but they tend to facilitate one's overall ability to effectively cope with daily demands and pressures.

Although the Bar-On model of emotional and social intelligence appears to be a promising approach to this construct, it is essential to continue its validation on additional, more diverse, and larger populations samples. It is particularly important to continue studying its discriminant and predictive validity in an effort to better examine its applicability in parenting, education, industry, and clinical work. By comparing and contrasting findings rendered by this and other approaches to emotional and social intelligence, we will be more effective in mapping out this construct. Encouraging continued empirical work in this area is the best way to discourage the proliferation of ungrounded "theorizing" that abets misconceptions and false claims of what emotional intelligence is and is not.

References

American Psychiatric Association (1994). *Diagnostic and statistical manual of mental disorders* (4th ed.). Washington, DC: Author.

Bagby, R., Taylor, G. J., & Parker, J.D.A. (1994). The twenty item Toronto Alexithymia Scale: I, Item selection and cross-validation of the factor structure. *Journal of Psychosomatic Research, 38,* 23–32.

Bar-On, R. (1985). *The development of an operational concept of psychological well-being.* Unpublished doctoral dissertation (first draft), Rhodes University, South Africa.

Bar-On, R. (1988). *The development of a concept of psychological well-being.* Unpublished doctoral dissertation (final draft), Rhodes University, South Africa.

Bar-On, R. (1996, August). *The era of the EQ: Defining and assessing emotional intelligence.* Poster session presented at the 104th Annual Convention of the American Psychological Association, Toronto, Canada.

Bar-On, R. (1997a). *The Emotional Quotient Inventory (EQ-i): A test of emotional intelligence.* Toronto, Canada: Multi-Health Systems.

Bar-On, R. (1997b). *BarOn Emotional Quotient Inventory (EQ-i): Technical manual.* Toronto, Canada: Multi-Health Systems.

Bar-On, R., & Parker, J.D.A. (2000). *The Bar-On EQ-i:YV: Technical manual.* Toronto, Canada: Multi-Health Systems.

Beck, A. T., & Steer, R. A. (1987). *Beck Depression Inventory manual.* San Antonio, TX: Psychological Corporation.

Butcher, J. N., Dahlstrom, W. G., Graham, J. R., Tellegen, A., & Kaemmer, B. (1989). *Minnesota Multiphasic Personality Inventory–2 (MMPI-2) manual for administration and scoring.* Minneapolis, MN: University of Minnesota Press.

Cattell, R. B., Eber, H. W., & Tatsuoka, M. (1970). *Handbook for the Sixteen Personality Factor Questionnaire (16PF).* Champaign, IL: Institute for Personality and Ability Testing.

Costa, P. T., Jr., & McCrae, R. R. (1991). *The NEO Five Factor Inventory: Manual.* New York: Psychological Assessment Resources.

Dawda, D. (1997). *The development and validation of an interview-based observer rating scale for alexithymia (SIFA).* Unpublished master's thesis, Simon Fraser University, Burnaby, British Columbia, Canada.

Dawda, R., & Hart, S. D. (2000). Assessing emotional intelligence: Reliability and validity of the Bar-On Emotional Quotient Inventory (EQ-i) in university students. *Journal of Personality and Individual Differences, 28,* 797–812.

Dayan, Y. (2000). *Stability reliability of the EQ-i.* Unpublished manuscript.

Denney, N. W., & Palmer, A. M. (1981). Adult age differences on traditional and practical problem-solving measures. *Journal of Gerontology, 36,* 323–328.

Derksen, J., Kramer, I., & Katzko, M. (1999). *Does a self-report measure for emotional intelligence assess something different than general intelligence?* Unpublished manuscript.

Derogatis, L. R. (1973). *SCL-90: Administration, scoring, and procedures.* Baltimore, MD: Johns Hopkins University School of Medicine.

Dupertuis, D. G. (1996). *The EQ-i and MMPI-2 profiles of a clinical sample in Argentina.* Unpublished manuscript.

Endler, N. S., & Parker, J.D.A. (1990). *Coping Inventory for Stressful Situations (CISS): Manual.* Toronto, Canada: Multi-Health Systems.

Eysenck, H. J., & Eysenck, S.B.G. (1975). *Manual for the Eysenck Personality Questionnaire.* San Diego, CA: EdITS/Educational and Industrial Testing Service.

Flesch, R. (1948). A new readability yardstick. *Journal of Applied Psychology, 32,* 221–233.

Fund, S. (2000). *Examining the contribution of emotional intelligence in occupational performance.* Unpublished manuscript.

Goleman, D. (1995). *Emotional intelligence.* New York: Bantam Books.

Goleman, D. (1998). *Working with emotional intelligence.* New York: Bantam Books.

Guilford, J. P., & Fruchter, B. (1978). *Fundamental statistics in psychology and education* (6th ed.). New York: McGraw-Hill.

Hee-Woo, J. (1998). *Emotional intelligence and cognitive ability as predictors of job performance in the banking sector.* Unpublished master's thesis, Ateneo de Manila University, Philippines.

Henner, T. (1998). *Comparing EQ-i and TMMS scale scores.* Unpublished manuscript.

Jackson, D. N. (1974). *Personality Research Form manual.* Goshen, NY: Research Psychologists Press.

Kobasa, S. C. (1979). Stressful life events, personality and health: An inquiry into hardiness. *Journal of Personality and Social Psychology, 37,* 1–11.

Kobasa, S. C. (1982). Commitment and coping in stress resistance among lawyers. *Journal of Personality and Social Psychology, 42,* 707–717.

Luria, O. (1999). *Comparing the emotional intelligence of asthmatics with a non-clinical sample.* Unpublished manuscript.

MacLeod, C. M. (1991). Half a century of research on the Stroop effect: An integrative review. *Psychological Bulletin, 109,* 163–203.

Marin, G., Sabogal, F., Marin, B., Otero-Sabogal, R., & Perez-Stable, E. (1987). The development of a Short Acculturation Scale for Hispanics. *Hispanic Journal of Behavioral Sciences, 9*(2), 183–205.

Mayer, J. D., Caruso, D., & Salovey, P. (forthcoming-a). *Mayer-Salovey-Caruso Emotional Intelligence Test (MSCEIT)*. Toronto, Canada: Multi-Health Systems.

Mayer J. D., Caruso, D., & Salovey, P. (forthcoming-b). *MSCEIT technical manual.* Toronto, Canada: Multi-Health Systems.

Møller, C. (1992). *Employeeship.* Hillerød, Denmark: TMI Publishing.

Møller, C., & Bar-On, R. (2000). *Heart work.* Hillerød, Denmark: TMI Publishing.

Morey, L. C. (1991). *The Personality Assessment Inventory professional manual.* Odessa, FL: Psychological Assessment Resources.

Naglieri, J. A., & Bardos, A. N. (1997). *General Ability Measure for Adults (GAMA).* Tucson, AZ: National Computer Systems.

Pallazza, R., & Bar-On, R. (1995). *A study of the emotional intelligence of convicted criminals.* Unpublished manuscript.

Parker, J. D. A. (1999). *An emotional Stroop task examination of the EQ-i.* Unpublished manuscript.

Parker, J. D. A., Taylor, G. J., & Bagby, R. M. (forthcoming). The relationship between emotional intelligence and alexithymia. *Journal of Personality and Individual Differences.*

Plake, B. S., & Impara, J. C. (Eds.). (1999). *Supplement to the thirteenth mental measurement yearbook.* Lincoln, NE: Buros Institute for Mental Measurement.

Salovey, P., Mayer, J. D., Goldman, S. L., Turvey, C., & Palfai, T. P. (1995). Emotional attention, clarity, and repair: Exploring emotional intelligence using the Trait Meta Mood Scale. In J. Pennebaker (Ed.), *Emotion, disclosure, and health* (pp. 125–154). New York: Bantam Books.

Seligman, M.E.P., Abramson, L. Y., Semmel, A., & von Baeyer, C. (1979). Depressive attributional style. *Journal of Abnormal Psychology, 88,* 242–247.

Shostrom, E. L. (1964). An inventory for the measurement of self-actualization. *Educational and Psychological Measurement, 24*(2), 207–218.

Suzuki, L. A., & Valencia, R. R. (1997). Race-ethnicity and measured intelligence. *American Psychologist, 52*(10), 1103–1114.

Thorndike, E. L. (1920). Intelligence and its uses. *Harper's Magazine, 140,* 227–235.

Wechsler, D. (1940). Nonintellective factors in general intelligence. *Psychological Bulletin, 37,* 444–445.

Wechsler, D. (1943). Nonintellective factors in general intelligence. *Journal of Abnormal Social Psychology, 38,* 100–104.

Wechsler, D. (1958). *The measurement and appraisal of adult intelligence* (4th ed.). Baltimore, MD: Williams & Wilkins.

Zung, W.W.K. (1965). A self-rating depression scale. *Archives of General Psychiatry, 12,* 63–70.

PART FOUR

PREVENTION STRATEGIES AND INTERVENTIONS

Criteria for Evaluating the Quality of School-Based Social and Emotional Learning Programs

Patricia A. Graczyk, Roger P. Weissberg, John W. Payton,
Maurice J. Elias, Mark T. Greenberg, and Joseph E. Zins

Educators and policy makers are becoming increasingly aware of the importance of providing all students with educational opportunities that enhance
their emotional development and social competence. Effective efforts to
address students' social and emotional needs can promote academic performance
and citizenship, and decrease the likelihood that students will engage in maladaptive and risky behaviors such as violence, substance use, and early and
unprotected sexual activities. Schools are a critical setting in which programmatic
competence-enhancing and preventative efforts could and should occur. Schools
have extended and intensive accessibility to the majority of children and can
facilitate ample opportunities for students to develop, practice, and receive recognition for emotionally appropriate and socially competent behaviors both within
and beyond the classroom setting (Consortium on the School-Based Promotion
of Social Competence, 1994; Weissberg, Caplan, & Sivo, 1989; Weissberg &
Greenberg, 1998). Yet, school-based programs addressing these competencies
can vary significantly in quality, scope, and effectiveness. Given the myriad of
programs currently available, how do educators select and effectively implement
quality programs that meet the needs of their students?

Note: The authors wish to acknowledge support for CASEL provided by the United States Department of Education, the Surdna Foundation, the Joseph P. Kennedy, Jr., Foundation, and the Fet-
zer Institute. The work of the first author has been supported, in part, by a postdoctoral
fellowship from the National Institute of Mental Health in Urban Children's Mental Health and
HIV/AIDS Prevention, #1-T32-MH19933).

To answer this question, we begin our discussion with background information about the current status of our youth as it relates to health-compromising and risk-taking behaviors; this serves to underscore the necessity of systematic and comprehensive school-based efforts to promote students' social and emotional learning (SEL) within the standard educational program. Then we discuss two conceptually different yet compatible prevention paradigms that, taken together, provide a solid conceptual foundation for school-based universal prevention programs (programs appropriate for *all* students) (Institute of Medicine, 1994), which forms the major focus of this chapter. A conceptual framework that elucidates critical elements in the design of quality school-based programs that promote social and emotional competence in our youth is presented within the context of recent efforts by the Collaborative to Advance Social and Emotional Learning (CASEL) to identify such programs. These critical elements are guided by both theory and sound educational practices and include (1) the promotion of effective teaching strategies, (2) both student- and environment-oriented interventions, (3) successful implementation of the program, and (4) care in planning and conducting ongoing and summative (outcome or product) evaluations. We further discuss how critical design features that contribute to successful implementation and institutionalization of programs also facilitate successful outcomes for students. The chapter concludes with a discussion of critical issues that need to be addressed more fully in the future relative to curriculum design, evaluation, implementation, and institutionalization.

CURRENT STATUS OF OUR YOUTH

Prevalence of Problematic Behaviors

Many of today's young people are engaging in behaviors that increase the likelihood they will personally experience poor health, social, academic, and emotional outcomes and consequently will have a negative impact on society. Information from the Youth Risk Behavior Surveillance System (YRBSS) survey conducted in 1997 by the United States Centers for Disease Control and Prevention (1998) and reviews of recent epidemiological findings (Dryfoos, 1997; Sells & Blum, 1996) illustrate some of these outcomes.

Aggressive behavior and the possession of weapons are prevalent among American high school students. According to YRBSS results, more than one-third of teens reported they had been in a physical fight within the preceding year, and approximately one-fifth indicated they had carried a weapon. Rates of drug use and early sexual activity are even higher. Slightly more than half of the adolescents surveyed reported they had consumed alcohol in the previous month, 33.4 percent had engaged in binge drinking, and 47.1 percent had used marijuana. Nearly one-half also described themselves as sexually active, and of these, 43.2 percent had not used a condom when they last had sexual intercourse. With respect to academic performance, Dryfoos's (1997) review found that by the time students reached the tenth grade, approximately 25 percent have been retained, and approximately 12 percent eventually drop out of school.

Many young people also fear for their personal safety and are at serious risk for suicide. One in twenty-five respondents to the YRBSS survey indicated that he or she stayed home from school at least one day of the previous month because of feeling unsafe either at school or traveling to and from school. Moreover, far too many young people contemplate, attempt, and commit suicide. According to YRBSS results, approximately 20 percent of high school students indicated they had seriously contemplated suicide, and 7.7 percent had made at least one suicide attempt in the preceding year. Homicide and suicide follow unintentional injuries as the second and third leading causes of death, respectively, for young Americans ages fifteen to twenty-four (United States Centers for Disease Control and Prevention, 1999).

Co-Occurrence of Problematic Behaviors

Health-compromising and risk-taking behaviors seldom occur in isolation (Dryfoos, 1997; Jessor, 1993). Rather, they tend to occur in what Dryfoos (1997) referred to as "packages," or clusters, of maladaptive behaviors. For example, of the 28 percent of high school students who engaged in antisocial behavior, many reported that they had been sexually active (72 percent), consumed alcohol (54 percent), smoked cigarettes (37 percent), and been depressed or contemplated suicide (34 percent). As would be expected, the higher the number of co-occurring problem behaviors present, the greater the likelihood an individual will experience poor adjustment outcomes. Unfortunately, more young people today are displaying packages of multiple risky behaviors than was the case in the 1980s (Dryfoos, 1997). Accordingly, Dryfoos concluded with this sobering note: 30 percent of fourteen- to seventeen-year-olds engage in multiple risky behaviors and are consequently at "high risk" for negative outcomes; 35 percent engage in one or two risky behaviors and are at "medium risk"; and 35 percent are currently at "low risk" or "no risk" for future adjustment difficulties. Thus, 65 percent of today's young people are at medium to high risk of experiencing maladaptive outcomes. In addition, the healthy status of the 35 percent who are currently "safe" could be compromised if their families, communities, or schools fail to continue to foster their healthy development.

The preceding discussion provides compelling evidence of the need for action to prevent our young people from experiencing poor outcomes. Although preventing negative outcomes is a critical goal in itself, "building wellness from the start, and promoting conditions that maintain and enhance it, is a promising strategy in its own right" (Cowen, 1998, p. 455). In fact, there is evidence to suggest that the more competent and supported adolescents feel, the less likely they are to engage in risk-taking behaviors and the more likely they are to maintain good health, be successful in school, care about themselves and others, and overcome adversity (Scales & Leffert, 1999). In concert, these findings underscore the importance of providing young people with opportunities to learn, practice, and receive recognition for displaying positive attitudes and values as well as health-enhancing and emotionally and socially competent behaviors. A natural forum for the provision of such opportunities exists within the context of students' school experiences. In the next section, a conceptual framework based on a review of the prevention and wellness enhancement literature is presented that is relevant to school-based prevention efforts and, ultimately, leads to identification of the key elements and design features practitioners should look for when considering programs for their schools.

RISK AND PROTECTIVE FACTORS PARADIGM

Over the past thirty years prevention scholars have expended considerable attention on the task of identifying risk factors (such as those that place individual children at risk for a variety of maladaptive outcomes). More recently preventionists have also focused their efforts on identifying protective factors (such as those that enhance an individual's resistance to risk factors and maladjustment). Three major findings from this line of research are noteworthy: (1) Rarely does a specific risk factor apply to only one form of maladjustment. Instead, multiple forms of maladjustment are typically associated with the same risk factor. This fact may in part explain the high rates at which health-compromising and risk-taking behaviors co-occur. (2) Any form of maladjustment is typically associated with multiple risk factors. (3) A common set of protective factors also appears related to the mitigation of multiple forms of maladjustment.

Common Risk Factors

A variety of maladaptive patterns of behavior share a set of risk factors (Coie et al., 1993; Dryfoos, 1997; Durlak, 1998) that are frequently targeted in school-based prevention programs focused on a single negative outcome (for example, violence, drug abuse, suicide, or HIV/AIDS). These generic risk factors are grouped here according to the five levels of analysis used by Durlak (1998): individual, family, peer group, school, and community.

Common risk factors related to the individual child include constitutional (for example, physical or genetic) handicaps, delays in skill development, emotional difficulties, and early onset of problematic behaviors. Family risk factors include parental psychopathology, marital tension, conflict among family members, disorganization in family structure, low social or economic status, large family size, high mobility, insecure attachment to parents, inadequate supervision, and harsh or inconsistent parenting. Problematic peer interactions leading to multiple poor outcomes include peer rejection, negative peer pressure, and negative peer modeling. At the school level, risk factors include attending ineffective schools, academic failure, and disaffection. Characteristics of communities that place young people at risk include disorganization, gang activity, accessibility to firearms, high levels of unemployment, and limited available resources.

Common Protective Factors

In comparison to risk factors, less is known about factors that facilitate a child's ability to cope with stress and achieve positive outcomes. Nonetheless, the information currently available suggests that there are two categories of protective factors: those pertaining to personal characteristics of the child and those pertaining to positive features of the child's environment (Coie et al., 1993; Doll & Lyon, 1998; Dryfoos, 1997; Durlak, 1998). Personal attributes of the child that serve as protective factors include social and emotional competencies such as strong interpersonal skills, a pleasant disposition, good problem-solving abilities, self-efficacy, a positive sense of self, effective communication skills, and high aspirations. Environmental factors that provide a supportive context and nurture the social and emotional development of children include a strong bond to at least one caring adult, adequate parenting, involvement in constructive organizations or activities, and access to good schools.

The identification of common risk and protective factors has important implications for effective prevention and competence-promotion efforts. These implications include the following: (1) A common framework for effective prevention and competence-promotion programs should focus on decreasing risk factors and increasing protective factors. (2) By targeting generic risk and protective factors, a single program could impact multiple outcomes. Accordingly, an efficient approach to school-based prevention or competence-promotion programming should target multiple adjustment outcomes rather than limit its scope to one category of problematic behavior (for example, violence prevention). (3) Effective prevention and competence-promotion programs should include interventions focused not only on the individual child, but also on the multiple contexts (such as family, peer group, school, and community) in which the child lives. (4) Social and emotional competencies are protective factors for a variety of adjustment outcomes, and their development should be targeted in comprehensive programmatic efforts.

COMPETENCE ENHANCEMENT PARADIGM

The competence enhancement perspective assumes that *all* children and adolescents can improve their well-being by becoming more responsible decision makers and problem solvers who can cope more effectively with life's daily challenges and stressful life events (Durlak & Wells, 1997). The compatibility of strategies and goals from a competence enhancement perspective with those of a more traditional "risk and protective factors" perspective can be seen in five strategies proposed by Cowen (1998) to advance wellness enhancement goals. These strategies include (1) encouraging the development of positive bonding between a child and primary caregiver, (2) helping children attain stage-salient developmental proficiencies (for example, making friends, communicating effectively), (3) teaching children how to cope with stressors, (4) helping children feel they are in control of their destinies, and (5) providing them with wellness-enhancing environments, such as effective schools. According to the classification system endorsed by the Institute of Medicine (1994), the competence enhancement perspective can most readily be viewed as a universal prevention approach (Weissberg & Greenberg, 1998) in that it pertains to all children and youth and is not limited to those students who are at risk or are already displaying early signs of maladaptive behavior.

Together the risk and protective factor paradigm and the competence-enhancement paradigm provide valuable guidance for the design of effective school-based programs that promote positive youth development. First, both perspectives suggest that school-based programs should provide students with the necessary tools to develop personal competencies in the cognitive, affective, and behavioral domains that in turn allow them to grow in a healthy manner and cope effectively with stress and negative influences. However, intervention strategies that focus solely on the individual child are not sufficient. Instead, as many scholars have argued, effective programming must consider the multiple contexts in which children live as appropriate and indeed necessary targets of intervention efforts (Bronfenbrenner, 1977; Scales & Leffert, 1999; Weissberg & Greenberg, 1998). Families, communities, peers, and schools all serve as settings that can facilitate or impede students' achievements in life by either providing or limiting their opportunities to develop the competencies they need to engage in constructive activities and receive recognition for such efforts (Hawkins, 1997). In addition, effective prevention programs should target multiple goals, rather than single categories of health-compromising or risky behaviors (Dryfoos, 1990; Durlak, 1998; Perry, 1999). Prevention and competence-promotion programs with these features require not only a multifaceted and comprehensive package of intervention strategies to accomplish their goals, but also a unifying framework to maintain the cohesiveness of the overall intervention. We contend that SEL can serve as that unifying framework.

SEL AS THE UNIFYING FRAMEWORK

Whether a school is focusing on the prevention of specific adjustment problems or risk-taking behaviors or the promotion of overall competence in their students, SEL is the key to effective school programming. SEL can serve as the framework for all prevention and wellness enhancement objectives because SEL focuses on promoting specific social and coping skills as well as providing the necessary environmental supports that are conducive to both prevention and wellness efforts.

Specifically, SEL is the process by which children and adults gain the ability to recognize and manage their emotions, make responsible decisions, establish positive relationships with others, and become healthy and productive individuals (Elias, Zins, et al., 1997). Social and emotional education (SEE) involves teaching a core group of cognitive, affective, and behavioral life competencies that promote positive development in children. SEE optimally occurs within safe and supportive environments and is facilitated through a process of modeling, observation, practice, constructive reinforcement, and guidance. SEE provides children with both the tools and opportunities to use their competencies to achieve a range of positive social and health outcomes such as effective interpersonal relationships, academic and career development, responsible citizenship, and emotional and physical well-being. To achieve these outcomes requires a child to become socially and emotionally competent, that is, to have the ability to understand, manage, and express the social and emotional aspects of his or her life in constructive ways, and to adapt to the complex demands of growth and development (Elias, Zins, et al., 1997). Indeed, there is a growing consensus of opinion that addressing a child's social and emotional "intelligences" is an essential ingredient to a happy and productive life (Gardner, 1993; Goleman, 1995; Mayer & Salovey, 1997; Sternberg, 1996).

Social and emotional competence is both complex and multifaceted. It is complex in that it involves the adaptive integration of emotions, cognitions, and behaviors to address critical developmental issues, transitions, and stressors at different points in life. Social and emotional competence is multifaceted in that it encompasses multiple domains of functioning (intrapersonal, interpersonal, academic) within multiple contexts (home, school, peer group, community). Consequently, fostering social and emotional competence requires intervention strategies targeted toward individual children themselves, the significant people in their lives, and the multiple contexts in which they live.

Thus, quality school-based programs that promote SEL can serve to integrate a variety of prevention and health-promotion efforts conducted by school personnel. Yet, how do school personnel identify "quality" school-based programs that promote SEL? The answer to this question has been the focus of a major initiative of CASEL. Both CASEL and its SEL Program Review initiative are the topics of the following sections.

CASEL AND THE SEL PROGRAM REVIEW

Overview of CASEL

CASEL was founded in 1994 and is a leading national and international organization committed to identifying the best educational practices to maximize children's healthy social and emotional development, academic achievement, ethical behavior, and citizenship. It is composed of a network of educators, scientists, policy makers, and concerned citizens that seeks to attain the following primary goals through research, scholarship, and advocacy: (1) advance the science of SEL, (2) translate scientific knowledge into effective school practices, (3) disseminate information about scientifically sound SEL educational strategies and practices, (4) enhance training so that educators effectively implement high-quality SEL programs, and (5) network and collaborate with scientists, educators, advocates, policy makers, and interested citizens to increase coordination of SEL efforts.

SEL Program Review

One of the most important ways for CASEL to achieve its goals is to develop a clear framework for evaluating SEL programs so that educators, program developers, scientists, policy makers, and the general public are more aware of the critical elements that should serve as standards for successful SEL programming. Such a framework can also provide assistance to educators who care and are inundated with a variety of programs and mandates to make informed decisions in selecting and implementing SEL programs. Having a common framework can facilitate schools' efforts to integrate and streamline interventions addressing multiple student needs and mandates (Elias, Zins, et al., 1997).

We believe this work can be done best through an effective program that is multiyear in duration, targets multiple outcomes (for example, health, citizenship, violence prevention, drug education), includes a classroom-based component conducted by well-trained teachers, is implemented with integrity, and involves coordinated efforts among schools, families, and communities. For schools with a single-outcome approach (such as violence prevention) to their prevention efforts, staff may want to look at the degree to which their current programs include these design features and where their programs need to be enhanced.

DESIGN FEATURES OF QUALITY SEL PROGRAMS

Four primary categories of design features can be used to distinguish quality SEL programs. These categories are (1) classroom curriculum features; (2) coordinated efforts involving entire schools, families, and the community; (3) evaluation and monitoring; and (4) training and other implementation supports. Within each category we have identified key elements necessary for successful SEL programming. These elements were distilled from a review of the scientific literature as well as interviews with fourteen experts in the field. A description of each category and its key elements follows. For illustration purposes, examples are provided from currently available programs.

Curriculum Features

Quality SEL programs have a strong theoretical framework that provides a clear rationale for program objectives and methods for achieving them. Several theories have made positive contributions to SEL program design. These theories include social learning theory (Bandura, 1977), the social development model (Hawkins, 1997; Hawkins & Weis, 1985), the ecological systems model (Bronfenbrenner, 1977), problem behavior theory (Jessor & Jessor, 1977), and the theory of reasoned action (Fishbein & Ajzen, 1975). Theoretical models can also serve as guides in identifying key SEL competencies, understanding the processes and factors involved in developing effective intervention strategies, and designing appropriate evaluation procedures. For example, social learning theory emphasizes the role of models in the learning process. Programs based on social learning theory typically include modeling as an instructional strategy and emphasize the ways in which various role models such as peers, media figures, teachers, and parents can influence young people's attitudes, beliefs, values, and behaviors.

Quality SEL programs include a focus on critical cognitive, affective, and behavioral competencies that can be grouped into five major categories: (1) awareness of self and others, (2) positive attitudes and values, (3) responsible decision making, (4) communication skills, and (5) social skills (Payton et al., forthcoming). Table 18.1 includes definitions for the SEL competencies within each category. Awareness of self and others includes awareness and management of one's feelings, perspective taking skills, and social norm analysis. However, awareness is insufficient to motivate young people to act in prosocial ways. Thus, the next category of competencies, positive attitudes and values, covers adaptive self-perceptions, responsibility, caring, and respect for others. Taken together, the first two categories lay the groundwork for the third category, responsible decision making, which includes the capacity to identify problems, set adaptive goals, and engage in constructive problem solving. The final two categories include skills needed to implement effective solutions to problems and engage others in positive and productive interactions. Communication skills include the ability to attend to and express both verbal and nonverbal messages accurately. Key social skills include cooperation, negotiation, refusal skills, and effective help-seeking behavior.

The identification of critical SEL competencies represents the first step in the process of facilitating students' social and emotional development. However, the way competencies are taught is also very important because students need to be motivated to learn about and to use the competencies in their everyday lives. Thus, quality SEL programs employ effective teaching strategies. These

Table 18.1. Key SEL Competencies by Category.

I. Awareness of Self and Others

1. *Awareness of feelings*: The capacity to accurately perceive and label one's feelings
2. *Management of feelings*: The capacity to regulate one's feelings
3. *Perspective taking*: The capacity to accurately perceive the perspectives of others
4. *Social norm analysis*: The capacity to critically evaluate social, cultural, and media messages pertaining to social norms and personal behavior

II. Positive Attitudes and Values

5. *Constructive sense of self*: Feeling optimistic and empowered in handling everyday challenges
6. *Responsibility*: The intention to engage in safe, healthy, and ethical behaviors
7. *Caring*: The intention to be fair, just, charitable, and compassionate
8. *Respect for others*: The intention to accept and appreciate individual and group differences and value the rights of all people

III. Responsible Decision Making

9. *Problem identification*: The capacity to identify situations that require a solution or decision and assess risks, barriers, and resources
10. *Adaptive goal setting*: The capacity to set positive and realistic goals
11. *Problem solving*: The capacity to develop positive and informed solutions to problems

IV. Communication Skills

12. *Receptive communication*: The capacity to attend to others both verbally and nonverbally to receive messages accurately
13. *Expressive communication:* The capacity to initiate and maintain conversations, express one's thoughts and feelings clearly both verbally and nonverbally, and demonstrate to other speakers that they have been understood

V. Social Skills

14. *Cooperation*: The capacity to take turns and share within both dyadic and group situations
15. *Negotiation*: The capacity to resolve conflict peacefully, considering the perspectives and feelings of others
16. *Refusal*: The capacity to make and follow through with clear "no" statements, to avoid situations in which one might be pressured, and to delay acting in pressure situations until adequately prepared
17. *Help seeking*: The capacity to identify the need for support and assistance and to access available and appropriate resources

strategies include modeling the targeted skill, presenting it in manageable parts to insure mastery, and providing students with ample opportunities to practice the newly acquired skill and receive feedback and reinforcement (Hawkins, 1997). In addition, quality programs provide students with instruction that systematically builds on previously learned material and lays the foundation for future learning.

Quality SEL programs view students as active learners and employ interactive teaching strategies. They utilize techniques such as group work, discussions, cooperative learning, and role plays, (Dusenbury, Falco, Lake, Brannigan, & Bosworth, 1997), as well as dialoguing, guided practice, and both teacher and peer reinforcement. Unlike traditional didactic approaches such as lectures, interactive strategies require students to be actively engaged with both teachers and peers as part of the learning process. A typical lesson involving interactive teaching strategies often includes the following sequence. The targeted skill is modeled by the teacher during the initial phases of instruction and then modeled again by peers in role plays. Through their own active participation in role plays that are constructed to be similar to real life, student actors are provided opportunities to practice the new skill. Immediately following the role play, actors are provided feedback from both teachers and peers to reinforce their performance of the skill and to guide them toward proficiency. They are then encouraged to practice the skill in real-life situations that arise.

Once a lesson is over, students do not automatically apply newly acquired competencies to other situations and settings. Consequently, to promote generalization, quality SEL programs are designed to provide ample opportunities for students to practice competencies both within and outside the classroom. Within the classroom, teachers may use dialoguing as a means of facilitating generalization. Through dialoguing a teacher can encourage students to reflect on a situation, become aware of their immediate feelings about it, and generate strategies they can then use to successfully resolve the issue at hand. Dialoguing can be used when a student is facing a situation that is an appropriate context in which to apply learned SEL competencies. Opportunities for dialoguing are not limited to the classroom, however. Many of the most meaningful interpersonal opportunities occur in less-structured settings such as hallways, playgrounds, or in the lunchroom. Homework assignments can also facilitate generalization when they offer explicit guidance to students about ways to apply skills to other settings such as their home or peer group. For example, in addition to dialoguing and homework as generalization strategies, the Promoting Alternative Thinking Strategies (PATHS) curriculum includes strategies to facilitate generalization across settings, individuals, academic subjects, and time (Kusche & Greeenberg, 1994).

Coordination with Schools, Families, and Community

For school personnel to determine whether they have a good SEL program, they need to consider how the program is connected with the multiple contexts in which students live. SEL programs are typically classroom based and facilitated by teachers. To be effective, programs need to connect with what is going on in the larger school context, in families, and in the community, because adults and peers in the school, family, and community can influence students' health-enhancing values and behaviors in several ways. First, adults and peers can serve as models of health-enhancing values and behaviors. In addition, they can convey norms and expectations that encourage students to adopt these values and behaviors. Finally adults and peers can provide support and opportunities for students to engage in health-enhancing behaviors (Perry, 1999). In other words, family members, peers, teachers, and other community members can all serve to either promote or impede a young person's adjustment. Thus, to promote positive outcomes for students, quality SEL programs coordinate classroom-based and teacher-directed interventions with interventions involving a broader range of contexts and individuals.

Examples of schoolwide interventions include the infusion of program lessons into other subject areas, schoolwide initiatives that encourage prosocial behavior such as showing respect for others, and the development of a positive school climate. Programmatic efforts to support school-family partnerships encourage parents to be supportive and involved in their children's education both at home and at school. They include parent participation in program selection and implementation efforts, parent newsletters, parent informational meetings, and linking classroom-based SEL lessons to family activities. School-community partnerships can be nurtured by coordinating school and community efforts to achieve common goals in promoting students' healthy development. For example, Project Northland is a drug abuse prevention program for students in grades six through eight that has a community component that involves the formation of a committee consisting of parents, school personnel, and community leaders to address community-level factors that contribute to community norms and standards regarding teen drinking (Perry, Williams, Forster, & Wolfson, 1993). It also includes a family component that is most prominent at grade six and a peer leadership component that is an integral part of the program at all grade levels.

Evaluation and Monitoring

When schools are considering the adoption of a program, they should be concerned about implementing the program accurately and successfully. Good programs provide guidance to schools about ways of doing this. Depending on the purpose, program evaluations can take multiple forms and occur at multiple points in time. Several major reviews of categorical school-based prevention programs (see, for example, Center for the Study and Prevention of Violence, 1998) and federal mandates have underscored the importance of empirical validation of program effectiveness through the posttreatment measurement of student outcomes. However, other facets of school-based SEL programs should be evaluated in order to (1) determine the program's fit with the target student population and the multiple contexts in which students live, (2) insure the program is implemented with integrity, and (3) increase the likelihood that positive student outcomes will be sustained.

In general education, Stufflebeam's (Stufflebeam & Shrinkfield, 1985) conceptual framework of evaluation has been widely used, and we propose that this model, frequently referred to as the CIPP model of evaluation, also holds relevance in guiding evaluation efforts for SEL programs. According to the CIPP model, evaluation efforts should include four major components: (1) context evaluations, (2) input evaluations, (3) process evaluations, and (4) product evaluations.

Context and input evaluations occur prior to program implementation and are predicated on the belief that planning decisions made prior to program implementation can have a significant effect on the success of the program. Context evaluations include an accurate assessment of the student population and its needs as well as a subsequent determination of the program's capability to address the needs of the targeted group of students. Such information is often obtained from student records. New information can also be obtained through other means such as student surveys, focus groups, and interviews (Perry, 1999). Without such information, it is difficult to assess the likely fit between what a program offers and what students need. School structure and resources are the issues addressed in input evaluations. Input evaluations encourage schools to analyze their infrastructure to determine if it is sufficient to handle programmatic needs. At this stage, analyses consider such factors as available and needed personnel and material resources, budgeting issues, and feasibility.

Process evaluations occur while a program is being implemented. The purposes of process evaluations include (1) monitoring the implementation process and the degree to which the program is being implemented as designed, (2) identifying and addressing problems in implementation so that integrity of implementation can occur or be reinstated, and (3) documenting the implementation process so that such information can be used in interpreting outcomes. Process evaluations need to occur in a systematic fashion so that accurate decisions can be made to either continue a program, revise the ways in which it is being implemented, or if necessary, abandon implementation efforts altogether (Elias, Gager, & Leon, 1997).

Finally, product evaluations are completed at the conclusion of a program and are intended to determine the extent to which students have attained particular outcomes. Also referred to as summative or outcome evaluations (Armstrong, 1989), product evaluations typically include the administration of the same student measures just prior to program implementation (preintervention), immediately following program implementation (postintervention), and at some follow-up point later in time. Product evaluations are conducted to (1) measure both short-term and long-term changes in student outcomes as a result of the intervention, (2) relate student outcomes to program objectives and design, and (3) determine the overall merit of the program for the targeted student population. When product evaluations are coupled with other forms of evaluation proposed by the CIPP model, potential threats to the attainment of positive student outcomes can be avoided at times. In addition, information accrued through other evaluation procedures may facilitate interpretation of outcome measures with greater clarity. For example, if a well-designed program is not implemented with integrity (for example, insufficient time is allotted for the program, or teachers lack the necessary skills to provide effective teaching to students), disappointing student outcomes may be a by-product of the implementation process rather than the program itself (Weissberg, Caplan, & Harwood, 1991). On the other hand, information gathered during the input evaluation stage can lead to planning that includes sufficient time for the program to be presented during the school year, and adequate teacher training and ongoing consultation. Such planning insures that the program is implemented as intended, which in turn can increase the likelihood that students will experience sustained positive outcomes. Consequently, programs should provide schools with the necessary resources to facilitate successful implementation. These resources are discussed in the following section.

Implementation Supports

For a program to be implemented successfully, good manuals and sufficient training opportunities for school personnel are necessary. Implementation supports can take multiple forms and may vary from one program to another. However, all programs should include provisions for the following: (1) user-friendly teacher manuals in which lessons are presented in a clear and logical sequence, (2) preimplementation training of implementers (for example, teachers, peer leaders), (3) on-going supervision and coaching of school personnel while the program is being implemented, and (4) adaptability of the program to the ecology of the school setting (Weissberg et al., 1989; Weissberg & Greenberg, 1998).

Teacher manuals are probably the single resource most widely used by teachers who are implementing SEL and other instructional programs. Consequently, the content and design of teaching manuals may have a significant impact on the quality of program delivery. Teacher manuals can be most conducive to implementation efforts when they include a comprehensive scope and sequence chart, provide the theoretical rationale for the program and explain its connection to lesson content and teaching strategies, clearly state the objectives of the program, and include detailed and well-organized lesson plans. As an example, lesson plans for the Teenage Health Teaching Modules (Education Development Center, 1991) include teacher background information, a statement of purpose, lesson agenda, objectives, listing of preparatory materials and readings, carefully delineated procedures, suggested way to conclude the lesson, and a homework assignment. Without quality teacher manuals, the day-to-day instructional aspects of a program can suffer significantly.

To some extent the amount of training required for successful implementation of an SEL program will vary according to the administrative and teaching staff's experience with similar types of programs and with the comprehensiveness of the program. The more knowledge administrators and teachers have of the theoretical underpinnings of a program, and the types of competencies and learning opportunities it employs, the less additional training may be warranted (Consortium on the School-Based Promotion of Social Competence, 1992). However, in general, three to five days of preimplementation training may be necessary for successful implementation of quality programs (Consortium on the School-Based Promotion of Social Competence, 1992). Once the program is initiated, ongoing consultation and monitoring of program integrity can be done in various ways. Program developers may either provide their own staff to furnish ongoing support to school personnel or offer a "training of trainers" model of support in which developers train a limited number of key school personnel who in turn train their colleagues who serve as program implementers. Having teachers within the same school or school district serve as peer coaches may be more effective than using outside trainers because local teachers are more sensitized to indigenous ecological issues of relevance to successful implementation for a particular school. Training should include effective teaching strategies and follow a sequence whereby trainees receive clear demonstrations of targeted skills, have their progress carefully monitored, and receive consistent support and reinforcement for their efforts to apply newly acquired skills (Durlak, 1995).

Program effectiveness can be impacted by both classroom-level and broader ecological factors that affect its implementation. At the classroom level, the way a particular teacher presents the program and general discipline problems present can influence student motivation and the degree to which the program is implemented as intended (Weissberg et al., 1989). Broader ecological issues that may impact the implementation of a new program include administrative support, the number of mandated categorical prevention programs already scheduled as part of the school day, perceived parental and community support for the program, and whether the program is being implemented in an elementary or secondary setting. Implementation is a crucial contributory factor to the success of a program in any school or classroom setting, and every effort should be made to insure its integrity.

CONCLUSION

There is a growing consensus from a number of different groups that suggests efforts to improve children's social and emotional development are critical in achieving a multitude of positive developmental outcomes (Gardner, 1993; Goleman, 1995; Mayer & Salovey, 1997; Scales & Leffert, 1999; Sternberg, 1996). Such thinking is helping to fuel a paradigm shift away from the traditional conceptualization of education in general and the mission of schools in particular.

Schools as institutions will always be charged with the responsibility of educating our young people in the basic skills of reading, writing, and mathematics. SEL programs will have greater staying power when they facilitate the mission of the school and conform to current school practices and structures. Indeed, there is growing evidence to suggest that well-designed, effectively implemented, comprehensive SEL programs can influence children's ability to stay focused on their studies, achieve better cognitive and learning skills, and remain in school (Elias, Zins, et al., 1997; Hawkins, 1997). In addition to enhancing academic performance, the mission of schools also involves preparing young people to be successful in the multitude of roles they currently face and those that await them in their future. With this charge, schools need to broaden their scope of efforts to include systematically helping young people develop personal attitudes, values, and interpersonal competencies that can serve as a foundation for their roles as students and workers, and also as classmates, friends, siblings, team players, community members, neighbors, spouses, and parents. SEL programs can assist schools in helping students acquire the competencies to be successful in these multiple roles. Therefore, it is of utmost importance that schools select the best possible programs and implement them with integrity.

The main purpose of this chapter has been to emphasize the most important criteria for SEL programs that schools can adopt and institutionalize as part of their standard curriculum. These criteria include an emphasis on basic SEL competencies; a clear rationale; effective teaching strategies; means to promote generalization; coordination of classroom-based instruction with schools, families, and communities; implementation supports; and tools for evaluation and monitoring.

As a school adopts an SEL program, it is also important to determine how to assimilate the program within the broader school context. Universal prevention programs should be coordinated with other school-based support systems including special education, health services, and mental health service providers such as school psychologists, social workers, and counselors. Together, these programs and personnel can provide an integrated network of services to meet the varying needs of individual students within the school. Therefore, programs should be evaluated on the extent to which they provide guidance about how to integrate them within the fabric of other school programs and reform initiatives.

In closing, we encourage school practitioners to familiarize themselves with the wealth of information currently available from a variety of sources that can facilitate their efforts to select and successfully implement effective SEL programs. Of particular note is the fact that excellent information can be obtained from Internet Web sites of such organizations as the United States Department of Education (www.ed.gov), where exemplary programs are identified through their Safe, Disciplined, and Drug-Free School Initiative; the Center for the Study and Prevention of Violence (www.colorado.edu/cspv/blueprints), where there is information on effective violence prevention programs identified through their Blueprints initiative; and CASEL (www.casel.org), where there is updated information about the SEL Program Review initiative and other helpful resources. Such information can help schools provide students with the competencies and opportunities to become knowledgeable, responsible, and caring members of their families, peer groups, schools, communities, and society at large.

NOTES

Correspondence concerning this chapter should be addressed to Patricia A. Graczyk, Department of Psychology (MC 285), University of Illinois at Chicago, 1007 W. Harrison St., Chicago, IL 60607–7137; e-mail: pgraczyk@uic.edu.

References

Armstrong, D. G. (1989). *Developing and documenting the curriculum.* Needham Heights, MA: Allyn and Bacon.

Bandura, A. (1977). *Social learning theory.* Englewood Cliffs, NJ: Prentice Hall.

Bronfenbrenner, U. (1977). Toward an experimental ecology of human development. *American Psychologist, 32,* 513–531.

Center for the Study and Prevention of Violence. (1998). *Blueprints for violence prevention* [On-line]. Available: http://www.colorado.edu/cspv/blueprints.

Coie, J. D., Watt, N. F., West, S. G., Hawkins, J. D., Asarnow, J. R., Markman, H. J., Ramey, S. L., Shure, M. B., & Long, B. (1993). The science of prevention: A conceptual framework and some directions for a national research program. *American Psychologist, 48,* 1013–1022.

Consortium on the School-Based Promotion of Social Competence. (1992). Drug and alcohol prevention curricula. In J. D. Hawkins & R. F. Catalano, Jr. (Eds.), *Communities that care: Action for drug abuse prevention* (pp. 129–148). San Francisco: Jossey-Bass.

Consortium on the School-Based Promotion of Social Competence. (1994). The school-based promotion of social competence: Theory, research, practice, and policy. In R. J. Haggerty, L. R. Sherrod, N. Garmezy, & M. Rutter (Eds.), *Stress, risk, and resilience in children and adolescents: Processes, mechanisms, and interventions* (pp. 268–316). New York: Cambridge University Press.

Cowen, E. L. (1998). Changing concepts of prevention in mental health. *Journal of Mental Health, 7,* 451–461.

Doll, B., & Lyon, M. A. (1998). Risk and resilience: Implications for the delivery of educational and mental health services in schools. *School Psychology Review, 27,* 348–363.

Dryfoos, J. G. (1990). *Adolescents at risk: Prevalence and prevention.* New York: Oxford University Press.

Dryfoos, J. G. (1997). The prevalence of problem behaviors: Implications for programs. In R. P. Weissberg, T. P. Gullotta, R. L. Hampton, B. A. Ryan, & G. R. Adams (Eds.), *Healthy children 2010: Enhancing children's wellness* (pp. 17–46). Thousand Oaks, CA: Sage Publications.

Durlak, J. A. (1995). *School-based prevention programs for children and adolescents.* Thousand Oaks, CA: Sage Publications.

Durlak, J. A. (1998). Common risk and protective factors in successful prevention programs. *American Journal of Orthopsychiatry, 68,* 512–520.

Durlak, J. A., & Wells, A. M. (1997). Primary prevention mental health programs for children and adolescents: A meta-analytic review. *American Journal of Community Psychology, 25,* 115–152.

Dusenbury, L., Falco, M., Lake, A., Brannigan, R., & Bosworth, K. (1997). Nine critical elements of promising violence prevention programs. *Journal of School Health, 67,* 409–414.

Education Development Center. (1991). *Teenage health teaching modules: Strengthening relationships with families and friends.* Newton, MA: Author.

Elias, M. J., Gager, P., & Leon, S. (1997). Spreading a warm blanket of prevention over all children: Guidelines for selecting substance abuse and related prevention curricula for use in the schools. *Journal of Primary Prevention, 18,* 41–69.

Elias, M. J., Zins, J. E., Weissberg, R. P., Frey, K. S., Greenberg, M. T., Haynes, N. M., Kessler, R., Schwab-Stone, M. E., & Shriver, T. (1997). *Promoting social and emotional learning: Guidelines for educators.* Alexandria, VA: Association for Supervision and Curriculum Development.

Fishbein, M., & Ajzen, I. (1975). *Belief, attitude, intention, and behavior: An introduction to theory and research.* Reading, MA: Addison-Wesley.

Gardner, H. (1993). *Multiple intelligences: The theory in practice.* New York: Basic Books.

Goleman, D. (1995). *Emotional intelligence: Why it can matter more than IQ.* New York: Bantam Books.

Hawkins, J. D. (1997). Academic performance and school success: Sources and conse-
quences. In R. P. Weissberg, T. P. Gullotta, R. L. Hampton, B. A. Ryan, & G. R.
Adams (Eds.), *Healthy children 2010: Enhancing children's wellness* (pp. 278–305).
Thousand Oaks, CA: Sage Publications.

Hawkins, J. D., & Weis, J. G. (1985). The social developmental model: An integrated
approach to delinquency prevention. *Journal of Primary Prevention, 6,* 73–97.

Institute of Medicine. (1994). *Reducing risks for mental disorders: Frontiers for preventive intervention research.* Washington, DC: National Academy Press.

Jessor, R. (1993). Successful adolescent development among youth in high-risk settings. *American Psychologist, 48,* 117–126.

Jessor, R., & Jessor, S. L. (1977). *Problem behavior and psychosocial development: A
longitudinal study of youth.* New York: Academic Press.

Kusche, C. A., & Greenberg, M. T. (1994). *Teaching PATHS in your classroom: The
PATHS curriculum instructional manual.* Seattle, WA: Developmental Research &
Programs.

Mayer, J. D., & Salovey, P. (1997). What is Emotional Intelligence? In P. Salovey & D. J.
Sluyter (Eds.), *Emotional development and emotional intelligence: Educational
implications* (pp. 3–31). New York: Basic Books.

Payton, J. W., Wardlaw, D. M., Graczyk, P. A., Bloodworth, M. R., Tompsett, C. J., &
Weissberg, R. P. (forthcoming). Social and emotional learning: A framework for
quality school-based prevention programs. *Journal of School Health.*

Perry, C. L. (1999). *Creating health behavior change: How to develop community-wide
programs for youth.* Thousand Oaks, CA: Sage Publications.

Perry, C. L., Williams, C. L., Forster, J. L., & Wolfson, M. (1993). Background, conceptualization, and design of a community-wide research program on adolescent
alcohol use: Project Northland. *Health Education Research, 8,* 125–136.

Scales, P. C., & Leffert, N. (1999). *Developmental assets: A synthesis of the scientific
research on adolescent development.* Minneapolis, MN: Search Institute.

Sells, C. W., & Blum, W. R. (1996). Current trends in adolescent health. In R. J.
DiClemente, W. B. Hansen, & L. E. Ponton (Eds.), *Handbook of adolescent health
risk behavior* (pp. 5–34). New York: Plenum Press.

Sternberg, R. J. (1996). *Successful intelligence: How practical and creative intelligence
determine success in life.* New York: Plume.

Stufflebeam, D. L., & Shinkfield, A. J. (1985). *Systematic evaluation.* Boston: Kluwer-
Nijhoff.

United States Centers for Disease Control and Prevention. (1998). CDC surveillance
summaries. *Mobidity and Morality Weekly Reviews, 47*(SS-3), 1–89.

United States Centers for Disease Control and Prevention. (1999). *Ten leading causes
of death by age group, 1993–1995* [On-line]. Available: http://www.cdc.gov
/ncipc/osp/leadcaus/chrtrqpg.htm.

Weissberg, R. P., Caplan, M., & Harwood, R. L. (1991). Promoting competent young people in competence-enhancing environments: A systems-based perspective on primary prevention. *Journal of Consulting and Clinical Psychology, 59,* 830–841.

Weissberg, R. P., Caplan, M. Z., & Sivo, P. J. (1989). A new conceptual framework for establishing school-based social competence promotion programs. In L. A. Bond & B. E. Compas (Eds.), *Primary prevention and promotion in the schools* (pp. 255–296). Newbury Park, CA: Sage Publications.

Weissberg, R. P., & Greenberg, M. T. (1998). School and community competence-enhancement and prevention programs. I. E. Sigel & K. A. Renninger (Eds.), *Handbook of child psychology: Vol 4. Child psychology in practice* (5th ed., pp. 877–954). New York: John Wiley & Sons.

CHAPTER NINETEEN

The Effectiveness of School-Based Programs for the Promotion of Social Competence

Keith Topping, Elizabeth A. Holmes, and William Bremner

Policy and practice in education have often been shaped by what "feels right" to teachers, by contagious fashions that sweep in and then leave without trace, and by the short-term expedients of politicians who feel the need to be seen to be doing something in order to secure votes. However, recent years have seen much talk of effectiveness, cost-effectiveness, and a movement to "evidence-based education." In this chapter we pursue this theme, offering an overview of more than 700 rigorous research reports of outcome evaluations of school-based programs designed to enhance social competence.

ORIGINS AND AIMS OF THE EFFECTIVENESS SURVEY

This effectiveness survey stemmed from the Promoting Social Competence project in Scotland, which was funded by the central government and based at the Centre for Paired Learning in the Department of Psychology at the University of Dundee. One of the project activities was a survey of the literature on the effectiveness of school-based programs designed to enhance personal, social, emotional, and behavioral competence and development for all children and young people in primary (elementary), secondary, and special schools.[1]

---

[1]More detailed information about this and parallel relevant products of the project are available on the project Web site (www.dundee.ac.uk/psychology/prosoc.htm), on CD-ROM, and in more traditional publications (Bremner & Topping, 1998a, 1998b, 1999; Topping & Bremner, 1998).

The aim of the effectiveness survey (Topping & Holmes, 1998) was to make available, directly to practitioners and in a brief and accessible way, information about the effectiveness of different school-based practices in promoting social competence. Access to this information needed to be interactive so that practitioners could seek answers to questions currently relevant to themselves and their contexts, framed in their own vocabulary and schema. The expectation was that this would help to increase the proportion of demonstrably effective practices established in schools, thereby improving educational outcomes for children and young people.

METHODOLOGY

The project team searched a number of on-line literature databases, then scrutinized and selected items for inclusion if they reported evaluations of school-based interventions to improve the social competence of school children. The ensuing final version of the survey contained more than 700 items. These items were made available in an electronic bibliographic database that enables users to carry out searches customized to their own particular needs and purposes.

A consistent overall set of descriptive keywords for the whole survey was developed, and the relevant ones attached to each item. Then, considering all the items in the survey, all the keywords used were categorized, to help users toward an organized overview, or mapping, of the whole field of social competence, as reflected in the literature.

Keywords describing different types of interventions were found to fall into seven categories of intervention (albeit with some inevitable arbitrariness), which thus constituted a typology of such interventions. The seven categories are behavior analysis and modification interventions, counseling and therapeutic interventions, social skills training, peer-mediated interventions, cognitive and self-managed interventions, multiple interventions, and miscellaneous.

The behavior analysis and modification category included interventions based on behavioral learning theory, usually primarily controlled by teachers. The counseling and therapeutic category included interventions that adopted a child-centered and humanistic approach, usually delivered by teachers or other professionals. Social skills training included interventions that gave pupils instruction to help increase their competence in using specific social skills, usually delivered by teachers. The peer-mediated category included all interventions, regardless of theoretical basis, in which the main mediators and deliverers of the program were pupils in the peer group, with some teacher coordination. The cognitive and self-managed category included interventions in which pupils had even greater control over the management of the intervention, often on an individual basis, with some teacher coordination (for example, self-management, self-monitoring, self-recording). The multiple category included interventions using a combination or range of the others. The miscellaneous category included interventions not classifiable as any of the others.

To exemplify the structure, a few sample keywords are given below, grouped according to their typology category. Some of the keywords cover a number of programs or interventions of a particular type or category (such as behavior contracts), whereas others refer to a particular program that asserts its own special or "brand" name (for example, CABAS).

Behavior analysis and modification. Assertive discipline, behavior recovery, CLASS (contingencies for learning academic and social skills), discrimination training, guided practice, positive teaching project, rules praise and ignore.

Counseling and therapeutic. Adlerian therapy, brief therapy, counseling, drama therapy, fantasy play, life space interviewing, music therapy, play therapy, psychotherapy, rational emotive therapy, reality therapy.

Social skills training. Assertiveness training, behavioral rehearsal, classwide social skills training program, dealing with conflict, enhancing emotional competence curriculum, PACT (positive adolescent choices training), resolving conflict creatively, SFA (skills for adolescence), social perception skills training.

Peer-mediated. Big Brothers/Big Sisters mentoring program, CHAMPS (children are making progress in school), circle time, peaceful solutions peer-mediation training program, peer counseling, peer education, peer-mediated conflict resolution, peer modeling, peer monitoring, peer reinforcement, peer tutoring.

Cognitive and self-managed. Anxiety management training, attribution training, choicemaker self-determination program, cognitive restructuring, generation of alternative behavior training, goal setting, ICPS (interpersonal cognitive problem solving), ISA-SPS (improving social awareness–social problem solving), PATHS (promoting alternative thinking strategies), perspective-taking skills training, problem solving with people program, self-instruction, self-modeling, self-monitoring, self-reinforcement, skillstreaming, stop think do, stress control and management, stress inoculation training, transactional analysis.

Multiple. Adolescent development program, Boys' Town, CLUE (creative learning in a unique environment), FAST Track (families and schools together), Project Turnaround, San Clemente Project, Superstart Plus.

Miscellaneous. Activity group therapy, ALAS (achievement for Latinos through academic success), bibliotherapy, COMP (Classroom Organization and Management Program).

INTERPRETING THE EFFECTIVENESS SURVEY LITERATURE

Despite the brave talk of effectiveness, cost-effectiveness, and evidence-based education, there are questions about the degree to which evidence really influences policy and practice. There are also questions about what constitutes "good" evidence. The randomized controlled trials that might be useful to evaluate a new drug in "evidence-based medicine" are much more difficult to establish in the more complex and subtle world of education and might have their own difficulties with ecological validity.

However, this effectiveness survey can help practitioners and policy makers move toward more soundly based decisions. As well as considering the contents of the survey, users should also reflect on what is *not* within it—what methods and programs that are already in use or being promoted do not appear to have any satisfactory evidence of effectiveness. Even where there is evidence within the survey of the effectiveness of an approach, that evidence must be interpreted thoughtfully and carefully by users because there are a number of pitfalls.

First, the effectiveness survey comprises research reports that are published, and the reports that are published are likely to be a biased sample of all the research done because publishers prefer to publish positive and significant results. Projects subject to intensive research might also be atypical—operated by particularly competent or committed people, or especially well resourced. This further source of sampling error might severely limit the generalizability of effects reported in the literature to average (or mediocre) real-world settings.

Second, users should not assume that programs or methods given the same name in the literature were actually the same in practice. One reason for this is that different workers often use the same vocabulary to describe different things, and different vocabulary to describe the same thing. Another reason is that even if identical programs or methods were actually deployed, the quality of program delivery (or implementation integrity) might have been very different in two different sites.

Even when two research reports seem to describe exactly the same program, implemented competently in both cases for the same length of time, users are likely to find other differences between the reports. Perhaps the two research reports had different objectives, focused on different age groups, targeted different types of children, involved different numbers of children, had different gender balances among the participants, were delivered in different locations, were set in different geographical or socioeconomic areas, or used different measures of effectiveness in different domains (cognitive, affective, behavioral). For these and other reasons, the two reports might not be directly comparable. The effectiveness survey includes additional keywords to enable users to search discriminantly in these respects.

However, not all research reports include information on all the things users want to know. For example, the reporting of how the program was actually implemented might not be detailed enough for users to decide how well it was implemented, or whether it was implemented in exactly the same way as in another report. When users inspect research reports systematically, it often becomes clear how much has *not* been reported, leaving the reader to wonder whether this was accidental or deliberate. Relatively few research reports include information about the generalization of any gains (to other situations, for instance) or the maintenance of any gains (over time after the end of the program), although both of these aspects are crucial to estimating practical effectiveness, and certainly to estimating cost-effectiveness. Regarding the latter, it is relatively unusual to find detailed information about the real total cost of implementing the program, let alone the calculation of unit cost per participant or overall cost-effectiveness.

When researchers look carefully at a number of different research reports on a topic or area, they might decide to make a personal interpretation of the significance of each report as they work toward some conclusion; this is the traditional style of literature review. Or they might first consider the quality of research design and method in each report, then give much more emphasis to the few studies that are of high quality; this is the "best evidence synthesis" approach. Or they might focus only on those reports that give outcomes in quantitative or numerical form and use statistical analysis to aggregate the "effect sizes" across all these studies (ignoring the rest); this is the "meta-analysis" method. All three approaches have different inherent biases and problems.

For all of these reasons, users need to read the detailed "small print" of the relevant research reports carefully and critically before arriving at conclusions or operational decisions. Users also need to be aware of their own potential bias: if one is already enthusiastic about a program or method, one may preferentially seek out those reports that describe it as effective and tend to ignore those that describe it as not effective.

Given these considerations, no attempt is made here to summarize the 700 or so research reports in the effectiveness survey into one convenient paragraph. Rather, an attempt is made to give the user a broad (and inevitably superficial) overview of the quantity and quality of research evidence available in each of the seven intervention categories. This general orientation mentions reviews of research, but rarely individual studies.

BEHAVIOR ANALYSIS AND MODIFICATION INTERVENTIONS

Behavior analysis and modification includes interventions based on behavioral learning theory (concerning the relationship between the antecedents of behavior, the behavior itself, and the consequences of the behavior, including reinforcement). In the literature, these interventions were usually primarily controlled by teachers.

An impressive, early large-scale evaluation (with 459 pupils) of a token economy system in one school by Boegli and Wasik (1978) recorded reduced suspensions, improved academic achievement, and reduced teacher turnover. Skiba and Casey (1985) reviewed 521 interventions for behavior problems, finding that those focused on behavior problems in the classroom and derived from a behavior analysis and modification framework tended to be the most powerful and robust (although cognitive-behavioral and peer-mediated approaches were in their infancy at that time). Pigott and Heggie (1986) reviewed twenty studies comparing the relative efficacy of individual and group reinforcement in classroom settings and found that group reinforcement for improved academic performance was more effective than individual reinforcement in improving academic behavior, and also more effective in improving social behavior than reinforcement targeted on social behavior.

More recently, a review by Williams, Williams, and McLaughlin (1991) noted generally high effectiveness for behavioral interventions, but higher effectiveness when such methods were used in combination with other methods. Elliott and Gresham (1993) similarly noted that behavioral (operant) methods were consistently associated with high effectiveness, although social learning and problem-solving approaches had also proved valuable.

However, it must be noted that although behaviorally oriented intervention studies tend to feature clear, firm, and cohesive research methodology and often show high effectiveness, the numbers of children involved in many studies are small. Additionally, the intervention sometimes seems rather simplistic and primitive by current standards, and there are questions about external (ecological) validity and transfer of effects into self-management (Palardy, 1992).

Interpreting the term *behavior management* more widely, Emmer and Aussiker (1990) reviewed research findings on four classroom management programs (assertive discipline, reality therapy, teacher effectiveness training, and Adlerian/Dreikurs approaches) but were dissatisfied with the quality of the evidence, noting that the context in which the program was embedded had more impact on outcomes than the program itself.

Wang, Haertel, and Walberg (1993) conducted a meta-analysis of the impact of various factors in school learning and found that the quality of classroom management was the most important. Freiberg, Stein, and Huang (1995) reported a controlled evaluation of their "consistency management school development program," noting substantial effect sizes on academic attainments and improved school ethos.

COUNSELING AND THERAPEUTIC INTERVENTIONS

Counseling and therapeutic approaches include interventions that adopt a child-centered and humanistic approach, usually delivered by teachers or other professionals. Establishing the nature and quality of counseling delivered is especially problematic because those who do not have specialist counseling training might interpret any "talking to" as "counseling."

The stereotypical counseling relationship is a series of nondirective, one-to-one encounters in schools, between a member of the pastoral care or guidance staff and a child with a problem. However, studies have found group counseling as effective as individual counseling (Downing, 1977; Shechtman, Gilat, Fos, & Flasher, 1996), peer counseling as effective as counseling by professional adults (Huey & Rank, 1984), behaviorally oriented counseling more effective than nondirective counseling (Gumaer & Myrick, 1974; Omizo, Hershberger, & Omizo, 1988), and contingent teacher approval in class more effective than counseling (Marlowe et al., 1978).

Much of the literature in this area is descriptive, and the quality of research is generally poor. Some of the few better quality studies have failed to find any effect for traditional counseling; Hayes, Cunningham, and Robinson (1977) found only a slight positive effect on some measures when the parents rather than the children received counseling. Topping (1983) noted that studies up to that point had rarely found the effectiveness of counseling better than the spontaneous remission rate, especially with children with the acting-out types of behavioral problems.

Good quality studies of the many forms of therapy are even rarer, although Glaser's reality therapy has had positive evaluations (Edens & Smryl, 1994). In the United Kingdom, Kolvin et al. (1981) reported positive long-term results from group therapy along Rogerian lines delivered by social workers in secondary schools—although no short-term effects were apparent. Twice-weekly activity therapy groups in primary schools in West Sussex failed to yield changes in teacher behavior ratings (Labon, 1974).

SOCIAL SKILLS TRAINING

Social skills training (SST) includes interventions that give pupils instruction to help increase their competence in using specific social skills, usually delivered by teachers. Many reviews of the research literature in this area have been published over the years. Using the phrase *promoting social competence*, Asher and Taylor (1983) focused on children who were isolated or rejected in their peer group, concluding that direct skill training studies had met with considerable success in terms of immediate change in sociometric status and in the maintenance of change. Beck and Forehand (1984) reviewed thirty-two studies with a behavioral approach more rigorously and less conclusively and declared the overall results encouraging. Training methods as well as outcomes in behavioral studies were considered by Elliott, Gresham, and Heffer (1987), who concluded that multimethod approaches that manipulated both antecedents and consequences, included modeling and coaching procedures, and programmed for generalization were most likely to be successful.

Hollin (1990) considered the application of social skills training to a more challenging population: delinquents. He concluded that although SST could be successful in changing some aspects of social behavior in delinquents, this tended not to have a direct effect on their rate of offending. In the same vein, Zaragoza, Vaughn, and McIntosh (1991) reviewed twenty-seven studies of SST with children with behavior problems, concluding that a number of interventions (but not all) had been successful, although outcome data often relied on teacher, parent, peer, and self perceptions.

In 1992, Schneider offered a meta-analysis of seventy-nine controlled studies of SST with children, describing the overall short-term effectiveness as moderate; withdrawn children generally responded better than aggressive children. The use of modeling and coaching was linked with larger effect sizes, which were higher for directly related outcomes (such as improved observed social interaction) than tangential outcomes (such as improved academic attainment). Effectiveness at follow-up was still considered to be substantial, although follow-up periods longer than three months were rare. Christopher, Nangle, and Hansen (1993) noted that studies were increasingly concerned with the generalization of SST effects to the natural ecology of the child, through general problem-solving training, training in the natural environment, peer-mediated training and monitoring, self-management training, and the use of video feedback. Ogilvy (1994) concluded that SST was necessary to effect generalized change but was not always sufficient by itself. Kavale and Forness (1995) conducted a meta-analysis of 152 studies of SST with children with learning disabilities, concluding that between 60 and 75 percent of participants showed subsequent improvement, a success rate that these authors felt was modest.

The development of broad-spectrum "ecobehavioral" SST packages deliverable to groups in the natural environment has continued apace, one of the best examples being the classwide social skills program (Hundert, 1995). However, even with well-structured programs, generalization is not automatic (Hundert & Houghton, 1992), and DuPaul and Eckert (1994) counsel against the "train and hope" approach. Greater emphasis is now being placed on the use of video-assisted training, modeling, and feedback (Lonnecker, Brady, McPherson, & Hawkins, 1994; McCurdy & Shapiro, 1988). Information technology seems to hold possibilities with respect to computer-assisted multimedia training programs (Thorkildesen et al., 1989) and virtual reality SST role playing (Muscott & Gifford, 1994).

PEER-MEDIATED INTERVENTIONS

Peer-mediated interventions are those in which, regardless of theoretical basis, the main mediators and deliverers of the program are pupils in the peer group, with some teacher coordination. The importance of the peer group in the development of social competence has been emphasized by many researchers. For example, Hallenbeck and Kauffman (1995) reviewed the evidence for observational learning of social behavior from peer models, and Cullingford and Morrison (1997) explored the importance of peer group pressure in deviance from adult norms of conventionally socially competent behavior.

However, peers have increasingly been seen as part of the solution rather than part of the problem. A classic review of the literature by Grace Kalfus on peer-mediated interventions appeared as long ago as 1984. The majority of the rigorous research literature at that time was behavioral in orientation, and she considered peers as tutors, peers as reinforcing agents, and peers as facilitators of generalization. The effectiveness of peer tutoring was well established. Peers had been found effective as reinforcing agents, although maintenance and generalization had been demonstrated in a minority of studies. The few studies of peers as facilitators of generalization were more equivocal.

The rapid development in this field is well illustrated in the much broader reviews that emerged in the 1990s. Van-Slyck and Stern (1991) reviewed the role of peer-mediated conflict resolution training in schools, considering the short- and long-term effects on the mediators and those with whom they intervened, set in the context of the ethos and disciplinary idiosyncrasies of individual schools. Powell, Muirmclain, and Halasyamani (1995) reviewed nine selected peer-mediated conflict resolution programs, noting evidence that some (but not all) reduced absenteeism and disciplinary incidents. However, implementation integrity varied widely, not least in terms of the amount and quality of teacher and pupil training and degree of external support for the school.

Reviewing peer-mediated conflict resolution programs particularly in relation to violence prevention in schools, Johnson and Johnson (1996) concluded that such programs in general demonstrated effectiveness. Trained students actually used the trained strategies, and this led to more constructive social outcomes and reductions in conflicts referred to school staff and in suspensions and exclusions. Only a few studies provided evidence of generalization and maintenance, at least in the short term. However, programs were varied widely, and many studies appeared to have methodological weaknesses, so this sweeping conclusion should be interpreted with caution. Johnson and Johnson (1996) emphasized the need for much better quality research in the area.

Peer-mediated interventions can have reflexive and recursive effects on all participants. This is certainly true of peer tutoring and related peer-assisted learning methods if properly organized (Topping & Ehly, 1998). For example, the "valued youth" program assigns high school pupils with behavior problems as tutors for primary school pupils, with positive effects on the former as well as the latter (Cardenas, Montecel, Supik, & Harris, 1992; Gable, Arllen, & Hendrickson, 1994).

Another current program widely adopted in the United States is the Resolving Conflict Creatively Program, coordinated by Linda Lantieri, involving twenty hours of training for teachers. An evaluation indicated that participating children showed significantly improved understanding of the conceptual content of the program curriculum. Furthermore, 66 to 71 percent of responding participant teachers had reduced verbal and physical violence in their classrooms, 69 to 78 percent noted more caring and cooperative student behavior, and 84 percent reported improvements in class and whole-school ethos. However, the teacher response rate was only 66 percent (Metis Associates, 1990).

By contrast, even remotely adequate evaluations of peer-mediated approaches widely adopted and adapted in the United Kingdom (such as Circle Time) are conspicuous by their absence (Curry, 1997).

COGNITIVE AND SELF-MANAGED INTERVENTIONS

The cognitive and self-managed category includes interventions in which pupils have even greater control over the management of the intervention, often on an individual basis, with some teacher coordination (such as self-management, self-monitoring, and self-recording). Following earlier reviews of behavioral self-management in education by Workman and Hector (1978), Roberts and Dick (1982), and Wilson (1984), Mace, Brown, and West (1987) reported that the self-monitoring and self-instruction components of self-management had yielded mixed results when deployed alone, often in rather small-scale studies. Of the other components (self-evaluation and self-reinforcement), self-reinforcement seemed the most consistently powerful. These authors offered practical guidelines for successful implementation.

In parallel, Gesten, Weissberg, Amish, and Smith (1987) reviewed the literature on social problem-solving training (arguably also within the cognitive-behavioral self-management category, although clearly also overlapping with the social skills training category). First developed by Spivack and Shure (1974) for use with preschool children, this approach has become increasingly popular across a wider age range (Shure, 1992, 1993). Pfeiffer and Reddy (1998) reported a recent five-year longitudinal study of the Shure and Spivack program that found reductions in impulsive and withdrawn behaviors and increases in prosocial behaviors, with gains sustained over three years.

Gesten et al. (1987) summarized six previous reviews, encompassing sixty studies, most of which incorporated a control group. Although some replications had failed to demonstrate effects, later studies had done so more consistently. The authors' research into their own program indicated some but not all effects endured at three year follow-up, even in the absence of booster sessions. However, Urbain and Kendall (1980) and Denham and Almeida (1987) noted that although effect sizes in the acquisition of social cognitive problem-solving skills were large, effect sizes in terms of changes in actual social behavior in the natural ecological settings were much smaller. However, Denham and Almeida (1987) and Carpenter and Apter (1988) concluded that the relationship between training and subsequent adjustment appeared robust, although follow-up data were relatively sparse.

A review of the use of behavioral self-management in mainstream primary school settings was carried out by Panagopoulou-Stamatelatou (1990), who noted many differences in the interventions thus labeled. Generally, however, positive effects were reported, although many studies were of small size. Nelson, Smith, Young, and Dodd (1991) reviewed studies of self-management with children exhibiting behavior disorders, a more challenging target group, but nevertheless reported moderate to large treatment effects overall. Although treatment effects were durable, generalization rarely occurred spontaneously and needed to be systematically programmed. Grossman and Hughes (1992) reviewed twenty-two studies and found the approach to be effective in general, but they pointed out a need for more evidence of lasting changes in actual behavior.

Ollech (1992) reviewed self-management approaches specifically targeted to anger control and reported modest effects and uncertainty regarding maintenance and generalization, with combined methods yielding the biggest effects. Lochman (1992) did the same, commenting that although effects were generally positive, this was more likely to be true on some variables than others. Coleman, Wheeler, and Webber (1993) reviewed nine studies and noted that cognitive gains were commonplace, but application to actual behavior was less certain. Webber, Scheuermann, McCall, and Coleman (1993) reviewed twenty-seven studies of self-monitoring, most results being positive.

Other current examples of "thinking skills for social competence" interventions are the Stop Think Do Program of Lindy Petersen (1992, 1995) (used with primary- and secondary-aged children and involving teachers, parents, or both), the PATHS (promoting alternative thinking strategies) curriculum (Greenberg, 1993; Greenberg, Kusche, Cook, & Quamma, 1995), skillstreaming and the prepare curriculum from Goldstein (1978, 1988), and the ISA-SPS (improving social awareness–social problem solving) Program (Battistich, Elias, & Branden-Muller, 1992; Elias & Clabby, 1992; Elias, Gara, Schuyler, & Branden-Muller, 1991). Most of these have shown positive evaluation results with school children. For example, Maurice Elias's two-year ISA-SPS Program showed positive effects that endured at four-year follow-up.

However, most of the studies in this area are still relatively small in scale. Although the majority show positive effects, there is still concern about generalization of effects to everyday behavior, especially in the longer term. Only the larger studies of well-established programs offer convincing evidence in this regard.

MULTIPLE INTERVENTIONS

The multiple category includes interventions using a combination or range of specific interventions. Reviews of broad-spectrum programs are often set in the context of epidemiological research on risk factors predisposing children to social or behavioral problems, with a view to identifying those most at risk and targeting interventions on them (Rutherford, Nelson, & Forness, 1988). Thus Haggerty, Sherrod, Garmezy, and Rutter (1994) considered processes, mechanisms, and interventions in stress, risk, and resilience in children and adolescents, Rutter and Smith (1995) reported on causes and time trends of psychosocial disorders in young people, and Fortin and Bigras (1997) reviewed risk factors for the development of behavior problems. Bear (1998) reviewed methods of promoting self-discipline in schools in the United States, and their implication for long-term social development. Moore (1996) discussed research on the role of parenting styles in developing social competence in children, considering the balance between authoritarianism and permissiveness. Mental health and violence prevention programs for children are prominent in the United States; Durlak and Wells (1997) conducted a meta-analysis on mental health programs, and Larson (1994) reviewed violence prevention programs. Withers (1995) reviewed the American, Canadian, and British literature on programs for at-risk youth from 1984.

Daniel Goleman's (1996) book on emotional intelligence has of course had enormous influence around the world. Its appendixes included a number of descriptions of programs and related references. Included are a number of projects headed by members of CASEL (Collaborative for the Advancement of Social and Emotional Learning), who have written widely on the topic of promoting social and emotional competence (for example, Weissberg, Shriver, Bose, & DeFalco, 1997; and see Chapter Eighteen in this volume). Weissberg and Greenberg (1997) produced a wide ranging review of school and community competence enhancement and prevention programs, which included some solely targeted on social competence. The key CASEL resource is, however, the book *Promoting Social and Emotional Learning: Guidelines for Educators* (Elias et al., 1997).

Earlier, Conoley (1989) compiled a wide ranging review, and Furman and Gavin (1989) and Erwin (1993) reviewed a range of methods of improving peer relationships. Cohen (1993) produced a handbook of school-based interventions, and Carter (1994) created a survey guide to seventy-seven interventions and systems to support competent social behavior. Walker, Colvin, and Ramsey (1995) reviewed strategies and practices for intervening in antisocial behavior in school. Hundert (1995) compiled an excellent book that reviewed school-based approaches to enhancing social competence. In Australia, Prescott (1995) produced a valuable practical guide to resources and materials. Walker, Colvin,

and Ramsey (1995) reviewed strategies and best practices for managing antisocial behavior in school, and Jones and Charlton (1996) discussed various methods for developing partnership with pupils to overcome learning as well as
behavior difficulties.

Moving to more rigorous reviews of research more tightly focused on social
competence, Beelmann, Pfingsten, and Loesel (1994) conducted a meta-analysis
of evaluation studies since 1980 of the effects of training social competence in
children, concluding that such programs were moderately effective in general,
although the limited evidence for generalization and maintenance of gains was
a cause for concern. Brown and Odom (1994) echoed this concern in their
review of strategies and tactics for promoting generalization and maintenance
of improvements in social behavior.

Considering more "special" populations, Singh, Deitz, Epstein, and Singh
(1991) had earlier conducted a quantitative analysis of twenty-eight social competence intervention programs with children who were classified as "seriously
emotionally disturbed," and found that the majority of the studies demonstrated
program effectiveness in terms of a reduction in problematic behavior of at least
50 percent. Hudley and Graham (1995) reviewed four very different school-
based interventions for aggressive African American youth. One intervention
yielded mostly positive and significant results, another mostly positive results
of which only some were significant, another descriptive outcomes of uncertain
reliability, and the fourth mixed results.

MISCELLANEOUS INTERVENTIONS

Miscellaneous interventions are not classifiable under any other category. By
definition such interventions are idiosyncratic and difficult to compare with each
other or indeed with any other intervention. They are not referred to further in
this chapter.

CONCLUSION

The somewhat arbitrary nature of the categorization of methods adopted here
will now be even more evident to the reader. Methods that have been placed in
one category on account of their main orientation might well include elements
of practice from another. However, notwithstanding the inexactitude of the categorization, this overview leads us to the following conclusions.

Behavior analysis and modification interventions. These programs are consistently reported to be effective and robust, especially when used in combination and focused on classroom behavior. However, many studies are of small

samples, and issues of generalization and maintenance are not ubiquitously addressed. Ease of implementation and durability might be an important factor because some research suggests that the quality and consistency of classroom management is more important than its type or style, and the context of implementation might have more effect than the program itself.

Counseling and therapeutic interventions. These approaches are characterized by very wide variety and by very poor quality evaluation research. Lengthy individual professional counseling seems no more effective than brief group counseling by nonprofessionals, although behaviorally oriented methods tend to perform better. One or two forms of therapy have shown some promise.

Social skills training. These approaches have shown moderate and variable effectiveness, higher for withdrawn children than those acting out or with learning difficulties. Multimethod approaches involving modeling and coaching that program for generalization over time and contexts tend to be most effective.

Peer-mediated interventions. These include peer tutoring and peer reinforcement, both of which have been found effective, with potential benefits for the helpers as well as the helped. Peer-mediated conflict resolution training encompasses widely varing approaches, where implementation integrity is sometimes in doubt and the quality of research very variable. Such programs show some evidence of moderate but mixed effectiveness, with very limited information about generalization and maintenance.

Cognitive and self-managed interventions. These approaches have shown moderate to large effects. More mixed results from small studies and some concern about transfer from knowledge to behavior and maintenance of gains are counterbalanced by large-scale, long-term studies that have shown substantial gains maintained over follow-up periods as long as four years. The Spivack-Shure and Elias programs have proved particularly impressive. Interventions focusing specifically on anger control have shown more mixed results.

Multiple interventions. This group of broad-spectrum programs to promote social competence have shown some effects, but programs are varied and difficult to compare. Overall, outcomes are mixed and moderate, statistical significance is not always attained, and evidence for generalization and maintenance of gains is limited.

As noted above, the amount of evaluation evidence on any particular program does not necessarily indicate the extent to which it is used by practitioners. There are a number of programs in widespread use that do not have a significant evaluation literature, and others that are well evaluated but not particularly well known or widely used.

Clearly, caution is needed when initiating programs in those categories where evidence of effectiveness has proved relatively elusive; building in performance indicators or more rigorous evaluation would seem essential if effort, time, and other scarce resources are not to be wasted.

Even for initiatives in categories where high effectiveness has been demonstrated in the research literature, it cannot be assumed that effectiveness in a specific initiative will automatically follow. Careful planning is needed to address the question, What do we need to do to make sure this initiative is effective? before the more obvious, And how will we know if it is effective?

Evaluation Begins at Home

A framework for school self-evaluation using performance indicators has been devised (Topping & Bremner, 1998). This is intended to help schools undertake an audit of their current approaches to promoting social competence, and also help schools develop locally relevant means for evaluating the impact of any innovations. It is a flexible framework, designed to be fleshed out by negotiation between the main stakeholders who are most familiar with the local needs and ecology, perhaps in the context of staff development meetings.

The framework begins with the consideration of obvious questions such as what is social competence and why is it important? Different teachers are likely to offer very different answers. Then teachers are encouraged to consider values clarification, ethos assessment, stakeholders and key players (internal and external) identification, and the identification of strengths, resources, and support (internal and external). Next is an outline of how to conduct a social competence audit, which covers the purposes of audit, primary and secondary sector differences, level (child, class, school), specification of observable behavior, performance indicators, and development of more refined indicators. This leads to identification of areas for improvement, the setting of objectives and priorities for action at various levels of operation (child, class, school), and linkage to school development plans, which is coupled with identification of resources and support (staff development, processes and packages, resources, support networks, and agencies).

Of course, alternative frameworks can be found in the literature, but some structure and framework within which to develop and negotiate shared vocabulary and concepts is definitely needed if schools are to move forward constructively in a coordinated and cost-effective way. Nor should this be a one-off exercise, but a renewing cycle of intervention, evaluation, intervention, and so on.

Updating

Even when a school has successfully built in iterative intervention and evaluation processes for the promotion of social competence within its own organization, it might still wish to keep up to date with the wider research literature. The existing effectiveness survey will of course slowly become dated. However, users should not assume that the latest research is necessarily the best.

Readers might well want to update the search within a specific area of interest. A number of electronic databases enable this (if only abstracts are wanted initially, rather than the full text). However, ease and cost of access to these varies considerably.

Some electronic literature databases are published in updated versions on CD-ROM for access via a computer. These are usually very expensive to buy but are available at some college and university libraries, which may let readers scan the CD-ROM and save the items that seem especially interesting.

Most on-line information services are available only on a subscription basis, with the expectation that institutions will pay the subscription. Readers might be able to access these within a local specialist library. Also, check if any department within the local school district already subscribes to these or any similar service—perhaps the research and evaluation office, the planning department, or the psychological service.

If Internet access is available, particularly the World Wide Web, there are other possibilities. For instance, the Education Resources Information Center has excellent free searching services on the World Wide Web, yielding abstracts where available. The ASKERIC service (http://ericir.syr.edu/) has a swift and efficient interface and is very useful for updating. If readers have time, it might be worth searching the whole World Wide Web using one of the usual search engines, (such as Yahoo or Alta Vista) or a meta-engine (such as Dogpile). Narrow and specify the search carefully, however, to avoid being overwhelmed with material of doubtful relevance.

References

Asher, S. R., & Taylor, A. R. (1983). Social skill training with children: Evaluating processes and outcomes. *Studies in Educational Evaluation, 8,* 237–245.

Battistich, V. A., Elias, M. J., & Branden-Muller, L. R. (1992). Two school-based approaches to promoting children's social competence. In G. W. Albee, L. A. Bond, & T. V. Monsey (Eds.), *Improving children's lives: Global perspectives on prevention* (pp. 217–234). Newbury Park, CA: Sage.

Bear, G. G. (1998). School discipline in the United States: Prevention, correction, and long term social development. *Educational and Child Psychology, 15,* 15–39.

Beck, S., & Forehand, R. (1984). Social skills training for children: A methodological and clinical review of behavior-modification studies. *Behavioral Psychotherapy, 12,* 17–45.

Beelmann, A., Pfingsten, U., & Loesel, F. (1994). Effects of training social competence in children: A meta-analysis of recent evaluation studies. *Journal of Clinical Child Psychology, 23,* 260–271.

Boegli, R. G., & Wasik, B. H. (1978). Use of the token economy system to intervene on a school-wide level. *Psychology in the Schools, 15,* 72–78.

Bremner, W. G., & Topping, K. J. (1998a). *Focus on social competence: Report on a meeting of expert witnesses.* Edinburgh: Scottish Office Education and Industry Department.

Bremner, W. G., & Topping, K. J. (1998b). *Promoting social competence: Practice and resources guide.* Edinburgh: Scottish Office Education and Industry Department.

Bremner, W. G., & Topping, K. J. (1999). *Promoting social competence: Practice and resources taster pack.* Edinburgh: Scottish Office Education and Industry Department.

Brown, W. H., & Odom, S. L. (1994). Strategies and tactics for promoting generalization and maintenance of young children's social behavior. *Research in Developmental Disabilities, 15,* 99–118.

Cardenas, J. A., Montecel, M. R., Supik, J. D., & Harris, R. J. (1992). The Coca-Cola valued youth program: Dropout prevention strategies for at-risk students. *Texas Researcher, 3,* 111–130.

Carpenter, R. L., & Apter, S. J. (1988). Research integration of cognitive-emotional interventions for behaviorally disordered children and youth. In M. C. Wang, M. C. Reynolds, & H. J. Walberg (Eds.), *Handbook of special education: Research and practice* (Vol. 2, pp. 155–169). Oxford, U.K.: Pergamon Press.

Carter, S. (1994). *Interventions: Organizing systems to support competent social behavior in children and youth.* Eugene, OR: Western Regional Resource Center. (ERIC Document Reproduction Service No. ED 380 971)

Christopher, J. S., Nangle, D. W., & Hansen, D. J. (1993). Social-skills interventions with adolescents: Current issues and procedures. *Behavior Modification, 17,* 314–338.

Cohen, J. J. (1993). *Handbook of school-based interventions: Resolving student problems and promoting healthy educational environments.* San Francisco: Jossey-Bass.

Coleman, M., Wheeler, L., & Webber, J. (1993). Research on interpersonal problem-solving training: A review. *Remedial and Special Education, 14,* 25–37.

Conoley, J. C. (1989). Cognitive-behavioral approaches and prevention in the schools. In J. N. Hughs & R. J. Hall (Eds.), *Cognitive-behavioral psychology in the schools: A comprehensive handbook* (pp. 535–568). New York: Guilford Press.

Cullingford, C., & Morrison, J. (1997). Peer group pressure within and outside school. *British Educational Research Journal, 23,* 61–80.

Curry, M. (1997). Providing emotional support through Circle-Time: A case study. *Support For Learning, 12,* 126–129.

Denham, S. A., & Almeida, M. C. (1987). Children's social problem-solving skills, behavioral adjustment, and interventions: A meta-analysis evaluating theory and practice. *Journal of Applied Developmental Psychology, 8,* 391–409.

Downing, C. J. (1977). Teaching children behavior change techniques. *Elementary School Guidance and Counseling, 11,* 277–283.

DuPaul, G. J., & Eckert, T. L. (1994). The effects of social skills curricula: Now you see them, now you don't. *School Psychology Quarterly, 9,* 113–132.

Durlak, J. A., & Wells, A. M. (1997). Primary prevention mental health programs for children and adolescents: A meta-analytic review. *American Journal of Community Psychology, 25,* 115–152.

Edens, R. M., & Smryl, T. (1994). Reducing disruptive classroom behaviors in physical education: A pilot study. *Journal of Reality Therapy, 13,* 40–44.

Elias, M. J., & Clabby, J. F. (1992). *Building social problem-solving skills: Guidelines from a school-based program.* San Francisco: Jossey-Bass.

Elias, M. J., Gara, M. A., Schuyler, T. F., & Branden-Muller, L. R. (1991). The promotion of social competence: Longitudinal study of a preventive school-based program. *American Journal of Orthopsychiatry, 61,* 409–417.

Elias, M. J., Zins, J. E., Weissberg, R. P., Frey, K. S., Greenberg, M. T., Haynes, N. M., Kessler, R., Schwab-Stone, M. E., & Shriver, T. P. (1997). *Promoting social and emotional learning: Guidelines for educators.* Alexandria, VA: Association for Supervision and Curriculum Development.

Elliott, S. N., & Gresham, F. M. (1993). Social skills interventions for children. *Behavior Modification, 17,* 287–313.

Elliott, S. N., Gresham, F. M., & Heffer, R. W. (1987). Social-skills interventions: Research findings and training techniques. In C. A. Maher & J. E. Zins (Eds.), *Psychoeducational interventions in the schools: Methods and procedures for enhancing student competence.* New York: Pergamon.

Emmer, E., & Aussiker, A. (1990). School and classroom discipline programs: How well do they work? In O. C. Moles (Ed.), *Student discipline strategies: Research and practice.* Albany, NY: State University of New York Press.

Erwin, P. (1993). Improving peer relationships. In P. Erwin (Ed.), *Friendship and peer relations in children.* Chichester: Wiley.

Fortin, L., & Bigras, M. (1997). Risk factors exposing young children to behavior problems. *Emotional and Behavioral Difficulties, 2,* 3–14.

Freiberg, H. J., Stein, T. A., & Huang, S. (1995). Effects of a classroom management intervention on student achievement in inner-city elementary schools. *Educational Research and Evaluation, 1,* 36–66.

Furman, W., & Gavin, L. A. (1989). Peers' influence on adjustment and development: A view from the intervention literature. In T. J. Berndt & G. W. Ladd (Eds.), *Peer relationships in child development* (pp. 319–340). New York: Wiley.

Gable, R. A., Arllen, N. L., & Hendrickson, J. M. (1994). Use of students with emotional/behavioral disorders as behavior change agents. *Education and Treatment of Children, 17,* 267–276.

Gesten, E. L., Weissberg, R. P., Amish, P. L., & Smith, J. K. (1987). Social problem-solving training: A skills-based approach to prevention and treatment. In C. A. Maher & J. E. Zins (Eds.), *Psychoeducational interventions in the schools: Methods and procedures for enhancing student competence.* New York: Pergamon.

Goldstein, A. P. (1978). Training aggressive adolescents in prosocial behavior. *Journal of Youth and Adolescence, 7,* 73–92.

Goldstein, A. P. (1988). *The Prepare curriculum: Teaching prosocial competencies.* Champaign, IL: Research Press.

Goleman, D. (1996). *Emotional intelligence.* London: Bloomsbury.

Greenberg, M. T. (1993). *Promoting social and emotional development in deaf children: The PATHS project.* Seattle, WA: University of Washington Press.

Greenberg, M. T., Kusche, C. A., Cook, E. T., & Quamma, J. P. (1995). Promoting emotional competence in school-aged children: The effects of the PATHS curriculum. *Development and Psychopathology, 7,* 117–136.

Grossman, P. B., & Hughes, J. N. (1992). Self-control interventions with internalizing disorders: A review and analysis. *School Psychology Review, 21,* 229–245.

Gumaer, J., & Myrick, R. D. (1974). Behavioral group counseling with disruptive children. *School Counselor, 21,* 313–317.

Haggerty, R. J., Sherrod, L. R., Garmezy, N., & Rutter, M. (1994). *Stress, risk and resilience in children and adolescents: Processes, mechanisms, and interventions.* Cambridge, U.K.: Cambridge University Press.

Hallenbeck, B. A., & Kauffman, J. M. (1995). How does observational learning affect the behavior of students with emotional or behavioral disorders? A review of research. *Journal of Special Education, 29,* 45–71.

Hayes, E. J., Cunningham, G. K., & Robinson, J. B. (1977). Counseling focus: Are parents necessary? *Elementary School Guidance and Counseling, 12,* 8–14.

Hollin, C. R. (1990). Social skills training with delinquents: A look at the evidence and some recommendations for practice. *British Journal of Social Work, 20,* 483–493.

Hudley, C., & Graham, S. (1995). School-based interventions for aggressive African-American boys. *Applied and Preventive Psychology, 4,* 185–195.

Huey, W. C., & Rank, R. C. (1984). Effects of counselor and peer-led group assertive training on black adolescent aggression. *Journal of Counseling Psychology, 31,* 95–98.

Hundert, J. (1995). *Enhancing social competence in young students: School-based approaches.* Austin, TX: PRO-ED.

Hundert, J., & Houghton, A. (1992). Promoting social interaction of children with disabilities in integrated preschools: A failure to generalize. *Exceptional Children, 58,* 311–320.

Johnson, D. W., & Johnson, R. T. (1996). Conflict resolution and peer mediation programs in elementary and secondary schools: A review of the research. *Review of Educational Research, 66,* 459–506.

Jones, K., & Charlton, T. (1996). *Overcoming learning and behavior difficulties: Partnership with pupils.* London: Routledge.

Kalfus, G. R. (1984). Peer mediated intervention: A critical review. *Child and Family Behavior Therapy, 6,* 17–43.

Kavale, K. A., & Forness, S. R. (1995). Social skill deficits and training: A meta-analysis of the research in learning disabilities. In T. E. Scruggs & M. A. Mastropieri (Eds.), *Advances in learning and behavioral disabilities* (Vol. 9, pp. 345–356). Greenwich, CT: JAI Press.

Kolvin, I., Garside, R. F., Nicol, A. R., MacMillan, A., Wolstenholme, F., & Leitch, I. M. (1981). *Help starts here: The maladjusted child in the ordinary school.* London: Tavistock.

Labon, D. (1974). Some effects of school-based therapy. *Journal of the Association of Educational Psychologists, 3,* 28–34.

Larson, J. (1994). Violence prevention in the schools: A review of selected programs and procedures. *School Psychology Review, 23,* 151–164.

Lochman, J. E. (1992). Cognitive-behavioral intervention with aggressive boys: 3-year follow-up and preventive effects. *Journal of Consulting and Clinical Psychology, 60,* 426–432.

Lonnecker, C., Brady, M. P., McPherson, R., & Hawkins, J. (1994). Video self-modeling and cooperative classroom behavior in children with learning and behavior problems: Training and generalization effects. *Behavioral Disorders, 20,* 24–34.

Mace, F. C., Brown, D. K., & West, B. J. (1987). Behavioral self-management in education. In C. A. Maher & J. E. Zins (Eds.), *Psychoeducational interventions in the schools: Methods and procedures for enhancing student competence.* New York: Pergamon.

Marlowe, R. H., et al. (1978). Severe classroom behavior problems: Teachers or counselors. *Journal of Applied Behavior Analysis, 11,* 53–66.

McCurdy, B. L., & Shapiro, E. S. (1988). Self-observation and reduction of inappropriate classroom behavior. *Journal of School Psychology, 26,* 371–378.

Metis Associates. (1990). *The Resolving Conflict Creatively program 1988–1989: Summary of significant findings.* New York: Author.

Moore, S. G. (1996). The role of parents in the development of peer group competence. ERIC Digest.

Muscott, H. S., & Gifford, T. (1994). Virtual reality and social skills training for students with behavioral disorders: Applications, challenges, and promising practices. *Education and Treatment of Children, 17,* 417–434.

Nelson, J. R., Smith, D. J., Young, R. K., & Dodd, J. M. (1991). A review of self-management outcome research conducted with students who exhibit behavioral disorders. *Behavioral Disorders, 16,* 169–179.

Ogilvy, C. M. (1994). Social skills training with children and adolescents: A review of evidence on effectiveness. *Educational Psychology, 14,* 73–83.

Ollech, D. (1992). Anger control for adolescents: Review of social skills and cognitive behavioral interventions. In I. G. Fodor (Ed.), *Adolescent assertiveness and social skills training: A clinical handbook* (pp. 151–164). New York: Springer.

Omizo, M. M., Hershberger, J. M., & Omizo, S. H. (1988). Teaching children to cope with anger. *Elementary School Guidance and Counseling, 22,* 241–246.

Palardy, J. M. (1992). Behavior modification: It does work, but . . . *Journal of Instructional Psychology, 19,* 127–131.

Panagopoulou-Stamatelatou, S. A. (1990). The use of behavioral self-management in primary school settings: A review. *Educational Psychology, 10,* 207–224.

Petersen, L. (1992). Stop-Think-Do: A systems based pro-social skills training program. *Guidance and Counseling, 8,* 24–35.

Petersen, L. (1995). Stop Think Do: Improving social and learning skills for children in clinics and schools. In H. P. J. G. van Bilsen, P. C. Kendall, & J. H. Slavenburg (Eds.), *Behavioral approaches for children and adolescents: Challenges for the next century* (pp. 103–111). New York: Plenum Press.

Pfeiffer, S. I., & Reddy, L. A. (1998). School-based mental health programs in the United States: Present status and a blueprint for the future. *Educational and Child Psychology, 15,* 109–125.

Pigott, H. E., & Heggie, D. L. (1986). Interpreting the conflicting results of individual versus group contingencies in classrooms: The targeted behavior as a mediating variable. *Child and Family Behavior Therapy, 7,* 1–15.

Powell, K. E., Muirmclain, L., & Halasyamani, L. (1995). A review of selected school-based conflict-resolution and peer mediation projects. *Journal of School Health, 65,* 426–431.

Prescott, K. (Ed.) (1995). *Teaching prosocial behavior to adolescents: A directory of processes and programs used in Australian schools.* Vermont, VIC: Australian Guidance and Counseling Association.

Roberts, R., & Dick, L. (1982). Self-control strategies with children. In T. R. Kratochwill (Ed.), *Advances in School Psychology.* Hillsdale, NJ: Erlbaum.

Rutherford, R. B., Nelson, C. M., & Forness, S. R. (Eds.). (1988). *Bases of severe behavioral disorders in children and youth.* Boston: College-Hill Press/ Little, Brown.

Rutter, M., & Smith, D. J. (1995). *Psychosocial disorders in young people: Time trends and their causes.* London: Wiley.

Schneider, B. H. (1992). Didactic methods for enhancing children's peer relations: A quantitative review. *Clinical Psychology Review, 12,* 363–382.

Shechtman, Z., Gilat, I., Fos, L., & Flasher, A. (1996). Brief group therapy with low-achieving elementary school children. *Journal of Counseling Psychology, 43,* 376–382.

Shure, M. B. (1992). *I Can Problem Solve. An interpersonal cognitive problem-solving program: Kindergarten and primary grades.* Champaign, IL: Research Press.

Shure, M. B. (1993). I Can Problem Solve (ICPS): Interpersonal cognitive problem solving for young children. *Early Child Development and Care, 96,* 49–64.

Singh, N. N., Deitz, D. E., Epstein, M. H., & Singh, J. (1991). Social behavior of students who are seriously emotionally disturbed: A quantitative analysis of intervention studies. *Behavior Modification, 15,* 74–94.

Skiba, R., & Casey, A. (1985). Interventions for behaviorally disordered students: A quantitative review and methodological critique. *Behavioral Disorders, 10,* 239–252.

Spivack, G., & Shure, M. B. (1974). *Social adjustment of young children: A cognitive approach to solving real-life problems.* San Francisco: Jossey-Bass.

Topping, K. J. (1983). *Educational systems for disruptive adolescents.* Beckenham, U.K.: Croom Helm; New York: St. Martin's Press.

Topping, K. J., & Bremner, W. G. (1998). *Taking a closer look at promoting social competence: Self-evaluation using performance indicators.* Edinburgh: Scottish Office Education and Industry Department.

Topping, K. J., & Ehly, S. (Eds.) (1998). *Peer-assisted learning.* Mahwah, NJ: Erlbaum.

Topping, K. J., & Holmes, E. A. (1998). *Promoting social competence: Effectiveness survey.* Edinburgh: Scottish Office Education and Industry Department.

Urbain, E. S., & Kendall, P. C. (1980). Review of social-cognitive problem-solving interventions with children. *Psychological Bulletin, 88,* 109–143.

Van-Slyck, M., & Stern, M. (1991). Conflict resolution in educational settings: Assessing the impact of peer mediation programs. In K. G. Duffy, J. W. Grosch, & P. V. Olczak (Eds.), *Community mediation: A handbook for practitioners and researchers* (pp. 257–274). New York: Guilford Press.

Walker, H. M., Colvin, G., & Ramsey, E. (1995). *Antisocial behavior in school: Strategies and best practices.* Pacific Grove, CA: Brooks Cole.

Wang, M. C., Haertel, G. D., & Walberg, H. J. (1993). Toward a knowledge base for school learning. *Review of Educational Research, 63,* 249–294.

Webber, J., Scheuermann, B., McCall, C., & Coleman, M. (1993). Research on self-monitoring as a behavior management technique in special-education classrooms: A descriptive review. *Remedial and Special Education, 14,* 38–56.

Weissberg, R. P., & Greenberg, M. T. (1997). School and community competence-enhancement and prevention programs. In: I. E. Sigel & K. A. Renninger (Eds.), *Handbook of child psychology* (5th ed., pp. 877–954). New York: Wiley.

Weissberg, R. P., Shriver, T. P., Bose, S., & DeFalco, K. (1997). Creating a districtwide social development project. *Educational Leadership, 5,* 37–39.

Williams, B. F., Williams, R. L., & McLaughlin, T. F. (1991). Classroom procedures for remediating behavior disorders. *Journal of Developmental and Physical Disabilities, 12,* 34–49.

Wilson, R. (1984). A review of self-control treatments for aggressive behavior. *Behavioral Disorders, 9,* 131–140.

Withers, G. (1995). *Programs for at-risk-youth: A review of the American, Canadian, and British literature since 1984.* A.C.E.R. Research Monograph No. 47. Melbourne, Australia: Australian Council for Educational Research.

Workman, E. A., & Hector, M. A. (1978). Behavioral self-control in classroom settings: A review of the literature. *Journal of School Psychology, 16,* 227–236.

Zaragoza, N., Vaughn, S., & McIntosh, R. (1991). Social skills interventions and children with behavior problems: A review. *Behavioral Disorders, 16,* 260–275.

CHAPTER TWENTY

Social and Emotional Competence in the Workplace

Cary Cherniss

W hen Daniel Goleman published his book *Emotional Intelligence* in 1995, many readers were particularly intrigued with the chapter on emotional intelligence at work. They immediately recognized how much the effectiveness of workers, work groups, and whole organizations is influenced by emotional and social competence. However, some people wondered whether such competencies could be improved once a person became an adult and entered the world of work.

In this chapter, I suggest that there actually is a long history of efforts to help workers improve their emotional intelligence, although that term usually has not been used. Furthermore, some training and development interventions that have been developed and evaluated in the past appear to be effective in improving emotional competence and work performance. These "best practices," along with a large body of research on training, development, and behavior change, suggest a number of guidelines that can help us design better programs in the future. The concept of emotional intelligence itself also suggests new directions for both practice and research on organizational training and development.

WHY FOCUS ON EMOTIONAL INTELLIGENCE AT WORK?

There are four primary reasons that the workplace is a logical setting for efforts to improve the competencies associated with emotional intelligence. First, such competencies are critical for effective performance in most jobs. Scores of studies in dozens of organizations suggest that about two-thirds of the competencies linked to superior performance are emotional or social qualities such as self-confidence, flexibility, persistence, empathy, and the ability to get along with others (Boyatzis, 1982; Lusch & Serpkeuci, 1990; McClelland, 1999; Rosier, 1994–1996; Spencer & Spencer, 1993). And in leadership positions, almost 90 percent of the competencies necessary for success are social and emotional in nature (Goleman, 1998).

Employers have long recognized that the competencies associated with emotional intelligence are crucial. In the mid-1980s, the U.S. Department of Labor conducted a national survey of what employers were looking for in entry level workers. The list was dominated by social and emotional qualities such as adaptability in the face of setbacks and obstacles, personal self-management, confidence, motivation to work toward goals, group and interpersonal effectiveness, teamwork, skill in negotiating disagreements, and leadership potential (Carnevale, Gainer, & Meltzer, 1988). People need those qualities even more today as the workplace increasingly is characterized by competitive pressures, constant change, and downsizing.

Second, workplace interventions to improve emotional intelligence are necessary because many adults now enter the world of work without the necessary competencies. Another national survey of employers found that more than half the people who work for them lack the motivation to keep learning and improving in their job. Four in ten are not able to work cooperatively with fellow employees. And only 19 percent of those applying for entry-level jobs have enough self-discipline in their work habits (Harris Education Research Council, 1991).

Third, workplace interventions make sense because many employers already have the means and the motivation for providing the necessary training experiences. American industry currently spends over $50 billion each year on training, and much of this training focuses on social and emotional abilities. When the American Society for Training and Development asked a group of fifty leading-edge companies whether they were trying to promote emotional intelligence in their employees through training and development activities, four out of five reported that they were (American Society for Training and Development, 1997).

There is one more reason why it makes sense to target the workplace as a site for intervention: most adults spend more of their waking hours at work than any other place. Whether the motivation is to promote greater organizational productivity and competitiveness, individual success and career advancement, or physical health and personal well-being, the workplace is the best setting for reaching adults.

PAST EFFORTS TO IMPROVE EMOTIONAL INTELLIGENCE

Although interest in the concept of emotional intelligence is rather new, efforts to improve the social and emotional competence of employees have a long history. Ever since the famous Hawthorne studies of the late 1920s, scholars and managers have been keenly interested in the social aspects of work (Roethlisberger & Dickson, 1939). Those studies showed that the social and emotional needs of workers were as important for work motivation as monetary incentives or threats. More specifically, they suggested that when managers pay more attention to employees and show more concern for their well-being, both satisfaction and performance increase. These findings ultimately led to the development of training programs that taught managers how to better manage human relations in their work groups.

Interest in human relations training for managers increased following World War II. Kurt Lewin's work on the effects of participation and autocratic versus democratic leadership styles formed the basis for much management training during the following five decades (Lewin, 1947, 1948). The National Training Lab, founded by some of Lewin's students and colleagues in 1947, also contributed to interest in social and emotional learning, particularly for supervisors, managers, and executives.

It was not long before studies of human relations–oriented training efforts began to appear in the literature. A doctoral dissertation on human relations training is recorded in *Dissertation Abstracts* in 1950, and there were 200 more such studies during the next twenty years. The earliest programs relied heavily on lecture and group discussion, with some role playing exercises to teach skills. In the 1960s, the t-group emerged as a new method for helping managers and other employees develop greater self-awareness and interpersonal sensitivity. As research and theory on leadership changed, the focus of training programs also shifted. However, a large percentage continued to emphasize social and emotional competence. A recent example was an effort to train managers in "transformational leadership" (Barling, Weber, & Kelloway, 1996).

Many other types of workplace training and development efforts have focused on enhancing social and emotional competence. In health care settings, for example, there have been a number of training programs directed to increasing the empathy and communications skills of physicians. Police officers also have received training in competencies associated with emotional intelligence. Stress management programs, which became particularly popular in the 1980s, teach employees self-management competencies.

Conflict management programs have also incorporated a skills training component that emphasizes social and emotional competencies. In fact, Morton Deutsch, a leading figure in the study of conflict resolution, has chastised his colleagues for not sufficiently emphasizing the role of "abilities and skills" in theoretical discussions of conflict resolution. In arguing that training in these skills "should be more widespread," he specifically mentioned emotional and social competencies such as the abilities to establish an effective working relationship with each of the conflicting parties, develop a creative group process, and establish a cooperative problem-solving attitude in the midst of conflict (Deutsch, 1994, pp. 25–26).

Diversity programs and training in "cultural competence" represent another area in which social and emotional learning has played an important role. For instance, one expert in this area wrote that multicultural competence refers to the "ability to demonstrate respect and understanding, communicate effectively, and work collaboratively with people from diverse backgrounds" (Garcia, 1995, p. 493). He proposed training that focuses on "personal knowledge and skills" as well as interpersonal competencies.

Thus, there are many areas of human resource development practice today that involve training in the competencies associated with emotional intelligence, and such training has a long history in both the private and public sectors. But how effective have these efforts been? And are there programs and intervention models that have been empirically validated?

WHAT WORKS?

One can find effective programs for improving emotional intelligence in a number of different areas associated with training and development. These include management training programs, communication and empathy training programs for physicians, programs to teach police how to handle conflict, stress management training, self-management training, and training for unemployed workers. In this section, I present some examples of each of these types of programs and then conclude with a brief discussion of negative findings.

Management Training

As I noted above, management training interventions focusing on the development of emotional and interpersonal competencies began to appear in the research literature in the early 1950s. By the mid-1980s, there had been scores of well-controlled studies evaluating different types of management training programs, including those focused on social and emotional competence. At that time, Burke and Day (1986) published a meta-analysis of management training programs in which they singled out for evaluation various types of programs, including those with either a human relations or a self-awareness focus. They found that human relations training with managers, as measured by objective results criteria (such as performance measures, absenteeism), was highly effective: the average effect size for human relations training as measured by objective results criteria was 1.01. Such training was also moderately effective as measured by subjective ratings of on-the-job behavior (such as ratings by coworkers or supervisors), with an average effect size of .39. Self-awareness training also had a moderately strong impact on on-the-job behavior as measured by subjective ratings: the average effect size was .61.

One of the earliest examples of successful human relations training for managers was a program offered to hundreds of supervisory and middle-level managers throughout the state of Pennsylvania during the 1960s (Hand & Slocum, 1972). The training consisted of twenty-eight weekly, ninety-minute sessions. The first phase of the training focused on discussions of leaders, leadership, followership, and leadership styles. The next phase, which was the largest component of the training, involved experiential learning exercises such as self-ratings on the managerial grid, a measure of leadership style, judgment and decision-making activities, in-basket exercises, and listening and interview exercises. The last phase of the training focused on theories of motivation. An evaluation of the program showed that managers who completed the training, compared to a control group, became more self-aware, more sensitive to the needs of others, and more trustworthy, as measured by behavior ratings completed by subordinates and superiors as well as self-ratings. Subordinates of the trained managers also reported that rapport and communication with the managers improved. Most of these changes persisted and were still apparent eighteen months following the completion of training.

In 1974, Goldstein and Sorcher (1974) published a book in which they suggested how social learning theory (Bandura, 1977) could be used as the basis for training supervisors to be more effective in handling the interpersonal aspects of their jobs. Since then, a training approach that combines modeling, role playing practice, feedback, and reinforcement has been used by a number of different consulting firms. Such training has involved more than a million supervisors in a wide range of industries including government, banking, insurance, manufacturing, and health care. In the typical version, the program designers begin by identifying several interpersonal situations that prove problematic for a group of supervisors. Then they make training videos in which actors model the most effective way of handling the interaction in each situation. When the trainers show the video to the trainees, they highlight a set of "learning points"—aspects of the model's behavior that are most important to study and learn. After watching the model and discussing the learning points, the trainees begin to work on emulating the model in role plays. After each attempt, they receive positive feedback and suggestions for improvement from the other participants and the trainers. The trainees continue to practice until they reach a certain level of mastery.

Several evaluation studies of behavior modeling training have been published since the late 1970s, and they suggest that this approach can be effective when implemented properly (Burnaska, 1976; Byham, Adams, & Kiggins, 1976; Latham & Saari, 1979; Moses & Ritchie, 1976; Russ-Eft & Zenger, 1997; Smith, 1976). For instance, in one case the program was implemented with a group of supervisors in a forest products company (Porras & Anderson, 1981). The results indicated that within two months following completion of the behavior modeling program, the trained supervisors had significantly increased their use of all five target behaviors. No comparable change occurred in a control group. Further, most of these improvements maintained themselves or increased during the following six months. Even more impressive, the work groups of the trained supervisors pulled ahead of the controls in several performance and productivity measures, such as increased monthly production, improved recovery rates, and decreased turnover and absenteeism.

Emotional intelligence involves more than just human relation competencies; self-motivation is another dimension that has been associated with the concept. One type of management training program that specifically targets self-motivation is achievement motivation training, based on the work of McClelland and his colleagues (Miron & McClelland, 1979). Versions of this program have been offered on numerous occasions, and there have been several evaluation studies documenting its effectiveness. The program uses a variety of methods, including self-assessment, lecture and discussion, case studies, and simulations to help participants become more aware of achievement-oriented thinking and to develop a stronger achievement drive. The results of one evaluation showed that program participants evidenced a significantly higher rate of advancement within their companies when compared to a control group (Aronoff & Litwin, 1971). In another evaluation study, an achievement motivation training program targeted at small business owners was shown to be effective in influencing business performance (Miron & McClelland, 1979). Results of a cost-benefit analysis of this government-sponsored program showed that the net increase in tax revenues due to the increased profitability of the targeted businesses more than paid for the program. The cost-benefit ratio after two years was more than five to one.

A more recent management development application is executive coaching. This approach, which has become quite popular, usually targets the whole range of emotional intelligence competencies. It is a highly individualized program targeted at executives and middle managers. Although executive coaching is being used in hundreds of organizations, there are few systematic evaluations of its efficacy. An exception is the Individual Coaching for Effectiveness program (Peterson, 1996). The typical participant in this program goes through an initial one-to-two-day diagnostic assessment and feedback session, followed by the coaching phase, which involves about one day of training per month for the next six months. The typical participant receives about fifty hours of intensive one-on-one work. Specific behavioral learning objectives are developed for each individual. These objectives are defined in terms of expected on-the-job behaviors. Each person's goals are unique, based on an integration of the organization's description of the person's needs and the results of a diagnostic assessment. In order to evaluate the program, ratings of each behavior are collected from the participant, the coach, and the participant's supervisor before coaching. These ratings are compared with scores immediately after training and six months after training is complete. Change on targeted behaviors is compared to change on behaviors that are rated but not targeted. In this way each participant serves as his or her own control. Results of one published evaluation of the program indicated that all three ratings showed improvement on behaviors targeted for coaching. There was no change on nontargeted behaviors. Moreover these improvements were maintained over time as evidenced by a follow-up evaluation (Peterson, 1993).

Some of the most important management training occurs in master's programs in business administration. In the past, such programs have emphasized cognitive and analytical skills while ignoring the development of emotional intelligence. For this reason, employers of these graduates are often critical of management schools (Dowd & Liedtka, 1994). One business administration program that is an exception is the competency-based program at Case Western Reserve University's Weatherhead School of Management (Boyatzis, Cowen, & Kolb, 1995). The curriculum makes the promotion of social and emotional competence an integral part of each student's education. All first-year students go through two weeks of in-depth assessment activities in which the social and emotional competencies associated with managerial success are assessed. Then they spend the next seven weeks studying the results of those assessments and using them to develop learning plans for the next two years. Several cohorts of students who have gone through the program have been evaluated longitudinally. Students who have participated in the competency-based program have been compared to those who went through the traditional program. These comparisons suggest that the program helps promote positive change in many different social and emotional competencies, including initiative, flexibility, achievement drive, empathy, self-confidence, persuasiveness, networking, self-control, and group management (Boyatzis, 1996).

Communication and Empathy Training with Physicians

Although many efforts to promote social and emotional competence occur in the context of management training and development, there are other contexts as well, and some of this work has also been evaluated. For instance, there is an accumulating body of research suggesting that well-designed training programs for physicians not only improve their social competence but also the quality of health care delivery (Evans, Stanley, Mestrovic, & Rose, 1991; Greco, Francis, Buckley, Brownlea, & McGovern, 1998; Roter et al., 1998). An example of such a program is the one developed and evaluated in the pediatrics ward at a large university hospital in Israel (Kramer, Ber, & Moore, 1989). The participants were fifth-year medical students. The training consisted of ten ninety-minute meetings held twice weekly for five weeks. Each meeting was structured around a particular topic, such as initial patient history taking, diagnosis of a severe disease, family counseling, or crisis intervention. Activities included role play in which the students played the parts of doctors, patients, and family members. The students also observed interviews in which live patients discussed their experiences with health care personnel and systems. An evaluation study indicated that students who went through the training showed a significant and lasting increase in supporting behavior during actual interviews with patients, as measured by independent observers, whereas students in the control group showed a significant decrease in supporting behavior. Evaluations of similar programs suggest that they also result in more efficient and productive interviews (for example, patients provide more information) and greater patient satisfaction (Evans et al., 1991; Greco et al., 1998; Roter et al., 1998).

Teaching Police to Handle Conflict

Recent protests over police brutality in many American cities point to the importance of emotional intelligence in police work. A police officer's emotional and social competence can literally mean the difference between life and death. For instance, a study of New York City traffic police showed that those who managed a calm response when faced with angry motorists had the fewest incidents escalate into violence (Brondolo, 1996). Such research has convinced a number of police departments to adopt training designed to help police officers better manage their own reactions and those of others in conflict situations. One of the earliest programs involved police officers assigned to the New York City Housing Authority (Zacker & Bard, 1973). Training procedures included group discussions, real-life simulations of interpersonal conflicts, role plays, and lectures. Evaluation research indicated that officers who completed the program performed significantly better than a control group on a number of performance criteria deemed important by police officials, such as clearance rates, total arrests, number of misdemeanors, and total crime.

Stress Management Training

Stress management training programs target the self-regulation dimension of emotional intelligence. Stress management programs, like some other human resource development initiatives, became popular in industry for a while and then seemed to lose their appeal. However, a number of studies suggest that when these programs are well designed and effectively implemented, they can produce significant improvements in coping and health outcomes. Furthermore, such improvement can have a measurable impact on the bottom line.

Stress management training can take many forms. The most effective programs teach participants a combination of techniques such as breathing, autogenic training (which involves thinking about the bodily sensations associated with physical and mental relaxation, such as warmth or heaviness), mental imagery, muscle relaxation, and cognitive restructuring. Lectures on stress and its consequences are typically followed by training in specific coping methods.

A number of evaluation studies have employed pretest and posttest control group designs with follow-ups of six to twelve months or even longer. They have also assessed change on a number of different types of outcomes. The most common has been self-reported stress and stress symptoms: several studies have shown that stress management training can produce significant improvements in measures of subjective well-being and physical symptoms (Backman, Arnetz, Levin, & Lublin, 1997; Cecil & Forman, 1990; Charlesworth, Williams, & Baer, 1984; Friedman, Lehrer, & Stevens, 1983; Monroy, Jonas, Mathey, & Murphy, 1997; Tsai & Crockett, 1993). A few studies also have shown a positive impact on objective physiological measures such as electromyograph results (Murphy & Sorenson, 1988), adrenaline levels (McNulty, Jefferys, Singer, & Singer, 1984), and blood pressure (Charlesworth et al., 1984). In one study, a ten-week program for hypertensive employees in a large corporation led to a sharp cut in health care claims; the average value of claims for the year following the program was half the annual average for the previous two and one-half (Charlesworth et al., 1984). In another study, a program for highway maintenance workers led to a significant improvement in attendance records (Murphy & Sorenson, 1988). And a study involving forty-four hospitals found that a comprehensive stress management program led to a significant reduction in malpractice claims (Jones et al., 1988).

Self-Management Training

Self-management training is another type of intervention that specifically targets the self-regulation dimension of emotional intelligence. Although the earliest applications were in clinical contexts (Kanfer, 1986; Kanfer & Phillips, 1970), self-management training has been used widely in work settings as well.

In one study, the participants were blue-collar employees, working for a state government, who had an abnormally high absenteeism record (Frayne & Latham, 1987; Latham & Frayne, 1989). They received eight weekly one-hour group sessions during which they were taught how to (1) set proximal and distal goals for job attendance, (2) write a behavioral contract with themselves for administering self-chosen reinforces and punishers, (3) self-monitor their attendance behavior, (4) administer these incentives, and (5) brainstorm potential problems in implementing their plan and come up with potential solutions. The group sessions were supplemented with one-hour per week individual sessions. An evaluation of the program suggested that it increased participant self-efficacy and job attendance. Participants in the program spent an average of thirty-eight hours per week on the job compared to the control group's thirty-three hours per week. Furthermore, this improvement was maintained for one year after employees completed the program.

Training for Unemployed Workers

Not all programs focus on those who already have a job. A particularly well researched program that targets a number of emotional intelligence competencies is the JOBS program (Caplan, Vinokur, & Price, 1996; Price & Vinokur, 1995). The main objective of this program is to enhance productive job-seeking skills and self-confidence for the unemployed. Short-term goals include fortifying job seekers' ability to resist demoralization and to persist in the face of barriers and setbacks. The long-term goal is to help persons seek employment in settings that maximize economic, social, and psychological rewards. The program helps participants to maintain high levels of motivation, become more adept at finding job leads and interviewing for jobs, and cope with the setbacks and frustrations associated with job seeking. Results of an evaluation indicated that program participants found employment sooner than a control group. A follow-up study showed continued beneficial effects on monthly earnings, level of employment, and episodes of employer and job changes. Four weeks after the intervention, the participants had earned, on average, $178 per month more than controls. At four months this advantage in earnings had increased to $227 per month, and by two and one-half years it had grown to $239 per month (Vinokur, van Ryn, Gramlich, & Price, 1991).

Personnel Selection Based on Emotional Intelligence Competencies

Although the focus of this chapter is on training and development, another workplace application that deserves mention involves emotional intelligence–based selection. The use of competency-based selection procedures for selecting high-performing employees has become a standard practice for many organizations, and a close inspection of the competency models that are used indicates that most of the competencies relate to emotional intelligence (Goleman, 1998). Several studies have shown that selecting employees based on emotional intelligence produces superior results compared to more traditional methods that may rely more on cognitive ability or technical knowledge (or simply how well a candidate performs in an unstructured job interview). An example is the competency-based selection program used by L'Oreal to hire sales people (Spencer & Spencer, 1993). The behavioral event interview was used to identify key competencies critical for success in sales. As used in this study, such an interview asked the individual to think of three situations at work in which the outcome was especially positive, and three situations in which the outcome was not positive. Then the interviewer asked a number of questions about each incident in order to get a full description of what happened and how the individual thought about it. The individual's answers were transcribed and later analyzed for themes relating to competencies. Once the competencies that distinguished the superior performers were identified, new salespeople were selected using the behavioral event interview. Data indicated that on an annual basis, the competency-selected salespeople sold $91,370 more than salespeople selected using the company's old selection procedure, for a net revenue increase of $2,558,360.

Selecting for emotional intelligence has produced even greater revenues when used for upper-level management positions. For instance, in one multinational beverage company, the average annual turnover among thirty-five divisional presidents was 25 percent (McClelland, 1999). When the company began to use behavioral event interviews to select divisional presidents based largely on social and emotional competencies, the turnover rate for the next one and one-half years dropped to 6.3 percent. Because the cost of replacing a divisional president was $250,000, selection based on emotional intelligence competencies saved the company almost $3.5 million during that one and one-half year period.

Negative Findings

Thus far I have focused on positive results. However, not all attempts to improve the emotional intelligence of employees in the workplace have been successful. Although researchers rarely publish negative findings, there are some to be found in the literature, and they can be as instructive as the successes. For instance, outdoor, experienced-based training programs such as Outward Bound have become popular in the business world, and many managers see them as a vehicle for enhancing social and emotional competence. However, two different studies could not find any positive effects on social and emotional competence for this type of program (Ibbetson & Newell, 1996; Stoltz, 1992). Other types of training programs have also been found lacking; for instance, a study that examined the impact of a human relations training program in a public bureaucracy found no evidence that it was successful in changing behavior (Miller, 1990). And when a large pharmaceutical firm evaluated a large number of its management training programs, it found that many were worthless (Morrow, Jarrett, & Rupinski, 1997).

These negative findings suggest that it is naive to assume that a training program, even one that is popular, such as Outward Bound, will necessarily be effective in enhancing social and emotional competence. They point to the need for evaluation that goes beyond the typical "smile sheets" that only tap participants' enjoyment of the training experience. Good evaluations must also assess whether a training experience has produced change in social and emotional competence, and whether that change transfers to meaningful behavior in the job situation. And there needs to be some kind of quasi-experimental control to ensure that positive changes are not the result of maturation, historical factors, or some other confounding variable.

These negative results also suggest that there may be certain ingredients that training programs need to incorporate in order to be effective. For instance, the evaluator of the unsuccessful human relations training program suggested that it may have been ineffective because it was too brief (only two days in length), it relied on massed practice rather than distributed practice, and there was insufficient posttraining support from management (Miller, 1990). Although we now have evidence that it is possible to help adults improve their emotional intelligence, and become more productive and successful workers in doing so, it is also clear that training and development efforts need to follow certain guidelines in order to be effective.

Ingredients of Effective Programs: Practice Guidelines

The Consortium for Research on Emotional Intelligence in Organizations recently sponsored a review of the research on training and development, counseling, psychotherapy, and behavior change in order to identify the factors that contribute to more effective social and emotional learning in work settings (Cherniss, Goleman, Emmerling, Cowan, & Adler, 1998). This review led to a set of empirically based practice guidelines, a modified version of which is summarized in the appendix at the end of this chapter. Although training and development efforts can be successful without adhering to all of the guidelines, chances for success are greatly improved as the number of guidelines that are followed increases. In fact, the impact of the guidelines may well be multiplicative.

Although many of the guidelines apply to all types of learning, they are especially crucial for efforts to improve emotional competence, because cognitive learning and emotional learning involve distinctly different neural processes (Goleman, 1998). In cognitive learning, new information is added to existing categories and maps, and new categories are formed. At the level of the brain, this involves adding to existing neural pathways. But in emotional learning, there are strong response habits that must be altered. Existing neural pathways must be weakened and eventually extinguished before new ones can be established (Edelman, 1987). What this means in practice is that the learning process requires repeated practice over a much longer time. Also, there will probably be many lapses and setbacks along the way. This means that the learners must enter the process with a high degree of motivation, and there must be considerable guidance and support to help them maintain that motivation until the new ways of thinking and acting become second nature. (Anyone who has tried to become less shy, more relaxed, or less prone to losing one's temper has discovered how difficult it can be to make a lasting change in social and emotional habits!)

Social and emotional learning also typically involves change that is much closer to the core of personal identity. We are what we *feel* much more than we are what we *think*. Being told, for instance, that one must learn a new word processing program involves less inner turmoil than being told that one must learn to be more assertive or to handle stress better. The need to improve emotional intelligence is more likely to generate defensiveness and resistance, and for this reason the change process must incorporate a number of practices that are less critical in cognitive learning situations.

The guidelines are grouped under the three major phases of the change process, which we have labeled (1) preparation for change, (2) doing the work of change, and (3) encouraging, maintaining, and evaluating change.

Preparation for Change

Some of the most important work in social and emotional learning occurs even before the process of active change begins. People are most likely to be motivated to improve an emotional competence if they are convinced that such a change will lead to desirable consequences. Many approach training and development experiences with a skeptical "show me" attitude. For this reason, as well as others that should be obvious, it is important to determine which competencies are critical for effectiveness in any particular job and organization. Supervisors, for instance, are more likely to be willing to learn how to become more empathic if they see evidence that greater empathy will lead to more motivated, committed, and productive employees. Thus, efforts to improve emotional competence should begin with an *assessment of the competencies that are most critical for organizational and individual effectiveness.* Methods for assessing competencies are reviewed by Spencer, McClelland, and Kelner (1997).

Once the learners recognize that a particular set of competencies is important for effective performance, they may remain unmotivated unless they see evidence that they are lacking in one or more of those competencies. Many people are unaware of their strengths or weaknesses in the emotional and social domain. For example, Davis and Kraus (1997) have found that there is no correlation between people's estimates of their empathy and their scores on objective tests of empathy. Thus another guideline is that *learners be assessed on the target competencies prior to starting the learning process.* But assessment is not enough. The way in which the assessment results are delivered to the learners is crucial. Learners need time to reflect on and assimilate the results, and they need to do so in a supportive, safe environment. It often is not enough, for instance, to be given only a printout with one's assessment results and a written description of what it means.

Once the learners are clear about their strengths and limits, motivation and commitment to change may be strong. But readiness for change should not be taken for granted. At this stage it is important to *gauge whether the learners are truly committed to embarking on an arduous change program.* If they are not, then it is probably unwise to proceed with training. A better course of action would be to make readiness for change the focus of activity (Prochaska, Norcross, & DiClemente, 1994). That means that energy should go into activities that might increase the learners' motivation to change.

Even if learners are ready to embark on the change process, motivation and commitment can be further strengthened by helping them to *set specific, meaningful, and realistic goals for change.* A number of studies have documented the motivating power of goals (Locke & Latham, 1990; Wexley & Baldwin, 1986). But not just any goal will do. The goal needs to be specific, not vague. And it needs to be challenging enough to engage the learner, but not so challenging that the learner is likely to fail. Most important, the goal needs to be meaningful to the individual. This means it needs to be linked to what the learner most values.

Goals are most meaningful when they are the *learner's* goals and not someone else's. Ideally, the decision to change, the change goals, and the way in which those goals are pursued will be determined by the learners themselves. It is difficult, if not impossible, to change someone who does not want to change (Kolb & Boyatzis, 1970; Sonne & Janoff, 1982). Thus, whenever possible, *change should be self-directed.*

The final guideline for the preparation phase concerns the learners' expectations. Particularly in social and emotional learning, these expectations are likely to become self-fulfilling prophecies. Unfortunately, even when people are convinced that they should change, they may not be sure that they can. Thus self-efficacy is crucial for effective social and emotional learning in adults (Bandura, Adams, & Beyer, 1977; Gist, Stevens, & Bavetta, 1991). Training programs will be more effective if they include activities designed to *help learners develop positive expectations for the training,* in other words, to realize that it is possible (although not necessarily quick and easy) to improve whatever competencies they are interested in improving.

Doing the Work of Change

The next set of guidelines relates directly to the training or development process. The first concerns *the trainer and the relationship between the trainer and the learners.* Although the teacher is important in any learning situation, the role of the teacher is crucial in social and emotional learning. Technical skill is not enough. The trainers themselves need to be emotionally intelligent, for they are models for the learners (Burns & Nolen-Hoeksema, 1992; Henry, Schacht, & Strupp, 1986). Also, social and emotional change needs to occur in a safe and supportive setting, and the relationship between trainers and learners becomes crucial in defining how safe and supportive the learning environment is for the learners. Thus, the trainers must be carefully selected for their social and emotional competencies. And they should be closely monitored and guided at least during the early part of their work to ensure that they use those competencies effectively in helping the learners to change.

Unlike cognitive learning, emotional learning occurs mostly at the nonverbal level because it involves neural pathways in the limbic system, a part of the brain that developed long before humans had language. Many of the guidelines relating to the change process are based on this fact. Thus, for instance, live *models* (which includes models depicted on videotape) that demonstrate the skills and competencies to be mastered are more effective than simply telling the learners what to do and how to do it (Bandura et al., 1977; Tannenbaum & Yukl, 1992). Most of the training also should involve *experiential learning* rather than lecture and discussion (Robins & Hayes, 1993). And there should be ample opportunity for the learners to practice the new skills repeatedly, both within the training setting and in as many other domains of their lives as possible. The principles of distributed rather than massed practice, and overlearning, are well established in the experimental research on learning, but they are often not followed in workplace training programs (Dempster, 1988). Research on the dose-response effect in psychotherapy also shows that the longer people work at changing, the more durable the change will be. Most people do not show stable changes until they have completed at least a dozen or more sessions (Howard, Kopta, Krause, & Orlinsky, 1986). These findings fit with what we know about brain function: the old, deeply embedded neural pathways in the emotional centers of the brain can be changed only through an experiential learning process that involves *repeated modeling, practice, and corrective feedback.*

Receiving feedback on practice is particularly invaluable. In a study of self-development groups conducted for students attending a business school, the amount of feedback individuals received from other group members during the last half of the group was one of two factors that predicted success. Improving the change method to enhance feedback increased the percentage of learners who successfully attained their goals from 5 percent to 61 percent (Kolb, Winter, & Berlew, 1968).

Even if the training process incorporates all of the guidelines I have presented, and the learners are highly motivated, setbacks and lapses in this kind of learning are inevitable. And such setbacks can undermine a learner's commitment to the change effort. Thus, one other guideline for the change phase involves *preparing the learners in advance for these setbacks.* Sometimes referred to as "relapse prevention," this type of training activity encourages the learners to anticipate what barriers and problems they might encounter when they begin to apply what they have learned in their day-to-day lives. Then they think about how those setbacks might affect them emotionally and what they might do to deal effectively with those problems and their emotional consequences when they occur. In this way, the learners can be inoculated against the demoralization that might undermine their efforts to maintain change.

A growing body of research points to the value of relapse prevention. For instance, one study showed that adding relapse prevention to a management training program helped increase transfer of skills to the job (Tziner, Haccoun, & Kadish, 1991). Several other studies have also documented the value of relapse prevention in training (Gist et al., 1991; Noe, Sears, & Fullenkamp, 1990; Vinokur & Schul, 1997).

Encouraging, Maintaining, and Evaluating Change

Just as much important work occurs even before the learning process formally begins, so too does much need to be done after training formally ends. In order to encourage people to use the social and emotional competencies they have developed, it often is helpful to *provide social support* through groups, coaching, or mentoring arrangements (Kram, 1996). Through periodic meetings with supportive individuals, learners are prompted and reinforced to think and act in ways that still may be somewhat foreign for them and others with whom they work. A like-minded group of people can help its members to maintain the changes that have recently occurred, as research on self-help groups amply demonstrates (Hinrichsen, Revenson, & Shinn, 1985; Levy, 1976; Lieberman & Borman, 1979; McCrady & Miller, 1993; Powell, 1994).

Although support groups or coaches can help maintain change, the effort will prove difficult if not impossible unless there is *a supportive environment in the learner's work group and organization.* Even prior to starting the training program, its developers should work on establishing organizational policies and procedures that support the development of social and emotional competence. The actions of the organization's leaders are especially important. Supervisors and the top leaders provide models that can encourage—or discourage—learners from using emotional intelligence at work (Manz & Sims, 1986; Weiss, 1977). Supervisors can also help learners apply these competencies through reinforcement of various kinds (Baldwin & Ford, 1988; Noe & Schmitt, 1986). Daily activities can also reinforce or undermine people's willingness to act in emotionally intelligent ways.

The final guideline concerns *evaluation.* All training efforts, of course, should be evaluated to determine not just whether people feel good about them but also whether they produce meaningful changes in on-the-job behavior (Kraiger & Jung, 1997). But this is especially important for emotional intelligence promotion efforts because there is often greater skepticism about whether such work is useful. Even managers who recognize that emotional intelligence is important for individual and organizational success may question whether a training initiative can bring about significant improvements in these competencies. Good evaluations with pretraining and posttraining assessments of meaningful outcomes, and comparisons between individuals who receive the training and those who do not, can provide a strong rationale for this type of effort. ("Meaningful outcomes" include not only competencies assessed through tests such as the ECI, EQ-i, or the Mayer-Salovey-Caruso Emotional Intelligence Test (MSCEIT) (Mayer, Caruso, & Salovey, forthcoming) but also hard measures relating to performance and productivity.) Equally important, evaluation research can, and should, be used to help program managers see why and how a training effort works and ways in which it can be improved in the future.

Unfortunately, evaluation of emotional intelligence programs in the corporate world has been rare. An October 1997 survey of thirty-five highly regarded benchmark companies conducted by the American Society for Training and Development found that of the twenty-seven companies that said they tried to promote emotional competence through training and development, more than two-thirds made no attempt to evaluate the effect of these efforts. Those that did attempt to evaluate their efforts relied primarily on measures such as reactions to training and employee opinion surveys (American Society for Training and Development, 1997).

CONCLUSION

Given that there is a long history of efforts to improve social and emotional competencies in the workplace, and there have been effective models available to practitioners, one might wonder whether the concept of emotional intelligence adds anything new. I believe it does, and its contribution is a conceptual one that could have great practical significance.

For instance, much of the previous work in this area has been guided either by a focus on social skills or a rather vague concern with personal growth and humanism. Behavioral modeling programs, for instance, focus on teaching supervisors the social behaviors that should lead to more effective interpersonal functioning. However, the concept of emotional intelligence, as elaborated by Goleman (1998), suggests that social skills in part depend on more fundamental emotional competence. When a supervisor finds it difficult to deal with a "problem employee," lack of listening skill on the supervisor's part may well contribute to the difficulty. However, it is likely that the supervisor's emotional reactions (anger, resentment, anxiety) also play a role. In order to listen well, the supervisor must be able to monitor and regulate his or her own emotional reactions. The concept of emotional intelligence thus suggests that training may be needed to help such a supervisor develop greater emotional self-awareness, self-management, and empathy, as well as social skills.

One can put this idea in the form of a hypothesis that can be the basis for future research and practice: training programs that help participants develop greater self-awareness, self-management, and empathy—along with social skills—will be more effective than programs that target only social skills.

Another area for future research and practice concerns the relationship between individual emotional intelligence and "organizational emotional intelligence." Can one think meaningfully about emotional intelligence on a group or organizational level? In other words, is there something analogous to emotional self-awareness or self-management in a group or an organization? If so, what does it look like and how can we measure it? And what are the most effective methods for improving group and organizational competence? Previous research on organizational effectiveness has led to the development of organizational surveys, which include dimensions that resemble some of the individual emotional intelligence competencies (Personnel Resources and Development Center, 1997). And there are other emotional intelligence competencies that have not been conceived of or measured on the group or organizational level but could be. This promising area for future research represents another contribution that the concept of emotional intelligence makes.

Emotional intelligence at the individual and group or organizational levels converges in the exercise of leadership. The emotional intelligence of a group's leader, for instance, will have a powerful impact on the group's climate and effectiveness (Kelner, Rivers, & O'Connell, 1994; Kozlowski & Doherty, 1989; Litwin & Stringer, 1968). Of course, groups also have a powerful impact on their leaders. But the emotionally intelligent leader is aware of those influences, recognizes when they become pernicious, and has the capability to manage them in a way that minimizes harm. Emotionally intelligent leaders understand group, intergroup, and organizational dynamics, particularly as they affect emotional functioning, and they are skillful in working with those dynamics for the benefit of individuals and their organization. Hopefully, the ideas and guidelines in this chapter will help schools and work organizations to develop leaders with just this kind of emotional intelligence.

APPENDIX

The Best Practice Guidelines

Phase 1: Preparation for Change

1. *Assess the organization's needs.* Determine the competencies that are most critical for effective performance in a particular job. In doing so, use a valid method, such as comparison of the behavioral events interviews of superior performers and average performers. Also make sure the competencies to be developed are congruent with the organization's culture and overall strategy.

2. *Assess each person's strengths and limits on the key competencies and deliver the results with care.* The data should come from multiple

sources using multiple methods to maximize credibility and validity. In delivering the results to the individual, try to be accurate and clear. Also, allow plenty of time for the person to digest and integrate the information. Deliver the results in a safe and supportive environment in order to minimize resistance and defensiveness. But also avoid making excuses or downplaying the seriousness of deficiencies.

3. *Gauge readiness of the learners before starting the development process.* If they are not motivated enough, make readiness a focus for change. Do not begin training and development until the learners are ready.

4. *Set clear goals, link them to personal values, and break them into manageable steps.* People need to be clear about what the competence is, how to acquire it, and how to show it on the job. Spell out the specific behaviors and skills that make up the target competence. Make sure that the goals are clear, specific, meaningful, and optimally challenging.

5. *Make learning self-directed.* People are more motivated to change when they freely choose to do so. As much as possible, allow people to decide whether they will participate in the development process, and have them set the change goals themselves. Let them continue to be in charge of their learning throughout the program, and tailor the training approach to the individual's learning style.

6. *Help learners build positive expectations for the training.* Show them that the social and emotional competencies can be improved and that such improvement will lead to valued outcomes.

Phase 2: Training

1. *Foster a positive relationship between the trainer and learner.* Carefully select trainers based on their warmth, empathy, and ability to relate to the learners, as well as their technical knowledge of the subject and their presentation skills. Once they begin to do the training, give the trainers ongoing evaluation and feedback on their competencies.

2. *Use "live" models to teach the competencies.* High status, highly effective people who embody the competence can be models who inspire change.

3. *Rely on experiential methods.* Emphasize active learning. Spend more time in demonstrations and practice of the competencies than in presenting lectures on them or having learners read about them.

4. *Provide opportunities for practice and give frequent feedback on practice efforts.* Encourage learners to use naturally arising opportunities for practice at work and in life, and to try the new behaviors repeatedly and consistently, over a period of months.

5. *Inoculate against setbacks so that they are not seen as signals of defeat.* Help learners anticipate and prepare for lapses. Use relapse prevention, which helps people use lapses and slip-ups as lessons to prepare themselves better for the next round.

Phase 3: Encouraging, Maintaining, and Evaluating Change

1. *Build in social support.* Encourage the formation of groups where people give each other support throughout the change effort. Even a single buddy or coach will help.

2. *Create an encouraging environment.* Organizational policies and procedures should reinforce people to work on improving their social and emotional competence. Supervisors also should provide encouragement and the necessary support. Help supervisors to value and exhibit the competencies and integrate emotional competence into the daily activities and culture of the organization.

3. *Conduct ongoing evaluation research.* Find unobtrusive measures of the competence or skill as shown on the job, ideally before and after training, and also at least two months (and, if possible, a year or more) later.

References

American Society for Training and Development. (1997). *Benchmarking forum member-to-member survey results.* Alexandria, VA: Author.

Aronoff, J., & Litwin, G. H. (1971). Achievement motivation training and executive advancement. *Journal of Applied Behavioral Science, 7,* 215–229.

Backman, L., Arnetz, B. B., Levin, D., & Lublin, A. (1997). Psychophysiological effects of mental imaging training for police trainees. *Stress Medicine, 13,* 43–48.

Baldwin, T. T., & Ford, J. K. (1988). Transfer of training: A review and directions for future research. *Personnel Psychology, 41,* 63–105.

Bandura, A. (1977). *Social Learning Theory.* Englewood Cliffs, NJ: Prentice-Hall.

Bandura, A., Adams, N., & Beyer, J. (1977). Cognitive processes mediating behavioral change. *Journal of Personality and Social Psychology, 35,* 125–139.

Barling, J., Weber, T., & Kelloway, E. K. (1996). Effects of transformational leadership training on attitudinal and financial outcomes: A field experiment. *Journal of Applied Psychology, 81,* 827–832.

Boyatzis, R. (1982). *The competent manager: A model for effective performance.* New York: Wiley.

Boyatzis, R. E. (1996). Competencies can be developed, but not in the way we thought. *Capability, 2,* 25–41.

Boyatzis, R. E., Cowen, S. S., & Kolb, D. A. (1995). *Innovation in professional education: Steps on a journey to learning.* San Francisco: Jossey-Bass.

Brondolo, E. (1996). Correlates of risk for conflict among New York City traffic agents. In G. R. VandenBos & E. Q. Bulatao (Eds.), *Violence on the job: Identifying risks and developing solutions.* Washington, DC: American Psychological Association.

Burke, M., & Day, R. (1986). A Cumulative Study of the Effectiveness of Managerial Training. *Journal of Applied Psychology, 71,* 232–245.

Burnaska, R. F. (1976). The effects of behavior modeling training upon managers' behaviors and employees' perceptions. *Personnel Psychology, 29,* 329–335.

Burns, D. D., & Nolen-Hoeksema, S. (1992). Therapeutic empathy and recovery from depression in cognitive-behavioral therapy: A structural equation model. *Journal of Consulting and Clinical Psychology, 60,* 441–449.

Byham, W. C., Adams, D., & Kiggins, A. (1976). Transfer of modeling training to the job. *Personnel Psychology, 29,* 345–349.

Caplan, R. D., Vinokur, A. D., & Price, R. H. (1996). From job loss to reemployment: Field experiments in prevention-focused coping. In G. W. Albee & T. P. Gullota (Eds.), *Primary prevention works: Issues in children's and families' lives* (Vol. 6, pp. 341–379). Thousand Oaks, CA: Sage.

Carnevale, A. P., Gainer, L. J., & Meltzer, A. S. (1988). Workplace basics: The skills employers want. *Training and Development Journal, 42,* 22–26.

Cecil, M. A., & Forman, S. G. (1990). Effects of stress inoculation training and coworker support groups on teachers' stress. *Journal of School Psychology, 28,* 105–118.

Charlesworth, E. A., Williams, B. J., & Baer, P. E. (1984). Stress management at the worksite for hypertension: Compliance, cost-benefit, health care and hypertension-related variables. *Psychosomatic Medicine, 46,* 387–397.

Cherniss, C., Goleman, D., Emmerling, R., Cowan, K., & Adler, M. (1998). *Bringing emotional intelligence to the workplace.* New Brunswick, NJ: Consortium for Research on Emotional Intelligence in Organizations, Rutgers University.

Davis, M., & Kraus, L. (1997). Personality and accurate empathy. In W. Ickes (Ed.), *Empathic accuracy.* New York: Guilford Press.

Dempster, F. N. (1988). The spacing effect: A case study in the failure to apply the results of psychological research. *American Psychologist, 43,* 627–634.

Deutsch, M. (1994). Constructive conflict resolution: Principles, training, and research. *Journal of Social Issues, 50,* 13–32.

Dowd, K. O., & Liedtka, J. (1994, Winter). What corporations seek in MBA hires: A survey. *Magazine of the Graduate Admission Council, 10,* 34–39.

Edelman, G. (1987). *Neural Darwinism: The theory of neuronal group selection.* New York: Basic Books.

Evans, B. J., Stanley, R. O., Mestrovic, R., & Rose, L. (1991). Effects of communication skills training on students' diagnostic efficiency. *Medical Education, 25,* 517–526.

Frayne, C. A., & Latham, G. P. (1987). Application of social learning theory to employee self-management of attendance. *Journal of Applied Psychology, 72,* 387–392.

Friedman, G. H., Lehrer, B. E., & Stevens, J. P. (1983). The effectiveness of self-directed and lecture/discussion stress management approaches and the locus of control of teachers. *American Educational Research Journal, 20,* 563–580.

Garcia, M. H. (1995). An anthropological approach to multicultural diversity training. *Journal of Applied Behavioral Science, 31,* 490–504.

Gist, M. E., Stevens, C. K., & Bavetta, A. G. (1991). Effects of self-efficacy and post-training intervention on the acquisition and maintenance of complex interpersonal skills. *Personnel Psychology, 44,* 837–861.

Goldstein, A. P., & Sorcher, M. (1974). *Changing supervisory behavior.* New York: Pergamon.

Goleman, D. (1995). *Emotional intelligence.* New York: Bantam.

Goleman, D. (1998). *Working with emotional intelligence.* New York: Bantam.

Greco, M., Francis, W., Buckley, J., Brownlea, A., & McGovern, J. (1998). Real-patient evaluation of communication skills teaching for GP registrars. *Family Practice, 15,* 51–57.

Hand, H. H., & Slocum, J. W. (1972). A longitudinal study of the effects of a human relations training program on managerial effectiveness. *Journal of Applied Psychology, 56,* 412–417.

Harris Education Research Council. (1991). *An assessment of American education.* New York: Committee for Economic Development.

Henry, W. P., Schacht, T. E., & Strupp, H. H. (1986). Structural analysis of social behavior: Application to a study of interpersonal process in differential psychotherapeutic outcome. *Journal of Consulting and Clinical Psychology, 54,* 27–31.

Hinrichsen, G. A., Revenson, T. A., & Shinn, M. (1985). Does self-help help? An empirical investigation of scoliosis peer support groups. *Journal of Social Issues, 41,* 65–87.

Howard, K., Kopta, S. M., Krause, M. S., & Orlinsky, D. E. (1986). The dose-effect relationship in psychotherapy. *American Psychologist, 41,* 159–164.

Ibbetson, A., & Newell, S. (1996). Winner takes all: An evaluation of adventure-based experiential training. *Management Learning, 27,* 163–185.

Jones, J. W., Barge, B. N., Steffy, B. D., Fay, L. M., Kunz, L. K., & Wuebker, L. J. (1988). Stress and medical malpractice: Organizational risk assessment and intervention. *Journal of Applied Psychology, 73,* 727–735.

Kanfer, F. H. (1986). Implications of a self-regulation model of therapy for treatment of addictive behaviors. In W. R. Miller & N. Heather (Eds.), *Treating addictive behaviors: Vol. II. Processes of change* (pp. 272–314). New York: Plenum Press.

Kanfer, F. H., & Phillips, J. S. (1970). *Learning foundations of behavior therapy.* New York: Wiley.

Kelner, S., Rivers, C., & O'Connell, K. (1994). *Managerial style as a behavioral predictor of organizational climate.* Boston: McBer.

Kolb, D., & Boyatzis, R. (1970). Goal-setting and self-directed behavior change. *Human Relations, 23,* 439–457.

Kolb, S. K., Winter, & Berlew, D. E. (1968). Self-directed change: Two studies. *Journal of Applied Behavioral Science, 4,* 453–471.

Kozlowski, S. W., & Doherty, M. L. (1989). Integration of climate and leadership: Examination of a neglected issue. *Journal of Applied Psychology, 74,* 546–553.

Kraiger, K., & Jung, K. M. (1997). Linking training objectives to evaluation criteria. In M. A. Quinones & A. Ehrenstein (Eds.), *Training for a rapidly changing workforce: Applications of psychological research* (pp. 151–175). Washington, DC: American Psychological Association.

Kram, K. E. (1996). A relational approach to career development. In D. T. Hall (Ed.), *The career is dead—long live the career* (pp. 132–157). San Francisco: Jossey-Bass.

Kramer, D., Ber, R., & Moore, M. (1989). Increasing empathy among medical students. *Medical Education, 23,* 168–173.

Latham, G. P., & Frayne, C. A. (1989). Self-management training for increasing job attendance: A follow-up and a replication. *Journal of Applied Psychology, 74,* 411–416.

Latham, G. P., & Saari, L. M. (1979). Application of social-learning theory to training supervisors through behavioral modeling. *Journal of Applied Psychology, 64,* 239–246.

Levy, L. H. (1976). Self-help groups: Types and psychological processes. *Journal of Applied Behavioral Science, 12,* 310–322.

Lewin, K. (1947). Frontiers in group dynamics: Concept, method, and reality in social science. *Human Relations, 1,* 5–13.

Lewin, K. (1948). *Resolving social conflicts.* New York: Harper.

Lieberman, M. A., & Borman, L. (1979). *Self-help groups for coping with crises: Origins, members, processes, and impact.* San Francisco: Jossey-Bass.

Litwin, G., & Stringer, R.A.J. (1968). *Motivation and organizational climate.* Boston: Harvard University, Graduate School of Business Administration, Division of Research.

Locke, E. A., & Latham, G. P. (1990). *A theory of goal setting and task performance.* Englewood Cliffs, NJ: Prentice-Hall.

Lusch, R. F., & Serpkeuci, R. (1990). Personal differences, job tension, job outcomes, and store performance: A study of retail managers. *Journal of Marketing, 54,* 85–101.

Manz, H. P., & Sims. (1986). Beyond imitation: Complex behavioral and affective linkages resulting from exposure to leadership training models. *Journal of Applied Psychology, 71,* 571–578.

Mayer, J. D., Caruso, D., & Salovey, P. (forthcoming). *Mayer-Salovey-Caruso Emotional Intelligence Test (MSCEIT).* Toronto, Canada: Multi-Health Systems.

McClelland, D. C. (1999). Identifying competencies with behavioral-event interviews. *Psychological Science, 9,* 331–339.

McCrady, B. S., & Miller, W. R. (1993). *Research on Alcoholics Anonymous: Opportunities and alternatives.* New Brunswick, NJ: Rutgers Center for Alcohol Studies.

McNulty, S., Jefferys, D., Singer, G., & Singer, L. (1984). Use of hormone analysis in the assessment of the efficacy of stress management training in police recruits. *Journal of Police Science and Administration, 12,* 130–132.

Miller, S. G. (1990). Effects of a municipal training program on employee behavior and attitude. *Public Personnel Management, 19,* 429–441.

Miron, D., & McClelland, D. C. (1979). The impact of achievement motivation training on small businesses. *California Management Review, 21,* 13–28.

Monroy, J., Jonas, H., Mathey, J., & Murphy, L. (1997). Holistic stress management at Corning. In M. K. Gowing, J. Quick, & J. D. Kraft (Eds.), *The new organizational reality: Downsizing, restructuring, and revitalization.* Washington, DC: American Psychological Association.

Morrow, C. C., Jarrett, M. Q., & Rupinski, M. T. (1997). An investigation of the effect and economic utility of corporate-wide training. *Personnel Psychology, 50,* 91–119.

Moses, J. L., & Ritchie, R. J. (1976). Supervisory relationships training: A behavioral evaluation of a behavior modeling program. *Personnel Psychology, 29,* 337–343.

Murphy, L. R., & Sorenson, S. (1988). Employee behaviors before and after stress management. *Journal of Organizational Behavior, 9,* 173–182.

Noe, R. A., & Schmitt, N. (1986). The influence of trainee attitudes on training effectiveness: Test of a model. *Personnel Psychology, 39,* 497–523.

Noe, R. A., Sears, J., & Fullenkamp, A. M. (1990). Relapse training: Does it influence trainees' post training behavior and cognitive strategies? *Journal of Business and Psychology, 4,* 317–328.

Personnel Resources and Development Center. (1997). *Individual and organizational competency linkages for high performance organizations.* Washington, DC: U.S. Office of Personnel Management.

Peterson, D. B. (1993, April). *Skill learning and behavior change in an individually tailored management coaching program.* Paper presented at the annual conference of the Society for Industrial and Organizational Psychology, San Francisco.

Peterson, D. B. (1996). Executive coaching at work: The art of one-on-one change. *Consulting Psychology Journal, 48,* 78–86.

Porras, J. I., & Anderson, B. (1981). Improving managerial effectiveness through modeling-based training. *Organizational Dynamics, 9,* 60–77.

Powell, T. J. (1994). *Understanding self-help: Frameworks and findings.* Newbury Park, CA: Sage.

Price, R. H., & Vinokur, A. D. (1995). Supporting career transitions in a time of organizational downsizing: The Michigan JOBS program. In M. London (Ed.), *Employees, careers, and job creation* (pp. 191–208). San Francisco: Jossey-Bass.

Prochaska, J. O., Norcross, J. C., & DiClemente, C. C. (1994). *Changing for good: The revolutionary program that explains the six stages of change and teaches you how to free yourself from bad habits.* New York: W. Morrow.

Robins, C. J., & Hayes, A. M. (1993). An appraisal of cognitive therapy. *Journal of Consulting and Clinical Psychology, 61,* 205–214.

Roethlisberger, F. J., & Dickson, W. J. (1939). *Management and the worker.* Cambridge, MA: Harvard University Press.

Rosier, R. H. (Ed.). (1994–1996). *The competency model handbook* (Vols. 1–3). Lexington, MA: Linkage.

Roter, D., Rosenbaum, J., de Negri, B., Renaud, D., DiPrete-Brown, L., & Hernandez, O. (1998). The effects of a continuing medical education programme in interpersonal communication skills on doctor practice and patient satisfaction in Trinidad and Tobago. *Medical Education, 32,* 181–189.

Russ-Eft, D. F., & Zenger, J. H. (1997). Behavior modeling training in North America: A research summary. In L. J. Bassi & D. F. Russ-Eft (Eds.), *What works* (pp. 89–109). Alexandria, VA: American Society of Training and Development.

Smith, P. (1976). Management modeling training to improve morale and customer satisfaction. *Personnel Psychology, 29,* 351–359.

Sonne, J. L., & Janoff, D. (1982). The effect of treatment attributions on the maintenance of weight reduction: A replication and extension. *Cognitive Therapy & Research, 3,* 389–397.

Spencer, L. M., Jr., & Spencer, S. (1993). *Competence at work: Models for superior performance.* New York: Wiley.

Spencer, L.M.J., McClelland, D. C., & Kelner, S. (1997). *Competency assessment methods: History and state of the art.* Boston: Hay/McBer.

Stoltz, P. G. (1992). An examination of leadership development in the great outdoors. *Human Resource Development Quarterly, 3,* 357–372.

Tannenbaum, S. I., & Yukl, G. (1992). Training and development in work organizations. *Annual Review of Psychology, 43,* 399–441.

Tsai, S.-L., & Crockett, M. S. (1993). Effects of relaxation training, combining imagery and meditation, on the stress level of Chinese nurses working in modern hospitals in Taiwan. *Issues in Mental Health Nursing, 14,* 51–66.

Tziner, A., Haccoun, R. R., & Kadish, A. (1991). Personal and situational characteristics influencing the effectiveness of transfer of training improvement strategies. *Journal of Occupational Psychology, 64,* 167–177.

Vinokur, A. D., & Schul, Y. (1997). Mastery and inoculation against setbacks as active ingredients in the JOBS intervention for the unemployed. *Journal of Clinical and Consulting Psychology, 65,* 867–877.

Vinokur, A. D., van Ryn, M., Gramlich, E. M., & Price, R. H. (1991). Long-term follow-up and benefit-cost analysis of the JOBS program: A preventive intervention for the unemployed. *Journal of Applied Psychology, 76,* 213–219.

Weiss, H. M. (1977). Subordinate imitation of supervisor behavior: The role of modeling in organizational socialization. *Organizational Behavior and Human Performance, 19,* 89–105.

Wexley, K. N., & Baldwin, T. T. (1986). Posttraining strategies for facilitation of positive transfer: An empirical exploration. *Academy of Management Review, 29,* 503–520.

Zacker, J., & Bard, M. (1973). Effects of conflict management training on police performance. *Journal of Applied Psychology, 58,* 202–208.

CHAPTER TWENTY-ONE

Emotional Intelligence, Adaptation to Stressful Encounters, and Health Outcomes

Gerald Matthews and Moshe Zeidner

"Indeed, keeping our distressing emotions in check is the key to emotional well-being" (Goleman, 1995, p. 56). The twentieth century has been variously called the age of stress and anxiety, and more recently, coping (Endler, 1996). Coping refers to a person's efforts to manage or control a situation viewed as stressful, or as overtaxing or challenging one's personal coping resources (Lazarus & Folkman, 1984). The relationship between coping processes and adaptational outcomes, such as psychological and physical health, has become a major concern among personality researchers (Lazarus, 1993; Zeidner & Matthews, 2000). Current transactional stress models (such as that of Lazarus & Folkman, 1984) view stress as a multivariate process involving inputs (person and environmental variables), outputs (immediate and long-term effects), and the mediating activities of appraisal and coping processes. Implicit in most descriptions of coping is the notion of effectiveness: "the prime importance of appraisal and coping processes is that they affect adaptational outcomes" (Lazarus & Folkman, 1984, p. 13). Furthermore, handling the aversive emotions evoked in a stressful encounter may be critical to the successful negotiation.

As our opening quotation suggests, effective coping is often seen as central to emotional intelligence (EI). Salovey, Bedell, Detweiler, & Mayer (1999, p. 161) claim that more emotionally intelligent individuals cope more successfully, because they "accurately perceive and appraise their emotional states, know how and when to express their feelings, and can effectively regulate their mood states." Similarly, Bar-On (1997) includes stress management and adaptability as two major components of EI. In other words, adaptive coping might be conceptualized as emotional intelligence in action, supporting mastery of emotions, emotional growth, and both cognitive and emotional differentiation, allowing us to evolve in an ever-changing world. There are also grounds for skepticism about the utility of EI as a scientific construct. Popular claims about the power of EI to predict real-world behaviors are overstated and unsupported by evidence (Mayer, Salovey, & Caruso, 2000). Furthermore, EI may be overly inclusive; it can seem that EI refers to just about every desirable characteristic other than general (cognitive) intelligence. The idea that life success requires more than cognitive ability is hardly new. Popular accounts of EI tend to neglect the well-established literature on personality and stress, which supports a more differentiated, multidimensional account of individual differences in coping and stress outcome.

In this article, we explore the prospects for establishing EI as a novel explanatory construct in stress research. We aim to delineate and evaluate some potential research strategies for conceptualizing and validating the EI construct within the stress domain. We conclude by adopting a critical stance, while recognizing that there is a paucity of empirical evidence on which to base definitive conclusions. The theoretical framework for our analysis is provided by the Lazarus and Folkman (1984) transactional model of stress. According to these authors, stress develops from unfolding person-environment interactions that tax or exceed the person's capacity to cope with environmental demands. Lazarus and Folkman distinguish *processes* such as appraisal and coping from *outcomes* such as emotional distress and health problems. Hence, for EI to have explanatory power, it must be distinguished from stress outcomes, as a set of competencies for adaptive processing in demanding, potentially stressful situations. In addition, EI, as a subset of the intelligence or personality domains (Mayer et al., 2000), should be viewed as a major individual difference variable and should therefore show some of the purported properties of individual difference constructs.

Next, we outline three complementary ways in which EI might be established as a scientifically useful construct akin to general intelligence *(g)*. First, there might be some master process, or processes that controls how adaptively the person copes with stressful transactions. If so, this process may operate more successfully in the individual with high EI. Potential problems for this approach include the multiplicity of processes that contribute to coping, and difficulties in conceptualizing the adaptiveness of encounters. Second, there may be preexisting individual difference constructs, such as personality variables, that play a critical role in controlling adaptive outcome. Perhaps key traits for handling stressful encounters may be identified. Problems here include, again, the multiplicity of relevant traits, and doubts over whether major traits relate to adaptiveness in any simple fashion. Third, EI might relate to the individual's ability to transfer competencies for handling stress to novel situations. It remains to be seen whether therapy and stress management techniques induce the transfer of competencies across disparate situations, as this definition of EI requires. We conclude by summarizing the difficulties that each of the approaches to conceptualizing EI must overcome. We focus primarily on the application of EI to studies of stress and coping, but given the centrality of handling negative emotions to EI in general, our analysis is relevant to the wider EI construct.

CONCEPTUALIZING EMOTIONAL INTELLIGENCE

Definitions of emotional intelligence differ (see, for example, Mayer et al., 2000). It is not always clear whether EI represents an *outcome* variable, that is, successful resolution of emotional challenges, or an *aptitude* for handling challenging situations, whose expression may vary according to environmental contingencies. As an aptitude, EI would operate through specific processes or behaviors that support coping with emotional challenge. For example, one of the core abilities contributing to EI is managing emotions (Salovey & Mayer, 1990), in other words, understanding one's feelings and managing their behavioral expression. Such a construct might be operationalized at several conceptually distinct levels: (1) the underlying *processes* that support emotional management, such as labeling somatic sensations, selecting verbal descriptors for emotions, and accessing memories of personal emotional experiences; (2) the *behaviors* that implement emotion management, such as expressing anger verbally or avoiding a perceived threat; and (3) the *outcomes* of instances of emotion management, such as the degree of personal harm resulting from the encounter, the person's feelings of satisfaction or dissatisfaction, and physical health problems that may develop in the longer-term.

It is expected that processes, behaviors, and outcomes are systematically related, but making the conceptual distinctions is important for clear operationalization of constructs, which in turn is required for hypothesis testing.

Figure 21.1 represents the conceptual starting point for this chapter, based on the Lazarus and Folkman (1984) transactional model of stress, and Wells and Matthews' (1994) account of self-regulation and emotion. These theories place cognitive processes at the center of emotional response, and we adopt a cognitive orientation here. Emotional intelligence is seen here as a quality of the person, that is, a set of competencies or skills for handling affectively loaded encounters, which might predict future adaptive outcomes. It is assumed that EI competencies are represented in long-term memory, although EI may change through experience and learning. In demanding or challenging environments, EI competencies influence selection and control of coping strategies directed toward the immediate situation. Regulation of coping operates in tandem with

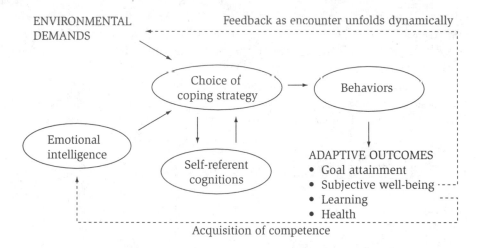

Figure 21.1. An outline model of the place of emotional intelligence within the transactional model of stress.

self-referent cognitions of the personal significance of events, and of internal stimuli (metacognitions). *Emotion-focused* coping comprises sequences of self-referent cognitions that aim to reconceptualize the problem. *Task-focused coping* is directed toward changing external reality and typically refers to behaviors intended to resolve the problem. The consequence of coping is a change in adaptive outcome, which may take various forms, as indicated in the figure. Maladaptation might be signaled by failure to attain a significant goal, subjective distress, acquisition of self-damaging beliefs or behaviors, or health problems.

The conceptualization of EI shown in Figure 21.1 assumes that people can be rank-ordered in terms of their personal coping efficacy, and that the rank-ordering reflects the underlying competencies described as emotional intelligence. There are several ways in which such a model might fail.

Competencies may be independent. For EI to represent a coherent psychological construct, different competencies should be correlated. Individuals who are competent in self-analysis should also be self-motivated, empathic, and adept at handling relationships. Gardner (1993), for example, identifies interpersonal and intrapersonal intelligences and proposes that different measures of these capabilities should be positively correlated in the same way that cognitive task intercorrelations support the construct of general intelligence. Mayer and Salovey's (1993) conception of EI subsumes these two intelligences such that interpersonal and intrapersonal skills should correlate with one another. However, competencies identified with EI might not in fact be mutually positively correlated: a ruthless chief executive officer might be highly self-motivated but lacking in empathy, for example. Conceivably, handling emotive situations might be influenced by a variety of unrelated competencies. If so, the term *EI* (like the term *stress*) might be a useful label for a broad area of enquiry, but the term would not identify a psychologically meaningful construct.

Adaptation may be situation specific. People with high EI should express it in a variety of situations. For example, individuals with good impulse control are able to resist qualitatively different impulses. Again, this is not necessarily the case: a patient with an eating disorder might be good at resisting all impulses except the desire to eat. The situation specificity of adaptation (the extent to which stable personal characteristics generalize across different situations) is one of the fundamental issues addressed by personality research (Matthews & Deary, 1998). Situational generality also implies transferability of skills. One of the hallmarks of general intelligence is that cognitive skills are adapted to new problems (Sternberg, 1985); EI should be associated with a similar flexibility of application.

Adaptation may be criterion specific. It is supposed that high EI brings all manner of benefits: personal fulfillment, popularity, wealth, and moral virtue (Goleman, 1995). However, specific forms of coping might be adaptive with respect to some criteria but maladaptive with respect to others. Furthermore, attributes of low EI may sometimes bring adaptive benefits. A criminal with low empathy might prosper materially without being troubled by remorse, for example. People may trade off adaptive benefits against one another: smokers and drinkers may believe that enhancement of mood and social functioning more than compensates for health risks, considering it better to have what seems to be a short, happy life than a long, miserable one.

The questions raised by this conceptual critique of EI are difficult, and empirical evidence is limited. In this chapter, we review three areas of research that provide some initial indications of the viability of EI as the construct controlling adaptive coping. The first area comprises research on coping with life events to determine whether we can differentiate adaptive and maladaptive strategies. The second research area is personality research. Is there a trait or traits that govern the adaptiveness of coping across diverse situations and criteria for adaptation? The third area is that of interventions for stress and emotional disorder. To what extent do interventions promote generalized improvement in emotional functioning? We conclude with a reassessment of whether research supports the existence of an integrated set of competencies for coping with emotional challenge, which generalize across situations and are unequivocally adaptive.

COPING AND ADAPTATION

Current psychological writings view coping as an active process, interacting with other factors such as personality and stress management skills (Zeidner &

Saklofske, 1996). The transactional model (Lazarus, 1993; Lazarus & Folkman, 1984) suggests a possible conceptualization of EI as the psychological basis for adaptive coping, but two steps are necessary to establish this conceptualization as valid. First, we must be able to discriminate adaptive and maladaptive coping. Within the context of coping research, the term *adaptive* refers to "the effectiveness of coping in improving the adaptational outcome" (Lazarus, 1993, p. 237). Adaptive or functional coping behavior both buffers the immediate impact of stress and ensures a sense of self-worth and wholeness with one's past and anticipated future. Deciding on whether particular coping strategies are adaptive requires an examination of situational factors (for example, nature of the stressor, degree, and chronicity), personal factors (for example, personality and beliefs about coping resources and their effectiveness), and the nature of the adaptational outcome.

The second step in conceptualizing adaptive coping as EI in action is to differentiate the two constructs. If EI is no more than a snapshot of the sum total of the person's coping efforts in a given encounter, the construct is redundant and adds nothing to the understanding offered by existing models of stress. Within Lazarus's (1991) model, coping is in dynamic interaction with appraisal of personal meaning, which in turn depends on the stable knowledge base the person brings to the taxing situation. The essence of the EI hypothesis is that some people acquire a knowledge base of competencies that affords a general facilitation of their handling of emotional encounters. To examine the hypothesis further, we next consider (1) conceptual issues raised by the transactional model, (2) criteria for assessment of adaptiveness, and (3) empirical studies of coping effectiveness.

Conceptualizing Adaptation Within the Transactional Model

Defining what is an effective way of handling emotions is determined mainly by the theoretical model or paradigm guiding research (Folkman et al., 1991). Psychodynamic models generally assume a hierarchy of coping and defense in which some processes are seen as superior to others. Haan (1977) categorized ego processes as adaptive or maladaptive depending on their relative freedom from reality distortion, their future orientation, and their allowance for impulse gratification and expression of affect. In contrast, the transactional stress model focuses on the changing cognitive and behavioral efforts required to manage specific demands appraised as taxing or exceeding the person's resources (Folkman et al., 1991). A contextual definition of effectiveness in handling an emotionally laden situation (for example, what is said, thought, or done in a specific situation) is demanded by interactional models. Thus, *in a given situation,* adaptive coping protects us by eliminating or modifying the conditions that produce stress or by keeping the emotional consequences within manageable bounds (Zeidner & Hammer, 1990). Effective coping may protect against physiological disturbance, emotional distress, and negative effects on health, all of which may be a result when a person engages in behaviors that involve risk taking (high-speed car racing) or substance abuse (alcohol).

The use of some strategies may impede rather than promote health-enhancing behaviors. Although denial and wishful thinking may delay seeking life-saving medical attention for chest pains, so might the overuse of information-seeking strategies. In many instances, however, we cannot prejudge particular strategies employed in dealing with managing stressful emotional encounters as being universally adaptive or maladaptive. Rather, the concern must be for whom and under what circumstances a particular mode of coping has adaptive consequences. The transactional model has additional implications for conceptualizing relationships between emotionally intelligent behaviors and outcomes.

Time-Course of Coping. As a stressful episode evolves and develops over time, there is a continuous interplay between appraisal, coping, and emotional and somatic responses, each response fluctuating as the transaction unfolds (Lazarus & Folkman, 1984). Thus, a particular coping strategy may be more effective at one stage of a stressful encounter or in one time period than another (Auerbach, 1989). For example, whereas emotion-focused behaviors might be more adaptive following an exam, active-oriented behaviors would probably be more adaptive prior to the exam, when something could be done to change the outcome (see, for example, Folkman & Lazarus, 1985). Also, certain strategies found useful in one time period may not be useful in a different period. For example, resigning from a tenured position in academia on account of conflictual encounters with the dean might be a more adaptive coping strategy in time of high institutional demand for academics than in a time of high unemployment, when academic positions are scarce.

Reciprocal Determinism. Causal relationships among emotionally intelligent strategies and outcome indices are likely to be multidirectional rather than linear, reflecting dynamic person-situation interactions (Lazarus & Folkman, 1984). Indices of effective behaviors, often seen as dependent variables, might also serve as independent variables in a complex process of reciprocal and unfolding transactions over time. Efforts at managing stress should not be confounded with outcomes (Lennon, Dohrenwend, Zautra, & Marbach, 1990), but it must also be acknowledged that coping and outcome factors may mutually influence one another as the transaction unfolds over time.

Manifold Functions of Coping Behaviors. Each act may have more than one function, depending on the psychological context in which it occurs. Problem-focused strategies, for example, may also regulate emotion, as in public speaking training that also decreases stage fright. Similarly, emotion-focused strategies (such as humor, relaxation exercises, tranquilizers) can have problem-focused functions if they are effective in decreasing anxiety or other aversive emotions that impede behavioral functioning. It is the specific function of the behavior rather than the act itself that indicates whether a strategy may be emotionally intelligent. It follows that current methods in stress research often fail to provide sufficient information. We may find we are comparing people who are not only grappling with different stressors and using different coping strategies, but also using the same behaviors for different purposes. It then becomes impossible to partition outcome variability among person, situation, and strategy factors, and the interactions between them.

Interactions between Coping Behaviors and Other Factors. Coping behaviors should interact with situational parameters in impacting on both adaptive and maladaptive outcomes. For example, avoidance-type behaviors (such as wishful thinking, distancing, or procrastination) would be ineffective when used by college students who are on academic probation—they should instead be attending to their study problems. On the other hand, distancing might be an adaptive response for these same individuals when confronted with a negative and unalterable situation, such as a serious illness in the family.

Context of Coping: Cultural and Social Factors. The evaluations of effectiveness of emotionally intelligent behaviors must be sensitive to broader social (Weidner & Collins, 1992) and cultural factors (Marsella, DeVos, & Hsu, 1985). Preferred coping methods and perceived effectiveness must be appraised relative to a social or cultural group, values, norms, world view, symbols, and orientation. Consider the case of the mother who devotes herself to her ill parents at the expense of her newborn baby. The evaluation of this approach is not merely a scientific but a moral matter and may differ in traditional versus modern child-centered societies. Evaluating the effectiveness of coping behaviors must be further addressed relative to people's normative response to a stressor. Virtually all bereaved persons manifest distress, with depression being a common feature, so that freedom from distress may not signal good coping skills. However, normative standards must be used cautiously when judging behaviors as emotionally intelligent, especially under extremely adverse conditions.

Choice of Outcome Criteria

Choosing criteria for adaptation is nontrivial, because conclusions about effectiveness of coping varies depending on the choice of outcome criteria selected (Meneghan, 1982). Coping behaviors are centered and structured around certain goals, issues, and patterns of challenges referred to as *coping tasks* (Cohen & Lazarus, 1979). For example, the tasks of children of divorced parents include acknowledging the marriage breakup, disengagement from parental conflict, coming to terms with multiple losses associated with divorce, and resolving feelings of self-blame and anger (Wallerstein, 1983). Coping generally centers on five main tasks (Cohen & Lazarus, 1979): to reduce harmful environmental conditions and enhance prospects of recovery; to tolerate or adjust to negative events or realities; to maintain a positive self-image; to maintain emotional equilibrium and decrease emotional stress; and to maintain a satisfying relationship with the environment. Ideally, successful coping should lead to satisfactory task completion with little additional conflict and few residual outcomes, while maintaining a positive emotional state (Pearlin & Schooler, 1978). The following are the most salient outcome criteria for judging coping effectiveness and problem resolution (Meneghan, 1982; Pearlin & Schooler, 1978; Taylor, 1986).

Resolution of the conflict or stressful situation. Coping with a problem should be instrumental in alleviating or removing the stressful situation, where possible.

Reduction of physiological and biochemical reactions. Coping efforts are judged to be successful if they reduce arousal and its indicators (such as heart rate, blood pressure, respiration, or skin conductivity), although active coping itself appears to be accompanied by physiological changes such as increased catecholamine secretion. In the longer term, effective coping should be associated with better physical health (Steptoe, 1991).

Reduction of psychological distress. Adaptive coping usually involves success in controlling emotional distress, and keeping anxiety within manageable limits.

Normative social functioning. Adaptive coping is assessed in relation to normative patterns of social functioning that reflect realistic appraisal of events. Deviation of behavior from socially acceptable norms is often a sign of maladaptive coping, although norms are also open to question, and personal and societal values may differ.

Return to prestress activities. To the extent that people's coping efforts enable them to resume their routine activities, coping may be judged effective. However, substantial life change following a stressful encounter may be a sign of successful rather than unsuccessful coping, particularly if the person's prior living situation was not in some sense ideal.

Well-being of self and others affected by the situation. This includes spouses, children, parents, coworkers, friends, and neighbors. Well-being might be expressed as positive affect and positive self-esteem.

Perceived effectiveness. Perceived effectiveness involves the respondents' claims that a particular strategy or approach was helpful to them in some way. Such testimonials, however, may have an uncertain relation to observed effects. Judgments of the effectiveness of emotionally intelligent behaviors in action should be context specific and related to the specific encounter. For example, relevant outcome measures of hospital patients undergoing first-time coronary bypass surgery might include length of stay in the hospital, progress toward walking, and pace of recovery (Carver, Scheier, & Pozo, 1992). However, there are no universal criteria for assessing coping effectiveness. Indeed, the resolution of one stressful encounter might even come at the expense of another (for example, working long hours for professional gain may contribute to marriage breakdown). Adaptation is a complex process that must be viewed as a multivariate construct and judged according to a number of criteria.

Empirical Research on Coping Effectiveness

In spite of recent advances in theory, research, and assessment, the issue of effectiveness of various coping strategies is still open to debate. Which emotionally intelligent behaviors are most effective in the short and long term, in which contexts, and for whom poses a conceptual and empirical puzzle. The behaviors people use in stressful conditions are often conceptualized in terms of basic categories of coping, such as the task- and emotion-focused strategies previously described. Endler and Parker (1990) proposed that avoidance of the problem through distracting oneself constitutes a third basic category.

Theorists have frequently emphasized the positive effects of problem-focused strategies and the negative effects of emotion-focused coping on psychological outcomes, especially when the threatening situation can be ameliorated by the subject's responses (Lazarus & Folkman, 1984). Although emotion-focused behavior or avoidance may help in maintaining emotional balance, an adaptive response to remediable situations still requires problem-solving activities to manage the threat. Active behaviors are preferred by most persons and are highly effective in stress reduction (Gal & Lazarus, 1975). Active behaviors provide a sense of mastery over the stressor, divert attention from the problem, and discharge energy following exposure to threat. Non-problem-solving strategies are increasingly used when the source of stress is unclear, when there is a lack of knowledge about stress modification, or there is little one can do to eliminate the stress (Pearlin & Schooler, 1978).

The research evidence on the adaptiveness of avoidance behaviors is mixed. On one hand, there is a wealth of data to indicate that avoidance in general is positively tied to concurrent distress and may have negative consequences (Aldwin & Revenson, 1987; Billings & Moos, 1984; Mullins et al., 1991). A review of the literature (Zeidner & Saklofske, 1996) suggested that avoidance types of coping (such as wishful thinking, escapism, overt effort to deny, and self-distraction and mental disengagement) typically work against people rather than to their advantage. Avoidance is related to impairments of objective performance (Matthews & Campbell, 1998). On the other hand, cognitive avoidance may be an effective way to cope with short-term stressors (such as noise, pain, and uncomfortable medical procedures) (Suls & Fletcher, 1985). Avoidance may give the person a psychological "breather" and an opportunity to escape from the constant pressures of the stressful situation (Carver et al., 1992). Roger, Jarvis, and Najarian (1993) claim benefits for "detached coping," which addresses the problem without the person feeling personally involved or threatened. Pearlin and Schooler (1978) found that distancing strategies were most successful for dealing with stressful impersonal situations. Conversely, strategies by which individuals remained committed and engaged with relevant others were most successful in reducing emotional distress in more personal situations.

Some strategies appear to be inherently maladaptive in managing stress. Although alcohol and drugs may provide brief relief, they ultimately leave the person worse off. Factor analytic studies suggest a cluster of theoretically adaptive strategies: active coping, planning, suppression of competing activities, restraint coping, positive reinforcement, seeking social support, and positive reappraisal. The second cluster included denial, behavioral disengagement, focus on emotions, and alcoholism (Carver, Scheier, & Weintraub, 1989). However, although some research supports the relationship between active coping and well-being (Aldwin & Revenson, 1987; Aspinwall & Taylor, 1992), the opposite effect has been reported with a focal stressor (Bolger, 1990; Mattlin, Wethington, & Kessler, 1990).

Similarly, some research suggests that emotion-focused coping is maladaptive and increases stress (Folkman, Lazarus, Gruen, & DeLongis, 1986), but the opposite pattern is also reported (Baum, Fleming, & Singer, 1983). Though many advocate that keeping one's emotional distress within manageable bounds reflects good adjustment, research shows that some (such as patients with cancer and those with spinal cord injuries) may be better off in the long run if they initially express their emotions rather than behaving in a restrained manner (Wortman, 1983). Baum et al. (1983) reported that emotion-focused behaviors were adaptive in dealing with technological disaster because they increased the sense of perceived control.

Emotion-focused coping may be too broad and heterogeneous a construct to characterize the various inner-directed strategies that people use. Emotion-focused strategies include both those that, superficially, would appear beneficial, such as coming to terms with an event or reappraising it as a learning experience, and those that are negatively-toned strategies, such as self-blame. Endler and Parker's (1990) emotion-focused coping scale relates more to self-blame than to positive reappraisal, and several studies suggest that this style of coping relates to negative outcomes (Deary et al., 1996). For example, Morgan, Matthews, and Winton (1995) found that flood victims with high scores on the Endler and Parker (1990) emotion-focus scale tended to report high levels of trauma symptoms, even with the appraised severity of the flood event statistically controlled. Matthews, Schwean, Campbell, Saklofske, and Mohamed (2000) suggest that emotion-focused strategies may be distinguished functionally in terms of their intended aims. They make conceptual distinctions between *palliative* coping, intended to reduce immediate negative feelings, *self-transformation*, which aims to produce long-lasting changes in attitudes toward the problem, and *ruminative problem solving*, which is intended to exhaustively review personal significance of the problem. Ruminative strategies tend to generate protracted worry states, which are often maladaptive (Wells & Matthews, 1994).

Salovey et al. (1999) claim that maladaptive coping may be a consequence of difficulties in processing emotional material (in other words, maladaptive coping is a result of low EI). For example, rumination may be a consequence of inability to make sense of one's emotional experience. Conversely, clarity of thought and experience seems to promote well-being and active regulation of mood. Emotional disclosure and availing oneself of social support may promote adaptive self-transformation (Pennebaker, 1997). The link between problems with handling emotion and ineffective coping is supported by work on alexithymia, a personal quality associated with difficulties in describing and identifying feelings. Alexithymia relates both to low EI, measured with the Bar-On scale (Parker, Taylor, & Bagby, forthcoming), and to a probably maladaptive pattern of coping: low problem-focus and high emotion-focus and avoidance or distraction (Parker, Taylor, & Bagby, 1998).

Some Tentative Generalizations About Adaptive Emotionally Intelligent Behaviors

Few unequivocal principles have been uncovered in three decades of research on coping, but we now put forward some tentative generalizations about adaptive behaviors gleaned from the coping literature (for a review of coping research, see Lazarus, 1993).

Strategies Work with Modest Effects, Sometimes, with Some People. Some kinds of responses to some kinds of situations and exigencies do make a difference. However, the magnitudes of such differences are frequently disappointing (Pearlin, 1991), offering little justification for the power of coping in the stress outcome process. Methodological difficulties and weaknesses in the research may account for some of these less than robust findings.

Responses are Not Uniformly Adaptive. The results of a given coping style are determined by the interaction of personal needs and preferences and the constraints of the current situation. Adaptive coping requires a good fit between the person-environment transaction, the person's appraisal of the transaction, and the consequent coping behavior (Lazarus & Folkman, 1984; Lazarus, 1993). Hence, strategies often viewed as maladaptive (for example, avoidance and distancing) may be adaptive under some circumstances and vice versa. Problem-focused coping is more adaptive in situations viewed as changeable, whereas emotion-focused coping is best used in unalterable situations (Lazarus & Folkman, 1984). Emotionally intelligent behaviors must also be matched to appraisals of control and personal factors (for example, values, goals, and beliefs), and to choosing whether to stay with or abandon goals depending on circumstances.

Adaptive Strategies Vary Between and Within Individuals. Task-focused efforts (such as studying) may be activated by certain individuals at the announcement of an exam. Others procrastinate or complain about the course or instructor, yet they may use adaptive methods to manage other stressors. Person-situation interactions also occur; for example, one student may use problem-focused strategies with little skill and be less successful than another who uses emotion-focused coping to alleviate anxiety.

Adaptive Behaviors Involve a Flexible Repertoire and a Combination of Coping Strategies. People tend to employ both emotion- and problem-focused coping in managing most stressful events. This would appear to be functional because it allows for both the regulation of emotion and the management of the stressor (Lazarus & Folkman, 1984). For example, theft of a personal possession may certainly cause some anger, and one may express this in conversation with friends while hoping for the "worst" to befall the culprit, but at the same time, report the theft to police, call the insurance company for compensation, and increase security. A large repertoire of coping resources and flexibility and creativity in their use may increase coping adaptiveness. A number of studies (for example, Mattlin et al., 1990; Pearlin & Schooler, 1978; Wethington & Kessler, 1991) suggest that having a versatile coping profile is associated with good adjustment, but the effects are rather modest. Although greater flexibility may relate to better emotional adjustment (Mattlin et al., 1990), multiple coping reactions within a given period may reflect ineffective coping (Carver et al., 1993).

Emotionally Intelligent Responses May Influence Some but Not Other Outcomes. A particular behavior may differentially influence various outcomes (Silver & Wortman, 1980). Various indices are not highly correlated. Further, each coping strategy has both its benefits and costs. For example, denying the seriousness of a partner's illness may reduce emotional distress but also negatively affect the care given to the spouse.

Adaptiveness of Particular Strategies May Vary Across Phases of a Stressful Encounter. The relevance and effectiveness of a particular reaction to a stressful encounter varies with the phase of the stressful transaction. Denial may interfere with the early detection and treatment of breast cancer. Following diagnosis, denial of one's emotional reaction or the life-threatening implications of the disease may have very different effects (Carver et al., 1993). Avoidance strategies may be effective for short-term stressors, but nonavoidant strategies may be effective for long term-stressors (Suls & Fletcher, 1985). A response positively associated with short-term well-being (for example, maintaining hope that a husband missing in action will be found) may be negatively associated with well-being if it persists for a number of years. Continued life stressors may themselves wear down the individual and lead to the use of less effective strategies while a person is under continued stress (Aldwin & Revenson, 1987). Coping may be less effective among people exposed to a chronic difficulty than to acute stressors (for example, Wethington & Kessler, 1991). Thus, the power of specific strategies to promote adjustment may become weaker as stress continues. Furthermore, some situations may be so intractable that endurance is more efficacious than action.

Coping with Emotional Reactions May Be Maladaptive. The emotions provoked in oneself and others by problematic encounters may hinder adaptive coping. Difficulties in understanding emotions may elicit maladaptive rumination (Salovey et al., 1999), and emotions may prime inappropriate action tendencies such as aggression in the case of anger (Lazarus, 1991). We might then attribute maladaptive coping to low EI, to the extent that it reflects difficulties in processing and regulating emotions. However, it is not established that difficulties in dealing with emotions are central to maladaptive coping, as opposed to being one of various contributory factors, or even a symptom rather than a cause. Rumination may be a consequence of faulty metacognitions and attention to self-referent cognitions (Wells & Matthews, 1994) rather than a direct response to emotional confusion. If a person has good problem-solving skills, unruly emotions may simply be a minor irritant that dissipates when effective task-focused coping resolves the encounter favorably.

Influences on Coping: Appraisal and Knowledge

Thus far, we have seen that adaptive and maladaptive coping strategies can sometimes be distinguished in the qualified sense discussed previously. Choice of a coping strategy does not just happen of its own accord: antecedent processes and knowledge structures determine strategy selection (Matthews & Wells, 1996). These issues are addressed most directly by research on self-regulation, following on from Carver and Scheier's (1981) pioneering cybernetic model, within which discrepancies between actual and preferred self-state initiate coping efforts intended to restore homeostasis. Coping is thus influenced by appraisal of current status and accessing the personal and societal norms with which current status is compared. Appraisal can be decomposed into primary appraisal of the disturbance of equilibrium, and secondary appraisal of the individual's potential for coping with the disturbance and personal controllability (Lazarus & Folkman, 1984). Appraisal and coping are in dynamic interaction: coping feeds back into reappraisal as the stressful encounter unfolds.

So far, the self-regulative analysis regresses the problem only one stage further back. If appraisal is a primary determinant of coping, what determines appraisal? Primary appraisal reflects multiple mechanisms: broadly, we can distinguish lower level and upper level processes in appraisal, although some authors make further subdivisions (van Reekum & Scherer, 1997). Lower-level evaluation is bottom-up, or stimulus-driven. Affective information is processed automatically at an early, preattentive stage of processing (Kitayama, 1997), which establishes an initial, coarse representation of stimulus significance, which in turn feeds into subsequent attention-demanding processing. Upper-level evaluation is top-down, or conceptually driven, and requires controlled processing of propositions accessed from long-term memory (van Reekum & Scherer, 1997). Typically, it is intimately related to self-regulation and secondary appraisal. The self-referent executive function model of Wells and Matthews (1994) identifies this level of processing as the principal determinant of coping and stress reactions. Controlled processing of stimulus significance and coping is driven by self-knowledge in long-term memory, represented as generic procedures for stimulus interpretation and action. Controlled processing compiles routines for coping that fit the immediate situation.

Hence, coping is a complex outcome of multiple levels of appraisal and proceduralized self-knowledge. It follows that there are multiple sources of coping effectiveness, and so maladaptive coping may have various sources.

Lower-level processing. This type of maladaptive coping misinterprets the personal significance of events. Anxiety disorders may be driven by oversensitivity in automatic threat evaluation, although the evidence is conflicting (Matthews & Wells, 1999). In addition, personal experience may lead to overlearned appraisals, which become maladaptive, as when a combat veteran misinterprets another person's movements as an immediate threat.

Controlled processing. This type tends to be error prone, especially when the person's attention is overloaded. Maladaptive coping may result from misinterpretation of a complex situation, as when a pilot misdiagnoses the source of an unusual instrument reading.

Self-knowledge. The normative self-knowledge accessed as the guide to self-regulation may be inappropriate to the situation, as when a person inadvertently transgresses the customs of an unfamiliar culture.

Lack of skills. The person may choose a coping strategy for which he or she lacks the skill to implement successfully. Confronting a coworker about a problem may aggravate matters unless the person has adequate social or assertiveness skills.

Processing limitations. The person may choose a potentially successful strategy but fail to implement it effectively because of processing limitations. In test-anxious individuals, attempts at problem-solving may be stymied by an insufficiency of attentional capacity (Zeidner, 1998).

In summary, success or failure in coping has many sources, related to qualitatively different mental processes and structures. It seems unlikely that EI resides exclusively in any single psychological source. A person may read a situation accurately but still fail to choose and implement an effective coping strategy. An examination candidate may know exactly what is required but still lack the test-relevant knowledge or the verbal skills to translate that knowledge into lucid answers. Conversely, advanced behavioral coping skills may be rendered useless by a fundamental misinterpretation of the situation. The Chernobyl power plant operators were highly skilled professionally but failed to control the nuclear reactor because they misdiagnosed the initial physical problem (Reason, 1987). It follows that there is no single EI process that controls adaptive success, analogous to the speed-of-processing factor that is sometimes (controversially) said to control general intelligence. The better-adapted person must be distinguished from the more poorly adapted individual across a number of distinct processes. Processes supporting analysis and regulation of emotions, seen as central to EI (Salovey et al., 1999), might constitute a subset of these processes, but they do not support the totality of adaptation. Even those who are "in touch with their feelings" may fail to cope successfully as a consequence of the various cognitive deficiencies listed above. The next question is then whether there is some interrelationship between the functioning of the emotional and nonemotional processes concerned that would afford coherence to the EI construct. This is a question about individual differences, which the next section of this chapter addresses.

PERSONALITY AND INDIVIDUAL DIFFERENCES IN ADAPTATION

The psychometric basis for the general intelligence construct is provided by the *positive manifold,* the tendency for all cognitive tests to intercorrelate positively. It is unclear whether there is a comparable positive manifold for all tests of emotion-related processing and response, and a general factor integrating adaptive coping with other facets of EI. Several authors have developed questionnaires that provide a statistically reliable global EI score. Bar-On (1997) used a self-report instrument to assess various personality-like dimensions thought to be related to stress and emotion, whereas Mayer, Caruso, and Salovey (1999) used a battery of behavioral tests to assess an ability for perceiving, understanding, and regulating emotion. These measures differ substantially in conception; for example, the Bar-On scale refers explicitly to stress and adaptation, but the Mayer et al. (1999) tests seem more narrowly focused on emotion per se.

Davies, Stankov, and Roberts (1998) found various dimensions related to emotion, including an emotion perception factor, corresponding to one of the theoretical key attributes of EI identified by Mayer et al. (1999). However, they also found no evidence for a general factor, and scales tended to correlate substantially with well-established personality factors, indicating a lack of divergent validity. Evidently, further empirical work on the assessment and validation of EI may contribute to stress research. An alternative approach is to ask whether there is in fact a single dimension of adaptability to stress, whose association with EI measures might be explored in further research. If there is no adaptability general factor, then clearly, we cannot identify EI with a global adaptability construct.

Individual Differences in Cognitive Stress Processes

In the stress context, there have been some studies of intercorrelations of coping and appraisal measures. Such studies address both intrasituational and intersituational relationships between cognitive stress processes. Schwarzer and Schwarzer's (1996) review of coping questionnaires shows that there is little consensus among researchers on the dimensionality of coping: models vary from two to twenty-eight dimensions. Folkman and Lazarus (1988), for example, have developed a questionnaire for eight dimensions of coping, although the Schwarzers point out difficulties in replicating factor structure. More general, and possibly higher-level, models of coping tend to command more widespread support. For example, Endler and Parker's three broad dimensions of task focus (also called problem focus), emotion focus, and avoidance appear to describe both general dispositions and coping with a specific situation (Endler, Kantor, & Parker, 1994; Matthews & Campbell, 1998). There appears to be no evidence for a general factor of coping; at the least the fundamental distinction between problem focus, or task focus, and emotion focus requires two near-orthogonal dimensions. Hence, there is no single overarching attribute of coping to which EI may be linked.

There have been few studies of individual differences in appraisal. Ferguson, Matthews, and Cox (1999) reported exploratory and confirmatory factor analyses that differentiated the Lazarus primary appraisal dimensions of threat, loss, and challenge. The confirmatory analyses showed very poor fit to the data for a single-factor model, and threat and challenge were correlated at .00 within the best-fitting three-factor model. There is no general factor of appraisal. Ferguson et al. (1999) also reported a study of relationships between coping and appraisal in a sample of 268 postgraduate students. Across two types of potentially stressful encounters, threat and loss appraisal were consistently associated with emotion-focused coping (range of r, .40 to .61) and avoidance (range of r, .24 to .43), and challenge appraisal was correlated with task-focused coping (range of r, .24 to .28). As expected from the transactional model, appraisal and coping were interrelated, but there was little indication of a general factor.

Matthews, Hillyard, and Campbell (1999) investigated individual differences in metacognition, that is, appraisal of one's own thoughts and their personal significance, in a study of test anxiety. They included scales for metacognition, worry, and coping with mentally demanding situations. Factor analysis of dispositional measures discriminated orthogonal factors related to (1) general metacognitive awareness, worry, and emotion focus; and (2) use of task-focused coping in preference to avoidance and emotion focus. The second factor was labeled *adaptive coping* but explained little of the variance in the person's appraisal of his or her own thought processes. Both factors independently predicted scores on Sarason's (1984) dispositional test anxiety measure.

Furthermore, the factor scores were only weakly predictive of individual differences in coping with a specific examination. Again, no single construct differentiated the individual with presumed adaptive cognitions from the person with presumed maladaptive cognitions. A person might report use of more adaptive coping strategies, simultaneously with high metacognitive awareness and worry (presumed maladaptive). In addition, a person might report typically using maladaptive coping strategies and high metacognition but also report using more adaptive strategies such as task focus in the specific examination setting.

Traits for Emotional Intelligence

So far, we have seen that although there are some relationships between functionally distinct processes, individuals characteristically show complex patternings of cognitive characteristics, which are neither universally adaptive nor maladaptive (Zeidner & Matthews, 2000). These data do not suggest any clear EI construct in the stress domain, but EI might be valid in a weaker sense if it could be shown that there was a personality trait or traits that were consistently associated with a variety of adaptive cognitions. Broad traits such as neuroticism and extraversion are distinguished by their correlations with a wide variety of disparate psychological indices, even though many of the correlation magnitudes might be small. Conceivably, adaptive stress processes A, B, and C might be independent of one another but correlated with a given trait. In this case, we might identify EI with the disposition to process stress-related stimuli adaptively, without linking EI to any specific process.

Contemporary personality trait theory (see Matthews & Deary, 1998, for a review) does not recognize any general factor. It adopts a hierarchical view within which traits may be described either in terms of a small number of broad superfactors, such as the dimensions of the Five Factor Model, or as a larger number of midlevel traits. Stress vulnerability has been linked both to the neuroticism (N) superfactor, and to various midlevel traits that tend to correlate with N, such as trait anxiety, pessimism, external locus of control, and self-consciousness (Matthews, Saklofske, Costa, Deary, and Zeidner, 1998).

There are some grounds for linking N to low EI, not least that N is substantially correlated with low scores on the Bar-On scale (R. Bar-On, personal communication, July 2, 1999), as are other negative affectivity constructs such as various measures of depression and anxiety (Bar-On, 1997). Broadly, individuals with high N appear to be disadvantaged within stressful situations. Subjects with high N report higher levels of acute and chronic emotional distress, and they appear to be more vulnerable to clinical emotional disturbance; there is also increasing evidence for causal effects of N on distress (Matthews & Deary, 1998). Other outcomes linked to N include health problems and impairment of attention and performance. Persons with high N also seem to experience a greater frequency of negative life events, possibly because their maladaptive handling of demanding encounters leads to difficulties with relationships with others (Magnus, Diener, Fujita, & Pavot, 1993). Individuals with high N also show styles of cognition that are at least loosely associated with ineffective adaptation. Emotion-focused coping, in the sense of self-blame and deliberate worry, is particularly strongly related to N (Deary et al., 1996). N relates more weakly to reduced task focus and increased avoidance: in general, the strategies favored by individuals with high N are rated as relatively ineffective (McCrae & Costa, 1986). Individuals with high N also tend to appraise the world and themselves more pessimistically. In four studies, Matthews et al. (2000) reported consistently significant correlations between N and threat appraisals (range of .17 to .44) and between N and lower perceived controllability of stressors (range of $-.17$ to $-.41$).

The evidence that more neurotic individuals find it difficult to handle threatening or unpleasant encounters is overwhelming, but we cannot necessarily infer that emotional stability (low N) is the basis for EI. To do so would entail establishing (1) that the influence of N far outweighs other personality factors in determining stress processes and outcome, and (2) that N is unequivocally related to emotional maladjustment. In fact, neither precondition holds up to scrutiny. At the level of broad superfactors, there is a tendency for extraversion, conscientiousness, and agreeableness to relate to lower emotional distress (Trull & Sher, 1994). These factors also correlate positively with EI scales in recent unpublished data (R. Bar-On, personal communication, July 2, 1999). Studies of personality disorders also show that different forms of maladjustment relate to different traits: dissatisfaction with self relates to neuroticism, stimulus seeking relates to extraversion, lack of concern for others relates to low agreeableness, and compulsiveness relates to conscientiousness (Schroeder, Wormsworth, & Livesley, 1992). There are multiple forms of emotional difficulty, which relate to multiple personality traits, with no indication of a unitary EI. The capacity to resist impulses, which Goleman (1995) describes as a master aptitude, seems to relate primarily to conscientiousness (Zuckerman, Kuhlman, Joireman, Teta, & Kraft, 1993). Midlevel traits such as pessimism and dispositional self-consciousness and contextualized traits such as test anxiety may contribute to stress vulnerability independently of N (Matthews et al., 1998).

The second precondition for linking neuroticism to EI is that the trait is, in fact, maladaptive. This hypothesis is loosely acceptable as a broad generalization in that N relates to unpleasant experiences in various areas of life, and to mental and possibly physical illness (Matthews & Deary, 1998). Those with high N do indeed seem to find it harder to form and maintain relationships with others and to perform well on demanding tasks (Matthews & Dorn, 1995). Other evidence shows that neuroticism is not all bad. Its effects on real-world job performance are surprisingly slight. Barrick and Mount (1991) report a meta-analysis that gives a mean corrected correlation of $-.08$ between N and occupational performance: oversensitivity to negative emotion is not necessarily disabling in the real world.

Individuals with high N may often be able to compensate for their vulnerability to distress. Studies of motivation and trait anxiety (which is highly correlated with N) show that anxious individuals exert additional effort to compensate for processing inefficiency, thereby maintaining performance effectiveness (M. W. Eysenck & Calvo, 1992). Mughal, Walsh, and Wilding (1996) found in two real-world studies that anxiety was positively correlated with number of sales closed by insurance sales consultants. Anxious consultants experienced more subjective stress but saw more prospective clients and worked a greater number of hours per month. In an academic setting, McKenzie (1989) has reviewed studies showing that the combination of N and motivation relates to a higher class of degree. In other words, even if N is associated with a general tendency toward presumed maladaptive coping, in certain key circumstances the person with high N is capable of coping more effectively than the person with low N, for example through greater job effort. Personal insecurity may act as a spur to achievement.

Negative affect may have some cognitive as well as motivational benefits. Studies of decision making (Forgas, 1995) show that both positive and negative moods have costs and benefits, depending on circumstances. Sometimes, positive mood may promote fast, decisive action. However, in some circumstances, people in negative moods are more likely to use extensive, substantive processing strategies, whereas people in positive moods are biased toward using heuristics, which require less processing effort. These are state rather than trait data, but they imply that the negative moods characteristic of individuals with high N may help them to avoid hasty, careless decisions. In sum, although high N has some obvious psychological costs, it may also facilitate effective handling of demanding encounters in circumstances that call for self-motivation and caution, and the trait cannot be equated with low EI.

Patterns of Adaptation

In fact, most personality traits may be associated with a blend of adaptive strengths and weaknesses (Zeidner & Matthews, 2000). We have seen already that extraversion, conscientiousness, and agreeableness broadly tend to be associated with resilience under stress, but all these personality qualities may have compensating disadvantages. Extraverts have difficulty in sustaining attention over time and on problem-solving tasks requiring reflection, insight, and restraint (Matthews, 1997a). Introverts appear to be better suited than extraverts to literary, artistic, and scientific occupations (H. J. Eysenck, 1995), which perhaps require skills in sustained attention and reflective thought. According to H. J. Eysenck (1995), creativity and genius are associated with the psychoticism trait, which is associated with tough-mindedness, impulsivity, and indifference to others. Agreeableness and conscientiousness are both associated with low psychoticism, and so may hinder creativity. Welsh (1975) found that creative students tended to possess low-conscientiousness traits such as irresponsibility, disorderliness, lack of control, and carelessness. In the workplace, conscientiousness promotes good job performance and integrity (Ones, Viswesvaran, & Schmidt, 1993). However, as shown by Adorno, Frenkel-Brunswick, Levinson, & Sandford's (1950) work on authoritarian personality, overconcern with order and control can increase vulnerability to frustration. Agreeableness seems to have mixed effects in the workplace: it is associated with better teamwork, but also with poorer managerial performance under conditions of high autonomy of action (chief executive officers appear to be notably disagreeable) (see Matthews, 1997b, for references).

Matthews (1997a) proposed that traits are associated with adaptations to specific environments. For example, the cognitive characteristics of extraversion support adaptation to social and high-information-flow environments, whereas the introvert's cognitive capabilities support success in environments requiring solitary, reflective thought. Broadly, persons with low N are adapted to handling stress, but high N represents an adaptation to subtle or disguised threat, for which sensitivity to threat and behavioral caution are beneficial. Implicit in the EI construct is the idea that persons are either globally better or worse at handling emotional situations. By contrast, personality studies suggest that people are characterized by patterns of strengths and weaknesses that allow them to thrive in some environments at the expense of others. The qualities that allow the person to appear emotionally intelligent in some settings elicit "emotional stupidity" in others. Some traits, such as low neuroticism and high conscientiousness, appear to be predominantly adaptive, but labeling these traits as constituents of EI does not add to the more sophisticated view of personality offered by contemporary research.

TRAINING ADAPTIVE BEHAVIORS

Studies of situational adaptive coping and of personality traits provide two possible avenues toward a rigorous definition of EI in the stress context. A further avenue is provided by studies of training adaptive behaviors. A key attribute of general intelligence is its transferability (Sternberg, 1985): the intelligent person adapts existing knowledge flexibly and pertinently to deal with a novel problem. By analogy, the same criterion should apply to EI. The individual with high EI should be able to apply the skills acquired in dealing with one type of stressor to other stressors or to novel stressors. We raise this issue largely as a question to be answered because there is very little relevant evidence available: does learning generalize across situations, or are acquired skills largely situation specific? The answer may depend on the specificity of the skills themselves. We can distinguish various levels of specificity.

Specific domain knowledge. As Lazarus (1991) points out, life events often require specific items of knowledge for successful coping. The person faced with divorce or bankruptcy must acquire legal knowledge, for example. It is hard to see factual information of this type as representing EI. In fact, understanding complex information, such as legal procedures, is likely to require general intelligence.

Specific transferable coping procedures. At a more general level, the person may acquire specific but potentially transferable coping routines. Counting up to five and taking a deep breath in moments of anxiety is a somewhat trivial example. More usefully, the person may be taught cognitive procedures, for reevaluating an event, for example, or for systematically formulating a plan of action. Problem solving can be taught explicitly (D'Zurilla & Goldfried, 1971; Janis & Mann, 1977). Problem-solving strategies have been incorporated into various cognitive-behavioral therapies and are defined as efforts to identify or create effective and adaptive coping behaviors (D'Zurilla & Goldfried, 1971). Nezu (1986) has reported that depressed patients benefit from social-problem-solving therapy. Training in problem-solving skills has been incorporated into programs for the prevention of health care problems (for example, concerning diet or tobacco use) among Native American youth (Schinke & Singer, 1994).

Packages of specific procedures. Training for individual coping procedures grades into training packages that teach integrated sets of skills, such as cognitive-behavioral programs ranging from specific techniques such as self-instruction training (Meichenbaum, 1977) to comprehensive health care programs (Schinke & Singer, 1994). Meichenbaum's (1977) stress inoculation training program includes skills acquisition and rehearsal phases in which participants are trained in both instrumental and palliative coping skills for the management of stress. The self-instruction component further includes the generation of self-statements designed to cope effectively with feelings of being overwhelmed. Training effective skills is important in successfully managing both old and new stressors that may cause a relapse of such behaviors as smoking (Baer, Karmack, Lichtenstein, & Ransom, 1989). Further, the use of multiple behaviors in smoking cessation programs appears to increase the effectiveness of the treatment, thereby reducing the likelihood of relapse (Bliss, Garvey, Heinold, & Hitchcock, 1989). A recent study of unaided smoking cessation suggested that quitters more often than nonquitters used problem-solving coping strategies and cognitive restructuring in contrast to wishful thinking, self-criticism, and social withdrawal (Carey, Kalra, Carey, Halperin, & Richards, 1993).

Training effective self-regulation. The most general approach is not to train coping, as such, but to train the person to make the most of his or her personal resources, for example, by boosting the person's confidence and self-efficacy. Somewhat outré techniques such as fire-walking and parachuting aim to do this, as do more conventional cognitive-behavioral methods such as cognitive restructuring (Ellis, 1977). In terms of the transactional model, the target is secondary appraisal—the persons' evaluations of their personal resources as more or less effective in managing perceived stress. As perceptions of one's own coping effectiveness increases, one is more likely to employ problem-focused coping (MacNair & Elliott, 1992). We might suppose that the more general the technique, the greater the likelihood of transfer across different types of stressful episode, but as previously indicated, this hypothesis awaits empirical tests. Stress management programs directed only toward training specific skills may not in fact be training EI. Matthews and Wells (1996) discuss five limitations of skill-based treatments.

Superficiality. The treatment may not address the underlying cognitions that hinder the person's acquisition of effective coping skills.

Prevention of disconfirmation of dysfunctional beliefs. Relaxation techniques, for example, may provide short-term relief but make it more difficult for people to confront nonveridical beliefs about the consequences of the stressor.

Loss of functional capacity. The need to allocate attention and effort to coping routines may divert attention from necessary tasks.

Priming of negative belief. Cognitive strategies that require attention to disturbing thoughts and feelings may actually enhance the intrusiveness of negative ideation.

Rationales for Training Effects

Techniques may work for reasons other than those claimed. For example, if a skill is trained, it may be the increased confidence that results that is beneficial, rather than the skill itself. Matthews and Wells (1996) further argue that for clinical patients, deeper cognitive restructuring that addresses generic self-knowledge is critical (Ellis, 1977). Because much of this knowledge is procedural rather than consciously available, a range of cognitive-behavioral techniques such as guided dialogue, systematic exploration and challenging of cognitions, and disconfirmatory behavioral experiments are required (Wells, 1997). Plausibly, patients with generalized anxiety have a wide-ranging problem that could be described as a lack of EI. Furthermore, cognitive-behavioral therapies, when successful, produce clinical improvements that generalize across situations; the patient is liberated from the self-defeating ruminative worries that produce widespread problems in living. In a restricted sense, we might say that emotional disorders impair EI, which is restored by therapy. It is much less clear that the stress management techniques used by persons with nonclinical conditions can be similarly described. Training coping skills may often elicit improvements in one area of life, but their cross-situational generality remains to be explored empirically.

CONCLUSION

Successful coping with stressful encounters is central to any construct of EI. However, it is difficult to infer a psychologically meaningful EI construct from research on stress. EI is of scientific interest only if it can be identified as a coherent quality of the person that underpins adaptive coping (and other manifestations of emotion regulation). Research on stress long predates the coining of the term *emotional intelligence;* stress models are imperfect, but they capture something of the processes driving a response. We can attempt to describe what differentiates persons varying in EI in terms of those models, notably the transactional model. For example, there might be a style of coping that promotes successful outcomes across a range of different encounters, which could be labeled as "intelligent." We can do so in a very approximate way: on average, successful adaptation follows from positive self-appraisal, coping through problem focus, and minimizing bouts of self-blame and ruminative worry. However, in our view, the disadvantages of describing cognitive stress responses in this way outweigh the advantages. It is often difficult to distinguish adaptive and maladaptive coping, in that what constitutes adaptiveness is highly dependent on the criterion adopted and the situation of interest. Furthermore, there are multiple processes, operating at different levels of the cognitive architecture, that feed into the coping outcome.

Similarly, studies of personality offer a highly differentiated view of individual differences in adaptation, which is not commensurate with the EI construct in any simple way. A variety of qualitatively different traits, operating through a variety of mechanisms, contribute to multifaceted outcomes of stressful encounters. Broadly beneficial traits such as conscientiousness and agreeableness have a downside, and traits related to emotional distress, such as neuroticism, have some adaptive benefits. The best hope for future research on stress and EI may be to show that individuals can be trained in generic self-regulation skills that facilitate adaptation to a variety of stressors. To some degree, cognitive-behavior therapy for anxiety and depression aims to effect training of this kind. It remains unclear whether comparable training programs might be effective for nonclinical groups, though there are some indications that conventional stress management techniques do not engender sufficiently wide-ranging benefits to be described as enhancing EI.

We emphasize that our conclusions are tentative, owing to the lack of direct evidence on EI and stress. High-quality scientific investigation of EI is only just beginning, and dismissing the construct at this stage would be premature (P. Salovey, personal communication, March 30, 1999). One of the key tests will be whether the new EI scales have superior predictive validity compared to existing individual difference measures. However, our current view is that the EI hypothesis fails to engage with three critical aspects of stress reactions. First, stress reactions are distributed, that is, supported by a diversity of functionally distinct cognitive and physiological reactions. There is no single master process for stress regulation, and hence, no clean mapping between EI and stress outcome. Second, stress outcomes are often more qualitative than quantitative. Typically, encounters may provoke a pattern of costs and benefits rather than an unequivocally positive or negative outcome. Even apparently successful coping may have costs such as loss of behavioral flexibility, fatigue, and resource depletion (Lepore & Evans, 1996). Personality data suggest that people may be differentiated by their fitness for different types of challenge and choice of adaptive tradeoff (Matthews, 1997a), rather than by some global adaptability. Fitness for dealing with some types of emotional challenge may necessarily entail costs in other contexts. For example, the career-minded executive may require a degree of insensitivity to others' feelings, and the creative artist seems to benefit from personal irresponsibility. We may not be able to "have it all" emotionally, though we can perhaps find (or construct) a niche in society that suits our strengths and weaknesses. Third, the EI construct implies a continuum of adaptability, which makes little qualitative distinction between normality and pathology. The construct seems more readily applicable to clinical patients, who show global deficits in emotion management—although different conditions relate to qualitatively different deficits. There is little evidence from research on stress to suggest that individuals without major problems in living can be differentiated on an emotional intelligence continuum.

References

Adorno, T. W., Frenkel-Brunswick, E., Levinson, D. J., & Sandford, R. N. (1950) *The authoritarian personality.* New York: Harper & Row.

Aldwin, C. M., & Revenson, T. T. (1987). Does coping help? A reexamination of the relation between coping and mental health. *Journal of Personality and Social Psychology, 53,* 337–348.

Aspinwall, L. G., & Taylor, S. E. (1992). Modelling cognitive adaptation: A longitudinal investigation of the impact of individual differences and coping on college adjustment and performance. *Journal of Personality and Social Psychology, 63,* 989–1003.

Auerbach, S. M. (1989). Stress management and coping research in the health care setting: An overview and methodological commentary. *Journal of Consulting and Clinical Psychology, 57,* 388–395.

Baer, J. S., Karmack, T, Lichtenstein, E., & Ransom, C. C., Jr. (1989). Prediction of smoking relapse: Analyses of temptations and transgressions after initial cessation. *Journal of Consulting and Clinical Psychology, 57,* 623–627.

Bar-On, R. (1997) *BarOn Emotional Quotient Inventory (EQ-i): Technical manual.* Toronto, Canada: Multi-Health Systems.

Barrick, M. R., & Mount, M. K. (1991) The Big Five personality dimensions and job performance: A meta-analysis. *Personnel Psychology, 44,* 1–26.

Baum, A., Fleming, R. E., & Singer, J. E. (1983). Coping with technological disaster. *Journal of Social Issues, 39,* 117–138.

Billings, A. G., & Moos, R. H. (1984). Coping, stress, and social resources among adults with unipolar depression. *Journal of Personality and Social Psychology, 46,* 877–891.

Bliss, R. E., Garvey, A. J. Heinhold, J. W., & Hitchcock, J. L. (1989). The influence of situation and coping on relapse crisis outcomes after smoking cessation. *Journal of Consulting and Clinical Psychology, 57,* 443–449.

Bolger, N. (1990). Coping as a personality process: A prospective study. *Journal of Personality and Social Psychology, 59,* 525–537.

Carey, M. P., Kalra, D. L., Carey, K. B., Halperin, S., & Richards, C. S. (1993). Stress and unaided smoking cessation: A prospective investigation. *Journal of Consulting and Clinical Psychology, 61,* 831–838.

Carver, C. S., Pozo, C., Harris, S. D., Noriega, V., Scheier, M. F., Robinson, D. S., Ketchan, A. S., Moffat, F. L., Jr., & Clark, K. C. (1993). How coping mediates the effect of optimism on distress: A study of women with early stage breast cancer. *Journal of Personality and Social Psychology, 65,* 375–390.

Carver, C. S., & Scheier, M. F. (1981). *Attention and self-regulation: A control-theory approach to human behavior.* Berlin: Springer-Verlag.

Carver, C. S., Scheier, M. F., & Pozo, C. (1992). Conceptualizing the process of coping with health problems. In H. S. Friedman (Ed.), *Hostility, coping, and health* (pp. 167–199). Washington, DC: American Psychological Association.

Carver, C. S., Scheier, M. F., & Weintraub, J. K. (1989). Assessing coping strategies: A theoretically based approach. *Journal of Personality and Social Psychology, 56,* 267–283.

Cohen, F., & Lazarus, R. (1979). Coping with the stresses of illness. In G. C. Stone, F. Cohen, & N. E. Adler (Eds.), *Health psychology: A handbook* (pp. 77–112). San-Francisco: Jossey-Bass.

Davies, M., Stankov, L., & Roberts, R. D. (1998). Emotional intelligence: In search of an elusive construct. *Journal of Personality and Social Psychology, 75,* 989–1015.

Deary, I. J., Blenkin, H., Agius, R. M., Endler, N. S., Zealley, H., & Wood, R. (1996). Models of job-related stress and personal achievement among consultant doctors. *British Journal of Psychology, 87,* 3–30.

D'Zurilla, T. J., & Goldfried, M. R. (1971). Problem solving and behavior modification. *Journal of Abnormal Psychology, 78,* 107–126.

Ellis, A. (1977). Rational-emotive therapy: research data that supports the clinical and personality hypotheses of RET and other modes of cognitive-behavior therapy. *Counseling Psychologist, 7,* 2–42.

Endler, N. S. (1996, August). *Advances in coping research: An interactional perspective.* Paper presented at the symposium Advances in Coping with Stress: Interactional Perspectives, International Congress of Psychology, Montreal, Canada.

Endler, N. S., Kantor, L., & Parker, J.D.A. (1994). State-trait coping, state-trait anxiety and academic performance. *Personality and Individual Differences, 16,* 663–670.

Endler, N. S., & Parker, J.D.A. (1990). Multi-dimensional assessment of coping: A critical review. *Journal of Personality and Social Psychology, 58,* 844–854.

Eysenck, H. J. (1995). Creativity as a product of intelligence and personality. In D. H. Saklofske & M. Zeidner (Eds), *International handbook of personality and intelligence* (pp. 231–247). New York: Plenum.

Eysenck, M. W., & Calvo, M. G. (1992). Anxiety and performance: The processing efficiency theory. *Cognition and Emotion, 6,* 409–434.

Ferguson, E., Matthews, G., & Cox, T. (1999). The Appraisal of Life Events (ALE) Scale: Reliability and validity. *British Journal of Health Psychology, 4,* 97–116.

Folkman, S., Chesney, M., McKussick, L., Ironson, G., Johnson, D. S., & Coastes, T. J. (1991). Translating coping theory into an intervention. In J. Eckenrode (Ed.), *The social context of coping* (pp. 239–260). New York: Plenum.

Folkman, S., & Lazarus, R. S. (1985). If it changes it must be a process: Study of emotion and coping during three stages of a college examination. *Journal of Personality and Social Psychology, 48,* 150–170.

Folkman, S., & Lazarus, R. S. (1988). Manual for the Ways of Coping Questionnaire. Palo Alto, CA: Consulting Psychologists Press.

Folkman, S., Lazarus, R. S., Gruen, R. J., & DeLongis, A. (1986). Appraisal, coping, health status, and psychological symptoms. *Journal of Personality and Social Psychology, 50,* 571–579.

Forgas, J. P. (1995). Mood and judgement: The affect infusion model (AIM). *Psychological Bulletin, 117,* 39–66.

Gal, R., & Lazarus, R. (1975). The role of activity in anticipation and confronting stressful situations. *Journal of Human Stress, 1,* 4–20.

Gardner, H. (1993). *Multiple intelligences: The theory in practice.* New York: Basic Books.

Goleman, D. (1995). *Emotional intelligence.* New York: Bantam Books.

Haan, N. (1977). *Coping and defending: Processes of self-environment organization.* New York: Academic Press.

Janis, I., & Mann, L. (1977). *Decision making.* New York: Free Press.

Kitayama, S. (1997) Affective influence in perception: Some implications of the amplification model. In G. Matthews (Ed.), *Cognitive science perspectives on personality and emotion* (pp. 193–258). Amsterdam: Elsevier Science.

Lazarus, R. S. (1991). *Emotion and adaptation.* New York: Oxford University Press.

Lazarus, R. S. (1993). Coping theory and research: Past, present and future. *Psychosomatic Medicine, 55,* 237–247.

Lazarus, R. S., & Folkman, S. (1984). *Stress, appraisal, and coping.* New York: Springer.

Lennon, M. C., Dohrenwend, B. P., Zautra, A. J., & Marbach, J. J. (1990). Coping and adaptation to facial pain in contrast to other stressful life events. *Journal of Personality and Social Psychology, 59,* 1040–1050.

Lepore, S. J., & Evans, G. W. (1996). Coping with multiple stressors in the environment. In M. Zeidner & N. S. Endler (Eds.), *Handbook of coping* (pp. 350–377). New York: Wiley.

MacNair, R. R., & Elliott, T. R. (1992). Self-perceived problem solving ability, stress appraisal, and coping over time. *Journal of Research in Personality, 26,* 150–164.

Magnus, K., Diener, E., Fujita, F., & Pavot, W. (1993). Extraversion and neuroticism as predictors of objective life events: a longitudinal analysis. *Journal of Personality and Social Psychology, 65,* 1046–1053.

Marsella, A. J., DeVos, G., & Hsu, F. (Eds.). (1985). *Culture and self: Asian and Western perspectives.* New York: Tavistock.

Matthews, G. (1997a) Extraversion, emotion and performance: A cognitive-adaptive model. In G. Matthews (Ed.), *Cognitive science perspectives on personality and emotion* (pp. 399–442). Amsterdam: Elsevier.

Matthews, G. (1997b) The Big Five as a framework for personality assessment. In N. Anderson & P. Herriot (Eds.), *International handbook of selection and appraisal* (2nd ed., pp. 175–200). London: Wiley.

Matthews, G., & Campbell, S. E. (1998). Task-induced stress and individual differences in coping. In *Proceedings of the 42nd Annual Meeting of the Human Factors and Ergonomics Society* (pp. 821–825). Santa Monica, CA: Human Factors and Ergonomics Society.

Matthews, G., & Deary I. (1998). *Personality traits.* Cambridge, U.K.: Cambridge University Press.

Matthews, G., & Dorn, L. (1995). Personality and intelligence: Cognitive and attentional processes. In D. Saklofske & M. Zeidner (Eds.), *International handbook of personality and intelligence* (pp. 367–396). New York: Plenum.

Matthews, G., Hillyard, E. J., & Campbell, S. E. (1999). Metacognition and maladaptive coping as components of test anxiety. *Clinical Psychology and Psychotherapy, 6,* 111–125.

Matthews, G., Saklofske, D. H., Costa, P. T., Jr., Deary, I. J., & Zeidner, M. (1998). Dimensional models of personality: A framework for systematic clinical assessment. *European Journal of Psychological Assessment, 14,* 35–48.

Matthews, G., Schwean, V. L., Campbell, S. E., Saklofske, D. H., & Mohamed, A.A.R. (2000). Personality, self-regulation and adaptation: A cognitive-social framework. In M. Boekarts, P. R Pintrich & M. Zeidner (Eds.), *Handbook of self-regulation* (pp. 171–207). New York: Academic.

Matthews, G., & Wells, A. (1996). Attentional processes, coping strategies, and clinical intervention. In M. Zeidner & N. S. Endler (Eds.), *Handbook of coping: Theory, research, application* (pp. 573–601). New York: Wiley.

Matthews, G., & Wells, A. (1999). The cognitive science of attention and emotion. In T. Dalgleish & M. Power (Eds.), *Handbook of cognition and emotion.* New York: Wiley.

Mattlin, J. A., Wethington, E., & Kessler, C. (1990). Situational determinants of coping and coping effectiveness. *Journal of Health and Social Behavior, 31,* 103–122.

Mayer, J. D., Caruso, D. R., & Salovey, P. (1999). Emotional intelligence meets traditional standards for an intelligence. *Intelligence, 27,* 267–298.

Mayer, J. D., & Salovey, P. (1993). The intelligence of emotional intelligence. *Intelligence, 17,* 433–442.

Mayer, J. D., Salovey, P., & Caruso, D. (2000). Emotional intelligence. In R. J. Sternberg (Ed.), *Handbook of intelligence* (pp. 117–137). New York: Cambridge University Press.

McCrae, R. R., & Costa, P. T. (1986). Personality, coping, and coping effectiveness in an adult sample. *Journal of Personality, 54,* 383–405.

McKenzie, J. (1989). Neuroticism and academic achievement: The Furneaux Factor. *Personality and Individual Differences, 10,* 509–515.

Meichenbaum, D. (1977). *Cognitive-behavior modification: An integrative approach.* New York: Plenum.

Meneghan, E. (1982). Measuring coping effectiveness: A panel analysis of marital problems and coping efforts. *Journal of Health and Social Behavior, 23,* 220–234.

Morgan, I. A., Matthews, G., & Winton, M. (1995). Coping and personality as predictors of post-traumatic intrusions, numbing, avoidance and general distress: A study of victims of the Perth flood. *Behavioural and Cognitive Psychotherapy, 23,* 251–264.

Mughal, S., Walsh, J., & Wilding, J. (1996) Stress and work performance: The role of trait anxiety. *Personality and Individual Differences, 20,* 685–691.

Mullins, L. L., Olson, R. A., Reyes, S., Bernardy, N., Huszti, H. C., & Volk, R. J. (1991). Risk and resistance factors in the adaptation of mothers of children with cystic fibrosis. *Journal of Pediatric Psychology, 16,* 701–715.

Nezu, A. M. (1986). Efficacy of a social problem solving therapy approach for unipolar depression. *Journal of Consulting and Clinical Psychology, 54,* 196–202.

Ones, D. S., Viswesvaran, C., & Schmidt, F. L. (1993) Comprehensive meta-analysis of integrity test validities: Findings and implications for personnel selection and theories of job performance. *Journal of Applied Psychology, 78,* 679–703.

Parker, J.D.A., Taylor, G. J., & Bagby, R. M. (1998). Alexithymia: Relationship with ego defense and coping styles. *Comprehensive Psychiatry, 39,* 91–98.

Parker, J.D.A., Taylor, G. J., & Bagby, R. M. (forthcoming). The relationship between emotional intelligence and alexithymia. *Personality and Individual Differences.*

Pearlin, L. I. (1991). The study of coping: An overview of problems and directions. In J. Eckenrode (Ed.), *The social context of coping* (pp. 261–276). New York: Plenum.

Pearlin, L. I., & Schooler, C. (1978). The structure of coping. *Journal of Health and Social Behavior, 19,* 2–21.

Pennebaker, J. W. (1997). Writing about emotional experiences as a therapeutic process. *Psychological Science, 8,* 162–166.

Reason, J. T. (1987). The Chernobyl errors. *Bulletin of the British Psychological Society, 40,* 201–206.

Roger, D., Jarvis, G., & Najarian, B. (1993). Detachment and coping: The construction of a new scale for measuring coping strategies. *Personality and Individual Differences, 15,* 619–626.

Salovey, P., Bedell, B. T., Detweiler, J. B., & Mayer, J. D. (1999). Coping intelligently: Emotional intelligence and the coping process. In C.R. Snyder (Ed.), *Coping: The psychology of what works* (pp. 141–164). New York: Oxford University Press.

Salovey, P., & Mayer, J. D. (1990). Emotional intelligence. *Imagination, Cognition, and Personality, 9,* 185–211.

Sarason, I. G. (1984). Test anxiety, stress, and cognitive interference: Reactions to tests. *Journal of Personality and Social Psychology, 46,* 929–938.

Schinke S. P., & Singer, B. R. (1994). Prevention of health-care problems. In D. K. Granvold (Ed.), *Cognitive and behavioral treatment: Method and applications* (pp. 285–298). Pacific Grove, CA: Brooks/Cole.

Schroeder, M. L., Wormsworth, J. A., & Livesley, W. J. (1992). Dimensions of personality disorder and their relationships to the big five dimensions of personality. *Psychological Assessment, 4,* 47–53.

Schwarzer, R., & Schwarzer, C. (1996) A critical survey of coping instruments. In M. Zeidner & N. S. Endler (Eds.), *Handbook of coping* (pp. 107–132). New York: Wiley.

Silver, R. L., & Wortman, C. (1980). Coping with undesirable life events. In J. Garber & M.E.P. Seligman (Eds.), *Human helplessness* (pp. 279–340). New York: Academic Press.

Steptoe, A. (1991). Psychological coping, individual differences and physiological stress responses. In C. L. Cooper & R. Payne (Eds.), *Personality and stress: Individual differences in the coping process* (pp. 205–233). Chichester: Wiley.

Sternberg, R. J. (1985). *Beyond IQ: A triarchic theory of intelligence.* New York: Cambridge University Press.

Suls, J., & Fletcher, B. (1985). The relative efficacy of avoidant and nonavoidant coping strategies: A meta-analysis. *Health Psychology, 4,* 249–288.

Taylor, S. E. (1986). *Health psychology.* New York: Random House.

Trull, T. J., & Sher, K. J. (1994). Relationship between the five-factor model of personality and Axis I disorders in a nonclinical sample. *Journal of Abnormal Psychology, 103,* 350–360.

van Reekum, C. M., & Scherer, K. R. (1997). Levels of processing in emotion-antecedent appraisal. In G. Matthews (Ed.), *Cognitive science perspectives on personality and emotion* (pp. 259–301). Amsterdam: Elsevier.

Wallerstein, J. S. (1983). Children of divorce: The psychological tasks of the child. *American Journal of Orthopsychiatry, 53,* 230–243.

Weidner, G., & Collins, R. L. (1992). Gender, coping, and health. In H. W. Krohne (Ed.), *Attention and avoidance: Strategies in coping with aversiveness* (pp. 241–265). Toronto, Canada: Hogrefe & Huber.

Wells, A. (1997). *Cognitive therapy of anxiety disorders: A practice manual and conceptual guide.* Chichester, U.K.: Wiley.

Wells, A., & Matthews, G. (1994). *Attention and emotion: A clinical perspective.* Hove, U.K.: Erlbaum.

Welsh, G. (1975). *Creativity and intelligence: A personality approach.* Chapel Hill, NC: University of North Carolina.

Wethington, E., & Kessler, R. C. (1991). Situations and processes of coping. In J. Eckenrode (Eds.), *The social context of coping* (pp. 13–29). New York: Plenum.

Wortman, C. (1983). Coping with victimization: Conclusions and implications for future research. *Journal of Social Issues, 39,* 195–221.

Zeidner, M. (1998). *Test anxiety: The state of the art.* New York: Plenum.

Zeidner, M., & Hammer, A. (1990). Life events and coping resources as predictors of stress symptoms in adolescents. *Personality and Individual Differences, 11,* 693–703.

Zeidner, M., & Matthews, G. (2000). Personality and intelligence. In R. J. Sternberg (Ed.), *Handbook of intelligence* (pp. 581–610). New York: Cambridge University Press.

Zeidner, M., & Saklofske, D. S. (1996). Adaptive and maladaptive coping. In M. Zeidner & N. S. Endler (Eds.), *Handbook of coping* (pp. 505–531). New York: Wiley.

Zuckerman, M., Kuhlman, D. M., Joireman, J., Teta, P., & Kraft, M. (1993). A comparison of three structural models for personality: the big three, the big five, and the alternative five. *Journal of Personality and Social Psychology, 65,* 757–768.

CHAPTER TWENTY-TWO

Emotional Intelligence

Clinical and Therapeutic Implications

James D. A. Parker

several of the chapters in this book have raised a number of clinical issues and concerns about emotional intelligence. In this chapter I explicitly examine the clinical and therapeutic implications of the emotional intelligence construct. To date, little research has been published on this topic. As noted in several chapters, the lack of reliable and valid measures for the emotional intelligence construct has prohibited clinical research from developing (see Chapters Fifteen, Sixteen, and Seventeen). Nevertheless, there are several constructs that overlap conceptually with emotional intelligence and have also generated a substantial clinical literature.

This chapter has three major sections. The first section I identify several constructs with widespread clinical implications that have conceptual overlap with emotional intelligence. Some of the more important empirical findings from this literature are also examined. In the second section I describe a number of specialized psychotherapeutic interventions that have relevance for treating individuals with limited (or less than average) levels of emotional intelligence. In the last section I examine the empirical evidence for the efficacy of some of these specialized psychotherapeutic interventions.

Note: This chapter was supported by research grants from the Social Science and Humanities Research Council of Canada and the Ontario Premier's Research Excellence Award program.

EMOTIONAL INTELLIGENCE AND RELATED CONSTRUCTS

Regardless of which emotional intelligence model one adopts (compare, for example, the models presented in Chapters Five and Seventeen), the construct has important clinical and therapeutic implications because it emerged from an amalgamation of research findings on how people appraise, communicate about, and use emotion (Salovey & Mayer, 1989–1990). For example, one would expect emotional intelligence to be associated with the motivation and interest to pursue particular types of clinical interventions (such as interpretive versus supportive forms of psychotherapy). One might also expect emotional intelligence to be linked with successful outcomes from specific psychotherapeutic interventions. For example, successful insight-oriented (or interpretive) psychotherapy frequently hinges on the patient's "ability to see relationships among thoughts, feelings, and actions, with the goal of learning the meanings and causes of his [or her] experiences and behavior" (Applebaum, 1973, p. 36). The ability to identify and describe internal mental states and the ability to link specific mental events with particular behaviors and situations are core dimensions in most models of emotional intelligence. It should be emphasized that these are also important abilities that are often linked with successful outcomes from psychotherapy (Greenberg & Safran, 1987; Krystal, 1988).

When we turn to the empirical literature for evidence of the clinical importance of emotional intelligence, however, we find almost no published information. Nevertheless, although the construct of emotional intelligence has a short history, it also has a long past. There are several related constructs that have generated considerable research on a variety of clinical issues. One of the oldest is the construct of psychological mindedness. (See Chapter Six for a detailed discussion on this topic.) This construct is part of a large literature that has resulted from the efforts to identify the personality factors that predict successful insight-oriented psychotherapy (Bachrach & Leaff, 1978). Other interrelated constructs that have attracted research interest include ego strength (Lake, 1985), need for cognition (Cacioppo & Petty, 1982), private self-consciousness (Fenigstein, Scheier, & Buss, 1975), and self-awareness (Bloch, 1979). In a subsequent section of this chapter I focus specifically on the clinical implications of psychological mindedness, because this construct appears to have generated more empirical literature than the other related constructs (McCallum & Piper, 1997).

Alexithymia (see Chapter Three for a detailed discussion on this topic) is another construct that has considerable clinical relevance and has generated a vast clinical literature (Taylor, Bagby, & Parker, 1997). In their conceptualization of emotional intelligence as a dimensional construct involving a set of skills related to the appraisal, expression, and regulation of emotion, Salovey, Hsee, and Mayer (1993) placed alexithymia at the extreme lower end of the emotional intelligence continuum. There is also empirical evidence to link together the alexithymia and emotional intelligence constructs (Schutte et al., 1998). In a recent study by Parker, Taylor, and Bagby (forthcoming), which used reliable and valid measures of alexithymia (the Twenty-Item Toronto Alexithymia Scale [TAS-20]; Bagby, Parker, & Taylor, 1994) and emotional intelligence (the BarOn Emotional Quotient Inventory; Bar-On, 1997), the total scores for the two measures had a correlation coefficient of −.72 in a large sample of adults who were not clinical patients. It is worth noting that alexithymia has also been found to correlate significantly and negatively with measures of psychological mindedness. Bagby et al. (1994) reported a correlation of −.68 between the total TAS-20 and the total Psychological Mindedness Scale (PMS; Conte et al., 1990).

Psychological Mindedness

The search for personality variables that identify individuals likely to benefit from insight-oriented psychotherapy has a long history (see, for example, Bachrach & Leaff, 1978; Barron, 1953; Piper, Joyce, McCallum, & Azim, 1998; Ryan & Cicchetti, 1985; Tolor & Reznikoff, 1960). As many clinicians have written (Krystal, 1982–1983; Silver, 1983; Taylor, 1977, 1984b), some individuals appear to respond very poorly to insight-oriented psychotherapy. From the start of treatment they are often difficult clients to manage. Quite often, these are the clients who terminate treatment after only a few sessions (Beckham, 1992; Saltzman, Luetgert, Roth, Creaser, & Howard, 1976). They become frustrated with what they believe to be the slow pace of therapy, and the perceived irrelevance (for their "problems") of the issues and questions raised in treatment sessions. Countertransference difficulties are not uncommon with these clients (Silver, 1983; Taylor, 1977). The clinician, too, runs the risk of becoming frustrated by the therapeutic process: "the therapist enters into a relationship expecting to be *fed* interesting fantasies and feelings only to encounter increasing frustration, dullness and boredom" (Taylor, 1977, p. 143).

The construct of psychological mindedness emerged in the clinical literature to refer to a set of abilities frequently linked with successful outcomes from psychotherapy. From a conceptual point of view, there is considerable overlap between psychological mindedness and emotional intelligence. Regardless of the conceptual models one might use to define these two constructs (or measurement models), an individual with limited psychological mindedness is generally expected to have limited emotional intelligence (Taylor et al., 1997). As noted by Silver (1983), in an early definition of the construct, psychological mindedness involves "the patient's desire to learn the possible meanings and causes of his internal and external experiences as well as the patient's ability to look inwards to psychical factors rather than only outwards to environmental factors" (p. 516). In a more recent definition, Conte et al. (1990) proposed that psychological mindedness involves four broad abilities: access to one's feelings, willingness to talk about one's feelings and interpersonal problems, capacity for behavioral change, and an interest in other people's behavior. Thus, for individuals with limited psychological mindedness, psychotherapy is often perceived as a confusing and frustrating experience (Piper et al., 1998). The proliferation of these kinds of negative emotions has the potential to impede, or even prevent, the therapeutic process from proceeding.

There are important practical implications from difficulties with the therapeutic process that need to be emphasized. Depending on the criteria and populations studied, drop-out rates from psychotherapy have been reported to be as high as 80 percent to 90 percent (Owen & Kohutek, 1981). Over one-third of adult outpatients terminated their psychotherapy after the first or second session (Pekarik, 1983; Sue, McKinney, & Allen, 1976). Baekeland and Lundwall (1975) reported that between 20 percent and 50 percent of clients attending general psychiatric clinics do not return for therapy after the first session. In a review of forty-eight published studies on premature termination from long-term psychotherapy, Reder and Tyson (1980) reported a median drop-out rate of 45 percent within two to five sessions. Although there are many reasons why individuals terminate psychotherapy (Luborsky, McLellan, Woody, O'Brien, & Auerbach, 1985), emotional and social competencies undoubtedly play an important role (Krystal, 1988; Mallinckrodt, King, & Coble, 1998; McCallum, Piper, & Joyce, 1992; Pierloot & Vinck, 1977; Piper et al., 1998; Taylor et al., 1997). Not all patients have the desire or the capacity to make use of psychotherapy. Knowing something about a particular client's level of emotional intelligence (or psychological mindedness) may be very useful to the therapist before the start of treatment. Armed with the knowledge that a particular client has limited imaginal or fantasy abilities, for example, a therapist might be able to spend more time than usual in the early stages of treatment working to improve these basic abilities. In a subsequent section of this chapter I describe a number of techniques thought to improve various emotional and social competencies.

Alexithymia

It is worth noting that the concept of alexithymia evolved from clinical observations of clients who responded quite poorly to insight-oriented psychotherapy. Working with individuals experiencing so-called psychosomatic disorders, Ruesch (1948) identified a cluster of personality variables in a subset of his patients. These individuals had a tendency to develop dependent relationships, seemed to be quite immature and unimaginative in their thinking, and had a tendency to use direct physical action for emotional expression. Writing just a few years later, Karen Horney (1952) described a similar set of personality characteristics in a group of clients who were responding quite poorly to insight-oriented psychotherapy. Horney, in fact, believed that psychotherapy was making her clients more frustrated and unhappy. She speculated that the reason these individuals were not responding to treatment was a profound lack of emotional awareness, minimal interest in their mental experiences (such as fantasies and dreams), and a rather concrete (or externalized) style of thinking.

The significance of these early clinical observations were appreciated two decades later when Sifneos (1967) and Nemiah and Sifneos (1970) investigated the personality characteristics of clients experiencing classic psychosomatic diseases (such as peptic ulcer, bronchial asthma, essential hypertension, thyrotoxicosis, ulcerative colitis, rheumatoid arthritis, and neurodermatitis). The results of this work revealed that many of these clients had great difficulty understanding and describing their internal mental states. Sifneos (1973) coined the word *alexithymia* (from the Greek: *a* meaning lack, *lexis* meaning word, *thymos* meaning emotion) to identify the particular cognitive and affective characteristics they found in many of their clients. Alexithymia, as the construct has come to be defined (Taylor, 1984a; Taylor et al., 1997), consists of the following features: difficulty identifying feelings and distinguishing between feelings and the bodily sensations of emotional arousal; difficulty describing feelings to other people; constricted imaginal processes; and a stimulus-bound, externally orientated cognitive style. A comparison of the definitions of alexithymia and emotional intelligence suggests that the two constructs are closely related (Taylor et al., 1997; Taylor, Parker, & Bagby, 1999), although alexithymia is a much more narrowly defined construct (see Chapter Three). Recent empirical evidence also suggests that individuals with alexithymia score very low on measures of emotional intelligence (Parker, Taylor, & Bagby, forthcoming; Schutte et al., 1998).

Although not part of the formal definition of the construct, there are several other characteristics associated with alexithymia that have important clinical implications: difficulties identifying emotions in the facial expressions of others (Lane et al., 1996; Parker, Taylor, & Bagby, 1993), limited capacity for empathizing with the emotional states of others (Krystal, 1979; McDougall, 1989; Taylor, 1987), and difficulty remembering or recalling dreams (Krystal, 1979; Nemiah, Freyberger, & Sifneos, 1976). Recent empirical evidence (Parker, Bauermann, & Smith, forthcoming) suggests that it is the quality of the dreams, rather than recall ability, that is associated with alexithymia. When individuals with alexithymia recall their dreams, the dreams frequently contain explicit mental content (such as scenes of violence) or replay relatively trivial daytime experiences (Levitan, 1989; Parker, Bauermann, & Smith, forthcoming; Taylor, 1987). Krystal (1979) reported that working dreams into psychotherapy tends to be very difficult for patients with alexithymia.

Although the alexithymia construct was associated initially with classical psychosomatic diseases, it soon became evident that the core features can be observed among patients experiencing a number of psychiatric disorders: somatization disorders (Catchlove, Cohen, Braha, & Demers-Desrosiers, 1985), posttraumatic stress disorder (Krystal, 1978), substance use disorders (Rybakowski, Ziólkowski, Zasadzka, & Brzezinski, 1988), and eating disorders (Garfinkel & Garner, 1982). As described in detail by Taylor et al. (1997), those with alexithymia may be vulnerable for developing these psychiatric disorders because of an inability to regulate distressing emotions through mental processes: "it is not surprising that alexithymia has been conceptualized as one of several possible personality risk factors for a variety of medical and psychiatric disorders involving problems in affect regulation. For example, hypochondriasis and somatization disorder might be viewed as resulting, at least in part, from the alexithymic individual's limited subjective awareness and cognitive processing of emotions, which leads both to a focusing on, and amplification and misinterpretation of, the somatic sensations that accompany emotional arousal" (p. 31). Because alexithymic individuals identify their subjective feelings very inaccurately, they communicate emotional distress to others very poorly. Thus, they are not likely to turn to other people for aid or comfort. Their restricted imaginal abilities also limit the extent to which they can modify negative mood states by fantasy or other mental activities (Krystal, 1979; Mayes & Cohen, 1992).

For health care professionals the presence of clients with alexithymia (or very low levels of emotional intelligence) has a number of important implications. The proneness of these individuals to somatize their distress is one cause for concern. Combined with a poor communication style, their tendency to somatize may result in medical overinvestigation. Physicians, trained to diagnose and treat somatic complaints, generally respond to client concerns about somatic problems with tests and interventions. The failure of these interventions to produce symptom relief in alexithymic individuals may initiate a round of more elaborate and expensive tests to find "the problem" (which may also add an iatrogenic component to the client's problems). Thus, unnecessary medical consultations and procedures are an additional social cost of alexithymia. A recent Finnish study found that adults with alexithymia used significantly more health care resources during a one-year period than adults without alexithymia (Jyvaesjaervi et al., 1999).

Although individuals with alexithymia may be vulnerable to experience a variety of health problems (Taylor et al., 1997), they are rarely suitable clients for traditional forms of insight-oriented psychotherapy. Krystal (1982–1983), who has written extensively about his experiences treating individuals with a variety of psychiatric problems (such as posttraumatic stress disorder and substance use disorders), suggests that alexithymia may be "the most important single factor diminishing the success of psychoanalysis and psychodynamic psychotherapy" (p. 364). A number of clinicians have written that those with alexithymia may actually be made worse as a result of psychotherapy (Sifneos, 1975; Taylor, 1987; Taylor et al., 1997). "Patients with active psychosomatic diseases may, instead of experiencing strong emotion, develop a serious or even life-endangering exacerbation of their illness. . . . In the addictive patients, the increase in intensity of their diffuse distress may drive them to drink, or whatever their usual form of drug abuse involves" (Krystal, 1982–1983, p. 363). Faced with the problem that conventional forms of psychotherapy might not work, or might make some clients worse, some clinicians have developed a number of therapeutic modifications for working with clients with alexithymia. The following section describes these therapeutic interventions.

PSYCHOTHERAPY AND THE ALEXITHYMIC CLIENT

Individual Therapy

Alexithymia, as noted above, appears to be a vulnerability factor for a number of psychiatric disorders. Not surprisingly, therefore, a number of clinicians have modified traditional forms of psychotherapy to treat clients with alexithymia who have various medical and psychiatric disorders. In general, these modifications attempt to increase the clients' awareness of their problems in the way they process and experience their emotions. This approach contrasts sharply with traditional psychotherapy because it "attempts to elevate emotions from a level of perceptually bound experience (a world of sensation and action) to a conceptual representational level (a world of feelings and thoughts) where they can be used as signals of information, thought about, and sometimes communicated to others" (Taylor et al., 1997, p. 252).

One of the first obstacles to be overcome by the therapist is the individual's tendency to form relatively poor interpersonal relationships. Individuals with alexithymia find close attachments quite aversive (Taylor et al., 1997) and have considerable fear of intimacy, with limited capacity to share personally significant feelings and thoughts with other people (Fischer & Good, 1997; Mallinckrodt et al., 1998). Not surprisingly, these such individuals often work to prevent close emotional relationships from developing with their therapist (Brown, 1985; Krystal, 1979; Taylor, 1987).

One of the more detailed accounts of an attempt to modify traditional psychotherapy for alexithymic clients is provided by Krystal (1979, 1988). The first step in treatment, according to Krystal (1979, 1988), is to explain to the clients that an important cause of their "problem" is a deficit in the way they understand and communicate emotional experiences. The clients need to be made aware that one consequence of this deficit is that they have a tendency (unlike most people) to experience their emotions as physiological reactions or sensations, rather than as feelings. The second step in treatment is to work to improve the clients' skills at recognizing and correctly labeling particular emotions, differentiating one emotional experience from another, and communicating these feelings to others (in this case, the therapist).

This type of modified psychotherapy, as several writers have noted (Krystal, 1979, 1988; Taylor, 1977, 1987), can be a slow and tedious process. Clients with alexithymia are quick to assume a dependent patient role; they frequently expect that their problems can be "cured" with specific medical interventions. Over time, however, these clients can learn to have a better understanding of their feelings, can learn to differentiate between different emotional states, and can develop a larger repertoire of verbal and behavioral expressions for communicating information about their emotional experiences (Krystal, 1988; Taylor et al., 1997). A number of therapeutic techniques can be used to facilitate this process. Greenberg and Safran (1987) have noted that directing the client's attention to behavioral (nonverbal) expressions of emotion, such as body movements, gestures, and sighs, provides important sources of information for communicating feelings. There is also some evidence (Cartwright, 1993) that teaching individuals with alexithymia to pay attention to their dreams leads to better progress in psychotherapy, in part because it teaches them to focus on inner feelings and experiences. For some clients it has also been found helpful to combine psychotherapy with behavioral techniques, such as relaxation training or biofeedback. These types of behavioral techniques help to foster greater introceptive awareness in alexithymic clients, especially the capacity to self-regulate different physiological states (Taylor, 1987).

As noted by several clinical writers (Krystal, 1982–1983; McDougall, 1989; Taylor, 1987; Wolff, 1977), the therapist can also foster the development of better emotional skills in clients with alexithymia by being more open about their own emotions than is usual in traditional insight-oriented psychotherapy. For example, the therapist may want to share humor and fantasy during therapeutic sessions. The therapist might also want to communicate feelings of boredom and frustration to the client when countertransference problems arise (which happen quite frequently with these clients; Krystal, 1979; Taylor, 1977). Such comments can help the client link specific inner experiences with particular interpersonal situations (for example, feelings of boredom from listening to trivial and repetitive details, or feelings of frustration because of missed or late appointments).

Group Therapy

Group therapy has been suggested as a useful and practical alternative to individual psychotherapy for some clients with alexithymia (Apfel-Savitz, Silverman, & Bennett, 1977; Swiller, 1988). Although individual sessions are well suited for educating particular clients about basic emotion abilities, there are some unique therapeutic benefits that can be achieved in a group situation. The group setting provides a structured social environment in which a broad range of new behaviors can be learned or modeled. "While it is essential that the alexithymic patients experience the group as a safe and supportive setting, candid feedback from other group members should be encouraged, to the extent that it does not threaten the patients' self-esteem, as this can help them learn about the impact of their lack of empathy on other people. At the same time, the group therapist can direct an alexithymic patient's attention to communications between other group members that demonstrate more successful and sensitive ways of relating" (Taylor et al., 1997, 253–254).

Swiller (1988) raises several practical issues about the use of the group therapy with alexithymic clients. The poor interpersonal skills of these individuals will, inevitably, generate feelings of frustration and boredom in other group members. This increases the likelihood that members without alexithymia will drop out of the group. Depending on the size of the group, therefore, it is important that there be only a small number of individuals with alexithymia in the group at any one time. When there is more than one in the group, Swiller (1988) recommends that he or she be at a different stage of the treatment process.

TREATMENT OUTCOME EFFECTIVENESS

Individual Therapy

Pierloot and Vinck (1977) conducted the first study to examine the relationship between alexithymia and different types of psychotherapy. Psychiatric outpatients presenting with a variety of anxiety symptoms were randomly assigned to two different interventions: behavior therapy (systematic desensitization) or short-term psychodynamic psychotherapy. Consistent with their expectations, Pierloot and Vinck found that "patients with more alexithymia characteristics are more likely to drop out from psychodynamic therapies, but in systematic desensitization they persist as well as those without alexithymic characteristics" (p. 162). According to the authors of this study, a drop out was considered to be either a therapeutic failure or an indication of an incompatibility between the client's communication style and the requirements of psychotherapy.

Keller, Carroll, Nich, and Rounsaville (1995) examined the response to psychotherapy in those with and without alexithymia who abused cocaine. Clients were randomly assigned to different treatment conditions: psychotherapy plus a placebo, or psychotherapy combined with the tricyclic antidepressant desipramine. Two types of psychotherapy were also used in this study (for a total of four different treatment groups): clinical management and cognitive-behavioral treatment. Clinical management included a supportive doctor-patient relationship, education, empathy, and medication management (which gave the therapist an opportunity to monitor the client's clinical status and treatment response). Thus, this therapeutic approach required very little internal focusing on the part of the client. The form of cognitive-behavioral therapy used by Keller et al. (1995) included asking clients to identify and communicate internal affect and cognitive states associated with their drug use. The therapist also encouraged clients to identify, monitor, and analyze their drug cravings and negative affects. After twelve weeks of treatment, the clients with and without alexithymia were found to have responded differently to the two types of psychotherapy. Those without alexithymia had better outcomes when treated with the cognitive-behavioral approach, whereas those with alexithymia had better outcomes when treated with clinical management.

Group Therapy

The effectiveness of group therapy for reducing alexithymic symptoms has been examined by Fukunishi, Ichikawa, Ichikawa, and Matsuzawa (1994). These researchers used a form of family psychotherapy with a group of patients who abused alcohol. Participants in the study met in small groups (with four to five members) once weekly for two hours. After six months of group therapy, alexithymia levels in the participants were found to be significantly lower, and communication abilities among family members were found to have improved.

Beresnevaite (1995) has also examined the effectiveness of group therapy for reducing alexithymic symptoms in a sample of patients who had experienced myocardial infarction. The patients attended the group once weekly for ninety minutes over a period of four months. A variety of therapeutic techniques were employed during the course of treatment. Patients were taught relaxation techniques to decrease stress and focus attention on inner experiences. To improve their abilities to identify and communicate subjective feelings, participants were also required to participate in various role-playing and nonverbal communication activities. To improve imaginal activity, participants listened to music while in a relaxed state and were encouraged to write down dreams and fantasies. When participants became preoccupied with the details of external events (a common alexithymic symptom), the therapist directed them to replace utilitarian statements with statements that expressed wishes or desires. Participants were encouraged to practice the techniques they were learning between sessions. Alexithymia levels were assessed at four different time points: before the start of treatment, four months later (at the end of treatment), six months later, and twelve months later. Compared to levels before treatment started, there was a significant reduction in alexithymic symptoms at the end of treatment. Alexithymia levels continued to be significantly lower than baseline levels at the six-month and twelve-month testing sessions.

CONCLUSION

Based on the literature related to several overlapping constructs, I have described a number of important clinical and therapeutic implications for emotional intelligence. There is considerable need for clinicians and researchers to investigate explicitly the relationship between emotional intelligence and various psychotherapy outcome variables. There is also the need for researchers and clinicians to examine the effectiveness of specific therapeutic interventions for enhancing or improving specific facets of the emotional intelligence construct. The development and proliferation of reliable and valid measures for emotional intelligence offers clinicians and researchers a number of useful and new clinical tools. The emotional intelligence instruments described in Chapters Fifteen, Sixteen, and Seventeen may help in the process of matching clients with appropriate therapeutic interventions, as well in monitoring the progress of clients during psychotherapy.

References

Apfel-Savitz, R., Silverman, D., & Bennett, M. I. (1977). Group psychotherapy of patients with somatic illnesses and alexithymia. *Psychotherapy and Psychosomatics, 28,* 323–329.

Applebaum, S. A. (1973). Psychological-mindedness: Word, concept, and essence. *International Journal of Psychoanalysis, 54,* 35–45.

Bachrach, H. M., & Leaff, L. A. (1978). "Analyzability": A systematic review of the clinical and quantitative literature. *Journal of the American Psychoanalytical Association, 26,* 881–920.

Baekeland, F., & Lundwall, L. (1975). Dropping out of treatment: A critical review. *Psychological Bulletin, 82,* 738–783.

Bagby, R. M., Parker, J.D.A., & Taylor, G. J. (1994). The Twenty-Item Toronto Alexithymia Scale: I, Item selection and cross-validation of the factor structure. *Journal of Psychosomatic Research, 38,* 23–32.

Bar-On, R. (1997). *BarOn Emotional Quotient Inventory (EQ-i): Technical manual.* Toronto, Canada: Multi-Health Systems.

Barron, F. (1953). An ego-strength scale which predicts response to psychotherapy. *Journal of Consulting Psychology, 17,* 327–333.

Beckham, E. (1992). Predicting patient dropout in psychotherapy. *Psychotherapy, 29,* 177–182.

Beresnevaite, M. (1995, May). Efficacy of alexithymia's correction and its relation with the course of ischaemic heart disease. Paper presented at the Annual Congress of Lithuanian Cardiologists, Kaunas, Lithuania.

Bloch, S. (1979). Assessment of patients for psychotherapy. *British Journal of Psychiatry, 135,* 193–208.

Brown, L. J., (1985). On concreteness. *Psychoanalytic Review, 72,* 379–402.

Cacioppo, J. T., & Petty, R. E. (1982). The need for cognition. *Journal of Personality and Social Psychology, 42,* 116–131.

Cartwright, R. D. (1993). Who needs their dreams? The usefulness of dreams in psychotherapy. *Journal of the American Academy of Psychoanalysis, 21,* 539–547.

Catchlove, R.F.H., Cohen, K. R., Braha, R.E.D., & Demers-Desrosiers, L. A. (1985). Incidence and implications of alexithymia in chronic pain patients. *Journal of Nervous and Mental Disease, 173,* 246–248.

Conte, H. R., Plutchik, R., Jung, B. B., Picard, S., Karasu, T. B., & Lotterman, A. (1990). Psychological mindedness as a predictor of psychotherapy outcome: A preliminary report. *Comprehensive Psychiatry, 31,* 426–431.

Fenigstein, A., Scheier, M. F., & Buss, A. H. (1975). Public and private self-consciousness: Assessment and theory. *Journal of Consulting and Clinical Psychology, 43,* 522–527.

Fischer, A. R., & Good, G. E. (1997). Men and psychotherapy: An investigation of alexithymia, intimacy, and masculine gender roles. *Psychotherapy, 34,* 160–170.

Fukunishi, I., Ichikawa, M., Ichikawa, T., & Matsuzawa, K. (1994). Effect of family group psychotherapy on alcoholic families. *Psychological Reports, 74,* 568–570.

Garfinkel, P. E., & Garner, D. M. (1982). *Anorexia Nervosa: A multidimensional perspective.* New York: Brunner/Mazel.

Greenberg, L. S., & Safran, J. D. (1987). *Emotions in psychotherapy.* New York: Guilford Press.

Horney, K. (1952). The paucity of inner experiences. *American Journal of Psychoanalysis, 12,* 3–9.

Jyvaesjaervi, S., Joukamaa, M., Vaeisaenen, E., Larivaara, P., Kivelae, S., & Keinaenen-Kiukaanniemi, S. (1999). Alexithymia, hypochondriacal beliefs, and psychological distress among frequent attenders in primary health care. *Comprehensive Psychiatry, 40,* 292–298.

Keller, D. S., Carroll, K. M., Nich, C., & Rounsaville, B. J. (1995). Alexithymia in cocaine abusers: Response to psychotherapy and pharmacotherapy. *American Journal on Addictions, 4,* 234–244.

Krystal, H. (1978). Trauma and affects. *Psychoanalytic Study of the Child, 33,* 81–115.

Krystal, H. (1979). Alexithymia and psychotherapy. *American Journal of Psychotherapy, 33,* 17–31.

Krystal, H. (1982–1983). Alexithymia and the effectiveness of psychoanalytic treatment. *International Journal of Psychoanalysis and Psychotherapy, 9,* 353–388.

Krystal, H. (1988). *Integration and self-healing: Affect, trauma, alexithymia.* Hillsdale, NJ: Analytic Press.

Lake, B. (1985). Concept of ego strength in psychotherapy. *British Journal of Psychiatry, 147,* 471–478.

Lane, R., Sechrest, L., Reidel, R., Weldon, V., Kaszniak, A., & Schwartz, G. (1996). Impaired verbal and nonverbal emotion recognition in alexithymia. *Psychosomatic Medicine, 58,* 203–210.

Levitan, H. (1989). Failure of the defensive functions of the ego in psychosomatic patients. In S. Cheren (Ed.), *Psychosomatic medicine: Theory, physiology, and practice* (Vol.1, pp. 135–157). Madison, CT: International Universities Press.

Luborsky, L., McLellan, A., Woody, G., O'Brien, C., & Auerbach, A. (1985). Therapist success and its determinants. *Archives of General Psychiatry, 42,* 602–611.

Mallinckrodt, B., King, J. L., & Coble, H. M. (1998). Family dysfunction, alexithymia, and client attachment to therapist. *Journal of Counseling Psychology, 45,* 497–504.

Mayes, L. C., & Cohen, D. J. (1992). The development of a capacity for imagination in early childhood. *Psychoanalytic Study of the Child, 47,* 23–47.

McCallum, M., & Piper, W. E. (1997). *Psychological mindedness: A contemporary understanding.* Mahwah, NJ: Erlbaum.

McCallum, M., Piper, W., & Joyce, A. (1992). Dropping out from short-term group therapy. *Psychotherapy, 29,* 206–215.

McDougall, J. (1989). *Theatres of the body: A psychoanalytic approach to psychosomatic illness.* New York: Norton.

Nemiah, J. C., Freyberger, H., & Sifneos, P. E. (1976). Alexithymia: A view of the psychosomatic process. In O. W. Hill (Ed.), *Modern trends in psychosomatic medicine* (Vol. 3, pp. 430–439). London: Butterworths.

Nemiah, J. C., & Sifneos, P. E. (1970). Affect and fantasy in patients with psychosomatic disorders. In O. W. Hill (Ed.), *Modern trends in psychosomatic medicine* (Vol. 2, pp. 26–34). London: Butterworths.

Owen, P., & Kohutek, K. (1981). The rural mental health dropout. *Journal of Rural Community Psychology, 2,* 38–41.

Parker, J.D.A., Bauermann, T. M., & Smith, C. T. (forthcoming). Alexithymia and impoverished dream content: Evidence from REM sleep awakenings. *Psychosomatic Medicine.*

Parker, J.D.A., Taylor, G. J., & Bagby, R. M. (1993). Alexithymia and the recognition of facial expressions of emotion. *Psychotherapy and Psychosomatics, 59,* 197–202.

Parker, J.D.A., Taylor, G. J., & Bagby, R. M. (forthcoming). The relationship between emotional intelligence and alexithymia. *Personality and Individual Differences.*

Pekarik, G. (1983). Follow-up adjustment of outpatient dropouts. *American Journal of Orthopsychiatry, 53,* 501–511.

Pierloot, R., & Vinck, J. (1977). A pragmatic approach to the concept of alexithymia. *Psychotherapy and Psychosomatics, 28,* 156–166.

Piper, W. E., Joyce, A. S., McCallum, M., & Azim, H. F. (1998). Interpretive and supportive forms of psychotherapy and patient personality variables. *Journal of Consulting and Clinical Psychology, 66,* 558–567.

Reder, P., & Tyson, R. (1980). Patient dropout from individual psychotherapy. *Bulletin of the Menninger Clinic, 44,* 229–252.

Ruesch, J. (1948). The infantile personality. *Psychosomatic Medicine, 10,* 134–144.

Ryan, E. R., & Cicchetti, D. V. (1985). Predicting quality of alliance in the initial psychotherapy interview. *Journal of Nervous and Mental Disease, 173,* 717–725.

Rybakowski, J., Ziólkowski, M., Zasadzka, T., & Brzezinski, R. (1988). High prevalence of alexithymia in male patients with alcohol dependence. *Drug and Alcohol Dependence, 21,* 133–136.

Salovey, P., Hsee, C. K., & Mayer, J. D. (1993). Emotional intelligence and the self-regulation of affect. In D. M. Wegner & J. W. Pennebaker (Eds.), *Handbook of mental control* (pp. 258–277). Englewood Cliffs, NJ: Prentice Hall.

Salovey, P., & Mayer, J. D. (1989–1990). Emotional intelligence. *Imagination, Cognition, and Personality, 9,* 185–211.

Saltzman, C., Luetgert, M. J., Roth, C. H., Creaser, J., & Howard, L. (1976). Formation of a therapeutic relationship: Experiences during the initial phase of psychotherapy as predictors of treatment duration and outcome. *Journal of Consulting and Clinical Psychology, 44,* 546–555.

Schutte, N. S., Malouff, J. M., Hall, L. E., Haggerty, D. J., Cooper, J. T., Golden, C. J., & Dornheim, L. (1998). Development and validation of a measure of emotional intelligence. *Personality and Individual Differences, 25,* 167–177.

Sifneos, P. E. (1967). Clinical observations on some patients suffering from a variety of psychosomatic diseases. *Acta Medicina Psychosomatica, 7,* 1–10.

Sifneos, P. E. (1973). The prevalence of "alexithymic" characteristics in psychosomatic patients. *Psychotherapy and Psychosomatics, 22,* 255–262.

Sifneos, P. E. (1975). Problems of psychotherapy of patients with alexithymic characteristics and physical disease. *Psychotherapy and Psychosomatics, 26,* 65–70.

Silver, D. (1983). Psychotherapy of the characterologically difficult patient. *Canadian Journal of Psychiatry, 28,* 513–521.

Sue, S., McKinney, H., & Allen, D. (1976). Predictors of the duration of therapy for clients in the community mental health system. *Community Mental Health Journal, 12,* 365–375.

Swiller, H. I. (1988). Alexithymia: Treatment utilizing combined individual and group psychotherapy. *International Journal of Group Psychotherapy, 38,* 47–61.

Taylor, G. J. (1977). Alexithymia and the counter-transference. *Psychotherapy and Psychosomatics, 28,* 141–147.

Taylor, G. J. (1984a). Alexithymia: Concept, measurement, and implications for treatment. *American Journal of Psychiatry, 141,* 725–732.

Taylor, G. J. (1984b). Psychotherapy with the boring patient. *Canadian Journal of Psychiatry, 29,* 217–222.

Taylor, G. J. (1987). *Psychosomatic medicine and contemporary psychoanalysis.* Madison, CT: International Universities Press.

Taylor, G. J., Bagby, R. M., & Parker, J.D.A. (1997). *Disorders of affect regulation.* Cambridge: Cambridge University Press.

Taylor, G. J., Parker, J.D.A., & Bagby, R. M. (1999). Emotional intelligence and the emotional brain: Points of convergence and implications for psychoanalysis. *Journal of the American Academy of Psychoanalysis, 27,* 339–354.

Tolor, A , & Reznikoff, M. (1960). A new approach to insight: A preliminary report. *Journal of Nervous and Mental Disease, 130,* 286–296.

Wolff, H. H. (1977). The contribution of the interview situation to the restriction of phantasy life and emotional experience in psychosomatic patients. *Psychotherapy and Psychosomatics, 28,* 58–67.

About the Authors

Reuven Bar-On is director of the Institute of Applied Intelligence in Denmark. He has been involved in defining, measuring, and applying emotional and social intelligence since 1980. Dr. Bar-On coined the term *EQ* and published the EQ-i, the first test of emotional intelligence.

James D. A. Parker is associate professor in the Department of Psychology at Trent University in Canada. He has been involved in extensive research on alexithymia and its relationship with emotional intelligence, personality, and psychopathology.

James R. Averill is professor of psychology at the University of Massachusetts, Amherst. His recent research has focused on individual differences in the ability to be emotionally creative and on emotional reactions to the natural environment.

R. Michael Bagby is professor of psychiatry at the University of Toronto, chief of psychology at the Centre for Addiction and Mental Health (CAMH, formerly the Clarke Institute of Psychiatry), and head of the Research Section on Personality and Psychopathology at CAMH. He has a long-standing interest in test construction theory and dimensional models of personality psychopathology.

Antoine Bechara is assistant professor of neurology at the University of Iowa Health Care. He has been investigating the neurological substrates of emotion and the influence of emotion on decision making and cognition in patients with focal brain lesions since 1992.

Richard E. Boyatzis is professor of organizational behavior at Case Western Reserve University. He has been researching the relationship of emotional intelligence competencies and performance since 1970 and has been conducting longitudinal studies on its development since 1987.

William Bremner is currently deputy principal of a large high school in Edinburgh, Scotland. He has had practical interests in social and emotional intelligence and competence for many years and served as National Curriculum Development Officer in Social Competence for Scotland.

David R. Caruso is a management psychologist who consults with individuals and organizations on career, team, and management development. Originally trained in intelligence research, he has worked most recently on emotional intelligence and its measurement. Dr. Caruso has a particular interest in applications of emotional intelligence to the workplace.

Cary Cherniss is professor of applied psychology at Rutgers University. He also is Cochair of the Consortium for Research on Emotional Intelligence in Organizations.

Antonio R. Damasio is the M. W. Van Allen Distinguished Professor and head of the Department of Neurology at the University of Iowa. He is internationally recognized for his research on the neuroscience of emotion, reason, and the mind. He is the author of two books on emotion and consciousness: *Descartes' Error* and *The Feeling of What Happens*.

Maurice J. Elias is professor in the Department of Psychology, Rutgers University, a member of the Leadership Team of the Collaborative to Advance Social and Emotional Learning (CASEL), and first author of *Emotionally Intelligent Parenting* (1999) and *Promoting Social and Emotional Learning: Guidelines for Educators* (1997).

Daniel Goleman is the author of numerous books, including two international best-sellers on emotional intelligence. His current research is focused on leadership, creating new assessment methods, developing emotional intelligence, and the emotionally intelligent organization.

Patricia A. Graczyk is director of research and operations for the Collaborative to Advance Social and Emotional Learning (CASEL) at the University of Illinois at Chicago. As a practitioner and researcher she has worked to promote students' emotional and social development for over twenty years.

Mark T. Greenberg is director of the Prevention Research Center for the Promotion of Human Development. He is one of the developers of the Promoting Alternative Thinking Strategies (PATHS) curriculum and has written extensively on emotional development.

Elena L. Grigorenko is research scientist in the Department of Psychology and Child Study Center at Yale University and Associate Professor of Psychology at Moscow State University.

Jennifer Hedlund is associate research scientist at Yale University. Her research focuses on practical intelligence and, in particular, the assessment and development of tacit knowledge in the domains of leadership and management.

Elizabeth A. Holmes was a high school teacher, with special responsibilities for personal and social development, who then trained as an educational (school) psychologist, undertaking doctoral research in social competence and anger management. She currently works in the Dundee Educational Psychology Service in the city of Dundee, Scotland.

Richard D. Lane is associate professor of psychiatry and psychology at the University of Arizona. His research is focused on individual differences in emotional awareness from the psychological and neuroanatomical perspectives.

Olivier Luminet is a postdoctoral researcher at the Belgian National Fund for Scientific Research. He works at the University of Louvain at Louvain-la-Neuve, Department of Psychology. He has been doing research on the aftermath of emotional episodes (rumination and social sharing of emotion) and on the relationship between emotion and personality.

Gerald Matthews is associate professor of psychology at the University of Cincinnati. He has been researching cognitive models of personality, stress, and intelligence since 1980.

John D. Mayer is professor of psychology at the University of New Hampshire. Dr. Mayer and Dr. Salovey's 1990 articles on emotional intelligence are widely credited with initiating contemporary scientific interest in the area. Since then, they and their colleague Dr. Caruso have published widely in scholarly journals and books on the theory and measurement of emotional intelligence. Dr. Mayer has a particular interest in the role of emotional intelligence in personality.

Mary McCallum is associate clinical professor in the Department of Psychiatry at the University of Alberta. She has researched psychological mindedness and its relation to associated concepts such as emotional intelligence.

Robert R. McCrae is research psychologist in the Laboratory of Personality and Cognition at the National Institute on Aging (United States). His research is focused on the five-factor model of personality, with a special emphasis on openness to experience.

John W. Payton is a certified health education specialist and licensed school social worker. He has conducted reviews of school-based violence prevention and comprehensive health education curricula and is currently Director of the Social and Emotional Learning Program Review of the Collaborative to Advance Social and Emotional Learning (CASEL) at the University of Illinois at Chicago.

William E. Piper is professor, Department of Psychiatry, University of British Columbia, and adjunct professor, Department of Psychiatry, University of Alberta. He is also editor of the *International Journal of Group Psychotherapy*.

Kenneth S. Rhee is assistant professor of Management at Northern Kentucky University. His research focuses on self-directed behavior change, learning, and development, including those competencies that constitute emotional intelligence.

Carolyn Saarni, professor of counseling at Sonoma State University, is a developmental psychologist specializing in emotional development. Her social constructivist theoretical orientation is evident in her approach to emotional competence, defined as the demonstration of self-efficacy in emotion-eliciting social transactions.

Peter Salovey is professor of psychology and of epidemiology and public health at Yale University. In 1990 he coauthored, with Dr. Mayer, the first articles that formally defined and measured the concept of emotional intelligence. In more recent years, he, Dr. Mayer, and Dr. Caruso have been investigating the measurement of emotional intelligence. Dr. Salovey has a particular interest in the role of emotions and emotional intelligence in health and illness.

Elaine Scharfe is assistant professor in the Department of Psychology at Trent University in Canada. She has been involved in extensive research on the stability and change of attachment patterns across the life span.

Robert J. Sternberg is IBM Professor of Psychology and Education in the Department of Psychology at Yale University. He studies practical intelligence as part of his research.

Graeme J. Taylor is professor of psychiatry at the University of Toronto and a staff psychiatrist at the Mount Sinai Hospital in Toronto. He has been developing theory and conducting research on alexithymia since 1977 and in recent years has related this work to the concept of emotional intelligence.

Keith Topping is director of the Centre for Paired Learning and of Postgraduate Educational and School Psychology at the University of Dundee, Scotland. He has researched social, emotional, and behavioral competencies and difficulties since 1980.

Daniel Tranel is professor of neurology and psychology at the University of Iowa. He is the author of several publications that demonstrate how certain patients with focal brain lesions can evoke emotional responses to familiar faces, despite the lack of explicit recognition of these faces, thus indicating the intactness of some aspects of emotional intelligence in these patients.

Roger P. Weissberg is professor at the University of Illinois at Chicago, where he directs the Prevention Research Training Program in Urban Children's Mental Health. He also is Executive Director of the Collaborative to Advance Social and Emotional Learning (CASEL).

Moshe Zeidner is professor of educational psychology at the University of Haifa in Israel and director of the Center for Interdisciplinary Research on Emotions. His research focuses on two main areas: (1) the interaction between intelligence and personality and (2) stress, coping, emotions, and adaptive outcomes.

Joseph E. Zins is professor at the University of Cincinnati and Editor of the *Journal of Educational and Psychological Consultation.* His research focuses on consultation, collaboration, and prevention.

Sabrina Zirkel is an executive faculty member of Saybrook Graduate School. Her research interests are the socially intelligent aspects of personality, particularly as they apply to goal setting and attainment.

SUBJECT INDEX

NAMES INDEX

Camras, L. A., 251
Cantor, N., 144
Carnochan, P., 84
Caron, R. F., 249
Carpenter, R. L., 421
Carroll, K. M., 498
Carstensen, L. L., 258, 292, 293
Carter, S., 422
Caruso, D. R., 32, 83, 92, 264, 306, 320, 474, 506
Carver, C. S., 472
Casey, A., 415
Caspi, A., 151, 217, 219
Cassidy, J., 257
Ceci, S. J., 150, 151, 221, 222, 230
Chapin, F. S., 140, 141
Charles, S. T., 258, 293
Charlton, T., 423
Charness, N., 219
Cherniss, C., xiv, 433, 506
Chi, M.T.H., 230
Christopher, J. S., 418
Clyman, R. B., 186
Cohen, D., 245
Cohen, J. J., 422
Cohen, N. J., 129
Coie, J. D., 30
Colby, A., 72
Cole, M., 150, 221
Cole, P. M., 253
Coleman, M., 421
Collingwood, R. G., 288
Colvin, G., 422
Combs, M. L., 30
Conoley, J. C., 422
Conte, H. R., 48, 492
Contrada, R. J., 50
Conway, B. E., 140
Cooper, R. K., 102, 112
Córcoles, A. E., 307
Cornelius, S. W., 151, 217, 219
Costa, P. T., Jr., 265
Cowen, E. L., 396
Cowen, S. S., 350, 351
Cox, T., 475
Crick, N. R., 31
Cullingford, C., 419
Cunningham, G. K., 417

Damasio, A. R., 181–182, 192, 193, 506

Damon, W., 72
Darwin, C., 326
Davidson, R. J., 247
Davies, M., 82, 83, 146, 149, 268, 328, 332, 474
Davis, M., 445
Davis, T. L., 254
Day, J. D., 143, 157
Day, R., 436
de M'Uzan, M., 41
Deaux, K., 16
Deiner, E., 80
Deitz, D. E., 423
Denham, S. A., 248, 252, 257, 420, 421
Denney, N. W., 151, 219, 225
Detweiler, J. B., 459
Deutsch, M., 435
DeVoe, M., 258
Dick, L., 420
Dickstein, S., 250, 257
Dixon, R. A., 224
Dodd, J. M., 421
Dodge, K. A., 31
Dondi, M., 249
Dörner, D., 223
Dryfoos, J. G., 393
Dunn, J., 84, 257
DuPaul, G. J., 418
Durlak, J. A., 394, 422
Dweck, C., 6, 18

Eccles, J. S., 8, 10
Eckert, T. L., 418
Ekman, P., 177
Elias, M. J., 391, 421, 506
Eliot, G., 294
Elliott, S. N., 416, 417
Emde, R. N., 250
Emmer, E., 416
Endler, N. S., 468, 469, 475
Epstein, M. H., 423
Epstein, S., 85, 112
Erasmus, D., 282
Erikson, E. H., 12–13, 14
Erwin, P., 422
Eslinger, P. J., 193
Estes, D., 257
Ethier, K. A., 16
Eysenck, H. J., 479

Faber, B. A., 124
Fenigstein, A., 126
Ferguson, E., 475

Field, T. M., 245, 246, 247, 249, 251, 256
Fischer, K. W., 84
Folkman, S., 460, 461, 475
Ford, M. E., 142
Forehand, R., 29
Forness, S. R., 418
Forsythe, G. B., 221
Fortin, L., 422
Fox, N. A., 247
Freiberg, H. J., 416
Frenkel-Brunswick, E., 479
Freyberger, H., 41
Fukunishi, I., 310, 499
Furman, W., 422

Garber, J., 254
Gardner, H., 44, 45, 48, 52, 58, 102, 106, 118, 138, 271, 343, 462
Garmezy, N., 422
Garonzik, R., 346
Gavin, L. A., 422
Gazzaniga, M. S., 53
Gelbard, H. A., 54
Gesten, E. L., 29, 420
Gibson, M., 10
Glod, C. A., 54, 58
Goldberg, S., 56
Goldstein, A. P., 437
Goleman, D., xi, 102, 106, 112, 118, 129, 146, 264, 265, 266, 343, 344, 345, 347, 363, 422, 433, 449, 506
Gollwitzer, P. M., 16
Gough, H. G., 140
Gougis, R. A., 9
Graczyk, P. A., xiv, 391, 507
Grafton, F. C., 143
Graham, S., 423
Greenberg, L. S., 497
Greenberg, M. T., 391, 422, 507
Greenberg, R., 245
Greenwood, J. D., 284
Gresham, F. M., 32, 416, 417
Grigorenko, E. L., xiii, 153, 154, 215, 233, 507
Guerra, V., 307
Guilford, J. P., 140, 141

Haan, N., 464
Haertel, G. D., 416
Haggerty, R. J., 422